CONSUMER BEHAVIOR & CULTURE

Sara Miller McCune founded SAGE Publishing in 1965 to support the dissemination of usable knowledge and educate a global community. SAGE publishes more than 1000 journals and over 800 new books each year, spanning a wide range of subject areas. Our growing selection of library products includes archives, data, case studies and video. SAGE remains majority owned by our founder and after her lifetime will become owned by a charitable trust that secures the company's continued independence.

Los Angeles | London | New Delhi | Singapore | Washington DC | Melbourne

Marieke de Mooij

3rd
EDITION

CONSUMER BEHAVIOR & CULTURE

Consequences for Global Marketing and Advertising

Los Angeles | London | New Delhi
Singapore | Washington DC | Melbourne

Los Angeles | London | New Delhi
Singapore | Washington DC | Melbourne

SAGE Publications Ltd
1 Oliver's Yard
55 City Road
London EC1Y 1SP

SAGE Publications Inc.
2455 Teller Road
Thousand Oaks, California 91320

SAGE Publications India Pvt Ltd
B 1/I 1 Mohan Cooperative Industrial Area
Mathura Road
New Delhi 110 044

SAGE Publications Asia-Pacific Pte Ltd
3 Church Street
#10-04 Samsung Hub
Singapore 049483

Editor: Matthew Waters
Editorial assistant: Jasleen Kaur
Production editor: Sarah Cooke
Marketing manager: Lucia Sweet
Cover design: Francis Kenney
Typeset by: C&M Digitals (P) Ltd, Chennai, India
Printed in the UK

Library of Congress Control Number: 2019931577

British Library Cataloguing in Publication data

A catalogue record for this book is available from
the British Library

ISBN 978-1-5443-1815-8
ISBN 978-1-5443-1816-5 (pbk)

At SAGE we take sustainability seriously. Most of our products are printed in the UK using responsibly sourced
papers and boards. When we print overseas we ensure sustainable papers are used as measured by the PREPS
grading system. We undertake an annual audit to monitor our sustainability.

Contents

Online Resources

Consumer Behavior and Culture 4th Edition is supported by a wealth of online resources for both students and lecturers to help support learning and teaching. These resources are available at: https://study.sagepub.com/cbc3e.

Lecturers can log in and access...

- Author-prepared PowerPoint slides for each chapter to support teaching
- Questions provided in the chapter discussions and other examples to encourage reflection and test understanding
- Videos of the black and white story boards in the book's illustrations to expand knowledge

Preface

It has been 15 years since the first edition of this book. Since then, increased research results have become available to support the understanding of culture's influence on consumer behavior. In these 15 years also the Internet has become integrated in people's lives worldwide, and differences in usage have become manifest. Increasing spending power of consumers worldwide runs parallel to increasing choice. Most consumers, wherever they live, are not rational in their choice behavior. With increased wealth, peoples' values become manifest in the decision-making process and these values vary across cultures. Western marketing managers are driven by the need for consistency, which is an innate need of their own culture, but they shouldn't project this need to other cultures where it isn't relevant. It is the fundamental error of consistency that makes Western marketing managers develop consistent brand identities and universal advertising campaigns for the rest of the world, where they don't apply or are not understood and thus are less effective.

This book is written for those who have understood that markets are people and that people are not the same everywhere. The focus of this book is consumption and consumer behavior; it is about people – what they buy, why they buy, and how they buy. The basic message is that there are no global consumers, and consumer behavior is not converging across countries. As a result, understanding the differences in behavior across countries is of utmost importance.

To provide evidence of how culture explains variance of consumption, I have collected and analyzed recent and past data on consumption. What I learned from these data is the importance of history. Consumer behavior appears very stable, and habits of the past often can best explain current and future behavior. Behavior that is considered new is often only a new format of old behavior.

In many models of consumer behavior, culture is viewed as an environmental factor, whereas it is in the heads of consumers. This book goes to the roots of culture's influence, the mind of the consumer. I have structured the various elements of consumer behavior in an – to users of US consumer behavior textbooks – unusual way, using a model that integrates culture in all aspects of the human being, in the self, in personality, and in people's relationships with others. I could do this thanks to the increasing evidence of how culture influences the self, gained from cross-cultural psychology. Much of this work has not yet been used for explaining consumer behavior across cultures; little has reached the academic world and marketing professionals.

The structure of the book follows this model. After the introductory Chapter 1, which reviews the current myths of global marketing and explains the structure of the book, Chapter 2 explains the concept of culture. This chapter compares several cultural models that are most used in theory and practice and explains my choice of the Hofstede model.

Chapter 3 deals with my findings of convergence and divergence of consumption and consumer behavior. It also reviews national income and sociodemographic variables that tend to be used to analyze cross-country differences.

Chapter 4 deals with the self, personality, and identity – concepts that are central for understanding human behavior and that are also used as metaphors in branding and corporate strategy. In particular, personality theories, developed mostly by Anglo-Saxon psychologists, have been adopted by Western brand managers. These theories are not as universal as generally thought, which has major implications for strategy development. I learned this myself when dealing with Japanese companies, who have very different perceptions than, for example, American companies of what makes a strong brand.

Chapter 5 deals with the self in the social environment. In a large part of the world, the context in which the self operates defines the self, which is very different from what Western psychology teaches.

Chapter 6 describes mental processes, such as perception, learning, language, and information processing. There is increased evidence that around the world people process information in different ways. How these processes vary is of great importance for marketing communications.

Chapter 7 extends the communication theories and advertising styles that were covered in Chapter 6 of the previous edition; it covers differences in media usage, both the classic media and the new electronic media.

Chapter 8 includes most statistical evidence of how culture influences product ownership and usage. In addition, it covers consumer behavior domains such as complaining behavior, brand loyalty, and shopping and buying behavior, including Internet shopping.

Many explanations of my findings are based on my own analysis and practical experience, statistical analysis of a growing database, and increased research results as found in literature. I hope this book, like the previous editions, will be a challenge for academics and researchers to do further research. Although availability of data from Latin America and Asia is improving, most data are still from the European Union. There is no other area that provides so many data that are also available in the public domain.

For this edition, Sage will have an updated companion website available for those who – according to the publisher – are qualified to receive additional information to aid teaching: this will include PowerPoint presentations; the films and print ads that are in black and white in the book; additional material to illustrate the cultural dimensions, questions and discussion points; and a few short cases.

With this third edition I would like to thank Sage in the United States for the years they published the previous editions. I have to say goodbye, and my thanks go to the many pleasant, dedicated and conscientious editors who assisted me in the past years. I am pleased that Sage UK has taken over, in particular as interest in Europe and Asia is growing faster than in the United States. I have encountered the same pleasantness and conscientiousness in the editing this book. For all editions Geert Hofstede always was stand-by. I am very grateful having known him for so many years. Increased usage of this book also has led to research in many areas covered in the book, resulting in a host of academic publications. I feel honored, and have used many to update this book. Thanks go to all who contributed.

Marieke de Mooij
Burgh-Haamstede
www.mariekedemooij.com

About the Author

Marieke de Mooij, (1943, the Netherlands) studied English literature at the University of Amsterdam and textile management at the school of Engineering Management in Enschede, the Netherlands where she graduated in 1966. She was PR and advertising manager for an international textile company, account executive at an advertising agency, was a director at the Dutch institute for professional advertising education, director of education of the International Advertising Association and managed BBDO College, the Educational program for BBDO Europe. She has worked on the application of the Hofstede model to cross-cultural consumer behavior and international advertising since 1990, doing research, conducting seminars, and teaching at various universities worldwide as visiting professor. As a consultant in cross-cultural communications she advised both companies and advertising agencies on international branding and advertising. As a *profesora asociada* she has been teaching international advertising at the University of Navarra, Spain. In 2001 she received her Ph.D. at that University, at the Department of Communication. The subject of her doctoral research was convergence and divergence in consumer behavior across countries. She is the author of several publications on the influence of culture on marketing, advertising, and consumer behavior. She is also the author of *Global Marketing & Advertising. Understanding Cultural Paradoxes. Fifth Edition*, also published by SAGE Publications. A book on communication theory and culture is titled *Human and Mediated Communication around the World: A Comprehensive Review and Analysis*, published by Springer International. Her books are used at universities worldwide. Her website: www.mariekedemooij.com

Consumer Behavior Across Cultures

When the Canadian media philosopher Marshall McLuhan[1] coined the concept of the global village, he was referring to Plato's definition of the proper size for a city – the number of people who could hear the voice of the public speaker. By the global village, McLuhan meant that the new electric media of his time, such as telephone and television, abolished the spatial dimension. By means of electricity, people everywhere could resume person-to-person relations, as if on the smallest village scale. Thus, McLuhan viewed the electronic media as extensions of human beings. They enhance people's activities; they do not make people the same. If you assume people are the same everywhere, global media extend homogeneity. If you realize that people are different, extensions reinforce the differences. McLuhan did not include cultural convergence in the concept of the global village. In fact, he said the opposite: that uniqueness and diversity could be fostered under electronic conditions as never before.

This is exactly what technological development has accomplished. Contrary to expectations, people have embraced the Internet and other new technology mostly to enhance and intensify their current activities. In the cold climates, where people used to preserve food in the snow, they have embraced deep-freeze technology most intensely. The colder the climate, the more deep freezers. In Korea, where people used to preserve the national dish *Kimchi* in pots in the ground, they developed a special refrigerator to be able to do this in the home. At the start the mobile phone penetrated fastest in countries that already had advanced fixed telecommunications infrastructures. The number of contacts people have with their friends increased and intensified by social media. It was assumed that the Internet would undermine authoritarian regimes, but in fact it is used to strengthen them. The Internet has not changed people. It has reinforced existing habits that, instead of converging, tend to diverge. There is no evidence of converging consumer behavior across countries. This phenomenon is a core topic discussed in this book that provides evidence of consumer behavior differences that are too large and too stable to ignore.

Technology and national wealth have converged in the developed world to the extent that the majority of people can buy enough to eat and have additional income to invest in new technology and other durable goods. As a result, countries may become similar with respect to penetration of many of such goods, but what people do with their possessions does not converge. Much of consumer behavior varies across borders. As national wealth converges across countries, its explanatory power declines, and mainly cultural variables can explain cross-country differences. Cultural values are at the root of consumer behavior, so understanding culture's influence is necessary for those who want to succeed in the global marketplace. Culture is pervasive in all aspects of consumption and consumer behavior and should be integrated into all elements of consumer behavior theory. That is what this book attempts to do. This first chapter reviews the assumptions of homogenization and the underlying causes of these assumptions.

Global Consumers in a Global Village?

One of the greatest myths of global marketing is of global consumers living in a global village. In a sense, new communication technology has made the world into a global city or village in which we, in theory, can hear and see everything at any time in any place. The question is whether in practice we *do* hear and see everything at any time and in any place. And then, even if we do, the core question is whether this makes us similar to each other. Jeremy Bullmore says, 'In many ways, consumers are growing more alike, and we all know why. Mass communications, travel, multinational companies, the whole apparatus of the global village.'[2] Because we adopt some consumption symbols, such as jeans and trainers, from people in other parts of the world, the assumption has been that other aspects of our behavior will likewise change. In particular, Western international news journals have made us believe that a homogenization process would work toward universal (American) values. A single youth culture was expected to form across Europe, mimicking a kind of American model because teenagers listen to the same music, surf the net, and talk to each other on their mobile phones.[3]

Also, in academia the belief is that convergence of technology, global media, increased trade, and travel act to bring people together. In textbooks of international marketing and consumer behavior, there are plenty of statements about convergence of lifestyles and values, but these statements are not accompanied by empirical evidence. Assael,[4] author of one of the leading textbooks on consumer behavior, states that world cultures are becoming closer in many respects, that tastes in music, fashion, and technology among the young are becoming more similar across the world. With more consumers craving American goods, consumption values abroad are Americanizing. In particular, teenagers across the world have become similar.

As teens across the world watch the same television shows and similar commercials, they begin to develop similar consumption patterns. . . . Teens in the United States, Europe, Latin America and the Far East find being with friends and watching TV to be the most enjoyable ways to spend time. . . . Greater travel, better global communications, and increased access to the web have spurred the development of common norms and values among teens worldwide.[5]

Another consumer behavior textbook, by Solomon[6] suggests

we shape our opinions and desires based on a mix of voices from around the world, which is becoming a much smaller place as a result of rapid advancements in communication and transportation systems. In today's global culture, consumers often prize products and services that 'transport' them to different places and allow them to experience the diversity of other cultures ....

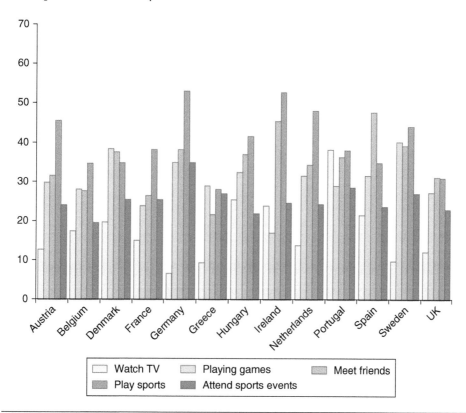

Figure 1.1   Leisure activities of young people in Europe: Percentages who watch TV, meet friends, play sports, attend sports events, or play games for two or more hours on weekdays

SOURCES: *Young Europeans: A Survey Among Young People Aged Between 15–30 in the European Union,* Flash EB 202 (2007); *Society at a Glance* (2016), OECD Social Indicators, OECD Publishing, Paris; *Physical Activity Statistics* (2015), British Heart Foundation (see Appendix B)

In our local supermarket we can buy blueberries from Argentina, wine from Chile, dates from Israel and kiwis from New Zealand, but that doesn't make us experience the diversity of the people of Argentina, Chile, Israel or New Zealand. In reality, relatively few people travel to an extent that they get insight into people's lives in other countries. Few people watch international (English language) television programs regularly. The English language cross-border channel CNN had to introduce national language versions. MTV has localized its content all over the world. The degree of exchange of people is limited, and there is no empirical evidence that global media make consumer behavior converge across countries. Generally people make blogs in their own language and thus limit their audience. Instead of globalization there is a trend of localization. Twitter trending topics are mostly local: about the weather, transport, politics etc.[7] This applies to most social media. At the start of 2018 with respect to the kind of posts, videos or photos, Facebook decided to start focusing on what people's friends and families share and de-emphasize content from publishers and brands.[8] Even across Europe, often thought to be a relatively homogeneous area, how young people spend their leisure time varies. Watching TV and meeting friends are activities of young people everywhere, but the degree to which they do this varies. Whereas 45% of Portuguese youngsters watch TV, only 8% of German youngsters do so. Also in some countries other activities like playing sports are preferred to watching TV or meeting friends. Attending sports events and playing games as leisure activities also vary across countries. Figure 1.1 illustrates some of the differences for 13 European countries.

Globalization and Global Consumer Culture

Globalization is a recurrent theme in the media, often with the focus on its negative effects. People are thought to feel dominated by large multinational corporations more than by their local and national governments. Global trade is supposed to result in a global consumer culture. What are *globalization* and *global consumer culture*?

Globalization

According to Robertson,[9] *globalization* became a common term in intellectual, business, media, and other circles with a number of meanings and with varying degrees of precision. In 1990 he related the term *globalization* to modernity and postmodernity. The concept of globalization per se should be applied to a particular series of developments concerning the structuration of the world as a whole. These are the spread of capitalism, Western imperialism, and the development of a global media system. The notion of Western imperialism in particular has linked negative connotations to the term *globalization*. Critics of globalization tend to protest against an emerging global monoculture consisting of McDonald's, Nike, Levi's, Barbie dolls, and American television. Use of the term *cultural imperialism* suggests a passive consumer who has no free will to withstand the attractive propositions of effective marketing techniques applied by a few American brands.

The definition by Unesco[10] covers this as follows:

> Globalization is a process in which the people and the countries of the world are being brought closer together, economically and culturally, through trade, information technology, travel, cultural exchanges, the mass media and mass entertainment. Globalization can be subdivided into three major areas: economic globalization, cultural globalization, and political globalization.

Relevant for this book are economic and cultural globalization. Globalization is largely visualized as a few ubiquitous global brands such as Coca-Cola, McDonald's, and Nike, and such brands are frequently targeted because of their symbolic function. This is partly caused by American marketing executives who would like us to believe that the global village means we drive the same cars, eat the same food, and watch the same television programs. This idea is reinforced by journalists and editors of international (mostly Anglo-American) newspapers who, whenever they discuss globalization, use pictures of Coca-Cola and McDonald's to illustrate the process, which is basically the spread of a small number of American brands across the world. These few global brands are neither representative of the total consumption package nor of transnational trade. The United Nations Conference on Trade and Development (UNCTAD) constructs an 'index of transnationality.' It works out the ratios of companies' foreign assets to total assets, foreign sales to total sales, and foreign employment to total employment; the index is the average of these three numbers. By this measure, Nestlé, the Swiss food company, is the world's most foreign-oriented company: 87% of its assets, 98% of its sales, and 97% of its workers are outside its homeland. Several of the most transnational companies are from small, advanced economies with small home markets. America's Coca-Cola and McDonald's, makers of the best-known global brands, rank only 31st and 42nd respectively.[11] Yet these brands have become the symbols of globalization.

Consumers have varying views on globalization. In 2003 a majority of inhabitants of the European Union were of the opinion that globalization has a positive effect on scientific and technological progress, employment, health, and cultural exchanges, although the degree of these positive responses varied across countries. Whereas 66% of the Irish viewed globalization as advantageous to themselves and their families, only 33% of the Greeks did so. In 2017 51% of all Europeans had a positive view on globalization (this was 65% in Ireland and 27% in Greece). In 2003 only 31% trusted the multinationals, but in 2013 48% of Europeans thought the large companies make efforts to behave responsibly towards our society.[12] Yet, the 2017 Edelman Trust Barometer showed a more negative picture of ongoing globalization and technological change that was weakening people's trust in global institutions.[13]

Global Consumer Culture

In the previous text the word culture was used in several different contexts with different meanings. The word culture is used for the expressions of culture, what Hofstede[14] refers to as the *hardware*, but also for the *software* of culture, the cultural values. Those who refer to the hardware – global symbols such as Coca-Cola and McDonald's – assume that global communications create a global, homogeneous consumer culture. This so-called Global Consumer Culture Theory, like Consumer Culture Theory (CCT) is the study of consumption choices and behaviors from a social point of view, as opposed to an economic or psychological one. CCT is based on a European critical philosophical tradition and American consumer research tradition.[15] In this book the concept of culture generally refers to shared values of groups of people (see Chapter 2), whereby groups refer to nations. Understanding differences in consumer behavior is best helped by understanding differences in values that are at the basis of differences in attitudes, motives, emotions, behaviour, etc.

Views on a global homogenization process are stronger in the United States than in other parts of the world. Alden and colleagues,[16] who analyzed the representation of global consumer culture in advertising, view global consumer culture as shared sets of consumption-related symbols (product categories, brands, and consumption activities) that are meaningful to segment members. Mass media programming, flowing primarily from the United States, has played a major role in the creation, learning, and sharing of such consumption symbols. As a result, the symbols of global consumer culture are basically American symbols that in the United States are viewed as local. In the sample of advertisements that was analyzed, only 5.5% were viewed as including global culture symbols compared with 25.6% in the other countries. The spread of global symbols does not necessarily include homogeneity of people's habits or values.[17]

In practice, notwithstanding the worldwide reach of television and the Internet, in many areas of people's lives, in consumption or entertainment habits, be it music or sports, the people of different nations continue to have different habits, tastes, and loyalties. Instead of causing homogenization, globalization is the reason for the revival of local cultural identities in different parts of the world.[18]

Increasingly, music is local. Local music has gained market share throughout most of the world. In many European markets, demand for local films is increasing. In Germany, 26.6% of cinema attendants choose national films.[20] There are a limited number of global products and global brands, and there are no global consumers. This book presents evidence that in the foreseeable future economic development and technology will not lead to homogenization of consumption.

Different nations play different sports: Cricket is the sport of Britain and its old dominions. Rugby is the sport of New Zealand. Cycling is an important sport of the Netherlands, France, and Spain. Badminton is strong in Malaysia. Maybe only football (soccer) can be considered to be a global sport, but it is by no means as popular in the United States as it is in Europe or Latin America. Even within Europe, interest in soccer varies from 49% in the United Kingdom to 65% in Portugal. Whereas 60% of Belgians are interested in tennis, only 15% of Norwegians share this interest. Interest in golf varies from 46% in Ireland to a meager 7% in Belgium. Of the Irish, 58% are interested in rugby, as compared to 2% of the Danes.[19]

Converging and Diverging Consumer Behavior

In his famous article, 'The globalization of markets,' Harvard professor Ted Levitt[21] argued that new technology would lead to homogenization of consumer wants and needs because consumers would prefer standard products of high quality and low price to more customized high-priced products. Levitt's argument was based on the assumption that consumer behavior is rational and that consumers always want to maximize profit. The assumption of rationality is increasingly regarded as unrealistic and places consumers outside of a cultural context.[22] No empirical evidence has been brought to show homogenization of tastes or the appearance of universal price-minded consumer segments.[23]

Empirical evidence of convergence is usually based on macro-developmental data, such as the numbers of telephones, television sets, or passenger cars per 1,000 population. The US sociologist Alex Inkeles[24] finds that such macro-level data often mask diversity at the micro level. Convergence at macro level (e.g., convergence of GNI [gross national income] per capita) does not necessarily imply convergence of consumer choice. As people around the globe become better educated and more affluent, their tastes diverge. With increased wealth, people increasingly accord greater relevance to their civilizational identity.

There is no support for the argument that increased global mobility for business and vacations will cause people to homogenize. People do not travel to an extent that they are frequently confronted with other cultures. Even if all people were to have enough money to travel abroad, they would not all travel to the same extent. Across European countries, the degree to which people travel varies widely. Whereas in 2008 only 11% of Swedes and 14% of the Irish had not made any short business or private trips, 54% of Hungarians and 47% of Portuguese had not made a business or private trip.[25] Also, young people do not travel to an extent that induces them to adopt different habits and values. In 2001 in Europe, 44% of young people age 15–24 had not visited another country in the previous two years. This was the same percentage as in 1997. Of those who have visited other European countries in the past two years, 86% went on vacation.[26] White[27] adds to this that people on vacation are not in a mood that has much to do with their domestic purchasing behavior, so the relevance of any advertising they see is limited. Annually, only 0.4% of Europeans (1.5 million) work in another European Union (EU) state, compared with 2.4% of Americans who work in a state other than where they grew up.[28] These data are hardly changing and the differences between countries are not disappearing. In Europe, in 2016 the total percentage of young people not willing to study or work in another EU country was 61%; this was 33% in Sweden, 67% in the United Kingdom, and 52% in Italy.[29]

In regions other than Europe, the trend is also toward divergence. Initially, with increased wealth, standards of living appear to converge, but a closer look makes clear that there are large differences. In Latin America, because of the large differences between rich and poor, the rich in each country have more in common with each other than with their poorer compatriots, but middle-income people differ from one country to another. They vary in the use of their discretionary income. All Latin Americans use toothpaste and shampoo each day, but there are varying brand preferences. Although 25% of Latin Americans eat cold cereal for breakfast, the national figures vary from 48% in Central America to 11% in the South.[30] Japan was the country that developed earliest and fastest of all Asian countries, and it was expected that development patterns of other countries in Asia would follow the pattern of Japan. This has not happened. The way other economies, like Malaysia and Indonesia, have developed is different.

What convergence can be found is at macro level and follows economic development–household penetration of products like refrigerators, washing machines, and color television sets. Only at a certain level of economic development, when people's stomachs are filled, when most people can afford proper housing and durable products such as cars and television sets, do people reach a higher level of unsatisfied needs. That is the moment when cultural values become manifest and are reflected in the different choices of products and brands. The interesting question is what people do with their incremental income, the extra money they have after they have bought the necessary durables to live a comfortable life. At that level, countries tend to diverge. (This phenomenon is further discussed in Chapter 3.)

Post-Scarcity Societies and the Culture Paradigm

A point of agreement among economists is that people will spend more as they become richer, so it would be surprising if there were no effect of increased national wealth on consumption. But the effect can take many different forms. One reason may be that consumption is a matter of habit. Much of consumer behavior is based on longtime habits.

An assumption by sociologists is that with increased wealth people's values will change. The idea is that with increased wealth, expenditures on education and media increase, resulting in more egalitarian values and democratic systems that in turn would lead to convergence of consumption. However, better education also makes people more aware of their value preferences. The expectations were that with increased openness and capitalism in China, the Chinese would turn to Western values. Instead, the Chinese have been rediscovering the teachings of Confucius, which for centuries have been the moral guidance of the Chinese people. The Chinese have become modern while retaining their core values.[31]

> Instead of homogenizing, continents are becoming more heterogeneous. In 1945, Europe had 31 independent countries. Today there are 51. In Africa, the number of countries grew over the same period from 21 to 53. The European Union has not harmonized people's values or national feelings. Consumers tend to feel most comfortable with their 'own' products or brands, the images and emotions they are used to.

The paradigm of economics is that consumers will maximize their own utility and will prefer low-priced, high-quality products to high-priced, added-value brands. This paradigm fits the old scarcity societies where people had to make either/or decisions, for example either a washing machine or holidays. In post-scarcity societies, people have more choices that make them less rational in their buying behavior. When comparing post-scarcity societies that have converged economically, one observes that national wealth is no longer a useful variable for explaining consumption differences. The new paradigm is culture, which becomes an increasingly important variable to explain consumption differences and brand preferences.

Chapter 3 presents data of longer time periods of consumption that demonstrate that people's habits do not converge and that with converging wealth some habits even diverge. For many new commodities, initially national income explains differences in ownership across countries. At some point in time, ownership across countries has reached maximum convergence. When that point is reached, ownership and usage start to diverge. The differences can be explained by culture. In Europe, around 1995, both ownership of television sets and cars per 1,000 inhabitants had converged. At the end of the century, countries had diverged with respect to the number of television sets owned per family, ownership of widescreen TVs, viewing time, and numbers of cars owned per family. The patterns followed by 'old' technology can be used to predict the pattern of 'new' technology. New technology (e.g., computers) has not reached the point of convergence, so differences between countries are related to national wealth, but future development can be predicted.

Generally speaking, the older the product category, the stronger the influence of culture. This explains why consumption of food products is persistently culture bound. The wealthier countries become, the more manifest the influence of culture on consumption. When people possess more or less enough of everything, they will spend their incremental income on what most fits their value patterns. Americans will buy more cars, the Dutch will buy more luxurious caravans (holiday trailers), and the Spanish will eat out even more than they do now. So greater wealth will not make people spend more on the same products in all countries. With converging wealth, the influence of income on consumption decreases. Cultural values are the main variable to explain differences in consumer behavior. (The convergence–divergence process is a major topic of Chapter 3.)

Global Communities?

One of the preconditions of global advertising is the existence of homogenous global segments across borders with similar values. Focus on similarities or marketing universals rather than the differences has led international marketers to search for market segments of people with similar lifestyles and values across countries that are called *global communities* or *global tribes*. The assumptions are that 18-year-olds in Paris have more in common with 18-year-olds in New York than with their own parents.[32] Business travelers and teenagers are most often cited as examples of such homogeneous groups. Samuel Huntington speaks of a 'Davos culture,' referring to people who speak fluent English, hold university degrees, who travel frequently outside their own country and dress alike.[33] These people are only superficially alike; their ways of thinking and behavior in the home country are not necessarily the same. It is the *hardware* that can go global, not the *software* of culture.

Young people worldwide are considered to form a homogeneous group because youngsters were reared on the same movies and global brands, like Coca-Cola and Levi's, and use the same technology and apps like YouTube, all of which have supposedly encouraged the development of a global teenager with common norms and values. By 2014 across Europe between 90% (Denmark) and 65% (Romania) of young people participated on social networking sites.[34] There is little evidence that this has led to a common youth culture. The way media are used by young people rather reinforces local connections. Several value studies show that between countries, young people vary as much as do grown-ups (see also Figure 2.1). General evidence is the fact that cross-cultural psychologists who measure value differences across cultures tend to use students as subjects. Youths from Stockholm to Seville may use the same type of mobile phone or computer, but they may have bought it for different reasons, and they use it in different ways and places. Young people may buy and use the same technology world-wide, but to a different degree, for different purposes, and in different ways. Everywhere young people may play sports, listen to music, or play videogames, but they do this to a different extent. These differences are related to culture.

Western magazines suggest that Asian teens, in the way they behave and dress and express themselves, increasingly resemble American and European teens and mistake it for Western individualistic behavior, but this behavior is not driven by individualistic values. Moreover, there is not one teenage culture in Asia; there is enormous diversity among Asian teenage lifestyles.[35] Young Asians may be typically Western on the surface, but traditional values like hard work remain next to aspiration toward money and display of success via branded goods.[36] If you take a typical Indian teenager in Bombay, Delhi, or Calcutta, he'd be wearing a Lacoste shirt or Nike shoes, but he is very much an Indian in his values. He respects his parents, lives together in a family, and removes his Nike shoes before entering a place of religion.[37] Many Westerners make a mistake when they think Japanese are chang-ing because students between 18 and 25 years old act in an extreme and revolutionary way. Westerners have to realize that these years are the only free years a Japanese has in his entire life. As soon as he gets a job, he conforms to typical Japanese behavior.[38] A study by ACNielsen found that, increasingly, Indonesian youth like to use traditional Indonesian products, pre-fer advertisements that use Indonesian models, and when sick would rather use Indonesian medicine than Western medicine.[39] In India, family and religion remain solid blocks of society, even as teens experiment with Western music, fashion, and brands. In India, pride in Indianness has increased hand in hand with globalization. Increasingly teens in Asia turn to Japan, not to the West, for their music, books, comics, and television programs.[40]

Often when new age groups are defined the question is asked if such groups are similar across borders.

During the first decade of the new millennium researchers defined a new age group consisting of those born after 1980, the first generation to come of age in the new millennium. These were thought to have similar values across countries. A study comparing three countries – the United States, New Zealand and Sweden – found similar values for the United States and New Zealand millennials, as could be expected because of similarity of American and New Zealand general values. Swedish millennials were considerably different, and their values represented simi-lar values as the general Swedish population. American millennials score highest on patriotism, achievement and self reliance, which is partly shared by New Zealand millennials. Swedish millennials score high on gender equality and a stronger role of government.[41]

Global homogeneous markets exist only in the minds of international marketing managers and advertising people. Even people with similar lifestyles do not behave as a consistent group of purchasers because they do not share the same values. Yes, there are young people and yuppies (young urban professionals), millennials, rich people and graying populations who have economic and demographic aspects in common, but marketing communications cannot use similar motives and arguments because their targets do not have the same values. This is demonstrated by ownership of luxury products as measured by the European Media and Marketing Survey. The high-income European target, consisting of people who read international media, is not one homogeneous, cross-border target group for high-touch and high-tech luxury articles. Expenditures on expensive luxury articles by this high-income group in Europe vary strongly. The differences can only be explained by cultural variables. (More about this is discussed in Chapter 8 of this book.)

Within nations, lifestyle segmentation is useful, as it adds value to economic and demographic segmentation. For cross-national marketing, the concept is less applicable because value differences of national culture are overriding. It may be that only very small groups of people, such as the NYLON[42] – jet setters who live between New York and London – have some common habits with respect to restaurants and theaters visited. This is relevant only for a limited number of products and services. Even if across countries certain groups of people can be defined by common ownership of some products, the motives for buying these products vary so strongly that for developing effective marketing programs across countries these lifestyle distinctions are not useful. (Differences in buying motives and their relationship with culture are discussed in Chapters 5 and 8 of this book.)

Business people are generally considered to be a 'culture-free group' because of assumed rational decision making as compared with consumer decision making, but decision making by business people, like many business habits, is also culture bound. Whereas the French and the Belgians will prefer meeting in a restaurant for lunch, the Dutch will prefer meeting in the office with some sandwiches.

Digital Media

The new media have facilitated doing business and intensified existing behavior. Satellites, mobile phones, and the Internet are helping people in developing countries to better their lives. Faster information by satellite (as in Figure 1.2) about prices for buying and selling has helped farmers in India, but it hasn't made them dress as farmers do in the United States.

Figure 1.2   **Information by satellite in India. Photograph Gerard Foekema**

Expectations of the Internet were that it would homogenize people's values. In the year 2000, Nicholas Negroponte of the Massachusetts Institute of Technology declared that 'thanks to the Internet the children of the future are not going to know what nationalism is.'[43] Bill Clinton was quoted as saying 'the Internet, with foreign involvement, would eventually bring democracy to the Middle Kingdom,' but as yet, that hasn't happened. Indeed, Internet diffusion has been correlated with democracy, but positive democratic effects of the Internet have primarily been observed in countries that were already developed and at least partially democratic. The Internet amplifies and modifies existing patterns of governmental conflict and cooperation. In many developing and non-democratic countries, access to the Internet is limited by filtration software, state laws, self-censorship, cost, speed, and other factors.[44]

Whereas in the Western world, the adoption of the Internet is bottom-up, in Asian countries it is pushed and controlled by governments. In 1999 the government of Taiwan wanted 50,000 companies to be online by 2001, and in Thailand a law was passed requiring all export and import documents to go online before 2000.[45] In Korea, the government saw to it that all Korean households have a broadband connection.

The Internet is not a homogenizing factor. Instead, there is growing demand for the ability to adapt language and advertising and to apply local laws based on the geographic locations of individual Internet users. The expectation of convergence has caused many to ignore that the basic principles of effective communication also apply to the new media.[46]

The Internet may change some of people's habits, but it does not change people's values. It confirms and enhances existing values, habits, and practices. Where people are used to many interpersonal contacts, they also use more social media. Like the old media, the new digital media can be viewed as extensions of human beings including their cultural values and behavior.

An Asian example of adoption of the Internet for a culture-specific activity was the Bandai i-service in Japan. In Japan, cartoon magazines have always been very popular. One of the first, most popular services to the subscribers of NTT DoCoMo's i-service (one of the early Internet services by mobile phone) was by Bandai, allowing subscribers to download cartoon characters to their mobile phones.[47]

Mobile communication carries the potential to enhance *economic development* by facilitating the circulation of useful information for business, education, healthcare or governance-related information. However, the idea that people use the phone to obtain useful information has been challenged. In many places mobile phones are just used for mundane communication and not to access so-called useful information. Expectations that the mobile phone would fundamentally change people's behavior or bring societal change have not been met. For example, some expected that the mobile phone would bring people to communicate outside their community.

In Africa the mobile phone can be best compared to the role of the 'talking drum'[48] and thus continues older modes of communication more than satisfying information hunger. Also in Africa the mobile phone is not necessarily used to bring about new connections; it often has merely intensified existing relations than created extended networks with new and far away relations. In Kerala in India mobile communication mainly has created cohesion within the sphere of the familiar, a phenomenon called *bounded solidarity*. A comparison of relationship contacts between 2002 and 2007 when the mobile phone penetration had increased from fewer than one-third having a mobile phone to 96 percent in 2007, found that relationships had become more concentrated among friends and family in the local area, and foreign ties had decreased. In this context the mobile phone is a tool of the intimate sphere, strengthening the bonds between family and friends.[49]

Online sellers are not changing people's preferences. They are selling things that people already buy. Online selling is mainly a new retail method. Across cultures similar differences in product buying via the Internet are found as via conventional retail channels.[50]

Universalism

At the root of many assumptions about convergence is universalistic thinking. By the term *convergence*, people often mean Westernization, whereby 'Western' usually is American. Trends spotted in the United States are indiscriminately extended to other areas where different circumstances and habits will prevent their materializing. An example is a statement like, 'In Western society 15% of meals eaten outside the home are in the car.'[51] Dashboard dining is a typical American habit that is alien to most people of Europe and is unlikely to become a European habit.

Americans, but also northern Europeans, tend to be universalistic in their perception and assumptions. They genuinely think that their values are valid for the whole world and should be shared by all.[52] In contrast, most Asians are particularistic and focus more on the differences than on the similarities. They think their own culture to be so unique that no outsider can understand it. The way the Japanese try to demonstrate their cultural uniqueness in the world is called *nihonjinron*, a body of discourse that demonstrates Japan's cultural identity. A survey by Kazufumi Manabe,[53] a Japanese professor of sociology, shows that 82% of the Japanese are interested in the subject and read about it in the media, and 63% think foreigners are incapable of completely understanding Japanese culture.

In an interview, *Newsweek*'s George Wehrfritz asked a journalist for the official Xinhua News Agency which stories upset Chinese young people. The answer was:

The Western press is always talking about human rights. To you in the United States, human rights mean the right to be elected president, change your government or establish a political party. But to 1.3 billion Chinese people, human rights means the right to be with family and friends, the opportunity to make money and go to school and have access to good health care.[54]

From the Western point of view, democracy and human rights should be universal, and these are the regular topics that pop up in many articles by American journalists. This selective focus annoys many Chinese. The reaction by the Chinese is that they are depicted as slaves with no freedom.

Many international marketing managers are convinced that their own ideas or practices represent universal wisdom and try to impose them on everybody. Most global advertising agencies and many multinational companies have Anglo-American management. Their universalism makes them focus on the similarities and ignore the differences. These similarities are often pseudo-similarities.

In advertising, American values are viewed as universally valid, whereas the values of other cultures are not acceptable for advertising in the United States. Although Americans easily export their marketing and advertising concepts abroad, they rarely take an ad campaign from abroad into the United States.

Universalism can also be the cause of mistaking habits or values of one European country for all of them, for example, taking the United Kingdom as representative of Europe or categorizing all European countries as hierarchical societies,[55] whereas the differences between European countries with respect to hierarchical thinking and acting are large. Another mistake is grouping Europe into Nordic and Latin, or Mediterranean, groups or grouping the countries of the Benelux. There are important cultural differences between countries in Europe that influence consumer behavior, also between the Mediterranean cultures, for example, Italy and Spain. In Europe no two countries are more different than Belgium and the Netherlands, although they share a language and a border. Yet companies tend to take the countries together, present them as the Benelux, and extend research findings for Belgium to the Netherlands or vice versa.

A problem that reinforces universalistic thinking is lack of knowledge of other countries and cultures. A previous boss of Coca-Cola, Doug Ivester, after a contamination incident in Belgium, was said to have dismissed the problem with the comment: 'Where the fuck is Belgium?'[56] CEOs, when traveling, hardly meet the average consumer. It is easy to pretend everybody is the same when you are at the top of a company and business partners are inclined to agree with you to avoid conflicts.

Lack of knowledge of separate countries makes people also see more similarities than there actually are. In international marketing, Americans tend to view all Europeans as similar; Europeans tend to view all Asians as similar; and Asians, when referring to Western culture, usually mean American culture.

Language is a related cause of misunderstanding. Some 380 million people speak English as their first language and perhaps two thirds as many as their second. Yet, understanding of English as a second language tends to be overestimated. In 2001 nearly half of all EU citizens spoke no language other than their own,[57] and 31% of young Europeans age 15–24 spontaneously claimed not to know any foreign languages.[58] Some expect that the advance of English as a global language will damage or destroy local culture. However, just adding English to one's native language doesn't change one's culture. The problem is actually the native English speakers who think that use of English by others elsewhere makes them also think like native English speakers. Although the English language is widely spoken in many countries, it often is not spoken well enough to understand a native English or American speaker, which can cause misunderstanding in international advertising.

An example of difficult to interpret use of the English language was a UK commercial for Bacardi Breezer in spring 2002 that was also aired in the Netherlands, referring to a 'tomcat.' The word for tomcat (*kater*) in the Netherlands is used for what is a 'hangover' in the English language. This was probably not intended to be the effect of the alcoholic beverage advertised. In addition, the tomcat is asked whether he has been 'chasing birds' (which means chasing women in English), the sort of word play that is beyond the understanding of most inhabitants of the Netherlands.

Although English language understanding across Europe generally is overestimated, apart from English language brand names, many commercials show English words, songs or short phrases in the body copy. But the degree to which English is used varies between countries.[59] (Language as one of the mental processes related to culture is a topic discussed in Chapter 6 of this book.)

Finally, universalism has led to the application of Anglo-American marketing theories worldwide. This is not due to American imperialism but to the fact that advanced marketing and advertising practice and theory originated in the United States. Not only have these theories been exported to other cultures, practitioners and academics elsewhere have enthusiastically copied practices and theories from the United States without realizing that not all these concepts and theories are equally valid in their own countries. This has happened in all regions of the world, both in Europe and in Asia. In developing countries in particular, because Western concepts are regarded as 'proven,' Western ideas are readily acceptable to clients of advertising agencies.[60] With increased marketing literacy, people in business have slowly started to understand that not all American concepts and theories can be applied to their own cultures.

Sense of History

Another cause of mistakes is lack of a sense of history. Many recent phenomena are perceived as new, whereas they are often only a new format of the past. Knowledge of history helps to understand phenomena that seem to be new but are not. Those who hadn't known people's behavior in the former European Eastern bloc prior to the Soviet occupation thought new behavior resulted from Western capitalism or globalization after the Communists had left, whereas, in reality, people just resumed their old ways.

The following is a reader's reaction to an article in *Newsweek* about patterns of Hungarian behavior that were seen to be the result of globalization:

In your insightful article, you write of the Hungarian executive who 'thinks nothing of popping over to Vienna to hear U2 or Whitney Houston.' This may not be as much a sign of globalization as a return to the way things were. In their day, our great-grandparents thought nothing of heading to Vienna for a night at the opera. They took the train, not their Alfa Romeo, and listened to Verdi, not Whitney. The difference is that back then not only the elite were able to afford this kind of entertainment.[61]

Mate Hegedus, Budapest, Hungary

Austrians and Hungarians have much in common because Austria and Hungary have belonged to one empire (the Habsburg Empire), which makes it understandable that people easily and frequently travel through each other's countries. Only the Communist occupation prevented that temporarily.

Behavior that is understandable in the context of history is often interpreted as new by the historically ignorant. Many differences between countries can be traced to history. What most people mean by globalization is increasing flows of trade and investment between parts of the world and between countries, but many nations have been global from their origin.

One of the most important themes in the history of world economy is the balance between nationalism and internationalism, not in the ideological sense but in organization. The historian George Holmes[62] states that the economic relationship of the modern world existed in embryo within late medieval Europe. The city-states of the fourteenth century, such as Venice, Florence, and Genoa, were republics, where state and commercialism were integrated. Venice provided its trading nobility with a state-controlled shipping service. There were Italian trading communities in every city from London to Alexandria. Marco Polo, who at the end of the thirteenth century described China for Westerners, was one of a family of Venetian merchants. At that time journeys by Italian merchants across Asia from the Black Sea to China were commonplace. Venice, a city without much industry, came to control an empire through trading enterprise. The most famous commercial family of the fifteenth century, the Medici, established a network of branches at Rome, Geneva, Bruges, London, Lyons, Naples, and Milan. They were experts in the international exchange business, transferring money by letters of exchange from one part of Europe to another.

Increased worldwide interconnectedness has intensified global trade, money exchange, and flow of information. Individuals like Bill Gates or Richard Branson, or families like the Wallenbergs or Guccis, can span the globe with their trade like the Medici did in their times on a smaller scale. What has changed is that modern branding and media have made the phenomena of globalization more visual. Family names have become brands.

Technological advances have always played a role in altering the economic importance of certain areas. Advanced technology came from the Silicon Valley in the twentieth century, and it came from China in the fifteenth century, where it may come from again in the twenty-first century. The degree to which some nations or areas have embraced new technology has changed their structural role in the world economy. During the Middle Ages, a reasonable trade balance existed between Christian Europe and the Arabian world. Gold and silver flowed eastward, and spices and precious stones went westward. However, a shortage of gold caused problems for Florence and Genoa, which needed gold to produce coins for their trade activities. Gold had to be obtained elsewhere. The Portuguese were the only people interested in traveling further afield than the usual kind of discovery voyages. Due to its geographical position, Portugal could only expand via the sea. Financed by Genoa, the Portuguese set out on their voyages of discovery. Europeans traveled the world in order to obtain exotic commerce and to trade. Looking at China during that same period, it seems that Europe and China had similar population levels between the thirteenth and sixteenth centuries. From the second century to the fifteenth century, China had a technological advantage. It was only around 1450 that Europe began to increase its technological development. One reason was political: Europe could not afford to lag behind in the development of its arms industry because of many wars between the different states. In China, on the other hand, the government decided to restrict the development of the arms industry in order to improve internal peace.

The Portuguese and the Chinese went on their voyages of discovery in the same period. After 18 years, however, the Chinese stopped abruptly with the death of eunuch-admiral Cheng Ho in 1434. The main reason lay in an important cultural difference: the Chinese did not travel to *obtain* something but to *bring* something. By bringing gifts of high quality to faraway countries, they wanted to assure those countries of their superiority. They were not interested in colonizing because they believed that they were already the whole world. When their treasuries were depleted due to the escapades of Cheng Ho, the discovery voyages were stopped and China cut itself off.[63]

Historical, political, and cultural factors explain the economic development of nations that have played an integrated role in global trade. That has not changed. Despite the existence of a World Trade Organization, there still are trade wars between nations. What has changed is that there are no more military wars between commercial communities. The armies of the government do not support the cola wars.

Many current global developments can be better understood by knowing the history of global trade and the varying national contexts in which global trade has developed. Habits of inhabitants of India can be explained by the former British colonial influence. How China in the far past dealt with technological development can explain how that country deals with new developments in the present. The Chinese people are, as in the past, eager to embrace new technology, but a historically strongly centralized government wishes to guide (control in Western eyes) the people in the way they adopt it.

When entering new markets with new products or brands, a sense of history can help. In a country like the Czech Republic, where people have been drinking fruit juice and herbal teas for centuries, it will not be easy to change their habits to drinking cola. Perceptions of brands are often formed by their history in the marketplace. In 1996 in China, Panasonic was seen as the leading electronics brand in Beijing, Shanghai, Guangzhou, and Chengdu, according to a survey by advertising agency Grey, but ironically, Panasonic was introduced to Chinese consumers when the manufacturer shipped a load of what were actually outdated cassette players to the country in the early 1980s. For many Chinese households, Panasonic was their first foreign brand.[64]

Branding and Advertising: From Global to Multi-Local

The discussion about the advantages and disadvantages of standardizing advertising across countries has been a long one. One of the most frequently heard advantages is cost reduction because of economies of scale. Other reasons are quality control and consistency in an era when many media reach various countries at the same time. It is good international business practice to want to control one's communications, but standardization of global branding and marketing communications is wrong in principle and impossible in practice. Global advertising can only be effective if there are global consumers with universal values. As consumers' values and behavior vary across cultures, global standardized advertising is not equally effective in all markets. Much of it is wasted in markets where consumer values are different from the values of the advertising campaign. Because of this, even Saatchi & Saatchi, the advertising agency that was first to embrace the concept of global advertising, changed their opinion. Kevin Roberts, CEO worldwide of Saatchi & Saatchi, stated in 2002,

Anyone who wants to go global has to understand the local—their own local and the locals of all their customers. People live in the local. I've never met a global consumer. I never expect to. We define ourselves by our differences. It's called identity—self, family, nation.[65]

In an interview in *BusinessWeek,* Martin Sorrell, CEO of WPP group, says that the idea that globalization would lead consumers to buy goods and services the same ways everywhere now looks to be flawed. According to Sorrell, truly global products and services such as soft drinks or computers only account for 15% of WPP's revenues. What has been going on may not have been globalization but the Americanization of markets.[66]

The old marketing paradigm says that markets are people. There may be global products, but there are no global people. There may be global brands, but there are no global motives for buying these brands. There may be global markets, but most consumption patterns are local. Douglas Daft, Coca-Cola's CEO, stated in 2000, 'People don't buy drinks globally.'[67] Coca-Cola is one of the brands that are frequently used as examples of longtime successful global advertising. Probably the most important success factor of Coca-Cola, however, has been its efficient distribution system, not its global advertising. For a long time Coca-Cola's main goal was 'to be within an arm's reach of desire,'[68] and its longtime slogan was 'Always, everywhere Coca-Cola.' In the year 2000 the Coca-Cola Company, which had until then been the prototype of a global advertiser, decided to get closer to local markets because of declining profitability. CEO Douglas Daft was quoted in the *Financial Times,* 'We kept standardizing our practices, while local sensitivity had become absolutely essential to success.'[69] According to Daft, the general direction is away from global advertising. 'We need to make our advertising as relevant as possible to the local market.'[70] This approach is a better way to control the marketing process than exporting universal brand values to global publics without knowing what the takeout will be. As the sociologist–anthropologist David Howes says,

> The assumption that goods like Coca-Cola, on entering a culture, will retain and communicate the values they are accorded by their culture of origin must be questioned. Often these goods are transformed in accordance with the values of the receiving culture.'[71]

Many of the large multinationals that have standardized their operations and brands since the 1990s have seen their profits decline because centralized control lacks local sensitivity. In the mid-1990s, Ford centralized global management. 'That move, Ford execs now say, took Ford of Europe's focus off local strategy. As a result it lacks competitive offerings in segments that make up 35 percent of the European market.'[72] The continental European clothing retailer C&A standardized buying and advertising in Europe in 1997. In June 2000 the company decided to close all 109 shops in the United Kingdom and Ireland because of substantial losses. The taste of the British and Irish consumers is different from that of continental

Europeans.[73] Also, tastes vary across continental Europe. Casual clothing, for example, sells better in the Netherlands than in Germany. At the end of the year 2000, C&A had relocalized both buying and advertising. The British retail chain Marks & Spencer, which until then had made different advertising campaigns for each country where it operated, changed to uniform advertising for the whole of Europe. At the end of 2001, Marks & Spencer withdrew from the European continent. Differences in local tastes not only prevent selling standard products; they also affect the way retailers sell their goods. In 1996 the American retailer Wal-Mart set up efficient, clean supercenters in Indonesia, only to find that Indonesians preferred Matahari, the shabbier shop next door, which reminded shoppers of a street market where they could haggle.[74] Many international companies underestimate the strength of local products in the markets they enter. And they overestimate the value of their reputations.

Perhaps one of the causes of success of McDonald's in foreign markets is the fact that, in addition to maintaining a strong brand image and consistent service standards around the world, its product offer has a local touch and its advertising has been mostly local. Examples are the Kiwi burger in New Zealand; the Maharaja Mac in India; the Prosperity burger in Malaysia; the Teriyaki burger in Japan; the McKroket in the Netherlands; McLaks, a grilled salmon burger, in Norway; and the Croque McDo in France that refers to the popular French 'Croque Monsieur,' a hot ham and cheese sandwich. Advertising by McDonald's tied into local habits, values, and symbols. In 2001, for example, advertising for McDonald's in France tied into 'Asterix and Obelisk,' the most famous historical cartoon of the nation. Figure 1.3 shows a few pictures from this commercial.

Figure 1.3 **McDonald's advertising in France**

In Asia, McDonald's follows cultural habits and uses celebrities. Figure 1.4 shows pictures from a Japanese commercial that is hardly understandable to outsiders. We see a young woman putting on all sorts of different hats and in the end eating a hamburger. What is special is that her name is Yuri Ebihara. McDonald's Japan annually has a special fillet-o-fish with shrimp inside, which is called *ebi fillet-o*. *Ebi* means shrimp in Japanese. Since Ebihara is such a famous model, and her name is actually a bit strange, including the word *ebi*, anybody in Japan can easily relate Ebihara to *ebi fillet-o*, even without saying anything about the hamburger.

Figure 1.4   **McDonald's advertising in Japan**

Instead of consistency, flexibility will become increasingly important in global market-ing. The strength of many national or multi-local brands is demonstrated by the *Reader's Digest* surveys, 'European Trusted Brands,'[75] conducted annually since 2000 and asking respondents which brands they trusted most for several product categories. There are sev-eral national brands that have remained strong in the face of the power of the large multi-nationals. These are national brands that are either old or include important national values in their advertising, or both. In France, in 2000 the French car brand Renault was most trusted; in Germany and Austria it was the German brand Volkswagen; and in the Czech Republic, it was Skoda, an originally Czech car brand. The most trusted car brand in India was the Indian brand Maruti. In 2017 the car best sold in France was Renault, in Germany and Austria it was Volkswagen, in Italy Fiat, and in India Maruti-Suzuki.[76]

The trend from global to local is reinforced by localization of media. Many originally global or pan-regional television channels have localized, that is, adapted to local languages and offered local ad windows to advertisers. In 2018 there were six variants of CNN Inter-national: CNN International Asia Pacific, CNN International Latin America, CNN Inter-national Europe/Middle East/Africa, CNN International Middle East, CNN International North America, CNN International South Asia. CNN is available on television in several different languages, such as in Spanish on CNN+, Spain; in Turkish on CNN Turk, Turkey; and in German on n-tv, Germany. On the web it is available in more languages.

Localization makes it increasingly important for marketing and advertising people to understand the influence of culture. Cultural effects are often less obvious and more diffi-cult to research than economic consequences, but they can be more pervasive and serious in the long run.

Consumer Behavior

Consumer behavior can be defined[77] as the study of the processes involved when people select, purchase, use, or dispose of products, services, ideas, or experiences to satisfy needs and desires. In this definition, consumer behavior is viewed as a process that includes the issues that influence the consumer before, during, and after a purchase. In some models of consumer behavior, the elements of consumer behavior are classified according to the academic disciplines of psychology and sociology, from which consumer behavior theory borrows. Whereas psychology studies human behavior at the individual level, sociology studies human behavior at group level. But culture operates at each level. Personality and culture are inextricably bound together. How people learn is studied at the individual level, but what and how human beings learn varies with the society in which they live.

Consumer behavior theories are rooted in Western psychology that has mostly limited its concepts and empirical findings to only a small part of the [Western] world and has largely ignored the influence of the role of culture.[78] Subjects in 96% of investigations are people from communities comprising only 12% of the world's population. Yet theories based on these investigations have been viewed as universally valid.[79] These theories are not necessarily applicable for understanding how consumers behave in other parts of the world. For example, much of Western psychology may be irrelevant in Asia.[80]

To understand culture's consequences for consumer behavior, culture must be integrated in the various aspects of consumer behavior theory. Ideally, theories of consumer behavior are developed within cultures, studying people's behavior within each nation. For comparing cultures, variables and constructs must be found that allow discovering how these cultures or groups of cultures are different from or similar to each other. Following this 'etic' approach (see also Chapter 2) includes the risk of overlooking some unique aspects of unique cultures, but it is the most practical approach and is common to current research in cross-cultural psychology and other comparative social sciences.[81] This book approaches consumer behavior across cultures by reviewing various existing theories and integrating culture in these theories. Instead of categorizing behavior aspects according to the separate disciplines, we need an integrated view of the individual, culture, and society. This approach is reflected in the model that structures the various components of consumer behavior process described in this book.

A Model of Cross-Cultural Consumer Behavior

The components of human behavior can be summarized as *what people are* ('Who am I?'), the *self* and *personality*, defined by people's attributes and traits ('What sort of person am I?'), *how people feel, how people think and learn,* and *what people do.* The terms of the social sciences for feeling, learning, and doing are *affect, cognition*, and *behavior*. These elements are included in the definition of consumer behavior of the American Marketing Association as 'the dynamic interaction of affect and cognition, behavior, and the environment by which human beings conduct the exchange aspects of their lives.'[82]

For understanding the influence of culture on consumer behavior, marketers must integrate culture in the various components of human behavior. US marketing scholars Manrai and Manrai[83] point out that in the definitions, culture is a complex concept. Many items defined as consequences of culture are also included in the definition of culture, either as artifacts (e.g., food, dress) or as abstract elements (e.g., values and norms). These must be separated, so that consumer behavior consequences of culture can be specified beyond other types of behavior that are implicitly included in the definition of culture itself. Cultural values should be included as an integrated part of the consumer and not as an environmental factor. In this book also *national income* is not viewed as an environmental factor as in so many textbooks, so I do not use the term *economic environment.* Income interacts with the consumer's values and culture, in particular in post-scarcity societies. In this I follow Süerdem,[84] who defines economic rationality as a 'value system' appropriate for a certain social system.

The model presented in Figure 1.5 structures the cultural components of the *person* in terms of consumer *attributes* and *processes,* and the cultural components of *behavior* in con-sumer *behavior domains.* Wealth is influenced by culture, but in turn it influences culture, so *income* is placed in a separate box, shown as interacting with the culture of the consumer.

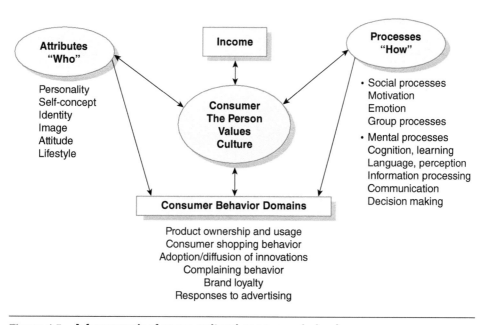

Figure 1.5   A framework of cross-cultural consumer behavior

SOURCE: Adapted from Manrai and Manrai (1996, 2001)[85]

Organization of the Book

This book is organized according to the framework shown in Figure 1.5. It discusses topics found in American consumer behavior textbooks, but it is structured in a different way.

Core differences in the approach of this book are with respect to the influence of culture on the self and information processing. In US-based textbooks, the self and information processing are described from the perspective of an individualistic culture only. The group is viewed as an external factor and not as part of the self. Information is described as an instrument that empowers consumers with the ability to make informed decisions.[86] Culture is usually viewed as merely an environmental influence on consumer behavior instead of interiorized in the person. Another major difference is that most textbooks start with the decision-making process, whereas this book views decision making as a mental process, and influences on decision making are found all through the book. Consumer behavior textbooks of US origin – apart from an introductory chapter that includes varying topics in different textbooks – generally consist of the following major parts: (1) consumer decision making; (2) the consumer as an individual; (3) group and cultural influences. Table 1.1 shows how these topics are covered in this book.

Table 1.1   **Comparison of organization of topics in US consumer behavior textbooks and in *Consumer Behavior and Culture***

General Consumer Behavior Textbooks	Topics	Consumer Behavior and Culture (Chapter Number)	
Consumer decision making	Buying, consumption	(8)	Consumer behavior domains
	Brand loyalty	(8)	Consumer behavior domains
	Individual decision making	(6)	Mental processes
	High-, low-involvement decision making/processing	(6)	Mental processes
	Situational influences on decision making	(5)	Social processes
		(8)	Consumer behavior domains
	Dissatisfaction	(8)	Consumer behavior domains
	Shopping behavior		
Consumer as individuals	Motivation and values	(5)	Social processes
	The self, personality, image, lifestyle	(4)	The consumer: Attributes
		(4)	The consumer: Attributes
	Attitude	(6)	Mental processes
	Perception, learning, memory	(6)	Mental processes

General Consumer Behavior Textbooks	Topics	Consumer Behavior and Culture (Chapter Number)	
Group and cultural influences	Categorization	(6)	Mental processes
	Information processing	(3)	Convergence/divergence in consumer behavior
	Demographics		
	Cultural values	(2)	Values and culture
	Group influence, roles of group members, reference groups	(5)	Social processes
		(5)	Social processes
	Influentials, opinion leaders	(7)	Culture and communication
	Household decision making	(7)	Culture and communication
	Group communication	(7)	Culture and communication
	Link values-behavior	(7)	Culture and communication
	Diffusion of innovations		
	Opinion leaders		

Conclusion

The topics reviewed in this chapter illustrate assumptions generally found in academic literature and in practice. The assumptions are that there are global consumers or global communities with universal values who can be reached by global advertising. Reality is different, and examples are given of companies that have standardized their products and communications with bad results. Global advertising was conceived from the assumption that consumer behavior across countries would converge with converging media, technology, and national wealth. There is little evidence to support this thesis. Instead, with converging wealth, when people increasingly live in post-scarcity societies, the differences become more pronounced. At the root of misunderstanding are universalism, the spread of the English language, and lack of a sense of history. For comparing post-scarcity societies, income can no longer serve as an explaining variable, and culture becomes the new paradigm.

Notes

1. M. McLuhan, *Understanding Media: The Extensions of Man* (McGraw-Hill, New York, 1964), pp. 225, 268, 276.
2. J. Bullmore, 'Alice in Disneyland: A creative view of international advertising,' in J.P. Jones (ed.), *International Advertising Realities and Myths* (Sage, Thousand Oaks, CA, 2000), p. 48.

3. J. Rossant, 'A common identity for Europe? You better believe it,' *BusinessWeek* (20 November 2000), p. 72.

4. H. Assael, *Consumer Behavior: A Strategic Approach* (Houghton Mifflin, Boston, 2004), p. 378.

5. Ibid., p. 386.

6. M.L. Solomon, *Consumer Behavior: Buying, Having and Being*, 12th edn (Pearson Education Limited, 2018), p. 28.

7. www.trendsmap.com shows a worldwide map of Twitter trending topics. This observation was of 17 January 2018.

8. M. Isaac, 'Facebook overhauls new Feed to Focus on what friends and family share,' *The New York Times* (11 January 2018). Available at: www.nytimes.com/2018/01/11/technology/facebook-news-feed.html (accessed 17 January 2018).

9. R. Robertson, 'Mapping the global condition: Globalization as the central concept,' in M. Featherstone (ed.), *Global Culture* (Sage, London, 1990), pp. 15–30.

10. *Unesco*. Available at: www.unesco.org/education/tisf/mods/theme_c/mod18.html (accessed 1 May 2017).

11. 'Financial indicators,' *The Economist* (27 September 1997), p.123; 'Worldbeater, Inc,' *The Economist* (22 November 1997), p. 108.

12. *Globalisation* (Flash Eurobarometer report 151b, October–November 2003); *Public Opinion in the European Union* (Standard Eurobarometer 87, Autumn 2017); *How Companies Influence Our Society: Citizens' View* (Flash Eurobarometer report 363, 2013).

13. R. Edelman, 'An implosion of trust, 6 AM' (March 7, 2017). Available at: https://www.edelman.com/post/an-implosion-of-trust

14. G. Hofstede, *Culture's Consequences*, 2nd edn (Sage, Thousand Oaks, CA, 2001).

15. S. Askegaard and L. Scott, 'Consumer culture theory: The ironies of history,' *Marketing Theory*, 13, 2 (2013), pp. 139–147.

16. D.L. Alden, J.B.E.M. Steenkamp, and R. Batra, 'Brand positioning through advertising in Asia, North America, and Europe: The role of global consumer culture,' *Journal of Marketing*, 63 (1999), pp. 75–87.

17. M. Featherstone, *Consumer Culture and Postmodernism* (Sage, London, 1991).

18. A. Giddens, *Runaway World* (Routledge, New York, 2000).

19. European Media and Marketing Survey (Synovate, Amsterdam, 2007).

20. *European Audiovisual Observatory*. Available at: www.obs.coe.int/about/oea/pr/berlinale2009.html (accessed 18 April 2009).

21. T. Levitt, 'The globalization of markets,' *Harvard Business Review*, May–June (1983), pp. 2–11.

22. A. Süerdem, 'Social de(re)construction of mass culture: Making (non)sense of consumer behavior,' *International Journal of Research in Marketing*, 11 (1993), pp. 423–443.

23. J.C. Usunier, 'Consommation: Quand global rime avec local (Consumption: When global rhymes with local),' *Revue Française de gestion*, 110 (1996), pp. 100–116.

24. A. Inkeles, *One World Emerging?: Convergence and Divergence in Industrial Societies* (Westview, Boulder, CO, 1998).

25. *Survey on the Attitudes of Europeans Towards Tourism* (Flash Eurobarometer report 258, 2008).

26. *Young Europeans in 2001* (Eurobarometer report 151, 2001).

27. R. White, 'International advertising. How far can it fly?,' in J.P. Jones (ed.), *International Advertising* (Sage, Thousand Oaks, CA, 1998), pp. 29–40.

28. S. Theil, 'Not made for walking,' *Newsweek* (1 November 2004), pp. 36–37.

29. J. Nancy, *European Youth in 2016* (Special Eurobarometer of the European Parliament, European Parliamentary Research Service PE 582.005, May 2016).

30. J. Allman, 'Variety is the spice of Latin life,' *M&M Europe* (January 1997), pp. 49–50.

31. P. Mooney, 'Learning the old ways,' *Newsweek* (27 May 2002), p. 29.

32. Assael, *Consumer Behavior*, p. 386.

33. S.P. Huntington, *The Clash of Civilizations and the Remaking of World Order* (Simon & Schuster, New York, 1996), p. 57.

34. Eurostat, *Being Young in Europe Today – Digital World* (European Commission, 2015).

35. S. Lau, 'I want my MTV, but in Mandarin, please,' *Admap* (March 2001), p. 34.

36. P. Cooper, 'Western at the weekends,' *Admap* (17 October 1994), pp. 18–21.

37. E. Malkin, 'X-ers,' *Advertising Age International* (17 October 1994), pp. 1–15.

38. M. Dijkgraaf, 'Interview with Amélie Nothomb,' *NRC Handelsblad* (17 December 1999), p. 5.

39. *Insights 88* (ACNielsen, New York, November 1998), p. 8.

40. 'Advance of the amazons,' *The Economist* (22 July 2000), p. 69.

41. C.D. Schewe, K. Debevec, T.J. Madden, W.D. Diamond, A. Parment, and A. Murphy, '"If you've seen one, you've seen them all!" Are young millennials the same worldwide?,' *Journal of International Consumer Marketing*, 25, 1 (2013), pp. 3–15.

42. 'High rollers,' *The Economist* (16 June 2001), p. 43.

43. 'What the Internet cannot do,' *The Economist* (19 August 2000), p. 9; 'Wired China,' *The Economist* (22 July 2000), pp. 24–25.

44. D. Groshek, 'The democratic effects of the Internet, 1994–2003: A cross-national inquiry of 152 countries,' *The International Communication Gazette*, 71, 3 (2009), pp. 115–136.

45. J. Moore and B. Einhorn, 'A biz-to-biz e-boom,' *BusinessWeek* (25 October 1999), pp. 30–31.

46. L. Percy, 'Marketing communication in evolution,' *Admap* (February 2001), p. 31.

47. *Nikkei Trendy* (March 2000).

48. J.S. Archambault, 'Breaking up "because of the phone" and the transformative potential of information in Southern Mozambique,' *New Media & Society*, 13, 3 (2011), pp. 444-456.

49. A. Palackal, P.N. Mbatia, D-B. Dzorgbo, R.B. Duque, M.A. Ynalvez, and W.M. Shrum, 'Are mobile phones changing social networks? A longitudinal study of core networks in Kerala,' *New Media & Society*, 13, 3 (2011), pp. 391–410.

50. K. Goodrich and M.K. De Mooij, 'New technology mirrors old habits: Online buying mirrors cross-national variance of conventional buying,' *Journal of International Consumer Marketing*, 23, 3–4 (2011), pp. 246–259.

51. C. Nuttall, 'Trend-spotters don't have to follow fashion,' *M&M Europe* (September 2001), p. 18.

52. N.J. Adler, *International Dimensions of Organizational Behavior*, 2nd edn (Wadsworth, Belmont, CA, 1991), p. 47.

53. K. Manabe, 'Cultural nationalism in Japan,' in H. Vinken, J. Soeters and P. Ester (eds), *Comparing Cultures: Dimensions of Culture in a Comparative Perspective* (Brill, Leiden-Boston, 2004), p. 46.

54. G. Wehrfritz, 'The great stone curtain. Do American journalists obscure the real China?', *Newsweek* (17 February 1997), p. 39.

55. J. Rossant, 'Old world, new mandate,' *Business Week* (31 January 2001), p. 49.

56. 'Who's wearing the trousers?', *The Economist* (8 September 2001), p. 29.

57. 'English is still on the march,' *The Economist* (24 February 2001), p. 33; 'A world empire by other means,' *The Economist* (22 December 2001), pp. 33–35.

58. *Young Europeans in 2001*.

59. M. Raedts, N. Dupré, J. Hendrickx, and S. Debrauwere, 'English in television commercials in Belgium, France, Italy, the Netherlands and Spain,' *World Englishes*, 34, 4 (2015). DOI: 10.1111/weng.12161.

60. 'Interview with Jimmy Lam, Regional Executive Creative Director and Chairman of D'Arcy Greater China,' *New Sunday Times (Malaysia)* (12 November 2000), p. 12.

61. 'Letters to the editor, re: "Globalization in Eastern Europe," September 25. Special Report on Prague's IMF summit,' *Newsweek* (23 October 2000).

62. G. Holmes, *Europe: Hierarchy and Revolt 1320–1450* (William Collins and Sons, Glasgow, 1975), p. 119.

63. I. Wallerstein, *The Modern World System* (Vol. I) (Academic Press, New York, 1974).

64. E. Liang, 'Solving the consumer jigsaw puzzle,' *Asian Marketing* (12 July 1996), p. 10.

65. K. Roberts, 'Running on empty,' *M&M Europe* (January 2002), p. 8.

66. K. Capell 'Martin Sorrell on the ad game,' *Business Week* (7 July 2003), p. 23.

67. 'Debunking Coke,' *The Economist* (12 February 2000), p. 74.

68. 'New Doug, old tricks,' *The Economist* (11 December 1999), p. 59.

69. D. Daft, 'Back to classic Coke. Personal view,' *Financial Times* (27 March 2000). Available at: http://news.ft.com (accessed 30 March 2000).

70. A.M. Crawford, 'New Coke chief cans "universal" message,' *M&M Europe* (March 2000), p. 8.

71. Ibid., p. 5.

72. D. Welch and C. Terney, 'Can the Mondeo get Ford back into the race?', *Business Week* (16 October 2000), p. 29.

73. 'C&A heft alle Britse winkels op,' *NRC Handelsblad* (15 June 2000).

74. 'Shopping all over the world,' *The Economist* (19 June 1999), pp. 73–75.

75. *European Trusted Brands* (Reader's Digest, London). Available at: www.rdtrustedbrands.com.

76. E. Cummins, 'This map shows Toyota really does rule the world,' *Inverse* (18 July 2017). Available at: www.inverse.com/article/34315-toyota-dominates-car-brands-by-country.

77. M. Solomon, G. Bamossy, and S. Askegaard, *Consumer Behaviour: A European Perspective* (Pearson Education, London, 1999), p. 8.

78. J.W. Berry, 'Distinguished scholar essay. Global psychology: Implications for cross-cultural research and management,' *Cross Cultural Management*, 22, 3 (2015), pp. 342–355.

79. V.V. Glebkin, 'The problem of cultural-historical typology from the four-level-cognitive-development theory perspective,' *Journal of Cross-Cultural Psychology*, 46, 8 (2015), pp. 1010–1022.

80. A.Miyahara, 'Toward theorizing Japanese interpersonal communication competence from a non-Western perspective,' in F.E. Jandt (ed.), *Intercultural Communication* (Sage, Thousand Oaks, CA, 2004), p. 181.

81. D. Luna and S. Forquer Gupta, 'An integrative framework for cross-cultural consumer behavior,' *International Marketing Review*, 18 (2001), pp. 377–386.

82. Ibid.

83. L.A. Manrai and A.K. Manrai, 'Current issues in cross-cultural and cross-national consumer research,' in L.A. Manrai and A.K. Manrai (eds), *Global Perspectives in Cross-Cultural and Cross-National Consumer Research* (International Business Press/Haworth Press, New York, 1996), pp. 9–22.

84. Süerdem, 'Social de(re)construction of mass culture.'

85. Manrai and Manrai, 'Current issues in cross-cultural'; L.A. Manrai and A.K. Manrai, 'Current issues in the cross-cultural and cross-national consumer research in the new millennium,' *Journal of East-West Business*, 7, 1 (2001), pp. 1–10.

86. Assael, *Consumer Behavior*.

Values and Culture

2

For some time it has been understood that different value orientations cause variations in preferences for products and brands.[1] Values of both consumers and marketers are defined by their culture, hence the importance of understanding the value concept and culture. To understand how culture operates, we have to vocalize it. Models of culture that enable observing and tabulating cultural differences facilitate this. This chapter deals with such models. It describes the value concept, culture, and the various dimensions of culture that can explain consumer behavior differences across nations.

Values

A *value* is defined by Rokeach, one of the early US researchers of values, as

> an enduring belief that one mode of conduct or end-state of existence is preferable to an opposing mode of conduct or end-state of existence. A *value system* is an enduring organization of beliefs concerning preferable modes of conduct or end-states of existence along a continuum of relative importance.[2]

In a value system, values are ordered in priority with respect to other values. This is why some authors use the term *value priority* interchangeably with *values*.

Because values are preferences of one state of being over another, they are often measured on polar scales, for example:

Healthy versus ill

Clean versus dirty

Active versus passive

Optimist versus pessimist

Modern versus traditional

A *value* refers to a single belief of a very specific kind, as opposed to an *attitude* that refers to an organization of several beliefs around a specific object or situation.[3] Values have cognitive, affective, and behavioral components. Although values are expressed in abstract terms, people generally *know* what their preferred 'state of being' is (e.g., being healthy, not ill). Values are *affective* in the sense that people can *feel* emotional about them. A value has a *behavioral* exponent in the sense that it is an intervening variable that leads to *action* when activated.

Rokeach distinguishes two levels of values: terminal values and instrumental values. *Terminal* values refer to desirable end-states of existence. *Instrumental* values refer to desirable modes of conduct; they are motivators to reach end-states of existence. Examples are the instrumental values 'ambitious' and 'capable' that lead to the terminal values 'a comfortable life' and 'a sense of accomplishment.'

The Rokeach Value Survey (RVS) has been used in other cultures, but with different results, in particular with respect to value priorities. Whereas in the United States being honest, ambitious, and responsible have been consistently shown as the most important instrumental values, in China being cheerful, polite, and independent appear to be the most important values. Being cheerful and polite are values of the doctrine of Confucianism.[4]

Values and Norms: The Desired and the Desirable

Values can be distinguished between the values of individuals and collectives or between micro- and macro-level values. Macro-level values are *collective values* – values shared by members of a group – or *cultural values*; micro-level values are individual values, also called *value orientations*.[5] *Cultural values*, the value priorities that characterize a society, are the aggregated value priorities of individuals. *Norms* or *social norms* are what in a society people in general do, or (think they) should do or should not do. In the scholarly literature a distinction is made between *descriptive social norms* that refer to perceptions of how the majority of group members actually behave, what *is* done; and *injunctive social norms* that are about what in-group members *think* what they *approve* of, what *should* or *should not* be done.[6] Norms can be imposed by others, and do not need to correspond with reality.

Value researchers have used varying conceptions of values: (1) values as guiding principles in life, and (2) a value as a preference for one mode of behavior over another. The distinction refers to the *desirable* and the *desired*, or what people think ought to be desired (following societal norms) and what people actually desire – how people *think the world ought to be* versus *what people want for themselves*.[7] The desirable refers to the general norms of a society, the correct ways to behave; it often is worded in terms of right or wrong. The desired relates to choice, to what is important and preferred; it relates to the 'me' and the 'you.' The desirable relates to what is approved or disapproved, to what is good, right, what one ought to do, and what one should agree with; it refers to people in general (see Table 2.1).[8]

Table 2.1   **The desirable versus the desired**

The Desirable	The Desired
The norm, what ought	What people want for themselves
Words	Deeds
Approval, disapproval	Choice
What is good, right	Attractive, preferred
For people in general	For me and for you
Ideology	Pragmatism

Rokeach states that conceptions of the desirable are deliberately excluded from his definition. In his definition of values, he refers to preferable states of being, not to moral principles. When measuring values, asking people for moral guidelines is likely to result in different answers than asking them, directly or indirectly, for their preferred state of being. An example is the question about equality. In some cultures inequality is implicitly accepted in relationships with higher-placed persons (e.g., bosses), yet people tend to say Yes when asked if there should be greater equality between people.

Market researchers Grunert and Muller[9] point at an additional type of interference in research. The desirable can signify something that guides one's day-to-day life, as well as something one wishes to have, but cannot attain given present circumstances. In research we have to distinguish between 'real' life values and 'ideal' life values.

The desired and the desirable do not always overlap, and often are seemingly opposing or paradoxical. Each society has its specific *value paradoxes* as a result of these opposing elements in values.[10] An example is a value found in many lists of values of the United States: 'belonging,' which seems paradoxical in view of the equally important value 'rugged individualism.' An example of a paradoxical element in Chinese culture is the combination of modernity and tradition that go together, whereas from the Western value perspective, it seems the two are opposing values.[11] Understanding the value paradoxes of cultures is of great importance when analyzing advertising, which may focus on the desirable, what should be, but also on what people want for themselves, the desired, for example concerning a value that is perceived to be lacking. For example, in collectivistic cultures where the family is an integrated part of the self, advertising need not focus so much on the importance of the family. In individualistic cultures where family values may be perceived to be lacking, advertising may focus more on the role products play in a desirable happy family life.

Values are Enduring

Values are among the first things children learn, not consciously, but implicitly. Development psychologists believe that by the age of 10, most children have their basic value systems firmly in place.[12] Values are stable through generations. Several studies demonstrate this stability. Yankelovich[13] found that many of Americans' most important traditional values have remained firm and constant over time. Examples are freedom, equality, fairness, achievement, patriotism, democracy, and religion. Since 1934, Gallup polls have measured the opinions and beliefs of American people that have remained stable over time. The United States, for example, remains much more religious than any other religious country. A Gallup poll of 1995 found that 61% of Americans say that democracy cannot survive without a widespread belief in a god of some kind.[14] According to a Pew Research study of 39 nations between 2011 and 2013, 53 percent of Americans say belief in God is a prerequisite for being moral and having good values, much higher than the 23 percent in Australia and 15 percent in France.[15] Time and again, Japan is expected to converge with the West, but Japanese values have remained relatively stable. Examples of Japanese stable values are pragmatism and hard work. In China, throughout the changes brought by the Cultural Revolution, Confucian values have remained important.[16]

Also, value differences across Europe have remained quite stable over time. Data from Eurobarometer surveys between 1973 and 2016 show that across countries the levels of satisfaction with life in general have remained more or less the same, and there are remarkable cross-cultural differences: consistently, the Danish, Dutch, and British publics show a higher level of satisfaction than the Italian, French, and German. These differences have remained stable over time.

Figure 2.1 illustrates the stability of the differences. An important finding is that similar differences are found for young people 15 to 24 years old. Eurobarometer also asked young people in Europe to what degree they are satisfied with their lives, and, as the chart shows, this line runs parallel to the one of the general publics.

Also, Chinese values appear to be resistant to change. Traditional moral values such as filial piety are still the top moral concerns among young people in Beijing and Hong Kong China.[17]

Scholars of advertising also have reported stability of values. Commercial communication has been relatively consistent in its cultural character, both in the Western world and in Asia. Despite the rapid changes in Chinese society, for example, people continue to hold many traditional attitudes that influence what they buy and how they respond to advertising messages.[18] Pollay and Gallagher[19] found strong consistency in values in advertising between 1970 and 1980 in the United States. Similar values were found in print advertising and in television advertising. Wiles et al.[20] compared US values found in a comparative study with a similar study conducted 20 years earlier and found the same values. People

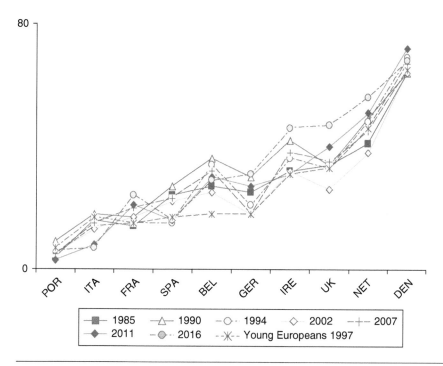

Figure 2.1 Values are stable: Satisfaction with life

SOURCES: Data from Eurobarometer (1985, 1990, 1994, 2002, 2008, 2016); *Young Europeans*, Eurobarometer (1997) (see Appendix B)

tend to think that inequality between males and females is decreasing, along with wealth and better education, but there is evidence of persistent or even increasing role patterns in the United States,[21] where between 1975 and 1993 the differences between the sexes with respect to certain duties, obligations, and beliefs in the roles of fathers had increased.[22]

Values in Marketing

The Rokeach Value Survey was one of the first value studies that served as an example for many others. A simpler approach to values, called list of values (LOV), was developed by Kahle and Goff Timmer.[23] LOV consists of nine values: sense of belonging, excitement, fun and enjoyment in life, warm relationship with others, self-fulfillment, being well-respected, a sense of accomplishment, security, self-respect. The nine items of LOV became the basis of the development of a measurement scheme by the United States Marketing Science

Institute, called MILOV (Multi-Item List of Values). Clawson and Vinson[24] were among the first scholars who applied the value concept to marketing and from there on several lists of US values have been used for value studies in marketing, also in other countries. So the value concept is often used in an ethnocentric way. Value studies developed in one culture are applied to other cultures where they do not fit. An example is the lists of values, applicable to advertising, as defined by Pollay,[25] that contains only American values. This is logical, as they result from analysis of American advertising. The cultural values extracted from an examination of hundreds of ads from more than 60 years reveal that these values are fundamental to American cultural life and have found their way into consumer culture. Yet, Pollay's list of values has also been used in cross-cultural advertising studies. Applying sets of values derived from one culture in cross-cultural contexts without regard to the substance of the cultures in question is called *ethnoconsumerism*.[26] One cannot assume that the same set of values will influence two different groups of consumers' responses for the same marketing stimuli, or that causes of behavior in one country are the same as in another.[27] Both values and related behavior vary by culture.

Cultures can overlap with respect to some values and related habits. Some values are found everywhere, but they are more prevalent in some cultures than in others. Figure 2.2 illustrates this overlap. The distribution of values of a culture follows the normal distribution. The averages of one culture are different from the averages of another culture, but they may overlap to a certain extent. For international marketers, such overlaps can be niches. A marketer's choice is to adapt the brand values and advertising to the target culture or stick to the specific values of the home culture. This will result in having only a niche market in the target market for what is a mass market of the home market. An example is the Italian car brand Alfa Romeo. Italians are more aggressive drivers than are the British or the Dutch, and the Alfa Romeo caters to aggressive drivers. In the Netherlands, there will be some people who like to drive aggressively, but this is a minority. Alfa Romeo, which can cater to a mass market in Italy, will, without adapting their positioning strategy, have only a niche market in the Netherlands.

Culture Defined

Culture is the glue that binds groups together. Without cultural patterns – organized systems of significant symbols – people would have difficulty living together. Culture is what defines a human community, its individuals and social organizations. The anthropologist Clifford Geertz[28] views culture as a set of control mechanisms – plans, recipes, rules, instructions (what computer engineers call 'programs') – for the governing of behavior.

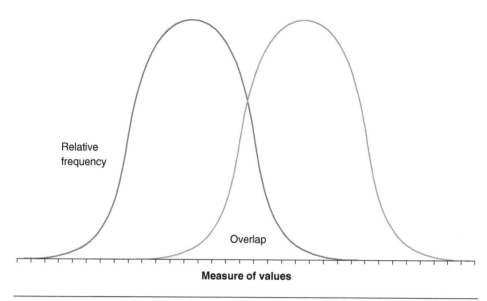

Relative frequency

Overlap

Measure of values

Figure 2.2   **Culture overlap**

People are dependent upon the control mechanisms of culture for ordering their behavior. In line with this, Hofstede defines culture as 'the collective mental programming of the people in an environment. Culture is not a characteristic of individuals; it encompasses a number of people who were conditioned by the same education and life experience.'[29]

Individuals are products of their culture and their social groupings; therefore, they are conditioned by their sociocultural environment to act in certain manners. Culture cannot be separated from the individual; it is not a system of abstract values that exists independently of individuals. Neither can culture be separated from the historical context. Culture is to society what memory is to individuals. It includes the things that have 'worked' in the past. It includes shared beliefs, attitudes, norms, roles, and values found among speakers of a particular language who live during the same historical period in a specific geographic region. These shared elements of subjective culture are usually transferred from generation to generation. Language, time, and place help define culture.[30]

The US sociologist Alex Inkeles[31] uses the term 'national character' because individuals make up societies, and patterned conditions of life in a particular society give rise to certain distinctive patterns in the personalities of its members. The national character is the set of psychosocial characteristics manifested by a given national population. Some of those characteristics are shared by some other populations. The total profile, however, is likely to be distinctive. The discussion of culture often leads to the question of which influence comes first: what we inherit from our parents, our genes, or the society of which we are part.

Nature or Nurture

Basically, there are two strands of thought: our behaviors, perception, and so forth are determined by our genes or by our learning in specific societies – or in popular terms, are we driven by *nature or nurture*? A recent area of research that confirms a link between biology and culture is *cultural neuroscience*, which by using MRI technology, has given novel insights into cultural influences and mental processes. Cultural neuroscientists investigate the mutual constitution of culture, brain, and genes, discovering how 'human culture' is manifested in neural activation patterns.[32] Findings have pointed at the interrelationship between cultural and neural processes. Cultural neuroscience has, for example, an explanation for differences between North Americans and East Asians in performing numerical tasks and in the perception of background information or context.[33] When an American thinks about whether he is honest, his brain activity looks very different from when he thinks about whether another person is honest. When a Chinese man evaluates whether he is honest, his brain activity looks almost identical to when he is thinking about whether his mother is honest.[34] Nature and nurture interact to produce variation in traits and behaviors.

> Genetic influences shape psychological and behavioral predispositions, and cultural influences shape how these predispositions are manifested in the form of social behaviors and psychological outcomes.[35]

Comparing Cultures

Cultural differences manifest themselves in several ways. Hofstede[36] distinguishes symbols, heroes, rituals, and values. Symbols, heroes, and rituals are the practices or expressions of culture that are the visible aspects of culture. The underlying values are invisible. Often when people suggest that cultures converge, they refer to the symbols of culture.

The Emic and the Etic

Two different ways to compare cultures are from the emic or from the etic point of view. The terms *emic* and *etic* are derived from the 'phonemic' and 'phonetic' classification in linguistics. The phonemic is the specific, the phonetic is the general. In line with this, the emic approach tries to describe behavior of one particular culture, while the etic approach uses external criteria to describe and compare behavior of different cultures. The usefulness of culture as an explanatory variable depends upon our ability to 'unpackage' the culture concept. To do so, the etic approach must be used, and cultural values must be arrayed along interpretable dimensions.[37] Differences in the locations of cultures along these dimensions can then be used to explain differences between cultures in their distributions of behavior patterns, norms, attitudes, and personality variables.

Measuring Cultural Values

The values that characterize a society cannot be observed directly. They can be inferred from various cultural products (fairy tales, children's books, or advertising) or by asking members of society to score their personal values by stating their preferences among alternatives and then calculating the central tendency of the answers. When value differences are derived from cultural products, or artifacts of culture, we run the risk of circular reasoning.[38] Values should be related to information about cultures derived from the study of individuals. This is not an easy job. Because values are learned unconsciously, people are only partly aware of them. They work as an automatic pilot and people can only describe them in an abstract way.[39] When measuring values at the individual level, culture always plays a role. Many (cultural) value studies use self-reflective reports; that is, they ask respondents to agree or not agree with statements about themselves (e.g., 'I tend to do my own thing'). However, people behave in actual social settings and when individuals make certain judgments about themselves, they implicitly draw comparisons with others. These referent others, however, are different for people in different cultures.[40] In a society where on average people are aggressive car drivers, an individual driver may not judge himself to be an aggressive driver, whereas he would notice his driving as being aggressive in a society where most people are more tolerant drivers.

Thus, values are abstract constructs that are measured by asking respondents in different societies to provide self reports on their attitudes, values or behaviors, and calculating differences in answers between groups of respondents. The questions and methodology depend on the purpose of the study. Governments or politicians want to monitor social issues and compare countries (e.g. European Union); international management studies want to compare in-company behavior and management styles across cultures; international marketing wants to understand value differences across nations that drive consumer behavior and influence strategy.

Many studies ask people's opinions of aspects of the societies in which they live or organizations in which they work. Such so-called group-referenced questions tend to concern the *descriptive norm*, for example 'In this society (or organization) people are generally assertive'; or the *injunctive norm*, for example 'I believe that in this society (or organization) people should be encouraged to be assertive.' The results depend on respondents' ability to express how they think the majority in their culture think or behave as well as the degree to which this relates to their own behavior or the degree to which they approve of such behavior. It is not always clear whether the norms derived from such questions reflect objective properties of the social system or individual's subjective perceptions.[41] Anyway, answers to questions about how people in general in a society *should* behave will be different from answers resulting from questions about *their own preferred state of being*. The personal desire to be a powerful leader does not include the wish that all others are or should also be powerful leaders.

Marketers are mostly interested in what people actually do or intend to do, what they want for themselves, and how they view themselves; not what they think of others and how others should behave. In marketing research questions usually refer to the self, not to society. Examples are agreement or disagreement with questions like 'I enjoy it when people see how successful I am' or 'I like to stand out in a crowd.' As compared to group referenced questions that force respondents to think about behavior of others in their society, self-referenced questions are closer to daily life and easier to answer.

Yet, in marketing we also have to distinguish between individual preferences and societal norms; what is typically done is often approved. There often is only a weak congruence between individual preferences and perceived descriptive norms; they may even show contrasting values or behaviors. The Japanese may express preference for status brands when in private, but when monitored by others, may decline such status brands[42]. The two types of norms are also capable of exerting opposite effects on the same behavior and this varies between societies. For example, people are more likely to litter in dirty than in clean environments – not because they think they should litter in such a place but because they believe that it is *commonplace*.[43]

So people do not always behave according to their personal preferences, but also to what is generally done, the descriptive norm. These do not always overlap. Generally advertising tends to depict the descriptive norm. Deviating too much runs the risk of alienating consumers. Across topics, brands or product categories, the influence of social norms may vary. For applying cross-cultural value studies to understand consumer behavior differences, the most useful studies are those that use self-referenced questions, referring to peoples' personal preferences in day-to-day life. The averages represent cultural values.

Questionnaires

For conducting value surveys following the etic approach, similar questionnaires have to be used and questions have to be translated. Language, however, is also an expression of culture. Questions about values must be translatable and meanings must have conceptual equivalence across all cultures where the questions are used. Some values that are specific for certain cultures alone cannot be measured directly by the etic method but only by interpreting the values included in the various etic scales. For culture-specific values there are often no linguistic or conceptual equivalents. An example is the concept of competitiveness linked with individuals. In the English language, one can say about an individual that he or she is 'a competitive person.' The Dutch language does not link competitiveness to a person. Some researchers may consider respondents' proficiency is enough to use all English language questionnaires. However, when using questionnaires with questions about cultural norms and values and other preferences, researchers observe that differences across countries are considerably smaller when the English-language questionnaire is used than when local languages are used.[44]

For making international comparisons, data should have the same meaning across countries – they must be equivalent – because biased information leads to ambiguous or even erroneous conclusions.[45] Three types of equivalence can be distinguished: *sample* equivalence, *linguistic* and *conceptual* equivalence, and *metric* equivalence. Similar people must be compared as to age, gender, profession, and so on. The questions must have the same meaning to all respondents. Translation and back-translation is not always sufficient. A scale that has been developed in one culture will not always have a similar effect in another culture. Response style and tendencies to use extreme points on verbal rating scales (Extreme Response Style, ERS), as well as yea-saying and nay-saying (Acquiescence Response Style, ARS) have been found to differ from country to country.[46]

Finally, whatever measurement system chosen, culture interferes in another way as researchers start with their own subjective cultural views, whether they study other cultures through firsthand experiences or from a distance by collecting and analyzing data. Researchers carry their own culture; what they observe and the questions asked in surveys are selected from the researchers' point of view. So culture influences both the respondent and the researcher. Even neurophysiological research that is supposed to be a neutral instrument can produce different behavioral results because of different cultural backgrounds.[47]

Individual and Culture Level

Cultural values are held by individuals and influence both individuals and society. For comparison across nations, the *average* value priorities of individual members of one society are compared with the *average* value priorities of individual members of other societies. The average value priorities of a group are what the members of that group or nation have in common. Individual values are partly a product of shared culture and partly a product of unique individual personality and experience. There is overlap between individual values and cultural values because institutions reflect the societal values shared by the individual members. If they would not do so, individuals would not be able to function adequately.

Individual members of a society have internalized values that help them conform to the requirements of societal institutions. Individuals are guided by their cultural priorities and in their behavior reinforce the social system.[48]

Consumer psychologists generally measure individual behavior within social systems (countries, cultures, states). Individuals are sampled from a population in order to reach conclusions on that population.[49] In comparative research, the properties of individuals as observed within a country (e.g., age or literacy) are aggregated and then treated as country-level variables. To find explanations for some phenomena at country level (e.g., differences in ownership of computers across countries) the aggregate data can be correlated to other country-level variables (e.g., gross national income [GNI] per capita). This is called 'between-system' or 'between-country' comparison, although data are used that were originally collected among individuals of countries. Because the data have been aggregated, we cannot use them anymore to explain within-system differences. Hofstede[50] states that cultures are wholes and their internal logic cannot be understood in the terms used for measuring individuals. Patterns observed at the culture level (also called *ecological level*) can be different from patterns at the individual level. Culture is no king-sized personality; cultures are formed through the interactions of different personalities, both conflicting and complementary, that create a whole that is more than the sum of its parts.[51] Thus, patterns of associations for specific values at the culture level can be different from those at the individual level. For example, Schwartz[52] has shown that patterns of associations with 'freedom' are different at the individual and at the cultural (national) level. Within countries, individuals who score high on the importance of 'freedom' also tend to score high on the importance of 'independence of thought and actions.' But if the scores for all individuals in each nation are averaged, the nations where on average 'freedom' is scored as more important than in other nations are not those scoring higher on the importance of 'independence,' but those scoring higher on 'protecting the welfare of others.' The individual associations are based on psychological logic, the national associations on the cultural logic of societies composed of different, interacting individuals.

Using a culture-level correlation to interpret individual behavior (for this the term *ecological fallacy* is used) can lead to misinterpretations. Within-system correlations can be different from between-system correlations. So, conclusions about individual-level relationships drawn from relationships between culture-level variables may be fallacious. A classic example was a strong correlation between the percentage of blacks and percentage of illiteracy across states in the United States, whereas the relationship between blacks and illiteracy might be nonexistent within each American state.[53] Reverse ecological fallacy is committed in the construction of ecological indexes from variables correlated at the individual level. Cultures cannot be treated and categorized as if they were individuals. An example of a reverse ecological fallacy is the use of a ready-made US scale for comparing cultures, for example, Rokeach's structure of central and instrumental values for comparing countries.

Because of their strong belief in the uniqueness of individuals, generally, individualists are in favor of individual-level studies; they feel reluctant categorizing people on the basis of group characteristics and insist that people should be treated, analyzed, and interpreted as individuals, not as group members. In more collectivistic cultures, the opposite bias can be found. Group differences are exaggerated and viewed as absolute. There is a tendency to treat people on the basis of the group that they belong to rather than as individuals.[54]

Searching for Similarities or for Differences

Studies that search for *similarities* across countries are studies that use culture-level (ecological) variables to determine types or subsets of cultures that are similar among themselves but differ from other types or subsets (e.g., the young, business people, or lifestyle groups). Studies that focus on the *differences* determine dimensions of societies consisting of societal variables. Next to dimensions, *typologies* are used, as in most value and lifestyle studies. A typology describes easy-to-imagine ideal types; hence typologies are popular among marketing and advertising people who develop messages for imaginary consumers. For such research, usually large numbers of questions on activities, interests, and opinions are reduced to two basic and bipolar dimensional structures resulting from factor analysis, and the resulting factors are given labels that cover the factor items, as interpreted by the creators of the studies. As a result, the labels will reflect the culture of the developers of the study. This leads to labels like 'strivers,' 'devouts,' or 'fun seekers' if the study is directed by Americans, or to labels like 'mythical' or 'emotional' by French researchers, whereas British researchers tend to include class-based segment labels. Both concepts and dimensions used in value studies reflect the culture of the home country and cannot be extended to other cultures without losing meaning.

The Stanford Research Institute's values and lifestyles (VALS) program was one of the first value and lifestyle studies. VALS, developed by SRI International, Menlo Park, California,[55] is based on the Rokeach value system. It uses a questionnaire asking motivations and demographic characteristics that are seen as predictors of consumer preferences. Later, a parallel system called RISC International (after the International Research Center for Social Change in Paris) emerged in Europe. Such studies were developed in several other countries as well.

The common aspect of these studies is the use of two-dimensional space in which consumption, respondents, and values are placed. The primary dimensions of VALS are motivations and resources. RISC distinguished three dimensions: *expansion–stability* (openness to new ideas versus resistance to change), *enjoyment–responsibility*, and *flexibility–structure*.[56] The VALS segmentation system was developed in the United States, and the values included are typical for the United States. Nevertheless, international research and advertising agencies apply it to other cultures.

CCA, a French system developed in the 1990s, worked with the dimensions 'progressive–conservative' and 'material–spiritual.' The Belgian market research agency Censydiam uses theories by the psychoanalyst Alfred Adler.[57] According to this theory, consumers develop basic strategies for the management of tension.

A commercial segmentation system developed by Gallup in Scandinavia, Kompas, works with the dimensions 'modern' versus 'traditional' and 'individual' versus 'social' values.[58] A Japanese model developed by Dentsu[59] used the dimensions 'achiever' versus 'membership dependent' and 'group merit' versus 'intelligent, nonconformist' that both reflect the individualism–collectivism paradox. An originally German study of social milieus extended its study to other markets in Europe.[60] Social milieus describe the structure of society in terms of social class and value orientations. Within cultures, groups of people are delineated who share a common set of values and beliefs about, for example, work, leisure, and relationships. Groups are labeled in terms of 'modern,' 'conservative,' 'proactive,' or 'materialist.' These groups are not necessarily similar across cultures.

The previous discussion may have demonstrated that most lifestyle studies have strong local roots. The cross-cultural validity of international lifestyle instruments remains to be demonstrated. The results of such studies are also often presented without saying that the findings are based on a study among respondents of one specific culture and are not applicable to subjects who are of a totally different culture.

National Cultures

A point of discussion is the delineation of cultural groups by national borders. A country is not necessarily equivalent to a culture or society in the anthropological sense. A country often contains more than one culture or society, anthropologically speaking. Conventionally, a culture is the set of customary beliefs and practices characteristic of a society, the latter being the population that occupies a particular territory and speaks a common language not understood by neighboring populations. There may be great variation in the learned behavior that may be found in 'the population that occupies a particular territory and speaks a common language.'[61]

Hofstede[62] states that indeed nations should not be equated to societies. Societies are, historically, organically developed forms of social organizations and, strictly spoken, the concept of a common culture applies to societies, not to nations. Nevertheless many nations do form historically developed wholes even if they consist of clearly different groups. Within nations that have existed for some time, there have been strong forces toward further integration: (usually) one dominant language, common mass media, a national education system, and national markets for products and services. Nations as political bodies also supply all kinds of statistics about their populations. To assess the potential of international markets, companies generally compare nations with respect to demographics, GNI per capita, and consumer usage and attitudes. The classic mass media, such as television, newspapers, and magazines, are important means of communication that mostly target national audiences. Also the various Internet applications have adjusted to different languages, communication styles, shopping habits, etc. that characterize different national cultures.

> Simon Anholt, one of the leading consultants in global advertising, bases his culture mapping on Hofstede's dimensions of national culture. He states:
>
> For advertising agencies and their clients, culture mapping [i.e., working with the Hofstede dimensions] really comes into its own: it's absolutely *made* for mass marketing, an area where individual personality is of very secondary importance, and what you really want is reliable, true, but *gross generalizations.* You need to know what *most people* in a country are like, and how most of them will behave in response to certain stimuli.[63]

Yet with respect to values, some nations are more homogeneous than others, although differences between nations are substantially larger than differences within nations. One of the most heterogeneous nations is the United States, where the white, Caucasian American population is decreasing and other groups, in particular Americans of Hispanic origin, are increasing. Previously so-called minority groups are becoming majorities. In 2015, Hispanics, African-Americans, and Asian-Americans accounted for more than 120 million people, representing 38% of the total US population. These cultural groups are projected to increase by 2.3 million each year before becoming a majority of the population by 2044, according to the US Census. Although differences in consumption and shopping behavior are observed, the cultural values of these groups appear to converge, rather than diverge.[64]

As we'll see throughout this book, neither Europe nor Asia are homogeneous regions with respect to national values, and heterogeneity within nations varies. Some nations are clearly more homogeneous than others. Cross-cultural consultant Arne Maas used regional data from the *European Social Survey*[65] to calculate a measure of cultural cohesion by cluster analysis of 21 value questions that were answered by people from all provinces in a country. The questions measured value preferences, like the importance of having friends, family, equality, the importance of work, or of being rich. These are not representative of the total value system of countries, but variety gives an indication of the degree of coherence of countries. The coherence measure found for 19 countries ranged from 1.4 for Norway to 14.9 for Spain, indicating that of these 19 countries, Norway is most homogeneous and Spain most heterogeneous. The score for the whole region, comprising the 19 countries, was 27.

The northern European countries are evidently culturally coherent. Their measures ranged from 1.4 for Norway to 2.4 for Sweden. Only Denmark appears to be less coherent, with a measure of 5.3. The United Kingdom seems to be somewhere in the middle, with 7.0, but this changes dramatically when Northern Ireland is left out of the analysis, and the measure changes from 7.0 to 1.6. A similar change occurs in Switzerland (coherence = 7.2) when Ticino, the Italian part of Switzerland, is left out. The figure then drops to 2.6. Spain is the least culturally coherent of all countries measured. It has a score of 14.9, the highest of all 19 countries. This is not so strange for a country with at least three regions with different languages and histories (Castilia, Cataluna, and Pais Vasco). Also, Greece is not very coherent (12.2), although the regions within Greece have more in common with other Greek regions than with regions in other countries. This means that Greek culture is quite different from other European cultures.

A third country that is culturally not very cohesive is Germany (8.5). It is interesting to see that the differences are especially large in former Western Germany (13.7) and that the former DDR is quite cohesive (4.3). Some southern German regions cluster with Austria and Switzerland rather than with other German regions. Also, Hamburg is quite different from the rest of Germany. Table 2.2 provides the measures for the 19 countries.

Table 2.2   **Measures of coherence for 19 countries**

1. Norway	1.4	11. Austria	5.7
2. Finland	1.9	12. Netherlands	5.7
3. Sweden	2.4	13. U.K	7.0
4. Hungary	2.9	14. Switzerland	7.2
5. Slovenia	3.0	15. Israel	7.5
6. Belgium	3.6	16. Portugal	8.3
7. Ireland	3.6	17. Germany	8.5
8. Poland	4.5	18. Greece	12.2
9. Czech Republic	5.0	19. Spain	14.9
10. Denmark	5.3	20. All 19 countries	27.0

Devinderpal Singh found regional cultures in India that were quite different with respect to cultural values. For example, the state of Gujarat in western India is far more hierarchical and power is distributed unequally as compared to the West Bengal in the east and Punjab in the north. Whereas Tamil Nadu is collectivistic, in West Bengal people are more individualistic.[66]

The consequences of heterogeneity of countries is that companies, when testing products or advertising, have to be careful which region to select as a test market in a country if it is a heterogeneous one. For international research, using a too homogeneous or too heterogeneous country as a test market is risky.

Dimensions of Culture

Cultures can be described according to specific *characteristics* or categorized into *value categories* or *dimensions* of national culture. Cultural characteristics distinguishing countries described by international management consultants Harris and Moran[67] are sense of self and space, communication and languages, food and feeding habits, time consciousness, values and norms, beliefs and attitudes, and work habits and practices. These characteristics are based on observations, and many of these are found in dimensional models derived from large surveys.

The advantage of dimensions over descriptions is the empirical base. Dimensions are generally developed from large numbers of variables by statistical data reduction methods (e.g., factor analysis) and provide scales on which countries are scored. Dimensions that order cultures meaningfully must be empirically verifiable and more or less independent.

Reducing culture to dimensions with numbers on scales has been criticized. But we have to understand that dimensions are useful constructs that explain behavior. As Hofstede states:

> We cannot directly observe mental programs. What we can observe is only behavior: Words or deeds. Mental programs are intangibles and the terms we use to describe them are *constructs*. A construct is a product of our imagination, supposed to help our understanding. Constructs do not 'exist' in an absolute sense: We define them into existence. In the same way values and dimensions do not exist. They are constructs, which have to prove their usefulness by their ability to explain and predict behavior ... Culture is not the only thing we should pay attention to. In many cases economic, political or institutional factors provide better explanations. But sometimes they don't, and then we need the construct of culture.[68]

The most common dimension used for ordering societies is their degree of economic evolution or modernity, from traditional to modern. One of two dimensions used by US political scientist Ronald Inglehart, who leads the *World Values Survey* (WVS), follows this order of societies. Inglehart[69] arranges world values in two broad categories. The first is 'traditional' versus 'secular-rational,' and the second looks at 'quality of life' attributes ranging from 'survival' to 'well-being,' the latter including so-called post-materialist values.

Increasingly more complex models are developed. Most of them define patterns of basic problems that are common to all societies and that have consequences for the functioning of groups and individuals. Few are true dimensions in the sense of being statistically independent. Such categories are better called *value orientations* or *value categories*.

The idea that basic common problems exist is not new. An early analysis by Alex Inkeles and Daniel Levinson[70] suggested that the following issues qualify as common basic problems worldwide: (1) relation to authority; (2) the conception of self, including ego identity; and (3) primary dilemmas of conflict and dealing with them. These basic problems have been found in many other studies. American anthropologists Kluckhohn and Strodtbeck[71] proposed five value orientations on the basis of their investigations of small communities in the southwestern United States: (1) perception of human nature (good/evil); (2) relationship of man to his environment (subjugation/mastery); (3) time orientation (past/present); (4) orientation toward the environment (being and doing); (5) orientation toward human relationships (hierarchical/individualistic). The five value orientations are recognized in later studies, for example, by Trompenaars[72] who applied these orientations to countries and presented seven categories of work-related values. These are universalism–particularism, achievement–ascription, individualism–collectivism, emotional–neutral, specific–diffuse, time orientation, and orientation to nature, but these categories were not combined into country scores. Trompenaars's database was analyzed by the British psychologist Peter Smith,[73] who only found two independent dimensions in the data that basically measured various intercorrelated flavors of individualism. Trompenaars's dimensions are not statistically independent and he produced no country scores, so his findings are not useful for analysis of consumption data.

Fiske[74] proposed four elementary forms of sociability that occur within and across cultures: (1) communal sharing, (2) authority ranking, (3) equality matching, and (4) market pricing. Fiske's theory was supported by ethnographic field work and experimental studies covering five cultures. Authority ranking and equality matching are similar to forms found in classifications by others, such as by Schwartz and by Hofstede, models that we deal with in more detail later.

The anthropologist Edward Hall[75] distinguished patterns of culture according to context, space, time, and information flow. In particular, the context concept is useful for understanding consumer behavior across cultures. Also, Hall did not develop country scores, but the context orientation is related to individualism–collectivism, one of Hofstede's dimensions that provides country scores. Differences between cultures with respect to the relationship between man and nature still are viewed as unique. The nature and context orientations are described in the following sections.

Only a few dimensional models provide country scores that can be used as independent variables for statistical analysis of consumption differences and other aspects of consumer behavior across cultures. These are the models by Geert Hofstede, by Shalom Schwartz, and the more recent GLOBE study. The Dutch scholar Geert Hofstede was the first who, starting in 1973, developed five independent dimensions of national culture that from the start have been used in this book to analyze and explain differences in consumer behavior.[76] His five dimensions are labeled: *power distance, individualism/collectivism, masculinity/femininity, uncertainty avoidance,* and *long-/short-term orientation.* Recently a sixth dimension, called *indulgence–restraint* was added.

The Israeli psychologist Shalom Schwartz[77] developed seven value types, labeled *embeddedness, intellectual and affective autonomy, hierarchy, mastery, egalitarianism,* and *harmony.*

The most recent large-scale dimensional model is GLOBE,[78] developed by Robert House of the Wharton School of Management and his associates, who initiated a cross-national project for the study of leadership and societal culture. They discovered nine cultural dimensions, labeled *uncertainty avoidance, power distance,* two types of *collectivism, gender egalitarianism, assertiveness, future orientation, performance orientation,* and *humane orientation.*

Of the three major models, several dimensions overlap conceptually, but each model has dimensions that measure specific cultural values that do not appear in other models or that are only part of a dimension of another model. The explanatory power of the different dimensions varies. They don't all equally contribute to understanding differences in consumer behavior and communication.

Of the three models, the Hofstede model has been applied most. A reason for widespread adoption of Hofstede's classification of culture lies in the simplicity of his dimensions, which are straightforward and appealing to both academic researchers and business people. Although Hofstede's work has been thought to be outdated, several reviews and analysis of the validity of different models for the purpose of measuring cultural distance for international marketing strategy show that the more recent cultural frameworks provide only limited advancements compared with Hofstede's original work.[79] In this chapter the three models will be summarized and compared. First, context, concepts of time and nature are described.

Relationship of Man with Nature

There are basically three types of relationship between man and nature: *mastery-over-nature* (man is to conquer nature), *harmony-with-nature* (man is to live in harmony with nature), and *subjugation-to-nature* (man is dominated by nature). In the Western world, man is viewed as separate from nature. The North American relationship to nature in particular is that it should be conquered and controlled for human convenience. To most North Americans the expression 'to move a mountain' is not a metaphor symbolizing the impossible but rather an optimistic challenge. The view of US culture is that it is the person's responsibility to overcome obstacles that may stand in his or her way. The Japanese experience of nature is one of communion, of exchange, characterized by a subtle intimacy. It is an experience of identification with nature. Westerners tend to explain the Asian reverence of nature as a relationship with God, which involves living in harmony with the world of nature. Takeo Doi,[80] a Japanese psychiatrist, says that in Japan, God as a creator is absent and, therefore, human beings seek comfort by attempting to immerse themselves completely in nature. Other cultures, such as many African cultures, see people as dominated by nature, and supernatural forces play a dominant role in religion. This subjugation-to-nature involves the belief that nothing can be done to control nature.

High-Context and Low-Context Communication Culture

In a high-context communication or message, most of the information is either part of the context or internalized in the person; very little is made explicit as part of the message. The information of a low-context message is carried in the explicit code of the message. In general, high-context communication is economical, fast, and efficient. However, time must be devoted to programming. If this programming does not take place, the communication is incomplete. To the observer, an unknown high-context culture can be completely mystifying because symbols, not known to the observer, play such an important role. Thus, high-context culture communication can also be defined as inaccessible to outsiders. Low-context communication cultures are characterized by explicit verbal messages. Effective verbal communication is expected to be direct and unambiguous. Low-context communication cultures demonstrate high value and positive attitudes toward words. Argumentation and rhetoric in advertising are more found in low-context cultures, whereas advertising of high-context cultures can be characterized by symbolism or indirect verbal expression.

For the purpose of shaping and maintaining corporate identity, companies develop an 'identity standards manual,' which is a guide to managing the application of the corporate identity visual system, or how an organization uses logotypes, typography styles, names, and architecture to communicate its corporate philosophy. In high-context cultures, these manuals include more nonverbal features (logo and symbol), traditions and customs (history, values), features defining the context of the communication, accessories or decorative elements and people (uniforms). In low-context cultures, these manuals include more textual features (name and publications) and direct messages (e.g., incorrect applications). Manuals are more prescriptive and simpler than in high-context cultures where manuals use more indirect language and are more complex because of use of indirect language and also have more sections.[81]

Hofstede suggested a correlation between collectivism and high-context in cultures. In collectivistic cultures, information flows more easily between members of groups, and there is less need for explicit communication than in individualistic cultures. Another explanation of high context is homogeneity of cultures. Homogeneous cultures have more in common with respect to cultural heritage, and thus their members, more than members of heterogeneous cultures, can rely on shared symbols.

Cultures are on a sliding scale with respect to context. Most Asian cultures are high-context, whereas most Western cultures are low-context, extremes being Japan and China (high-context) on the one end of the scale and Germany, Switzerland, and the United States (low-context cultures) on the other end.

Dimensions of Time

Time is more than what the clock reads. Different cultures have different concepts of time. Western advertisers tend to use clocks in their international advertising to symbolize efficiency. Clocks are not recognized as symbols of efficiency in cultures where people have a different sense of time. Time is a core system of cultural, social, and personal life.

Each culture has its own unique time frame which influences how people deal with specific aspects of time in daily life. For example, different cultural groups have different norms or practices regarding punctuality. In some cases this has resulted in metaphors like *Rubber time*, as used by Indonesians to refer to a laid-back attitude about appointments, or *Mañana* which refers to a Latin-American time frame in which 'the business of today is put off to tomorrow.'[82]

Hall's[83] important study of time as an expression of culture provides an explanation of differences in behavior and language. He distinguishes different types of time, among others biological time (light–dark/day–night, hot–cold/summer–winter), personal time (how time is experienced), and sync time (each culture has its own beat). Hall developed his theories during his stay with Native Americans, discovering how differently they dealt with time than Anglo-Americans. Different concepts of time can explain significant differences in behavior. A few aspects of time that are relevant to consumer behavior – closure; linear versus circular time; and monochronic versus polychronic time – are summarized below.

Closure

Americans are driven to achieve what psychologists call 'closure,' meaning that a task must be completed or it is perceived as 'wasted.' What Hall saw as characteristic of Hopi (Native Americans of the Southwest) villages was the proliferation of unfinished houses. The same can be seen in Turkey, in southern Europe, and in other collectivistic cultures where additional rooms will be built only when family needs arise. American novels or films always have a 'happy ending,' including solutions to problems, which are rare in Japanese novels.

Time is Linear or Circular

Time can be conceived as a line of sequential events or as cyclical and repetitive, compressing past, present, and future by what these have in common: seasons and rhythms. The latter time orientation is linked with Asian culture; the former is the Western time orientation. The linear time concept causes people to see time as compartmentalized, schedule dominated. Americans have a linear time concept with clear structures, such as beginning, turning point, climax, and end. Time is used as a measuring instrument and a means of controlling human behavior by setting deadlines and objectives. Time is tangible, like an object; it can be saved, spent, found, lost, and wasted. Temporal terms such as *summer* and *winter* are nouns; they are treated as objects. For Native Americans, summer is a condition: hot. The term is used as an adverb, not related to time but to the senses.

In Japan, time is circular and is related to the special meaning of seasons. Japanese time thinking is not in terms of today, tomorrow, or the day after tomorrow. The seasons form an automatic, upward spiral; everything returns automatically. Saying 'back to the old values' in Japan does not imply a step backward but a step forward. It means progressing through an upward spiral, using what was good in the past for progress.

Monochronic and Polychronic Time

Another distinction by Hall[84] of how people handle time is between monochronic (M-time) and polychronic (P-time) cultures. People from monochronic cultures tend to do one thing at a time; they are organized and methodical, and their workdays are structured to allow them to complete one task after another. Polychronic people, on the other hand, tend to do many things simultaneously. Their workday is not a chain of isolated, successive blocks; time is more like a vast, never-ending ocean extending in every direction. The Germans adhere to the more rigid and compartmentalized way of dealing with time. To people who do many things at the same time, however, such as the Spanish, Arabs, Pakistani, or South Americans, punctuality is nice but by no means an absolute necessity in the middle of a hectic day. This polychronic behavior that is so natural to polychronic cultures, has received a special term in monochronic cultures: *multi-tasking*. In monochronic cultures, time spent on the Internet takes time from other activities, such as TV viewing. In polychronic cultures, people do both at the same time.

> In Latin American countries that are mostly polychronic, the PC is next to the TV set because people use them simultaneously. Data from Ipsos (2010) on media behavior show that in the Philippines 15–24 year-olds spend 31.3 hours per 24 hours on media activities.[85]

When two people of different time cultures meet, they may easily offend each other because they have different expectations of time. In particular, the fact that in polychronic cultures people interfere during meetings is very annoying to people of monochronic cultures. Not all M-time cultures are the same, however. In Japan, tight M-time is for business, and P-time is for private life.

Time Orientation Toward the Past, Present, or Future

North Americans tend to be future oriented; the future is a guide to present action, although the time horizon is short term. The old is easily discarded, and the new embraced. Most things are disposable, from ideas, trends, and management fads to marriage partners. Even the 'old' is treated as new. Many Europeans are past oriented; they believe in preserving history and continuing past traditions.[86] Japan has a very long-term future time horizon, as have the Chinese, but they look to the past for inspiration. Destiny as an aspect of time and referring to a future is part of the Indian magic-cosmic world that the Western world has regarded as superstition and ignorance.[87]

Most cultures in sub-Saharan Africa are short-term oriented. To many Africans the concept of time is simply a composition of events that have occurred, events that are taking place now, and events that are immediately to occur. The future is absent because events which lie in it have not taken place. Time is not abstract but part of the present that includes manifestations of the ancestral, the living and the unborn. The best quoted passage of the Bible in South Africa is Matthew 6:34: 'Therefore do not worry about tomorrow, for tomorrow will worry about itself. Each day has enough trouble of its own.' Related to this are African characteristics like patience and generosity, both important values to the Hausa of Nigeria. Open-handed generosity is a much-admired virtue and the big spender is admired and derives respect and status from being generous.[88]

Generally most Latin American cultures are short-term oriented. The Nahuas of Mexico were more concerned with the now than with a distant future. They knew that some day they had to go, descend in the region of mystery, and the answer to that was to live life on earth to the fullest; to derive the maximum pleasure possible by 'enjoying ourselves and sing before we go.'[89] The old Nahua time concept seems to be repeated in the Mexican saying *Salud, dinero, amor y tiempo para disfrutarlos* (Health, wealth, love and time to enjoy them).[90] Short-term vs long-term orientation will be further discussed under dimensional models.

The Three Major Large-Scale Dimensional Models

Dimensional models that offer country scores for large numbers of countries can be used to provide indications of relations between cultural values and specific aspects of consumption or consumer behavior across nations, which in turn can help develop meaningful marketing strategies. A significant correlation between product usage per capita or a particular brand attitude and one or two cultural dimensions can point at specific values related to this attitude or brand. As this book shows, there are many areas of consumption and consumer behavior that can be analyzed this way. Country scores also allow us to make cultural maps for cross-cultural segmentation because often a configuration of two dimensions explains differences in product usage or other consumption-related phenomena. It makes more sense to cluster countries based on cultural closeness than on geographical closeness.

When researchers want to select one of several models, they have to take into account that cultural dimensions are human constructs. Although they are based on objectively existing phenomena, they are not the phenomena themselves but ways of describing them. One and the same reality can be explained and presented in different ways, through different constructs.[91] Not all models and dimensions within models contribute equally well to understanding differences in consumer behavior, marketing and advertising. This may be due to the different purpose, design and structure of the models, most of all the different types of questions used.

The purpose of the Hofstede model[92] was to understand differences in work motivations of all levels of employees, caused by the nationality of the employees. Schwartz, as a psychologist, searched for basic values on which individuals in all cultures differ and from there developed a theory of cultural values on which societies differ.[93] House,[94] the initiator of GLOBE was interested in the effectiveness of leadership styles; he wanted to find out if charismatic leader behavior is universally acceptable and effective.

The samples used for the three models are different. Hofstede used matched groups of employees in seven occupational categories within one global company in 66 countries in order to understand differences in work-related behavior. By doing this within one global company, he eliminated the influence of corporate culture. Schwartz used students and teachers in 54 countries. GLOBE surveyed middle managers in 951 local organizations in food processing, financial services, and telecom services in 62 societies.

Hofstede's and GLOBE's scales are bipolar; they include a positive and negative pole for each dimension. The Schwartz scales are unipolar that are seemingly opposites; but a negative correlation with one does not imply a positive correlation with the opposite scale, and results are often difficult to interpret.

The types of questions used follow different patterns. Both GLOBE and Schwartz in their questions refer to the society in which the respondents live (the norm, group-referenced ratings), whereas Hofstede asked respondents for personal behavioral preferences, referring to the self, not to society (self-referenced ratings). The averages represent cultural values. Schwartz asked respondents for guiding principles in people's lives with respect to social issues.[95] This type of question requires respondents to evaluate the importance of abstract values, which makes the questions easier to answer by educated people than by less educated people. This aspect has implications for the universality of the method. According to Schwartz and Bardi,[96] such an abstract task is likely to be inappropriate for some of the world's populations and is likely to elicit unreliable and invalid value ratings. The GLOBE researchers ask respondents to report on how things are actually done in their society and how they should be done. The items contain the phrase 'in this society.' With this approach, collective culture is measured through respondents' perceptions of values or practices in their social group.[97] What is measured are ideological abstractions, about society *as it is* and *as it should be,* which the researchers call *practices* and *values*; these are descriptive and injunctive norms and based on group-referenced ratings. A cause of confusion can be use of the term practices by GLOBE, which is not the same as what Hofstede calls practices that refer to the *expressions* of culture. What the GLOBE researchers call *values* are in fact *norms,* how people state the way other people behave or should behave. As values and norms often are opposed, for seven of the nine GLOBE dimensions, the values and practices are negatively correlated.[98] This highlights the discrepancy between value and norms approaches. Only for in-group collectivism and gender egalitarianism do the two correlate positively, which may be due to the fact that the questions for these dimensions are more closely related to people's daily lives than those for the other dimensions.

Several studies have applied selected dimensions to aspects of consumption and consumer behavior. Examples of findings with the Hofstede model are explaining differences in buying life insurance,[99] Internet shopping,[100] consumer innovativeness,[101] international new product take-off,[102] and international growth of new products.[103] The Hofstede dimensions also have been used for comparing the use of appeals in advertising,[104] status motives,[105] or the use of celebrities in advertising.[106]

Some international marketing researchers have used the other two dimensional models. Terlutter and colleagues[107] suggested using GLOBE's dimension assertiveness to help explain differences in advertising appeals. Diehl and colleagues[108] found that an identical advertisement expressing performance orientation was perceived differently across countries. They also found a significant relationship between the perceived level of performance orientation and the overall evaluation of the advertisement. Czarnecka and Brennan[109] found a negative relationship between the community appeal in advertising and GLOBE's dimension Institutional Collectivism.

Comparing Dimensions

As his model was the first one, the Hofstede model has been used most, and in this book most examples are based on his work and the descriptions are of his dimensions.[110] As the other models partly overlap with the Hofstede model, short descriptions of the relevant dimensions of the other models are added. When describing or using the GLOBE dimensions, we refer to the practices, not the values (that measure what people think other people should do), as the latter result in confusing relationships with consumer behavior.

The tables help compare the dimensions by showing partial correlations between the dimensions of the three models and data on values, usage or attitudes. Partial correlations, controlling for GNI/capita at PPP were used because for this group of countries several dimensions correlated significantly with GNI/capita.[111] Next to this, there are significant correlations between some of the GLOBE dimensions, e.g. between in-group collectivism and power distance and gender egalitarianism, which tend to cause confusing results.

Power Distance

Power distance can be defined as 'the extent to which less powerful members of a society accept and expect that power is distributed unequally.' It is reflected in the values of both the less powerful and more powerful members of society. It influences the way people accept and give authority. In large power distance cultures (those scoring high on the power distance index), everyone has his or her rightful place in a social hierarchy, and as a result acceptance and giving of authority come naturally. To the Japanese, behavior that recognizes hierarchy is as natural as breathing. It means 'everything in its place.' In cultures scoring low on the power distance index, authority can have a negative connotation; focus is on equality in rights and opportunity. In high power distance cultures, there are strong dependency relationships between parents and children, bosses and subordinates, professors and students. In low power distance cultures, children are raised to be independent at a young age. Americans will avoid becoming dependent on others, and they do not want others, with the possible exception of immediate family members, to be dependent on them. In high power distance cultures, one's social status must be clear so that others can show proper respect. Global brands and luxury goods serve that purpose.

> Power distance explains, for example, differences in the way people behave in the public and private domains and the importance of appearance as well as luxury articles and status brands. It explains differences in communication behavior, such as information gathering for making a buying decision and reading newspapers as well as differences in usage of the Internet and mobile phones. It explains differences in complaining behavior of consumers and behavior of personnel in retail. Examples of values reflected in advertising are independence/dependence of children, importance of authority, and social status.

Although the name pretends similarity to GLOBE's dimension, the explanatory power of Hofstede's power distance dimension is more similar to Schwartz's hierarchy than to GLOBE's power distance. Both Hofstede's power distance and Schwartz's hierarchy present power distance as *acceptance* and *expectance* of power and authority. GLOBE's power distance[112] is about control of others, maintenance of inequality, prestige, status and material possessions. Hofstede's power distance and Schwartz's hierarchy explain similar phenomena, but the Schwartz dimension explains more items, although some Internet-related items show an unexpected negative correlation with egalitarianism, which may serve as an example of the effects of questions asking for the desirable. Hierarchy relates to status needs, as expressed by owning or buying expensive shoes and the importance of clothing. Egalitarianism includes equality, honesty, loyalty, responsibility and helpfulness. It appears to be the opposite to hierarchy when observing the negative correlation with 'I enjoy it when people see my success.' Hierarchy correlates positively with viewing family as woman's first priority, which also is negatively correlated with egalitarianism. With this respect the two Schwartz dimensions seem to be true opposites. The relationships between GLOBE's power distance and many aspects of computer ownership and Internet usage are similar – though less significant – to the relationships between these items and in-group collectivism, which is not surprising in view of the significant correlation between both dimensions ($r = .74^{**}$), next to the fact that both dimensions are also related to GNI/cap. In sum, Hofstede's power distance is similar to Schwartz's hierarchy, but very different from GLOBE's power distance, which is more similar to GLOBE's in-group collectivism.

Table 2.3 shows a few examples of significant partial correlations between answers to questions about computers, Internet, the function of clothing, status, and conservative attitudes towards the role of women.

Table 2.3 **Comparing power distance and hierarchy/egalitarianism**

Pearson partial correlation coefficient one-tailed, controlled for GNI/cap at PPP 2013, $*p < 0.05, **p < 0.01$ Percentages of respondents who use, own, bought or agree with statement	*Power distance GLOBE*	*Power distance Hofstede*	*Hierarchy*	*Egalitarianism*
Have Internet connection at home	−.53*			−.61**
If used, use it every day	−.65**			
Bought expensive fragrance in past year		.64**		
Bought expensive shoes in past year			.49*	
With my clothing I express who I am		.59*	.65**	
I enjoy it when people see my success			.77**	−.52*
A woman's first priority should be her family			.59*	−.63**

SOURCES: *E-communications and Telecom Single Market Household Survey*, EBS 414, 2014; *Consumers in Europe*, EBS, 2009; *European Media and Marketing Survey*, Ipsos, 2012 (see Appendix B)

Individualism/Collectivism

'People look after themselves and their immediate family only, or people belong to in-groups who look after them in exchange for loyalty.' In individualistic cultures, values are in the person, and people want to differentiate themselves from others. In collectivistic cultures, identity is based in the social network to which one belongs. In individualistic

cultures people are 'I' conscious and express private opinions; self-actualization is important. Individual decisions are higher valued than group decisions. Individualists attach priority to variety and adventure, whereas collectivists prefer harmony. There is more explicit,
verbal communication. In collectivistic cultures people are 'we' conscious – their identity
is based on the social system. Harmony with in-group members and avoiding loss of face
is important. People enjoy themselves more in groups, meet each other in the public
domain more than at home. Between 70% and 80% of the world's population is more or less
collectivistic. All of Asia, Africa, and Latin America are collectivistic. In Italy, the data were
collected in the north, where people appeared to be individualistic. Other studies[113] indicate that the Italians as a whole are collectivistic. Individualistic cultures are universalistic
cultures, whereas collectivistic cultures are particularistic.

Individualism is increasing worldwide because it is linked with wealth, but it remains
a relative concept. If it is said that Japanese society is individualizing, that does not mean
Japanese values will come close to American values. The relative difference is expected to
remain. Through analysis of birth cohorts of the *World Values Survey*, Beugelsdijk et al.[114]
found that individualism increased over time, but the differences between countries
remained the same. The scale had moved but the positions of the countries hadn't.

Individualism/collectivism explains, for example, many differences in communication
behavior, both interpersonal and mass communication. It is related to high/low context
communication, so explains differences in direct versus indirect communication, information gathering from the media or word-of-mouth communication. It partly explains
differences in adoption of innovations such as adoption of computers and the Internet,
Internet buying, owning insurances and cars. It explains differences in Internet usage
such as e-mailing or blogging. It explains differences in the importance of pleasure
and adventure for spending leisure time and fun shopping. It explains differences in
demonstrating uniqueness versus wanting to conform, which can be recognized in
the importance of one's appearance and buying behavior of fashion and luxury articles. Examples of values reflected in advertising are self-confidence, self-expression
versus conformance, and sharing.

Individualism–collectivism is the most used dimension in cross-cultural research, for
which also other terms are used, such as independent versus interdependent self-construal,
idiocentrism–allocentrism, and private–collective self. There are more than 100 competing
instruments for measuring individualism–collectivism and the same label is used for many
conceptual variations. Taras et al.[115] analyzed six instruments that are most used: those by
Gudykunst and colleagues,[116] Kim and Leung,[117] Oyserman,[118] Singelis,[119] Takata,[120] and

Triandis.[121] Gross variations exist depending on the specific instrument used to collect the data, the level of analysis, the sample characteristics and region where data are collected. Vargas and Kemmelmeier[122] analyzed an even larger number of studies and also found that the results differ with the type of scale used, questions asked, and topics covered.

Of the other models, GLOBE's dimension in-group collectivism covers similar values as Hofstede's dimension, and so does Schwartz's embeddedness, contrasted by intellectual and affective autonomy. In the descriptions by the researchers,[123] in-group collectivism includes strong family ties, loyalty, interdependence versus focus on the self and need for adventure. Embeddedness includes tradition, social order, family security, obedience, reciprocation of favors. Intellectual autonomy includes freedom, curiosity, creativity, broadmindedness. Affective autonomy includes pleasure, enjoy life, exciting life.

Table 2.4 **Comparing individualism–collectivism, in-group collectivism, embeddedness, and intellectual and affective autonomy**

*Pearson partial correlation coefficient one-tailed, controlled for GNI/cap at ppp 2013, *p < 0.05, **p < 0.01* Percentages of respondents who use, own, bought or agree with statement.	*In-group collectivism*	*Individualism – Collectivism*	*Embed-dedness*	*Intellectual autonomy*	*Affective autonomy*
Have internet connection at home	−.65**				.48*
Individuals using internet	−.66**				.51*
I follow developments of new technology	.57*	−.48*			
I take care of my appearance	.62**	−.55*			
Pay regular visits to the cinema	.47*	−.70**			
I enjoy it when people see my success			.46*	−.63**	.77**
A woman's first priority should be her family			.70**	−.54*	

SOURCES: World Development Indicators 2013, 2014; E-communications and Telecom Single Market Household Survey, EBS 414, 2014; Consumers in Europe, EBS, 2009; European Media and Marketing Survey, Ipsos, 2012

In our exercise, GLOBE's in-group collectivism showed significant negative correlations with several computer and Internet-related items. Several other items correlate with both GLOBE's and Hofstede's dimensions, such as the importance of appearance (upholding face) and visits to the cinema. In-group collectivism appears to be an important explaining variable. Embeddedness seems not to include the values as in individualism–collectivism with respect to computers and Internet usage, but it does for other values such as traditional values and status. The significant correlation between embeddedness and the statement that family should be woman's first priority points at traditional values. The negative correlation with intellectual autonomy corresponds with this. Intellectual and affective autonomy appear to include different values and conceptually cannot be compared with Hofstede's individualism. Table 2.4 compares the four dimensions with respect to several characteristics that are specific for individualism–collectivism.

Masculinity/Femininity and Assertiveness

Several dimensions measure differences with respect to the degree of assertiveness, average performance orientation of people, and relationships between males and females, such as gender equality and male–female roles in household and family. Hofstede's dimension *masculinity–femininity* is a complex dimension as it measures the degree of assertiveness or achievement orientation (masculinity pole) versus quality of life (femininity pole) as well as role differentiation versus overlapping roles of males and females. GLOBE measures several aspects of Hofstede's masculinity–femininity dimension through different dimensions. The *assertiveness* dimension[124] measures the degree of assertiveness and *gender egalitarianism*[125] measures gender equality. Schwartz's mastery pole of his dimension *mastery/harmony* also has some conceptual overlap with masculinity. Both emphasize assertion and ambition[126] but the harmony pole is not similar to Hofstede's femininity pole.

Hofstede's masculinity/femininity dimension can be summarized as follows. 'The dominant values in a masculine society are achievement and success, the dominant values in a feminine society are caring for others and quality of life.' In masculine societies, performance and achievement are important. Status is important to show success. Big and fast are beautiful. Societies that score low on the masculinity index are more service oriented, have a people orientation, and regard small as beautiful. There is a tendency to strive for consensus. Quality of life is more important than competition. Status is not so important to show success. Being a 'winner' is positive in masculine cultures and negative in feminine cultures. In masculine cultures, children learn to admire the strong, whereas in feminine cultures children learn sympathy for the underdog. A consequence of this dimension is variation in the degree of role differentiation: small in feminine societies, large in masculine societies. In feminine cultures, a male can take a typical female job without being seen as a 'sissy'. It explains differences in household roles such as cleaning, child care, cooking, and shopping as well as differences in working part-time, by both males and females. Much advertising depicts children because it makes advertising more likeable. Yet advertising also should depict the right relationships between children and their parents. Two dimensions are important in this respect: power distance (degree of authority of parents) and masculinity–femininity, that depicts the caring role of parents. Showing mothers or fathers with children is an essential difference that should reflect the roles in different societies. Data from the European time survey by Eurostat and the OECD family database[127] show for domestic care activities by males and females significant correlations with masculinity (time allocated to domestic and caring activities by females) and with gender egalitarianism (time allocated to domestic and caring activities by males).

In masculine cultures, people consume more for show; in feminine cultures people consume more for use. The masculine/feminine dimension also discriminates between cultures with respect to values related to winning, success, and status as used in advertising appeals, so it is an important dimension for marketing and advertising.

Masculinity/femininity explains, for example, differences in household roles like cleaning, child care, cooking, and shopping. It explains differences in frequency of Internet access and using the Internet for leisure and other personal reasons, to enhance the quality of life. It explains differences in buying status brands, luxury goods, jewelry and taking care of one's appearance. In masculine societies people want to show their success more than in feminine societies where people are more modest. In the masculine cultures of Latin America, men must be real men. In a Latin American survey across seven countries, the percentages of answers agreeing with the statement 'Real men don't cry' correlated with masculinity.[128] Examples of values reflected in advertising are winning and success as compared to modesty, as well as role differences. In feminine cultures, the Internet is used more to enhance the quality of life than to be more productive and this influences the purposes and frequency of usage.

In view of the descriptions of the GLOBE model by the authors, gender egalitarianism and assertiveness cover similar values as the Hofstede model, and so do Schwartz's dimensions of mastery and harmony. High scores of gender egalitarianism point at the same opportunities for females and males; low scores indicate greater male domination. This is, however, more about equal opportunity in education and in the workplace than about the existence or absence of specific male–female roles in society and in family life and households. The female–male ratio of enrollment in tertiary education and adult literacy rates correlate positively with gender egalitarianism whereas the percentage of women in parliament correlates negatively with Hofstede's masculinity dimension, and there is no relationship with gender egalitarianism. The percentage of women in parliament is more a matter of roles in society as it is not only about women's opportunities but also about men, for example, whether they are willing to vote for women.

Assertiveness implies being tough, dominant, aggressive in social relationships, enterprising, taking initiative. Mastery includes being capable, daring, successful, ambitious, influential, and social recognition. Harmony implies protecting the environment, unity with nature, a world at peace, and a world of beauty.

Several computer and Internet-related items connect with quality of life values as in low masculinity and high gender egalitarianism, in particular frequency of usage. Some items also correlate with harmony, less with mastery; generally a negative correlation with harmony is not necessarily a positive one with mastery.

Apparently all dimensions include values related to relationships between males and females as well as assertiveness, achievement and success orientations, except mastery that seems to be more limited to achievement. With respect to male and female roles, the Hofstede dimension is most important for understanding various differences in cross-cultural consumer behavior, such as shopping behavior, decision making in families, activities related to child care, cooking, cleaning and depictions of such behavior in advertising. Of the GLOBE dimensions both gender egalitarianism and assertiveness explain related differences.

This is confirmed by our exercise with items concerning role differences (family is woman's first priority, university education is for boys, a father must put his career ahead of his small child, and balanced decision making when buying expensive goods) which correlate significantly with all dimensions, be it that Schwartz's dimension harmony explains more than mastery which doesn't contribute much in this area.

Items pointing at the need to demonstrate one's success (taking care of appearance, enjoy when people see my success) mostly correlate with masculinity and assertiveness. Enjoying the fun of shopping relates to both masculinity and assertiveness. Table 2.5 shows several relationships related to the typical values of role differentiation or overlapping roles of males and females.

Uncertainty Avoidance

'The extent to which people feel threatened by uncertainty and ambiguity and try to avoid these situations.' Some people do not mind ambiguity, whereas others hate uncertainty or ambiguity and try to cope with it by making rules and prescribing behavior. In cultures of strong uncertainty avoidance (those scoring high on the index), there is a need for rules and formality to structure life and belief in experts. People are more interested in the process of how a product works than in the results. Purity is an important value. There is more

Table 2.5 Comparing masculinity–femininity, assertiveness, gender egalitarianism, mastery and harmony

*Pearson partial correlation coefficient one-tailed, controlled for GNI/cap at PPP 2013, *p < 0.05, **p < 0.01*

Percentages of respondents who use, own, bought or agree with statement	Masculinity–Femininity	Gender egalitarianism	Assertiveness	Mastery	Harmony
If Internet is used, every day	-.82**	.73**	-.57*		
I enjoy the fun of shopping	.77**		.50*		
I enjoy it when people see my success	.69**		.57*		-.59*
I take care of my appearance	.53*		.49*	.60*	
A woman's first priority should be her family	.78**		.60*		-.57*
Agree with a university education is more for a boy than for a girl	.68**	-.54*	.69**		.50*
A father must put his career ahead of looking after his young child	.83**	-.55*	.61**		
Buy expensive goods: balanced decision between you and your partner	-.49*				.59**

SOURCES: *E-communications and Telecom Single Market Household Survey*, EBS 414, 2014; *Consumer Empowerment*, EBS 342, 2011; *Gender Equality*, EBS 428, 2014; *European Media and Marketing Survey*, Ipsos, 2012 (see Appendix B)

formal communication. People in high uncertainty avoidance cultures have a higher level of anxiety and aggressiveness, and showing emotions is accepted. Conflict and competition are threatening. Weak (low-scoring) uncertainty avoidance cultures feel that there should be as few rules as possible. They are more result oriented than process oriented. They believe more in generalists and common sense, and there is less ritual behavior. Conflict and competition are not threatening. The uncertainty avoidance dimension discriminates between cultures where innovations are adopted early and cultures where people lag in the adoption process.

Risk avoidance is not included in this dimension. Only in some specific product categories risk perception may be related to high uncertainty avoidance. An example is food-related risk. In 2010 Eurobarometer[129] asked for the degree to which people worry about the potential risk of food damages to one's health. The percentages of respondents who worried correlated significantly with high uncertainty avoidance.

Uncertainty avoidance explains, for example, differences in the adoption of innovations, differences in access to the Internet and ownership of personal computers. It explains differences in the degree to which people read books and newspapers. It explains differences playing sports, in use of medication, numbers of physicians per 1,000 people, and consumption of mineral water. It explains differences in traveling, foreign language speaking, and contacts people have with foreigners. Examples of values reflected in advertising are details and precision versus use of humor.

The GLOBE dimension uncertainty avoidance[130] is very different from Hofstede's dimension with the same name. Both the researchers' descriptions and relationships with consumer-related items include quite different values: on the one end orderliness, consistency, importance of formal law and procedures; high importance of in-groups, and lack of interest in out-groups; satisfaction with life and importance of science and technology. On the low end is mainly less religious dogma. Whereas Hofstede's dimension *uncertainty avoidance* points at consumer innovativeness in adopting new technology (smartphone, tablet, laptop, use of Internet) and following technology, GLOBE's dimension doesn't do so. Also not traveling (fear of the unknown), an item that relates to high uncertainty avoidance, does not correlate with the GLOBE dimension. Although interest in technology is included in the researchers' description, this is not found in our exercise. Many different studies of satisfaction with life in general show negative correlations only with Hofstede's dimension, not with GLOBE's. There are only two significant correlations with the GLOBE dimension and these are difficult to interpret. Part of GLOBE's description includes high importance of in-groups and relative lack of interest in out-groups, which are collectivistic values.[131] This explains why several items that were expected to relate to GLOBE's uncertainty avoidance show more significant correlations with GLOBE's in-group collectivism. The two dimensions are significantly correlated (r = -.82**). Table 2.6 shows correlations with a few of the items from our set of items used to compare dimensions. None were found for GLOBE's uncertainty avoidance, apart from 'my clothing expresses who I am.'

Table 2.6   **Comparing uncertainty avoidance by GLOBE and Hofstede**

Pearson partial correlation coefficient one-tailed, controlled for GNI/cap at PPP 2013, *p < 0.05, **p < 0.01 Percentages of respondents who use, own, bought or agree with statement	Uncertainty avoidance GLOBE	Uncertainty avoidance Hofstede
Very satisfied with life in general		−.71**
I personally own a smartphone		−.70**
Never used Internet		.62**
My clothing expresses who I am	−.59*	
I never exercise		.47*
I never travel abroad in EU		.46*
I follow developments of new technology		.75**
I will not make a decision if I am not well informed		.56*

SOURCES: World Development Indicators 2014; *Social Climate*, EBS 408, 2013; *E-communications and Telecom Single Market Household Survey*, EBS 414, 2014; *Consumer Empowerment*, EBS 342, 2011; *Sport and Physical Activity*, EBS 412, 2014; *European Media and Marketing Survey*, Ipsos, 2012 (see Appendix B)

Long-/Short-Term Orientation

The fifth dimension was originally discovered in cooperation with Michael Bond.[132] Bond, who called it 'Confucian Work Dynamism,' sampled a domain of values formulated by Chinese scholars. He assembled a group of researchers, named the Chinese Culture Connection (CCC), who presented these values to students from 23 countries. The resulting dimension referred to a long-term versus a short-term orientation in life.

Consequences of long-term orientation are that there is not one truth; there is perseverance, thrift, and pursuit of peace of mind, elements of Confucian philosophy. The opposite is a short-term orientation in which spending now is more important than saving for tomorrow. Most East Asian countries scored high on this fifth dimension, particularly the ones with large Chinese populations. Anglo-Saxon societies scored low. Because measurements started later than for the other dimensions, scores were available for fewer countries. One of Michael Minkov's[133] dimensions, called 'monumentalism versus flexhumility,' appeared to share common values with the original LTO dimension, but it also included other values that are not linked with Confucian philosophy.[134] Country scores are available for nearly all countries for which scores of the other dimensions are available. Included in short-term orientation are values of national pride, tradition, low thrift, self-enhancement, appeal of folk wisdom and witchcraft, and talent for theoretical, abstract sciences. Included in long-term orientation are thrift, perseverance, pragmatism, and talent for applied, concrete sciences. In short-term-oriented cultures, there is a need for the absolute truth. Important elements are also tradition, self-esteem and self-enhancement. In long-term-oriented cultures, parents are more lenient toward children than in short-term-oriented cultures. The country scores for LTO in Appendix A refer to this new dimension.

Long-/short-term orientation explains, for example, differences in use of cosmetics, deodorants, and convenience products such as soft drinks, all sorts of processed food, microwave ovens, and dishwashing machines. It explains differences in time spent eating and shopping and visits to museums. It explains adoption of all sorts of applications of the Internet as well as relationships between parents and children. It explains differences in communication styles and Internet usage. The number of friends people have in social media is related to short-term orientation; having many friends is a form of self-enhancement. Examples of values reflected in advertising are long-term symbols like thick trees or other time-related references versus convenience.

GLOBE's dimension future orientation includes persistence, thrift and looser ties with family and friends; low scores include pleasure, importance of customs and traditions; and procrastination – altogether a content that is very different from Hofstede's dimension. Only a few meaningful correlations are found with these dimensions.

In our exercise an interesting correlation is between Hofstede's long-term orientation and personally own a desktop. This points at thrift. Whereas many people may throw out the desktop when buying newer gadgets like tablets and smartphones, probably in the more thrifty cultures people may longer adhere to the good old desktop. The more modern versions of a computer correlate negatively with long-term orientation. Following technology may be viewed as a reflection of longer-term values. There are only two significant correlations with future orientation, of which never travelling abroad seems to reflect the opposite of the values included in the description of this dimension. Not traveling is in contrast with values of pleasure. Because Hofstede's indulgence–restraint (IVR) also includes values like pleasure and thrift, in some cases these dimensions overlap, so in Table 2.7 we also include IVR correlations with the same items.

Table 2.7   Comparing long-/short-term orientation, future orientation and indulgence/restraint

*Pearson partial correlation coefficient one-tailed, controlled for GNI/cap at PPP 2013, *p < 0.05, **p < 0.01* Percentages of respondents who use, own, bought or agree with statement	*Future orientation*	*Long- vs short-term orientation*	*Indulgence vs restraint*
I personally own a desktop		.61*	
I personally own a laptop		−.63**	.63**
I personally own an i-phone		−.53*	.56*
Individuals using Internet	.55*		.59*
I never travel abroad in EU	−.54*		−.54*
I follow developments of new technology		.47*	−.59*

SOURCES: World Bank, 2014; *E-communications and Telecom Single Market Household Survey*, EBS 414, 2014; *European Media and Marketing Survey*, Ipsos, 2012 (see Appendix B)

Other Dimensions

Other dimensions that are included in the Hofstede, GLOBE, and Schwartz models are *indulgence/restraint, performance orientation* and *humane orientation*.

Indulgence includes the degree of happiness people experience, the control they have over their own lives, and the importance of leisure. *Restraint* includes values like hard work and thrift. Examples of correlations have been included in Table 2.7. As this dimension was introduced only recently, it will take more analysis to understand its full explaining power.

Performance orientation[135] includes valuing education, learning and taking inititative. None of the items correlated significantly with this dimension.

Humane orientation is defined as the degree to which an organization or society encourages and rewards individuals for being fair, altruistic, friendly, generous, caring, and kind to others versus self-interest, self-enjoyment and self-enhancement.[136]

Validation of Hofstede's Work

Hofstede's dimensions are increasingly used as independent variables for comparative cross-cultural studies and have led to many useful explanations of cross-cultural differences in consumer behavior. An often-posed question is whether his country scores, produced in the late 1960s and early 1970s are valid to use some 40/50 years later. Also, because Hofstede's dimensions were derived from answers by IBM employees only, often the question is asked whether the same dimensions are found among other matched samples of respondents. Several replications of Hofstede's study on different matched or nonmatched samples have proved that his data are still valid. Søndergaard[137] analyzed applications and replications of Hofstede's work in the 1980s, which showed that the differences predicted by Hofstede's dimensions were largely confirmed. There are remarkably few nonconfirmations. In the second edition of his book *Culture's Consequences*, Hofstede describes more than 200 external comparative studies and replications that have supported his indexes.

Hofstede's dimensions are increasingly used as a conceptual framework outside their original setting and are used to classify and explain the influence of culture on various research topics.

Several inventories of cultural classifications applied to international marketing show that of available models the Hofstede model has been used most frequently to understand differences across markets. It has been used for analyzing market entry modes, for innovation, research and development, for personality and for motivation studies, for understanding emotions across cultures as well as for analyzing advertising. Marketing managers have a need to estimate cultural differences between the firm's home and host markets, for which the Hofstede model is used.[138] It is useful to segment the world on a country level so international marketers can adopt similar advertising campaigns in a country segment.[139]

Culture Relationships

Because the Hofstede model is the most robust, it is used in this book to explain culture's influence on consumer behavior. The model was developed for people's behavior in organizations, so the relationship with behavior of consumers needs some additional analytical skills. It is easy to draw the wrong conclusions of cause and effect of culture. Problems can arise in the formulation of hypotheses and in selecting countries or groups of countries for analysis. A few general points of caution are dealt with in the following sections.

Cause-Effect

A frequently asked question is about the cause–effect relationship between culture and social phenomena. Are the characteristics of a social system (e.g., legal, political, or economic system) produced by the personal qualities of the population, or are the personal qualities of people generated by the nature of the social system in which they live? In many cases, common historical learning that has shaped national culture is the best factor to explain variance. But problems of determining whether what is observed is caused by history or is a functional relationship are frequent. A classical controversy of this nature concerns the meaning of the Weberian hypothesis relating Protestant values to capitalist orientations. Is it a 'functional' relationship between Protestant values and entrepreneurship, or is it based on shared contacts or common historical learning?[140] The latter is probably the case. Capitalism thrived in countries of a specific cultural configuration that also harbored Protestantism.[141] Religious affiliation by itself is less culturally relevant than it is often assumed. If we trace the religious history of countries, what religion a population has embraced seems to have been a result of previously existing cultural value patterns more than a cause of cultural differences.[142]

Another example is the relationship (in continental Europe) between low English-speaking skills and low usage of the Internet. Both are related with Hofstede's dimension uncertainty avoidance. In strong uncertainty avoidance cultures, people avoid difficulties of language learning[143] as well as innovative behavior with respect to new technology (see also Chapter 7). So the functional relationship is with uncertainty avoidance.

Another assumed cause–effect relationship is between economic development and culture. Some theorists see culture as a major determinant of socioeconomic success, whereas others see national wealth as a determinant of culture. Schwartz[144] states that socioeconomic and cultural variables powerfully influence each other. Inglehart's findings suggest that economic development is related to culture change away from traditional values and toward self-expression values. However, further analysis of the WVS data by Van de Vliert[145] led to the conclusion that higher levels of economic growth are not related to decreases in traditional values and increases in secular-rational values.

The anthropologist Fricke[146] notes that correlations merely measure covariation and that their usefulness for explaining behavior depends on interpretation. Strict causality is difficult to prove. 'Procedures that work well in natural sciences that do not deal with human beings may be too confining for the study of causality in human beings.'

However, if companies find significant differences in sales or usage of their products or brands in countries that have a similar level of purchasing power and no other variables can be found that explain variance it is appropriate to examine the explanatory function of cultural values. Generally, when cross-cultural researchers find consistent relationships between aggregate data on various aspects of consumer behavior and cultural values, they view these values as variables that can explain and predict.

Comparing Groups of Cultures

Evolutionary theory states that only cultures in the same stage of development can be meaningfully compared.[147] Comparisons that include both modern and developing countries produce differences that are very hard to interpret – if they make sense at all. In youth surveys, for example, one observes young people in developing countries such as India reacting with high degrees of optimism that are factually completely inappropriate. By way of contrast, young people in Sweden or in the Netherlands exude gloom in the wake of incomparably greater opportunity.[148] So, the choice of which nations to compare can influence the validity of the findings and reduce the possibility of generalizing findings. It is not easy to get subclasses of cultures for which valid comparison is possible. Correlations of different groups of countries will have different results. Hofstede's dimension power distance can serve as an example of how different groups of countries show different relationships. Worldwide, for a group of 33 countries of mixed levels of development, power distance is correlated with wealth; that is, the higher the GNI per capita, the lower countries score on power distance, so there is a negative correlation between national wealth and power distance. This relationship does not exist among a group of developed countries.

The relationships between dimensions can also vary for different regions. For example, Hofstede's dimension uncertainty avoidance correlates positively with power distance in a wealthy subgroup of countries, but this correlation is nonexistent in a poorer subgroup of countries.[149] This may be related to findings that in richer countries uncertainty avoidance is negatively related to the penetration of new products, but this relationship tends to be positive under poorer economic conditions.[150]

Different selections of countries can result in different significance of correlations. For several communication technology products, our finding is that the wealthier the group of countries, the more significant the correlations with culture. When comparing cultural relationships over time, the same groups of countries have to be selected.

Comparing Groups Within Cultures

In line with the distinction individual-level and culture-level, comparing subgroups (within-country groups) can lead to different results than when countries are compared. Power distance, measured by Hofstede at the culture level, can only be used as a characteristic of social systems, not of individuals or groups within countries. When for the group of 33 countries worldwide, populations are segmented in subgroups of different levels of wealth, these subgroups show different correlations with power distance. The groups that have the 20% highest share of national wealth, for example, correlate positively with power distance, whereas at national level, GNI per capita correlates negatively with power distance. If the 20% highest income groups correlate positively with power distance, and the 20% lowest correlate negatively, such results demonstrate that the subgroups are not functionally equivalent. The findings say that in high power distance cultures, differences in income equality are larger than in low power distance cultures. Similar effects are found when comparing groups of students as students from some countries belong to the elites in their countries.

Value Shift

Although values are enduring, some values may change in the long term. Value shift can be caused by economic change, modernization, maturation and generation effects, zeitgeist, and seniority effects.

Economic change, like increased wealth, can lead to individualism, and poverty leads to collectivism. With better education, the level of power distance goes down. Yet relative differences remain, and some differences may even become stronger. At face value, people tend to become more individualistic, but individuation follows different patterns.

Modernization, including industrialization and urbanization, is assumed to turn collectivistic societies into individualistic societies. Although urbanization tends to break up the joint household of the extended family in favor of more nuclear households, this does not imply decreasing extended family values.

Maturation effects[151] mean that people's values shift as they grow older. Stress, for example, is highest at middle age. Masculinity decreases with increasing age. Young people who want to make it in life generally adhere more to masculine values than do those who have already made it. Youngest and oldest age categories are less individualistic.

Generation effects occur when values are fixed in the young from a certain period and then stay with that age cohort over its lifetime. Drastic changes in the conditions of life during youth may lead to generations having different fixed values. The value shift of the generation of the 1960s in Europe and the United States is an example of a generation effect.

Zeitgeist effects occur when drastic systemwide changes in conditions cause everyone's values to shift, regardless of age. In times of recession, the degree of power distance may increase because equality is less functional, or it may lead to increased bureaucracy and shift to a stronger level of uncertainty avoidance. *Seniority effects* occur when the values of people who are more senior in an organization are measured. Seniority and age effects cannot be separated easily.

The degree of uncertainty avoidance of countries can change with environmental factors. Natural disasters and war will cause higher levels. When in 1996 we measured the dimensions in the EMS survey, Finland's score on uncertainty avoidance had lowered and the score of the United Kingdom had become higher. The United Kingdom was in an economic crisis at that time, and Finland had been delivered from the pressure of the Soviet Union.

Conclusion

People of different countries have different value orientations that cause variation in preferences of products and brands. For effective international marketing and communications, people must understand these differences. Much consumer behavior research is conducted at the individual level. This chapter discussed comparative research at the culture level. Models that distinguish value categories or dimensions of culture can help to analyze differences at culture level. They allow statistical analysis that can discover relationships between country scores on cultural dimensions and data on consumption and consumer behavior. Not all models are equally practical. Several models were reviewed in this chapter. The model that is most applied to marketing and advertising is the model of national culture developed by Geert Hofstede. Analysis of the effect of culture becomes increasingly important, because value differences are stable over time and become manifest with increased wealth. This is the topic that will be further pursued in Chapter 3.

Notes

1. D.E. Vinson, J.E. Scott, and L.M. Lamont, 'The role of personal values in marketing and consumer behavior,' *Journal of Marketing* (April 1997), pp. 44–50.
2. M. Rokeach, *The Nature of Human* Values (Free Press, New York, 1973), p. 5.
3. Ibid., p. 18.
4. Z. Wang, C.P. Rao, and A. D'Auria, 'A comparison of the Rokeach Value Survey (RVS) in China and the United States,' in J.A. Cote and S.M. Leong (eds), *Asia Pacific Advances in Consumer Research*, Vol. 1 (Association for Consumer Research, Provo, UT, 1994), pp. 185–190.
5. W. Jagodzinski, 'Methodological problems of value research,' in H. Vinken, J. Soeters, and P. Ester (eds), *Comparing Cultures: Dimensions of Culture in a Comparative Perspective* (Brill, Leiden/Boston, 2004), p. 105.
6. C-M.Vauclair, R. Fischer, M.C. Ferreira, V. Guerra, U. Hößler, S. Karabati, M.K. De Carvalho Filho, J. Porto, M. Lopez Reyes, J. Rytkönen, and E. Spieß, 'What kinds of value motives guide people in their moral attitudes? The role of personal and prescriptive values at the culture level and individual level,' *Journal of Cross-Cultural Psychology*, 46, 2 (2014), pp. 211–228.
7. G. Hofstede, G.J. Hofstede, and M. Minkov, *Cultures and Organizations: Software of the Mind* (McGraw-Hill, London & New York, 2010).
8. G. Hofstede, *Culture's Consequences*, 2nd edn (Sage, Thousand Oaks, CA, 2001), pp. 6–7.
9. S.C. Grunert and T.E. Muller, 'Measuring values in international settings: Are respondents thinking "real" life or "ideal" life?,' in L. Manrai and A. Manrai (eds), *Global Perspectives in Cross-Cultural and Cross-National Consumer Research* (International Business Press/Haworth Press, New York and London, 1996), pp. 169-186

10. M. De Mooij, *Global Marketing and Advertising, Understanding Cultural Paradoxes*, 5th edn (Sage, Thousand Oaks, CA, 2018).

11. H. Cheng and J.C. Schweitzer, 'Cultural values reflected in Chinese and US television commercials,' *Journal of Advertising Research*, May/June (1996), pp. 27–45.

12. G. Hofstede, *Cultures and Organizations: Software of the Mind* (McGraw-Hill, London & New York, 1991), p. 8.

13. D. Yankelovich, 'How changes in the economy are reshaping American values,' in H.J. Aaron, T.E. Mann, and T. Taylor (eds), *Values and Public Policy* (Brookings Institution, Washington, DC, 1994), pp. 23–24.

14. 'Dr Gallup's finger on America's pulse,' *The Economist* (September 1997), p. 102.

15. G. Gao, 'For a rich country, America is unusually religious and optimistic,' Wonkblog, *The Washington Post* (12 March 2015). Available at: www.washingtonpost.com/news/wonk/wp/2015/03/12/for-a-rich-country-america-is-unusually-religious-and-optimistic/?utm_term=.1cb0404c6f33 (accessed 16 February 2018).

16. A. Inkeles, *Continuity and Change in Popular Values on the Pacific Rim* (Hoover Institution, Stanford University, Stanford, CA, 1997).

17. J.H.Y. Fu and C.Y. Chiu, 'Local culture's responses to globalization. Exemplary persons and their attendant values,' *Journal of Cross-Cultural Psychology*, 38, 5 (2007), pp. 636–653.

18. S.H.C. Tai and J.L.M. Tam, 'A comparative study of Chinese consumers in Asian markets – a lifestyle analysis,' *Journal of International Consumer Marketing*, 9 (1996), pp. 25–42.

19. R.W. Pollay and K. Gallagher, 'Advertising and cultural values: Reflections in the distorted mirror,' *International Journal of Advertising*, 9 (1990), pp. 359–372.

20. C.R. Wiles, J. Wiles, and A. Tjernlund, 'The ideology of advertising: The United States and Sweden,' *Journal of Advertising Research*, May/June (1996), pp. 57–66.

21. A. Inkeles, *One World Emerging?* (Westview, Boulder, CO, 1998), p. 173.

22. P. Cafferata, M.I. Horn, and W.D. Wells, 'Gender role changes in the United States,' in L. Kahle and L. Chiagouris (eds), *Values, Lifestyles, and Psychographics* (Lawrence Erlbaum, Mahwah, NJ, 1997), pp. 249–262.

23. L.R. Kahle and S. Goff Timmer, *A Theory and Method for Studying Values and Social Change: Adaptation to Life in America* (Praeger, New York, 1983).

24. C.J. Clawson and D.E. Vinson, 'Human values: A historical and interdisciplinary analysis,' in H.K. Hunt (ed.), *Advances in Consumer Research*, Vol. 5 (Association for Consumer Research, Ann Arbor, MI, 1978), pp. 396–402.

25. R.W. Pollay, 'The identification and distribution of values manifest in print advertising 1900–1980,' in R.E. Pitts Jr. and A.G. Woodside (eds), *Personal Values and Consumer Psychology* (Lexington Books, Lexington, MA, 1984), pp. 111–135.

26. A. Venkatesh, 'Ethnoconsumerism: A new paradigm to study cultural and cross-cultural consumer behavior,' in J.A. Costa and G.J. Bamossy (eds), *Marketing in a Multicultural World* (Sage, Thousand Oaks, CA, 1995), pp. 26–67.

27. A.C-T. Lowe and D.R. Corkindale, 'Differences in "cultural values" and their effects on responses to marketing stimuli: A cross-cultural study between Australians and Chinese from the People's Republic of China,' *European Journal of Marketing*, 32 (1998), pp. 843–867.

28. C. Geertz, *The Interpretation of Cultures* (Basic Books, New York, 1972), p. 44.

29. Hofstede, *Cultures and Organizations*, p. 5.

30. H. Triandis, *Individualism and Collectivism* (Westview, Boulder, CO, 1995).

31. A. Inkeles, *National Character* (Transaction, New Brunswick, NJ, 1997), pp. 3–17.

32. M. Martínez Mateo, M. Cabanis, N. Cruz de Echeverría Loebell, and S. Krach, 'Concerns about cultural neurosciences: A critical analysis,' *Neuroscience and Biobehavioral Reviews*, 36 (2012), pp. 152–161.

33. N. Ambady and J. Bharucha, 'Culture and the brain,' *Current Directions in Psychological Science*, 18, 6 (2009), pp. 342–345.

34. B. Azar, 'Your brain on culture,' *American Psychological Association Science Watch*, 41, 10 (2010), pp. 1–3. Available at: www.apa.org/monitor/2010/11/neuroscience.aspx (accessed 4 October 2012).

35. J.Y. Sasaki and H.S. Kim, 'Nature, nurture, and their interplay: A review of cultural neuroscience,' *Journal of Cross-Cultural Psychology*, 48, 1 (2017), pp. 4–22.

36. Hofstede, *Culture's Consequences*, p. 11.

37. S.H. Schwartz, 'Beyond individualism/collectivism: New cultural dimensions of values,' in U. Kim, H.C. Triandis, Ç. Kâgitçibasi, S.-C. Choi, and G. Yoon (eds), *Individualism and Collectivism* (Sage, Thousand Oaks, CA, 1994), pp. 85–119.

38. Inkeles, *National Character*, p. 103.

39. Hofstede, *Cultures and Organizations*, p. 8.

40. S. Kitayama, 'Culture and basic psychological processes: Toward a system view of culture: Comment on Oyserman et al.,' *Psychological Bulletin*, 128 (2002), pp. 89–96.

41. R. Fischer, 'Congruence and functions of personal and cultural values: Do my values reflect my culture's values?,' *Personality and Social Psychology Bulletin*, 32, 11 (2006), pp. 1419–1431.

42. X. Zou and A.K.-y Leung, 'Enriching cultural psychology with research insights on norms and intersubjective representations,' *Journal of Cross-Cultural Psychology*, 46, 10 (2015), pp. 1238–1244.

43. J.T. Jost, J.L. Sterling, and M. Langer, 'From "Is" to "Ough" and sometimes "Not": Compliance with and resistance to social norms from a system justification perspective,' *Journal of Cross-Cultural Psychology*, 46, 10 (2015), pp. 1287–1291.

44. A.W. Harzing, 'Does the USE of English-language questionnaires in cross-national research obscure national differences?,' *International Journal of Cross Cultural Management*, 5, 2 (2005), pp. 213–224.

45. H. Van Herk, Y.H. Poortinga, and T.M.M. Verhallen, 'Equivalence of survey data: Relevance for international marketing,' *European Journal of Marketing*, 39, 3/4 (2005), pp. 351–364.

46. S.P. Douglas and C.S. Craig, *International Marketing Research* (Prentice-Hall International Editions, Englewood Cliffs, NJ, 1983), p. 192.

47. G. Isabella, J.A. Mazzon, and A. Dimoka, 'Culture differences, difficulties, and challenges of the neurophysiological methods in marketing research,' *Journal of International Consumer Marketing*, 27, 5 (2015), pp. 346–363.

48. Hofstede, *Culture's Consequences*, pp. 15–17; Schwartz, 'Beyond individualism/collectivism,' pp. 92–93.

49. W.F. Van Raaij, 'Micro and macro economic psychology,' in M. Lambkin, G. Foxall, F. van Raaij, and B. Heilbrunn (eds), *European Perspectives on Consumer Behaviour* (Prentice Hall, London, 1998), pp. 335–347.

50. Hofstede, *Culture's Consequences*, pp. 16–17.

51. Hofstede, *Culture's Consequences*, p. 463.

52. Schwartz, 'Beyond individualism/collectivism,' p. 104.

53. A. Przeworski and H. Teune, *The Logic of Comparative Social Inquiry* (Wiley-Interscience, New York, 1970), pp. 59–60.

54. M. Minkov, *What Makes Us Different and Similar* (Klasika I Stil, Sofia, Bulgaria, 2007), p. 35.

55. R.H. Holman, 'A values and lifestyles perspective on human behavior,' in R.E. Pitts Jr. and A.G. Woodside (eds), *Personal Values and Consumer Psychology* (Lexington Books, D.C. Heath, Lexington, MA, 1984), pp. 35–54.

56. RISC International, *Why People Buy* [Brochure] (Paris, 1995). Available at: www.risc-int.com.

57. J. Callebaut, M. Janssens, D. Lorré, and H. Hendrickx, *The Naked Consumer: The Secret of Motivational Research in Global Marketing* (Censydiam Institute, Antwerp, 1994), p. 106.

58. F. Hansen, 'From lifestyle to value system to simplicity,' *Advances in Consumer Research*, 25 (1998), pp. 181–195.

59. M. De Mooij, *Advertising Worldwide*, 2nd edn (Prentice Hall International, London, 1994), pp. 178–183.

60. N. Homma and J. Ueltzhoffer, *The Internationalization of Everyday-Life Research Markets and Milieus*. ESOMAR Conference on America, Japan and EC '92: The Prospects for Marketing, Advertising and Research. Venice, Italy (18–20 June 1990); See also: www.motivaction.nl

61. T. Denton, 'Unit of observation in cross-cultural research: Implications for sampling and aggregated data analysis,' *Cross-Cultural Research*, 41, 1 (2007), pp. 3–31.

62. G. Hofstede and G.J. Hofstede, *Cultures and Organizations Software of the Mind*, 2nd edn (McGraw Hill, New York, 2004).

63. S. Anholt, *Another One Bites the Grass* (Wiley, New York, 2000), p. 66.

64. M. De Mooij and J. Beniflah, 'Measuring cross-cultural differences of ethnic groups within nations: Convergence or divergence of cultural values? The case of the United States,' *Journal of International Consumer Marketing*, 29, 1 (2017), pp. 2–10.

65. *European Social Survey*. See Appendix B. This study provides answers to value questions that can be isolated for the various provinces of the participating countries. In the cultural cohesion analysis, France and Italy could not be included, as the respondents hadn't answered the particular set of questions.

66. D. Singh, *Cross Cultural Comparison of Buying Behavior in India*, Doctoral thesis (University Business School, Panjab University, Chandigarh, 2007).

67. P.R. Harris and R.T. Moran, *Managing Cultural Differences* (Gulf Publishing, Houston, TX, 1987), pp. 190–195.

68. G. Hofstede, 'Dimensions do not exist: A reply to Brendan McSweeney,' *Human Relations*, 55, 11 (2002), pp. 1355–1361.

69. R. Inglehart, M. Basañez, and A. Moreno, *Human Values and Beliefs* (University of Michigan Press, Ann Arbor, 1998).

70. Inkeles, *National Character*, pp. 45–50.

71. F. Kluckhohn and F. Strodtbeck, *Variations in Value Orientations* (Row, Peterson, Evanston, IL, 1961).

72. F. Trompenaars, *Riding the Waves of Culture: Understanding Cultural Diversity in Business* (Nicholas Brealey, London, 1993).

73. P.B. Smith, S. Dugan, and F. Trompenaars, 'National culture and the values of organizational employees: A dimensional analysis across 43 nations,' *Journal of Cross-Cultural Psychology*, 27 (1996), pp. 231–264.

74. A.P. Fiske, 'The four elementary forms of sociality: Framework for a unified theory of social relations,' *Psychological Review*, 99 (1992), pp. 689–723.

75. E. Hall, *Beyond Culture* (Doubleday, New York, 1976); E. Hall, *The Dance of Life* (Doubleday, New York, 1984), pp. 85–128.

76. Analysis is through correlation and regression analysis. Throughout this book for correlation analysis, the Pearson product-moment correlation coefficient is used. Correlation analysis is one-tailed. Significance levels are indicated by * $p < .05$, ** $p < .01$, and *** $p < .005$. When regression analysis is used, multiple linear regression analysis is done stepwise. The coefficient of determination or R^2 is the indicator of the percentage of variance explained. The examples in the charts are of significant correlations between secondary data and one or more dimensions. Usually, for presentation clarity not all countries are included. If more countries are available than presented in the chart, the original number of countries with the related correlation coefficient are included in an endnote.

77. S.H. Schwartz and W. Bilsky, 'Toward a universal psychological structure of human values,' *Journal of Personality and Social Psychology*, 53 (1987), pp. 550–562.

78. R.J. House, P.J. Hanges, M. Javidan, P.W. Dorfman, and V. Gupta (eds), *Culture, Leadership, and Organizations: The GLOBE Study of 62 Societies* (Sage, Thousand Oaks, CA, 2004).

79. P. Magnusson, R.T. Wilson, S. Zdravkovic, J.X. Zhou, and S.A. Westjohn, 'Breaking through the cultural clutter: A comparative assessment of multiple cultural and institutional frameworks,' *International Marketing Review*, 25, 2 (2008), pp. 183–201.

80. T. Doi, *The Anatomy of Self* (Kodansha International, Tokyo, 1985).

81. B. Jordá-Albiñana, O. Ampuero-Canellas, N. Vila, and J.I. Rojas-Sola, 'Brand identity documentation: A cross-national examination of identity standards manuals,' *International Marketing Review*, 26, 2 (2009), pp. 172–197.

82. L.T. White, R. Valk, and A. Dialmy, 'What is the meaning of "On Time"? The sociological nature of punctuality,' *Journal of Cross-Cultural Psychology*, 42, 3 (2011), pp. 482–493.

83. Hall, *The Dance of Life*, pp. 16–27, 32–34.

84. Hall, *The Dance of Life*, pp. 17–24.

85. M. De Mooij, *Human and Mediated Communication Around the World. A Comprehensive Review and Analysis* (Springer, Champaign, 2014), p. 191.

86. N.J. Adler, *International Dimensions of Organizational Behavior* (Wadsworth, Belmont, CA, 1991), pp. 30–31.

87. A. Roland, *In Search of Self in India and Japan* (Princeton University Press, Princeton, NJ, 1988), p. 302.

88.   De Mooij, *Human and Mediated Communication*, p. 152.

89.   S.L. Lindsley and C.A. Braithwaite, 'US Americans and Mexicans working together: Five core Mexican concepts for enhancing effectiveness,' in L.A. Samovar and R.E. Porter (eds), *Intercultural Communication: A Reader*, 10th edn (Wadsworth, Belmont, CA, 2003), pp. 293–299.

90.   De Mooij, *Human and Mediated Communication*, p. 94.

91.   Minkov, *What Makes Us Different and Similar*, p. 23.

92.   Hofstede, *Culture's Consequences*; Hofstede et al., *Cultures and Organizations*.

93.   S.H. Schwartz, 'Studying values: Personal adventure, future directions,' *Journal of Cross-Cultural Psychology*, 42, 2 (2011), pp. 307–319.

94.   House et al., *Culture, Leadership, and Organizations*.

95.   S.H. Schwartz, 'Mapping and interpreting cultural differences,' in H. Vinken, J. Soeters, and P. Ester (eds), *Comparing Cultures: Dimensions of Culture in a Comparative Perspective* (Brill, Leiden, Netherlands, 2004).

96.   S. Schwartz and A. Bardi, 'Value hierarchies across cultures: Taking a similarities perspective,' *Journal of Cross-Cultural Psychology*, 32 (2001), pp. 268–290.

97.   G. Sun, S. D'Allessandro, L. Johnson, and H. Winzar, 'Do we measure what we expect to measure? Some issues in the measurement of culture in consumer research,' *International Marketing Review*, 31, 4 (2014), pp. 338–362.

98.   M. Javidan, R.J. House, P.W. Dorfman, P.J. Hanges, and M. Sully de Luque, 'Conceptualizing and measuring cultures and their consequences: A comparative review of GLOBE's and Hofstede's approaches,' *Journal of International Business Studies*, 37 (2006), pp. 897–914.

99.   A.C.W. Chui and C.C.Y. Kwok, 'National culture and life insurance consumption,' *Journal of International Business Studies*, 39, 1 (2008), pp. 88–101.

100.   K.H. Lim, K. Leung, C.L. Sia, and M.K.O. Lee, 'Is eCommerce boundary-less? Effects of individualism-collectivism and uncertainty-avoidance on Internet shopping,' *Journal of Internet Business Studies*, 35 (2004), pp. 545–559.

101.   S. Yeniurt and J.D. Townsend, 'Does culture explain acceptance of new products in a country?,' *International Marketing Review*, 20, 4 (2003), pp. 377–396.

102.   G.J. Tellis, S. Stremersch, and E. Yin, 'The international take-off of new products: The role of economics, culture, and country innovativeness,' *Marketing Science*, 22, 2 (2003), pp. 188–208.

103.   S. Stremersch and G.J. Tellis, 'Understanding and managing international growth of new products,' *International Journal of Research in Marketing*, 21 (2004), pp. 421–438.

104.   N.D. Albers-Miller and B.D. Gelb, 'Business advertising appeals as a mirror of cultural dimensions: A study of eleven countries,' *Journal of Advertising*, 15, 4 (1996), pp. 57–70; K. Chan and Y.S. Moon, 'Cultural values manifest in Hong Kong and Korean television commercials,' *International Marketing Review*, 22, 1 (2005), pp. 48–66; C. Emery and K.R. Tian, 'China compared with the US: Cultural differences and the impacts on advertising appeals,' *International Journal of China Marketing*, 1, 1 (2010), available at: www.na-businesspress.com/ijcm/emery-web.pdf (accessed 30 January 2014); D.L. Rhodes and C.R. Emery, 'The effect of cultural differences on effective advertising: A comparison between Russia and the US,' *Academy of Marketing Studies Journal*, 7, 2 (2003), pp. 89–105.

105. L. Zheng, J. Phelps, and M. Hoy, 'Cultural values reflected in Chinese Olympics advertising,' in H. Li, S. Huang, and D. Jin (eds), *Proceedings of the 2009 American Academy of Advertising Asia-Pacific Conference* (American Academy of Advertising in conjunction with China Association of Advertising of Commerce and Communication University of China, 2009), pp. 26–27.

106. C.L.C. Praet, 'National wealth or national culture? A multi-country study of the factors underlying the use of celebrity endorsement in television advertising,' in P. De Pelsmacker and N. Dens (eds), *Research in Advertising: The Medium, the Message, and the Context* (Garant, Antwerp, 2009), pp. 383–392.

107. R. Terlutter, S. Diehl, and B. Mueller, 'The GLOBE study – applicability of a new typology of cultural dimensions for cross-cultural marketing and advertising research,' in S. Diehl and R. Terlutter (eds), *International Advertising and Communication. Current Insights and Empirical Findings* (Gabler Edition Wissenschaft, Wiesbaden, 2006), pp. 421–438.

108. S. Diehl, R. Terlutter, and B. Mueller, 'The influence of culture on responses to the GLOBE dimension of performance orientation in advertising messages – Results from the US, Germany, France, Spain, and Thailand,' *Advances in Consumer Research*, 35 (2008), pp. 269–275.

109. B. Czarnecka and R. Brennan, 'How well does GLOBE predict values in advertising? A content analysis of print advertising from the UK, Ireland, Poland and Hungary,' *Proceedings of 8th EAA International Conference on Research in Advertising*, 26–27 June 2009, Klagenfurt, Austria.

110. The descriptions of the dimensions are summaries of the dimension descriptions from Hofstede et al., *Cultures and Organizations*; and Hofstede, *Culture's Consequences*. With permission.

111. The author of this book has compared the three models by correlation analysis of relevant items from a number of large databases using all 21 dimensions of the three models. This draws from a study reported in: M. De Mooij, 'Comparing dimensions of national culture for secondary analysis of consumer behavior data of different countries,' *International Marketing Review*, 34, 3 (2017), pp. 444–456.

  In the tables are the correlations with the percentage answers to survey questions. For the Hofstede dimensions, the country scores are published in Hofstede et al., *Cultures and Organizations,* as well as in this book (Appendix A). The GLOBE scores are available from House et al., *Culture, Leadership, and Organizations*, and Shalom Schwartz personally provided the most recent scores for his model. For the GLOBE model, only the practices were used as the value data are too far from reality. The dimension institutional collectivism practices didn't provide any meaningful results, in contrast to in-group collectivism, so only the latter was used. The examples in the tables are for 16 European countries.

  The 16 countries used of the World Development Indicators database, Special Eurobarometer surveys and Eurostat are Austria, Denmark, Finland, France, Germany, Greece, Hungary, Ireland, Italy, Netherlands, Poland, Portugal, Slovenia, Spain, Sweden, UK. The 15 countries of the *European Media and Marketing Survey* are Austria, Denmark, Finland, France, Germany, Hungary, Ireland, Italy, Netherlands, Poland, Portugal, Spain, Sweden, Switzerland, UK.

112. D. Carl, V. Gupta, and M. Javidan, 'Power distance,' in R.J. House, P.J. Hanges, M. Javidan, P.W. Dorfman, and V. Gupta (eds), *Culture, Leadership, and Organizations. The GLOBE Study of 62 Societies* (Sage, Thousand Oaks, CA, 2004), pp. 513–563.

113. Michael Hoppe, a German American management educator, replicated the IBM study on a population of political and institutional elites and found that Italy is much more collectivistic than the IBM scores lead one to believe. Hoppe's study (*A Comparative Study of Country Elites: International Differences in Work-related Values and Learning and their Implications for Management Training and Development* [Unpublished doctoral dissertation, University of North Carolina, Chapel Hill, 1990]) also found differences with respect to Finland, which may be more individualistic than the IBM scores indicate. Contradictory information about the level of individualism or collectivism in Italy is probably due to the fact that Italy is bicultural: the north is individualistic, but the rest of the country is collectivistic. Hofstede's IBM data were mainly collected in the north, and he found strong individualism. Consumption and media behavior data are based on a country average; where these relate to individualism or collectivism, Italy tends to score similar to Spain, which is much more collectivistic.

114. S. Beugelsdijk, R. Maseland, and A. Van Hoorn, 'Are scores on Hofstede's dimensions of national culture stable over time? A cohort analysis,' *Global Strategy Journal*, 5 (2015), pp. 223–240.

115. V. Taras et al., 'Opposite ends of the same stick? Multi-method test of the dimensionality of individualism and collectivism,' *Journal of Cross-Cultural Psychology*, 45, 2 (2014), pp. 213–245.

116. W.G. Gudykunst, Y. Matsumoto, S. Ting-Toomey, and T. Nishida, 'The influence of cultural individualism-collectivism, self-construals, and individual values on communication styles across cultures,' *Human Communication Research*, 22 (1996), pp. 510–543.

117. M.S. Kim and K. Leung, *A Revised Self-Construal Scale* (unpublished manuscript, University of Hawaii at Manoa, Honolulu, 1997).

118. D. Oyserman, 'The lens of personhood: Viewing the self and others in a multicultural society,' *Journal of Personality and Social Psychology*, 65 (1993), pp. 993–1009.

119. T.M. Singelis, 'The measurement of independent and interdependent self-construals,' *Personality and Social Psychology Bulletin*, 20 (1994), pp. 580–591.

120. T. Takata, 'Social comparison and formation of self-concept in adolescent: Some findings about Japanese college students,' *Japanese Journal of Educational Psychology*, 41 (1993), pp. 339–348.

121. H.C. Triandis, *INDCOL* (unpublished research scale on individualism and collectivism, University of Illinois, Champaign, 1994).

122. J.H. Vargas and M. Kemmelmeier, 'Ethnicity and contemporary American culture: A meta-analytic investigation of horizontal-vertical individualism-collectivism,' *Journal of Cross-Cultural Psychology*, 44, 2 (2013), pp. 195–222.

123. M.J. Gelfand, D.P.S. Bhawuk, L.H. Nishi, and D.J. Bechtold, 'Individualism and collectivism,' in R.J. House, P.J. Hanges, M. Javidan, P.W. Dorfman, and V. Gupta (eds), *Culture, Leadership, and Organizations. The GLOBE Study of 62 Societies* (Sage, Thousand Oaks, CA, 2004), pp. 437–512.

124. D.N. Den Hartog, 'Assertiveness,' in R.J. House, P.J. Hanges, M. Javidan, P.W. Dorfman, and V. Gupta (eds), *Culture, Leadership, and Organizations. The GLOBE Study of 62 Societies* (Sage, Thousand Oaks, CA, 2004), pp. 395–436.

125. C.G. Emrich, F.L. Denmark, and D.N. Den Hartog, (2004). 'Cross-cultural differences in gender egalitarianism: Implications for societies, organizations, and leaders,' in R.J. House, P.J. Hanges, M. Javidan, P.W. Dorfman, and V. Gupta (eds), *Culture, Leadership, and Organizations. The GLOBE Study of 62 Societies* (Sage, Thousand Oaks, CA, 2004), pp. 343–394.

126. Schwartz, 'Mapping and interpreting cultural differences.'

127. *Harmonised European Time Use Survey* (Eurostat report, European Commission, 2007). Availaable at: http://epp.eurostat.ec.europa.eu/portal/page/portal/eurostat/home

128. R. Soong, 'Argentina, Brazil, Chile, Colombia, Ecuador, Mexico and Peru,' message posted to TGI Latina, 23 December 2003. Available at: www.zonalatina.com/Zldata332.htm.

129. *Food-related Risks* (Special Eurobarometer report 354, 2010).

130. M. Sully de Luque and M. Javidan, 'Uncertainty avoidance,' in R.J. House, P.J. Hanges, M. Javidan, P.W. Dorfman, and V. Gupta (eds), *Culture, Leadership, and Organizations. The GLOBE Study of 62 Societies* (Sage, Thousand Oaks, CA, 2004), pp. 602–653.

131. M. Minkov and V. Blagoev, 'What do project GLOBE's cultural dimensions reflect? An empirical perspective,' *Asia Pacific Business Review* (2011), pp. 1–17.

132. G. Hofstede and M.H. Bond, 'The Confucius connection: From cultural roots to economic growth,' *Organizational Dynamics*, 16, Spring (1988), pp. 4–22.

133. Minkov, *What Makes Us Different and Similar.*

134. Hofstede et al., *Cultures and Organizations.*

135. M. Javidan, 'Performance orientation,' in R.J. House, P.J. Hanges, M. Javidan, P.W. Dorfman, and V. Gupta (eds), *Culture, Leadership, and Organizations. The GLOBE Study of 62 Societies* (Sage, Thousand Oaks, CA, 2004), pp. 239–281.

136. H. Kabasakal and M. Bodur, 'Humane orientation in societies, organizations, and leader attributes,' in R.J. House, P.J. Hanges, M. Javidan, P.W. Dorfman, and V. Gupta (eds), *Culture, Leadership, and Organizations. The GLOBE Study of 62 Societies* (Sage, Thousand Oaks, CA, 2004), pp. 564–601.

137. M. Søndergaard, 'Research note: Hofstede's consequences: A study of reviews, citations and replications,' *Organization Studies*, 15 (1994), pp. 447–456.

138. Magnusson et al., 'Breaking through the cultural clutter.'

139. J. Vanderstraeten and P. Matthyssens, 'Country classification and the cultural dimension: A review and evaluation,' *International Marketing Review*, 25, 2 (2008), pp. 230–251.

140. Przeworski and Teune, *The Logic of Comparative Social Inquiry*, pp. 51–56.

141. Hofstede, *Culture's Consequences*, p. 114.

142. Hofstede et al., *Cultures and Organizations.*

143. Several data on foreign language speaking show a relationship with uncertainty avoidance: the higher countries score on this dimension, the fewer foreign languages people speak. With respect to the English language, the argument can be that the countries with a language structure that is similar to the English language (all Germanic languages) have an advantage in

learning English. Quite a few Germanic languages are spoken in cultures of low uncertainty avoidance. However, also within the group of Germanic language countries (United Kingdom and Ireland excluded), a significant correlation is found between English speaking and low uncertainty avoidance.

144. Schwartz, 'Mapping and interpreting cultural differences,' p. 65.

145. E. Van de Vliert, 'Climatoeconomic roots of survival versus self-expression cultures,' Journal of *Cross-Cultural Psychology*, 38, 2 (2007), pp. 156–172.

146. T. Fricke, 'Culture and causality: An anthropological comment,' *Population and Development Review*, 29, 3 (2003), pp. 470–479.

147. W.F. Van Raaij, 'Cross-cultural research methodology as a case of construct validity,' in K. Hunt (ed.), *Advances in Consumer Research*, 5 (1978), pp. 693–701.

148. E.K. Scheuch, 'Theoretical implications of comparative survey research: Why the wheel of cross-cultural methodology keeps on being reinvented,' in A. Inkeles and M. Sasaki (eds), *Comparing Nations and Cultures* (Prentice Hall, Englewood Cliffs, NJ, 1996), pp. 57–73.

149. H.P. Müller and P. Ziltener, 'The structural roots of values: An anthropological interpretation of Hofstede's value dimensions,' in H. Vinken, J. Soeters, and P. Ester (eds), *Comparing Cultures. Dimensions of Culture in a Comparative Perspective* (Brill, Leiden/Boston, 2004), pp. 122–140.

150. S. Yeniurt and J.D. Townsend, 'Does culture explain acceptance of new products in a country?,' *International Marketing Review*, 20, 4 (2003), pp. 377–396.

151. Hofstede, *Culture's Consequences*.

Convergence and Divergence in Consumer Behavior

Chapter 1 reviewed the assumptions of converging consumer behavior and the counterarguments. The universalism of Western marketing professionals presupposes the emergence of a unique world culture following the maturity of consumer markets in which the United States leads the world. As American advertising professor John Philip Jones states, 'Logic points to similar patterns emerging in other countries when their per capita income levels approach that of the United States.'[1] Also, consumer behavior theorists follow this idea – that consumers in all parts of the world want American goods as status symbols – and in the process they adopt American consumption values. This chapter reviews the underlying socioeconomic phenomena of assumed convergence of consumer behavior, such as modernization, urbanization, rising education levels, changing demographics, and convergence of national wealth. Convergence theory and forms of convergence and divergence in consumer behavior are discussed.

Convergence Theory

Convergence theory proposes that, along with industrialization and modernization, nations are becoming increasingly alike despite different cultural and historical legacies and diverse political and economic systems.[2] Aspects of socioeconomic convergence are patterns of social relationships, increasing dependence on science and technology, popular attitudes, and systems of political and economic control.[3] Almost every society on Earth has at least begun to industrialize, and it seems likely that within the next century most of humanity will live in predominantly urban industrialized societies. This does not mean that all societies will be identical. Industrial societies have a wide variety of cultures and institutions. But their common characteristics are also striking; virtually without exception, they are characterized by high degrees of urbanization, the use of science and technology, and high levels of formal education.[4] However, the assumption that industrialization and modernization will bring a universal civilization, including universal values and consumption patterns, is a distinctive product of Western thinking.[5]

The convergence debate is not new; it resulted from modernization theory of the 1960s. Advocates of convergence argued that all or nearly all societies were, at different speeds, moving toward the same point, mainly as a result of industrial man,[6] whereas adherents to the divergence thesis emphasized the idea of there being different forms of modernity and that in that sense there is no convergence.[7] In order not to mistake the spread of American consumption symbols for cultural convergence, we have to understand the various aspects of modernization that underlie the global convergence hypothesis.

Modernization

Taken literally, the word *modern* refers to anything that has more or less recently replaced something that in the past was the accepted way of doing things.[8] Being modern is opposed to being traditional, whereby the modern is viewed as positive and the traditional as negative. The terms are used to characterize individuals and nations. When societies or nations are defined as modern, they are characterized by mass education, urbanization, industrialization, bureaucratization, and rapid communication and transportation. Some add to these cultural homogeneity and the secularization of belief.[9] *Economic modernization* includes intense application of scientific technology and inanimate sources of energy, high specialization of labor, interdependence of impersonal markets, large-scale financing combined with concentration of economic decision making, and rising levels of material well-being. The *socio-psychological* approach to modernization treats it mainly as a process of change in ways of perceiving, expressing, and valuing.

American social scientists Alex Inkeles and David Horton Smith[10] developed dimensions of individual modernity, including personal qualities such as openness to new experience, readiness for social change, a disposition to form or hold opinions and acknowledge differences of opinion, information, sense of time, control of the environment, orientation toward planning, calculability versus trust, educational and occupational aspirations, sense of dignity, and respect for others. The dimensions were developed to measure individual modernity in order to find scientific knowledge as to how far the qualities of a nation's people are important in fostering development. With the exception of Japan, all the major nations that can be considered modernized according to these dimensions are part of the European tradition. Although business people and the elites in most of the (from the Western point of view) developing societies have adopted the Western businessman's suit and shoes, the societies to which they belong are considered to be traditional societies.

This approach demonstrates that the term *modern* is often equated with *Western,* and the assumption is that with modernity people also will adopt Western values. This also applies to popular thought in marketing and advertising. According to the French marketing professor Jean-Claude Usunier,[11] some researchers, even though they acknowledge national differences, envision multinational marketing activities merely as processes of innovation and change that would bring worldwide convergence, with 'traditional' cultures being progressively replaced by 'modern' ones.

Although technological modernization is an important force to societal change, it does not wipe out variety. It may even increase differences, as on the basis of preexisting value systems societies cope with technological modernization in different ways.[12] Varying use of the Internet demonstrates this thesis. Associations with modernization vary. Whereas Westerners view modernization as a matter of changing values, Asians view modernization as involving technology, behavior, or material progress, without cultural implications.[13]

From Premodern to Postmodern

The distinction of societal stages of development from premodern to modern to postmodern and the effects on people's behavior and values reflects the development of Western societies. *Premodern times* tend to be characterized by agriculture as the dominant means of sustaining life, households containing three-generation extended families, feudal societies with landowners and nobility, and a cyclical perception of time. Industrialization brought *modern times*, characterized by increased urbanization, the nuclear family of husband, wife, and children, mass production, and a linear time orientation. A third societal development stage is postindustrialization, when most professions deal with obtaining, transforming, and integrating information. A variety of names using the prefix *post-*, meaning 'after,' are used to describe a new social order after the industrial development phase. Examples are *postmodern* or *post-scarcity society, postindustrial society, information society, service society,* or *knowledge society.* The term *postmodernism* is not a well-defined concept. It is used in many different ways. For example, postmodernity is a condition of Western society after modernity, and postmodernism is a movement that reacts to earlier modernist principles. According to Inglehart and colleagues,[14] in postmodern society, emphasis on economic achievement is giving way to an increasing emphasis on quality of life.

Modernization is often equated with individualism in the sense of increased autonomy of individuals and decreasing sense of community that could even lead to the disintegration of society. However, modernization should be distinguished from individualism/collectivism. Equating individualism with modernization amounts to psychologizing a sociological phenomenon.[15]

In the economic development process of nations, the change from agriculture to indus-trialization is a universal process, including changing living conditions, although different countries are passing through these phases at different speeds. The assumption that these changes have similar societal implications and consequences for the behavior of individuals is a product of Western thinking. In the strongly urbanized and modern Japan, planning and the linear time concept have not become mainstream. They are restricted to business practice. Many manifestations of Japanese culture, such as strong focus on the seasons (spring blossoms and autumn leaves), indicate that circular thinking has not disappeared with modernization.

Modernization, frequently mentioned as a cause of convergence, is not synonymous with convergence of values. Perkin refers to modernization as just 'one of the neologisms like postmodernism that tend to conceal a preference for the values and practices of an author's own national culture.'[16]

Convergence: Macro and Micro Level

For the analysis of convergence, we have to distinguish between convergence at macro and micro level, although the macro/micro dichotomy is not well defined. The following sec-tions describe definitions of the macro/micro dichotomy.

The Macro/Micro Dichotomy

Various fields of study define the dichotomy macro/micro in different ways. In interna-tional marketing textbooks, *macro information* generally includes population data, gross national income (GNI) per capita, and growth rates of production and consumption.[17] Another term used is the *macro environment,* which includes political, legal, economic, social, cultural, and technological dimensions.[18] Descriptions of the macro-economic environment also can include, in addition to purely economic factors, human, techno-logical, and natural resources, skills of a country's population (education), infrastructure (traffic, communication, and technology), and level of technology.

Measurements of economic advancement at macro level can be energy available, GNI per capita, consumption, transportation and communication facilities, urbanization, capital for investment, technology, media, and the structure of consumption. The *micro-economic environment* generally refers to the environment surrounding a product and/or market of interest to a company and essentially concerns competition. Different compet-itors may satisfy different types of demand (existing, latent, incipient). This description points only partly at the consumer.

Hunt distinguishes between macro and micro at the level of aggregation. 'Micro refers to the marketing activities of individual units, normally individual organizations (firms) and consumers or households. Macro suggests a higher level of aggregation, usually marketing systems or groups of consumers.'[19]

According to Peterson and Malhotra[20] macro criteria are typically traditional and stereo-typical and represent features of the country that can be counted, recorded, and shared as secondary data. The micro criteria are generally measured in consumer surveys. Consumer behavior researchers are typically concerned with micro and 'somewhat macro' processes of consumption behavior. At the micro level is the study of how individuals seek information, evaluate alternatives, develop affective responses, plan actions, and then decide, act, and evaluate. At the 'somewhat macro' level is the attempt to understand group behavior of households, neighborhoods, or lifestyle segments.[21]

For comparative analysis at the national level, the distinction between macro and micro at the level of aggregation is not useful, as all data are at the aggregate level. What the descriptions of Hunt, and Peterson and Malhotra have in common is that they point at micro-level data being more concerned with buying behavior of consumers, as opposed to macro-level data being indicators of the macro-economic environment of countries. This rough distinction is followed in this book. Statistical indicators of a country's development, which often are also composites or summaries of other phenomena, are indicated as macro-level data. Examples are numbers of telephone main lines, cars, personal computer and television sets per 1,000 people. Most other data are at micro level and represent differences in consumption, consumer behavior, attitudes, values, and so on. Examples include product usage, such as time spent watching television, what people do on the Internet or with their computers, and liters per capita mineral water consumed.

Convergence and Divergence at Macro Level

The convergence thesis at macro level deals with aspects of national income, infrastructure, health, social welfare, education levels of countries, possession of communication means such as telephone lines, computers, cars, television sets, newspapers, and increased leisure and physical security. The macro variables generally are the characteristics of the industrial but even more of the postindustrial world.

National wealth converges in the rich regions of the world, but not on a worldwide basis. This goes against popular thinking that with increased free trade and international access to information and technology, developing economies will catch up with the developed world. Analysis of longer historical periods questions this simple convergence hypothesis. Hollanders et al.[22] analyzed longer-term trends in economic development both in the developing and the developed world. They found that, whereas the period up to

1973 was characterized by a period of rapid growth and catching up between European and US consumption patterns, in the 1973–1991 period this catching up disappeared. Between 1991 until 1998, growth diverged among the United States, Europe, and Japan, with the United States leaping forward as compared with Europe and Japan. An explanation is that the US economy has benefited faster from the implementation of new technology. Global inequality is reinforced by what is called the 'digital divide.' In the year 2000, about 87% of people online lived in postindustrial societies.[23] Worldwide data on ownership of computers and use of the Internet still correlate positively with national wealth.

World income distribution has become much more unequal in the past several decades. The World Bank publishes for each country a so-called Gini coefficient, a commonly used measure of inequality: zero signifies perfect equality; 100 means that one person holds all the income. In the short period between 1988 and 1993, world inequality increased from a Gini coefficient of 62.5 to 66. In 2003 it was 68.7, but ten years later, in 2013 it was 64.9.[24] The implications are that the majority of the populations of poor countries are able to buy fewer and fewer of the goods and services that enter into the consumption patterns of rich-country populations.[25] Generally, in low-income countries, Gini coefficients are high. Worldwide GNI per capita explains 50% of variance. Examples of Gini coefficients of 2015 are 46 for Mexico, 34 for Spain, 33 for Japan, 29 for France and 26 for Denmark.[26] In the developed world, it is the degree of power distance that explains variance. High power distance means inequality. In economically homogeneous Europe, however, the differences are small and there is no relationship with income or culture.

At the end of the twentieth century, the North–South divide had increased. Between 1950 and 1992, the gap in the standards of living between the richer countries in the Northern Hemisphere and the poorer countries in the Southern Hemisphere had widened. Countries of the North experienced convergence among themselves. The bottom 16 countries of the North (real GNI/cap < US$5,000) experienced a catching up with the average standard of living of the top nine countries (real GNI/cap > US$5,000).[27]

International market researchers Craig, Douglas, and Grein[28] found that rather than converging in terms of macro-environmental characteristics, countries are becoming more divergent. They examined a set of 15 macro-environmental variables of the years 1960–1988 (e.g., infant mortality, cost of living, passenger motor vehicles, telephones in use, students, book production, daily newspaper circulation) among a set of industrialized nations. The results suggest that despite increased interaction and communication between industrialized nations, they were not becoming more similar in terms of macro-economic characteristics.

Convergence of Markets?

Most of the developments accelerating the trend toward global market unity are macro developments. For example, in some world regions, demographic convergence takes place with respect to age distribution and household size. Often-mentioned converging aspects in marketing are increased buying of services, increased demand for health and convenience products, convergence of distribution systems, and convergence of advertising expenditures.[29] Next to macro-level convergence, there is increasing evidence that at micro level there is not so much convergence. Infrastructural and economic integration usually occur at a higher speed than the cultural and mental integration of consumers. As people around the globe become well educated and more affluent, their tastes diverge. With increased wealth, people increasingly accord greater relevance to their civilizational identity.[30]

Forms of Convergence

Inkeles[31] reviewed various societal convergence effects of industrialization and modernization, such as of educational systems and family patterns. He did not find univocal evidence of convergence, but instead a variety of forms and levels of convergence and divergence. He summarized several patterns.

- Change may stop short of actual convergence, and a critical threshold of stable differences may remain. Moreover, on some dimensions there is a ceiling that most of the advanced countries reached long ago, leaving no room for further convergence. An example is the percentage of primary school enrolment.
- Movement toward a common point does not necessarily mean movement in the same direction. An example is convergence of age of marriage, which may come down in some countries, but move upward in others. Convergence and crossover take place when two converging lines meet, fuse, cross, and start to diverge.
- There may be thresholds that are more important than absolute differences. An example is education. Once a modern school system has been introduced, further expenditures in education seem not to produce any significant improvements.
- Parallel change takes place without convergence. An example is the remaining gap in wealth separating the less developed and more industrialized countries.
- Convergence masks diversity. Macro-level statistical indicators are by definition summaries of many single, discrete subsystems. These statistics are composites of several different indicators. Such summary indicators may become more alike with economic development, but they may mask diversity or actual divergence in the component elements of the summary indicator. An example

is convergence of the percentage of GNI devoted to public expenditure on education in the West. Underneath this common convergence there was a marked divergence in how the extra money was apportioned among the three levels of education.

- Change patterns may vary by subsystem and within subsystems. Some types of clothing may diffuse and converge fast (blue jeans), while this is not representative for the clothing category.
- With respect to consumption, some patterns converge significantly, whereas others do not, and the rate of convergence varies between product categories.[32]

Measuring Convergence/Divergence

Convergence or divergence can be measured by computing the coefficients of variation (the ratio of the standard deviation to the mean) and comparing them over time. The coefficient of variation (CV) is explained in Williamson and Fleming, who prefer the coefficient of variation rather than

> the more common alternatives such as the standard deviation or variance because the coefficient of variation is adjusted for shifts in the mean (i.e., a 10-point spread is likely to have a different interpretation around a mean of 150 than around a mean of 15). The greater the decrease in the coefficient of variation over a specified period of time, the greater the convergence.[33]

When data from one source are available for different time periods, the mean convergence per year can be calculated. Williamson and Fleming express the mean convergence per year symbolically as follows:

$$MC / year = \frac{\left(CV_{t1} - CV_{t2} \right)}{CV_{t1}} \times 100 / \left(t_2 - t_1 \right)$$

where MC/year = mean convergence per year, CV_{t1} = coefficient of variation at the earlier date, CV_{t2} = coefficient of variation at the later date, t_1 = the earlier date, and t_2 = the later date. Implicit in this statistic is the simplifying assumption that any 10-, 20-, or 30-year period is equivalent to another. When comparing convergence trends for different length time spans, one will notice some variation in the rate of convergence from one period to another.

If convergence is calculated for the degree of industrial and economic development of countries, rates of convergence or divergence will vary for different groups of countries.

In order to analyze the varying influence of national wealth, several groups should be assembled of economically heterogeneous and homogeneous countries. Examples provided in this book usually are for two groups of countries: an economically heterogeneous group of 44 or more countries worldwide,[34] and economically homogeneous groups of countries in Europe.[35] If no time series are available, differences in convergence can be demonstrated by comparing CVs of heterogeneous and homogeneous economic regions.

Convergence/Divergence in Consumer Behavior

Analysis of time series data on consumption and ownership of various product categories demonstrates that at macro level and at micro level both convergence and divergence take place, but to varying degrees in different regions. If products converge across countries, convergence is weakest in economically heterogeneous regions and strongest in economically homogeneous regions. But even in economically homogeneous regions, such as Europe, only a few cases of true convergence can be demonstrated. In many cases differences are stable over time or countries diverge. If ownership of products converges, it does not imply that usage also converges. People may own modern technology, but they do not use it the same way and for the same purposes across countries. So, even if convergence is found at macro level, substantial differences are likely to exist at micro level.

In Europe, for 20 product categories reviewed[36] in 1997, the coefficients of variation (CVs) varied from 0.66 for sales of real jewelry per capita to 0.11 for television sets per 1,000 people. Only three product categories had a CV below 0.20, which suggests a threshold of convergence across countries. These were television sets per 1,000 people (0.11), fixed telephone lines per 1,000 people (0.17), and automobiles per 1,000 people (0.18).

A few examples illustrate the convergence/divergence process. Between 1960 and 1997, in Europe the CV for television sets owned per 1,000 people decreased from 1.00 in 1960 to 0.30 in 1975 and to 0.11 in 1997, with the mean rate of convergence per year being 2.4%. Between 1996 and 2000 (the last year the World Bank published data on ownership of TV sets per 1,000 people), ownership diverged, with a mean rate of divergence per year being 5.77%. The CV for radios was 0.33 in 1960 and decreased to 0.24 in the next 10 years. After that year it increased to 0.38 in the year 2000, with mean divergence per year being 1.94%. In the 40 years between 1960 and 2000, the average annual rate of divergence of radios per 1,000 people was 0.38%. After the year 2000, no more data on radio ownership were published, because nowadays people listen to radio broadcasts in many different ways. The differences between countries with respect to newspaper circulation have remained more or less stable in the past 50 years and have slightly diverged in Europe. The examples are illustrated in Figures 3.1, 3.2, and 3.3, for 12 countries.

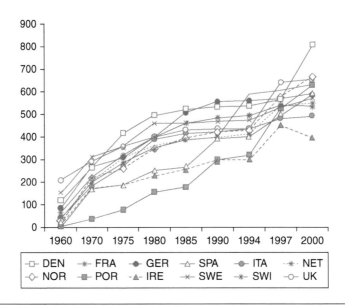

Figure 3.1   TV sets per 1,000 population

SOURCES: United Nations Statistical Yearbooks and World Bank Development Indicators (see Appendix B)

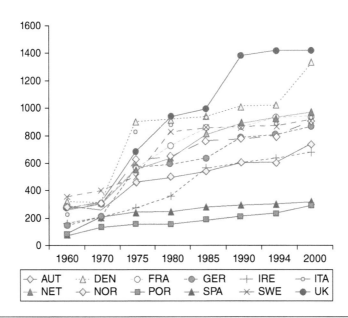

Figure 3.2   Radios per 1,000 population

SOURCES: United Nations Statistical Yearbooks and World Bank Development Indicators (see Appendix B)

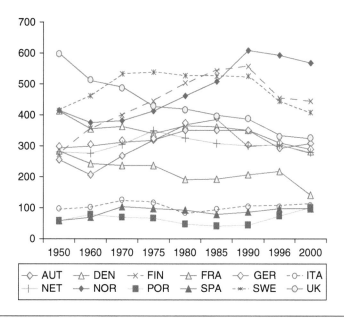

Figure 3.3   Newspaper circulation per 1,000 population

SOURCES: United Nations Statistical Yearbooks and World Bank Development Indicators (see Appendix B)

Table 3.1   Mean convergence or divergence per year (%) at macro level

		Worldwide (44 countries)	Europe (15 countries)
GNI/capita	1994–2006	−0.57	1.39
	2005–2015	.83	−3.13
Passenger cars per 1,000 population	1960–1990	1.52	1.96
	1990–2009	1.79	2.79
Television sets per 1,000 population	1960–1996	1.83	2.42
	1996–2000	0	−5.77
Radios per 1,000 population	1960–2000	0.75	−0.38
Newspapers per 1,000 population	1950–2000	0.18	−0.04
PCs per 1,000 population	1996–2006	0.75	1.91
Internet users per 100 population	2002–2007	5.32	9.00
	2007–2016	5.49	5.50

SOURCES: UN Statistical Yearbooks; World Bank Development Indicators; ITU: ICT Development Index (see Appendix B)

Table 3.1 presents the means of convergence or divergence per year at macro level for GNI per capita and six product categories (passenger cars, television sets, radios, newspapers, PCs per 1,000 population, and Internet users per 100 people) for several time periods, for a group of 44 countries worldwide and for the 15 most developed countries in Europe. In the long term, in economically homogeneous Europe, at macro level the more expensive products that are linked with economic development converged fastest, whereas older, cheaper products such as radios and newspapers diverged.[37]

Nowak and Kochkova[38] did similar calculations for 15 EU member countries and found more divergence than convergence between 1996 and 2006, in particular for food and non-alcoholic beverages, housing, furnishing and household equipment, and recreation and culture.

The previous examples are all at macro level. More interesting are micro-level data – what people actually do with the products they own. Data for calculating convergence/divergence at micro level are not readily available worldwide. Some data are available for Europe, but only for shorter time spans. These data provide evidence of both convergence and divergence. There may be 100% or higher penetration of TV sets, but viewing time varies considerably and diverges across Europe. This is illustrated in Figure 3.4.

Between 1960 and 2009 countries have converged for the total number of passenger cars per 1,000 people, but the distribution across populations, numbers owned per household, or type of car owned diverge. Table 3.2 presents convergence and divergence at micro level for a few product categories in 15 European countries, as measured in the *European Media and Marketing Survey*. Between 1997 and 2007 countries diverged with respect to having 'only one' car in the family, but converged with respect to having two cars and three cars. Between 2007 and 2012 there was divergence only for 3 or more cars.[39]

General data on daily TV viewing minutes show that countries converged between 1991 and 1993 and diverged after 1993. Between 1999 and 2008 the differences were stable, but after that year divergence took place. EMS data on TV viewing show that with respect to heavy viewing countries diverged between 1997 and 2007 as well as between 2007 and 2012. With respect to visits to the cinema, countries also diverged in both time periods.

Examples of divergence are noted in many other product categories, for example, consumption of milk and ice cream diverging in the past 20 years. For many food products, the differences have remained more or less the same.

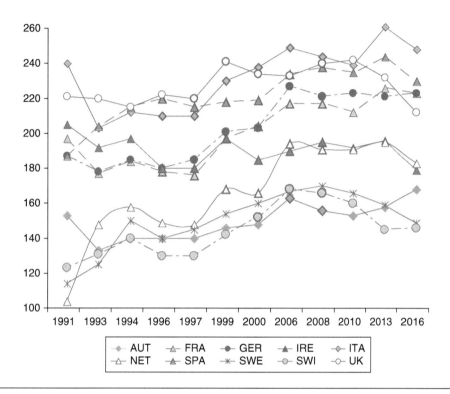

Figure 3.4   **Viewing minutes Europe**

SOURCE: IP TV (see Appendix B)

Table 3.2   **Convergence/divergence per year at micro level (Europe, 15 countries)**

	Convergence or divergence per year (%)			
Cars: One car in family	1997–2007	–4.70	2007–2012	11.12
Cars: Two cars in family	1997–2007	3.30	2007–2012	6.88
Cars: Three cars in family	1997–2007	1.14	2007–2012	–1.06
TV: Daily viewing minutes	1999–2008	0	2008–2016	–2.06
Heavy TV viewing	1997–2007	–0.60	2007–2012	–2.78
Three to five visits to cinema past year	1997–2007	–0.50	2007–2012	–1.90

SOURCES: EMS 1997, 2007 and 2012; IP TV *Key Facts 2017*; Euromonitor (see Appendix B)

Stability

In addition to convergence or divergence, in many cases differences are stable over time. In Chapter 2 we pointed at the stability of cultural values over time. The percentages of general life satisfaction as presented in Chapter 2 are consistently correlated with low uncertainty avoidance. In some cases cultural relationships are even becoming stronger.

An example of how value differences can increasingly be explained by cultural variables could be found in the *Reader's Digest* (2001) report (see Appendix B), *European Trusted Brands*. In the survey, a few questions about the degree of trust in institutions such as the police and the legal system were repeated from an earlier survey by *Reader's Digest* (1991). Differences in trust in the police and the legal system correlate significantly with Hofstede's cultural dimension power distance: in cultures of high power distance there is less trust than in cultures of low power distance. Regression analysis shows that for the 13 countries[40] involved in both surveys, in 1991 the percentage of variance explained by power distance was 52% for trust in the police and 41% for trust in the legal system. In 2001 the figures were 72% and 69%. In 10 years, with increased wealth, the differences between countries increased and the explanation by culture became more pronounced.

Table 3.3   **Mineral water consumption (Europe, 15 countries)**

	Product moment correlations					Step-wise regression
	GNI/cap	PDI	IDV	MAS	UAI	Predictors
1970	.31	.32	−.21	.24	.46*	None
1991	.21	.32	−.05	.53*	.57*	UAI+ (R^2 = .32)
1997	.04	.56*	−.10	.57*	.73***	UAI+ (R^2 = .53)
2003	−.23	.60*	−.14	.56*	.73***	UAI+ (R^2 = .53); MAS (R^2 =.69)
2015	−.11	.26	−.06	.48**	.60***	UAI+ (R^2 = .36); MAS (R^2 =.52)

NOTE: 1970: Drink taken in the past year: mineral spring water; 1991: Drinking mineral water almost every day; 1997: Mineral water sales, liters per capita; 2003 and 2015: sales bottled water in liters per capita.

SOURCES: *Reader's Digest* Surveys 1970 and 1991; Euromonitor, 1997; Bottled Water Corporation, 2004; European Federation of Bottled Water (see Appendix B)

With respect to some consumption differences, we also find stable or increasing cultural relationships. The Belgians drink 10 times as much mineral water as the British and 6 times as much as the Dutch, their neighbors in Europe. Although the quality of tap water has improved all over Europe, consumption of mineral water has increased, and differences have remained similar since 1970 or have become larger. These differences are related to Hofstede's dimension uncertainty avoidance, which includes values of purity. The significance of the correlations has become stronger over time. In France, Germany, Italy, and Belgium, all high uncertainty avoidance cultures, people drink increasing volumes of mineral water, as compared to the United Kingdom and Scandinavia, cultures of low uncertainty avoidance. Table 3.3 presents the correlation coefficients and percentages of variance explained in stepwise regression analysis for 15 European countries.

Convergence/Divergence: A Pattern

There is a pattern of convergence/divergence. For durable products – in particular those related to wealth, such as passenger cars, television sets, and computers – initially, with increased wealth, countries converged, but in the developed world, at a certain level of wealth, convergence reached a ceiling after which there is no further convergence, and differences remained more or less stable or increased. With converging wealth, convergence of consumption turns into divergence. For 'old' products such as newspapers and radio, that ceiling was reached long ago; for numbers of TV sets, the ceiling was reached in 1997. Some new products have not yet reached a ceiling, and differences between countries are still large. The point of convergence lies in the future. But it can be predicted by understanding the pattern of the old products.

At macro level, products linked with economic development of countries have converged fastest in the economically converging Europe, whereas older, cheaper products such as radios and circulation of newspapers have diverged. However, this convergence at macro level is not accompanied by convergence at micro level, what people do with products they own. New media and technology are converging at macro level, but differences at micro level emerged soon after introduction. Internet penetration converges, but the way the Internet is used varies, as is described in Chapter 7.

National Wealth as an Explaining Variable

The assumed strongest influence on consumer behavior is income. The amount of disposable income is expected to determine buying behavior once basic needs are fulfilled. This sounds logical, yet what must be considered to be basic needs are not the same all over the world. In affluent societies, basic needs may include television-watching capability in the home; in others it is just limited to food and shelter. In the developed world, what is viewed as a necessity will not only vary by country but also will change over time.

In 1999 the standard package of items considered as necessity in the United States consisted of an answering machine, a cordless phone, at least one television, cable TV, a VCR, a stereo cassette player and CD player, a microwave oven, dishwasher, washer and drier, air conditioning, two cars.[41]

In 2006, on top of the list of things Americans said they couldn't live without were a car (91%), a clothes washer (90%), a clothes dryer (83%), home air conditioning (70%), a microwave (68%), TV set (64%), car air conditioning (59%), and a home computer (51%).

In 2010 again a car came first (86%) after which a landline phone (62%), a clothes dryer (59%), home air conditioning (55%), home computer (49%), cell phone (47%), microwave (45%), TV set (42%), high speed Internet (34%), cable or satellite TV (23%), dishwasher (21%), flat screen TV (10%).[42]

A commonly used measure to compare national wealth is the *gross domestic product* (GDP) or the similar measure *gross national product* (GNP). In 2001 the terminology was changed to *gross national income* (GNI).[43] There are some problems when comparing countries using GNP data. First, for comparison, the data must be converted into a common currency. The US dollar is commonly used for this purpose. Fluctuations in the exchange rates disturb the picture. A second problem with the conventional GNP calculations is that it includes all efforts in a country. That does not, however, necessarily reflect the exact welfare of the community. In an effort to improve comparability, the United Nations and the World Bank developed a method to calculate a 'real' GNP on an internationally comparable scale. Originally this 'new' GNP was called ICP, named after the UN International Comparison Program. Later it was called 'GNP measured at PPP' (purchasing power parity). The World Bank publishes the data in the annual World Development Reports. The World Bank definition of GNP measured at PPP is 'GNP converted to US dollars by the purchasing power parity (PPP) exchange rate.' At the PPP rate, one dollar has the same purchasing power over domestic GNP that the US dollar has over US GNP; dollars converted by this method are sometimes called 'international dollars.'[44] Because differences between countries with respect to purchasing power parity are expected to better explain product consumption than GNP per capita, PPP data of the relevant years should ideally be used. As these data are only available from 1990 onward, they cannot be used for time-series analysis starting at an earlier date. However, income per capita at PPP and GNP per capita are closely related. The correlation coefficients between GNP and PPP vary between .93 and .95 for the group of 44 countries worldwide. For the 15 countries in developed Europe, the correlation coefficients vary between .90 and .95. In this book we use GNI, and in all calculations in this book GNI per capita at PPP is used.

Between 1995 and 2005 worldwide, 62 countries converged with respect to GNI per capita (1.07% mean convergence per year), but convergence was less strong between 2005 and 2015 (0.83% per year). Whereas in Europe and Asia countries converged, in Latin America they diverged. In 2016 worldwide individualism explained 38% of variance and low power distance an additional 5%.

Composite Development Indicators

Much cross-national consumer research uses macro-environmental indicators of economic development. Countries tend to be classified on a single dimension (e.g., GNI per capita) or on composite variables consisting of other developmental variables, for example, resource development, economic and demographic mobilization, and societal development, such as urbanization, literacy, or energy consumption. In such studies,[45] researchers form comparative clusters of countries and compute economic development factors from a large number of phenomena related to economic development. Examples of variables used are electricity production, urbanization, school enrollment per capita, imports and exports per GNI, number of air passengers/km, life expectancy, literacy, percentage of population in agriculture, average work week, percentage employed in service, physicians per capita, manufacturing percentage of GNI, and private spending as a percentage of GNI. Examples of consumption-related macro variables used in comparative studies are per capita ownership of cars, radios, television sets, telephones, energy consumption, hospital beds, foreign visitors per capita, tourist's expenditure per capita, newspaper circulation, and other aspects of media availability.[46] Such composite macro indicators are used for many purposes, for example, to study patterns of media use in Europe,[47] to measure the degree of materialism,[48] or for calculating modernity.[49] Most of such indicators that make up composite variables (e.g., possession of cars, TVs, PCs, video cameras, and the like) are interdependent and are each correlated with per capita GNI. Such factors are basically a function of economic development and an indirect measurement of national wealth. Consumer researcher Alladi Venkatesh points out:

> Many economically oriented consumer studies are conducted without regard to the intrinsic values studied … Poverty is studied abstractly as a condition related to lack of education, infrastructure, or adequate housing … The object … [of a] study

may be poverty, but it is never poor people. In particular, economists trained in the neoclassical tradition cannot deal with the whys and wherefores of their questions, either in historical or cultural terms, and they avoid, therefore, culture-theoretical explanations.[50]

Over Time, Culture Replaces Income as an Explanatory Variable

Europe is an interesting area for analyzing the effects of converging wealth. The region can serve as an example of how, with convergence of national wealth, cultural variables can better explain differences in consumption than income or related demographic variables. Analysis of historical time series data reveals that country-level ownership of many products and services is initially best predicted by national wealth. At a certain point in time, culture replaces wealth as a predictor variable for ownership and/or usage. The same effect is found when selecting a group of wealthy countries from a worldwide database. Several examples demonstrate this process.

Radios, TV Sets, and Cars

Consider the adoption of radio, television sets, and automobiles in Europe in the past. Table 3.4 contains CVs for these products for 15 European countries for selected years from 1960 to 2000 as well as the proportion of variance (R^2) respectively explained by national wealth or Hofstede's dimensions individualism and long-term orientation. Time series data for radios per 1,000 population show a breaking point between 1980 and 1990, when culture replaced income as an explanatory variable. In 1990 individualism explained 72% of variance of radio ownership, and radios per 1,000 people were no longer significantly correlated with national wealth.

In 1960, country differences in ownership of television sets per 1,000 people were related to individualism, not to income. From 1970 to 1994, country differences in television ownership were related to GNI per capita, after which this relationship disappeared. After 1990, the differences between countries became so minor that neither national wealth nor individualism was an effective predictor.

A similar pattern was found for passenger cars. Until 1970, differences in the numbers of automobiles per 1,000 people across 15 countries in Europe were explained by national wealth only. After 1970, individualism became another explaining variable. After 1997 in Europe, only long-term orientation explained differences in ownership.

Table 3.4 CV and R² values for durable products over time (Europe, 15 countries)

	Radios/1,000			TV sets/1,000			Passenger cars/1,000		
	CV	GNI/cap R²	IDV R²	CV	GNI/cap R²	IDV R²	CV	GNI/cap R²	IDV/LTO R²
1960	.33	.81		1.00		.37	.56	.80	
1970	.24	.69		.30	.61		.34	.82	IDV .91
1980	.36	.58		.24	.55		.23	.69	IDV .82
1990	.35		.72	.17	.35		.18	.47	LTO .66
1997	.36		.48	.11	none		.17	none	LTO .61
2000*	.38		.42	.16	none		.12	none	LTO .46

*Data for passenger cars are from 2003

SOURCES: Hofstede et al. (2010) (see Appendix A); United Nations Statistical Yearbooks; World Development Indicators (see Appendix B)

If we look at a larger scale, worldwide (41 countries[51], see Table 3.5) from 1960 to 1970 GNI is the main explaining variable for ownership of cars. From 1970 onward, individualism is the second explaining variable, and in 1980 individualism becomes the first explaining variable, with after 1998 uncertainty avoidance being an additional predictor.

Table 3.5 Passenger cars per 1,000 people 1960–2003: CVs and explaining variables (worldwide, 41 countries)

Year	CV	Pred.1	R²	Pred.2	R²	Pred.3	R²
1960	1.39	GNI	.81				
1970	1.04	GNI	.88	IDV	.91		
1980	.90	IDV	.79	GNI	.88		
1990	.84	IDV	.76	GNI	.87		
1998	.77	IDV	.70	GNI	.82	UAI	.87
2009	.58	IDV	.72	GNI	.77	UAI	.82

SOURCES: Hofstede et al. (2010) (see Appendix A); World Development Indicators (see Appendix B)

Next to this, many aspects of cars are culture related. Consumers in masculine cultures are more interested in the size and power of the engine than are consumers in feminine cultures. In high power distance cultures, consumers are particularly interested in the design of an automobile (for car motives, see Chapter 5).

Information Technology

Another example is how information technology developed at the end of the twentieth century when ownership of new technology was concentrated in developed countries. In 2000, the 29 OECD (Organisation for Economic Cooperation and Development) member states representing the postindustrial economies contained 97% of all Internet hosts, 92% of the market in production and consumption of computer hardware and services, and 86% of all Internet users. The whole of sub-Saharan Africa contained less than 1% of the world's online community.[52] Since then computer ownership worldwide has remained related to GNI per capita. Yet, as we'll see later in this book, preference for the different types and the applications vary with culture.

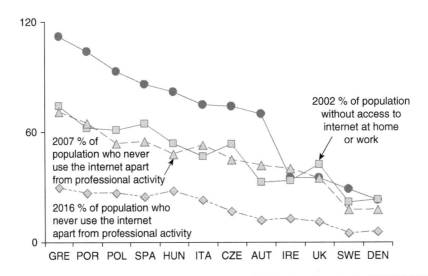

Figure 3.5 **Internet and uncertainty avoidance**

SOURCES: Data from Hofstede et al. (2010) (see Appendix A); *European Social Survey,* 2002; Eurobarometer, *European Cultural Values,* 2007; Eurobarometer report 86, 2016 (see Appendix B)

In the developed world, low uncertainty avoidance, a measure of innovativeness, tends to explain variance of penetration of new technology products. Countries scoring low to medium on the uncertainty avoidance index were the first to embrace the Internet and still are leading with respect to usage of it.

In 2002, differences in the percentage of population without access to Internet, neither at home nor at work, were related to high uncertainty avoidance, which across 20 countries explained 46% of variance.[53] The relationship is illustrated in Figure 3.5 for 12 countries ($r = .91$***). The same chart illustrates data of 2007: the percentage of people who never use the Internet apart from professional activity.[54] For 24 European countries, uncertainty avoidance explains 59% of variance ($r = .77$***). For these 12 countries $r = .94$***. In 2016 Eurobarometer[55] asked the same questions related to the Internet. For the same 12 countries the percentages were lower, but the differences still correlated quite significantly with uncertainty avoidance ($r = .93$***).

With increasing penetration of the Internet, several differences in usage are also found. Frequent usage is related to low masculinity. In feminine cultures, people use new technology to enhance quality of life more than productivity. Collectivists prefer person-to-person contact, have been late adopting the Internet for personal communication, but embraced social media even stronger than individualists. Chapter 7 will deal with Internet developments in more detail.

In sum, when countries have converged with respect to national wealth, cultural variables start to explain more of the differences in country-level consumer behavior.

With Increased Wealth, Cultural Values Become Manifest

The previous data have shown that the wealthier countries become, the more manifest is the influence of culture on consumption and consumer behavior. This phenomenon is reflected in many changes of the past decades.

Higher levels of wealth do not change traditional values. Longitudinal comparisons of economy and culture by Van de Vliert show that higher levels of economic growth are not related to decreases in traditional values.[56] More discretionary income gives people more freedom to express themselves, and that expression will be based in part on their national value system. Wealth brings choice. It enables people to choose leisure time or buy status products or devote free time to charitable work or to self-education. Two distinct philosophies on what people are expected to do with their incremental income are (1) that increased wealth leads to greater materialism and overconsumption, or (2) that with increased wealth people turn away from more consumption. Inglehart's[57] study of changing values from materialist to postmaterialist values follows the latter line. According to Inglehart, with prosperity and economic security, further income does not lead to higher levels of subjective well-being. People take their prosperity for granted and transfer their focus to other parts of life, such as politics and the quality of physical and social environment. However, no evidence can be found that people consume less with increased wealth.

New Manifestations of 'Old' Values

Whereas in many East Asian countries with economic development and modernity some practices changed dramatically, important cultural values have not changed or have become even stronger. Inkeles[58] measured change and stability in five countries on the Pacific Rim (Japan, Taiwan, Singapore, Korea, and China). Whereas in Chengdu in China in 1933, 68% of marriages still were 'arranged' by the parents, in the 1980s it was only 2%. A similar change was found in Taiwan. At the same time there are indications that some Asian populations are reinvigorating traditions. With increased wealth, people also seek outward signs of social respectability, which is expressed by participating in rituals such as ancestor worship and religious practices. An important East Asian value is 'filial piety,' a son's obligations of duty that affiliate him to his father. In surveys in Japan, the preference for filial piety has been rising year after year. In 1963, the first year this question was asked, filial piety was selected by 61% of the respondents, but by 1983 it had risen in popularity to 73%; it held its rank as the number one value in subsequent surveys through 1993. In the early 1990s, in Baoding, China, approximately 95% of both elders and adult children stressed their commitment to filial piety. Also among young people, both in Beijing and Hong Kong China, Chinese moral values such as filial piety are still heavily emphasized.[59]

With modernity, values don't change but manifestations, or expressions of these values, may change in such a way that it reflects collectivistic values. In collectivistic cultures extended families used to live together in more family housing. With modernity and changing living circumstances, people may live in separate apartments in the same apartment building, still close together, or stay in contact on a regular basis via the mobile phone. Everywhere women's roles change, but they change more in some cultures than in others. With economic development, variance in role differentiation becomes manifest. Cultural values influencing role behavior, which are latent in the more traditional societies, become manifest when countries modernize. An example is for shopping behavior. In 1991 the *Reader's Digest* survey divided main food shoppers into males and females. For 16 countries in Europe, there was a significant correlation between cultural masculinity and the proportion of main food shoppers who are women ($r = .50^*$). Because of stronger role differentiation, more females will do the daily food shopping in masculine cultures than in feminine cultures. In feminine cultures, males will be relatively more involved in the daily household chores than in masculine cultures. When the more traditional countries of Spain, Portugal, and Greece are excluded from the calculation, significance becomes much stronger ($r = .77$***).

Other Measurement Variables

Economic development is linked to a syndrome of changes that include urbanization, mass education, and communications development that are interdependent. Such socioeconomic variables are frequently used in cross-cultural studies, but they are indirect measures of economic development. Levels of education are indicators of economic development, and education influences income levels. Education also indoctrinates people to learn specific values.[60] In the following sections, several sociodemographic variables are discussed: urbanization, population density, education, age distribution, household and family, social class, and ethnicity. Also, the function of climate as an explanatory variable is discussed.

Urbanization

There is no universally accepted standard for distinguishing *urban* and *rural*. The World Bank's definition for urban population is the midyear population of areas defined as urban in each country and reported to the United Nations.[61] The measurement used by the World Bank is the 'population in urban agglomerations of more than one million.'[62] Most countries have adopted an urban classification related to the size or characteristics of settlements, others have based their definition on certain infrastructure, and some are based on administrative characteristics.

The distinction *urban/rural* is mainly important for understanding differences within large developing economies, such as China, where consumer spending still is concentrated in a number of key cities and provinces, and urban household disposable income is much higher than rural income. Populations of the world's largest metropolitan conglomerations have been growing.

The divide, urban/rural, is less pronounced in developed economies, and there is not one pattern. In Luxemburg, Denmark, and the United Kingdom, for example, in 1999, in sparsely populated areas average household expenditure was higher than in densely populated areas. In Portugal, Italy, and Spain, with larger rural areas, it was the other way around.[63] In the developed world, urbanization differences have little explaining power. With economic development in some parts of the world, for example in China, urbanization is increasing, but this is not a worldwide phenomenon. For 54 countries worldwide between 1990 and 2015 there was a mean convergence per year of only 0.37. Both in 1990 and in 2015 the differences in percentages of people living in urban agglomerations were explained by GNI/cap and collectivism and to a lesser degree by short-term orientation.

Urbanization and Housing

There are relationships between urbanization and type of housing, but this relationship rarely has explanatory power. An important difference that is influenced by culture is between people living more in one-family houses with private gardens and living in apartment blocks. In individualistic cultures, people live more in one-family houses and have more private gardens, whereas living in apartment blocks generally is correlated with collectivism. The type of housing in Britain and in the United States can be viewed as an expression of the individualistic lifestyle in general.[64]

Increased urbanization is assumed to turn collectivistic societies into individualistic societies because people cannot live anymore in the extended household. As yet, there is no evidence to support this assumption. Although urbanization tends to break up the joint household of the extended family in favor of more nuclear households, this does not imply decreasing extended family values. Despite changing living conditions, the Indian family always remains an extended one. The extended family maintains strong family ties, gets together on holidays, makes mutual decisions on important matters, and sometimes maintains joint ownership.[65] Close emotional bonds between generations may continue even though material interdependence weakens.[66] There is no evidence of convergence of family and kin patterns resulting from increased urbanization. Analysis of social relationships between parents and children, brothers and sisters, and friends has not shown a declining frequency of contact with relatives. The mobile phone has become an important communication means to maintain these social relationships. Across Europe an important argument for using the mobile phone is to keep contact with family and friends, and in 2008 this correlated negatively with individualism.[67]

Urbanization and Retail Structure

One would expect that the degree of urbanization would influence the retail structure of countries. But there is not one single pattern. Preferences for shopping in large shopping malls or small local shops are not related to degrees of urbanization, but more based on history and culture. Low urbanization would be expected to influence remote buying methods such as mail order or cyber-shopping. Data of 2000[68] on the percentage share of mail order in total retail trade sales, however, do not show such a relationship. The only relationship is with GNI per capita. It is not a lack of infrastructure that makes people adopt new distance buying opportunities. Increased wealth offers more choice that people, irrespective of urbanization, want to exercise. Additional facilities mainly attract people to do more of what they were used to do. If people like shopping and buying, they will try all sorts of new types of distribution. Findings from Roper Starch Worldwide[69] confirm this phenomenon. A survey of 1997 found that people who live in countries with well-established infrastructures are most likely to buy things in a remote fashion. Japanese and Britons, for example, ranked high in their propensity to buy things over the phone, followed by Americans and the Dutch. There are few meaningful significant correlations between urbanization and consumption or consumption-related phenomena. Other variables usually are better predictors.

Population Density

Another variable that is thought to be useful for measuring country-level differences is population density. *Population density* is defined as 'midyear population divided by land area.'[70] A more simple definition is the number of people per square kilometer. There are large differences between countries. In Europe, for example, in 2016 the Netherlands population density was 505, as compared with 14 for Norway and 93 for Spain. For Australia it is 3 and for Singapore 7,909.[71]

The degree of population density might influence various habits and product ownership, such as housing, the use of cable versus satellite television, and mobile phones. However, there are few significant correlations between consumer behavior data and population density. Worldwide (61 countries, 2016), population density correlates significantly with GNI/cap and uncertainty avoidance ($r = -.38***$ and $r = -.35***$). In partial correlation controlling for GNI/cap, correlations are with low individualism and high power distance ($r = -.57***$ and $r = .46***$), a configuration found both in Asia and Latin America. This relationship does not – as far as our knowledge goes – explain the differences. Because of the interdependence with other variables, population density is not a useful measurement of consumption differences.

Education

Education levels of countries are a function of national wealth. With respect to secondary education, worldwide (44 countries), countries converged until 1980, but after that year convergence stopped. There still are differences between countries, and these remain stable. A threshold of convergence has been reached at a CV of 0.35 worldwide and of 0.06 in Europe, which demonstrates that with respect to education levels, Europe is a truly homogeneous area. Convergence also takes place with respect to tertiary education. GNI per capita consistently explains variance of education levels, so wealth is the driver of education. Only in Europe, the relationship disappeared after 1990. Because of the interdependence with economic development, education is not a meaningful explaining variable at the national level.

Age Distribution

The age distribution of populations influences buying patterns of societies. In economically developed countries, senior citizens generally have a sizeable disposable income that is spent on goods that are often of little interest to the younger generation.

Age distribution is related to economic development and to culture. Worldwide (62 countries),[72] the percentages of people under 15 years old are negatively correlated with GNI per capita ($r = -.60^{***}$), and the percentages of people over 60 years old are positively correlated with GNI per capita, but there is a more significant correlation with individualism ($r = .64^{***}$). The wealthier nations are, the longer the life expectancy of people. In particular in Europe, where economies have converged, in all countries people have increasingly longer life expectancy and lower birthrates, although the decline of birthrates varies by culture. Birthrates are lower in long-term orientation cultures, but also in higher uncertainty avoidance cultures. Worldwide (62 countries), partial correlations controlling for GNI/cap show significant correlations with LTO for four different age groups: for 0–14 year olds r is $-.44^{***}$; for 15–24 year olds $r = -.46^{***}$; for 25–29 year olds $r = .34^{***}$ and for 60+ year olds $r = .37^{***}$. Only for the 60+ age group the correlation with UAI is more significant: $r = .49^{***}$. It looks like in the long-term oriented cultures parents have deeper thoughts about the consequences of having children. Michael Minkov offers the following quote about this:

> When my father worked in Algeria (whose birth rate is second only to some equatorial countries in Africa), he asked some poor people why they had so many children and who would feed them. Their answer was 'Who feeds the birds in the sky? Allah takes care of everything as he sees fit.'[73]

Figure 3.6 illustrates differences and similarities in age distribution for four sets of four countries each. Figure 3.6a shows the age distributions for Mexico, the United States, United Kingdom, and Spain. It shows a clear difference between Mexico and the other

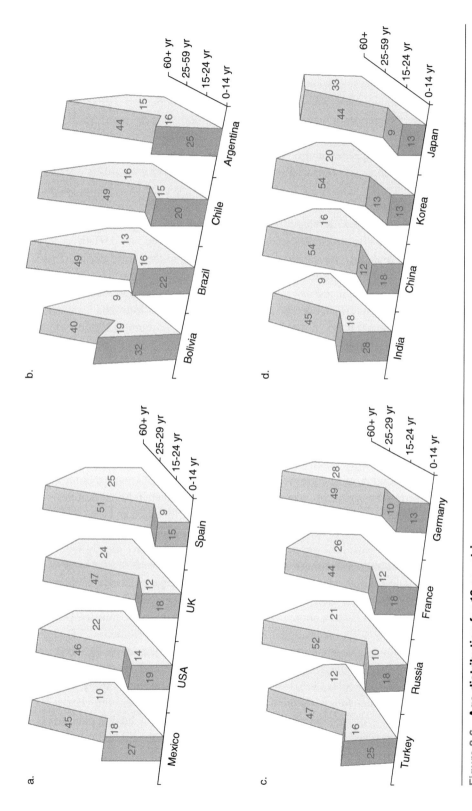

Figure 3.6 Age distribution for 16 countries

SOURCES: *World Population Prospects: The 2017 Revision, Key Findings and Advance Tables*, United Nations Department of Economic and Social Affairs/ Population Division. The numbers in the figures are the percentages of age groups of total populations

three countries with their large percentages of people over 60 years old. Mexico is an example of a developing economy with a large percentage of young people and a small percentage of old people. Differences in economic development can also be recognized when comparing four Latin American countries in Figure 3.6b, with Bolivia showing the typical age distribution of a developing economy with a small percentage of old people and a large percentage of young people, as compared with Chile and Argentina with an age distribution of a more developed economy, be it with a quite large proportion of young people. Figure 3.6c shows three European countries and Turkey. The age distribution of Germany and France represent the typical developed 'old' countries, comparable to Spain and Japan. Turkey shows the shape of a developing economy. Russia, however, has a relatively low percentage of older people for a developed country. According to the World Health Organization,[74] this is due to alcoholism in Russia. Alcohol not only affects mortality from cirrhosis of the liver and cardiovascular disease, but also through violence and road accidents caused by alcohol abuse. Finally, Figure 3.6d illustrates the pattern for four Asian countries that show similar differences between developed and developing economies as in the other regions. It clearly shows the particularly large 60+ group in Japan.

Household and Family

Household structures vary worldwide. Generally in lower-income and collectivistic cultures household sizes are larger. Small average household sizes, of fewer than three persons per household, are found in most countries of Europe and Northern America, but also in some Asian countries like Japan. In collectivistic cultures, multigenerational families are common, where children care for their parents in their homes. In Africa and Asia the largest average household sizes are found, including at least one child. Most households with children include two parents; lone-parent households with children are mostly found in Africa, North America and Latin America.[75]

The age at which people marry for the first time varies. In particular in Europe, couples are waiting longer to get married, if they get married at all. Living alone and cohabitation, even if a couple has children, has become more popular in northern European countries. Data of 2014–2015 show that in Sweden, for example, the age of first marriage of women is 33.5, but in Poland this is 26.9. Also Asia shows differences between countries, for example 29.3 in Japan and 22.3 in Indonesia. Most of the differences are explained by differences in GNI/cap.[76]

The different stages of people's lives, from single to married, raising a family, and old age, are lifestyle stages that follow different age levels across countries. The classical – typically individualistic – distinction of lifestyle stages that influence buying behavior is young singles, newly married or cohabitating, full nest (parents with children), and empty nest (children have left home). Developments like increased divorce rates add other distinctions, such as divorced single parents with children. In collectivistic cultures, there is a greater reliance on extended families for household chores and child care, and many children live with parents after they are married. In some European countries, children also remain living at home longer, but more in the collectivistic South than in the North. In particular for financial reasons children keep living with their parents longer. Of the 25–29 year olds in Italy in 2015 80% kept living with their parents, as compared with 76% of the Greeks, 55% of the Germans and only 34% of the Danes. Whereas in the United States 67% of young adults remained with their parents, in Canada it was 32%, and in Mexico 54%. A cultural explanation is found from positive correlations with uncertainty avoidance and masculinity, fear of the unknown and the more dominant roles of mothers.[77]

In all societies, women have traditionally performed roles of mother, carer, and home provider more than do men. In the various phases of economic development, some of these roles were more pronounced than others. In the developed world, 'housewives' used to be a category to be targeted by companies because of the sole involvement in the household by a majority of women. From the economic point of view, women could afford to stay home and dedicate themselves solely to doing household chores and raising children, whereas in the developing world working was a necessity, which was facilitated by the existence of an extended family that took care of the children.

In developed economies, increased education levels made women look for work outside the home, and the housewife in the old sense does not exist anymore. Increasingly, women have entered the labor force. The percentages of working women[78] of countries have converged between 1970 and 2004, but there still are differences.

Worldwide, until 1998, variance of female share of the labor force was mainly explained by national wealth. In that year, low masculinity started explaining variance. In order to become wealthy, women have to work. In turn, wealth leads to higher levels of education that lead to a greater drive for women to enter the labor force. However, in some cultures more women will work than in others. Table 3.6 shows how over time cultural variables take over income's explaining function. Gender equality of the low masculine cultures facilitates working by women because men share the caring roles. This is demonstrated by variance of working part-time by men, which is also explained by low masculinity. In Europe from 1990 onwards low masculinity starts explaining variance of female share of labor force. Working part-time by men is highest in the Netherlands and Denmark and lowest in Italy. In poor countries, part-time work by women is a luxury. In the wealthy masculine cultures, the majority of men work full time and women part time, so the female share of part-time work is higher.[79] Data of 2008 show that in the masculine cultures, females preferred to stay home to look after the children.[80] In Italy and Germany, women tend to choose between work and children, whereas in the northern European countries women are more able to compromise and combine children and work because partners help more in the house. The percentages who say it is difficult to find the right work–life balance relates to high uncertainty avoidance.

Table 3.6 **Women's share of labor force 1970–2016: Income and cultural variables**

Worldwide (44 countries)	GNI/cap	PDI	IDV	MAS	UAI	Predictors	R^2
1970	.47***	−.32*	.51***	−.00	−.31*	IDV	.26
1980	.59***	−.37**	.54***	−.17	−.40***	GNI/cap	.35
1990	.62***	−.47***	.58***	−.17	−.29*	GNI/cap	.34
1998	.63***	−.45***	.61***	−.24	−.29*	GNI/cap MAS- IDV	.40 .46 .52
2004	.64***	−.51***	.51***	−.03	−.14	GNI/cap	.41
2016	.51***	−.42***	.42***	−.20	−.01	GNI/cap	.26

Europe (15 countries)	GNI/cap	PDI	IDV	MAS	UAI	Predictors	R^2
1970	.55*	−.44*	.27	.09	−.31	GNI/cap	.30
1980	.47*	−.35	−.03	−.37	−.26	none	
1990	.39	−.26	.08	−.56*	−.35	MAS-	.32
1998	.29	−.08	.02	−.63**	−.21	MAS-	.40
2004	.46*	−.30	−.04	−.50*	−.35	None	
2016	−.04	−.09	−.49*	−.54*	−.03	MAS- IDV IVR	.29 .56 .72

SOURCES: Hofstede et al. (2010) (see Appendix A); World Bank Development Reports (see Appendix B)

Social Class

Definitions of class structure vary from country to country. Next to changeable categorizations, there are more permanent, organized class structures. For marketing purposes, people are categorized in groups that are *not organized*. Classifications can be by gender (male–female), age, education, income, or occupation. Basically for marketing purposes, the Western social class system categorizes people according to wealth, which provides an indication of disposable income. However, with increased wealth, disposable income is decreasingly a factor that can explain variance. Other categorizations are by age group (e.g., teenagers, gray populations) or by life stage, such as yuppies (young urban professionals) or DINKs (double income, no kids) or millennials. Not only do class systems differ in various parts of the world, the relative sizes of the classes vary with the relative prosperity of countries. Some class systems have a greater explanatory power of buying behavior than others.

An example of *organized* class is the Indian caste system that, although officially non-existent, determines a person's rank in all areas of life. In developing economies that tend to be collectivistic and of high power distance, income inequality goes together with social inequality. Whereas in individualistic cultures individuals can categorize themselves according to social strata, in collectivistic cultures class does not belong solely to oneself but also to one's group, usually one's family, relatives, and kinship clan.[81]

The social class structure most often used in marketing in developed economies is that of the United States or adaptations of it. American society is usually described as a three-tier society, divided into upper, middle, and lower classes. Another distinction is between blue-collar and white-collar, a simple classification by occupation.

In the developed world, many class distinctions have become irrelevant with increased wealth. In the developing world, growing middle classes with increased spending power are expected to become new markets for multinational companies. However, both within countries and across countries, income inequality, popularly said as the gap between the haves and have-nots, is increasing. In Latin America, the proportion of society considered to be middle class has shrunk since the 1990s. Real wages and purchasing power for the middle and lower classes have steadily declined, whereas the top 8–10% of its citizens hold a disproportionate amount of its wealth. In Brazil the median income of the wealthiest 10% of the population is almost 30 times greater than that of the poorest 40%, and their disposable income (after taxes, food, and housing are paid) is 80–100 times greater.[82]

Measuring Class

There are different ways to measure social class, and they produce different results. Consumers can be asked to self-assign themselves to social classes, people can be asked to assign others to class, or social class can be objectively measured. A most used objective measurement is by occupation, referring to the household head. An example is a measurement system of the United Kingdom, distinguishing among (a) upper middle class, consisting of professional, higher-managerial, senior civil servants; (b) middle class, consisting of middle managers or principle officers in local/central government; (c1) lower middle class, consisting of junior managers, routine white-collar or non-manual workers; (c2) skilled working class, consisting of skilled manual workers; (d) semiskilled and unskilled working class, consisting of manual workers, apprentices to skilled workers; (e) residual, consisting of those dependent on long-term state benefits. A more recent version is the National Statistics Socio-Economic Classification (NS-SEC), also consisting of occupational categories. This sort of classification can be useful for understanding different habits, but not necessarily all consumption, because some working-class people may have more disposable income than higher-class categories. Linking class to profession implies that people may move from one class to another, but in particular in Great Britain, social mobility is relatively low. Wealth of a child's parents strongly influences the child's prospects of higher education and a good salary.

How people classify themselves can produce different results from objective measurements. Whereas in the United Kingdom in 1949, 43% said they were working class, in 1989 67% said they were working class. The percentages for middle class changed from 52% in 1949 to 30% in 1989. When people classify themselves to specific class categories, they may assume a class position that may be different from the position others would ascribe them to. In the United Kingdom in 1993, of 1,004 people questioned, 3 in 10 said they thought of themselves as belonging to a particular class. Nearly 4 in 10 of those in occupational classes (a) or (b), such as judges, professors, stockbrokers, and psychiatrists, described themselves as working class. Conversely, 1 in 7 in classes (d) or (e), including unskilled, manual workers, were convinced they were middle class.[83] In 2011 a survey initiated by the BBC, called the Great British Class Survey (GBCS) measured economic (including occupation), social (social contacts) and cultural capital (highbrow and emerging, referring to classical arts versus Internet related), which resulted in seven main classes, labeled Elite, Established middle class, Technical middle class, New affluent workers, Traditional working class, Emergent service sector, and Precariat. The latter referred to the poorest and most deprived social group.[84] One of the findings was that the elite are most obsessed with class: whereas around 6% of the population are elite, 22% of the people who took the original survey conducted by the BBC categorized themselves as elite.[85]

Whereas the need to categorize the self and others is strong in cultures of the configuration individualism/masculinity, it is much weaker in feminine cultures where people are less inclined to consider themselves better than others. Asking people to place themselves in a category that may be higher than others is suspect. Whereas, for example, in the United States (a masculine culture), students know their rank in class, this is not viewed as interesting knowledge in feminine cultures like the Netherlands and Scandinavian countries.

Class is a sensitive subject. So are ethnicity and race, and, to a lesser degree, religion and age. In the United States, people are categorized according to race, and people are asked to define their own race. Asking people to do so in the Netherlands would be unthinkable. This applies to many countries in Europe, where asking people to categorize themselves according to race and religion is illegal. In France, in 2007 an effort to make official records on ethnic, religious, or racial backgrounds of immigrants was overturned as unconstitutional.[86] In this book the word race is not used, as scientifically it is viewed as an invalid genetic or biological designation when applied to human beings.

In the United States one does not ask another's age, whereas this is usually a lesser problem in most of the countries in Europe. Another sensitive area in the United States is the male–female categorization. Usage of the terms *sex, masculine,* or *feminine* is considered not to be politically correct. The term used for the social functions of sex is *gender.* As a result, another term that is used for Hofstede's dimension masculinity/femininity is the 'gender of nations,' on which scale countries can score high ('tough') or low ('tender').[87]

Ethnicity

In many countries, ethnic minorities have become interesting marketing target groups. The term *ethnic* is used for minority groups that are culturally or physically different from the dominant cultures of societies. Minorities in the world include a great variety of groups, from original populations overrun by immigrants (Native Americans, Australian Aborigines), to descendants of imported labor (African Americans, Turkish Germans), to natives of former colonies (Indians and Pakistanis in Britain), to international nomads (Roma or 'Gypsies'), to ethnic migrants or refugees.[88] Ethnicity can be viewed as a catchall collective term that has replaced several other identifiers – race, religion, language, nationality – as a way to determine the social identity of groups.[89]

In consumer behavior, research interest in ethnicity is increasing because of the changing ethnic landscapes in the United States and in Europe. In the United States, the metaphor describing the American ethnic landscape as a 'melting pot' is supplanted by the 'tossed salad' metaphor. In some states, minorities have become majorities, which makes them attractive as market segments. Examples are California with 38% whites and 39% Hispanics; Washington with 46% blacks vs 38% whites and New Mexico with 46% Hispanics and 37% whites.[90] The top four ancestry groups in the United States are German, Irish, English, and African American.[91]

In the United States newcomers are expected to retain their cultural identities and integrate less in mainstream America than earlier generations did. For understanding their behavior, analysis of the values of their country of origin can be helpful, but it may be questioned if the ethnic minorities within the United States resemble the cultural groups outside of the United States from which they originated. As discussed in Chapter 2, several studies have suggested that African Americans and Asian Americans are higher in collectivism compared to European Americans,[92] but it is unclear whether African Americans resemble Africans in their cultural orientation. In other respects African Americans are as, or even more, individualistic than European Americans, as they emphasize their own uniqueness and independence.[93] This may be due to the fact that African Americans, more than other ethnic groups, have been the targets of stereotyping and prejudice.[94] A replication of Hofstede's research (see also Chapter 2) comparing the values of four different ethnic groups within the United States showed that with respect to values of second generation immigrants there were no significant differences between the groups, except Chinese Americans whose values, more than the other groups, still lightly resembled the original values of their forefathers.[95] Yet, marketers tend to find differences in shopping behavior between the various groups that should be taken into account.

In Europe most ethnic minorities originate from collectivistic cultures, and related values are in contrast with the strong individualism of most receiver cultures. In some European cities, ethnic minorities are large groups. In Amsterdam in 2016, approximately 48% of the population was born in the Netherlands. The largest immigrant groups were from Morocco, Turkey, Surinam and the Antilles.[96] Many behavioral differences can be explained by the difference individualism/collectivism, but this is due to decrease with increased integration.

Acculturation

A question for the future is about the degree to which minorities will adapt to, or acculturate to, the values of the receiver culture. Berry[97] distinguished four acculturation strategies by which minority individuals adapt to a new society. These are 1) *Integration*, also called *biculturalism*, as opposed to segregation – individuals take part in all aspects of society, but retain (some of their) their values; 2) *Assimilation*, high new cultural and low ethnic preference; 3) *Separation*, high ethnic and low new cultural preference; 4) *Marginalization*, low on both ethnic and new cultural endorsement.

Integration is found to be the most occurring acculturation strategy among immigrant youth across countries, but integration may be moderated by the degree of cultural diversity of the receiving society and the cultural background of the acculturating group.[98]

A rule of thumb is that full integration takes three generations, but this depends on various factors, for example, the degree to which integration is stimulated by the receiver culture. Assimilation does take place at longer term. In a study of consumption-related values among students of a number of European countries and black and white students in South Africa, I found that the values of white (English and Afrikaans speaking) students were more similar to the values of black students (Nguni and Sotho) than to the originally English or Dutch values.

Understanding the effects of the different acculturation processes is important for all sorts of consumer behavior. It influences what one buys, where and how. Do individuals quickly shop with a shopping list or view it as a form of entertainment. It influences the relationships between family members and, most important, the relationship between parents and children. For example, Chinese parents living in New Zealand have different perceptions of children's influence on family purchase decision making than their counterparts living in China.[99]

Climate

Climate has a direct and indirect influence on consumption. *Climate* is typically defined as 'average meteorological conditions specific to a geographic region over a period of several years or decades.'[100] The Earth's climates originate from solar radiation that varies in relation to one's absolute latitude from the equator. No two countries have identical climates. A large portion of countries, however, has similar climates across broad classifications (e.g., mostly desert or tropical). Geographical latitude is an unambiguous measure of a country's geographical position and a crude measure of climate. At face value, average temperature may be a better indication, but in some countries extreme temperatures may vary widely between low and mountainous areas. Another problem is the 'average' character of the data, which makes them not very credible for large countries like the United States, Russia, and China.

Parker[101] sees climate as the primary cause of behavioral differences. His findings are that solar climate (absolute latitude squared, to account for the Earth's curve), explains the largest variances in behavior. Cultural differences can be traced back to ecological differences,[102] and there is a relationship between temperature and wealth.[103] Countries with colder climates are wealthier than countries with warm climates.

A direct effect of climate is on energy consumption. In hotter climates people will use less fuel for heating and eat less, especially of foods that require high energies to digest such as meat. The indirect effect is via the relationship with wealth and cultural variables. Although worldwide, total calories consumed per day are correlated with climate, they are more significantly correlated with GNI per capita and individualism. The relationships with wealth and climate do not exist in economically homogeneous Europe where the only explaining variable is masculinity. The more masculine cultures consume more calories as well as confectionery products. Eurostat[104] data on everyday consumption of chocolate and soft drinks by students show significant correlations with masculinity. Individualism explains variance of calorie intake best. In the developed collectivistic world, people take time for meals and have them at regular times, together with other people. They eat less in between meals, whereas in individualistic cultures people seem to eat all the time, both meals and snacks.

A climate-related process is *homeostasis*,[105] a system of controls in the hypothalamus. The hypothalamus mediates the effects of sunlight and temperature on the production of hormones and neurotransmitters. Changes in levels of hormones and neurotransmitters are theorized to influence consumer behavior. Certain stimulants, such as alcohol, cigarettes, coffee, and tea, are assumed to mediate the effects of climate. In cold climates, with less sunshine, its stimulating effect is stronger than in warm climates, which should explain higher consumption of coffee, tea, alcohol, and cigarettes in colder climates than in warmer climates. According to Parker, the ability to institutionalize climate (heating, air conditioning) can reduce the effects of the physical environment and may decrease psychological differences across cultures in the future.

Against this reasoning goes the working of collective memory. Consistently in the colder climates people drink more milk, eat more ice cream, and own more deep freezers than in the warm climates. In Europe, consistently in the warmer climates, fresh milk is not trusted. The differences in trust in food across the countries in Europe are explained by uncertainty avoidance, a dimension that includes purity needs in several consumption domains. Fresh milk, as well its modern replacement ice cream, is a perishable product; and in the past, without refrigerators, fresh milk perished faster in the warm climates than in cold climates. With a nearly 100% penetration of refrigerators throughout Europe, there is no need whatsoever to have less trust in fresh milk in warm climates than in cold climates. This looks more like an indirect effect of climate than a direct effect. Because milk cannot be kept in warm climates, people have historically not consumed as much fresh milk in the warm climates as in the cold climates, and a fresh milk industry has not developed. And still, in the collective memory of people, there is an attitude toward milk (and related products) that it cannot be trusted, because it is perishable. This distrust in perishable food products has become a cultural factor. The phenomenon also demonstrates the stability of people's habits. Logically one would expect more deep freezers in warm climates than in cold climates, but it is the other way round. The colder the climate, the more people were used to preserving food in the snow, and the more they keep doing that, helped by the latest technology.

Consumer Behavior, National Wealth, and Culture

The previous sections described how at country level, the explanatory role of income decreases and culture becomes an increasingly important variable that can explain cross-country differences in consumption. Table 3.7 shows the division of household expenditures by the different purposes and the relationships with income and culture. In 2016 there were negative correlations with GNI/cap for three items: food, alcohol and tobacco, and communications. This points at the lower income countries spending a relatively large percentage of their income on food, drink and communications. The food and drink percentages also correlate negatively with indulgence. Of the other categories only housing and recreation correlate significantly with GNI/cap. Variance of the other categories can only be explained by culture.

Table 3.7 **Income, culture and household expenditure by consumption purpose 2016, percentages of total expenditures. Zero order correlations with income and culture**

	GNI/cap	PDI	IDV	MAS	UAI	LTO	IVR
Food and non-alcoholic beverages	−.87***	.51**	−.43*		.44*		−.67***
Alcoholic beverages, tobacco	−.55***						−.51**
Clothing and footwear							−.38*
Housing, water, electricity, gas	.65***		.49**		−.50**		.52**
Furnishing, household maintenance						.49**	
Health					.51**		
Transport				−.37*			
Communications	−.53**	.41*	−.42*				
Recreation and culture	.45*		.41*		−.68***		.36*
Education						−.43*	
Restaurants and hotels						−.37*	

SOURCES: Hofstede et al. (2010) (see Appendix A); OECD *Household Expenditure by Consumption Purpose, Share of Total Expenditure* (2016) (see Appendix B)

When observing the relationship between national income and penetration of some new products at macro level, one may be tempted to conclude that the richer countries become, the more their inhabitants will spend on these products. We have seen that for some investment-type products, income is the initial explaining variable, but over time cultural variables better explain variance. Analysis at micro level often points at relationships with culture. For many products, income differences have no explanatory power at all, and only cultural variables can explain variance. So greater wealth will not make people spend more equally in all countries.

The Concept of the Rational Consumer

Economists have viewed the consumer as a rational human being or *homo economicus* whose decisions are based on the principle of maximizing utility and profit in an environment of perfect knowledge. Individuals are assumed to be able to use reason to make personal choices. Scholars from various disciplines have objected to the overstated influence of income, also at national level. 'Differences, which, toward the end of the fifties, seemed to social scientists to be characteristics of countries – such as variations in the value of GNI and living standards – are viewed over time as quite unreliable indicators.'[106] In Chapter 6 we will see that information-based decision making is not universal.

There are many consumption differences across nations that cannot be explained by income differences. *Homo economicus* is a social construct of the Western world, assuming people spend their income in a rational way, first deciding on primary needs, and only when these are met considering luxury goods. This is not the case. For example, in the poorer countries, income often is an irrelevant criterion for buying luxury goods. Poorer consumers in developing economies may buy symbolic products (of little functional value in the eyes of Western economists) for social status needs that are not viewed as a necessity to Western economists. The importance of the symbolic function of brands is not limited to the wealthy. In 2009, low GNI per capita was the main explaining variable of differences in answers to the question about the importance of brand or brand name for making a buying decision.[107]

Another assumption is about the influence of education on consumer behavior. Information technology is expected to cause better-educated consumers. Better-educated consumers are assumed to be better informed. Better-informed consumers are assumed to make better (i.e., more rational) buying decisions. In Chapter 6 we will see that in collectivistic and high power distance cultures people don't search for information the way they do in individualistic and low power distance cultures. The concept of a rational consumer, consciously searching for information to make an informed buying decision – if it ever was a valid concept – is less valid in other than individualistic and low power distance cultures.

Engel's Law

Another economic theory that needs justifying for cross-cultural use is Engel's law, which has tried to generalize consumers' spending patterns. Engel states that as a family's income increases, the percentage spent on housing will be roughly constant and the amount saved or spent on other purchases will increase. The percentage of private consumption spent on food should decrease with increasing incomes. The theory was developed for single countries. Indeed, in all countries in Europe, the percentage of total household expenditure spent on food has been higher in the 20% lowest-income households than in the 20% highest-income households.[108] Between countries, however, at the national level, the differences remain large over time and are culture bound. The percentage of consumption expenditures dedicated to food[109] over time have been correlated not only with GNI/cap but also with low individualism, as we also see in Table 3.7. In collectivistic cultures in Europe, people allocate a higher percentage of consumption expenditure to food than do people in individualistic cultures. Generally, in collectivistic cultures food has an important social function. Providing food and having food in the home for any guest who drops by is an important social value. So expenditures on food are likely to remain relatively high in collectivistic cultures as compared with individualistic cultures.

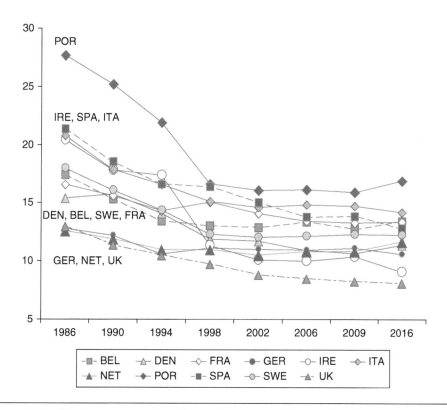

Figure 3.7 **Private consumption: Percentage expenditure on food**

SOURCE: Eurostat Yearbooks (see Appendix B)

Figure 3.7 illustrates how in each of the 11 European countries over time the percentage of private consumption spent on food has decreased. But after 1998 the percentages do not converge; the differences remain more or less the same. Thus, the universality of Engel's law is in the fact that for each separate country the percentage spent on food decreases with increased wealth. The modification is in the fact that the differences at country level remain the same. In the collectivistic cultures (e.g., Portugal, Spain), people continue to spend a relatively large amount of their income on food. With increased wealth, the percentage is even likely to increase. Whereas in individualistic cultures fast food is an increasingly important phenomenon, in collectivistic cultures increasing time and money is spent on quality and variety of food as well as on eating out. Food carries cultural meaning. It provides emotional and social security. It provides comfort and may also be used to relieve anxiety or cope with stress. It may be used to gain acceptance, friendship, to influence others, to establish communication with others.[110]

How Engel's law operates across countries is demonstrated by the development in Ireland. Ireland was, until the mid-1990s, a relatively poor country but it has developed remarkably fast at the end of the past century. Although Ireland is an individualistic culture, the percentage spent on food in Ireland used to be similar to that of a more collectivistic culture like Spain, because levels of wealth were similar. After 1995, however, with increased wealth, Ireland's percentage spent on food became similar to the percentage of the other individualistic cultures.

Conclusion

This chapter discussed convergence, divergence, and stability of consumption. It provided evidence of the stability of values and behavior. Instead of expected convergence, people's behavior is rather stable, and this is reflected in socioeconomic and consumption differences across countries. One of the assumed causes of convergence is modernization. When countries go through development stages from premodern to modern and postmodern, whatever convergence takes place is at macro level and rarely at micro level. It was argued that with converging wealth across countries, value differences become manifest and consumer behavior diverges. With disappearing income differences at country level, cross-country differences in consumption and consumer behavior cannot anymore be explained by GNP per capita. Because other demographic variables such as urbanization are related to national wealth, these variables cannot be used as explaining variables. Cultural variables are the best variables to explain differences.

Notes

1. J.P. Jones, 'Introduction, the vicissitudes of international advertising,' in J.P. Jones (ed.), *International Advertising, Realities and Myths* (Sage, Thousand Oaks, CA, 2000), pp. 1–10.

2. J.B. Williamson and J.J. Fleming, 'Convergence theory and the social welfare sector: A cross-national analysis,' in A. Inkeles and M. Sasaki (eds), *Comparing Nations and Cultures* (Prentice Hall, Englewood Cliffs, NJ, 1996), pp. 348–355.

3. A. Inkeles, *One World Emerging?: Convergence and Divergence in Industrial Societies* (Westview, Boulder, CO, 1998), pp. 20–23.

4. R. Inglehart, *Modernization and Postmodernization: Cultural, Economic, and Political Change in 43 Societies* (Princeton University Press, Princeton, NJ, 1997), p. 18.

5. S.P. Huntington, *The Clash of Civilizations and the Remaking of World Order* (Simon & Schuster, New York, 1996), p. 58.

6. D. Kerr, F.H. Harbison, and C.A. Myers, *Industrialism and Industrial Man* (Heinemann, London, 1960). Quoted in R. Robertson, *Globalization* (Sage, London, 1992), p. 11.

7. R. Robertson, *Globalization* (Sage, London, 1992).

8. A. Inkeles and D.H. Smith, *Becoming Modern* (Harvard University Press, Cambridge, MA, 1999), p. 15.

9. A. Giddens, *Introduction to Sociology* (W.W. Norton, New York, 1991), p. 795.

10. Inkeles and Smith, *Becoming Modern*, pp. 16–25.

11. J.-C. Usunier, 'Atomistic versus organic approaches,' *International Studies of Management and Organization*, 26 (1996/1997), pp. 90–112.

12. G. Hofstede, *Culture's Consequences*, 2nd edn (Sage, Thousand Oaks, CA, 2001), p. 34.

13. J.H.Y. Fu and C.Y. Chiu, 'Local culture's responses to globalization: Exemplary persons and their attendant values,' *Journal of Cross-Cultural Psychology*, 38, 5 (2007), pp. 636–653.

14. R. Inglehart, M. Basañez, and A. Moreno, *Human Values and Beliefs* (University of Michigan Press, Ann Arbor, 2001).

15. Ç. Kagitçibasi, 'Individualism and collectivism,' in J.W. Berry, M.H. Segall, and Ç. Kagitçibasi (eds), *Handbook of Cross-Cultural Psychology*, Vol. 3 (Allyn & Bacon, Boston, 1997), pp. 2–49.

16. H. Perkin, 'Review: One World Emerging? Convergence and Divergence in Industrial Societies by Alex Inkeles,' *Journal of Social History*, 33 (1999), pp. 461–462.

17. S.C. Jain, 'Standardization of international marketing strategy: Some research hypotheses,' *Journal of Marketing*, 53 (1989), pp. 70–79.

18. H. Mühlbacher, L. Dahringer, and H. Leihs, *International Marketing: A Global Perspective*, 2nd edn (International Thomson Business Press, London, 1999), pp. 50, 85.

19. S.D. Hunt, 'The nature and scope of marketing,' *Journal of Marketing*, 40 (1976), pp. 17–28.

20. M. Peterson and N. Malhotra, 'Country segmentation based on objective quality-of-life measures,' *International Marketing Review*, 17 (2000), pp. 56–73.

21. A.R. Andreasen, 'Cultural interpenetration: A critical consumer research issue for the 1990s,' in M. Goldberg and R.W. Pollay (eds), *Advances in Consumer Research*, Vol. 7 (Association for Consumer Research, Provo, UT, 1990), pp. 847–849.

22. H. Hollanders, L. Soete, and B. Ter Weel, *Trends in Growth Convergence and Divergence and Changes in Technological Access and Capabilities*, paper presented at the Lisbon Workshop on Cliometrics, Econometrics and Appreciative History in the Study of Long Waves in Economic Development, Lisbon (11–13 March 1999).

23. P. Norris, *Digital Divide: Civic Engagement, Information Poverty and the Internet in Democratic Societies* (Cambridge University Press, New York, 2001).

24. M. Roser, *Global Economic Inequality* [Online, 2017]. *Available at:* https://ourworldindata.org/global-economic-inequality.

25. R. Wade, 'Winners and losers,' *The Economist* (April 2001), pp. 79–82.

26. *Income Distribution Database*, OECD (2015). Available at: www.oecd.org.

27. P. Sarkar, 'Theory of convergence and real income divergence 1950-1992,' *Economic and Political Weekly* (20 February 1999).

28. C.S. Craig, S.P. Douglas, and A. Grein, 'Patterns of convergence and divergence among industrialized nations: 1960–1988,' *Journal of International Business Studies*, 23 (1992), pp. 773–786.

29. J.-C. Usunier, 'Consommation: quand global rime avec local (Consumption: when global rhymes with local),' *Revue Française de gestion*, 110 (1996), pp. 100–116.

30. S.P. Huntington, 'The goals of development,' in A. Inkeles and M. Sasaki (eds), *Comparing Nations and Cultures* (Prentice Hall, Englewood Cliffs, NJ, 1996), pp. 469–483.

31. Inkeles, *One World Emerging?*, pp. 30–45.

32. M. Van Mesdag, 'Culture-sensitive adaptation of global standardization: The duration-of-usage hypothesis,' *International Marketing Review*, 17 (2000), pp. 74–84.

33. J.B. Williamson and J.J. Fleming, 'Convergence theory and the social welfare sector: A cross-national analysis,' in A. Inkeles and M. Sasaki (eds), *Comparing Nations and Cultures* (Prentice Hall, Englewood Cliffs, NJ, 1996), pp. 348–355.

34. In most calculations the 44 countries of this group are Argentina, Australia, Austria, Belgium, Brazil, Canada, Chile, Colombia, Costa Rica, Denmark, Ecuador, El Salvador, Finland, France, Germany, Great Britain, Greece, Indonesia, India, Ireland, Israel, Italy, Japan, South Korea, Malaysia, Mexico, Netherlands, Norway, New Zealand, Pakistan, Panama, Peru, Philippines, Portugal, South Africa, Singapore, Spain, Sweden, Switzerland, Thailand, Turkey, Uruguay, United States, Venezuela.

35. When I refer to calculations for Europe, these are generally for 15 countries: Austria, Belgium, Denmark, Finland, France, Germany, Ireland, Italy, Netherlands, Norway, Portugal, Spain, Sweden, Switzerland, United Kingdom. When Eurostat data (available only for EU countries) are used, calculation sometimes is for 13 countries (Norway and Switzerland excluded). (See Appendix B.)

36. The examples of convergence and divergence are computed from data from annual reports of the World Bank, Eurostat, the United Nations, Euromonitor, and data from surveys like Eurobarometer, *Reader's Digest*, and the European Media and Marketing Surveys (EMS), as in Appendix B. The 20 product categories are telephony, passenger cars, television, radio, the press (newspapers, books), food, mineral water, soft drinks, alcoholic drinks, cigarettes, jewelry, personal computers, Internet, audio, household appliances, watches, cameras, personal care products, household cleaning products, and financial products. The amount of data that are free to

download from the public domain is decreasing, so this book cannot always present the most recent data.

37. The varying time spans for these calculations are due to the fact that data definitions and measurements tend to change over time or data are not available in the public domain. For example, until 2000 data for mobile phones were based on ownership, and after 2000 data are for mobile phone subscribers. For Internet I used data on usage, not on Internet connections, which data were used earlier. Several data provided for free by the Worldbank, now have to be paid for by the original owners of the data. An example is data for passenger cars, owned by IRF World Road Statistics.

38. J. Nowak and O. Kochkova, 'Income, culture, and household consumption expenditure patterns in the European Union: Convergence or divergence?', *Journal of International Consumer Marketing*, 23 (2011), pp. 260–275.

39. Data EMS 1997, 2007 and 2012.

40. Belgium, Denmark, Finland, France, Germany, Italy, Netherlands, Norway, Portugal, Spain, Sweden, Switzerland, United Kingdom.

41. J. Helm, *Advertising's Overdue Revolution*, paper presented to the *Adweek* creative conference, San Francisco (1 October 1999).

42. Pew Research Center. Available at: http://pewresearch.org/assets/social/pdf/Luxury.pdf; Data 2010: www.pewsocialtrends.org/2010/08/19/the-fading-glory-of-the-television-and-telephone (accessed 21 November 2009).

43. I use GNI consistently in this book in order not to confuse the reader. Information on this terminology change from the World Bank can be found at www.worldbank.org/data/changinterm.html

44. Technical Notes. *World Development Report 1998/99* (World Bank, Washington, DC).

45. S.P. Sethi, 'Comparative cluster analysis for world markets', *Journal of Marketing Research*, 8 (1971), pp. 348–354; C.S. Craig, S.P. Douglas, and A. Grein, 'Patterns of convergence and divergence among industrialized nations: 1960–1988', *Journal of International Business Studies*, 23 (1992), pp. 773–786.

46. K. Helsen, K. Jedidi, and W.S. DeSarbo, 'A new approach to country segmentation utilizing multinational diffusion patterns', *Journal of Marketing*, 57 (1993), pp. 60–71.

47. T. McCain, 'Patterns of media use in Europe: Identifying country clusters', *European Journal of Communication*, 1 (1986), pp. 231–250.

48. G. Ger and R.W. Belk, 'Cross-cultural differences in materialism', *Journal of Economic Psychology*, 17 (1996), pp. 55–77.

49. M.S. Roth, 'The effects of culture and socioeconomics on the performance of global brand image strategies', *Journal of Marketing Research*, 32 (1995), pp. 163–175.

50. A. Venkatesh, 'Ethoconsumerism: A new paradigm to study cultural and cross-cultural consumer behavior', in J.A. Costa and G.J. Bamossy (eds), *Marketing in a Multicultural World* (Sage, Thousand Oaks, CA, 1995), pp. 26–67.

51. For three countries of the group of 44 countries no LTO data are available, so these calculations are for only 41 countries.

52. P. Norris, *The Worldwide Digital Divide: Information Poverty, the Internet and Development*, paper presented at the annual meeting of the Political Association of the United Kingdom, London School of Economics and Political Science (10–13 April 2000).

53. *European Social Survey* (2003) (see Appendix B).

54. *European Cultural Values* (Special Eurobarometer report (EBS 278), 2007) (see Appendix B).

55. Eurobarometer report 86 (2016) (see Appendix B).

56. E. Van de Vliert, 'Climatoeconomic roots of survival versus self-expression cultures,' *Journal of Cross-Cultural Psychology*, 38, 2 (2007), pp. 156–172.

57. Inglehart, *Modernization and Postmodernization*, pp. 603–604.

58. A. Inkeles, *Continuity and Change in Popular Values on the Pacific Rim* (Hoover Institution, Stanford, CA, 1997), pp. 8–10, 14–15.

59. Fu and Chiu, 'Local culture's responses to globalization.'

60. P.R. Abrahamson and R. Inglehart, *Value Change in Global Perspective* (University of Michigan Press, Ann Arbor, 1995), p. 84.

61. *World Development Indicators – Urbanization Table 3.10* (World Bank, Washington, DC, 2007), p. 165.

62. *World Population Prospects: The 2017 Revision, Key Findings and Advance Tables*, Working Paper No. ESA/P/WP/248 (Population Division, Department of Economic and Social Affairs, United Nations, 2017).

63. *Consumers in Europe: Facts and Figures: Data 1996–2000*, Eurostat (Office for Official Publications of the European Communities, Luxembourg, 2001), p. 21.

64. F. Höllinger and M. Haller, 'Kinship and social networks in modern societies: A cross-cultural comparison among seven nations,' in A. Inkeles and M. Sasaki (eds), *Comparing Nations and Cultures* (Prentice Hall, Englewood Cliffs, NJ, 1996), pp. 147–170.

65. A. Roland, *In Search of Self in India and Japan* (Princeton University Press, Princeton, NJ, 1988), p. 302.

66. Kagitçibasi 'Individualism and collectivism,' p. 35.

67. *Information Society* (Flash Eurobarometer 241, 2008).

68. *Consumers in Europe*, p. 36.

69. Roper Starch Worldwide, 'The global marketplace,' *The Public Pulse*, 10, 11, 12 (1997), p.7.

70. *World Development Report 1998/99 – Technical Notes* (World Bank, Washington, DC).

71. *World Development Indicators 2017*.

72. *World Population Prospects, 2017 Revision* (Population Division, Department of Economic and Social Affairs, United Nations, 2017).

73. Personal communication, 17 November 2009.

74. *Dying Too Young* (Europe and Central Asia Human Development Department, World Bank, 2005). Available at: http://siteresources.worldbank.org/INTECA/Resources/DTY-Final.pdf (accessed 26 April 2009)

75. *Population Facts* (United Nations Department of Economic and Social Affairs, October 2017). Available at: www.unpopulation.org.

76. *UN Demographic Yearbook 2016* (United Nations Statistics Division, 2016).

77. *Society at a Glance* (OECD, 2016).

78. Female share of labor force data, World Bank Development reports for 1994 and 2006.

79. *United Nations Statistics*. Available at: http://unstats.un.org/unsd/demographic/products/indwm/tab5b.htm (accessed 16 November 2009).

80. *Satisfaction with Family Life* (Flash Eurobarometer report 247, 2008).

81. J.C. Usunier, *Marketing Across Cultures*, 3rd edn (Pearson Education, Harlow, UK, 2000), pp. 60–61.

82. J. Price, 'Mining for opportunities in Latin America,' *ESOMAR Research World*, 7 (July/August 2000), p. 5.

83. G. Hadfield and M. Skipworth, *Class: Where do you Stand?* (Bloomsbury, London, 1994), pp. 10–18.

84. M. Savage, F. Devine, N. Cunningham, M. Taylor, Y. Li, J. Hjellbrekke, B. Le Roux, S. Friedman, and A. Miles, 'A new model of social class? Findings from the BBC's Great British Class Survey Experiment,' *Sociology*, 47, 2 (2013), pp. 219–250.

85. H. Horton, 'The seven social classes of 21st century Britain – where do you fit in?,' *The Telegraph* (7 December 2015). Available at: www.telegraph.co.uk/news/uknews/12037247/the-seven-social-classes-of-21st-century-britain-where-do-you-fit-in.html (accessed 17 June 2018).

86. C. Dickey, 'Reflecting on race barriers,' *Newsweek* (24 November 2008), pp. 26–30.

87. See also Hofstede, *Culture's Consequences*, pp. 279–280.

88. Hofstede, *Culture's Consequences*, p. 429.

89. Venkatesh, 'Ethoconsumerism,' pp. 31–35.

90. Henry J. Kaiser Family Foundation, *Population Distribution by Race/Ethnicity* (2016). Available at: www.kff.org.

91. J. Berry, 'America's family tree,' *Brandweek* (19 July 1993), p. 19.

92. H.M. Coon and M. Kemmelmeier, 'Cultural orientations in the United States,' *Journal of Cross-Cultural Psychology*, 32 (2001), pp. 348–364.

93. D. Oyserman, H.M. Coon, and M. Kemmelmeier, 'Rethinking individualism and collectivism: Evaluation of theoretical assumptions and meta-analyses,' *Psychological Bulletin*, 128 (2002), pp. 3–72.

94. Coon and Kemmelmeier, 'Cultural orientations in the United States.'

95. M. De Mooij and J. Beniflah, 'Measuring cross-cultural differences of ethnic groups within nations: Convergence or divergence of cultural values? The case of the United States,' *Journal of International Consumer Marketing*, 29, 1 (2017), pp. 2–10.

96. *Kerncijfers Gemeente Amsterdam* (2016). Available at: www.ois.amsterdam.nl.

97. J.W. Berry, 'Immigration, acculturation, and adaptation,' *Applied Psychology: An International Review*, 46 (1997), pp. 5–34.

98. H. Abu-Rayya and D.L. Sam, 'Is integration the best way to acculturate? A re-examination of the bicultural-adaptation relationship in the "ICSEY Dataset" using the bilineal method,' *Journal of Cross-Cultural Psychology*, 48, 3 (2017), pp. 287–293

99. G.S. Shergill, H. Sekhon, and M. Zhao, 'Parents'perception of teen's influence on family purchase decisions,' *Asia Pacific Journal of Marketing and Logistics*, 25, 1 (2013), pp. 162–177.

100. P.M. Parker, *National Cultures of the World* (Greenwood, Westport, CT, 1997), pp. 23–34.

101. Ibid.

102. U Kim, H.C. Triandis, Ç. Kâgitçibasi, S.C. Choi, and G. Yoon, *Individualism and Collectivism* (Sage, Thousand Oaks, CA, 1994).

103. E. Van de Vliert, E.S. Kluwer, and R. Lynn, 'Citizens of warmer countries are more competitive and poorer: Culture or chance?,' *Journal of Economic Psychology*, 21 (2000), pp. 143–165.

104. *Consumers in Europe*, p. 73.

105. P.M. Parker and N.T Tavassoli, 'Homeostasis and consumer behavior across cultures,' *International Journal of Research in Marketing*, 17 (2000), pp. 33–53.

106. E.K. Scheuch, 'Theoretical implications of comparative survey research: Why the wheel of cross-cultural methodology keeps on being reinvented,' in A. Inkeles and M. Sasaki (eds), *Comparing Nations and Cultures* (Prentice Hall, Englewood Cliffs, NJ, 1996), pp. 57–73.

107. *Europeans' Attitudes Towards the Issue of Sustainable Consumption and Production* (Flash Eurobarometer report 256, 2009).

108. *Consumers in Europe*, p. 25.

109. Eurostat annual yearbooks (see Appendix B).

110. F.M. Magrabi, Y.S. Chung, S.S. Cha, and S.J. Yang, *The Economics of Household Consumption* (Praeger, New York, 1991), p. 211.

The Consumer: Attributes

The attributes of the person refer to *what people are*. The central question is, 'Who am I?', or the *self*, and in what terms people describe themselves, their personalities, traits, and identities. Related to the *who* are attitudes and lifestyles, because they are a central part of the person.

The concepts of self, personality, identity, and image are central to consumer behavior and are also used as metaphors in branding strategies. They have been derived from psychological studies in the United States and northwest Europe, so these and other psychological models presented in consumer behavior textbooks are derived from an individualistic worldview. Increasingly, other models are being developed for other groups.[1] Both attitude formation and the relationship between attitude and behavior vary across cultures. Whereas in Western models attitude can be used to predict behavior, this is much less the case in other parts of the world.

Although ideally the emic approach should be followed for the study of consumer behavior in different countries, for the purpose of international marketing it is more pragmatic to evaluate the cross-cultural usefulness of existing constructs. In this chapter, findings from cross-cultural psychology are presented to help understand the differences of the various aspects of the person across cultures.

The Concept of Self

Psychologists agree that self-concept plays a central role in behavior and psychological processes. It consists of whatever individuals consider to be theirs, including their bodies, families, possessions, moods, emotions, conscience, attitudes, values, traits, and social positions.[2] The cross-cultural psychologists Markus and Kitayama state:

> The self or the identity is critical because it is the psychological locus of cultural effects. It functions as a mediating, orienting and interpretative framework that will systematically bias how members of a given socio-cultural group will think, feel and act.[3]

The self is shaped by the cultural context, and in turn it strongly influences social behavior in various ways, including an individual's perceptions, evaluations, and values.[4] This mediating role of the self makes it an intermediary variable for understanding behavior.

The concept of self, as used in consumer psychology, is rooted in individualism. It includes the following ideas about a person: A person is an *autonomous entity* with a distinctive set of attributes, qualities, or processes. The configuration of these internal attributes or processes causes behavior. People's attributes and processes should be expressed consistently in behavior across situations. Behavior that changes with the situation is viewed as hypocritical or pathological.

In the collectivistic model of the self, persons are fundamentally interdependent with one another. The self cannot be separated from others and the surrounding social context. This concept of self is characteristic of Asia, South America, Russia, the Middle East, Africa, and the south of Europe. The interdependent view of human nature includes the following ideas about a person: A person is an *interdependent entity* who is part of an encompassing social relationship. Behavior is a consequence of being responsive to the others with whom one is interdependent, and behavior originates in relationships. Individual behavior is situational; it is sensitive to social context and varies from one situation to another and from one time to another.[5] People follow different norms and values at different places, times and with different people. For example, the behavior norm in public space (e.g., work) is different from the norm in private space (e.g., family).[6]

Next to the term *interdependent* self in collectivistic cultures, the term *familial*[7] self is used. It is a 'we' self, relational in different contexts. It includes a private self and a public self. The *private self* operates in interdependence with others of a person's in-group. There is emotional connectedness, empathy, and receptivity to others. It is through the *public self* that the social etiquette of relationships with the outer group is maintained in varying interpersonal contexts. These different concepts of self define what is considered social or pro-social behavior.

Hasegawa et al.[8] content analyzed Japanese fictional TV programs and found much less pro-social behavior depicted in such TV programs in Japan (twice per hour) than other such studies had found in the United States (between 20 and 40 times within an hour). The US definition of pro-social behavior included 'reparation for bad behavior,' 'control of aggressive impulses,' and 'resistance to temptation.' Whereas in Japan pro-social behavior is understood as ordinary formal behavior, it appears to be remarkable behavior in the United States.

In individualistic cultures focus is on individual autonomy. A youth has to develop an identity that enables him or her to function independently in a variety of social groups, apart from the family. In collectivistic cultures youth development is based on encouragement of dependency needs in complex familial hierarchical relationships, and the group ideal is being like others as opposed to being different.[9]

The very first words of children in China are people related, whereas children in the United States start talking about objects.[10] In Japan, feeling good is more associated with interpersonal situations such as feeling friendly, whereas in the United States feeling good is more frequently associated with interpersonal distance, such as feeling superior or proud. In the United Kingdom, feelings of happiness are more related to a sense of independence, whereas in Greece, good feelings are negatively related to a sense of independence.[11] In self alone drawings as well as in family drawings, Cameroonian children draw themselves significantly smaller than German children of the same age.[12]

Kagitçibasi[13] distinguished between a *relational self,* a *separated self,* and the *family model of emotional interdependence,* which is a combination of the first two. The relational self develops in collectivistic cultures in rural areas, where intergenerational interdependence functions for family livelihood. It is the family model of emotional and material interdependence. The separated self develops in the family model of independence in the urban context of Western, individualistic cultures, where intergenerational interdependence is not required for family livelihood. The third category of self combines a relational orientation with autonomy. It develops the family model of emotional interdependence in the developed urban areas of collectivistic cultures, where material interdependency weakens, but emotional interdependence continues.

The word 'individualism' is often translated into Chinese as *geren zhuyi,* which conveys a negative, rather than positive, connotation like 'self-centeredness' or 'selfishness.' Most Chinese would not want to be associated with this connotation.[14] This doesn't imply that a Chinese person doesn't have internal integrity, but the ability to properly function in society has priority. The two are symbolized by squareness (a person's internal integrity) and roundness, the external flexibility necessary to deal with other people.[15]

Although the relational self is characteristic of collectivistic cultures, a different type of relationship orientation exists in individualistic cultures that are also feminine.[16] This relationship orientation is called *horizontal individualism* by the cross-cultural psychologist

Harry Triandis,[17] who distinguishes between two types of individualism: vertical (independent and different) and horizontal (interdependent and different) individualism. What he calls horizontal interdependent is the relationship orientation of individualistic and low masculine cultures that are on the one hand characterized by self-reliance but on the other hand by interdependence, which translates to needs for consensus, low social status needs, and not wanting to 'stick out.' Whereas 'family values' are part of the self-concept in collectivistic cultures, comparable social aspects characterize the self-concept in individualistic cultures that are also feminine.[18] Both collectivism and femininity can explain variance in relationship orientation. Across seven countries in Latin America, in the more feminine cultures young people think the Internet is isolating. Low masculinity explains 59% of variance.[19]

The collectivistic concept of self is expressed in many different ways across the world. In much of Africa, the term *ubuntu* expresses the basic philosophy that to be a human being is to affirm one's humanity by recognizing the humanity of others, and on that basis, establish humane relations with them. An individual owes his or her existence to the existence of others. 'I am' because 'you are,' and 'you are' because 'I am.' We can only be human through others.[20]

The Buddhist idea of the self is an interconnected personhood – a personhood that is connected with others in society; not a free-floating autonomous self enjoying total and absolute freedom. It is shaped by the law of karma that guides human action.[21]

Although the interdependent self is a characteristic of collectivism, individuals from African and East-Asian countries (all collectivistic cultures) differ in levels of interdependence. Independence and interdependence are not necessarily conflicting but may vary with situational demands. In particular East-Asians are also self reliant and ambitious (a characteristic of long-term oriented cultures). In some situations the social oriented self may become more influential; in others individual oriented needs are prioritized. The superficial observer may confuse the latter with individualism.[22]

Adapting to situations suggests different self-concepts across contexts. Singh[23] writes that Indians tolerate inconsistency more than Westerners, and their thinking is more contextual, which leads to contradictory self-concepts. Zhang[24] suggests young Chinese, next to their local identity, may develop a global identity that allows them to communicate with people from other cultures either face to face or through interactive media. Their local identity is likely to be used most in daily interaction with family and friends and community members.

In the eyes of Westerners, behavior of Chinese or Japanese when in the West may suggest they are like Westerners because they are able to adapt so much to the situation and norms of the hosting country. This doesn't mean they share the same values, but they are much more than Westerners able to adapt to the situation.

Self-Descriptions and Self-Evaluations

In order to develop a distinctive, unique self, in individualistic cultures people learn to describe themselves in terms of psychological characteristics, but reporting one's distinctive characteristics is not a natural task in collectivistic cultures. Individualistic Westerners seem relatively more practiced in describing themselves in abstract and global ways than are members of collectivistic cultures. Individuals with interdependent selves may have difficulty describing themselves in absolute terms without any contextual or situational references. To the Japanese, abstract categorizations of the self seem unnatural or artificial because they reflect a claim of being a separate individual without the constraints of specific roles or situations.[25] So collectivists are more likely to refer to social roles and present themselves as a relational part of a greater whole. Markus and Kitayama[26] describe studies that demonstrate that Korean and Japanese students twice as often as American students use context-specific and social self-descriptions or refer to some features of the situation or social context. People may, for example, describe themselves as 'I am in the gymnastic club.' This difference has consequences for opinion or attitude research. In collectivistic cultures, opinions are much less individual opinions, and references to group membership or situational aspects should be included in questions.

In particular, American descriptions of the self tend to contain almost only positive self-evaluations. Whereas American adults tend to rate themselves as more attractive and intelligent than average adults, Japanese adults rate about 50% of others as higher on a given trait or ability. In American psychology it is said that Americans display a 'false uniqueness bias,' whereas Japanese and Chinese tend to show a 'modesty bias.'[27] Within Japanese culture, self-criticism (*hansei*) serves a functional purpose. It aids individuals in pointing at the areas in which they need to improve themselves. Self-improvement serves to aid Japanese in fulfilling their role obligations. This modesty bias is a reflection of collectivistic culture and in sharp contrast to North American practice, where negative self-features would symbolize lack of the ability to be self-sufficient, autonomous, and to make one's own unique mark in the world.[28]

Implications for Marketing, Branding, and Advertising

A central aspect of Western marketing is the focus on product attributes that are to distinguish the user's self from others. People will buy products that are compatible with their self-concepts or rather that enhance their 'ideal self' images.

Ownership of products or brands transfers the meaning of products to consumers. By owning an item, the item can become part of the 'extended self.' The product's image should contribute to the consumer's self-concept.[29] This process is likely to vary with the different self-concepts. Whereas product ownership in individualistic cultures can express uniqueness and independence, in collectivistic cultures the extended self is the group, and product ownership may have the function of demonstrating life stage and group identity. In Japan, brands do not enhance a unique personality but confirm social status. The extreme brand-related behavior of Japanese youths is often falsely interpreted as Japanese youths becoming individualistic. It is the context that allows such behavior. When one is a student one can behave in specific autonomous ways; in other roles one cannot.

> Key associations for fashion in France are individuality, symbolism, meaning, interpretation, pleasure, and seduction. In Japan, to be fashionable is to be dynamically integrated in a community that defines the self and proves that it exists by its ability to adapt to all new expressions of fashion.[30] To be fashionable in the United States is to demonstrate your unique individuality.

The Self-Concept and Branding

To many collectivists, abstract self-descriptions seem unnatural; characteristics can only be asked in the context of specific situations and relationships, for example, 'Describe yourself at home with your family.' An important lesson for branding is that if people are not able to describe *themselves* in abstract terms, they are likely not able to do so for *brands* either. For members of collectivistic cultures, the brand concept is too abstract to be discussed in a comparable manner as in individualistic cultures. The *Reader's Digest* Trusted Brands survey in 2002 asked people in 18 different countries[31] in Europe about the probability of buying a brand they had heard of but not tried before. In individualistic cultures people are more likely to buy unknown brands than in collectivistic cultures. The responses 'Extremely/quite likely to consider buying a brand which I've heard of but haven't tried before' correlate significantly with individualism ($r = .82***$). The relationship is illustrated in Figure 4.1. A brand out of context is less relevant to members of collectivistic cultures than to members of individualistic cultures.

The context specificity of the self in collectivistic cultures may imply that, in contrast to individualistic cultures, where a brand is supposed to be consistent with respect to its attributes and values, in collectivistic cultures one brand can have different attributes and/ or values in different contexts. The innate need for cross-situational consistency of Western

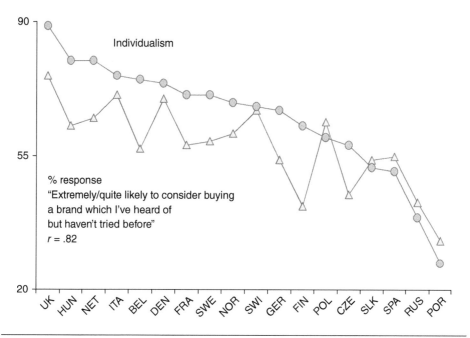

Figure 4.1   **The brand concept and individualism**

SOURCES: Hofstede et al. (2010) (see Appendix A); *Reader's Digest* Trusted Brands (2002) (see Appendix B)

marketing managers induces them to develop consistent brand identities across countries. This is a fundamental error that may limit cross-cultural success.

In Asia, marketing managers are not inclined to develop brands or brand strategies by adding abstract characteristics to brands, the way it is done in the West. Hu[32] analyzed the content of 30 issues of the Chinese professional advertising magazines *Modern Advertising* and China *Advertising*, including 10,000 titles, and found zero articles including *brand* as a keyword.

Another limitation is the Western concept of creativity that is historically based on originality and uniqueness. The practices of Western branding and design are a reflection of the uniqueness concept that is seen as a precondition to differentiation. That is why marketers and designers insist that their brands should be *unique*. In Asian cultures the concept of originality does not

Figure 4.2   **Wella advertisement**

exist as it does in the West. Instead, everything comes from somewhere else, because everything and everybody is part of a greater whole, out of which everything can be taken, assimilated, and remade even while it retains its own cultural origins and code.[33] The wish to be consistent is reflected in the ubiquitous use of standard – often English language – logos and pay-offs. What might, for example, for a Chinese consumer be the meaning of the pay-off 'Wella, perfectly you' under a logo for a shampoo brand consisting of stylized waving hair?[34] (see Figure 4.2).

The Self-Concept and Advertising

The difference between the independent and interdependent self has its impact on advertising. In collectivistic cultures, such as China and Korea, appeals focusing on in-group benefits, harmony, and family are more effective, whereas in individualistic cultures like the United States, advertising that appeals to individual benefits and preferences, personal success, and independence is more effective.[35] A commercial in which a guy breaks out from a group and starts doing something on his own that the group hasn't thought of would be seen as positive in the individualistic cultures of the West but negative in collectivistic Asian cultures.[36] For collectivists, one's identity is in the group. Depicting someone alone may imply he or she has no identity. A pan-European campaign by Vodafone depicted a lone individual, but the Vodafone brand Airtel in Spain depicted the group identity, as illustrated in Figure 4.3.

Members of individualistic and collectivistic societies will respond differently to advertisements emphasizing individualistic or collectivistic appeals. In the United States, people will be more persuaded by ads emphasizing individualistic benefits such as personal success and independence, whereas in Korea people will be more attracted to ads emphasizing collectivistic benefits, such as in-group benefits, harmony, and family.[37]

Advertising appeals that present a brand in a way that matches consumers' self-concepts appear to result in more favorable brand attitudes. This was confirmed in a study by Wang et al.,[38] who use the terms *separated* versus *connected* for appeals that are attractive for people in individualistic cultures or collectivistic cultures. A connected advertising appeal stresses interdependence and togetherness. A separated advertising appeal stresses independence and autonomy.

The importance of both context and the relationship orientation of the self in collectivistic cultures can explain the frequent use of celebrities in Japanese advertising. The use of celebrities in advertising varies across cultures. There are indications that in Western societies these variations are related to the degree of masculinity (need for success), which is likely to explain why in the United States the cult of personality and obsession with celebrity and

Figure 4.3 **Vodafone and Airtel advertisements**

stardom is pronounced. However, in the collectivistic Japan, the use of celebrities in advertising is even stronger than in the United States. In his description of the celebrity phenomenon in Japan, Praet[39] provides explanations that refer to two collectivistic aspects: the relational self and context. In Japan, unlike in most countries, celebrity appearances are not limited to famous actors, singers, sports stars, or comedians. Advertising is a stage for established celebrities to capitalize their fame; it also is the steppingstone for models and aspiring actors toward fame. In Japan, the word *talent* (*tarento*) is used to describe most celebrities in the entertainment world, and *star* is reserved for those who are seen to have long-lasting popularity. Many of these talents are selected on the basis of their cute looks. First, in the context of entertainment and advertising, this phenomenon seems not to pose problems of distinctiveness, which it might give in the context of the family or a work-related environment. Second, the function of using such *tarento* is to give the brand 'face' in the world of brands with similar product attributes. Instead of adding abstract personal characteristics to the product, it is linked to concrete persons. This is also explained as part of the creative process, in which a creative team in the advertising agency prefers to explain a proposed campaign by showing the client a popular talent around whom the campaign is to be built rather than talking about an abstract creative concept. In a large study comparing 25 countries, Praet found that mainly collectivism explains differences in the use of celebrities in advertising, where the function of a celebrity is to give face to the brand in a world of brands with similar product attributes.[40]

Self-Enhancement and Self-Esteem

European Americans show a general sensitivity to positive self-relevant information, which is named *self-enhancement*.[41] To Americans, self-enhancement leads to *self-esteem*, and self-esteem is a natural and valid barometer of human worth and psychological health, a belief that is unheard of in many other cultures. To Americans, self-esteem is important for a general sense of well-being, whereas in Japan, as well as in many other collectivistic cultures, subjective well-being depends on the appraisal of the self as actively responding to and correcting shortcomings. For collectivists, absence of negative features is more important for their well-being than presence of positive features.[42]

> How much self-esteem is integrated into the concept of self in Anglo-American culture is demonstrated by the definition of self-concept by Eysenck:
>
> Self-concept is all the thoughts and feelings about the self; it combines self-esteem and self-image (the knowledge an individual has about himself or herself). Self-esteem is the evaluative aspect of the self-concept; it concerns how worthwhile and confident an individual feels about himself or herself.[43]

Self-enhancement and self-esteem have been thought to be a phenomenon typical of individualistic cultures, because associated with individualism and the independent self is the tendency to maintain and enhance self-esteem through efforts to stand out or be superior to others.[44] Cross-cultural studies have shown that the self-enhancement tendency is indeed weaker in collectivist cultures but also in cultures that score low on cultural masculinity. However, we have to take into account that the measurement method of self-esteem is Western-based.[45] Virtually all empirical research has been undertaken in the United States or other Western industrialized countries. A large number of such studies have found evidence that men tend to have higher self-esteem than women and that self-esteem increases from adolescence to middle adulthood. A study across 48 nations found that gender differences in self-esteem were larger in wealthy, developed, egalitarian and individualistic cultures. One of the causes might be the cultural emphasis of girls' and women's physical appearance. Both males and females who feel physically attractive tend to have higher self-esteem. However, in cultures with greater gender equality, gender differences in self-esteem tend to become smaller with age.[46]

The recent data for the long-/short-term orientation dimension also show a relationship with feelings of pride and self-esteem that in particular are strong in short-term-oriented cultures. This explains the self-enhancement phenomenon in the United States, which is individualistic, short-term oriented and scores high on masculinity.

Among Americans, success situations are considered to be more important than failure situations, whereas the opposite is true for Japanese. The independent self-system, typical of Western individualistic societies, stresses the uniqueness and well-being of the individual, whereas the interdependent self stresses the importance of fitting in, restraining oneself, and maintaining social harmony. Having self-attributes that are more positive (the main advantage of self-enhancement) seems to be less central to the interdependent self than to the independent self.[47]

Self-enhancement practices like ego boosting, performance, and showing off are integrated aspects of the North American self. American sociologist Erving Goffman saw the structure of self in terms of 'how we arrange for performances in Anglo-American society.' He described the individual as 'a harried fabricator of impressions involved in the all-too-human task of staging a performance.'[48]

Making pictures of themselves in celebrations or other self-enhancing situations is what people historically have done more in individualistic and masculine cultures than in collectivistic and/or feminine cultures. In some countries people indeed make more photographs than in others. Usage of films (more than six used in the past 12 months) in 1995 (data EMS) correlated with masculinity, which explained 38% of variance. In 2007, 44% of variance of interest in photography was explained by short-term orientation. With respect to selfies there will be differences in the number of selfies people make, selfies of people alone or in groups, and style. Differences may be explained by the same three dimensions.

Acceptance of advertisements appealing to personal status and self-enhancement differs as much between the United States and Denmark, both individualistic cultures, as between the United States and Korea. This is because self-enhancement appeals may be judged in poor taste in the self-reliant yet egalitarian societies of Scandinavia, whereas they may be rejected for being too self-focused in Korea.[49]

Differences in how women judge their own bodies, beauty, or appearance, in an enhanced way or more critical, is related to differences in self-enhancement.

For the Dove campaign for Real Beauty, Unilever sponsored a study[50] on the self and beauty, asking questions to young girls about satisfaction with their own beauty and opinions on beauty in ten different countries worldwide. Individualism and short-term orientation were the main predictors of variance. The percentage of girls who were satisfied with their beauty correlated with short-term orientation, which explained 58% of variance;

short-term orientation also explained 69% of agreement with the statement 'Society expects women to enhance their physical attractiveness.' Agreement with the statement 'It would be better if the media depicted women of different shapes' varied with individualism, explaining 53% of variance and short-term orientation explaining an additional 25%. One statement to a larger group of women (18–64 years old) was, 'My mother has positively influenced my feelings about myself and beauty.' Sixty-five percent of variance of the percentages who agreed was explained by short-term orientation. Self-enhancement goes from generation to generation.

The international campaign targeted younger women with very different body shapes. Whereas the main pictures of this campaign in the United States and Europe focused on the differences in body shapes, including a variety of underwear styles, the campaign in Japan showed different Asian women, but they were all dressed in exactly the same underwear, so to preserve an image of group harmony.

Across 14 wealthy European countries, short-term orientation explains differences between countries with respect to consumers' relationships with brands, like finding that some brands are worth paying more for (42% explained) and consumers' desire to be among the first to try new brands (40% explained).[51] In short-term-oriented cultures, brands appear to be self-enhancing phenomena.

A need for self-esteem may exist across cultures, but people arrive at self-esteem in various ways. Self-esteem is not necessarily the cause of behavior; behavior can be the cause of self-esteem. Because different cultural behavioral practices lead to self-esteem, the content of self-esteem can vary across cultures. In individualistic and masculine cultures, self-esteem means being competent, talented, able to take care of oneself, and able to compete successfully. The pursuit of self-esteem is facilitated by self-enhancing motivations. In contrast, in collectivistic and high power distance cultures, in particular in East Asia, self-esteem is tied to maintaining face, implying meeting the consensual standards associated with their roles. The pursuit of face is facilitated by self-improving motivations.[52]

In collectivistic cultures, respect from others is more important than self-esteem. This can be recognized in answers to a question in the *European Social Survey*[53] that asks respondents across western and eastern European countries to mark the importance of getting respect from others. Collectivism explains 47% of variance, and masculinity explains an additional 13% of variance. The relationship between respect from others and collectivism is illustrated in Figure 4.4, which also shows that feminine cultures like Sweden, Norway, and Finland score lower than masculine cultures like Ireland, Switzerland, and Poland.

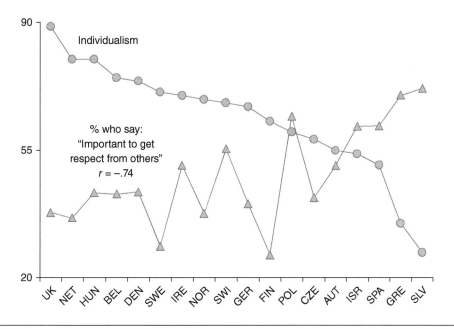

Figure 4.4 Importance of getting respect from others

SOURCES: Hofstede et al. (2010) (see Appendix A); *European Social Survey* (2002/2003) (see Appendix B)

The differences in self-enhancement are mapped in Figure 4.5. The X-axis contains Hofstede's country scores for individualism, and the Y-axis for short-/long-term orientation. In the cultures in the lower quadrants, we find need for respect from others, feelings of pride and self-enhancement. In the upper quadrants, maintaining face, self-improvement, and self-criticism are more common. Figure 4.5 shows that, although self-enhancement is often thought to be a universal human characteristic, the countries where it is strongest are the United States, United Kingdom, Ireland, and Australia, a limited number of countries.

Self-enhancement and self-esteem are essential concepts for marketing and advertising, as many consumption activities can reinforce both. The concepts are also important for understanding differences in the functioning of social media because of the different ways people tend to present themselves. Perceptions of self in relation to others and society are related to self-esteem. Yet different routes have been found to reaching self-esteem. To North Americans, *self-enhancement* leads to self-esteem, whereas in East Asian cultures it is *self-improvement*. Self-enhancement or a general sensitivity to positive self-relevant information, confirms competence to European Americans.[54] In East Asia, self-esteem is tied to maintaining face, which implies that meeting the consensual standards associated with their roles and the pursuit of face is facilitated by self-improvement motivations.[55]

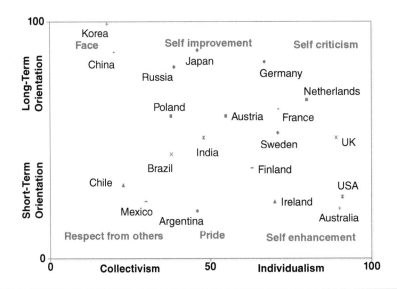

Figure 4.5   **Self-enhancement**

SOURCE: Hofstede et al. (2010) (see Appendix A)

Personality

Broadly defined, *personality* is the sum of the qualities and characteristics of being a person. Generally, the person is defined in the European–American psychological context in which the person is viewed as an 'independent self-contained, autonomous entity who comprises a unique configuration of internal attributes (e.g., traits, abilities, motives, and values) and who behaves primarily as consequence of these internal attributes.'[56] Definitions of personality in consumer behavior and marketing textbooks reflect this. Persons have distinct personalities that influence their buying behavior.

What is meant by *personality* are the person's distinguishing psychological characteristics that lead to relatively consistent and enduring responses to his or her environment. Like the self, the personality is assumed to be cross-situationally consistent. Increasingly, cultural psychologists argue that consistency is greater in individualistic cultures than in collectivistic cultures, because in the latter behavior is more strongly influenced by contextual factors.[57] Descriptions of the concept of personality generally include three Western-based elements: (1) People should distinguish themselves from others; (2) Consistency is an integral part of the concept; (3) Personality is described in terms of abstract personal traits.

This concept of personality as an autonomous entity separate from the social environment includes the characteristics of an independent self of individualistic cultures. In collectivistic cultures, people's ideal characteristics vary by social role. Behavior is more strongly influenced by contextual factors.[58] East Asian thinking does not make a sharp person–situation distinction and has a more holistic notion of the person without a boundary between the person and the situation. Easterners believe in the continuous shaping of personality traits by situational influences.[59] Among speakers of Nguni languages in South Africa, personality characteristics vary with situation and relational context; Nguni languages also have fewer words for traits, and personal descriptions referring to pro-social or antisocial behavior are larger in number than found in Western personality traits descriptions. The fact that there is no consistency in personality, which is the essence of the Western concept, implies that the personality concept is not universal.[60]

According to the Western view, the study of personality should lead to understanding, predicting, and controlling behavior. In individualistic cultures, because of consistency between personal traits and behavior, these traits are used to predict behavior. Collectivists place a higher value on situational cues and upholding 'face.' Emphasis on behavior that should not bring public shame to one's family and social group suggests that individuals behave irrespective of their individual characteristics. As a result the utility of personal traits may not be as strong in collectivistic cultures as it is in individualistic cultures.[61]

In individualistic cultures, once people have chosen to comply with a request, they will more than will collectivists comply with subsequent, similar requests. Comparison of consistency in compliance among Americans and Asians showed some differences. Differences in compliance were measured by (a) compliance with an initial request, (b) willingness to comply with future, related requests, and (c) compliance with a larger subsequent request. Although in both cultures participants were more likely to comply with a request if they had chosen to comply with a similar request one month earlier, this tendency was more pronounced among the US participants than among Asian participants. Despite their lower rate of compliance with an initial request, once committed, the US respondents were more likely than Asian respondents to agree to a larger, related request.[62]

Western individualists view personal traits as fixed; they are part of the person. East Asian collectivists view traits as malleable; traits will vary with the situation. When individualists describe themselves or others, they use elements of the personal self in objective, abstract words, out of context (I am kind, she is nice). People from collectivist cultures tend to use mostly elements of the collective self or describe actions of people in context (My family thinks I am kind, she brings cake to my family).[63] Easterners believe in the continuous shaping of personality traits by situational influences.[64]

People in Eastern cultures often use a 'tree' as a metaphor for a person, which emphasizes the endless shaping of internal dispositions by the external environment. For instance, in Korea a person is believed to be like a white root that takes on the color of the soil in which it grows. If a white root is planted in red soil, it becomes red. In China a person is likened to a white silk cloth. If placed in red dye, it becomes red; if placed in green dye, it becomes green. Once the self is likened to a plant, it is evident that the environment is essential for the development, nourishment, and cultivation of the person.[65]

The Brand Personality Concept

The human personality is used as metaphor in branding strategies. The *brand personality* concept is rooted in Anglo-American presumptions. The core of a sophisticated advertising campaign is the brand positioning statement, including a description of the brand personality in terms of human characteristics. In international marketing, the descriptions are usually in Anglo-American terms. A brand personality that can be recognized by or is attractive to the average public of one culture will not necessarily be recognized or found attractive to the average public of another culture. As a result, advertising campaigns that are effective in one culture because they are based on a strong brand personality are not necessarily as effective in another culture. Brands acquire their personalities over time, and these are largely derived from the market context in which they develop. This context consists of a series of peculiarities that might not repeat itself in the same ways in other intended markets.[66]

Whereas in individualistic cultures brands have to be unique, distinct, and contain consistent characteristics, in collectivistic cultures the brand personality should be viewed as being part of a larger whole, being a person in the world of other brands. In Asia a brand is probably better defined as being part of a *brand world* rather than being a *unique personality*.

Because of the nonexistence of the Western personality concept in Asia, Asian languages such as Japanese and Chinese do not have linguistic equivalents for the term *personality* as a person separate from the social environment. As a result the Western brand personality metaphor is not well understood in Asia, and brand personalities are more corporate personalities. This is recognized in the branding practice of Asian companies. Whereas American companies have concentrated on promoting product brands, Japanese companies have generally emphasized company brands. In essence this means inspiring trust among consumers in a company and so persuading them to buy its products. Western companies that tend to insist on consistency in their uniqueness, using one logo worldwide, run the risk of being perceived as arrogant or even insulting. In line with the idea of a brand world, another option may be to use the concept of *face of the brand,* a visual representation of the company's attributes that is more like a mosaic than a logo. It consists of a unified set of visual symbols that is tailored to depict the brand. 'A global "face of the brand" can have the same graphic roots but appear somewhat different depending on the local markets targeted. The idea is to depict unity, without forcing sameness.'[67]

A study by Linda Derksen at the advertising agency PPGH/JWT Amsterdam surveyed the practice of brand personality in four countries in Europe. The JWT agencies in Germany, United Kingdom, France, and Spain were asked to what extent they worked with the brand personality concept when developing advertising campaigns. One of the questions was to select a definition of brand personality from a choice of three possible definitions: (1) the unique characteristics of a brand that distinguish it from other (competitive) brands; (2) the brand as a 'human being' with human characteristics that are associated with a brand; (3) the reflection of a brand in its environment, just like people who are part of their environment, their family, and work. The British and Germans viewed the brand as a person who is characterized by unique qualities that differentiate it from other brands. The French saw the brand as a human being with human characteristics associated with the brand. The Spanish opted for the definition of brand personality as a reflection of how a brand fits in its environment, family, and work.[68]

Personal Traits

The Western habit of describing people in terms of abstract characteristics has led to the development of characterization systems of personal traits. *Traits* can be defined as 'dimensions of individual differences in tendencies to show consistent patterns of thoughts, feelings, and actions.'[69] Examples of traits are *altruism* (helpfulness and generosity to others), *modesty* (self-effacing attitudes and behaviors), and *trust* (beliefs about others' actions and intentions).[70] In the Western world it has been argued that there are only a relatively small number of universal trait dimensions.[71]

Personality traits can be found in the natural language used when people describe themselves. Such natural language adjectives are used in questionnaire scales for developing trait dimensions. Factor analysis is used to develop trait structures. The five-factor model (FFM or 'Big Five') is one of the most used models to organize personality traits. It was developed in the United States and based on analyses of the colloquial usage of the English language, on people's descriptions of themselves and others.

There are various problems when developing trait structures across cultures. Whereas American descriptions include psychological trait characteristics, self-descriptions in collectivistic cultures tend to refer to social roles. A difficulty when using scales across cultures is finding linguistic equivalents for the trait descriptions. Nevertheless, with the cooperation of psychologists of many different cultures, the FFM has developed into a universal model for measuring personality trait structure across cultures, using a scale called the NEO-PI-R facet scale. The universal five-trait factors have been named *neuroticism*, *extraversion*, *openness to experience*, *agreeableness*, and *conscientiousness*. These five basic trait factors are supposed to capture the many meanings of personality characteristics. Table 4.1 shows the factors and components of each factor.[72]

Table 4.1 Five-factor model of personality traits

Neuroticism	Extraversion	Openness to Experience	Agreeableness	Conscientiousness
Anxiety	Warmth	Fantasy	Trust	Competence
Angry hostility	Gregariousness	Aesthetics	Straight forwardness	Order
Depression	Assertiveness	Feelings	Altruism	Dutifulness
Self-consciousness	Activity	Actions	Compliance	Achievement striving
Impulsiveness	Excitement seeking	Ideas	Modesty	Self-discipline
Vulnerability	Positive emotions	Values	Tender-mindedness	Deliberation

SOURCE: R.R. McCrae, 'NEO-PI-R data from 36 cultures,' in A.J. Marsella and R.R. McCrae (eds), *The Five-Factor Model of Personality Across Cultures* (Kluwer, Dordrecht, The Netherlands, 2002), pp. 105–125.

Across cultures, several variations were found. There were, for example, more within-culture differences in European than in Asian cultures. A cause of this may be that in collectivistic cultures, individual differences are muted because individuals avoid emphasizing their distinctive personal attributes. Another reason can be more homogeneity of personality among Asians than among European groups.[73]

In particular, Asian psychologists have been eager to find whether the model applies to collectivistic cultures. Chinese psychologists Cheung et al.[74] developed an indigenous scale for China (Chinese Personality Assessment Inventory) and merged it with the five-factor model. They found similar five factors, but the components varied across the factors. A cause can be that the trait adjectives, when translated, get different meanings. The Chinese researchers also found a sixth dimension, which they called *interpersonal relatedness*, that included the components optimism versus pessimism, *Ren Qing* (relationship orientation), flexibility, *Ah-Q* mentality (defensiveness), harmony, face, and logical versus affective orientation. The interpersonal relatedness factor addresses the interdependent aspects of personality that are important to the Chinese as well as to other collectivistic cultures. If Chinese researchers had dominated personality research, the leading theory would have excluded the openness factor, which is a decidedly non-Asian factor.[75] For measuring an open person in collectivistic cultures, interpersonal tolerance and social sensitivity are more relevant than the items included in the Western scales.[76] Generally, in collectivistic cultures openness may take on a different form or function. Differences may be caused by translating concepts for which there are no linguistic equivalents. Openness also is difficult to translate in African languages, such as Shona and Xhosa, in which there is a shortage of openness-related terms. The Korean language version of the NEO-PI-R scale submitted to Korean respondents also produced differences between Korean and American respondents.[77]

From longitudinal studies psychologists find increasing evidence that our personality traits are partly biologically inherited and partly shaped by the interaction of the individual with the environment, at the broadest level. One of these environments is the culture of the country where we were raised.[78] The relationship with culture was found by correlating Hofstede's cultural variables with culture-level means of individual-level scores on the NEO-PI-R factors for 36 cultures.[79] Neuroticism scores are higher in cultures of strong uncertainty avoidance and high masculinity. This fits with other findings that anxiety, stress, and expression of emotion are more found in high uncertainty avoidance cultures than in low uncertainty avoidance cultures. Masculinity stands for focus on ego and money orientation, whereas femininity stands for focus on relationships and people orientation. The latter orientation probably relates to lower neuroticism. Impulsiveness, one of the elements of this dimension, does not necessarily include impulse buying. Data by TGI[80] among consumers in seven Latin American countries show a relationship with low, not high, uncertainty avoidance, with buying on impulse ($r = -.70^*$). Extraversion score levels are higher in individualistic cultures, where autonomy, variety, and pleasure are valued over expertise, duty, and security. Furthermore, they correlate with low power distance. Openness to experience was correlated with high masculinity and low power distance. In cultures of high masculinity, people tend to overrate their own performance, and low power distance stimulates independent exploration. Agreeableness correlated with low uncertainty avoidance, so in cultures with higher tolerance, people score themselves as more agreeable. Conscientiousness correlated with high power distance, but it is even stronger related to gross national income (GNI) per capita. Hofstede concludes that 'prosperity allows people to behave less conscientiously or more wasteful.'[81]

How consumer experiences reflect elements of personality is demonstrated by find-ings of a pan-European (13 countries) study of ecological awareness among drivers by the tire company Goodyear.[82] A typology of European drivers was developed from questions about attitudes toward driving and driving behavior. Respondents could categorize themselves in terms of personal driving characteristics. Considerable cul-ture-related differences were found between countries. The percentages of respon-dents who considered themselves to be *responsible drivers* (= conscientiousness) correlated positively with power distance. The percentages of respondents who con-sidered driving their car as an *adventure* (= extraversion) correlated with individual-ism. The percentages of respondents who considered themselves to be *social drivers*, who considered their car as a means of supporting their social life (= agree-ableness), correlated with low uncertainty avoidance and low power distance. The percentages of respondents who considered their car to be a means to *show off,* a status symbol, saying something about themselves (= openness to experience), cor-related with masculinity.

The problem with trait studies is that instead of factors emerging from native concep-tions of personhood across cultures, findings mainly confirm that when the same set of English items that form five factors are translated into other languages, they result in simi-lar five-factor structures across cultures. This doesn't imply that these are the only existing conceptions of personhood. It merely shows that a set of English language questions, when translated, result in similar five-dimensional structures.[83]

As in value studies, in addition to translation problems when measuring personal traits, there are other measurement problems. When individuals make judgments about themselves, they implicitly draw comparisons with others. These referent others, how-ever, are different for people in different cultures. This is particularly relevant for mea-suring personality traits. In a large study of the geographic distribution of the 'Big Five' personality traits, the researchers were surprised to find Chinese, Korean, and Japa-nese people in the very bottom on the conscientiousness scale. It seems unlikely that most people would think of individuals of these cultures as extremely undisciplined and weak willed – a profile indicative of low conscientiousness. However, where the stan-dards for being punctual, strong willed, and reliable are very high, a respondent may report that he or she is less disciplined than is generally the case in the particular culture.[84] A similar phenomenon can be recognized when measuring Spanish *simpatía* (agreeableness), which is associated with striving to promote harmony in relationships by showing respect toward others, avoiding conflict, emphasizing positive behaviors, and deemphasizing negative behaviors. However, self-report data show that Hispanics rate themselves lower on agreeableness than do European Americans. When *simpatía* is the norm, people will not score themselves high on this trait.[85]

Brand Personality Traits

Marketing people tend to develop trait dimensions for brands as if brands are human beings. Thus, brand personality is defined as a set of humanlike attributes associated with a particular brand. An example is a study by Aaker et al.[86] that developed personality dimensions in several countries by asking individuals to rate a representative set of commercial brands on a battery of personality attributes. In the United States, five dimensions were found and labeled *sincerity* (down-to-earth, real, sincere, honest); *excitement* (daring, exciting, imaginative, contemporary); *competence* (intelligent, reliable, secure, confident); *sophistication* (glamorous, upper class, good looking, charming); and *ruggedness* (tough, outdoorsy, masculine, and Western). The authors noted that three of the dimensions – sincerity, excitement, and competence – resemble personality dimensions that are also present in human personality models such as the Big Five model, relating respectively to agreeableness, extraversion, and conscientiousness. Sophistication captures aspirational images associated with wealth and status, and the ruggedness dimension represents typical American values such as strength, masculinity, and ruggedness. Similar studies were conducted in Japan and Spain, which resulted in two more sets of five dimensions. The five Japanese dimensions overlapped with the American ones with respect to excitement, competence, sincerity, and sophistication. One dimension, named *peacefulness,* was defined by a unique blend of attributes (e.g., shy, peaceful, naïve, dependent), which was assumed to be indigenous for Japan. Of the five dimensions found in Spain, three overlapped with the American dimensions sincerity, excitement, and sophistication. The latter included some of the competence associations. One dimension was similar to the Japanese dimension peacefulness, and one dimension seemed to be an indigenous Spanish one. It was named *passion* and included components like fervent, passionate, spiritual, and bohemian. The dimension peacefulness that Spain and Japan have in common is likely related to the collectivistic aspects they share. A Korean study of brand personalities[87] of well-known global brands like Nike, Sony, Levi's, Adidas, Volkswagen, and BMW found two specific Korean brand personalities. The first, labeled *passive likeableness*, included traits like easy, smooth, family oriented, playful, and sentimental. The second was labeled *ascendancy* and included traits like strict, heavy, intelligent, and daring. These findings suggest that, even if companies wish to be consistent, having connected one specific personality trait to a global brand, across cultures consumers attach different personalities to these brands. These are the traits that are viewed as fitting by consumers, but they can be very different from what the company wanted.

Comparison of the image of Red Bull in the United Kingdom, Singapore, Austria, Germany, the Netherlands, and the United States show differences in perceptions of the Red Bull brand personality. Although the global advertising campaign pushed competence and excitement as brand characteristics, these seem mostly to appeal to the UK public.[88]

A cross-cultural brand value study[89] showed that a brand characteristic like friendly is most attributed to strong global brands in high uncertainty avoidance and low power distance cultures. This fits with findings from a Eurobarometer study asking for the importance of friends. The percentages of answers saying that friends are very important correlate with low power distance ($r = -.59^{***}$).[90] Prestigious is a characteristic attributed to global brands in high power distance, and trustworthy is most attributed to strong brands in high uncertainty avoidance cultures. In the low power distance and low uncertainty avoidance cultures, people attributed innovative and different to these brands. Figure 4.6 presents a map of different brand personalities attributed to strong global brands.

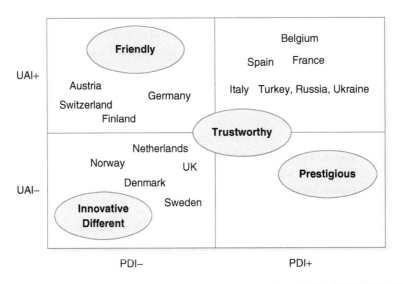

Figure 4.6   **Brand personality traits attributed to strong global brand**

Similar brand personality dimensions may exist across cultures, but the similarities are often based only on partial equivalents, meaning that superficially similar dimensions consist of different associations. Constructs tend to shift in meaning when examined in different cultural contexts. Excitement, for example, is associated with being young, contemporary, spirited, and daring, but in the United States and Spain it also conveys imaginativeness, uniqueness, and independence, whereas in Japan it includes talkative, funny, and optimistic. Sophistication takes on a different meaning in Spain than it does in Japan.

The previous discussion may demonstrate the difficulty in using personality descriptors for brand positioning across cultures. First, there are culture-specific personality dimensions, such as ruggedness in the United States and peacefulness in Japan. Brand personalities fitting in such indigenous dimensions are not likely to be as successful in other countries as they are in the home country. Second, although some studies suggest that there are similar personality dimensions across countries, similar labels can have different associations, so the meaning of seemingly similar trait descriptions can be very different.

One reason for developing consistent brand personalities may be the need for *control*. If consumers elsewhere perceive these global brands as having different personality traits than the company intended, the process is *out of control*, and to keep control, it may be better to define specific brand personality traits for the various cultures in which the company operates.

Identity and Image

Identity is the idea one has about oneself, one's characteristic properties, one's own body, and the values one considers important. *Image* is how others see and judge a person.[91] The importance of a unique identity for individualists emerges from a Eurobarometer[92] survey asking respondents to what degree people believe in a shared cultural identity. The percentages of respondents who agreed correlated negatively with individualism, whereas the percentages disagreeing correlated positively with individualism. Figure 4.7 illustrates this relationship for 12 countries in Europe.

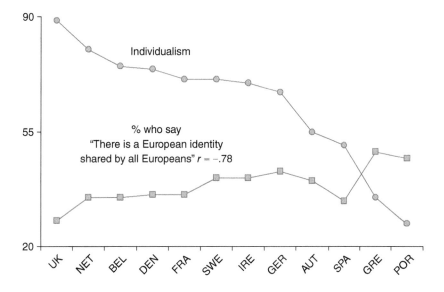

Figure 4.7 Identity and culture

SOURCES: Data from Hofstede et al. (2010) (see Appendix A); Eurobarometer report, *How Europeans See Themselves* (2001) (see Appendix B)

Identity among collectivists is defined by relationships and group memberships, whereas individualists base identity on what they own and their experiences. Identity also is one's capacity to fulfill expectations. When a person is asked what her identity is, she can categorize herself in terms of desirable values ('I believe that . . .'), as a member of social groups (e.g., a mother, a student), or by personality traits (e.g., ambitious, cheerful).[93] In most Western cultures, people tend to assess the identity of self and others based on personality traits, on other individual characteristics such as age and occupation, and on material symbols.[94] In collectivistic cultures, people are not used to doing so. They will assess themselves in terms of their ability to maintain harmonious relationships with others. One's identity is the group: the family, neighborhood, school, or the company where one works. In Africa people were – and many still are – assigned to a clan, tribe or ethnic group even before they are born, on the strengths and origins of their ancestors. Identity at this level is not easily shaken off or lost,[95] and certainly not easily replaced by a national identity.

A distinction can be made between achieved identity and ascribed identity. *Achieved identity* means one is judged by what one does, one's being; one is a 'good father,' a 'good student.' *Ascribed identity* involves fixed expectations based on non-chosen traits such as gender, age, and inherited position. The perception of people having fixed, ascribed identities is stronger in high power distance cultures, where people have more clearly defined positions in society than in cultures of low power distance. In Western societies, the possession of tangible goods provides achieved identity. Housing, transportation, and other visible consumption are assumed to reflect one's values, career success, and personality. In the United States social standing is fluid – one *buys* one's status – whereas 'the French still believe that it is noble to inherit a fortune and dirty to earn one.'[96]

Individuals can be pleased with personality traits that form a part of their *real identity*, or they may want to change them, as a function of an image they would like to have. This produces an identity that reflects what psychoanalysts have termed the 'ideal self.' These two dimensions of identity can be close or far apart from each other. If they are far apart, efforts are usually made to reduce the gap.[97] In individualistic cultures, material possessions can serve this purpose.

The Body and Identity

In Western psychology the body is viewed as part of the identity. Body esteem is related to several constructs of the self, such as self-esteem, body consciousness, and social anxiety. One of the central terms in the field is *body image*, which is the picture of our own body that we form in our mind.[98] In Western societies, people attribute more desirable characteristics to physically attractive persons. This is called the 'physical attractiveness stereotype.'[99]

What is considered attractive varies. The Japanese, for example, rate large eyes and small mouths and chins as attractive, whereas Koreans prefer large eyes, small and high noses, and thin and small faces.[100] The vast majority of research on what constitutes physical attractiveness has been conducted in Western societies, but mostly in the United States, where physical attractiveness of women is judged according to strict criteria, which leads to dissatisfaction. The typical American woman begins to voice dissatisfaction with her body early in life and continues to do so into the adult years. The general idea is that a desirable appearance leads to greater self-esteem. In Japan, where people attribute success more to external than to internal sources, there is less emphasis on the body as a source of esteem.[101] Confucian belief suggests that external physical appearance is less important than success in social role performance in the development of self-esteem and happiness.[102]

Attractiveness does not result in similar conclusions about people's characteristics across cultures. In Korea, for example, attractiveness is seen as being associated with lineage: high-status families are expected to produce better-looking children because their greater financial and social resources would permit considerable selection in mating.[103]

Each cultural group has its own unique definition of physical attractiveness (human beauty), and its own set of bodily ideals, that shape its collective body image.

> Chinese women view Caucasian men as wealthy, and this presumed wealth makes Caucasian men attractive. Chinese women's views on what makes men attractive differ completely from the South Korean perspective that overwhelmingly prefers images of immature young men who have a 'pretty face with big eyes and fair skin and a moderately masculine body.' It is a criterion also shared by young Japanese women. In contrast, Chinese women are adamant in their rejection of immature males. Chinese women prefer a more serious pose associated with an integrated or well-balanced character.[104]

Body image concerns, weight concerns, and eating disorders are more prevalent among Western women than among non-Western women.[105] Within the United States, disordered eating and dieting behaviors are more frequent among European Americans than among Asian and African Americans.[106] A study in 1995 found that 90% of white schoolgirls were dissatisfied with their weight, whereas 70% of African American teens were satisfied with their bodies.[107] Body images as displayed in the media are assumed to influence ideal body images. The continual exposure of good-looking, thin models creates pressure to have an attractive body. This thought is most pronounced in Western individualistic culture, although a relationship between TV viewing and body image dissatisfaction was also found in Hong Kong China.[108] In particular in the United States, the ideal is to be thin, and advertising shows thin people. Yet, the United States also is the country with the highest percentage of obese people. Obesity is – as yet – a problem of individualistic cultures. In 1999, in 18 countries of the developed world, the differences between countries with respect to the percentage of population with a body mass index (BMI) over 30[109] correlated significantly with individualism ($r = .59***$). So, in the individualistic cultures the discrepancy between the real and ideal body image is largest.

Although both Japanese and American young adults are concerned with physical attractiveness, female body images in the Japanese media are different from those in American media. Poses of American (thin) models are rebellious or defiant, offering a sultry facial expression, to represent the individual self, independent from and equal to others, whereas poses of Japanese (also thin) models emphasize youthful 'girlishness' reflecting dependence needs. The faces show happy, broad smiles reflecting non-challenging innocence.[110] Figure 4.8 illustrates the differences. These are covers of a British magazine (*Harpers*) for adult women, an American magazine (*Cosmopolitan*) for young women, a Japanese magazine (*Madam*) for adult women, and a Chinese language magazine from Malaysia (*Nuyou*) for young women.

Figure 4.8   **Magazine covers**

A comparison of covers of the magazine *Elle* in the United States and China[111] found more differences. For example, models in Chinese fashion photographs use more hand gestures than US fashion photographs. These hand gestures follow old examples as found in old caves. US *Elle* covers show more smiling faces. In China smiling isn't necessarily being friendly. Models' faces in China are often ¾ whereas USA models are looking straightforward with direct eye contact.

Finally, also how people identify themselves in terms of feeling young, middle-aged or old (cognitive age), varies across cultures. A 'young-at-heart' philosophy for older people as promoted in the United States is not a universal desire.[112]

Corporate Identity, Brand Identity, and Brand Image

Like the self, identity in individualistic cultures is supposed to be unique and consistent, as opposed to a collectivist's identity, which can change according to varying social positions and situations. This is reflected in the definitions of *corporate identity* that are based on the Western identity concept. The British communication consultant Nicholas Ind defined *corporate identity* as 'an organization's identity in its *sense of self*, much like our own individual sense of identity. Consequently, it is unique.'[113] Corporate identity is concerned with the impressions, the image, and the personality projected by an organization.

The individualistic identity metaphor is probably not well understood in collectivistic cultures. Like the personality concept, identity doesn't have a linguistic equivalent in many Asian languages like Japanese and Chinese.

Usually the task of creating a corporate identity begins with the selection of an appropriate corporate name. Other factors that contribute to corporate identity include the logo of the organization and marketing communications. All this, including language, lettering, and associations, is logically a reflection of the home country of the organization. Western organizations in particular prefer worldwide consistency of all these elements, without realizing that this is not an equally effective approach to business in all countries.

Ideally brands have clearly defined images created by advertising, packaging, and other positioning elements, and theory says that these brand images should be congruent with consumers' self-images. The question is whether people buy brands because they are similar to the self, or whether people assume that these brands are similar to the self because they bought them. There is general agreement in (American) marketing literature that consumers tend to favor brands they perceive as similar to themselves, so self-image should match brand image, and similarity of the self-image and brand image should lead to attraction. The Dutchman Bosman,[114] however, found evidence that it works the other way around. In his study the causal flow is not from liking brands because they are similar to the self, but liking a brand for other reasons leads to perceiving it as similar to the self. The subjects in the study were probably Dutch,[115] so his findings may apply to Dutch respondents, whereas the findings presented in American marketing literature may apply to American respondents. Within the Western world, the relationship between brand image and self-image may vary, and even more so between individualistic and collectivistic cultures, where the self-image is likely to be more situational.

Culture does influence how consumers organize the brand image in their minds, in particular the associations consumers have when perceiving a brand. The brand image is a set of perceptions about a brand as reflected by the brand associations held in the consumers' memories. Three main types of brand associations can be distinguished:

(1) the product attributes; (2) the benefits; and (3) the brand attitude, including values. Benefits and attitudes are at a higher level of abstraction than the attributes and are assumed to have a closer relationship with the consumer self than do product attributes. Culture influences how consumers perceive and organize these abstract associations. For some, 'latest technology' may be associated with 'prestige,' for others it may be negatively related with 'fuel economy.'[116]

Attitude

Western consumer behaviorists view *attitudes* as learned predispositions to respond to an object or class of objects in a consistently favorable or unfavorable way.[117] This reflects an individualistic worldview, including the assumption that attitudes lead people to behave in a fairly consistent way. Attitudes drive behavior, but behavior also drives attitudes. In collectivistic cultures, attitudes may vary along with the context in which they operate. A more neutral definition of *attitude* is the individual predisposition to evaluate an object or an aspect of the world in a favorable or unfavorable manner. Attitudes have affective and cognitive components. The affective component includes the sensations, feelings, and emotions one experiences in response to an attitude object. The cognitive component includes various attributes and functions of the object.[118]

In the Western definitions, attitudes serve as knowledge function, helping to organize and structure one's environment and to provide consistency in one's frame of reference. Individualists want consistency across their attitudes, feelings, and behaviors.[119] In collectivistic cultures, people are supposed to form attitudes that fulfill their social identity functions.

Western theory distinguishes three components of attitudes: cognitive, affective, and behavioral, which for attitudes toward brands translate as brand belief, brand evaluations, and intention to buy. The relationship among these three components is known as a *hierarchy of effects*, as if consumers consistently step from one component to another. The sequence varies with the degree of involvement with the product. Brand belief and brand evaluations are knowledge and information based. The role of information in this process will vary with culture as well. (This is discussed further in Chapter 6.)

In Western theory, many attitudes are supposed to serve a utilitarian function, helping to maximize the rewards and minimize the punishments obtained from objects in the environment. An example is one's attitude toward ice cream, which serves a utilitarian function because it can be based on the rewards (enjoyment) and punishment (weight gain). The cross-cultural relevance of this functional theory has not been tested.[120] The reward–punishment effects are a reflection of the typical Western value of guilt.

Attitude and Behavior

Consistency between attitude and behavior in individualistic cultures implies that under certain conditions, the behavior of consumers can be predicted from their attitudes toward products, services, and brands, and a purchase prediction is derived from a positive attitude. In collectivistic cultures, however, people form attitudes that fulfill their social identity functions, and there is not a consistent relationship between attitude and future behavior. It may be a reverse relationship: usage comes first and defines attitude. In collectivistic cultures, shared experiences influence brand attitude positively, more than in individualistic cultures.[121]

For measuring advertising effectiveness, the attitude to the advertisement (Aad) tends to be measured, which in turn is used as an indication of buying intention. This practice is logical in individualistic cultures where individuals want consistency between their personal attitudes and behaviors. In collectivistic cultures, where situational factors can influence the various elements of attitude and behavior, the practice may not work the same way.

> Behavior of Japanese youngsters is not consistent with their attitudes to life in general.
>
> Japanese kids like to shop, they curl their hair, they wear this really outrageous clothing that's really influenced by the West, but if you talk to these girls with piercing everywhere, they say that what they really want to do is get married, have a nice house and have kids.[122]

The most widely known model that measures the relationship between attitude and behavior is the Fishbein behavioral intentions model, also referred to as the theory of *reasoned action*. Fishbein hypothesizes that a person's behavioral intentions are determined by an *attitudinal* or *personal component* and a *normative* or *social component*. The personal attitude component, or *attitude toward the act*, refers to personal judgment of behavior, whereas the normative or social component refers to social pressures on behavior such as expectations of others. Cross-cultural findings are that attitude toward the act is the primary determinant in the United States, whereas social norm is more important in Korea. What in Western terms is called *social pressure*, put on Korean consumers, has relatively weak influence on Americans, who refer to their own personal attitudes as having influenced their buying decisions.[123] What is called *social norm* in American theory has a different loading in collectivistic cultures. The social component in the theory does not capture 'face.' Face motivates collectivists to act in accordance with one's social position. If one acts contrary to expectations of one's social position, a shadow is cast over one's moral integrity.[124] Thus, in collectivistic cultures face pressure is more like a personal norm, capturing personal perceptions of living up to the standards of one's position, whereas the social norm component included in the Fishbein model mainly measures perceptions of opinions of other persons.

Attitudes and intentions are what we feel and know and are derived from what we say. Intentions are often poor predictors of behavior, with large variance across cultures. Intentions must be measured, and differences in response styles are a cause of varying relationships between buying intention and actual buying. For example, if 55% of the people who try a new product in Italy say they will definitely buy it, the product will probably fail. If in Japan 5% say they will definitely buy it, the product is likely to succeed. If people are used to external, uncontrollable factors, such as fate or power holders interfering at any time in the realization of an expressed intention, people will more readily express positive intentions that will not transform into behavior. This difference is reflected in the way people answer in semantic scales in survey research.

Italians like extremes and mark toward the end of any semantic scale, whereas the Germans are more restrained and mark toward the middle. The effect is that a 'Completely agree' answer in Italy is not worth the same as a 'Completely agree' answer in Germany. This tendency to use extreme points in verbal rating scales is called Extreme Response Style (ERS). One cause of ERS is the type of Likert scale. If high-ERS participants are given a survey using a 7-point Likert-type scale, their responses tend to be either 1 (Strongly agree) or 7 (Strongly disagree). If low-ERS participants are given the same survey, their responses will tend to cluster around 4 (Neither agree nor disagree).[125] Another difference occurs when one group systematically gives higher or lower responses than another group, resulting in a scale displacement. This is called Acquiescence Response Style (ARS). To American respondents a response of 3 on a 5-point Likert scale may mean 'No opinion,' whereas it may mean 'Mild agreement' to Korean respondents. As a result of this scale displacement, Korean 3s are equivalent to American 4s, and Korean 4s are equivalent to American 5s. Overall, ERS and ARS will influence most traditional quantitative marketing techniques, and a strong bias can make market researchers draw wrong conclusions. Market researchers may be erroneously reporting differences in product preferences, consumer attitudes, or perceptions across countries that are wholly or partially attributable to ERS.

When attitudes are measured and compared at national level, there are examples of congruence and incongruence of attitudes and behavior. An example of congruence of national-level attitudes, knowledge, and self-reported behavior is attitude toward the environment among drivers. The tire company Goodyear[126] measured general ecological attitude and knowledge across 13 countries in Europe by asking a number of questions about what is good or bad for the environment (e.g., burning coal, the effects of nuclear waste, human-made chemicals, and the greenhouse effect). The percentages of respondents who answered all questions correctly correlated positively ($r = .61^*$) with questions about attitudes to environmental developments (e.g., worry about the destruction of the rain forest, global warming, and environmental pollution). So knowledge and attitudes matched. There was also a significant positive correlation between attitudes and self-reported behavior ($r = .53^*$) from questions about how people handle their cars (e.g., rapid acceleration, proper maintenance of their cars, or avoiding use of their cars for short distances).

An example of incongruence of attitudes and behavior is with respect to the euro, the European currency. Whereas the collectivistic and high uncertainty avoidance cultures have shown positive attitudes toward the euro[127] during the years before its introduction on January 2002, after introduction these were the cultures where people still calculated more in their own currencies than in the euro. In some restaurants in Spain, in 2003, the bills were still written in pesetas. The gap between expressed intention and actual behavior is also culture related and may vary by product category or social phenomenon. An example is provided in the section on attitude towards the environment.

Analysis of differences in attitudes can help explain differences in consumer behavior across cultures. Different attitudes toward the press explain differences in press readership. Attitudes toward technology and information explain differences in acceptance of computers and related technology. In the mid-1990s in Germany, consumers had lots of reservations against the computer. In contrast, US consumers saw the computer mainly as a means to success and prestige.[128] These differences reflected actual penetration differences of computers. Differences in confidence in specific food categories parallel consumption differences. In the following sections of the chapter, several examples of specific culture-bound attitudes are discussed. These are attitudes toward food, health, materialism, national pride, country of origin, environmentalism, and sex- and love-related attitudes.

Attitudes Toward Food

Attitudes toward food vary across cultures. There are in particular differences in the degree to which food is considered to be safe. In 2010 Eurobarometer[129] asked respondents for the potential risk that the food they eat will damage their health. The percentages correlated negatively with GNI/capita and positively with uncertainty avoidance. Together these variables explained 65% of variance. In 1998 Eurobarometer asked questions about confidence in food for more specific product categories. The question asked was, 'For each of the following food products, please tell me if you think it is safe or not safe.' Products were bread and bakery products, fresh fruit, fresh vegetables, fresh fish, fresh meat, fresh milk, cheese, eggs, canned foods, frozen foods, precooked meals and other prepacked food. Variance among the 13 countries of the European Union was considerable. A number of responses to confidence in food products correlate with actual consumption. Confidence in fresh milk is significantly, positively, correlated with actual consumption of fresh milk, so in countries where people drink more fresh milk, they also have more confidence in fresh milk. There is also a positive relationship between confidence in frozen food and consumption of frozen food. The common explaining factor is uncertainty avoidance. Whereas low confidence in several processed food categories correlates with high uncertainty avoidance, consumption of processed food products correlates with low uncertainty avoidance. Table 4.2 shows the relationships with three cultural variables for the answers 'Not safe' for five food products and for consumption data of related products.

Table 4.2 **Confidence in food and consumption of processed food**

	PDI	IDV	UAI	Predictor	R^2
Not Safe (13 countries)					
Fresh milk	.72***	−.31	.71***	PDI	.51
Cheese	.58*	−.34	.64**	UAI	.42
Frozen foods	.54*	−.60*	.75***	UAI	.56
Precooked meals	.43	−.50*	.67**	UAI	.45
Other prepacked	.49*	−.45	.64**	UAI	.40
Consumption, Liters or Kilograms per Capita (15 countries)					
Milk	−.65*	.11	−.79***	UAI (−)	.63
Ice-cream	−.57*	.45*	−.76***	UAI (−)	.57
Frozen food	−.33	.45*	−.69***	UAI (−)	.48
Frozen ready meals	−.31	.41	−.62**	UAI (−)	.57

SOURCES: Hofstede et al. (2010) (see Appendix A); EBS 120 (1998); Euromonitor (1997) (see Appendix B)

Low trust in processed food explains the aversion to genetically modified food (GMF) that is stronger in high than in low uncertainty avoidance cultures. The strong protests against genetically modified food in Europe originated in France, a culture of high uncertainty avoidance.

Attitudes Toward Health

People's attitudes toward their health are related to behavior. People's concern for health can be recognized in consumption patterns, in expenditures on health, and in the variations of fitness practice across countries. In Chapter 3 (section on stability), we mentioned the consistent relationship between mineral water consumption and uncertainty avoidance. Whereas in Europe people of high uncertainty avoidance cultures search for health in the purity and quality of their food, in low uncertainty avoidance cultures people's attitudes toward health make them pursue fitness activities. People's positive perception of their health is related to being actively involved in sports. The 1990 *World Values Survey* asked people to describe their health and also asked questions about membership in

Table 4.3   **Attitudes toward health: Active and passive**

	Uncertainty avoidance (r)
1990: Health very good (Worldwide, 26 countries)	−.74***
1990: Member Sports Organization (Worldwide, 26 countries)	−.68***
2000: Member Sports Organization (Europe, 18 countries)	−.56**
1999: Expenditures on recreational and sports services (Europe, 12 countries)	−.71***
2001: Play sports as leisure activity (Europe, 13 countries)	−.47*
2001: Member sports organization (Europe, 13 countries)	−.71***
2007: % active in sports club (Europe, 24 countries)	−.63***
1990: % who neither play sport nor exercise (Europe, 15 countries)	+.69***
2004: % who never play sport (Europe, 21 countries)	+.68***
2008: % who say health most important in connection with idea of happiness (Europe, 26 countries)	+.48**
2008: % of household consumption spent on health (Europe, 25 countries)	+.48**
2006: Number of physicians per 10,000 people (Worldwide, 18 countries GNI/cap 17,000+)	+.38*
2013: % who never exercise or play sports (EU, 28 countries)	+.65***
2016: Part of household expenditures spent on health (EU, 28 countries)	+.51**

SOURCES: 1990 data: Inglehart et al. (1998); 1999 data: Eurostat (2001); 2001 data: EB 151 *Young Europeans in 2001* (2001); 2007 data: EBS 273 (2007); 1990 data: *Reader's Digest* Eurodata (1991); 2004 data: EBS 213 (2004); 2008 data: Standard EB 69 (2008); Eurostat (2008); 2006 data: World Health Organization (2002/2009); 2013 data: British Heart Foundation (2015); 2016 data: Eurostat, *Healthcare Share of Household Expenditures* (2016) (see Appendix B)

sports organizations. There is a significant correlation between the percentages of respondents who describe their health as good or very good and membership in a sports organization. The common explaining variable is uncertainty avoidance. All sorts of data measuring an active attitude toward health, such as involvement in sports, correlate negatively with uncertainty avoidance, whereas all sorts of data relating to a passive orientation, such as use of antibiotics[130] and numbers of physicians per 100,000 people, correlate positively with uncertainty avoidance. An inventory of the results is provided in Table 4.3.

Attitudes Toward Consumption: Materialism

Materialism is described as an attitude toward consumption, an enduring belief in the desirability of acquiring and possessing things. Materialism can also be viewed as a function of one's personality, reflecting traits of possessiveness, envy, nongenerosity, and preservation. Another approach is to view materialism as a value, as a desirable goal in life. It can also be viewed as part of a self-concept, when people use material possessions to construct personal identities. More often than not materialists tend to judge their own and others' success by the number (of) and quality of possessions accumulated. The value of possessions stems not only from their ability to confer status but from their ability to project a desired self-image and identify one as a participant in an imagined perfect life.[131]

As a consumption orientation,[132] materialism is the importance a consumer attaches to worldly possessions. Materialism is also a competitive striving to have more than others. Possessions make people happy and things are more valued than people. Materialistic people display an excessive desire to acquire and keep possessions, including objects, people, and memories (photographs). Materialism consists of three belief domains.

1. Acquisition centrality: Materialism brings meaning to life and provides an aim for daily endeavors.
2. Acquisition as the pursuit of happiness: Materialists view their possessions and their acquisitions as essential to their satisfaction and well-being in life.
3. Possession-defined success: The number and quality of possessions accumulated form a basis for judgment of the materialist's own and others' success.[133]

Attitudes toward materialism vary across cultures. A study among American, British, German, and Austrian students showed that *success* played a vital role in attitudes toward materialism, but also differences in associations with materialism were found related to job matters, personal development, health, and happiness. For the Germans and Austrians, for example, happiness was more related to stability and social security than to materialism. Because all four groups score high on cultural masculinity, the similar associations with success are understandable. The differences are likely related to the differences in uncertainty avoidance.

> Chiagouris and Mitchell describe how much materialism is ingrained in American society:
>
> Materialism is the foundation of an inherently competitive humanity. A philosophy ingrained in the history of the United States of America and the capitalist society we hold so dear. We strive to accumulate goods, products, things that carry with them the external status symbolism that fosters perceived power and influence. It is the core of consumer behavior that has, throughout time, evolved through numerous phases of development.[134]

With increased wealth, materialism should increase. Inglehart,[135] however, assumes that after a certain level of affluence is reached, materialism declines as consumers turn to higher-order needs, and so-called postmaterialist values become more important. He defines *materialist* values as emphasizing economic and physical security above all, whereas *postmaterialist* priorities include emphasis on the quality of life. If this assumption were true, there would be evidence of ownership of expensive luxury articles becoming less important with increased wealth. This cannot be demonstrated at the national level. Inglehart's country scores for postmaterialist values do not show any significant correlations with data on ownership of luxury articles, such as watches, PCs, cars (three or four owned), expensive clothes, shoes, and handbags, and spending on cosmetics, skin care, and perfume.[136] In Europe, Inglehart's postmaterialist country scores are correlated with individualism ($r = .47^*$). In sum, at the culture level there is no relationship between Inglehart's postmaterialist values and ownership of luxury articles. Instead, the relationship between individualism and postmaterialist values leads us to conclude that Inglehart's definitions of postmaterialism and materialism are mainly reflections of values of individualistic cultures.

Analysis of other data supports this conclusion. Ger and Belk[137] developed scales to measure various aspects of materialism across nations, which were labeled *nongenerosity, possessiveness, envy,* and *preservation* (the conservation of events, experiences, and memories in material form). The four together were thought to be the underlying views of materialism.

When the country scores of the four scales (factors) were correlated with the cultural variables,[138] nongenerosity correlated with individualism ($r = .60*$), and envy correlated with power distance ($r = .53*$). Preservation correlated with GNI per capita ($r = .69**$), small power distance ($r = -.72***$), and individualism ($r = .67**$), a configuration of dimensions that fits the Western world. From the various studies, it looks like materialism is a specific Western concept, although the various separate elements of materialism are related to different cultural values.

Findings from another study, comparing Australia, France, Mexico, and the United States, suggest that materialism is indeed less strong in collectivistic than in individualistic cultures. Across cultures, the values associated with materialism also vary. For example, security is a value more related to materialism in individualistic cultures than in collectivistic cultures.[139]

National Pride and Consumer Ethnocentrism

Countries vary with respect to the importance people attribute to their own national identities, their attitudes toward their nations. National identity is the extent to which a given culture recognizes and identifies with its unique characteristics. 'National pride designates the positive affective bond to specific national achievements and symbols.'[140] According to the *World Values Survey* data from the years 1995–2004, Venezuelans are the most patriotic people in the world: 92% say they are very proud of their country. Americans and Australians also score high, with respectively 72% and 73%. In Asia, the Philippines scored high with 87%. In Europe, feelings of national pride are strong in Portugal and Ireland. In Portugal, 80% said that they were very proud to be Portuguese, and in Ireland 73% of respondents said they were proud to be Irish. National pride is weakest in Germany, where only 14% said they were proud to be German, and in Belgium, where 23% said they were proud to be Belgians. Feelings of national pride are not strong in Japan (23%) and Korea (17%) but are high in Thailand (85%). There is a strong relationship between national pride and short-term orientation, which explains 82% of variance. In short-term-oriented cultures, self-enhancement is strong, and so are feelings of pride that are associated with the country one belongs to.

When consumers prefer products or brands from their own country to products or brands from other countries, this is called consumer *ethnocentrism*. Generally, in developed countries preferences for domestic products are stronger than in developing countries.[141] The inclination to favor in-groups over out-groups in collectivistic cultures would suggest a relationship with collectivism,[142] but among consumers in developing countries that are usually also collectivistic – for reasons that go beyond quality assessments – nondomestic brands are attitudinally preferred to brands viewed as local. Brands from other countries, especially from the West, are seen as endowing prestige and cosmopolitanism and thus enhancing the buyer's social identity.[143] Status seeking by buying international brands is also a phenomenon of collectivistic cultures.

The essence of ethnocentrism is that purchasing foreign products is unpatriotic as it may harm the domestic economy and cause the loss of jobs.[144] The study of consumer ethnocentrism started in the United States where historically consumers evaluated imported products, which often were considered inferior. American professors Shimp and Sharma[145] developed a research instrument, the so-called CETSCALE to measure consumer ethnocentrism, which has been used for measuring consumer ethnocentrism in many other countries.

Consumer ethnocentrism is related to the degree of national pride, which is measured by Hofstede's long-term orientation dimension. Across Latin America, where feelings of national pride generally are strong, 67% agree with the statement 'I prefer to buy products manufactured in my own country.'[146]

Most studies of consumer ethnocentrism have been done within specific countries which limits the generalisability of the results. A few examples are of New Zealand and Indonesia. In New Zealand ethnocentric consumers have more favorable attitudes toward products from culturally similar countries than from culturally dissimilar countries if no domestic product is available.[147] In Indonesia, consumers who scored high on consumer ethnocentrism preferred to purchase television sets designed in Indonesia to those designed in Japan and the Netherlands. They perceived domestic brands that were locally designed and assembled to be of higher quality than imported brands.[148] Park[149] found differences within the United States, China, Japan, Korea and Taiwan. In all countries consumer ethnocentrism was found to be stronger among older individuals than younger ones and it varied by region. Overall ethnocentrism was strongest among consumers in the United States and it was strongest among less educated consumers. Helgeson et al.[150] found lower ethnocentrism in Norway than in the United States.

Across Latin America, where feelings of national pride generally are strong, 67% agree with the statement 'I prefer to buy products manufactured in my own country.'[151] Thai consumers have an overall preference for national brands, and they are willing to pay a premium for brands with strong reputations.[152]

Feelings of national pride can be reinforced after political turbulence. In 1995, a study of consumer patriotism and attitudes toward purchasing in Eastern Europe found that Czech, Slovakian, and Polish consumers considered their goods to be better value for money than those of Western countries. Hungarian consumers had the best opinion of their own food production, closely followed by consumers in the Czech Republic and Poland. Domestic brands had more loyal buyers than foreign brands.[153] Over time, preferences for domestic products had become stronger. By 1998, local brands had gained significant share from international brands. In Poland, when asked, 'If you have two similar products at the same price which one do you prefer: a local one or a foreign one?', the majority (77%) of adults said they would prefer the local product.[154]

In the year 2000, in the European car market, national brands dominated. The top three brands in the United Kingdom were Ford, Vauxhall, and Rover, all three British made. In Germany the top five car brands were Volkswagen, Ford (German made), Opel, BMW, and Audi. In France, the top three brands were Renault, Peugeot, and Citroen, all three of French heritage. In Spain, the third brand was Seat, the Spanish-made Volkswagen brand.[155] The extreme patriotism that motivates Americans to support national business and to continue buying in difficult economic or political times does not exist in Europe.

Attitudes Toward Country of Origin (COO)

Consumers are sensitive to the country of origin of products and brands. Country of origin of products or brands or foreign-sounding brand names influence consumer perceptions.[156] Consumers use country of origin as stereotypical information in making evaluations of products.[157] Consumers who have positive or negative attitudes toward a particular country will show favorable or unfavorable responses to country-related advertisements.[158]

Attitudes toward foreign products vary by country of origin of the product. Whereas Japan is judged best for technologically advanced and attractively priced products, Germany is the home of reliable, solid products. France and Italy share the preeminence for style, design, and refinement.[159]

Attitudes are related to the combination of the product category and country of origin. 'Fashionable' for clothes will relate to French origin, whereas 'quality' for cars will relate to Germany. A positive product–country match exists when a country is perceived as very strong in an area (e.g., design or technology), which is also an important feature for a product category (e.g., furniture, cars). Such product–country match is called *prototypicality*. Views of what product categories are prototypical for which countries vary. The role of the country image acts differently in different target countries.[160] Whereas, for example, in Korea refrigerators are viewed as prototypical for the United States,[161] this is not the case in Europe.

Country of origin can reflect on specific product categories or on a variety of products when a country represents a *way of life*. Both effects can change over time. In the past, Japan stood for shoddy, cheap products, but that image has changed into one of quality and technology. For Asian youth, 'American' has long represented an aspirational lifestyle. It used to offer freedom, independence, and opportunity, but in 2000, this attitude was changing, and European goods became more popular. Europe represents a more understated style, compared with the brashness of America.[162]

Attitudes toward developed countries are more favorable than attitudes toward developing countries, although in some cultures people tend to prefer anything from outside to domestic products. In the eyes of Nigerian consumers, for example, mere foreignness is a reason for product preferences. Even products from Ghana, which is economically and technologically not superior to Nigeria, are preferred to Nigerian products.[163]

Whereas consumer ethnocentrism refers to a preference of domestic products instead of products from *all* foreign nations, *consumer animosity* refers to the reluctance to purchase products of a *specific* country because of military, political, or economic events. Hence, someone low in ethnocentricity may still avoid purchasing products from a specific country as a form of punishment for that country's past (or current) military, political, or economic behavior. Examples of such consumer animosity are those against Japanese products in Nanjing, China, due to brutal treatment during the 1931 to 1945 Japanese occupation and against French products in Australia due to the French nuclear testing in the South Pacific. In ex-colonial countries, consumer animosity is found to turn to the ex-colonizing countries. Animosity has not been shown to affect the perception of the quality of products from the target country, but it does affect willingness to buy products from that country.[164]

Religious animosity has been a strong cause for consumer boycotts in some Muslim dominant markets.

> The publication in the Danish newspaper *Jyllands-Posten* of cartoons depicting the Prophet Mohammed in an insulting manner to the worldwide Muslim community affected Danish companies by a consumer boycott in several countries in the Middle East, in particular the dairy giant Arla Foods that manufactures in Saudi Arabia. Analysis of the effects showed that the impact of boycotting on brand image and customer loyalty was negative, but had not destroyed the perceived quality of Arla Foods' products, although consumers continue to refuse to buy them. Such macro-boycotts are difficult to avoid as the targeted companies have nothing directly to do with the cause of the boycott.[165]

According to Magnusson et al.[166] the importance of COO tends to be overestimated. Information on brand origin has become more ambiguous and difficult to ascertain. Most studies have found that brand origin perceptions are not accurate and even incorrect perceptions of brand origin are more important to consumers than correct ones. Another question is if consumer ethnocentrism may be understood differently in smaller countries that are dependent on imports because of having few domestic manufacturers.[167]

Attitudes Toward the Environment

Across countries, people vary with respect to their attitudes toward the environment. Only in the past decades have environmental problems become widespread matters of concern among the general publics. But attitudes to the environment vary. In the less wealthy countries, economic development usually has higher priority than the environment. In 2008, the percentage of inhabitants of European Union countries who said that 'economic growth must be a priority for our country, even if it affects the environment' correlated with low GNI per capita and high power distance.[168] In 2017, after the economic crisis, an average of 56% said protecting the environment was very important for them personally, varying between Sweden (87%) and Austria (41%). Few of the different issues were still related to GNI/cap.[169]

The associations people have with the concept of the environment vary. The word *environment* is associated with a wide variety of thoughts that, in equal measure, suggest negative images (pollution, disasters) and positive ideas (pleasant landscapes, protecting the natural world). German consumers tend to adopt a holistic perspective (i.e., humans are seen very much as a part of the ecological system). In Britain, environmentalism has been very much about the destruction of the inner cities, the preservation of the fabled English countryside, and the war on waste. In France, environmentalism is mostly about the depletion of the rain forests or problems stemming from the use of harmful products like aerosols.[170] Differences in associations are culture bound.[171] Whereas in high power distance cultures people think first of pollution in towns and cities, in low power distance cultures a first association is with climate change. Loss in biodiversity, depletion of natural resources, and consumption habits are worries of rich countries.

Over time results from Eurobarometer measurements of attitudes toward the environment (2008, 2014 and 2017) show similar relationships with culture. Associations with agricultural pollution and shortages of drinking water are more found in collectivistic cultures. In high uncertainty avoidance cultures, larger percentages of people agree with the statement that environmental problems have a direct effect on their daily life and health, which specifically applies to air pollution and the impact of plastic products. One of the pro-environmental actions taken in high uncertainty avoidance cultures is cutting down on water consumption, whereas in the feminine cultures actions are a more environmentally friendly way of travel, cutting down on energy consumption, using the car less and buying environmentally friendly products. Avoiding waste by over-packaging is related to long-term orientation.

With respect to some of the pro-environmental actions taken there are differences between intention and actual behavior. The gap can be quite large in high power distance and high uncertainty avoidance cultures. For example, the differences between intention to buy environmentally friendly products and actual buying are large. But overall the gaps have become smaller. Table 4.4 presents the results of Eurobarometer surveys of 2008 and 2014, measuring attitudes towards the environment.

Table 4.4 **Relationships between buying intention and actual buying of environmentally friendly products**

	Ready to buy environmentally friendly products (%)		Bought environmentally friendly products (%)		Gap between ready to buy and bought	
	2008	**2014**	**2008**	**2014**	**2008**	**2014**
Greece	88	72	13	17	75	55
Portugal	75	62	7	9	68	53
Poland	77	71	13	14	64	57
Germany	76	80	18	21	58	59
Austria	81	83	33	44	48	39
Sweden	88	94	42	60	46	34
Denmark	86	87	41	48	45	39

SOURCES: EBS 295, *Attitudes of European Citizens Towards the Environment* (2008); EBS 416, *Attitudes of European Citizens Towards the Environment* (2014) (see Appendix B)

Whether people take responsibility for the environment themselves or expect their governments to take responsibility varies by culture. The *World Values Survey* of 1990 asked questions to find whether people refer to the government as the responsible institution for caring for the environment or whether they want to pay for the environment themselves and accept higher taxes for this purpose. Viewing the environment as a government responsibility was significantly correlated with high uncertainty avoidance, both for 25 countries worldwide ($r = .61***$) and for Europe ($r = .75***$). In the low masculine cultures, people think they should pay for the environment themselves (worldwide $r = -.61***$, in Europe $r = -.71***$). In 2017 across European countries people still hold their governments responsible. The percentages who say their national governments are not doing enough vary between 88% for Greece and 45% for Estonia. The differences correlate with power distance that explains 25% of variance.

Sex- and Love-Related Attitudes

Although love is often mentioned as a universal value, attitudes toward romantic love vary widely across cultures. Generally, romantic love is valued highly in individualistic cultures and is less valued in collectivistic cultures where strong family ties reinforce the relationship between marriage partners. Asians are more friendship oriented in their love relationships than are Americans.[172] Japanese value romantic love less than Germans. Comparative research on intimacy shows that Americans conceptualize intimacy more concretely than do Japanese, especially in ways that are associated with direct behavioral manifestations. Americans also prefer to express intimacy through a greater variety of means and channels than do Japanese, who prefer high-contextual interaction in intimate relationships.[173] Compared with Swedish young adults, American young adults differentiate love and sex more strongly.[174] In feminine cultures the distinction between love and sex is less rigid than in masculine cultures. In spite of the sexual revolution of the 1950s, culturally masculine countries continue to manifest a stronger taboo on addressing sexual issues openly than culturally feminine ones.[175]

In some cultures nudity is related to sex, whereas in others nudity symbolizes purity or beauty. Whereas nudism is popular in Germany, it is unthinkable in the United States, where people are extremely sensitive to nudity, which tends to be confused with sex. In Sweden and Finland, on the other hand, people do not confuse nakedness with sexiness. That is why schoolchildren can see a naked boy or say 'penis' without collapsing into giggles. The fact that the Swedes tend to be matter-of-fact about both nudity and sex does not mean they are sexually more promiscuous than people elsewhere in Europe or America.[176] In Scandinavia and in the Netherlands, in the sauna one is nude. In Britain, a bathing costume is obligatory. While 'streaking' was trendy in several countries in Europe in the 1970s, it still is done in the United Kingdom because it shocks. In countries where nudity is not viewed as shocking, there is no fun in streaking. In Europe, toddlers commonly run around naked on the beach and nobody pays attention, whereas in the United States, people are easily shocked, and parents are told to cover the kids up. Americans tend to categorize nudity in advertising as sex appeal and may hypothesize a relationship with cultural masculinity, but such a relationship is not found.[177]

Likewise, the use of nudity in advertising varies across countries. Germans don't perceive female nudity in advertising as an affront or as sexist exploitation. They might see it as nothing more than a cheap advertising trick. In France naked women are more or less acceptable icons of the advertising language. The female body is used as a metaphor for beauty. The British, on the other hand, think it is sexist and exploitative first, and bad advertising second. Italy is probably the closest to Britain. Although on TV images of scantily clad women are commonplace, full nudity is rare.[178]

Lifestyle

Lifestyle is described in terms of shared values or tastes as reflected in consumption patterns. Personal characteristics are viewed as the 'raw' ingredients to develop a unique lifestyle.

In an economic sense, one's lifestyle represents the way one allocates income, but lifestyle is more viewed as a mental construct that explains but is not identical with behavior.[179] A comprehensive definition by Dutch consumer psychologists Antonides and Van Raaij shows how the lifestyle concept is embedded in culture: 'Lifestyle is the entire set of values, interests, opinions and behavior of consumers.'[180] Lifestyle descriptions tend to include attitudes, values, and behavioral elements that often are a reflection of culture. Lifestyles transcend individual brands or products but can be specific to a product class. Thus, it makes sense to talk about a food-related lifestyle, or a housing-related lifestyle.

An example of an American lifestyle description is one of the 'new materialists' from a study by Backer Spielvogel Bates as described by Chiagouris and Mitchell.

> The youthful materialists referred to as 'New Materialists' are financially independent, have acquired 'spending ability' and have compulsion toward its exercise. As the children of the decade of greed, they have grown accustomed to immediate gratification. They are not conscious of the ethics of saving. They want to consume as much as they can, even if it is sometimes beyond their means. Possession is the central concern of proving one's independence and success … They view themselves as opinion leaders and trendsetters. It is ingrained in their quest to make an impression in society. They have an unbridled desire to be the first to discover, purchase, and possess the newest in material goods. Material goods comprise a central and defining part of their identity.[181]

In the professional world, lifestyle research originated from what is called *psychographic* research, as a response to the decreased usefulness of *sociodemographic* and *economic* variables to explain differences in behavior. Classical psychographic segment descriptions could be in terms of behavior and attitudes or could relate to a particular consumer activity. An early example of five motorist segments in terms of attitudes and behavior by Esso was (1) the uninvolved, (2) the enthusiast, (3) the professional or business driver, (4) the tinkerer, and (5) the collector.[182] Generally lifestyle studies search for attitudes, interests, and opinions (AIOs) that do not relate directly to specific product characteristics. Examples of such AIOs are 'sense of fashion,' attitude toward money, or opinions on roles of males and females.[183] Working with AIO variables, segments were identified such as 'the happy housewife,' 'the affluent consumer,' or 'the price-conscious consumer.'[184]

Today many lifestyle studies and systems exist across countries. (A few examples were given in Chapter 2.) In academia, the lifestyle research instruments developed and used by most of the larger market research firms are criticized on several grounds. We mention five:

1. There is no agreement on what lifestyle actually means.
2. The methods used are purely inductive and not guided by theory. Lifestyle types come about based on dimensions derived by exploratory data analysis techniques like factor analysis or correspondence analysis.
3. The derivation of the underlying dimensions is unclear and unsatisfactory. Because commercially marketed instruments are proprietary, the information necessary to evaluate statistical soundness of the derived dimensional solutions is often missing.
4. The explanatory value of lifestyle types or dimensions with regard to consumer choice behavior is low and not well documented.
5. The cross-cultural validity of the international lifestyle instruments remains to be demonstrated.[185]

Lifestyles Across Cultures

Lifestyle may be a useful within-country criterion; it is less useful for defining segments across cultures because lifestyles are country specific. No one has ever produced an empirical base to support the argument that lifestyle similarities are stronger than cultural differences. In contrast, increasingly evidence is found that culture overrides lifestyle.

An early example of a cross-cultural lifestyle study is by Douglas and Urban,[186] who compared lifestyles of women in the United States, the United Kingdom, and France. They found similarities in the degree to which women accepted or rejected their traditional homemaking job. They also found large differences in underlying values of lifestyle elements. French women identified their own self-concepts relative to those around them, suggesting less self-reliance than found among US and UK women. Whereas in the United Kingdom and United States innovativeness primarily took the form of willingness to experiment and try new things, in France innovativeness and interest in buying new products was strongly associated with interest in fashion and in being well dressed.

In a comparative study in France, Brazil, Japan, and the United States, Eshgi and Sheth,[187] using the modern/traditional dichotomy as a lifestyle variable, demonstrated that more than lifestyle, national and cultural influences determine consumption patterns of stereo equipment, soft drinks, fruit juices, alcoholic beverages, automobiles, and deodorants.

Studies among consumers in different countries in Asia also demonstrate the continuing impact of culture on lifestyle. When comparing, for example, Singapore and Hong Kong China – lifestyles that are superficially similar – Singaporeans are more home oriented and place a higher value on family relationships and education, whereas Hong Kong consumers are more fashion conscious and concerned about their personal appearance, but they also adhere strongly to specific traditional cultural values.[188]

Although lifestyle studies are popular among advertising agencies, they are very general, which is their major weakness. To understand consumer behavior across cultures it is necessary to go beyond lifestyle and distinguish value variations by product category. Even if across cultures certain groups of people can be identified with respect to ownership of specific products, the motives for buying these products vary so strongly that, for developing advertising, these lifestyle groups are not useful.

Global Communities?

Pan-European or global lifestyle studies aim at identifying similar lifestyle segments across borders, assuming that national and cultural influences on consumption patterns are less significant than modern lifestyle patterns. Certain lifestyle groups are assumed to be so similar between countries that their behavior is more similar to the same group across borders than to other groups within borders. Ownership of similar products or brands across countries would create consumption communities that, like neighborhoods, provide a sense of community with other people who own the same products. Even though there is some evidence for psychological feelings of community in relation to people engaging in common consumption behaviors, the individuals sharing these feelings do not constitute a community.[189] Usually groups that are given one label across countries are very different as to content. The British TGI (Target Group Index),[190] for example, categorized age categories of women and labeled the 15- to 24-year-old group as the '@ generation.' What members of this group have in common is that they are mostly single women. However, young Italian and Spanish women mostly live at home with their parents, whereas young Germans start to live as a couple early on. All spend money on pleasure articles: CDs, makeup, sportswear, or snack products. However, Italians and Spaniards – probably because they live at home and have more spending power – spend more on personal and luxury goods and going out. They live in larger households and share products and brands, so brands must address the collective, not individual. Italian and British women are more involved in appearance. Snack consumption is high among this age group, but snacks are consumed in different situations. In Britain potato chips are an around-the-clock, individual snack product, but in Spain they are used as *tapas,* when people are socializing.

The difference between Western and Asian lifestyles of young people is even more pronounced. Teenagers of different countries live in different social and cultural environments with shared historical events that shape their lives. The promotion of products based on the typical youth themes of rebellion, individuality, freedom, confidence, sexiness, and even Americanness, as typified by brands such as Levi's, may communicate very little to teenagers in Asia.[191]

Conclusion

This chapter discussed the relationship among values, culture, and personal attributes: personality, the self, attitude, and lifestyle. Personality and trait structure are Western concepts. For marketing and branding, understanding these cultural variations is necessary because the concepts are used as metaphors for brand personality. Similarly, the concepts of self and identity vary across cultures. The most pronounced difference is between individualistic and collectivistic cultures, where the self is independent or interdependent. The Western approach is that the self and personality are consistent and unchangeable. Because the self is a relational self in collectivistic cultures, it varies along with the context and situation. Similarly, attitudes vary across cultures. Several examples of culture-related attitudes were given in this chapter. Finally, the concept of lifestyle was discussed as a not-so-well-defined concept that is used worldwide to find and describe similar segments. These are pseudo-similarities. There is little evidence that there are culture-free lifestyle groups that can be targeted in similar ways. On the contrary, there is evidence that cultural differences override lifestyle similarities.

Notes

1. D. Oyserman, 'High power, low power, and equality: Culture beyond individualism and collectivism,' *Journal of Consumer Psychology*, 16, 4 (2006), pp. 352–356.
2. R. Díaz-Loving, 'Contributions of Mexican ethnopsychology to the resolution of the etic-emic dilemma in personality,' *Journal of Cross-Cultural Psychology*, 29 (1998), pp. 104–118.
3. H.R. Markus and S. Kitayama, 'Culture and the self: Implications for cognition, emotion and motivation,' *Psychological Review*, 98 (1991), pp. 224–253.
4. T.M. Singelis, 'Some thoughts on the future of cross-cultural social psychology,' *Journal of Cross-Cultural Psychology*, 31 (2000), pp. 76–91.
5. Markus and Kitayama, 'Culture and the self.'
6. D. Singh, *Cross Cultural Comparison of Buying Behavior in India*, Doctoral thesis (University Business School, Panjab University, Chandigarh, 2007).
7. A. Roland, *In Search of Self in India and Japan* (Princeton University Press, Princeton, NJ, 1988), pp. 3–13.
8. M. Hasegawa, Y. Horiuchi, K. Suzuki, M. Sado, and A. Sakamoto, 'Characteristics of depiction of pro-social behaviour in Japanese television programmes,' *Media Asia*, 35, 3 (2008), pp. 170–178.
9. Roland, *In Search of Self in India and Japan*; H.C. Triandis, *Individualism and Collectivism* (Westview, Boulder, CO, 1995).
10. T. Tardif, P. Fletcher, W. Liang, Z. Zhang, N. Kaciroti, and V.A. Marchman, 'Baby's first ten words,' *Development Psychology*, 44, 4 (2008), pp. 929–938.

11. J.B. Nezlek, K. Kafetsios, and V. Smith, 'Emotions in everyday social encounters,' *Journal of Cross-Cultural Psychology*, 39, 4 (2008), pp. 366–372.

12. H. Rübeling, H. Keller, R.D. Yovsi, M. Lenk, S. Schwarzer, and N. Kühne, 'Children's drawings of the self as an expression of cultural conceptions of the self,' *Journal of Cross-Cultural Psychology*, 42, 3 (2011), pp. 406–424.

13. Ç. Kagitçibasi, (1997). 'Individualism and collectivism,' in J.W. Berry, M.H. Segall, and Ç. Kagitçibasi (eds), *Handbook of Cross-cultural Psychology*, Vol. 3 (Allyn & Bacon, Boston, 1997), pp. 2–49.

14. L.M. Mao, 'Reflective encounters: Illustrating comparative rhetoric,' *Style*, 37, 4 (2003), pp. 401–425.

15. P. Hessler, *Country Driving. A Chinese Road Trip* (Harper, New York, 2010).

16. Y. Kashima, S. Yamaguchi, U. Kim, S.C. Choi, M.J. Gelfand, and M. Yuki, 'Culture, gender, and self: A perspective from individualism-collectivism research,' *Journal of Personality and Social Psychology*, 69 (2001), pp. 925–937; G. Hofstede, *Culture's Consequences*, 2nd edn (Sage, Thousand Oaks, CA, 2001), p. 294.

17. Triandis, *Individualism and Collectivism*.

18. D. Watkins, A. Akande, J. Fleming, M. Ismail, K. Lefner, M. Regmi, et al., 'Cultural dimensions, gender, and the nature of self-concept: A fourteen-country study,' *International Journal of Psychology*, 33 (1998), pp. 17–31.

19. *Ibero-America Interactive Generation* (2008). See Appendix B.

20. M.B. Ramose, 'The philosophy of *ubuntu* and *ubuntu* as a philosophy,' in P.H. Coetzee and A.P.J. Roux (eds), *The African Philosophy Reader*, 2nd edn (Routledge, London, 2003), pp. 230–238.

21. W.Dissanayake, 'Personhood, agency, and communication: A Buddhist viewpoint,' *China Media Research*, 9, 1 (2013), pp. 11–25.

22. C. Cheng, P.E. Jose, K.M. Sheldon, T.M. Singelis, M.W.L. Cheung, H. Tiliouine, A.A. Alao, J.H.M. Chio, J.Y.M. Lui, W.Y. Chun, A. Golec de Zavala, A. Hakuzimana, J. Hertel, J-T. Liu, M. Onyewadume, and C. Sims, 'Sociocultural differences in self-construal and subjective well-being: A test of four cultural models,' *Journal of Cross-Cultural Psychology*, 42, 5 (2011), pp. 832–855.

23. Singh, *Cross Cultural Comparison of Buying Behavior in India*.

24. J. Zhang, 'The effect of advertising appeals in activating self-construals: A case of bicultural generation X consumers,' *Journal of Advertising*, 38, 1 (2009), pp. 63–81.

25. C. Harb and P.B. Smith, 'Self-construals across cultures: Beyond independence-interdependence,' *Journal of Cross-Cultural Psychology*, 39, 2 (2008), pp. 178–197.

26. H.R. Markus and S. Kitayama, 'The cultural psychology of personality,' *Journal of Cross-Cultural Psychology*, 29 (1998), pp. 63–87.

27. T.M. Singelis, M.H. Bond, W.F. Sharkey, and C.S.Y. Lai, 'Unpackaging culture's influence on self-esteem and embarrassability,' *Journal of Cross-Cultural Psychology*, 30 (1999), pp. 315–341.

28. S. Heine, S. Kitayama, and D.R. Lehman, 'Cultural differences in self-evaluation,' *Journal of Cross-Cultural Psychology*, 32 (2001), pp. 434–443.

29. M. Barone, T.A. Shimp, and D.E. Sprott, 'Product ownership as a moderator of self-congruity effects,' *Marketing Letters*, 10 (1999), pp. 75–85.

30. C. Becker, 'Hair and cosmetic products in the Japanese market,' *Marketing and Research Today* (1997), pp. 31–36.

31. Belgium, Czech Republic, Denmark, Finland, France, Germany, Hungary, Italy, Netherlands, Norway, Poland, Portugal, Russia, Slovakia, Spain, Sweden, Switzerland, United Kingdom.

32. X. Hu, 'Mainstream and trends: Brand research in China,' in H. Li, S. Huang, and D. Jin (eds), *Proceedings of the 2009 American Academy of Advertising Asia-Pacific conference* (American Academy of Advertising in conjunction with China Association of Advertising of Commerce, and Communication University of China, 2009), p. 44.

33. M. Gagliardi, 'Alchemy of cultures: From adaptation to transcendence in design and branding,' *Design Management Journal*, Fall (2001), pp. 32–39.

34. Personal observation by the author when traveling through Henan province, China.

35. S-P. Han and S. Shavitt, 'Persuasion and culture: Advertising appeals in individualistic and collectivistic societies,' *Journal of Experimental Social Psychology*, 30 (1994), pp. 326–350; Y. Zhang and B.D. Gelb, 'Matching advertising appeals to culture: The influence of products' use condition,' *Journal of Advertising*, 25 (1996), pp. 29–46.

36. J. Bowman, 'Commercials rise in the East,' *Media and Marketing Europe Pocket Guide on Asian TV* (Emap Media, London, 2002), p. 8.

37. Han and Shavitt, 'Persuasion and culture.'

38. C.L. Wang, T. Bristol, J.C. Mowen, and G. Chakraborty, 'Alternative modes of self-construal: Dimensions of connectedness-separateness and advertising appeals to the cultural and gender-specific self,' *Journal of Consumer Psychology*, 9 (2000), pp. 107–115.

39. C.L.C. Praet, 'Japanese advertising, the world's number one celebrity showcase? A cross-cultural comparison of the frequency of celebrity appearances in TV advertising,' in M. Roberts and R.L. King (eds), *Proceedings of the 2001 Special Asia-Pacific Conference of the American Academy of Advertising* (2001), pp. 6–13.

40. C.L.C. Praet, 'The influence of national culture on the use of celebrity endorsement in television advertising: A multi-country study,' in *Proceedings of the 7th International Conference on Research in Advertising (ICORIA)* (Antwerp, Belgium, s.1., CD-ROM, 2008).

41. S. Kitayama, H.R. Markus, H. Matsumoto, and V. Noraskkunkit, 'Individual and collective processes in the construction of the self: Self-enhancement in the United States and self-criticism in Japan,' *Journal of Personality and Social Psychology*, 72 (1997), pp. 1245–1267.

42. S. Kitayama, 'Culture and basic psychological processes – toward a system view of culture: Comment on Oyserman et al.,' *Psychological Bulletin*, 128 (2002), pp. 89–96.

43. M.W. Eysenck, *Psychology: A Student's Handbook* (Psychology Press, Hove, East Sussex, UK, 2000), p. 458.

44. J.M. Twenge and J. Crocker, 'Race and self-esteem: Meta-analyses comparing whites, blacks, Hispanics, Asians and American Indians and comment on Gray-Little and Hafdahl,' *Psychological Bulletin*, 128 (2000), pp. 371–408.

45. G.P. Moschis, F.S. Ong, M. Abessi, T. Yamashita, and A. Mathur, 'Cultural and sub-cultural differences in reliability. An empirical study in Japan and Malaysia,' *Asia Pacific Journal of Marketing and Logistics*, 25, 1 (2013).

46. W. Bleidorn, R.C. Arslan, J.J.A. Denissen, J.E. Gebauer, J. Potter, P.J. Rentfrow, and S.D. Gosling, 'Age and gender differences in self-esteem – A cross-cultural window,' *Journal of Personality and Social Psychology*, 111, 3 (2015), pp. 396-410.

47. J. Kurman, 'Measured cross-cultural differences in self-enhancement and the sensitivity of the self-enhancement measure to the modesty response,' *Cross-Cultural Research*, 36, 1 (2002), pp. 73–95.

48. E. Goffman, *The Presentation of Self in Everyday Life* (Penguin, Harmondsworth, Middlesex, UK, 1959), p. 244.

49. D. Maheswaran and S. Shavitt, 'Issues and new directions in global consumer psychology,' *Journal of Consumer Psychology*, 9 (2000), pp. 59–66.

50. N. Etcoff, S. Orbach, J. Scott, and H. Agostino, *Beyond Stereotypes: Rebuilding the Foundation of Beauty Beliefs* (February 2006). Available at: www.campaignforrealbeauty.com/DovebeyondStereotypesWhitePaper.pdf (accessed 4 November 2008).

51. *Reader's Digest* Trusted Brands, 2005 and 2007.

52. S. Heine and T. Hamamura, 'In search of East Asian self-enhancement,' *Personality and Social Psychology Review*, 11, 1 (2007), pp. 4–27.

53. R. Jowell et al., *European Social Survey 2002/2003* (technical report) (Centre for Comparative Social Surveys, City University, London, 2003).

54. S. Kitayama, H.R. Markus, H. Matsumoto, and V. Norasakunkit, 'Individual and collective processes in the construction of the self: Self-enhancement in the United States and self-criticism in Japan,' *Journal of Personality and Social Psychology*, 72 (1997), pp. 1245–1266.

55. Heine and Hamamura, 'In search of East Asian self-enhancement.'

56. Markus and Kitayama, 'The cultural psychology of personality.'

57. A.T. Church et al., 'Implicit theories and self-perceptions of traitedness across cultures,' *Journal of Cross-Cultural Psychology*, 37, 6 (2006), pp. 694–716.

58. Ibid.

59. A. Norenzayan, I. Choi, and R.E. Nisbett, 'Cultural similarities and differences in social influence: Evidence from behavioral predictions and lay theories of behavior,' *Personality and Social Psychology Bulletin*, 28 (2002), pp. 109–120.

60. V.H. Valchev, F.J.R. Van de Vijver, J.A. Nel, S. Rothmann, D. Meiring, and G.P. De Bruin, 'Implicit personality conceptions of the Nguni cultural-linguistic groups of South Africa,' *Cross-Cultural Research*, 45, 3 (2011), pp. 235–266.

61. S. Eap, D.S. DeGarmo, A. Kawakami, S.N. Hara, G.C.N. Hall, and A.L. Teten, 'Culture and personality among European American and Asian American men,' *Journal of Cross-Cultural Psychology*, 39, 5 (2008), pp. 630–643.

62. P.K. Petrova, R.B. Cialdini, and S. Sills, 'Consistency-based compliance across cultures,' *Journal of Experimental Social Psychology*, 43 (2006), pp. 104–111.

63. H.C. Triandis, 'Dimensions of culture beyond Hofstede,' in H. Vinken, J. Soeters, and P. Ester (eds), *Comparing Cultures: Dimensions of Culture in a Comparative Perspective* (Brill, Leiden and Boston, 2004), p. 37; Y. Kashima, E.S. Kashima, U. Kim, and M. Gelfand, 'Describing the social world: How is a person, a group, and a relationship described in the East and the West?,' *Journal of Experimental Social Psychology*, 42 (2005), pp. 388–396.

64. Norenzayan et al., 'Cultural similarities and differences in social influence.'

65. I. Choi, R.E. Nisbett, and A. Norenzayan, 'Causal attribution across cultures: Variation and universality,' *Psychological Bulletin*, 125 (1999), pp. 47–63.

66. P.R. Campana Carramenha, 'Evaluating the value of global brands in Latin America,' *Marketing and Research Today* (November 1999*)*, pp. 159–167.

67. D. Blumenthal, '"Face of the Brand": A design methodology with global potential,' *Design Management Journal*, Fall (2001), pp. 65–71.

68. L. Derksen, *Brand Personality Study*, unpublished report (PPGH/JWT, Amsterdam, 2002).

69. R.R. McCrae and P.T. Jr. Costa, *Personality in Adulthood* (Guildford, New York, 1990), p. 23.

70. R.R. McCrae, P.T. Jr. Costa, G.H. Del Pilar, J.P. Rolland, and W.D. Parker, 'Cross-cultural assessment of the five-factor model,' *Journal of Cross-Cultural Psychology*, 29 (1998), pp. 171–188.

71. A.T. Church and W.J. Lonner, 'The cross-cultural perspective in the study of personality,' *Journal of Cross-Cultural Psychology*, 29 (1998), pp. 32–62.

72. R.R. McCrae, 'NEO-PI-R data from 36 cultures,' in A.J. Marsella and R.R. McCrae (eds), *The Five-Factor Model of Personality Across Cultures* (Kluwer, Dordrecht, The Netherlands, 2002), pp. 105–125.

73. Ibid.

74. F.M. Cheung, K. Leung, J.X. Zhang, H.F. Sun, Y.Q. Gan, W.Z. Song et al., 'Indigenous Chinese personality constructs: Is the five-factor model complete?,' *Journal of Cross-Cultural Psychology*, 32 (2001), pp. 407–433.

75. K. Yoon, F. Schmidt, and R. Ilies, 'Cross-cultural construct validity of the five-factor model of personality among Korean employees,' *Journal of Cross-Cultural Psychology*, 33 (2002), pp. 217–235.

76. F.M. Cheung, S.F. Cheung, J. Zhang, K. Leung, F. Leong, and K.H. Yeh, 'Relevance for openness as a personality dimension in Chinese culture,' *Journal of Cross-Cultural Psychology*, 39, 1 (2008), pp. 81–108.

77. Yoon et al., 'Relevance for openness as a personality dimension in Chinese culture.'

78. G. Hofstede and R.R. McCrae, 'Personality and culture revisited: Linking traits and dimensions of culture,' *Cross-Cultural Research*, 38, 1 (2004), pp. 52–88.

79. McCrae, 'NEO-PI-R data from 36 cultures.'

80   Data provided by TGI, United Kingdom. Available at: www.tgisurveys.com. © TGI—All Rights Reserved. Countries: Argentina, Brazil, Chile, Colombia, Mexico, Peru, and Venezuela.

81. Hofstede. Personal communication.

82. *Pan-European Market Research Into Ecological Awareness Amongst Drivers* (September 2001). Received from Goodyear Dunlop Tires Nederland BV, Merwedeweg 4c, 3621 LR Breukelen.

83. D.P. Schmitt, J. Allik, R.R. McCrae, and V. Benet-Martínez, 'The geographic distribution of big five personality traits,' *Journal of Cross-Cultural Psychology*, 38, 2 (2007), pp. 173–212.

84. Ibid.

85. N. Ramírez-Esparza, S.D. Gosling, and J.W. Pennebaker, 'Paradox lost: Unraveling the puzzle of simpatía,' *Journal of Cross-Cultural Psychology*, 39, 6 (2008), pp. 703–715.

86. J.L. Aaker, V. Benet-Martínez, and J. Garolera, 'Consumption symbols as carriers of culture: A study of Japanese and Spanish brand personality constructs,' *Journal of Personality and Social Psychology*, 81 (2001), pp. 492–508.

87. Y. Sung and S.F. Tinkham, 'Brand personality structures in the United States and Korea: Common and culture-specific factors,' *Journal of Consumer Psychology*, 15, 4 (2005), pp. 334–350.

88. T. Foscht, C. Maloles III, B. Swoboda, D. Morschett, and I. Sinha, 'The impact of culture on brand perception: A six-nation study,' *Journal of Product and Brand Management*, 17, 3 (2008), pp. 131–142.

89. Crocus (Cross-Cultural Solutions) was a cross-cultural study that measured brand value (called 'brand pull') and provided a cultural explanation of strong or weak brand value in different countries. Conducted by the research agency chain Euronet, in cooperation with the advertising agency chain Interpartners.

90. *European Social Reality* (Special Eurobarometer report 225, 2007).

91. G. Antonides and W.F. Van Raaij, *Consumer Behaviour: A European Perspective* (Wiley, Chichester, UK, 1998), pp. 162–163.

92. *How Europeans See Themselves* (Eurobarometer, 2001).

93. C. Camilleri and H. Malewska-Peyre, 'Socialization and identity strategies,' in J.W. Berry, P.R. Dasen, and T.S. Saraswathi (eds), *Handbook of Cross-Cultural Psychology*, Vol. 2 (Allyn & Bacon, Boston, 1997), pp. 41–67.

94. R.W. Belk, 'Cultural and historical differences in concepts of self and their effects on attitudes toward having and giving,' in T.C. Kinnear (ed.), *Advances in Consumer Research* (Association for Consumer Research, Provo, UT, 1984), pp. 753–760.

95. W.E. Abraham, *The Mind of Africa* (Weidenfeld and Nicolson, London, 1962).

96. G. Edmondson, 'France: A CEO's pay shouldn't be a secret,' *BusinessWeek* (9 August 1999), p. 24.

97. Camelleri and Malewska-Peyre, 'Socialization and identity strategies,' p. 48.

98. R. Kowner, 'Japanese body image: Structure and esteem scores in a cross-cultural perspective,' *International Journal of Psychology*, 37 (2002), pp. 149–159.

99. D.R. Shafer, N. Crepaz, and C-R. Sun, 'Physical attractiveness stereotyping in cross-cultural perspective,' *Journal of Cross-Cultural Psychology*, 31 (2000), pp. 557–582.

100. D. Matsumoto, *Culture and Psychology: People Around the World*, 2nd edn (Wadsworth Thomson Learning, Delmar, CA, 2000), p. 411.

101. Kowner, 'Japanese body image.'

102. G. Prendergast, Y. Leung Kwok, and D.C. West, 'Role portrayal in advertising and editorial content, and eating disorders: An Asian perspective,' *International Journal of Advertising*, 21 (2002), pp. 237–258.

103. L. Wheeler and Y. Kim, 'What is beautiful is culturally good: The physical attractiveness stereotype has different content in collectivistic cultures,' *Personality and Social Psychology Bulletin*, 23 (1997), pp. 795–800.

104. W. Jankowiak, P.B. Gray, and K. Hattman, 'Globalizing evolution: Female choice, nationality, and perception of sexual beauty in China,' *Cross-Cultural Research*, 42, 3 (2008), pp. 248–269.

105. F. Wan, R.J. Faber, and A. Fung, 'Perceived impact of thin female models in advertising: A cross-cultural examination of third person perception and its impact on behaviors,' in *Proceedings of the 8th Cross Cultural Research Conference*, Association for Consumer Research and American Psychological Association, Hawaii (12–15 December 2001), pp. 13–16.

106. Matsumoto, *Culture and Psychology*.

107. M. Ingrassia, 'The body of the beholder,' *Newsweek* (24 April 1995), p. 50.

108. Prendergast et al., 'Role portrayal in advertising.'

109. 'Data OECD,' *The Economist* (15 December 2001), p. 88.

110. M.L. Maynard and C.R. Taylor, 'Girlish images across cultures: Analyzing Japanese versus US *Seventeen* magazine ads,' *Journal of Advertising*, 28 (1999), pp. 39–48.

111. X. Chen, *A Comparison of the Covers of Elle magazine for Mainland China and US*, Graduate Theses and Dissertations, Paper 13843 (Iowa State University, 2014).

112. L. Sudbury-Riley, F. Kohlbacher, and A. Hofmeister, 'Boomers of different nations. Identifying horizontal international segments based on self-perceived age,' *International Marketing Review*, 32, 3/4 (2015), pp. 245–278.

113. N. Ind, *The Corporate Image: Strategies for Effective Identity Programmes* (Kogan Page, London, 1992), p. 19.

114. J. Bosman, 'The relation between self image and brand image: An alternative perspective,' *Communications*, 21 (1996), pp. 27–47.

115. Unfortunately the author – like more authors of such studies do – assumes his findings to be universal because he does not mention the culture of the participants, which may have explained the outcome.

116. M.H. Hsieh and A. Lindridge, 'Universal appeals with local specifications,' *Journal of Product and Brand Management*, 14, 1 (2005), pp. 14–28.

117. This is the definition by Gordon Allport, in H. Assael, *Consumer Behavior: A Strategic Approach* (Houghton Mifflin, Boston and New York, 2004), p. 216.

118. M.C. Cervellon and L. Dubé, 'Assessing the cross-cultural applicability of affective and cognitive components of attitude,' *Journal of Cross-Cultural Psychology*, 33 (2002), pp. 346–357.

119. W.B. Gudykunst, Y. Matsumoto, S. Ting-Toomey, T. Nishida, K. Kim, and S. Heyman, 'The influence of cultural individualism-collectivism, self construals, and individual values in communication styles across cultures,' *Human Communication Research*, 22 (1996), pp. 10–543.

120. S. Shavitt and M.R. Nelson, 'The role of attitude functions and social judgment,' in J.P. Dillard and M. Pau (eds), *The Persuasion Handbook: Theory and Practice* (Sage, Thousand Oaks, CA, 2002), pp. 137–154.

121. P.L. Chang and M.H. Chieng, 'Building consumer-brand relationship: A cross-cultural experiential view,' *Psychology and Marketing*, 23, 11 (2006), pp. 927–959.

122. Bowman, 'Commercials rise in the East,' p. 11.

123. C. Lee and R.L. Green, 'Cross-cultural examination of the Fishbein behavioral intentions model,' *Journal of International Business Studies*, 22 (1991), pp. 289–305.

124. N.K. Malhotra and J.D. McCort, 'A cross-cultural comparison of behavioral intention models,' *International Marketing Review*, 18 (2001), pp. 235–269.

125. G.W. Cheung and R.B. Rensvold, 'Assessing extreme and acquiescence response sets in cross-cultural research using structural equations modelling,' *Journal of Cross-Cultural Psychology*, 31 (2000), pp. 187–212.

126. Goodyear Dunlop Tires, *Pan-European Market Research into Ecological Awareness Amongst Drivers*.

127. Data from Eurobarometer and EMS of various years (see Appendix B.)

128. N. Mundorf, R.R. Dholakia, N. Dholakia, and S. Westin, 'German and American consumer orientations to information technologies: Implications for marketing and public policies,' in L.A. Manrai and A.K. Manrai (eds), *Global Perspectives in Cross-cultural and Cross-national*

Consumer Research (International Business Press/Haworth Press, New York, London, 1996), pp. 125–144.

129. *Food–Related Risks* (Special Eurobarometer 354, 2010).

130. American Medical Association (AMA), in K. De Rijck, 'Vlaming grijpt naar antibiotica, Nederlander "ziekt uit" [Belgian people take antibiotics while the Dutch just wait till they recover without antibiotics],' *De Standaard* (2 April 2002).

131. R. Kamineni and A. O'Cass, 'The effect of materialism, gender and nationality on consumer perception of a high priced brand,' *ANZMAC 2000 Visionary Marketing for the 21st Century: Facing the Challenge* (2000), pp. 614–618.

132. G. Ger and R.W. Belk, 'Cross-cultural differences in materialism,' *Journal of Economic Psychology*, 17 (1996), pp. 55–77.

133. R.R. Sinkovics and H.H. Holzmüller, 'National differences in materialism: Using alternative research strategies to explore the construct,' *Journal of International Consumer Marketing*, 13 (2001), pp. 103–134.

134. L. Chiagouris and L.E. Mitchell, 'The new materialists,' in L.R. Kahle and L. Chiagouris (eds), *Values, Lifestyles and Psychographics* (Lawrence Erlbaum, Mahwah, NJ, 1997), pp. 263–282.

135. R. Inglehart, *Modernization and Postmodernization: Cultural, Economic, and Political Change in 43 Societies* (Princeton University Press, Princeton, NJ, 1997), p. 4.

136. Data EMS, various years.

137. Ger and Belk, 'Cross-cultural differences in materialism.' The 12 countries were Romania, United States, New Zealand, Ukraine, Germany, Turkey, Israel, Thailand, India, United Kingdom, France, and Sweden.

138. Ukraine excluded.

139. I. Clarke III and K.S. Micken, 'An exploratory cross-cultural analysis of the values of materialism,' *Journal of International Consumer Marketing*, 14, 4 (2002), pp. 65–89.

140. A. Müller-Peters, 'The significance of national pride and national identity to the attitude toward the single European currency: A Europe-wide comparison,' *Journal of Economic Psychology*, 19 (1998), pp. 702–719.

141. J.C. Usunier, *Marketing Across Cultures*, 3rd edn (Pearson Education, Harlow, UK, 1999), p. 158.

142. G. Balabanis, R. Mueller, and T.C. Melewar, 'The relationship between consumer ethnocentrism and human values,' *Journal of Global Marketing*, 15 (2002), pp. 7–37.

143. R. Batra, V. Ramaswamy, D. Alden, J.B. Steenkamp, and S. Ramachander, 'Effects of brand local and nonlocal origin on consumer attitudes in developing countries,' *Journal of Consumer Psychology*, 9 (2000), pp. 83–95.

144. Y-A. Huang, I. Phau, and C. Lin, 'Effects of animosity and allocentrism on consumer ethnocentrism: Social identity on consumer willingness to purchase,' *Asia Pacific Management Review*, 15, 3 (2010), pp. 359–376.

145. T. Shimp and S. Sharma, 'Consumer ethnocentrism: Construction and validation of the CETSCALE,' *Journal of Marketing Research*, 24 (1987), pp. 280–289.

146. *Patriot Games: Consumer Preferences for National Products* (May 2004). Available at: www.zonalatina.com/Zldata19.htm (accessed May 2004).

147. J.J. Watson and K. Wright, 'Consumer ethnocentrism and attitudes toward domestic and foreign products,' *European Journal of Marketing*, 34, 910 (2000), pp. 1149–1166.

148. Hamin and G. Elliott, 'A less-developed country perspective of consumer ethnocentrism and "country of origin" effects: Indonesian evidence,' *Asia Pacific Journal of Marketing and Logistics*, 18, 2 (2006), pp. 79–92.

149. J. Park, 'Comparison of consumer ethnocentrism in developed and developing countries,' *Journal of Global Media Studies*, 20 (2017), pp. 49–61.

150. J.G. Helgeson, L.H.V. Kurpis, M. Supphellen, and A. Ekici, 'Consumers' use of Country-of-Manufacture information? Norway and the United States: Ethnocentric, economic, and cultural differences,' *Journal of International Consumer Marketing*, 29, 3 (2017), pp. 179–193.

151. *Patriot Games: Consumer Preferences for National Products* (May 2004). Available at: www.zonalatina.com/Zldata19.htm (accessed May 2004).

152. R. Mandhachitara, R.M. Shannon, and C. Hadjicharalambous, 'Why private label grocery brands have not succeeded in Asia,' *Journal of Global Marketing*, 20, 2/3 (2007), pp. 71–87.

153. 'Home-grown appeal,' special report, *M&M Europe* (June 1995), p. 6.

154. M. Bartonova, 'Consumer attitudes to brands,' *ESOMAR Newsbrief*, 10 (1998), p. 7.

155. M. Mareck, 'The European car market: National brands dominate,' *M&M Europe* (March 2000), p. 49.

156. A. Diamantopoulos, B.B. Schlegelmilch, and J.P. Du Preez, 'Lessons for pan-European marketing? The role of consumer preferences in fine-tuning the product-market fit,' *International Marketing Review*, 12 (1995), pp. 38–52; B.D. Keillor and G.T. Hult, 'A five-country study of national identity: Implications for international research and practice,' *International Marketing Review*, 16 (1999), pp. 65–82.

157. D. Maheswaran, 'Country of origin as a stereotype: Effects of consumer expertise and attribute strength on product evaluations,' *Journal of Consumer Research*, 21 (1994), pp. 354–365.

158. B.J. Moon and S.C. Jain, 'Consumer processing of foreign advertisements: Roles of country-of-origin perceptions, consumer ethnocentrism, and country attitude,' *International Business Review*, 11 (2002), pp. 117–138.

159. B. Dubois and C. Paternault, 'Does luxury have a home country? An investigation of country images in Europe,' *Marketing and Research Today* (May 1997), pp. 79–85.

160. C.W. Lee, Y.G. Suh, and B.J. Moon, 'Product-country images: The roles of country-of-origin and country-of-target in consumers' prototype product evaluations,' *Journal of International Consumer Marketing*, 13 (2001), pp. 47–62.

161. Moon and Jain, 'Consumer processing of foreign advertisements.'

162. G. Murphy, 'From geisha to Gucci,' *M&M Europe* (August 2000), pp. 24–25.

163. B.A. Agbonifoh and J.U. Elimimian, 'Attitudes of developing countries towards country-of-origin products in an era of multiple brands,' *Journal of International Consumer Marketing*, 11 (1999), pp. 97–116.

164. G.G. Mosley and D.K. Amponsah, *The Effect of Consumer Animosity and Ethnocentrism on Product Evaluations and Willingness to Buy: An Example from Ghana* (2011). Available at: http://business.troy.edu/Downloads/Publications/TSUSBS/2006SBS/2006Consumer Animosity.pdf (accessed 10 July 2011).

165. I. Abosag and M.F. Farah, 'The influence of religiously motivated consumer boycotts on brand image, loyalty and product judgment,' *European Journal of Marketing*, 48, 11/12 (2014), pp. 2262–2283.

166. P. Magnusson, S.A. Westjohn, and S. Zdravkovic, '"What? I thought Samsung was Japanese": Accurate or not, perceived country of origin matters,' *International Marketing Review*, 28, 5 (2011), pp. 454–472.

167. S. Durvasula and S. Lysonski, 'Probing the etic vs. emic nature of consumer ethnocentrism,' *Innovative Marketing*, 10, 1 (2014), pp. 7–16.

168. *Europeans' State of Mind* (Standard Eurobarometer 69.3, 2008).

169. *Attitudes of European Citizens Towards the Environment* (Special Eurobarometer report 468, 2017).

170. N. Homma, 'The continued relevance of cultural diversity,' *Marketing and Research Today* (1991), pp. 251–259.

171. *Attitudes of European Citizens Towards the Environment* (Special Eurobarometer report 295, 2008).

172. Matsumoto, *Culture and Psychology*, p. 416.

173. K. Seki, D. Matsumoto, and T.T. Imahori, 'The conceptualization and expression of intimacy in Japan and the United States,' *Journal of Cross-Cultural Psychology*, 33 (2002), pp. 303–319.

174. D. Best and J.E. Williams, 'Sex, gender, and culture,' in J.W. Berry, M.H. Segall, and Ç. Kagitçibasi (eds), *Handbook of Cross-Cultural Psychology*, Vol. 3 (Allyn & Bacon, Boston, 1997), pp. 163–212.

175. G. Hofstede, 'Comparative studies of sexual behavior: Sex as achievement or as relationship?,' in G. Hofstede (ed.), *Masculinity and Femininity: The Taboo Dimension of National Cultures* (Sage, Thousand Oaks, CA, 1998), pp. 106–116.

176. 'Naked truths for Swedes,' *The Economist* (28 February 1998), p. 31.

177. M.R. Nelson and H.J. Paek, 'Nudity of female and male models in primetime TV advertising across seven countries,' *International Journal of Advertising*, 27, 5 (2008), pp. 715–744.

178. B. Archer, 'Sex in advertising,' *M&M Europe* (September 2000), pp. 44–45.

179. K.G. Grunert, K. Brunsø, and S. Bisp, 'Food-related lifestyle: Development of a cross-culturally valid instrument for market surveillance,' in L.R. Kahle and L. Chiagouris (eds), *Values, Lifestyles and Psychographics* (Lawrence Erlbaum, Mahwah, NJ, 1997), pp. 337–354.

180. Antonides and Van Raaij, *Consumer Behavior*, p. 377.

181. Chiagouris and Mitchell, 'The new materialists,' pp. 272–273.

182. P. Sampson, 'People are people the world over: The case for psychological market segmentation,' *Marketing and Research Today* (November 1992), pp. 236–244.

183. P. Vyncke, *Imago-management: Handboek voor reclamestrategen* [Image Management: Handbook for Advertising Strategists] (Mys & Breesch, Uitgevers & College Uitgevers, Gent, Belgium, 1992).

184. F. Hansen, 'From life style to value systems to simplicity,' *Advances in Consumer Research*, 25 (1998), pp. 181–195.

185. Grunert et al. 'Food-related lifestyle,' pp. 337–338.

186. S.P. Douglas and C.D. Urban, 'Lifestyle analysis to profile women in international markets. Can the same segmentation strategies be used?,' *Journal of Marketing* (July 1977), pp. 46–54.

187. A. Eshgi and J.N. Sheth, 'The globalization of consumption patterns: An empirical investigation,' in E. Kaynak (ed.), *Global Perspectives in Marketing* (Praeger, New York, 1985), pp. 133–148.

188. S.H.C. Tai and J.L.M. Tam, 'A comparative study of Chinese consumers in Asian markets: A lifestyle analysis,' *Journal of International Consumer Marketing*, 9 (1996), pp. 25–42; R. Wei, 'Emerging lifestyles in China and consequences for perception of advertising, buying behavior and consumption preferences,' *International Journal of Advertising*, 16 (1997), pp. 261–275.

189. M. Friedman, P. Vanden Abeele, and K. De Vos, 'Boorstin's consumption community concept: A tale of two countries,' *Journal of Consumer Policy*, 16 (1993), pp. 35–60.

190. TGI, *European Women Report*. Available at: www.bmrb.co.uk.womensreportch2.htm.

191. T.T.T. Wee, 'An exploration of a global teenage lifestyle in Asian societies,' *Journal of Consumer Marketing*, 16 (1999), pp. 365–375.

Social Processes

A human is human because of other people, according to the African concept of *ubuntu*.[1] In Chapter 4 this illustrated collectivism, but also in individualistic cultures the self is not an isolated unity; it is always part of a social environment, but in some cultures the self is less integrated into the social environment than in others. The self in the social environment is the topic of this chapter, which deals with the processes, or the *hows* of consumer behavior, that mostly are derived from social and cognitive psychology. Social psychology examines how we relate to other people, and cognitive psychology is concerned with internal processes, or what goes on in the mind. This chapter covers the social processes that include motivation, needs and drives, emotion, and group processes. All are processes that steer behavior. Although some emotions are internal, many relate to interaction with the social environment. Motivation theories such as those developed by Abraham Maslow, or Sigmund Freud's theories of structure and functioning of the mind, implicitly carry the culture of the country of origin because they were formed in the social environment of the theorists.

Motivation, Needs, and Drives

The study of motivation, the mixture of wants, needs, and drives within the individual, is of prime importance to understanding behavior. Motivation research seeks to find the underlying *why* of our behavior; it seeks to identify the attitudes, beliefs, motives, and other pressures that influence our purchase decisions. Understanding the variation of what motivates people is important for explaining product behavior, brand preference, media behavior and for developing effective advertising.

Motivation can be defined as the internal state of an organism that drives it to behave in a certain way.[2] *Drives* are the motivational forces that cause individuals to be active and to strive for certain goals. There are three main types of explanations of motivation:

1. Physiological explanations that emphasize the importance of *internal* drives or needs, also called *primary* drives, because of their importance to the organism.

Hunger and thirst are the primary drives for food or drink. Internal physiological drives are based on the process of *homeostasis* by which we maintain a reasonable constant internal (biological/physical) environment.

2. Behavioral explanations that rely on acquired drives through learning are called *external* drives. We have learned to adapt to external circumstances, for example, avoiding extreme temperatures.

3. Psychological explanations tend to apply to complex human behaviors. 'Motivation in the psychological sense is generally conceived in terms of process, or a series of processes, which somehow start, steer, sustain and finally stop a goal-directed sequence of behavior.'[3]

In Chapter 3 the relationship between climate and homeostasis was discussed. Both external drives, because they are based on learning, and psychological drives, because they concern the self, are culture bound.

Freud

Many motivation theories are based on Freud's idea of anxiety. In consumer behavior theory, Freud's theory is applied to motivation and needs.[4] Freud assumed that the mind is divided into three parts. First, there is the *Id* that contains sexual and aggressive instincts and is located in the unconscious mind. The sexual instinct is known as libido. The Id works in accord with the pleasure principle. Second, there is the *Ego*, or the conscious rational mind. It works on the reality principle. Third, there is the *Superego* that is partly conscious and partly unconscious. It consists of the conscience and ego ideal. Conscience makes people feel guilt. The ego ideal is formed through the use of reward. The Id contains basic motivational forces.

In developing his concepts of the Id, Ego, and Superego, Freud was a true product of Austrian–Hungarian culture. Austria and Hungary score extremely low on power distance and high on uncertainty avoidance. Strong uncertainty avoidance implies that parents raise their children with the message that life is threatening and dangerous, so the children have to create structures to cope with threat. If combined with large power distance, this attitude does not pose a problem for children, as parents will create the structures for them. Parents guard and guide their children. Low power distance, however, implies that children become independent at an early age and have to structure reality themselves. This leads to frustration. Freud's Superego is meant to control the Id, thus take the role of the parent. It serves as an inner uncertainty-absorbing device.[5] One conclusion is that if Freud's theory is true or useful, it will be most useful for Austrians and Hungarians and other cultures of a similar configuration of dimensions. It will be less useful for cultures of weak uncertainty avoidance, such as the UK and Scandinavia, or for cultures of large power distance, such as France and most Asian cultures.

Maslow

Maslow[6] arranged human needs in a hierarchy of importance: physiological needs, safety needs, social needs, esteem needs, and self-actualization. His *hierarchy of needs* concept is based on the assumption that a person's behavior is directed at satisfying needs and that some needs take precedence over others when the individual is faced with choices as to which needs to satisfy. *Physiological* needs will take precedence over *security* or *safety,* the need for *group membership* or *esteem* needs. The ultimate need then is *self-actualization.* Figure 5.1 depicts Maslow's hierarchy of needs.

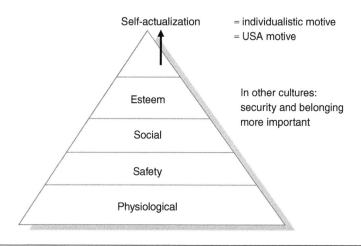

Figure 5.1   Maslow's hierarchy of needs

This order is generally presented as universal for mankind, but several authors have argued that it is defined by culture. A universal human pattern may be that physiological needs take precedence over higher-order needs, but the nonphysiological needs as such and their ranking varies across cultures. Self-actualization is a highly individualistic motive. In collectivistic cultures, what will be actualized is the interest and honor of the in-group rather than its individual members. In collectivistic cultures, belonging and safety will converge; it is very unsafe to distinguish oneself from the group.[7]

How much *self-actualization* is defined from the individualistic, Anglo-American perspective can be understood from the description of self-actualized individuals by the British psychologist Eysenck: 'Self-actualized individuals are characterized by an acceptance of themselves, spontaneity, the need for privacy, resistance to cultural influences, empathy, profound interpersonal relationships, a democratic character structure, creativeness and a philosophical sense of humor.'[8]

McClelland

According to David McClelland, there is a theory of motivation to go with every field of human endeavor. 'People do various things frequently and infer that therefore they must want to do them. People eat, so they must want to eat. Some people do well in school, so we infer they have a need for academic success.'[9] McClelland distinguished three specific needs: achievement, power, and affiliation. He defined the need for *achievement* as a desire to do things better or to surpass standards of excellence. If food is the reward or incentive for the hunger drive, 'doing something better' is the natural incentive for the achievement motive. A high need for achievement is assumed to affect performance. The goal of the *power* motive is exerting influence. One way individuals can appear powerful in a socially acceptable way is to collect symbols of power or *prestige* possessions. At the time of measurement (1975) in the United States, such prestige objects included a color television set, a rifle or pistol, and a convertible car for adults. Prestige possessions for students were cars, wine glasses, college banners, a tape recorder, wall hangings, and an electric typewriter. *Affiliation* was linked with harmonious relations, fear of rejection, and intimacy.

Like Maslow's theory, McClelland's theory of achievement motive is directly related to two cultural dimensions relevant for the United States: high masculinity and low uncertainty avoidance. People of this cultural configuration are motivated by the expectancy of some kind of result from their acts, and by extrinsic reasons and rewards.[10] In collectivistic cultures the motivation to achieve includes the self and others. When one's group succeeds, the success accrues to the self, and, similarly, when the self succeeds, so does the group. In a study that compared Turkish and Belgian participants, the Turkish motivation for achievement included a component of loyalty (to their families and the larger society) as well as a component of self-realization, which was the sole motivating factor among the Belgian participants.[11] Group achievement need in collectivistic cultures of high masculinity explains the problems that arise when Japanese companies merge, where groups of workers of the original companies remain hostile for a long time. Workers of one company have historically competed with workers of the other company's collectivities. Nelson and Shavitt[12] relate achievement needs to vertical individualism, rather than to horizontal individualism (see Chapter 4, section on the concept of self).

Culture-Related Consumer Needs and Motives

Consumption can be driven by functional or social needs. Clothes satisfy a functional need; fashion satisfies a social need. A house serves a functional need; a home serves a social need. A car may satisfy a functional need, but the type of car can satisfy a social need. Products can be distinguished between those that are products bought mainly for utilitarian reasons and those that are bought for more symbolic reasons, but often there is no clear-cut distinction between the two types. In some countries, high quality has a symbolic function, and in others a utilitarian function. For a car, latest technology may be viewed as a universal motive, but the associations linked to technology may be different across individuals and across cultures. *Latest technology* may be associated with *sporty* in one culture, with *fuel economy* in another culture, and with *prestige* in again another culture.[13]

People's behavior is not only determined by their needs and motivations but also by their surroundings and the context in which they make decisions. These contextual variables vary considerably from one country to another. 'People across cultures can do the same thing for different reasons or motives, and people in different countries may do different things for the same reasons.'[14] Buying motives are strongly related to the social environment. Many global standard products, assumed to be culture free, are bought for different reasons across cultures.

Already in 1975 differences were found in product attribute appeals of soft drinks and toothpaste in the United States, France, India, and Brazil. Even though the basic products essentially served the same need in each country, several cultural and environmental factors influenced the characteristics of the product that people emphasized in its purchase. For soft drinks, people from Brazil, France, and India rated the attribute 'contains no artificial ingredients' higher than did the US sample. Americans placed high importance on 'taste' and 'convenience.' For toothpaste the French rated high 'kills germs in the mouth.' Americans placed greater emphasis than the French on attributes not directly associated with the primary function of the product, such as 'well-known brand,' 'freshens the mouth,' and 'brightens teeth.' For the Brazilians other nonfunctional attributes were important, such as 'color of toothpaste' and 'tube squeezes easily.' In addition, the Brazilians rated the family-oriented attribute 'children like it' higher than the US sample did.[15]

Differences in sensitivity to certain product attributes and varying buying motives can be explained by the underlying cultural values that vary by product category. In some cultures certain motives may be considered 'prototypical' for a specific product category. For example, for mineral water, in the high uncertainty avoidance cultures a generic motive is purity; for luxury alcoholic beverages it may be social status in high power distance cultures and self-enhancement in short-term-oriented cultures. For cars, motives vary among safety, status, design, and prestige, all based on different cultural values. A comparative study of clothing motives of professional women in New York and Bangkok, found differences in motives that influence fashion clothing decisions. For example, professional women in New York were more motivated to conform to the norms for business clothes than their counterparts in Bangkok. Bangkok business women scored higher than their New York counterparts in variety seeking in fashion clothing decisions.[16]

Buying motives can be recognized in the appeals used in advertising. Several scholars have developed lists of consumption motives by analyzing advertising. Pollay's[17] list of values in advertising is one of the early inventories. Some motives may exist across cultures, but the degree of importance will vary. One product attribute that seems appealing across different markets cannot be generalized, as it may differ as to level of importance.[18] Examples of motives that vary by culture are the status motive, environmentalism, purity, and convenience.

The Status Motive

There are substantial differences in status needs across countries, and income differences have no explanatory power. In India, for example there is demand for high-status consumption goods among the low-income groups.[19] Status motives vary with power distance, individualism/collectivism, and masculinity, for different reasons. Comparison across nations has not shown a relationship between preferences for status articles and GNI/cap. A study comparing five countries (Saudi Arabia, Germany, Poland, Turkey and Portugal) found no relationship between the use of status symbols and market development. In so-called mature markets status needs were not stronger than in developing markets. The most important dimension found that explained differences in status needs was power distance.[20]

Because luxury articles can be used as manifestations of one's material success, they are more attractive to members of masculine cultures than to members of feminine cultures who are more reluctant to show off. They can serve as symbols to express success and achievement. In the United States, a masculine culture, the need for success and the search for status symbols is strong. Differences in status needs are also explained by power distance, but the type of status need is different. In high power distance cultures, positions and social status are not fluid, and people want to demonstrate their position in society.

Many Western brands have served the purpose of social status in high power distance and collectivistic cultures. Indians, for example, tend to drink Coca-Cola for the image, not for the taste. The choice is dependent on the context. Whereas in a simple restaurant one might just choose an orange- or lemon-flavored drink, in a more expensive hotel or restaurant one would order a cola.

Table 5.1 gives an overview of the correlations among masculinity, power distance, and a few luxury articles. EMS provides data on ownership of various luxury articles across Europe that may serve as status symbols. These are expensive clothes, shoes, fragrance, watches and jewelry. Euromonitor provides sales data for real jewelry. Even for this category national wealth has no explaining power in any part of the world. None of the items in Table 5.1 correlated significantly with GNI/cap. The only significant correlations were with masculinity or power distance.

Table 5.1   **Status needs and masculinity: Correlation coefficients for selected products**

Watches owned	PDI	Mas/Fem
1997 Value main watch over $1,600		.56*
2007 Value main watch over €750		.62**
1997 Own suit or dress over $800		.68***
2007 In past year bought suit or dress over €750		.58*
2012 In past year bought suit over €1,000	.61**	
2007 In past year bought shoes or boots over €300	.61**	
2012 In past year bought shoes or boots over €500	.64***	
2007 In past year bought fragrance over €75	.64***	.50*
2012 In past year bought fragrance over €75	.86***	
2007 In past year bought jewelry over €1,500		.77***
Sales real jewelry (in value)		
Worldwide 44 countries		.44*
26 developed countries worldwide (GNP/cap > $8,000)		.61***
Europe 15 countries		.51*

SOURCES: Hofstede et al. (2010) (see Appendix A); EMS 1997, 2007 and 2012; Euromonitor, 1997 (see Appendix B)

Also the wish to wear the latest fashion is a matter of status. As early as 1970,[21] the percentage of answers 'wholly true' to the statement 'I dress as far as possible according to the latest fashion' correlated with high masculinity ($r = .53*$). Generally brands are more important in masculine cultures than in feminine cultures, where fewer people say that the brand name is an important factor that influences food choice.[22]

Whereas in masculine cultures cars have high status value for young men, this is less so in feminine cultures. In Japan, young men need a car to attract girlfriends. In Malaysia, attitudes to cars are different. In 1995, a commercial for a new sports car, the Bufori, showed four women going to a marriage bureau in search of an ideal husband, and ended with the line by a model who said, 'I don't care who you are, or what you look like, if you drive a Bufori, I am yours.' Two women's organizations objected and the campaign had to stop. The advertising agency reacted saying the commercial was intended to be funny, cheeky and entertaining.[23] Playing with important cultural values can cause resistance.

In collectivistic cultures a high price delivers status. A high price is associated with quality, and high quality contains social meaning for consumers in collectivistic cultures more than in individualistic cultures. This also explains the success of pricey luxury brands in Asian markets, in which price not only signals high quality but also social status, prestige, and belonging. Some perfume companies have reported that in Asia they sell more perfumes by increasing prices than by lowering prices.[24] Also in Russia, which scores very high on power distance, luxury brands have become very popular.

A retail study in 2007 showed that for East Europeans, in particular Russian women, the most important criteria to select a retail store were style and quality of clothing/merchandise. Estimates from the European Fashion and Textile Export Council indicated that Russian women were one of the biggest evolving consumer markets for high-end fashion and accessories. These customers were also found to be very label conscious. Highly visible items are chosen to be 'status symbols' of wealth, sophistication, or success. More 'value for the dollar' variables were not ranked among the top attributes in the shopping criteria for the retail stores in Eastern European countries.[25]

An example of a luxury product that fulfills the desire for the latter type of status in Europe is Scotch whisky. For 13 countries in continental Europe,[26] there is a significant correlation between regular consumption of Scotch whisky and power distance ($r = .74***$). Also, drinking aperitifs and champagne are social status-reinforcing habits.

Luxury brands generally have a status-enhancing function, but luxury is a multi-faceted concept with strong cross-cultural differences in the meanings of luxury, and the product or brand features that represent these various meanings. For the individualistic cultures it is *exclusivity*, for high power distance cultures it is *prestige*; for the feminine cultures it can be *quality*, for the masculine cultures it can be *expensive*. [27]

Figure 5.2 shows how cultures can be mapped according to the different status motives.

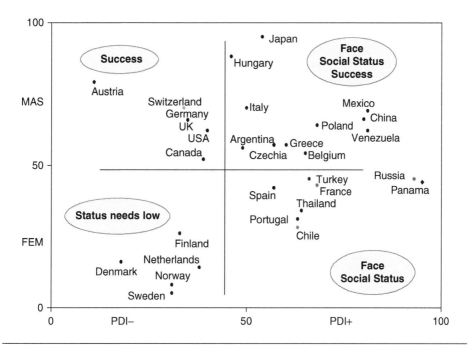

Figure 5.2 **Status needs and motives**

SOURCE: Data from Hofstede et al. (2010) (see Appendix A)

Face

An expression related to social status that entered the English language from the Chinese is *face*, a characteristic of collectivistic cultures. In general, *face* describes the proper relationship with one's social environment, which is as essential to a person (and that person's family) as the front part of his or her head. Social roles shape people's identities and constitute desirable images, and the more a person is expected to fulfill his or her social role, the more he or she is perceived as losing face when failing to do so. Face is lost when an individual, either through his action or that of people close to him, fails to meet essential requirements placed upon him by his social position.[28] Other collectivistic cultures have linguistic equivalents, for example, the Japanese *tatemae* or Greek *philotimos*.

The original Chinese concept of face (*mianzi*) includes social self-esteem and social recognition. *Mianzi* can be lost, maintained or enhanced during interaction. Another Chinese concept is *guanxi*, a type of relationship that bonds through reciprocal obligations. These concepts remain relevant, also for younger people.[29]

Avoiding loss of face is of overriding concern. Losing face is a damaging social event in which one's action is publicly and negatively judged by others, resulting in a loss of moral or social standing. Failure to maintain or protect one's face has adverse implications for social functioning. Consumption of luxury goods is regarded as a behavior to maintain and enhance one's face.[30] In 2004, 29% of the total turnover of LMVH and 58% of turnover of Cognac producer Rémy Martin was concentrated in Asia.[31] In China, status appeals are heavily used in advertising.[32] Yet, next to face saving, also group orientation is an important driver of luxury among East Asian consumers. Some aspects of luxury, such as hedonism and the perception of conspicuousness do not contribute to positive group orientation. Face saving also does not influence quality perceptions of luxury products.[33]

Upholding face goes with avoiding social embarrassment. Social embarrassment occurs when seen by others when buying, for example, intimate products. Avoidance of social embarrassment has been used in India as advertising appeals for several product categories such as deodorants or detergents, for example, being punished by your teacher for not wearing clean clothes.[34]

Green Motives, the Environment

Awareness of the environmental impact of consumption is increasing, but more in some areas than in others. (Some of the attitudes toward the environment were discussed in Chapter 4.) Overall awareness of environmental issues is relatively high, but it varies by country. Across 25 European countries, the percentages of people who say they are *fully aware* of the impact vary between 4.4% in Finland and 32.4% in France. In most countries the majority of people agree with the importance of taking into account a product's impact on the environment for making a buying decision, which is more than the percentage of people who attribute the same importance to the product's brand or brand name for making a buying decision. The environment is viewed of greater importance in collectivistic cultures of high uncertainty avoidance, which explains 32% of variance.[35] However, various data show that in the low power distance and low uncertainty avoidance cultures, people's behavior is more active with respect to environmental behavior. In cultures where people think the environment of high importance, they don't necessarily act accordingly.

In Chapter 4 we saw that across Europe, willingness to buy environmentally friendly products has not increased in the past years and attitudes and associations with the environment vary. As a motive, environmentally friendliness may also vary by product category as well as by culture. We have seen that actually having bought environmentally friendly products relates to low power distance and low uncertainty avoidance.

Purity

The need for purity is manifested in different ways and related to the product categories food, drink, and cleaning products. Cross-cultural variations in purity needs are explained by uncertainty avoidance. In Japan, high on uncertainty avoidance, cleanliness has historically been an important need. European visitors already reported it around the turn of the sixteenth century. The Japanese have a horror of filth. Most people have at least one bath a day.[36] Modern technology, providing all sorts of antibacterial products, has reinforced this need for purity. Shops sell germ-free pens, bicycle handles, telephones, tea towels, toothpaste, and underwear, all impregnated with antiseptic chemicals. Such products are called *kokin guzzu*, or antibacterial goods designed to get rid of germs on things with which people come into contact.

Varying purity needs are reflected in the differences in consumption of mineral water and all sorts of processed foods, as well as in the varying volume of soap powder used. In Europe, in high uncertainty avoidance cultures, people drink more mineral water and use more soap powder and household cleaning products. Data of 2015 for 25 European countries show a significant correlation between bottled water consumption and uncertainty avoidance ($r = .60**$).[37] The need for purity in food is related to perceived food safety. In 1998 Eurobarometer measured the elements that determine food safety. The responses 'absence of preservatives' correlated with high uncertainty avoidance ($r =. 67***$).[38] The purity motive is recognized in advertising for many beverages, but also for soap powder. Figure 5.3 gives examples from various countries.

Freshness in food is another culture-bound motive but is also related to individualism/collectivism. What is considered fresh in food merchandise varies. In the south of Europe, what is considered fresh is what people prepare themselves, so the whole salad or fish, not fresh fish cut into pieces and presented in a Styrofoam dish covered with plastic. In the North of Europe, anything that is not tinned or frozen is considered fresh.

Figure 5.3 **Purity in advertising**

Convenience

The convenience motive refers to the value placed on, and the active search for, products and services that provide personal comfort and/or save time in performing various activities. Convenience-driven demand is assumed to exist for products and services like frozen food, food processors, microwave ovens, and drive-in restaurants. The need for convenience is related to individualism, low uncertainty avoidance, and short-term orientation, but the relationships vary by product type. Short-term orientation (LTO-), correlates significantly with usage of ready-made food products such as breakfast cereals and potato crisps, but there is a stronger relationship with IVR. Use of deodorants and headache remedies have a stronger relationship with short-term orientation. For usage of electric dishwashers and microwave ovens comparison worldwide still shows the strongest relationship with GNI/cap.[39] In 2001, 41% of variance of convenience as a motive for food choice was explained by low uncertainty avoidance, and an additional 25% by low masculinity.[40] Low uncertainty avoidance explains 36% of variance of convenience that influences food choice.[41] Thirty percent of variance of minutes spent on eating is explained by long-term orientation.[42] Figure 5.4 illustrates the latter relationship for 14 countries.

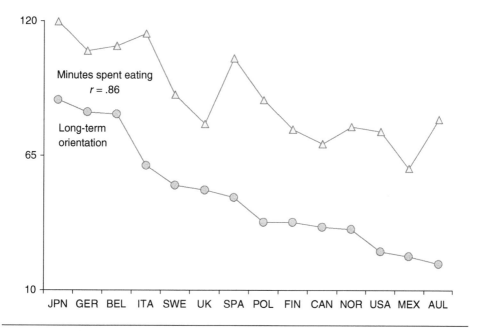

Figure 5.4   **Minutes spent eating**

SOURCE: Hofstede et al. (2010) (see Appendix A); *Society at a Glance* (2009) OECD Social Indicators (see Appendix B)

The configuration of dimensions explaining convenience orientation is the opposite of the cultural configuration of Italy, the country that harbors the propagators of 'slow food.' In 1986 in Rome, the Slow Food International Movement was founded. It claims 60,000 members, holds conferences, and protests fast food through education and information.[43]

One function of convenience is saving time, but this is not a universal motive for buying microwave ovens. Whereas in the United States, a nation of snack food and dashboard dining, the buying motive for microwave ovens may be the timesaving feature, in other cultures the motive is different. Similar to food processors, in cultures where food consumption is considered to be a social event, the microwave oven is a device that enables people to prepare more refined dishes, so people can spend even more time on cooking. Whereas in the United States people tend to think of food as something to pop into the microwave oven, in Spain much attention is given to cooking two meals a day or at least the main meal or *comida*. Microwave ovens are used to make meals even more perfect. Even on vacation, people cook meals. At some Spanish camping sites, every section has a special tent for placing your oven.

Car-Buying Motives

Several surveys have asked consumers questions about car-buying motives. EMS, for example, asks respondents, 'Which of the following factors are the most important in choosing your main car?' Four of the response choices in 1997 were 'safety,' 'fuel economy,' 'enjoyable to drive,' and 'distinctive design.' Another four in 1999 were 'car interior,' 'environmentally friendly,' 'importance of an international image,' and 'I would always choose a European make of car.' In 2007 these motives were repeated, adding a few others like

Table 5.2 **Factors of importance for the choice of car, Europe, significant correlations 1997/2007**

	PDI	IDV	MAS	UAI	LTO
Factor to choose car					
Progressive styling	−.69***				
Design		.49*			
Car interior					.76***
Engine performance					−.66**
Price					−.57*
Technology				.51*	
Country of origin				.58*	
Car security			.71**		.50*

SOURCES: Hofstede et al. (2010) (see Appendix A); EMS 1997, 1999 and 2007 (see Appendix B)

'engine performance,' 'price,' and 'technology.' Few of these motives were related to GNI/ capita, only fuel economy, enjoyment to drive, design (1997) and international image (1999). Some have no relationship at all with either GNI/cap or culture. These motives may be generic and valid everywhere. Several motives vary by culture and are related to different dimensions. Table 5.2 shows the correlation coefficients of the cultural variables with the different factors of car choice.

Fuel economy was related to GNI/cap and to short-term orientation in 1997, but these relationships had disappeared in 2007. Safety generally is viewed to be a universal attribute, because everybody wants a safe car, and nowadays basically all cars are safe so this may have become a generic motive. Design can be associated with status feelings but also be an expression of individuality, expressing uniqueness of the owner. Environmental friendliness obviously is not a culture specific motive anymore. Engine performance and price are specifically important in short-term-oriented cultures, whereas car security and car interior are more important in long-term oriented cultures. Technology is an issue of most importance in high uncertainty avoidance cultures. Other data have shown that car safety also is related to low masculinity, when it concerns the wish to protect the weak. The EMS

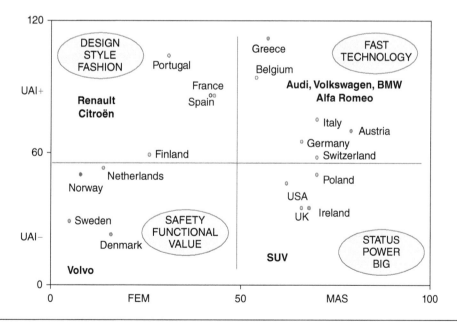

Figure 5.5   **Car buying motives**

SOURCE: Hofstede et al. (2010) (see Appendix A)

questions were referring to safety accessories such as airbags, which have become standard in cars. Safety is a multi-faceted motive.

Figure 5.5 shows motives for buying automobiles by cultural clusters according to two of Hofstede's dimensions, masculinity and uncertainty avoidance. These motives are recognized in the design of cars and in the appeals used by advertisers of successful car brands, found from content analysis of advertising.

The lower left quadrant shows the configuration of low masculinity and weak uncertainty avoidance. In this culture cluster, people have a preference for safety to protect the family and value for money. Safety (to protect the weak) and the functional aspects of a car are more important than technology or design. The Swedish Volvo car brand is well known for the safety claim. In feminine cultures, people have little interest in the motor of their car. Data from several surveys show that they don't even know the size of their car engines, as compared with masculine cultures. The lower right quadrant shows a cluster of cultures with the configuration masculinity and weak uncertainty avoidance. People in these cultures have status needs to show their success and prefer cars with big, powerful motors. This is the culture cluster where people will be most attracted to the sturdy SUV (sport utility vehicle). The upper right quadrant shows the cluster of cultures with the configuration of masculinity and strong uncertainty avoidance. People in these cultures are aggressive drivers, and they prefer cars with rapid acceleration. Speed of a car is an important motive. This seems paradoxical, as one would expect to see risk aversion translated into a safety motive. Not so: the explanation is that people of strong uncertainty avoidance cultures build up stress, which they also want to release. Fast and aggressive driving serves as an emotional safety valve. It demonstrates that uncertainty avoidance is not the same as risk avoidance. But cars must also be technologically advanced, well designed, and well tested. These are the cultures where people prefer the German brands like Audi and BMW and the Italian Alfa Romeo. Volkswagen's claim, *Vorsprung durch Technik* ('Headstart through technology'), reflects the technology motive. In the upper left quadrant, in the combination of low masculine and strong uncertainty avoidance, one sees the need for 'sporty' driving, fast acceleration but not so aggressive. This is combined with a preference for design (but more in the art/fashion sphere), pleasure, and enjoyment. This is the area where the stylish brands like Renault and Citroën originate. Most of the countries in the upper quadrants are also high power distance, so social status is a motive in both quadrants.

Emotion

Emotion is not a well-defined concept, neither in psychology nor in advertising. In psychology, emotion is generally described as a process that involves interaction between cognition and physiology, meaning the mind influences the body and vice versa. Emotion involves bodily (physiological) changes and, on the mental side, a state of excitement or disturbance marked by a strong feeling.[44] The basic emotions concept includes the notion that emotions form independent and integral wholes in which various components (e.g., experience, facial expression, and physiological response) are closely linked together.

In Anglo-Saxon literature, emotions and thinking are classified as different kinds of phenomena. Emotions appear to be natural phenomena governed by biological mechanisms that are beyond control. In contrast, thinking appears to be voluntary, learned, controlled, and dependent upon cultural symbols and concepts. Emotions are associated with art, beauty, poetry, and music. Thinking is associated with logic, science, calculation. Clear thinking supposedly requires eliminating emotions. Other cultures have different concepts of emotions.

Numerous peoples have no word or concept for emotions, per se. They regard emotions as integrated with thinking, attitudes, motives, behavior, and fate/fortune rather than being something distinct. Western parents indulge children's emotions and encourage them to pay a great deal of attention to their emotions, while non-Western parents usually do not. American mothers tend to encourage their children to introspect about, analyze, and discuss their feelings, which Chinese mothers don't do.[45]

Emotions are affective responses that are learned. This aspect of emotion makes it culture bound. It is unlikely that people in all cultures have learned to express their own feelings and to recognize feelings of others in the same way. Yet, emotion psychologists have argued that many emotions are universal, although the components of emotion are embedded in the sociocultural environment.[46] Matsumoto and Hwang[47] state that not all affective states should be called 'emotion' and a distinction should be made between biological versus cultural emotions. Emotions that may be biologically innate are different from those that are not and different domains of emotion are more relatively influenced by biology or culture. Across cultures we create meanings about emotion via concepts, attitudes, values and beliefs. Not all emotion terms in one language have an equivalent in another. This also applies to the word emotion that in American-English refers to an internal state that focuses on affect, but in other languages to relationships among people or between people and events.

Whereas in European–American culture, emotions, such as joy and anger, are constructed primarily as internal experiences, they are inherently more social and relational in non-Western cultures.[48] The psychologists Mesquita and Frijda[49] reviewed various elements of emotions across cultures and concluded that global statements about cross-cultural universality of emotion, or about their cultural determination, are inappropriate. Several elements of emotion, but not all, are related to culture. For example, among individualistic independent selves, 'ego-focused' emotions (e.g., anger, frustration, and pride) are more marked than among collectivistic, interdependent selves where 'other-focused' emotions (such as sympathy, shame, and feelings of interpersonal communion) are more marked.

Whereas in the United Kingdom happiness is positively related to feelings of independence, in collectivistic Greece happiness is negatively related to independence.[50] The very concepts, definitions, understandings, and meanings of emotion can differ across cultures.

American prize-winning TV commercials tend to display the quintessential American type of feelings and emotions as described by the Japanese American psychologist David Matsumoto.

> In the United States, we place a premium on feelings. We all recognize that each of us is unique and that we have our own individual feelings about the things, events, situations and people around us. We consciously try to be aware of our feelings, to be 'in touch' with them, as we say. To be in touch with our feelings and to understand the world around us emotionally is to be a mature adult in society … Much psychotherapeutic work is focused on helping individuals freely express the feelings and emotions they may have bottled up inside.[51]

Happiness is one of the strongest American emotions. 'Life, liberty and the pursuit of happiness' is one of the most famous phrases in the US Declaration of Independence, and Americans are obsessed by the pursuit of happiness. In 2008, 4,000 books were published on happiness, up from 50 in the year 2000.[52]

Universal, Basic Emotions?

Much research on emotions has been designed to test the hypothesis of the universality of basic emotions. Basic emotions were supposed to be a part of the human potential and therefore universal. One argument in favor of universal basic emotions is that most languages possess limited sets of central *emotion-labeling* words, referring to a small number of commonly occurring emotions. Examples of such words in the English language are *anger, fear, sadness*, and *joy*. Another argument is based on research on *recognition of facial expressions*. People from different cultures can recognize facial expressions in similar ways. From this it was concluded that there is also similarity in showing facial expressions, but there is no evidence that these facial expressions actually occur across cultures.[53] The question is whether it is justified to take facial expression as an index of the presence of emotions, because it is possible that in some societies emotions occur without facial expressions whereas in others facial expressions occur without emotions.[54] Seeing a facial expression allows an observer to draw a conclusion about a situation, but one specific facial expression is not necessarily connected to one specific emotion. For example, a smile is generally viewed as an expression of happiness. However, seeing a friend can make a person smile, but this does not imply that the person is happy. He or she can, in fact, be sad or lonely.

Facial expressions are only a crude measurement of emotions, and labeling a facial expression is not the same as conceptualizing emotion. Yet, many people in Western cultures implicitly believe that certain categories of emotion are natural kinds and that specific facial actions express these emotions.

Emotion and Language

English words are the core of psychologists' theories of emotion, but words for emotions vary from one culture to another. English words often assumed to denote natural basic categories of emotion have no equivalents in some other languages, and other languages provide commonly used emotion words that have no equivalent in English.[55]

Lists of English language emotion words do not cover the important emotions that exist worldwide. Examples are emotions like shame and guilt, important East Asian emotions that are generally lacking in lists of emotion words. The concept of emotion per se is not universal either. In a culture that lacks the concept of emotion, it is difficult to find out whether words refer to emotions. For many emotion words, there are no linguistic equivalents, or seemingly linguistic equivalents cover different concepts. Anger, for example, appears to be natural in Western cultures, but even across Western cultures the content varies. The American experience and organization of anger is American specific, stressing the expression of one's rights, goals, and needs. Anger occurs when these are blocked, and the person has a sense of 'I was treated unfairly.' By contrast, in collectivistic cultures anger would be a different experience because it produces separation and disconnection where connection and interdependence are so important.[56] The fact that anger is related to the concept of fairness makes it all the more culture bound because concrete notions of what is considered fair in a specific situation also vary among cultures.[57] Americans usually interpret behavior as motivated by personal traits that are consistent and persistent. Consequently, when someone hurts them they assume that this person is 'an injurious person' who warrants continued anger to defend against likely new attacks.[58]

Whereas the dominant American associations with anger identify the *causes* of anger, the Korean associations center on the *consequences* of anger,[59] which obviously implies disturbing harmony. In many English-language emotion words, the cause and situation are incorporated. *Fear* implies that a danger has appeared. *Anxiety* implies that the cause is vague or unknown. *Guilt* implies that you yourself are the causal agent of a bad outcome.

Anger implies that another has caused some harm. In collectivistic cultures emotion words are often seen as statements about the relationship between a person and an event, rather than as statements about introspection on one's internal states.

There are important cross-language differences in the meaning of *disgust*, in particular in conceptions of disgust toward the body and its products. For the Germans, the word for disgust, *Ekel,* means 'what leads to vomiting,' which also is included in the Swedish word for disgust, but not in the Dutch word. To Americans the common understanding of the word *disgust* reflects both disgust and anger. Causes of disgust are also shaped by culture. Whereas spiders are a source of disgust in many Western countries, this is not the case in China, where they are eaten as a delicacy.[60]

Some emotion terms can superficially include similar emotions, but that can be misleading. A desire typical of Japanese culture is *amae,* the desire to be dependent upon another's love and kindness, which is accepted in the context of family and other group members, in interactions between children and parents, spouses, siblings, friends and lovers, and even to a certain extent in a Japanese organizational context, but tends to be inappropriate outside a non-*amae* interaction when it is viewed as manipulative. Although in a Midland English dialect the term *mardy* suggests similar emotional elements of dependency, it comprises mainly unacceptable components, like spoilt, sulky, whining, and moody.[61]

Face and shame are typical East Asian emotions. The idea of face is Chinese in origin. In Chinese as well as Japanese, the idea of losing face is found in numerous expressions. Linguistic representation of shame and embarrassment is far richer in Chinese than in English. Chinese people are better equipped to make refined discriminations between nuances of these emotions. Avoiding shame is of overriding concern – as is the avoidance of losing face.[62]

In some cultures emotion words include multiple emotions or feelings. An example is from Japan, where *jodo* includes several emotional states, such as angry, happy, sad, and ashamed. However, *jodo* also includes what might not be called emotions: considerate, motivated, lucky, and calculating. In African languages one word covers both anger and sadness. There is no word for depression among many non-Western cultural groups. Anger is missing in some cultures. Guilt is missing in many Asian and Pacific languages. About 20% of the world's languages make no distinction between envy and jealousy, which in the United States are two different concepts.[63]

The commonly given examples of culture-specific emotion words are the German words *Schadenfreude* and *Angst. Schadenfreude* means malicious delight, enjoying other people's suffering or bad luck. In Dutch we have a similar word: *leedvermaak.* The German *Angst* is more related to anxiety than the English word *fear.* Korean words that have no linguistic equivalents in German are *uulhada* and *dapdaphada,* which can be interpreted as subcomponents of sadness. *Dapdaphada* is a feeling of loneliness resulting from the inability to express oneself in a foreign environment. *Uulhada* expresses a sort of depressive feeling, not wanting to laugh, but not wanting to cry either because there is no reason for it.[64]

Expression of Emotions

Much research in the field of human emotions is on facial expressions. For more than 100 years the argument has been whether facial expressions are innate and thus universal or socially learned and culturally controlled. The *neuro-cultural* position[65] states that there are distinctive movements of the facial muscle for each of a number of primary affect states, and these are universal for mankind. However, the emotion-eliciting stimuli, the linked feelings, the display rules, and the behavioral consequences all can vary from one culture to another. The *universalists* argue that the face reveals emotion in a way that is universally understood because a number of universal emotions, such as happiness, surprise, fear, anger, contempt, disgust, and sadness, are universally recognized from facial expressions. They base their ideas on studies of recognition of facial expressions against lists of basic emotions, based on a standard set of English terms. In the major studies, respondents have been asked to categorize the basic emotions against still photographs of facial expressions of Caucasian actors, who posed according to instructions by Anglo-American researchers (e.g., a smile for happiness, crying face for grief, wide open mouth and eyes for surprise, frown for anger, and wrinkled nose or tongue protrusion for disgust). Usually the choice respondents have to make is forced, meaning that they have to select basic emotions from a fixed list and options are mutually exclusive. This sort of study has led to high levels of recognition rates for several basic emotion categories across countries. Accuracy rates have been reported ranging from 86% for Americans down to 53% for tribes people in New Guinea (judging American facial expressions).[66] Cultural differences have been found in the level of recognition and ratings of intensity.

An alternative approach is free choice, when respondents can freely use their own descriptions of an emotion related to each facial expression. In free choice studies, facial expressions are rarely interpreted in terms of one specific category, more often in a broad range of overlapping categories that are not always emotions but are often situations. In particular, free responses by members of collectivistic cultures tend to include non-emotions, more situations.

In the process of measuring emotion by facial expression, several aspects can go wrong: the correct *recognition* of facial expressions, the *judgment of intensity,* and the *labeling* of the related emotion. Another aspect of the measurement of facial expression is the *absence of context or situation,* as such studies tend to be conducted in a laboratory setting, with no other communication or contextual cues.[67] People may judge expressions differently according to the context or event surrounding the emotion. The problem is that operationalizing context is a difficult task. Edward Hall states, 'Context never has a specific meaning. Yet the meaning of a communication is always dependent on context.'[68]

Several researchers have contributed to the understanding of the role of emotions in advertising across cultures. Many such studies try to measure the difference in persuasiveness of emotional appeals in individualistic and collectivistic cultures. An experimental approach is to use alternative (mock) advertisements with different emotions that are hypothesized to be more appealing to members of one culture than to members of another culture. An example is the measurement of the effectiveness of ego- versus other-focused emotions, using varying appeals, featuring, for example, *pride* (ego-focused emotion) or *empathy* (other-focused emotion) or *happiness*-related emotions (e.g., happy, cheerful, delighted) versus *peacefulness*-related emotion (calm, peaceful, serene). The logical approach to such studies is to keep other variables constant in order to be able to isolate the effect of the different appeals. So ads are made as similar as possible, varying only in the target emotion.[69] However, the constant variables provide the context of the emotion. Unlike individualists, collectivists have difficulties understanding the emotion properly outside the context. It is nearly impossible to find a culture-free context. Variation of copy only leaves out the role of context, which is so important in advertising. An example of background used in such studies is a beach, which is not culture free. Whereas a beach to Westerners is a place to relax, to play active sport, or have fun and adventure, in Asian countries it has different connotations. It is associated with many different activities and events, varying from special celebrations or funerals, to taking wedding pictures, to even use as a public toilet. So a beach is likely to be associated with different emotional events.

Recognition and Judgment of Expressions of Emotions

Both recognition of expressions of emotion and judgment vary across cultures. How people express their emotions, but also how people judge the expressions of emotion, are learned behavior. People of different countries and cultures learn culture-specific rules of decoding the meaning of emotion expressions. This can be due to the difference in meanings and associations of the emotion terms used as response alternatives. It can also be related to differences in *intensity* in the expression of emotions. When the Japanese express emotions, they express them less intensely than do Americans, which leads to lower intensity ratings when judging expressions.

Across cultures, people weigh facial cues differently. When interpreting emotions of others, the Japanese focus more on the eyes, whereas Americans focus on the mouth. This difference may explain why stylized facial icons seem to differ between Japan and the United States. In Internet text mails, Americans use emoticons that vary the direction of the mouth, e.g., :) and :(. Japanese emoticons vary the direction of the eyes and may not vary the direction of the mouth, e.g., ^_^ and ;_; .[70] A later, large cross-cultural study of emoticons on Twitter confirmed that when users of Twitter deliberatively select emoticons to convey intended emotions, people from collectivistic cultures will emphasize the shape of the eyes and people from individualistic cultures will highlight the shape of the mouth. This fits in a general pattern where vertical emoticons are more popular among countries with collectivistic cultures and less in individualistic cultures, but the masculinity–femininity dimension explains more. Horizontal emoticon use is less popular among countries that emphasize competition and assertiveness. Vertical emoticons are detected more frequently among countries that score high on masculinity.[71] Naturally, emotion recognition of emoticons also is not culturally universal. Japanese people were found to be sensitive to the emotion of emoticons to the same extent as the emotion of real faces, but while Cameroonian and Tanzanian people tend to discriminate the emotion of real faces, they hardly read emotion of emoticons.[72]

In China people do not generally correlate facial expressions with a discrete emotion category. Many Chinese phrases that describe facial expressions refer to more than one part of the face, for example, 'eyes wide open (with strength), mouth dumbstruck,' suggests that the speaker's mind goes blank and they are unable to say anything ('I can't say anything'); sticking out one's tongue may indicate that someone wants to say something now, but does not know what to say as if still being in a state of disbelief. [73]

Matsumoto[74] correlated the Hofstede dimensions with recognition accuracy levels and found that in individualistic cultures people are better at recognizing negative emotions than in collectivistic cultures. Hofstede explains differences in emotion recognition by the level of uncertainty avoidance. In low uncertainty avoidance cultures, where emotions are less expressed, people have learned to take cues from faces, as compared with high uncertainty avoidance cultures, where emotions are expressed in more powerful ways. There also is a relationship with the personality trait dimensions of the five-factor model.[75] (See Chapter 4, section on personal traits.)

> The ability to correctly interpret the emotional expression of customers is essential in service failure situations. A study comparing Anglo and East-Asian cultures found that service providers of different cultures were prone to misreading anger, happiness and shame expressed by dissatisfied consumers.[76]

The Canadian psychologist James Russell[77] reviewed a number of studies and summarized many discrepancies in recognition of emotions. The hypothesis that happiness, surprise, fear, anger, disgust, and sadness would be universally recognizable from facial expressions fit the data only for *happiness*. There are many examples of confusion of the other basic emotions. In particular, non-Western subjects tend to categorize expressions incorrectly. Examples are 'disgust' being confused with *contempt*, 'sadness' with *contempt* and *fear*, 'anger' with *contempt, frustration*, and *disgust*, and 'fear' being confused with *surprise*. In a study using a set of photographs of facial expressions of emotion posed by Chinese people living in Beijing, 'anger' expressions were also rated as *disgust* (and vice versa), 'surprise' as *fear*, and 'sadness' as *disgust* and *fear*.[78]

Researchers from Waseda University in Japan teamed up with Kyushi-based robot manufacturer tmsuk to develop a humanoid robot, called Kobian, that uses its entire body to express a variety of emotions. Kobian expresses seven different feelings, including delight, surprise, and disgust, as depicted in Figure 5.6.[79] The journalists who reported on this expressed difficulties in recognizing these expressions.

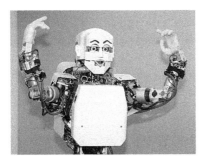

Delight

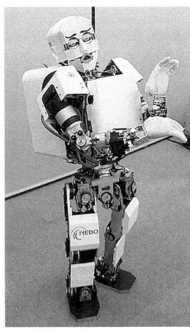

Surprise

Disgust

Figure 5.6   **Kobian: Delight, surprise, disgust**

Other studies have demonstrated that the match between the cultural background of expresser and judge is important. When members of a cultural group judge emotions expressed by members of that same cultural group, cross-cultural significance is higher. This suggests that emotions may be more accurately understood when members of the same national, ethnic, or regional group that express the emotion judge them. In heterogeneous societies, minority groups are better able to judge the emotions of majority group members than majority group members are able to judge the emotions of minority group members.[80] Emotional experience and linguistic expression are culture specific; they are learned either by growing up in a culture or by later exposure to the culture. The match between the emotional expressor and perceiver has implications for communication effectiveness. For effective advertising, the facial expression should be interpretable by the target group. This implies that for a culturally correct interpretation for each cultural group, the correct expression must be found. An example was described in Chapter 4 in the section on the body and identity. A sultry facial expression of American models is meant to express independence, whereas Japanese models present happy broad smiles to express dependence needs.

If emotions are better understood from faces of the same national or ethnic group, it should be important for advertisers to select not only the right expressions but also the right faces. In international advertising, for efficiency reasons companies tend to select faces that they think are recognizable to people of various countries in a region. An example is the Egyptian advertisement for Nivea (Figure 5.7), showing a Lebanese face. The differences may not be easily recognizable for Europeans or Americans, but I have been told by Egyptians that they recognize this face instantly as being not Egyptian.

For a long time international advertising strategies have tried to make their ads more international by depicting models of different national or ethnic backgrounds. Ethnicity of models influences responses to advertising. In the United States using models of diverse ethnicity in advertising doesn't improve likeability. In China, however, likeability improves when advertisements show models of diverse ethnicity. In East Asia, Western magazine advertisements have used Western models far more frequently than they used Asian models. Chinese consumers even perceived Western models in advertising as signs of status, success, cosmopolitanism, modernity and beauty. This is changing with the rapid economic development. So-called multi-cultural advertising, using models of diverse ethnicity emphasizes differences in physical appearance reinforcing ethnic stereotypes.[81]

Emotions are also expressed vocally. Comparative analysis of expression of emotions from voices shows that happiness is least recognizable from vocal portrayals. In a study in Germany, Switzerland,

Figure 5.7 **Nivea ad**

Great Britain, the Netherlands, United States, Italy, France, Spain, and Indonesia, the accuracy of recognition of emotions was related to the similarity of languages. The best recognitions of German speakers were by the Dutch and English speakers, also Germanic languages. This was followed by Romance languages (Italian, French, and Spanish). The lowest recognition was obtained for Indonesia.[82] People are not just faces. Other senses are likely to play an additional and complementary role in recognizing emotions. Whereas happiness is the most accurately understood emotion in the face, it is the least accurately understood emotion in the voice. Anger is the most accurately understood in the voice, whereas it is relatively less understood in the face.[83]

Recognition of facial expressions may be a human capacity, but it does not imply universality of emotions. In some cultures people hide their emotional states according to the social norms of their culture, called *display rules*. Cultural display rules also cause people of different cultures to attribute different meanings to emotional expressions. Americans, for example, rate smiling faces as more intelligent than neutral faces, whereas Japanese do not.[84]

Display Rules

The degree to which people display their emotions (and how) is culturally defined. *Meaning* and *intensity* of emotions vary. Emotions are, for example, more subdued in hierarchical, high power distance and collectivistic cultures.[85] In individualistic cultures personal feelings and their free expression are more important than in collectivistic cultures. A comparison of emotion expression across 32 countries showed a significant correlation with individualism for overall emotion expressivity, and in particular expressing happiness and surprise.[86] East Asian collectivists try to display only positive emotions and tend to control negative emotions. Probably this is the reason why in emotion recognition studies Chinese people are less able to identify expressions of fear and disgust.[87] To the Chinese the eyes and the eyebrows can convey rich emotions. However, such expressions of emotion are discouraged. Thus, when one speaks, one generally should not move one's eyebrows or one's eyes, otherwise the risk is being considered frivolous. As in other East Asian cultures, Chinese people are discouraged from having very dramatic facial expressions.[88]

Within Europe, members of cultures of weak uncertainty avoidance are less inclined to show emotions than cultures of strong uncertainty avoidance. The British 'stiff upper lip' can serve as an example. Also the vocal expression of emotion by Chinese young adults is more restrained than by Italian young adults.[89]

The same expressions may have different meanings in different cultures. Children in Western societies who protrude their tongue show *contempt*; among Chinese it means *surprise*. A smile may be an expression of pleasure or friendliness everywhere, but showing friendliness may be arrogant in one culture, a reason for distrust in another, and a requirement in social interaction in a third.[90] East Asian collectivists, instead of suppressing expression of displeasure, may display an expression of polite intercourse, what Westerners may perceive as a smile.[91] Matsumoto[92] mentions that in collectivistic cultures the expression of shame is more often accompanied by laughter and smiles than in individualistic cultures. In personal encounters, the author of this book has often seen Chinese or Indonesians smile or even laugh to hide their embarrassment. This sort of smile is certainly not a reflection of happiness. Not knowing this phenomenon can lead to misunderstanding.

> In the United States a smile means showing a happy face to the world. In line with the power of positive thinking expressions of positive emotion are encouraged and expected. In Russia, people may feel happy or content, but that is not necessarily shown to the outside world. Unexpected or unexplained positive expressions are viewed with suspicion.[93]

Members of individualistic cultures display a wider variety of emotional behaviors than do members of collectivistic cultures, who will also emphasize emotional displays that facilitate group cooperation, harmony, and cohesion. For collectivists, the specific emotions displayed depend on the context and target of the emotion. In a public context in a collectivistic culture, it would be inappropriate to display a negative emotion because it would reflect negatively on the in-group. If the emotion is a reaction to an out-group member, it would be acceptable to express it because this would foster cohesion in the in-group.[94] So the group and the context influence the display of emotions.

> Mesquita and Frijda[95] reported an experiment by Friesen,[96] who compared display of emotions between Americans and Japanese. When watching disgusting films, both Americans and Japanese displayed disgust when filmed outside the presence of the scientist, whereas the Japanese no longer indicated disgust but were found to smile more instead when the scientist was present.

Hofstede[97] reports studies that show significant correlations between uncertainty avoidance and the expression of embarrassment. In low uncertainty avoidance cultures, people control their emotions, claim not to express embarrassment and guilt, whereas in high uncertainty avoidance cultures, display of emotions is normal and people claim the expression of embarrassment and guilt. Individualistic cultures tolerate the expression of individual anger more easily than do collectivistic cultures.

Display of emotion is also influenced by social motivation. Evidence comes from observation of Olympic gold medal winners. Experiencing some of the happiest moments in their lives, the winners smiled much during specific social presentations, but little before or after.[98]

Emotion-Eliciting Events

Emotions are usually the results of specific events, and the events that cause similar emotions vary across cultures. Happiness may be a universal emotion, but what makes us happy can be very different across cultures. Whereas Americans, for example, relate achievement goals to happiness, what makes Danes most happy is time spent with friends and family.[99]

In 2008, Eurobarometer[100] asked the question, 'Which is the most important in connection with your idea of happiness?' Respondents had to make a choice of various options. Respondents in low power distance cultures most selected friendship ($r = .51***$) and love ($r = −.43*$). In high individualistic cultures they selected tolerance ($r = .33*$) and pleasure ($r = .42*$). In low individualistic cultures the choice was money ($r = −.49**$). In high masculine cultures it was tradition ($r = .43*$) and self-fulfillment ($r = .38*$). In low uncertainty avoidance cultures they selected love ($r = −.54***$), friendship ($r = −.63***$), and freedom ($r = −.51***$), and in high uncertainty avoidance cultures they chose solidarity ($r = .44*$). In short-term-oriented cultures, the choice was equality ($r = −.61***$).

Mesquita et al.[101] point at three variations in the effects of emotion-eliciting events: (1) the same situations are interpreted differently across cultures, and therefore lead to different emotions; (2) living conditions vary across cultures, resulting in different events; or (3) events derive their significance from certain culture-specific events. For example, various cultures interpret the condition 'being alone' differently. In collectivistic cultures being alone can mean not being among kin and not showing or being shown affection, implying unhappiness. Sitting alone can mean that the relationships between the individual and those considered as kin are not running smoothly. In contrast, in individualistic cultures being alone can serve the need for privacy, leading to happiness, or it can mean relaxation from stress.

Events that have an impact on the family or in-group will have greater importance in collectivistic cultures than in individualistic cultures. To reach an emotional state of happiness, Americans are more likely than Japanese to seek 'fun' situations, and Japanese are more likely than Americans to seek situations that produce harmonious interpersonal atmospheres.

The same type of situation or event will not necessarily trigger the same emotion in people across cultures. *Sadness* is more produced by problems in relationships for the Japanese than for Americans or Europeans. Strangers and achievement-related situations elicit more *fear* for Americans, whereas novel situations, traffic, and relationships are more frequent elicitors of fear for the Japanese. Situations involving strangers are more frequent elicitors of *anger* for the Japanese than for Americans or Europeans.[102]

Mesquita et al.[103] state that cross-cultural similarities in emotional phenomena are more likely to be found when these phenomena are described at a high level of abstraction. The differences are found when the more concrete features of emotions are taken into account. This is exactly what happens in global advertising. The argument for standard global advertising – that there are universal emotions such as love, pride, and motherhood – only holds for emotions described at a highly abstract level. When expressed in advertising, emotions must be made concrete; they must be displayed and placed in the cultural context. Universality of emotions exists only in theory, not in practice.

Emotions and expressions of emotion elicited by romantic love vary. In China romantic love is more 'embedded' than in the United States, where love is based on personal preferences and intense desire. *Embedded* means it is incorporated in a larger context, namely the natural world and long-term aspects of the relationship, including devotion, commitment, loyalty, and enduring friendship. This is in contrast to the Euro-American style of love characterized by physical attraction, intense feelings of desire, and dependency in the relationship. Whereas Chinese dependency needs are diffused into a web of multiple close relationships, including their relationship with nature, Americans' dependency needs are focused on their sexual partners. This can be recognized by the characteristics of love songs. Many American songs reflect sexual dependency by using the term *baby.* In Chinese love songs, contextual forces play a role, including harmony with both society and nature, expressed by flowers, rivers, and stars. This is recognized in expressions in songs, for example, 'having you, me, feelings, heaven, sea, and earth.' Chinese songs also include aspects of suffering and more negative expectations about the future of the relationship.[104]

In sum, cultural variations in emotion are relative to the cultural orientations from which they derive. The culture-specific American patriotism, with the American flag as a symbolic device, may serve as an example. The ubiquitous emotional reaction of individuals after the terrible events of 11 September 2001, was carrying the national flag, in whatever sort of form: big, small, or lapel pins. Emotional reactions to ETA killings in Spain are always collective marches. In 2002 the Dutch football coach Guus Hiddink helped the Korean football team win several matches in the World Cup finals, played in Korea and Japan.

The Koreans were extremely emotional about this, and thankful, because he had given them 'face' to the world. Soon, groups of Koreans even went to visit his birthplace Varsseveld, an until-then insignificant village in the Netherlands.

Emotions in Advertising

For a long time international advertising strategists have thought that emotional or 'feeling' appeals would travel better than 'thinking' ones because of the assumption that certain emotions are shared around the world.[105] Thus, international advertising has been dominated by emotional appeals such as love and happiness.[106] This is caused by the assumed universality of emotions, in particular happiness. A global brand like Coca-Cola uses happiness in global advertising worldwide showing happy people and using the pay-off 'open happiness' next to the bottle. Figure 5.8 shows a few pictures from a Coca-Cola commercial.

Figure 5.8 **Pictures from a Coca-Cola commercial**

The thought of universality of emotions in advertising has been stimulated by consumer behavior theorists like Morris Holbrook,[107] who used a number of basic emotions to categorize emotional responses in advertising in the United States. 'Disgust' would be an appropriate basic emotion related to cleaning products, 'anger' and 'frustration' would be recognized in a commercial for a bank, and 'joy' would be recognized in a commercial for a telephone company. The use of Anglo-American basic emotions in advertising may have been effective for advertising in the United States; the use of the typical American emotions, and in particular the way these emotions are expressed, is not likely to be equally effective in many other cultures.

An example of the use of disgust is a commercial for Johnson Flushable wipes. The commercial shows a woman throwing away a nonflushable wipe and after that she walks past the dustbin, acting in a disgusted way, viewed from inside the dustbin. The solution is Johnson Flushable wipes. This problem-solution approach may be less effective in collectivistic cultures where people avoid negative emotions and also don't want to be confronted with problems. Figure 5.9 shows a few pictures from the commercial.

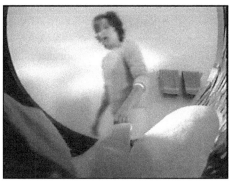

Figure 5.9   **Problem-solution and use of disgust**

Emotional Versus Rational Advertising

In (American) advertising theory, the concept of emotion is used in the rough classification of advertising in 'rational' and 'emotional,' where 'emotional' means *feeling, pleasure*, or *mood*, whereas 'rational' advertising includes mainly information about the product. The simple distinction is between 'thinking' ads and 'feeling' ads. Basically, any claim or appeal that is not rational is considered to be emotional. Examples of emotional appeals are sex appeals, humorous appeals, and fear appeals. The distinction represents the two schools of thought about advertising strategy in the United States: the 'head' and the 'heart.' *Head* stands for rational argumentation, whereas *heart* stands for emotional or image advertising, 'which doesn't barrage the consumer with words, facts, or claims.'[108] The distinction is typical of American advertising. The strong focus on feelings and emotions in the United States is related to the values of American culture, where emotions are highly personalized and individual, and being in touch with one's feelings is a condition for mental health. This helps to understand the impact of emotional appeals in American advertising, like 'Reach out and touch someone' as in the classic campaign for Bell Telephone long distance and use of phrases like 'The heartbeat of America.' In other parts of the world such emotional statements may be viewed as exaggeration or pure sentimentality.

The distinction 'rational/emotional' is also used to distinguish simply between the direct and the indirect approach in advertising or even between verbally and visually oriented advertising. Because much of advertising in Asia is more visual and indirect than American advertising, advertising in Asia tends to be characterized as emotional as opposed to more rational Western advertising. However, what is labeled as emotional in Japanese or French advertising is merely high-context, indirect style (see Chapter 7). Jean-Marie Dru, cofounder of the international advertising agency BDDP, observes, 'Japanese advertising is not simply emotional. It taps into the richness of imagination.'[109] Using the concept of emotion to classify advertising across cultures is often more confusing than clarifying, leading to obscure statements like 'Even when Japanese commercials use an informational strategy, such as hyperbole or a unique selling proposition, their executions are emotional in appeal.'[110]

Facial Expressions: Application to Advertising

In order to understand the emotional responses to advertising, researchers of advertising agencies apply the facial expression recognition method, a system based on the assumption that emotion can be recognized from facial expressions. An example is the emotional measurement system developed by BBDO in the United States that followed the method of still photographs of posed facial expressions. For developing such instruments, enormous investments have to be made as a pool of facial expressions ('photo decks') must be developed. At BBDO, 26 categories of emotion were selected and six professional actors, representing 20-, 30-, and 40-year-old age groups, were hired to pose for all the emotional categories. This resulted in the production of 1,872 facial expressions. Samples of consumers rated these in order to arrive at the best selection. This provided a standard for discussing the facial expressions in terms of the emotional meaning ascribed to them by consumers. Such emotional photo decks are useful instruments for nonverbally assessing the emotional impact of advertising. Consumer respondents who view television ads can select photographs from the deck that represent how the commercial makes them feel. The advantage of the method is that respondents do not have to verbalize the emotions elicited by advertising. The disadvantage is that it is only useful for international advertising if for each country different photo decks are made. Experience at BBDO in Europe has taught that photographs of facial expressions produced in the United States could not be transplanted to Europe. European respondents could not recognize the way American actors expressed specific moods. The same is true within Europe: no useful single 'photo deck' could be developed for the whole of Europe.[111]

Similar experiences are reported from New Zealand, where photographs of people's faces or stylized faces (smiley faces) are frequently used in projective techniques. Several groups other than the New Zealand Europeans, for example Tongans and Koreans, cannot associate easily with pictures of European faces. New Zealand Europeans can better associate brands with photographs that are similar to themselves. Also Koreans identify more closely with Korean photographs if they have the appropriate expressions. Cues in smiley faces developed for Koreans and Tongans tend to be viewed as offensive because the characteristics, such as eye shapes, are seen as offensive caricatures. Both Koreans and Tongans view representing the mouth as a straight horizontal line – meant to be a neutral cue – as indicating a negative reaction. Peripheral cues, such as distinctive hairstyles, tend to distract attention away from the expression of the face, which demonstrates the importance of context.[112]

Group Processes

According to Western consumer behavior theory, the behavior of individuals is based partly on their personal characteristics and partly on their group memberships. The group influences individual consumer behavior. Norms concerning perceptions, opinions, attitudes, and behaviors frequently develop within a group. A distinction is made between *formal* (associations) and *informal* groups (family and friends) that may influence behavior and decision making. Other groups that are distinguished as influencing consumer behavior are *reference group* and *aspirational group*.

Western examples of reasons why people are part of or join a group are (1) to achieve a task that cannot be completed alone; (2) to obtain friendship, companionship, and support; (3) to get a source of warmth and psychological security; (4) because we have no choice – we are born male or female and we are born in a particular family. The first three are Western-centric reasons. The basic assumption is that people can choose group membership, which is true for individualistic cultures, whereas in collectivistic cultures group membership is a central aspect of identity.

The degree to which group members depend on others in consumer decision making varies. In collectivistic and high power distance cultures, dependence on others is stronger than in individualistic and low power distance cultures. Comparative content analysis of Chinese and American advertising demonstrates that group consensus and conformity to family preference rather than individual choice is found more in Chinese than in American advertising.[113] Differences in family relationships and interdependence, however, are quite complex. Studies within the United States found that European Americans equated obligation to family with relationship quality and closeness to family members, and therefore viewed obligation to family as personal choice; whereas for Mexican Americans, obligation related to the social role of being family or group. As compared with Chinese American students, European American undergraduate students saw their parents as more respectful of their independence, felt supported in their independence, and rated their relationship with their parents as emotionally supportive and mutual and felt more comfortable asking their parents for support.[114] For understanding group influences on consumer behavior the in-group versus out-group distinction is important.

In-Group and Out-Group

Triandis defines in-groups as 'groups of individuals about whose welfare a person is concerned, with whom that person is willing to cooperate without demanding equitable returns, and separation from which leads to anxiety.'[115] Members of collectivistic cultures are born as part of a group, which defines their identity. In-group behavior can be different from out-group behavior. The Japanese divide their lives into inner and outer sectors, each with its own different standards of behavior. In the inner circle the individual is automatically accepted, there is interdependence and automatic warmth, love, or *amae,* the best translation of which is 'passive love' or dependency. Members of the inner circle experience this *amae* between each other, but it does not exist in the outer circle. You lose *amae* when you enter the outer circle. You don't expect *amae* in the outer circle.[116] In-group relationships in collectivistic cultures are more intimate than in individualistic cultures. Members of individualistic cultures belong to many specific in-groups, which they join willingly. Because of this, these in-groups have less influence than in-groups do in collectivistic cultures.[117]

In collectivistic cultures there is a sharp distinction between in-group and out-group. People in collectivistic cultures interact more frequently, more widely, more deeply, and more positively with in-group members than members of individualistic cultures do in their in-groups. Processes of mutual influence, harmony enhancement, and in-group favoritism are stronger in collectivistic cultures than in individualistic cultures.

Several elements of the McDonald's brand play a role in the evaluation of McDonald's in China. These are the way the food is ordered and delivered, the price, the decor, the noise, and the way the tables are set up. What makes McDonald's unique is the standardized menu and low price, cleanliness, and tables for two. These are exactly the reasons why McDonald's is not the place to go for a typical event celebrated in a restaurant, such as birthday parties with several generations of family. The tables are not right. There is too little choice of food and the price is too low to give proper face to the honoree. There is too much noise from out-groups. At Chinese birthday parties people order special food that sets them apart from other restaurant guests. They also get a special section where they are not disturbed by the noise of outsiders. The standardized approach of McDonald's does not allow for that sort of service. However, because of the two-person tables, McDonald's is a place that enables a couple on a date to find privacy. It offers social space outside of the home in which two people can be 'alone' and sit for a long time. This is in contrast to Chinese restaurants where people typically eat and leave immediately afterward. So in China, McDonald's offers the opposite of fast food.[118]

Studies among students have shown that Japanese and Hong Kong China students spend more time with in-groups than with out-groups. A within-US study showed that European Americans spend equal time with in- and out-groups and have more freedom to decide which groups to belong to than Indian or Asian Americans. Americans also belong to more groups than do Indian students.[119] The difference between in-group and out-group is particularly visible in Chinese restaurants that generally have round tables for eight or ten persons and where families or other in-groups can have their own sections in restaurants. Family birthday parties are characterized by a lot of noise, which is why restaurants have several special rooms to host celebrating groups. In-group noise is part of the celebration, but out-group noise can have a negative influence on the goals of the in-group. Figure 5.10 shows a restaurant in Shanghai.

Figure 5.10 **Large round tables in Chinese restaurants. Photograph: Gerard Foekema**

Interaction with strangers (out-groups) varies with uncertainty avoidance. In high uncertainty avoidance cultures people tend to think what is strange or unknown can be threatening. Behavior toward strangers may be ritualized and/or very polite, or strangers can be ignored, treated as if they don't exist. In low uncertainty avoidance cultures there is more interaction with foreigners. A Eurobarometer survey asked for the degree to which respondents interacted with foreigners, such as e-mailing with foreigners or having job contacts with foreigners. Variance of answers to both questions was explained by low uncertainty avoidance (respectively, 37% and 45%).[120]

Collectivistic cultures vary with respect to the type and rank-order of importance of in-groups. In-groups vary from the extended family (whether they live in joint or unitary households is not relevant) with neighborhood and school friends absorbed in the extended family, to the larger community such as the Indian *jati* or Spanish *barrio*, or the occupational unit.[121] Some put kinship organizations (family) ahead of all other in-groups, whereas others put their companies ahead of other in-groups. In-group relationships in collectivistic cultures are usually limited to three groups: brother/sister (family group), coworker and colleague (company in-group), and classmate (university in-group). In Japan, modernization has made the occupational unit more important than kinship links.

Even in the medium collectivistic cultures in Europe, one's city or region is an important part of one's identity, more than in individualistic cultures. This is demonstrated by correlation between individualism and the attachment to one's town ($r = -.66^{***}$) or region ($r = -.79^{***}$).[122] This relationship is quite stable. Also in 2017 the degree of attachment to one's city, town or village was significantly correlated with low individualism ($r = -.53^{***}$).[123]

Members of the collectivistic in-group are implicitly what in individualistic cultures are called your 'friends.' Members of individualistic cultures have to invest time in friendship, and they belong to many specific in-groups that may change over time. Across Europe, the percentages who state that friendship is very important correlate with individualism, low power distance, and low uncertainty avoidance.[124] Friendship is important because people have to make an effort to get and preserve friendship, other than in collectivistic cultures where people automatically belong to a group. Seven out of ten Americans belong at least to one club or association,[125] whereas membership in associations is not very popular in Japan. Also, Spaniards do not tend to subscribe in great numbers to clubs and associations, political or otherwise. Although many Americans have close friends to whom they feel special attachments and strong obligations, such friendships are small in number. Many other people are labeled 'friends' without the element of mutual obligations that comes so natural in the collectivistic in-group. In collectivistic cultures there is more communication and interaction between friends than in individualistic cultures; they meet each other much more frequently. Across 25 European countries, the percentages who say they meet their friends every day correlate negatively with individualism ($r = -.41^{*}$) but also with short-term orientation ($r = -.53^{***}$).[126] In short-term-oriented cultures people spend more money on enjoying themselves with others. This is included in an aspect of short-term orientation called 'service to others' by Minkov, who developed this long-/short-term orientation and labeled it *flexhumility* versus *monumentalism*.[127] This same dimension was adopted by Hofstede (see Chapter 2).

Giving gifts is much more important for in-group members than for out-group members. When the self is group based rather than individual based, gift giving within the group or family takes on a unique meaning. Giving to others can be seen as giving to self.[128] Gift buying for members of the in-group is a special art in Japan, and even pets are part of that group. In 2001, 'Posh dog products and accessories have become hot items, and Hermes, Louis Vuitton, Gucci, Prada and others sold 175,000 yen bags, 200,000 yen beds, and 50,000 yen collars for their canine clients.' Buyers say, 'He's family, so I don't mind spending up to 15,000 yen on things for him.'[129] The advantage of branded pet articles is that customers can match their own fashions with those of their pets, be in harmony. Also in Europe there is a relationship between gift giving and collectivism. Annual spending on cosmetics and skin care, as measured by EMS, correlates with low individualism. Of the respondents of EMS, 68% are males. So, the answers are likely to refer to buying perfume, cosmetics, and skin care as gifts when traveling.

Family and Relationships: Parents–Children

The traditional definition of a *family* is two or more people living together who are related by blood or marriage. What is called the *nuclear family* is one couple with children. If more generations are living together, it is called the *extended family*. In the individualistic Western world there are many varieties to the traditional family, and increasing numbers of babies are born with parents who are not married. In the OECD countries childbearing out of wedlock has increased enormously. In 1964 in these countries no more than 10 percent of births were out of marriage. By 2014 in only five countries (Greece, Israel, Japan, South Korea and Turkey) were the proportions of births out of wedlock below 10 percent. There is no relationship with GNI/cap. For 34 countries the percentages of births out of wedlock are significantly correlated with low masculinity ($r = -.30*$) and high IVR ($r = .31*$). Many of the children born out of wedlock live in single-parent households, but more in developing countries than in the developed world, where getting a child out of marriage doesn't necessarily translate into a single parent household and women continue cohabiting instead of marrying. In Sweden, for example 26% of children live with two cohabiting parents and 17% with sole parents. In Austria these percents are respectively 10% and 21%. These percentages are significantly correlated with individualism (sole parents, $r = .49**$) and low masculinity (two cohabiting parents, $r = -.45**$).[130] Increasing divorce rates in the Western world also lead to more single parents. In collectivistic cultures, economic development has led to the decrease of the extended family with a weakening of material interdependence, but that has not led to decreasing psychological interdependence.

Generally speaking children are raised to be able to properly function in the society in which they grow up and this is reflected in the type of relationships with their parents. Whereas in individualistic cultures, children are reared to develop an autonomous, independent identity, in collectivistic cultures parents tend to foster a high level of dependence in their children, to socialize them to successfully adapt to an interdependent society; children to some extent are allowed autonomy, without desiring separateness in the child. This influences the way parents and children relate to each other. Indian parents are found to be more authoritarian, whereas Japanese parents are more permissive.[131] Korean parents grant autonomy to their children, but they must accept in-group obligations. From the Western point of view in collectivistic cultures, the way young children are raised looks like permissiveness, with little interference by parents. But in collectivistic cultures small children get more freedom to learn to conform and preserve harmony with their siblings. Parental control also is more 'order setting' than 'dominating.'[132] This is confirmed by a study among young people 10–18 years old across seven Latin American countries that showed that in the more individualistic cultures, fathers and mothers more decide which program children watch on TV than in the more collectivistic cultures. Also the percentages who say they use the Internet with their mothers correlate with individualism.[133]

Another dimension that explains differences in parental control is long-/short-term orientation. In short-term-oriented cultures there are more strict rules to which people adhere in raising children. Long-term-orientation cultures are more pragmatic and lenient. Parents place fewer restrictions on their children's media exposure.[134] In long-term-oriented cultures children also have more say in important family decisions.[135]

In high power distance cultures, adults and children tend to live in different worlds, the world for children and the world for grown-ups. This has implications for the type of toys that are popular. LEGO, for example, developed in Denmark, is meant for parents and children to play together. Parents teach their children how to construct LEGO buildings. In France, a high power distance, dependency culture, LEGO never became as popular as in Denmark. In communications, children are also addressed in the context of their own world. This is a likely explanation of the fact that Chinese children's commercials are less likely to use an adult spokesperson or voice-over than are those in the United States.[136]

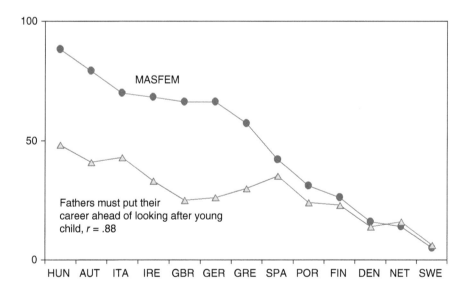

Figure 5.11   **Fathers must put career ahead of looking after young child**

SOURCES: Hofstede et al. (2010) (see Appendix A); Gender Equality, EBS 428, 2014 (see Appendix B)

Worldwide, parents have to find solutions to combining work and child care. As we have seen in Chapter 3, the degree to which women work varies with the degree of masculinity/femininity of their cultures. This is also the case for their view on how they ideally organize child care. In the masculine cultures, the general norm is that fathers must put their career ahead of looking after his young child (26 countries, $r = .70***$), woman's first priority is the family ($r = .67***$)[137] and women are responsible for running the household. Also data from the harmonized time use survey by Eurostat shows a significant correlation between women's (30-49 yr) share of daily time spent on housework and masculinity ($r = .64**$). This relationship is not found for young women aged 25–29 years.[138] The Japanese housewife manages household budget, decides on the choice of school of the children, the house, holidays, and often also the car to buy. In the Indian family, hierarchy, age and gender are the main ordering principles, and men have more decisive authority and property rights. The elders and both parents enjoy more respect and woman as a mother is more respected.[139]

Conformity

In collectivistic cultures, people conform more to others, both of in-groups and of out-groups, than they do in individualistic cultures. A famous experiment by Asch[140] measured the degree of conformity in the United States by showing participants a stimulus line and a set of three lines, in which one line was the same length as the stimulus line. The participants had to say which of the three lines was similar to the stimulus line. All but one participant were told to give the same wrong answer. Individuals, who had to judge in a group where the other participants all gave the same wrong answer, also gave the wrong answer, while this was not the case in groups where no such pressure took place. Hofstede[141] reports cross-analysis of Asch-like studies in the United States and 36 studies in 16 other countries that point at greater conformity in collectivistic cultures than in individualistic cultures. Young people conform more to their peers. For young girls in collectivistic and high power distance cultures, the most powerful influences on beauty and body image are their girlfriends.[142] Singh reports that young people in India are more influenced by their peers than by family members. Conformance to peers may be more important than family influence.[143]

Branded luxury products like Vuitton purses fulfill the need to conform. In Japan, 1 in 3 women and 1 in 6 men own a Vuitton product. Teenaged girls want Vuitton because 'Everyone has it.'[144] Vuitton's sales have risen by double digits every year since 1990. Japanese sociologists state that by owning a Vuitton purse, anonymous young women can feel kinship with other Vuitton owners and not feel the stigma of being excluded.[145] The Japanese term is *wa,* meaning to be similar to others, look the same as others.

In China, friendship circles or people living in the same area (e.g., apartment building) often consume similar product categories, select the same brands within a category, and purchase them in the same department store.

The need for conformity is also related to low masculinity. Feminine cultures can be characterized by a need for leveling; they are also said to be 'jealous' societies. Envy can be a motive to buy or not buy products or brands. In 2001, in Korea, a feminine culture, 70% said buying imported cars would lead to greater 'social disparity,' and nearly half avoided imports for fear of 'dirty looks' from fellow Koreans.[146]

The typical individualistic definition of conformity is 'yielding to group pressure,' but in collectivistic cultures conformity is not a matter of 'yielding' to pressure. Group conformity is an automatic process caused by the need for social harmony. Whereas conformity, obedience, and compliance are viewed negatively in American culture, they generally are positively valued behavior in collectivistic cultures. The American bias can be recognized when conformity-related values are discussed, like using the phrase 'yielding to group pressure' or 'sacrificing the self for the common goal' as done by Oyserman et al.[147] and Lee.[148]

Unilever found that the Chinese bought ice cream mainly when they saw other people eat ice cream. As a result, Unilever marketers intensified the distribution of ice cream in order to make it more visible in the streets.[149] In China/Taiwan people may line up when they see a line, even when they don't know what it is for. When so many people spend time standing in line, it must be good.[150]

The Heineken beer distributor in Hong Kong tapped into this key value by asking on-premise staff to leave Heineken bottles on the table. The key to marketing in Asia is perceived popularity. The bottles on the table, the restaurant with the queues. The 'Be like others' appeal works.[151]

In 2000, in Japan, cheaper 'chic' was challenging the Western luxury labels the Japanese had come to embrace as symbols of prosperity. People were increasingly wearing casual clothes. In an interview by *Newsweek*'s Kay Ito in Tokyo with Tadashi Yanai, president of the Fast Retailing Company, the parent of the successful casual brand Uniqlo, Ito referred to *Newsweek* stories that the Japanese are becoming more diverse and asked whether Yanai believed this. Yanai was quoted saying:

Japanese people are extremely interested in how different they are from each other. They want to be a little different, but they hate to be very different. Most people receive the same education, read the same magazines and watch the same television programs.

They couldn't be different even if they wanted to. In the US and Europe, there is more diversity in incomes people earn and how much information they receive.[152]

Whereas in individualistic cultures women are more fashion conscious, in collectivistic cultures there is more dress conformity. Fashion consciousness deals with an individual's interest in and attention to the latest fashion trends. It is about being up to date with respect to dressing. Dress conformity refers to dressing in line with the associative group, wearing the 'right' clothes.[153]

Inner-, Outer-Directedness

In the VALS (values and lifestyles) typology, people are described as outer directed who look more to the expectations of others and societal norms to fulfill their psychological needs, and inner directed when their personal needs and priorities take precedence over the expectations of others.[154] Collectivists can be characterized as more outer directed whereas individualists are more inner directed. Outer-directedness applies to the concept of *self-monitoring* – the degree to which a person takes his or her behavioral cues from the behavior of others. The self-monitoring individual is particularly sensitive to the self-presentations of others in social situations that are used as guidelines for monitoring his or her own self-presentation.[155] In individualistic cultures, prototypic individuals are used as examples, whereas in collectivistic cultures context and status relationships are more taken into consideration when deciding how to behave in a particular situation.

Public and Private Self-Consciousness

A concept related to the inner/outer distinction is *self-consciousness*. A distinction is made between *public* and *private* self-consciousness. The latter is defined as a discomfort in the presence of others. Private self-consciousness is concerned with attending to inner thoughts and feelings, and involves introspection about the self. Public self-consciousness involves a general awareness of the self in relation to others, as a social object.[156] Hofstede views public self-consciousness (measured by answers to the question 'I am concerned about what other people think of me') as presenting oneself as an individual, which is related to individualism.[157] In individualistic cultures self-consciousness implies concern for the self as viewed by unknown others, a concept that is not very well developed in collectivistic cultures where the self exists only in relation to known others, involving the concept of face. Introspection about the self is most relevant in masculine cultures that value performance and ambition, both of which require introspection about individual abilities. Research by cross-cultural communication researchers Gudykunst and Ting-Toomey[158] revealed that people in Japan are higher on private self-consciousness than those in Korea, whereas the United States fell in between. Both private and public self-consciousness are involved in the need for status luxury articles and may serve as an explanation of the extreme dependence on foreign, status-enhancing brands by the Japanese.

> The market research agency Salles D'Arcy in São Paulo[159] conducted a survey among 14- to 24-year-old girls and women in Latin America. There were several answer categories to the question 'What are the three things that Latin girls can't be without when going out?' Fifty-nine percent of Mexican respondents and 60% of Venezuelan respondents said, 'Trendy clothes,' as compared with 27% of respondents from Chile and 36% from Brazil. The responses correlated significantly with masculinity ($r = .98***$). To the question what sort of women they related to, the percentages answering 'Liberated' correlated significantly with low masculinity ($r = -.99***$).

Public and Private Space

Some products are used more privately (toothpaste, deodorants), others more in public (drinks, luxury articles). Next to culture, public or private use affects advertising appeals across countries. In general, advertising in individualistic cultures appeals more to individualistic values such as self-reliance and personal rewards, whereas advertising in collectivistic cultures tends to appeal more to values like family well-being, in-group goals, and interdependence. This difference, however, is not uniform across products. The differences are larger for products that are shared and used in public than for personal products that are more used in private. So the type of product advertised moderates the cultural differences. For example, Han and Shavitt[160] found that individualistic appeals were more effective in the United States and collectivistic appeals were more effective in Korea, but for personal products that are used privately, individualistic appeals were generally favored in both countries.

> Zhang and Gelb[161] compared the acceptance of culture-bound appeals in the United States and China for two different products: toothbrushes and cameras. The cultural dimension used was individualism/collectivism. They found that for cameras, a product used for self-expression, in China the collectivistic appeal worked better, whereas the individualistic appeal worked better in the United States. For the toothbrush it did

(Continued)

(Continued)

not make a difference. The product use condition made the difference: a toothbrush is a product used for personal purposes and not meant to show in public, so in the collectivistic China the individualistic appeal worked equally well as the collectivistic appeal. The collectivistic appeal did not work in the individualistic United States, but the individualistic appeal did work in China.

Behavior in private space can be different from behavior in public space. Members of individualistic cultures have a greater need for privacy than have members of collectivistic cultures, which has implications for usage of various products. Originally the mobile phone was only used for talking, which was ubiquitously done in public space in the collectivist cultures in the south of Europe, but this was not tolerated in the North. In 2001, some 56% of those over age 50 in the United Kingdom thought that mobile phones should be banned in public places.[162]

Culture influences the type of houses people live in and the activities in and around people's homes. In individualistic cultures people prefer one-family houses with private gardens. Every home should have its own garden, however small. Members of collectivistic cultures prefer to live in apartment buildings and own relatively few private gardens. In 1970 and 1991 possession of private gardens correlated significantly with individualism (1970: $r = .74$***; 1991: $r = .72$***).[163] As a result, mean consumption expenditures on garden plants and flowers is also significantly correlated with individualism (2001: $r = .65$**; 2005: $r = .53$***), as is the proportion of European inhabitants who do gardening during a typical week ($r = .49$*), but there also is a relationship with low power distance ($r = -.78$***).[164] In high power distance and collectivistic cultures a private garden is more viewed as public space, and not tended the way the house is tended inside, whereas in individualistic cultures the garden is viewed as an extension of the house. More recent data show that in 2012 still 41.3% of Europeans lived in flats, ranging from 4.7% in Ireland, 13.4% in Norway and 14.5% in the United Kingdom to 65% in Spain.[165]

Whereas in Europe, in individualistic cultures people get together with friends and family in the home or garden, in collectivistic and/or high power distance cultures people get more together in public places such as parks and bars and keep the home mainly for the family. Preferences for spending nearly all of one's free time out of home correlate with high power distance ($r = .67$**) and low individualism ($r = -.56$*), whereas preferences for spending free time mostly in the home are correlated with low power distance ($r = -.77$***).[166] The percentages of people who have a meal in a restaurant or visit a bar every day correlate with low individualism ($r = -.76$***), which explains 58% of variance.[167] Expenditures in restaurants and cafés correlate with low individualism ($r = -.38$*), but also with short-term orientation ($r = -.40$*).[168]

Mixing home and work life is also related to individualism. Whereas in individualistic cultures people may want to take work into their homes, this is not the usual behavior in collectivistic cultures. Another dimension that explains differences is cultural masculinity. The task orientation of high masculine cultures versus needs for quality of life of low masculine cultures explains the division between public work life and private home.

In an interview by Bill Powell of *Newsweek* with Seijiro Yokoyama, NEC executive vice president, the latter expressed his doubts about the emergence of virtual offices in Japan resulting from the possibilities of the Internet.

Far more so than in the West, business in Japan is a powerful social phenomenon. For 100 years Japanese businessmen have been coming to offices to work. Technology isn't going to change that any time soon. In Japan – and indeed, throughout much of East Asia – personal contact is still critically important, digital revolution or no digital revolution. Personal relationships matter more than contracts, and personal relationships are established within groups. No matter how good the latest technology, you can't go out and get drunk with your customers or your suppliers on the Infobahn. . . . In Japan, many men have two families. Their families at home and their families at the office. Both are very important. In Japan, this is the bottom line that doesn't appear on any balance sheet. For a lot of men, business and social life are simply one and the same. Many salary men have no interest in 'telecommuting.' They would be at a loss if they didn't have an office to go to – no matter what they actually do while they are there.[169]

Appearance

How people deal with their appearance is very much related to variations of the self in the social environment as discussed in the previous sections of the chapter. Three cultural dimensions can explain variance of people's needs for appearance: uncertainty avoidance, power distance, and individualism/collectivism. Strong uncertainty avoidance makes people want to be well groomed when they go out into the streets. It helps to structure an ambiguous world. This is confirmed by the relationship between uncertainty avoidance and the percentage of private consumption spent on clothing and footwear. In collectivistic cultures people dress well in order to preserve harmony, and in high power distance cultures dependence on others makes people more other-directed in their self-presentation. In collectivistic cultures being properly dressed when going out into the streets, facing out-groups, is important for not causing loss of face to the in-group. The psychoanalyst Alan Roland[170] notes that urban Indian women spend much more time and effort on personal grooming and dress when they go out in public in India than they would do when going out in public in New York.

In India, your position in society is defined by the clothes you wear, your shoes, your posture, your facial expression, and the volume of your voice. The combination provides you with your rightful place in the endless hierarchy of class and power. It defines the type of seat, the number of pillows, or the height of seat you are offered when shopping.[171] In the United States the workplace is the only place left that asks for role-consistent and situation-specific public clothing: the suit – which stands for tradition, hierarchy, conformity, and money.[172] In all other places there are few situation-specific ways of dressing. People wear in public whatever they wear in private. Presidents go jogging in shorts and baseball caps, film stars walk in the streets in jeans and T-shirts, and people go to church barefoot in shorts. Shanghai is known for, among other things, its middle-aged women who saunter onto the street in their sleepwear. Some even venture as far as the subway or the shopping mall. They view their pajamas as casual wear.[173]

Particularly for social occasions – and there are many in collectivistic and high power distance cultures – people buy new clothes. It is not a necessity to be dressed according to the latest fashion, which is more related to individualistic self-enhancement.

Several surveys have measured interest in fashion by asking positive or negative confirmation to the statement, 'I like to dress according to the latest fashion,' or 'I like to be well-dressed,' or 'I try to look stylish all the time.' Table 5.3 shows the correlations with three dimensions and percentages of variance explained in regression analysis. The relationship between individualism and fashion consciousness was confirmed by Manrai et al.,[174] who

Table 5.3 **Appearance**

	PDI	IDV	UAI	Predictor	R2
No to latest fashion 1970 (15 countries)	.57*	−.56*	.59**	UAI	.35
No to latest fashion 1997 (15 countries)	.22	−.51*	.22	IDV-	.26
				MAS-	.48
Well-dressed 1997 (15 countries)	.39	−.60**	.48*	IDV-	.36
Physical attractive women are more valued by men (2006, 10 countries)	.87***	−.60*	.71**	PDI	.75
Try to look stylish all the time (2007, 20 countries)	.63***	−.60***	.69***	UAI	.47
				PDI	.70

SOURCES: Hofstede et al. (2010) (see Appendix A); *Reader's Digest* Surveys 1970 and 1991; EMS 1997; Dove Report *Beyond Stereotypes*, 2006; Nielsen, 2007 (see Appendix B)

compared fashion consciousness of consumers in Hungary, Romania, and Bulgaria. Hungarian (individualist) consumers scored higher in fashion consciousness than (collectivist) Bulgarian and Romanian consumers.

Thus, the various aspects of appearance relate to different values across cultures. Appearance is important in collectivistic cultures as it is face preserving, but it is more meant to preserve group harmony and not to stand out by following the latest fashion, which is related to individualism. The relationship with individualism is confirmed by a GfK[175] survey of consumers in 20 countries asking for the time spent on grooming. This correlated with individualism ($r = .56^{**}$), but also with short-term orientation ($r = -.43^*$), which points at self-enhancement. Power distance implies that one's appearance follows one's social position, and uncertainty avoidance adds to that.

Group processes as discussed in the previous sections play a role in explaining variance of the importance of appearance. Countries can be clustered according to these variations, using the dimensions individualism–collectivism and uncertainty avoidance (see Figure 5.12).

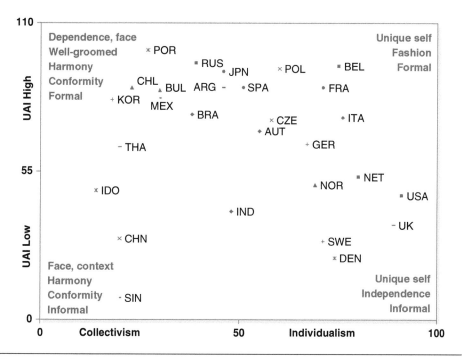

Figure 5.12   Appearance

SOURCE: Data Hofstede et al. (2010) (see Appendix A)

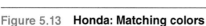

Figure 5.13   **Honda: Matching colors**

Figure 5.14   **Prior, Norway: No special attention to appearance**

Dependence needs are found in the two left-hand quadrants that are collectivistic. Face and context are important, as well as conformity. The differences between the two left-hand quadrants are in the degree of uncertainty avoidance. In the upper left-hand quadrant, of high uncertainty avoidance, people need structure – they ritualize life by the way they dress. This is where people want to match colors of shoes and handbags or the designer brand of their own clothes and even the attributes of their pets. The Spanish ad for Honda (Figure 5.13) refers to this need for matching colors. In the lower left-hand quadrant anything goes, but social context must be taken into account.

In the two right-hand quadrants of Figure 5.12 the unique self operates. In the upper right-hand quadrant it is combined with structure and ritualization. In this corner is a small group of countries that combine individualism with high power distance and high uncertainty avoidance. The self must be presented in a unique, but ritualized way, and social context is important. This leads to high importance of fashion, design, and art-orientation. In the lower right-hand quadrant are the countries where the unique self is combined with low ritualization needs. Anything goes – people don't dress up in the public domain; they don't care what they look like. The Norwegian ad for Prior (Figure 5.14) illustrates this.

Reference Groups

A *reference group* is a group that serves as a reference point in forming people's attitudes and behavior. In Western consumer behavior theory, three reference group influences are distinguished: informational, utilitarian, and value-expressive. *Informational* influence comes from groups or associations of professionals or experts (formal groups), from friends, or neighbors. *Utilitarian* influence comes from preferences of family members or other people with whom one has social interaction. *Value-expressive* influence is on the image, when the individual feels that the purchase or use of a particular product or brand will enhance the image others have of him or her.

The strongest cultural determinant of reference groups is individualism/collectivism. All aspects discussed in the previous sections of this chapter, such as dependency, harmony, or self-consciousness, will influence the role of reference individuals or groups. In collectivistic cultures, people do not belong to associations to the degree they do in individualistic cultures, so the influence of information from associations is less relevant. The influence of professionals and associations is strongest in individualistic and high uncertainty avoidance cultures. Consumer organizations may also be viewed as authorities, which is appealing to members of high power distance cultures. Whereas companies are mentioned as favorite sources of information in the low power distance cultures, consumer organizations are more mentioned in high power distance cultures. Colleagues and relatives are consulted more in individualistic cultures than in collectivistic cultures.[176] Expert groups will have a stronger reference function in high uncertainty avoidance cultures.

An indication of the influence of different types of reference groups across cultures is provided by a Eurobarometer survey on risk issues that asked who would be most trusted to inform people if a serious food risk would occur. The answer 'public

(Continued)

(Continued)

authorities' correlated with low power distance ($r = -.54^{***}$) and short-term orientation ($r = -.56^{***}$); 'food manufacturer' correlated with low uncertainty avoidance ($r = -.37^{*}$); 'the media' correlated with short-term orientation ($r = -.45^{*}$); 'consumer groups' correlated with individualism ($r = .49^{**}$); 'physician/doctor' correlated with high uncertainty avoidance ($r = .59^{***}$).[177]

Because members of high uncertainty avoidance cultures have respect for expertise and professionalism, formal or professional reference groups are likely to have greater influence in high than in low uncertainty avoidance cultures. The degree of dependency on elders and other family members will be stronger and different in collectivistic cultures than in individualistic cultures. In high power distance cultures experts are viewed as authorities.

The importance of others influencing a buying decision will vary with the type of product. If a product is consumed privately (e.g., necessities), the opinions of others are viewed to be less important than if a product is used publicly (e.g., luxury goods). In China friends and colleagues have a particularly strong influence on buying cosmetics. Friends (particularly girlfriend/boyfriend) and sisters are viewed as being appealing in cosmetics advertisements. The mother and daughter relationship, like the husband and wife relationship, has less relative influence.[178]

Opinion Leaders

In Western decision-making theory, specific individuals are assumed to influence the decision-making process through word-of-mouth communication, generally within a certain product category. Rogers,[179] in his theory of diffusion of innovations, called these people *opinion leaders*. Opinion leaders are strong, informal sources of product information. Opinion leaders get their status because of technical competence and social accessibility. They serve as role models and play an important role in the process of diffusion of innovations (to be discussed in Chapter 8). Rogers's concept of opinion leadership is basically an American concept. The concept as marketers know it today was derived from the diffusion of innovation theory, which resulted from investigation of the speed and pattern of the spread of new farming techniques across the United States. Herein lies a trap for non-US practitioners of marketing, for the assumption typically made is that the US-developed theory has universal applicability. This is doubly dangerous in that foreigners may assume that (at least) the basic theoretical constructs of opinion leadership can be applied without adjustment in other countries.

The roles of opinion leaders, like reference groups, vary across cultures. For example, people with technical competence or competent people in general, are likely to be favored in strong uncertainty avoidance cultures.

An important difference is in the way opinion leaders get their information. Whereas they get their information from the media in individualistic cultures, they obtain their information from the social network in collectivistic cultures. However, some doubts arise if in collectivistic cultures the opinion leader phenomenon is as relevant as it is in individualistic cultures. In collectivistic cultures, information gathering is an unconscious process. There is a strong flow of information between people with so much informal communication that people are not aware of the fact they are getting information or from whom they got the information. So when asked which sources of information they consult, collectivists tend to say 'none' much more than do individualists. Information is like air; it is there and you don't know where you got it. (This is further discussed in Chapter 6, information processing.)

In a comparative study in eight countries worldwide that tested the roles of opinion leaders, some characteristics of opinion leaders appeared to vary across cultures. In 3 of 8 countries, marketers tended to select opinion leaders from an older age group. All three countries were Asian.[180] Green and Langeard[181] found differences in opinion leadership between US and French consumers. The US sample indicated a significantly higher level of group membership than the French sample. Thirty-two percent of the members of the US sample belonged to more than three formal organizations, as compared with only 3% of the members of the French sample. Conversely, only 22% of the US respondents said they did not belong to any formal organizations, as compared with 56% of the French respondents.

Worldwide social media have become platforms for influencing consumers via blogs and, as in advertising, the roles of social media influencers will vary with culture. To a certain point, these social media influencers may serve as opinion leaders, but often there is insufficient transparency over payment of influencers, which reduces their believability.[182]

Conclusion

In this chapter a number of aspects related to the self in the social environment were discussed. Most motivations are not innate, but formed by culture. Motivation theories are culture bound, and they tend to reflect the culture of the theorist who developed the theory. That doesn't mean these theories are useless, but the user must be aware of the cultural bias. Buying motives are not only culture bound, they are also product-category related. Different cultural dimensions explain specific motives for specific product categories. For example, status motives are relevant for luxury goods. Purity is a motive that is most relevant for food and household cleaning products. Needs for dependence and harmony relate to how people dress in public space.

Emotions are not universal, although many students of psychology have learned they are. The emotions referred to as universal are of Anglo-Saxon origin. Although many can be found in other cultures, the connotations with these emotions vary across cultures. In particular, display rules vary. This is important for the service industry as well as advertising. Even if there would be universal emotions, advertising that would display such emotions would not be very relevant or effective in countries where people are not supposed to display them.

Group processes include the functions of in-groups and out-groups and the need to conform to others. With respect to conformity the big difference is between the West and the East, but also between the countries in the south and west of Europe and between the east and the west of Europe. Such differences are important for the marketing of many products.

Notes

1. M.B. Ramose, 'The philosophy of *ubuntu* and *ubuntu* as a philosophy,' in P.H. Coetzee and A.P.J. Roux (eds), *The African Philosophy Reader*, 2nd edn (Routledge, London, 2003), pp. 230–238.
2. M. Cardwell, *The Complete A-Z Psychology Handbook*, 2nd edn (Hodder & Stoughton, London, 2000), p. 160.
3. M. Eysenck, *Psychology: A Student's Handbook* (Psychology Press, Hove, East Sussex, UK, 2000), pp. 127–134.
4. G. Antonides and W.F. Van Raaij, *Consumer Behaviour: A European Perspective* (Wiley, Chichester, UK, 1998), p. 165.
5. G. Hofstede, *Culture's Consequences* (Sage, Thousand Oaks, CA, 2001).
6. A.H. Maslow, *Motivation and Personality* (Harper & Row, New York, 1954).
7. N.J. Adler, *International Dimensions of Organizational Behavior* (Wadsworth, Belmont, CA, 1991), pp. 30–31.
8. Eysenck, *Psychology: A Student's Handbook*, p. 28.
9. D.C. McClelland, *Human Motivation* (Cambridge University Press, Cambridge, UK, 1988), p. 32.
10. J.-C. Usunier, *Marketing Across Cultures*, 3rd edn (Pearson Education, Harlow, UK, 1999), p. 67.
11. T.M. Singelis, 'Some thoughts on the future of cross-cultural social psychology,' *Journal of Cross-Cultural Psychology*, 31 (2000), pp. 76–91.
12. M.R. Nelson and S. Shavitt, 'Horizontal and vertical individualism and achievement values,' *Journal of Cross-Cultural Psychology*, 33 (2002), pp. 439–458.
13. M.H. Hsieh and A. Lindridge, 'Universal appeals with local specifications,' *Journal of Product and Brand Management*, 14, 1 (2005), pp. 14–28.

14. J. Williams, 'Constant questions or constant meanings? Assessing intercultural motivations in alcoholic drinks,' *Marketing and Research Today* (August 1991), pp. 169–176.

15. R.T. Green, W.H. Cunningham, and I.C.M. Cunningham, 'The effectiveness of standardized global advertising,' *Journal of Advertising*, 4 (1975), pp. 25–30.

16. R. Mandhachitara and T. Piamphongsant, 'Professional women's fashionable clothing decisions in Bangkok and New York City,' *Journal of International Consumer Marketing*, 28, 2 (2016), pp. 135–149.

17. R.W. Pollay, 'The identification and distribution of values manifest in print advertising 1900–1980,' in R.E. Pitts Jr. and A.G. Woodside, *Personal Values and Consumer Psychology* (Lexington Books, D.C. Heath, Lexington, MA, 1984), pp. 111–135.

18. N. Papavassiliou and V. Stathakopoulos, 'Standardization versus adaptation of international advertising strategies: Towards a framework,' *European Journal of Marketing*, 31 (1997), pp. 504–527.

19. D. Singh, *Cross Cultural Comparison of Buying Behavior in India*, Doctoral thesis (University Business School, Panjab University, Chandigarh, 2007).

20. B. Stępień, A. Pinto Lima, L. Sagbansua, and M.B. Hinner, 'Comparing consumers' value perception of luxury goods: Is national culture a sufficiently explanatory factor?,' *Economics and Business Review*, 2, 16 (2016), pp. 74–93.

21. *Reader's Digest, A Survey of Europe Today* (1970).

22. *Risk Issues* (Special Eurobarometer report no. 238, 2005), 16 wealthy countries.

23. 'Malaysian feminists drive car ad off air,' *Asian Marketing and Advertising* (24 February 1995), p. 6.

24. M.S. Jo and E. Sarigollu, 'Cross-cultural differences of price-perceived quality relationships,' *Journal of International Consumer Marketing*, 19, 4 (2007), pp. 59–74.

25. D.W. White and K. Absher, 'Positioning of retail stores in Central and Eastern European accession states: Standardization versus adaptation,' *European Journal of Marketing*, 41, 3/4 (2007), pp. 292–306.

26. EMS (1997).

27. B. Godey, D. Pederzoli, G. Aiello, R. Donvito, K-P. Wiedmann, and N. Hennigs, 'A cross-cultural exploratory content analysis of the perception of luxury from six countries,' *Journal of Product and Brand Management*, 22, 3 (2013), pp. 229–237.

28. C-C. Lin and S. Yamaguchi, 'Under what conditions do people feel face-loss? Effects of the presence of others and social roles on the perception of losing face in Japanese culture,' *Journal of Cross-Cultural Psychology*, 42, 1 (2011), pp. 120–124.

29. J. Chen and S. Kim, 'A comparison of Chinese consumers' intentions to purchase luxury fashion brands for self-use and for gifts,' *Journal of International Consumer Marketing*, 25, 1 (2013), pp. 29–44.

30. Y. Jiang and N. Li, 'An exploratory study on Chinese only-child-generation motives of conspicuous consumption,' in H. Li, S. Huang, and D. Jin (eds), *Proceedings of the 2009 American Academy of Advertising Asia-Pacific Conference* (American Academy of Advertising in conjunction with China Association of Advertising of Commerce and Communication University of China, 2009), pp. 121–129.

31. M. Roll, *Asian Brand Strategy* (Palgrave McMillan, London, 2006), pp. 50–51.

32. L. Zheng, J. Phelps, and M. Hoy, 'Cultural values reflected in Chinese Olympics advertising,' in H. Li, S. Huang, and D. Jin (eds), *Proceedings of the 2009 American Academy of Advertising Asia-Pacific Conference* (American Academy of Advertising in conjunction with China Association of Advertising of Commerce and Communication University of China, 2009), pp. 26–27.

33. L.L. Monkhouse, B.R. Barnes, and U. Stephan, 'The influence of face and group orientation on the perception of luxury goods,' *International Marketing Review*, 29, 6 (2012), pp. 647–672.

34. Information from Vivek Gupta, Senior Vice President IMRB BrandScience at Kantar Group, Bangalore, India.

35. *Europeans' Attitudes Towards the Issue of Sustainable Consumption and Production* (Flash Eurobarometer report 256, April 2009).

36. 'Very clean people, the Japanese,' *The Economist* (2 August 1997), pp. 70–71.

37. European Federation of Bottled Water (see Appendix B).

38. *Consumers in Europe: Facts and Figures: Data 1996–2000*, Eurostat (Office for Official Publications of the European Communities, Luxembourg, 2001), p. 63.

39. *TGI Product Book 2009*. Data used for 22 wealthy countries worldwide, GNI/capita > US$17,000; *TGI Product Book 2013*, data for 46 countries worldwide; *TGI Global Product Usage Guide 2013*, 46 countries.

40. *Consumers in Europe*, p. 733.

41. *Risk Issues.*

42. *Society at a Glance*, OECD Social Indicators (2009).

43. C. Power, 'McParadox,' *Newsweek* (10 July 2000), p. 15.

44. Eysenck, *Psychology: A Student's Handbook*, p. 137.

45. C. Ratner, 'A cultural-psychological analysis of emotions,' *Culture and Psychology*, 6, 1 (2000), pp. 5–39.

46. H. Markus, S. Kitayama, and G.R. VandenBos, 'The mutual interactions of culture and emotion. Psychology Update,' *Psychiatric Services*, 47 (1996), pp. 225–226.

47. D. Matsumoto and H.S. Hwang, 'Culture and emotion: The integration of biological and cultural contributions,' *Journal of Cross-Cultural Psychology*, 43, 1 (2012), pp. 91–118.

48. S. Kitayama, H.R. Markus, H. Matsumoto, and V. Norasakunkit, 'Individual and collective processes in the construction of the self: Self-enhancement in the United States and self-criticism in Japan,' *Journal of Personality and Social Psychology*, 72 (1997), pp. 1245–1266.

49. B. Mesquita and N.H. Frijda, 'Cultural variations in emotions: A review,' *Psychological Bulletin*, 112 (1992), pp. 179–204.

50. J.B. Nezlek, K. Kafetsios, and C.V. Smith, 'Emotions in everyday social encounters: Correspondence between culture and self-construal,' *Journal of Cross-Cultural Psychology*, 39, 4 (2008), pp. 366–372.

51. D. Matsumoto, *Culture and Psychology: People Around the World*, 2nd edn (Wadsworth, Belmont, CA, 2000), pp. 305–310.

52. C. Flora, 'The pursuit of happiness,' *Psychology Today* (15 December 2008). Available at: www.psychologytoday.com/articles/200812/the-pursuit-happiness (accessed 1 January 2009).

53. B. Mesquita, N.H. Frijda, and K.R. Scherer, 'Culture and emotion,' in J.W. Berry, P.R. Dasen, and T.S. Saraswathi (eds), *Handbook of Cross-Cultural Psychology*, Vol. 2 (Allyn & Bacon, Boston, 1997), pp. 258–260.

54. J.A. Russell, 'Facial expressions of emotion: What lies beyond minimal universality?,' *Psychological Bulletin*, 118 (1995), pp. 379–391.

55. J.A. Russell, 'Culture and the categorization of emotions,' *Psychological Bulletin*, 110 (1991), pp. 426–450.

56. Markus et al., 'The mutual interactions of culture and emotion.'

57. K.R. Scherer, 'The role of culture in emotion-antecedent appraisal,' *Journal of Personality and Social Psychology*, 73 (1997), pp. 902–922.

58. Ratner, 'A cultural-psychological analysis of emotions.'

59. H-J.J. Kim and R.B. Hupka, 'Comparison of associative meaning of the concepts of anger, envy, fear, romantic jealousy, and sadness between English and Korean,' *Cross-Cultural Research*, 36, 3 (2002), pp. 229–255.

60. B. Olatunji et al., 'Confirming the three-factor structure of the disgust scale-revised in eight countries,' *Journal of Cross-Cultural Psychology*, 40, 2 (2009), pp. 234–255.

61. J.R. Lewis and R. Ozaki, '*Amae* and *Mardy*: A comparison of two emotion terms,' *Journal of Cross-Cultural Psychology*, 40, 6 (2009), pp. 917–934.

62. D.Y.F. Ho, W. Fu, and S.M. Ng, 'Guilt, shame and embarrassment: Revelations of face and self,' *Culture and Psychology*, 10, 1 (2004), pp. 64–84.

63. Kim and Hupka, 'Comparison of associative meaning of the concepts of anger, envy, fear, romantic jealousy, and sadness between English and Korean.'

64. L. Schmidt-Atzert and H.S. Park, 'The Korean concepts *dapdaphada* and *uulhada*: A cross-cultural study of the meaning of emotions,' *Journal of Cross-Cultural Psychology*, 30 (1999), pp. 646–654.

65. P. Ekman, 'Strong evidence for universals in facial expressions: A reply to Russell's mistaken critique,' *Psychological Bulletin*, 115 (1994), pp. 268–287.

66. H.A. Elfenbein and N. Ambady, 'Cultural similarity consequences: A distance perspective on cross-cultural differences in emotion recognition,' *Journal of Cross-Cultural Psychology*, 34 (2003), pp. 92–110.

67. M. Biehl, D. Matsumoto, P. Ekman, V. Hearn, K. Heider, T. Kudoh, and V. Ton, 'Matsumoto and Ekman's Japanese and Caucasian facial expressions of emotion (JACFEE): Reliability data and cross-national differences,' *Journal of Nonverbal Behavior*, 21 (1997), pp. 3–21.

68. E.T. Hall, *Beyond Culture* (Doubleday, New York, 1976), pp. 81–82.

69. J.L. Aaker and P. Williams, 'Empathy versus pride: The influence of emotional appeals across cultures,' *Journal of Consumer Research*, 25 (1998).

70. M. Yuki, W.W. Maddux, and T. Masuda, 'Are the windows to the soul the same in the East and West? Cultural differences in using the eyes and mouth as cues to recognize emotions in Japan and the United States,' *Journal of Experimental Social Psychology*, 43 (2007), pp. 303–311.

71. J. Park, Y.M. Baek, and M. Cha, 'Cross-cultural comparison of nonverbal cues in emoticons on Twitter: Evidence from big data analysis,' *Journal of Communication*, 64 (2014), pp. 333–354.

72. K. Takahashi, T. Oishi, and M. Shimada, 'Is Smiling? Cross-cultural study of recognition of emoticon's emotion,' *Journal of Cross-Cultural Psychology*, 48, 10 (2017), pp. 1578–1586.

73. Z. Ye, 'The Chinese folk model of facial expressions: A linguistic perspective,' *Culture and Psychology*, 10, 2 (2004), pp. 195–222.

74. Matsumoto, *Culture and Psychology*, p. 286; Hofstede, *Culture's Consequences*, p. 157.

75. D. Matsumoto, J. LeRoux, C. Wilson-Cohn, J. Raroque, K. Kooken, P. Ekman, et al., 'A new test to measure emotion recognition ability: Matsumoto and Ekman's Japanese and Caucasian brief affect recognition test (JACBART),' *Journal of Nonverbal Behavior*, 24 (2000), pp. 179–209.

76. A. Tombs, R. Russell-Bennett, and N.M. Ashkanasy, 'Recognising emotional expressions of complaining customers. A cross-cultural study,' *European Journal of Marketing*, 48, 7/8 (2014), pp. 1354–1374.

77. J.A. Russell, 'Is there universal recognition from facial expression? A review of the cross-cultural studies,' *Psychological Bulletin*, 115 (1994), pp. 102–141.

78. L. Wang and R. Markham, 'The development of a series of photographs of Chinese facial expressions of emotion,' *Journal of Cross-Cultural Psychology*, 30 (1999), pp. 397–410.

79. Available at: http://pinktentacle.com/2009/05/emotional-robot-kobian-pics-video/ (accessed 30 November 2009).

80. H.A. Elfenbein and N. Ambady, 'On the universality and cultural specificity of emotion recognition: A meta-analysis,' *Psychological Bulletin*, 128 (2002), pp. 203–235.

81. Z. Gao, J. Xu, J.H. Kim, 'The effect of racial cues on the reader's response to advertisements. A US-China comparative study,' *Asia Pacific Journal of Marketing and Logistics*, 25, 3 (2013), pp. 510–532.

82. K.R. Scherer, R. Banse, and H.G. Wallbot, 'Emotion inferences from vocal expression correlate across languages and cultures,' *Journal of Cross-Cultural Psychology*, 32 (2001), pp. 76–92.

83. Elfenbein and Ambady, 'On the universality and cultural specificity of emotion recognition.'

84. Matsumoto, *Culture and Psychology*, p. 287.

85. C. Kagitçibasi, 'Individualism and collectivism,' in J.W. Berry, M.H. Segall, and C. Kagitçibasi (eds), *Handbook of Cross-Cultural Psychology*, Vol. 3 (Allyn & Bacon, Boston, 1997), pp. 2–49.

86. D. Matsumoto et al., 'Mapping expressive differences around the world: The relationship between emotional display rules and individualism versus collectivism,' *Journal of Cross-Cultural Psychology*, 39, 1 (2008), pp. 55–74.

87. K. Wang, R. Hoosain, T.M.C. Lee, Y. Meng, J. Fu, and R. Yang, 'Perception of six basic emotional facial expressions by the Chinese,' *Journal of Cross-Cultural Psychology*, 37, 6 (2006), pp. 623–629.

88. Ye, 'The Chinese folk model of facial expressions.'

89. L. Anolli, L. Wang, F. Mantovani, and A. De Toni, 'The voice of emotion in Chinese and Italian young adults,' *Journal of Cross-Cultural Psychology*, 39, 5 (2008), pp. 565–598.

90. B. Mesquita, N. Frijda, and K.R. Scherer, 'Theoretical and methodological issues,' in J.W. Berry, P.R. Dasen, and T.S. Saraswathi (eds), *Handbook of Cross-Cultural Psychology*, Vol. 2 (Allyn & Bacon, Boston, 1997), pp. 255–297.

91. H.C. Triandis, *Individualism and Collectivism* (Westview, Boulder, CO, 1995).

92. Matsumoto, *Culture and Psychology*, p. 295.

93. K.M. Sheldon, L. Titova, T.O. Gordeeva, E.N. Osin, S. Lyubomirsky, and S. Bogomaz, 'Russians inhibit the expression of happiness to strangers: Testing a display rule model,' *Journal of Cross-Cultural Psychology*, 48, 5 (2017), pp. 718–733.

94. W.B. Gudykunst and M.H. Bond, 'Intergroup relations across cultures,' in J.W. Berry, M.H. Segall, and C. Kagitçibasi (eds), *Handbook of Cross-Cultural Psychology*, Vol. 3 (Allyn & Bacon, Boston, 1997), pp. 119–161.

95. Mesquita and Frijda, 'Cultural variations in emotions.'

96. W. Friesen, *Cultural Differences in Facial Expression in a Social Situation*, unpublished doctoral dissertation (Department of Psychology, University of California, San Francisco, 1972).

97. Hofstede, *Culture's Consequences*, pp. 156, 157, 160.

98. Russell, 'Facial expressions of emotion.'

99. Nelson and Shavitt, 'Horizontal and vertical individualism and achievement values.'

100. *Values of Europeans* (Standard Eurobarometer 69.1, November 2008).

101. Mesquita et al., 'Theoretical and methodological issues,' p. 270.

102. Matsumoto, *Culture and Psychology*, p. 300.

103. Mesquita et al., 'Theoretical and methodological issues,' p. 287.

104. F. Rothbaum and B.Y.P. Tsang, 'Lovesongs in the United States and China,' *Journal of Cross-Cultural Psychology*, 29 (1998), pp. 306–319.

105. T.J. Domzal and J.B. Kernan, 'Creative features of globally-understood advertisements,' *Journal of Current Issues and Research in Advertising*, 16 (1994), pp. 29–47.

106. M.H. Huang, 'Exploring a new typology of advertising appeals: Basic versus social, emotional advertising in a global setting,' *International Journal of Advertising*, 17 (1998), pp. 145–168.

107. M.B. Holbrook and R.A. Westwood, 'The role of emotion in advertising revisited: Testing a typology of emotional responses,' in P. Cafferata and A.M. Tybout (eds), *Advertising and Consumer Psychology* (DC Heath, Lexington, MA, 1998), pp. 353–371.

108. S.E. Moriarty, *Creative Advertising, Theory and Practice* (Prentice-Hall, Englewood Cliffs, NJ, 1991), p. 79.

109. J.-M. Dru, *Disruption* (Wiley, New York, 1996), p. 9.

110. J. Ramaprasad and K. Hasegawa, 'Creative strategies in American and Japanese TV commercials: A comparison,' *Journal of Advertising Research*, 32 (1992), pp. 59–67.

111. Majorie Dijkstal, advertising researcher at FHV/BBDO, the Netherlands (personal communication, 1995).

112. H.R. Cooper, A. Holway, and M. Arsan, 'Cross-cultural research – should stimuli be psychologically pure or culturally relevant?,' *Marketing and Research Today* (February 1998), pp. 67–72.

113. C. Lin, 'Cultural values reflected in Chinese and American television advertising,' *Journal of Advertising*, 30 (2001), pp. 83–94.

114. D. Oyserman, H.Coon, and M. Kemmelmeier, 'Rethinking individualism and collectivism: Evaluation of theoretical assumptions and meta-analyses,' *Psychological Bulletin*, 128 (2002), pp. 3–72.

115. Triandis, *Individualism and Collectivism*, p. 9.

116. T. Doi, *The Anatomy of Dependence* (Kodansha International, Tokyo, 1973).

117. W.B. Gudykunst and S. Ting-Toomey, *Culture and Interpersonal Communication* (Sage, Newbury Park, CA, 1988), pp. 42–43.

118. G.M. Eckhardt and M.J. Houston, 'Cultural paradoxes reflected in brand meaning: McDonald's in Shanghai, China,' *Journal of International Marketing*, 10 (2002), pp. 68–82.

119. Oyserman et al., 'Rethinking individualism and collectivism.'

120. *European Cultural Values* (Special Eurobarometer report 278, 2007).

121. A. Roland, *In Search of Self in India and Japan* (Princeton University Press, Princeton, NJ, 1988), pp. 134, 149.

122. Standard Eurobarometer 55, 2001.

123. Standard Eurobarometer 87, 2017.

124. *European Social Reality* (Special Eurobarometer Survey 273, 2007).

125. 'America's strange clubs: Brotherhoods of oddballs,' *The Economist* (23 December 1995), p. 63.

126. *Information Society* (Flash Eurobarometer 241, 2008).

127. M. Minkov, *What Makes us Different and Similar* (Infopartners, Sofia, Bulgaria, 2007), p. 175.

128. R.W. Belk, 'Cultural and historical differences in concepts of self and their effects on attitudes toward having and giving,' in T.C. Kinnear (ed.), *Advances in Consumer Research* (Association for Consumer Research, Provo, UT, 1984), pp. 753–760.

129. 'Dog accessories go through the "woof"', *The Asahi Shimbun*. Available at: www.asahi.com (accessed 16 September 2002).

130. *OECD Family Database* (Directorate of Employment, Labour and Social Affairs, OECD Social Policy Division, 2016). Available at: www.oecd.org/els/family/database.htm; J. Chamie, 'Out-of-wedlock births rise worldwide,' *YaleGlobalOnline* (2017). Available at: https://yaleglobal.yale.edu/content/out-wedlock-births-rise-worldwide.

131. G.M. Rose, V. Dalakas, and F. Kropp, 'Consumer socialization and parental style across cultures: Findings from Australia, Greece, and India,' *Journal of Consumer Psychology*, 13, 4 (2003), pp. 366–376.

132. C. Kagitçibasi, 'Autonomy and relatedness in cultural context. Implications for self and family,' *Journal of Cross-Cultural Psychology*, 36, 4 (2005), pp. 403–422.

133. X. Bringué Sala and C. Sádaba Chalezquer, *The Interactive Generation in Ibero-America: Children and Adolescents Faced with the Screens* (Colección Fundacion Telefónica, 2008).

134. *Towards a Safer Use of the Internet for Children in the EU: A Parents' Perspective* (Flash Eurobarometer report 248, December 2008).

135. *Family Life and Decision Making* (Future Foundation, 2009). 12 countries in Europe.

136. F.J. Mindy and J.U. McNeal, 'How Chinese children's commercials differ from those in the United States: A content analysis,' *Journal of Advertising*, 30 (2001), pp. 79–92.

137. EMS (2007).

138. *Youth in Europe* (Eurostat, 2014).

139. Singh, *Cross Cultural Comparison of Buying Behavior in India*.

140. S. Asch, S. (2000). 'Studies of independence and conformity: A minority of one against a unanimous majority,' *Psychological Monographs*, 70 (Whole no. 416) (2000). Quoted in Eysenck, *Psychology: A Student's Handbook*, p. 556.

141. Hofstede, *Culture's Consequences*, p. 232.

142. N. Etcoff, S. Orbach, J. Scott, and H. D'Agostino, *Beyond Stereotypes: Rebuilding the Foundation of Beauty Beliefs*, findings of the 2005 Dove Global Study (February 2006).

143. Singh, *Cross Cultural Comparison of Buying Behavior in India*.

144. D. Thomas, 'Addicted to Japan,' *Newsweek* (14 October 2002), p. 48.

145. M. Zielenziger, 'Young Japanese gobble up luxury items,' *Free Press* (2002). Available at: www. free com/news/nw/japan (accessed 6 September 2002).

146. B.J. Lee, 'Invisible barriers,' *Newsweek* (25 June 2001), pp. 38–39.

147. Oyserman et al., 'Rethinking individualism and collectivism.'

148. J.A. Lee, 'Adapting Triandis's model of subjective culture and social behavior relations to consumer behavior,' *Journal of Consumer Psychology*, 9 (2000), pp. 117–126.

149. M. De Bruyne, 'Het verschil zit in de smaakpapillen [The difference is in the taste],' *Nieuwstribune* (25 September 1997), p. 25.

150. C.A. Warden, S.C.T. Huang, T.C. Liu, and W.Y. Wu, 'Global media, local metaphor: Television shopping and marketing-as-relationship in America, Japan, and Taiwan,' *Journal of Retailing*, 84, 1 (2008), pp. 119–129.

151. C. Robinson, 'Asian culture: The marketing consequences,' *Journal of the Market Research Society*, 38 (1996), pp. 55–62.

152. K. Itoi, 'Dress down for success,' *Newsweek* (13 November 2000), pp. 40–44.

153. L.A. Manrai, D.N. Lascu, A.K. Manrai, and H.W. Babb, 'A cross-cultural comparison of style in Eastern European emerging markets,' *International Marketing Review*, 18, 3 (2001), pp. 270–285.

154. R.H. Holman, 'A values and lifestyles perspective on human behavior,' in R.G. Pitts and A.G. Woodside (eds), *Personal Values and Consumer Psychology* (DC Heath, Lexington Books, Lexington, MA, 1984), pp. 35–54.

155. Gudykunst and Ting-Toomey, *Culture and Interpersonal Communication*, pp. 138–141.

156. Ibid., p. 143.

157. Hofstede, *Culture's Consequences*, p. 231.

158. Gudykunst and Ting-Toomey, *Culture and Interpersonal Communication*, p. 143.

159. G. Rocha, 'What women want,' *M&M Europe, Latin America* (December 2001), pp. xii–xiii. Countries surveyed were Argentina, Brazil, Chile, Mexico, and Venezuela.

160. S.P. Han and S. Shavitt, 'Persuasion and culture: Advertising appeals in individualistic and collectivistic societies,' *Journal of Experimental Social Psychology*, 30 (1994), pp. 326–350.

161. Y. Zhang and B.D. Gelb, 'Matching advertising appeals to culture: The influence of products' use conditions,' *Journal of Advertising*, 25 (1996), pp. 29–46.

162. 'Research watch,' *M&M Europe* (May 2001), p. 41.

163. *Reader's Digest* surveys 1970 and 1991.

164. *Consumers in Europe* (2001), p. 251.

165. *Living Conditions in Europe* (Eurostat Statistical Books, 2014).

166. *Family Life and Decision Making in the Household* (Future Foundation, 2009).

167. *Information Society* (Flash Eurobarometer 241, 2008).

168. *Structure of Consumption* (Eurostat, 2005).

169. B. Powell, 'But we like it at the office,' *Newsweek* (6 June 1994), p. 25.

170. Roland, *In Search of Self in India and Japan*.

171. A. Ramdas, 'Onbegrijpelijke democratie [Incomprehensible democracy],' *NRC Handelsblad* (2 October 2000).

172. J. Adler, 'Is America a nation of slobs?', *Newsweek* (20 February 1995), pp. 42–49.

173. R. Zhou, 'In defense of pajamas,' *China Daily* (11 November 2009). Available at: www.china-daily.com.cn/opinion/200911/06/content_8923160.htm (accessed 27 November 2009).

174. L.A. Manrai, D.N. Lascu, A.K. Manrai, and H. Babb, 'A cross-cultural comparison of style in Eastern European emerging markets,' *International Marketing Review*, 18 (2001), pp. 270–285.

175. 'People average 4 hours on personal grooming. What motivates them?', *GfK* (2016). Available at: www.gfk.com/insights/press-release/people-average-4-hours-a-week-on-personal-grooming-what-motivates-them/ (accessed 31 March 2018).

176. *Consumer Survey* (Flash EB 117, 2002).

177. *Risk Issues*.

178. R. Bradley, B.R. Barnes, P.J. Kitchen, G. Spickett-Jones, and Q. Yu, 'Investigating the impact of international cosmetics advertising in China,' *International Journal of Advertising*, 23 (2004), pp. 361–387.

179. E.M. Rogers, *Diffusion of Innovations* (Free Press, New York, 1962).

180. R. Marshall and I. Gitosudarmo, 'Variation in the characteristics of opinion leaders across cultural borders,' *Journal of International Consumer Marketing*, 8 (1995), pp. 5–22.

181. R.T. Green and E. Langeard, 'A cross-national comparison of consumer habits and innovator characteristics: What makes French and US consumers different?', *Journal of Marketing*, 39 (1975), pp. 34–41.

182. A. Nicolaou, 'How to win friends online and influence people,' FT Special Report Global Brands, *Financial Times* (8 June 2016). Available at: www.ft.com/reports.

Mental Processes

How people see, what they see and do not see, how they think, how language structures their thinking, how they learn, and how they communicate are mental processes that apply to consumer behavior. These processes – in psychology called *cognitive processes* – deal with understanding of several *how*s of behavior. Consumer behavior is learned in the context of a specific social system. Consumer learning theories generally focus on repetition and the creation of simple associations between elements (e.g., a brand name becomes associated over time with a picture or a slogan), whereas more sophisticated approaches to learning are concerned with how advertising messages are stored in memory. These processes of storage and retrieval are the major focus of the dominant perspective in cognitive approaches to advertising, that of information processing.[1] With the acceptance of the person as a carrier of culture, cognitive processes are also considered as being shaped by culture. They will systematically vary as a function of the manner in which the self is culturally constituted.[2]

Cognition and Cognitive Styles

Cognition covers the main internal psychological processes that are involved in making sense of the environment and deciding what action might be appropriate. These processes include thinking and reasoning, understanding and interpreting stimuli and events, attention, perception, learning, memory, language, and problem solving. *Cognitive styles* are defined as 'characteristic, self-consistent modes of functioning that individuals show in their perceptual and intellectual activities.'[3] This definition reflects the Western, individualistic approach that views cognitive styles typically as part of relatively stable personality traits. But variations of the self influence how people think and process information, either as an independent self, isolated from the context, or context dependent.[4]

Americans are individual centered; they expect their environment to be sensitive to them. Chinese are more situation centered; they are obliged to be sensitive to their environment. Whereas the West is object focused, the East is context focused. This difference underlies different thinking styles, namely abstract versus concrete and analytic versus holistic.

In collectivistic cultures, more concrete styles of thought are found, because thought is more contextual and concrete as compared with individualistic cultures in which thought can be more abstract because it is not necessarily linked to the social environment. The implication for marketing communications is that the Chinese place relatively greater emphasis on the more concrete product attributes when evaluating products than on abstract affective (emotion) aspects.[5] It is not only East Asians who have a holistic cognitive style, but also many Latin Americans. A comparison between US Americans, Brazilians and Chinese found several examples of differences between the three cultures. Brazilian and Chinese images include more background relative to the main person than American images. Brazilians, more than Americans, include more context in photographs, they are more likely to sort objects by relationship than by category, and they are more likely to vary their expressivity based on context. Also the Chinese were found to be more holistic than Americans, but to a lesser extent than Brazilians.[6]

In the West, context dependent thinking is viewed as opposite to logic. The way collectivists, and in particular Asians, think and communicate in symbols and metaphors is viewed as illogic. Most theories of consumer behavior, their spending and decision making, are based on Western, logical thinking. From the early 1900s onward, economists have assumed that consumers have a stable and consistent set of preferences that they try to satisfy, and their decision making is based on rational evaluation of alternatives. Consumers are supposed to make self-interested choices, but they are limited by lack of information. As a result, much attention is paid to trying to understand information behavior.

Culture also influences how people categorize objects. Whereas Americans are likely to group objects on the basis of category membership or on the basis of shared features, Chinese are more likely to group objects or people on the basis of relational contextual criteria. For example, when shown a picture of a man, a woman, and a child, Chinese are likely to group the woman and the child together, because the woman takes care of the child. Americans would group the man and the woman because they are both adults. The American orientation may inhibit the perception of objects in terms of relationships or interdependence. Americans see the behavior of an individual fish moving in various ways in relation to a group of fish as due to internal properties of the individual fish; Chinese are more likely to see the behavior of the individual fish as a reaction to the behavior of the group.[7]

Inhabitants of European countries have distinctly different information wants for car purchases. Germans look out for detailed product specification data for car purchase research (categorization), whereas Italians are more interested in car images and subjective editorial (i.e., the context in which the car is used).[8]

Categorization differences can explain differences in company structure and marketing strategy. Many Asian companies produce a variety of product categories, all under the same company brand name. Companies and marketing departments in Western societies are split into divisions by product category. In the West, specific advertising styles have been developed for specific product categories. Whereas much Western advertising is structured analytically, following rules for the placement of headline, brand name, and pay-off, the total picture is more important for the holistically thinking Asians.

Learning and Memory

Most human behavior is learned. When people act, they learn. *Learning* describes changes in an individual's behavior arising from experience. Consumers learn from past experience. A person's learning is produced through the interplay of needs, stimuli, and reinforcement. Reinforcement results from product usage and satisfaction with the product, and this continuous reinforcement leads to habitual buying.

Culture is learned behavior. It is learned unconsciously. That unconscious process is called *socialization*. Socialization is the process whereby the young of a society learn the values, ideas, practices, and roles of that society. The socialization process is a semiconscious one, in that the major participants in socialization of young people, the family, would not see themselves consciously in this role, whereas others, such as educators, function deliberately for this purpose.

Education systems as well as the concepts behind education vary by culture. In the West, intelligence assumes a key role in human learning, and intelligence involves mostly logical–mathematical and verbal skills. African conceptions of intelligence focus on wisdom, trustworthiness, social attentiveness, and responsibility. Japanese conceptions include different kinds of social competence, such as individuals' sociability and ability to sympathize with others. The Western theoretical framework focuses on the outcome of learning (achievement) rather than on learning itself. This is different from the Chinese people's orientation to lifelong learning, which does not have achievement as an objective, although in the long term it will result in higher levels of achievement.[9]

Memory involves acquiring information and storing it for later retrieval. Learning and memory have great practical significance for many activities in life. Culture also affects memory. There is evidence for better recall of stories consistent with people's own cultural knowledge.[10]

The information a person has acquired must be *organized* in order for it to be placed in one's memory. The human memory is arranged according to *schemata*, structures of knowledge a person possesses about objects, events, people, or phenomena. To place the acquired

A Chanel No. 5 television commercial with a fairy tale moral based on the Little Red Riding Hood fairy tale, well understood by Europeans, had limited meaning for Asian immigrant populations. The narrative advertisement referred to the European fairy tale of Little Red Riding Hood and the Wolf. There are multiple close-ups of a young woman wearing a short red dress and hooded cape. Rich colors (red and gold) are repeatedly used throughout the advertisement, which is set in Paris. It deploys a strong linear narrative technique and the story is essentially a multilayered allegory where, paradoxically, a wolf is under the control of a young woman who is wearing Chanel No. 5 perfume.[11]

information in memory, it must be *encoded* according to the existing schemata. A schema relating to activity is called a *script*. One's generic schema for a product would include what to do with the product, the consequences of using it, and the environment in which it is used.[12] The independent self of individualistic cultures forms context-independent schemata, whereas the interdependent self of collectivistic cultures forms context-dependent schemata.[13]

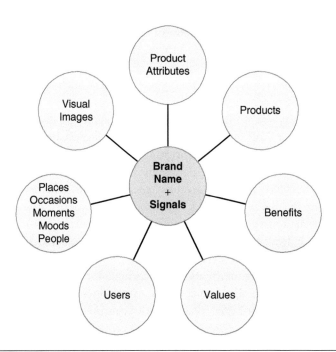

Figure 6.1 **Elements brand association network**

The information we gather about products or brands consciously and unconsciously form networks of associations in our memories related to usage, people, places, occasions, and so on. The associations in the consumer's mind will relate to a number of aspects of the brand (see Figure 6.1):

- The brand name and the brand's visual images: the package, logo, brand properties, and other recognizable aspects
- The product or products linked with the name
- Product attributes: what the product is or has (characteristics, formula)
- Benefits or consequences: rewards for the buyer or user, what the product does for the buyer
- Places, occasions, people, moments, moods when using the product
- Users: users themselves or referent persons or groups
- Values

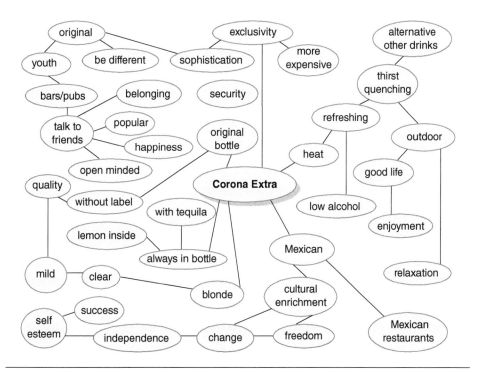

Figure 6.2   **German and Spanish associations with Corona Extra**

Associations are structured in the human mind: attributes and benefits will be linked with users and may be specific for the product category or for the brand. An example is an association network for the beer brand Corona Extra, a Mexican beer exported to many countries in the world. It distinguishes itself by its transparent white bottle with a long neck and the ritual of drinking from the bottle with a slice of lime pushed into the neck. A mixed group of Spanish and German students developed the association network presented in Figure 6.2. This association network includes attributes and benefits as well as values. Two clusters of values can be distinguished. Those of the Germans are success, self-esteem, independence, and freedom; those of the Spanish are belonging, happiness, and sophistication.

Many of the elements of an association network will vary across countries, depending on the people one associates with, places and occasions, and the product's benefits and values. One problem is that values are abstract properties, which people in individualistic cultures can formulate better than people in collectivistic cultures. When brand values are measured in surveys, respondents may find it hard to discriminate their responses when the questions are using relatively abstract expressions like 'the brand has strong associations.' Such associations may be individual, brand specific or culture-specific. In this respect, Western measurement systems that rely on answers to abstract questions are not adequate to measure global brand equity.[14] As associations with brands are part of the method for measuring brand equity, the results of these measurements will vary with individualism/collectivism. Hsieh[15] demonstrated that the brand value calculated based on brand associations for 19 car brands in 16 countries varied significantly. In Europe, the average brand value of the 19 brands was higher than in the Asian countries. These differences appear to correlate with individualism ($r = .68***$). Different cultural conditions lead consumers to different brand evaluations.[16] The associations conveyed in advertising may be different from the associations consumers derive from their own cultural environments.

Diesel, the Italian clothing manufacturer, developed an advertising campaign called 'Global warming ready.' Sophisticated models are posing in Diesel clothing in a world affected by raised water levels and temperatures. The models were shown in several world cities, such as New York, Paris, Rio, London, and Venice. We see the Chinese wall covered by desert sand and Antarctica in the sun with models in swim suits. Figure 6.3 shows New York in high water and Paris as a tropical jungle[17] as well as a picture of a young boy wearing a Diesel T-shirt in Tobolsk, Siberia. Associations with the Diesel brand will be quite different in New York, Paris, and Tobolsk.

Different learning conditions also lead to differences in the way people communicate with each other – to different communication styles. Consumption behavior is part of the society in which people live; it is learned behavior. As consumers gain experience in purchasing and consuming products, they learn not only what brands they like and do not like but also the features they like most in particular brands. Communication and advertising draw on a shared visual vocabulary and a learned system of pictorial conventions.[18] These

Figure 6.3   **Diesel advertising: New York and Paris; Diesel T-shirt Tobolsk. Photograph: Gerard Foekema**

are based on letters, words, pictures, maps, and models that are all part of what people have learned in a particular culture and what has become part of the collective memory of a culture.

Cognition and Affect

Emotions, feelings, and moods are viewed as affective responses to stimuli, whereas knowledge, meanings, and beliefs are cognitive responses to stimuli. Usually the combination of affective and cognitive components contributes to one's general disposition or attitude toward objects, goods, events, persons, or brands.

Western consumer psychology states that the cognitive and affective systems interact, and affective responses (e.g., emotions, feelings) are interpreted by the cognitive system (e.g., 'I wonder why I am so happy'). Examples of cognitive interpretation of a *physical stimulus* are 'This toilet paper is soft,' 'There are no artificial ingredients in this food product,' or 'Ice cream is fattening.' An example of cognitive interpretation of a *social stimulus* is 'The salesperson was helpful.' An example of cognitive interpretation of an *affective response* is 'I love this ice cream.'[19] Research on the cognitive and affective components of attitudes has mainly been done in the Western world. Cross-cultural psychologists have found that the idea that people interpret feelings, emotions, and mood – and even attribute these to phenomena, personal behavior, or personal characteristics – is not a universal phenomenon. The cognition–affect interaction varies across cultures and product categories.

In Western branding strategy, creating a favorable brand attitude, increasing the already favorable brand attitude, or modifying a brand attitude are viewed as basic objectives of advertising. Brand attitude consists of cognitive and affective components. Buying intention models include affective and cognitive components of attitudes to predict buying behavior. Understanding how the two components function across cultures is important for developing measurement tools to assess consumers' attitudes and buying intentions.

Cognitive and Affective Components of Attitudes Toward Food

An example of a product category that in the West involves a different interaction of cognition and affect than in the East is food. In the food domain, examples of affective

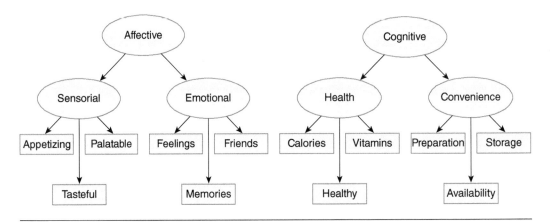

Figure 6.4   **Affective and cognitive components of attitude toward food**

SOURCE: M.C. Cervellon and L. Dubé, 'Assessing the cross-cultural applicability of affective and cognitive components of attitude,' *Journal of Cross-Cultural Psychology*, 33 (2002), pp. 346–357

components are hedonism, pleasure, and sharing food with family and friends. Examples of cognitive components are nutrition, health consequences, and convenience. Cervellon and Dubé[20] use food as an object of study of how affective and cognitive components vary among France, China, and Chinese immigrants in French-speaking Canada. They present a model (Figure 6.4) of attitude, including at the higher level affect and cognition, and at the lower level the object-specific attributes and consequences.

Food attitudes in Western cultures reflect ambivalence between affective and cognitive components. The French value the pleasure of food but also are conscious of possible negative effects on their health. The English and American focus is on health consequences, but this includes paradoxical aspects. Lots of unhealthy fast food is consumed – together with diet drugs and vitamins to compensate for bad eating. So in each cultural group people are convinced that hedonism and health are incompatible, but across Western cultures this phenomenon varies. Whereas Americans combine bad eating with a fitness culture and/ or drugs, the French look for purity in their food. So the affective and cognitive components of attitudes toward food seem to be inconsistent and conflicting. When taste or other affective beliefs attached to food are positive, health and other cognitive beliefs tend to be negative. For the Chinese, however, food attitudes do not reflect ambivalence between affective and cognitive components. Health value and sensory pleasure are viewed as necessary to a person's equilibrium. Food intake reflects a balance in filling and nutritional properties to satisfy physiological and taste properties. For the Chinese, the affective and cognitive components are positively linked. The difference is likely related to individualism/ collectivism because of the difference between guilt and shame cultures. In individualistic cultures, people can develop guilt feelings after doing something incompatible, like enjoying unhealthy food. People of collectivistic cultures lack this sense of guilt.[21] The more recently found dimension of Indulgence–Restraint (IVR) may be related to this specific example, as China scores low on this dimension and Canada high, but as yet this relationship has not been studied.

Cognitive Dissonance

In individualistic cultures, the choice between two desirable alternatives can lead to *cognitive dissonance*. The theory of cognitive dissonance is based on the premise that people have a need for order and consistency in their lives and that tension is created when beliefs or behaviors conflict with one another.[22] A state of dissonance occurs when there is a psychological inconsistency between two or more beliefs or behaviors, and people tend to reduce this dissonance by finding arguments to convince themselves their behavior was right. A frequently used example is cigarette smoking. People know that smoking cigarettes causes cancer, so cigarette smoking will cause dissonance. This dissonance is reduced by referring to examples of people who have grown old while smoking 25 cigarettes per day all of their lives. An effect of cognitive dissonance is that people will collect more information after they have bought a product than before because they want to confirm that they made a good decision. People may also like the product even more after than before buying it because of the need to prevent dissonance.

The cognitive dissonance effect is typical for individualistic cultures where people are driven by a need to classify their emotions, to evaluate them as positive or negative, and do not tolerate conflicting emotions. Seeking internal causes and consistency need generates the dissonance effect. Collectivists realize that people behave differently under different circumstances and may be aware that their behavior often is caused by situational constraints.[23] They can cope with the two types of emotions simultaneously without needing to resolve the incongruity between them. Individualists tend to react to incongruity by discounting one piece of information in favor of another, whereas collectivists tend to give weight to both pieces of information.[24]

Language

Language is an abstract system of rules and a medium of communication. Abstract rules are translated into a channel (spoken, written, sign language) in order to create messages. When the channel is the spoken word, speech is involved.[25] One of the most powerful generalizations discovered about language is that all known writing systems encode spoken language. Writing is speech put into visible form.[26]

Language is a manifestation of culture. At different language acquisition stages, children do not learn language per se; rather they learn the various patterns and styles of language interaction that enable them to function as competent communicators in different situational contexts. They develop a culture-specific communication style that is, for example, direct and explicit in individualistic cultures or indirect and implicit in collectivistic cultures. Examples of words linked with the direct style are categorical words like *absolutely*, *certainly*, or *positively*. By contrast, the cultural assumptions of interdependence and harmony require that collectivists limit themselves to implicit and even ambiguous use of words, using terms like *maybe*, *perhaps*, or *probably*.[27] The English language is the only language in the world that spells *I* with a capital letter. This phenomenon may reflect the fact that the roots of individualism are in England.[28] There is no Japanese equivalent for the English *I*. Different words are used to refer to the self, depending on the social situation, the speaker's gender, age, and the other social attributes relative to the listener. The terms reflect status differences, and the speaker usually attempts to elevate the status of the other, while reducing his or her own status, by choosing the correct wording. Similarly, *you* changes wording, depending on the social context.[29]

Language reflects values, and the expression of values varies by the language used. Several studies have shown that 'forcing' bilinguals to complete a test in their second language can often mean that they will express the values stereotypically associated with that language. In a projective test in both languages, the narratives of French American bilinguals were more romantic and emotional in French than in English. The reverse can operate with respondents who strongly identify with their cultural group. When students in Hong Kong were asked to complete a values test in either English or Cantonese, they expressed more traditional Chinese values in English than in Chinese.[30]

How the structure of language is a reflection of culture was demonstrated by Kashima and Kashima,[31] who studied the relationship between pronoun drop and culture. In some languages – including English – the use of subject pronouns is obligatory: *I* or *you* must be mentioned. By contrast, other languages do not require the utterance of subject pronouns, and these words can be dropped by the speaker's choice. In some Indo-European languages (e.g., Spanish), personal pronouns are not obligatory, partly because the referents can be recovered from the verb inflections. This phenomenon is called *pronoun drop.* Explicit use of *I* signals highlights the person. Its absence reduces the prominence of the speaker's person. Pronoun-drop languages are more associated with a contextualization of the person than languages that do not allow pronoun drops. Drop of the subject pronoun (*I*, *we*, or *you*) was found to correlate significantly with low individualism. Thus, languages licensing pronoun drop are associated with lower levels of individualism than those that require the obligatory use of personal pronouns such as *I* or *you*.

Language reflects culture. Expressions of culture are particularly recognizable in the use of metaphors. Examples are expressions like 'He is a team player,' 'He drives me up the wall,' a 'ballpark estimate,' 'the sweet spot,' all derived from American baseball in the American language, whereas British English has a number of expressions relating to cricket. The elements used in metaphors will vary. In Egypt, for example, the sun is perceived as cruel, so a girl will not be described as 'my sunshine,' but may be compared with moonlight.[32] *Moonlighting* in English means having a second job in the evening.

Some languages have more words for a phenomenon than other languages have, for example, for the different substances of ice or rain in Nordic countries. The Norwegian language reflects a historic seafaring nation, having one strong word for 'wind in your favor': *bør*. Some languages have words that do not exist in others. The English *pith*, the archaic word for 'marrow,' refers to the white under the skin of oranges and other citrus fruit. This seems to be directly linked with the British 'marmalade culture.' There is no equivalent in the Dutch language for the English *to fudge* (empty talk, refusing to commit oneself). The Dutch are not inclined to fudge, which may explain their image of being blunt.

Some culture-specific words migrate to other languages if they express something unique. Examples of such words are *management, computer, apartheid, machismo, perestroika, geisha, sauna, Mafia,* and *kamikaze.* Often, these words reflect the specific values of a culture. They cannot easily be translated into words of other cultures, or they have been borrowed from another culture from the start. The English language does not have its own words for *cousin* and *nephew.* These were borrowed from French (*cousin* and *neveu*). The way a person describes kin is closely connected with the way he or she thinks about them. In extended families, a father and a father's brother may both be termed 'father.' The Hungarians differentiate between a younger sister (*húg*) and an older sister (*növér*). The Russian language has different names for the four different brothers-in-law. In Indonesian, *besan* is the word for 'parents of the children who are married to each other.'[33] Even terms of abuse vary: whereas the most used term of the Germans, Spanish, Italians, and Greek is related to lack of mental capabilities, the French, Brits, Americans, and Dutch use sexually loaded terms. Norwegians use the devil.[34]

The Dutch language shows frequent use of diminutives; so does the Spanish language. In both languages, use of the diminutive suffix reflects something positive, whereas using the enlargement suffix turns it into something negative.

The English language reflects the way Anglo-Saxons deal with action and time. They have a rich vocabulary expressing this, such as 'down to earth,' 'feedback,' 'deadline.' The English word *upset* expresses the way the English handle their emotions, with self-constraint. *Upset* is not translatable into most other languages. The Dutch and the Scandinavians have words for 'togetherness' that express much more than 'being together' and that do not exist in the Anglo-Saxon world. The words are *gezellig* (Dutch), *hyggelig* (Danish), *mysigt* (Swedish), and *kodikas* (Finnish). The Danes use it even in combinations like *hyggetime* ('together time') and *hyggemad* ('together food'). It means sharing your feelings and philosophies in a very personal way while being together in a small group. To an Englishman, this sort of behavior is too intrusive. The concept means preferring a dinner party for four people to a larger group, whereas a small group is not considered to be a dinner party by the British or the Americans. For the Dutch and the Scandinavians, the concept can be used very effectively in advertising for the type of product used during such meetings, such as coffee, sweets, and drinks. The concept will not be understood by members of other cultures. Swedes even have a word for the combination of this feeling together with drinking coffee: *kafferep.*

German examples include the word *Reinheit,* which has a wider meaning than the word *purity.* The word *ergiebig* is another example, meaning delivering quality and efficiency, or more for the same money. The Spanish word *placer* means much more than the translation *pleasure*. It includes pleasure while eating, enjoyment, sharing a social event, softness, warmth, the good life, contentment, and satisfaction. Some words represent interpersonal relations of one culture that do not exist in others. The French notions of *savoir faire* and *savoir vivre* include a vast array of values specific to French culture and cannot be properly translated. The Japanese expression for 'computer graphics' carries the meaning of a picture, a drawing, and illustration or sketch, but not of a graph. Another example is the Japanese word for 'animation,' which in translation carries the meaning of 'comics' or 'cartoons.'[35] In Japan, the word for 'heart' associates with 'warmth,' not necessarily with 'love,' as love is not expressed the same as in the Western world. There are no proper equivalents to the words *identity* and *personality* in the Japanese language, as the concept of personality separate from the social environment is alien to the Japanese people.

Untranslatable concepts often are so meaningful to members of a specific culture that they are effective elements of advertising copy. They refer to collective memory. This implies that words that are labels of culturally meaningful concepts are too ambiguous to use in international campaigns.

A European campaign for the KitKat candy bar was based on the concept of the 'break': 'Take a break, take a KitKat.' The break was an English institution: the 11 o'clock morning tea break, when working people had their morning tea, and brought a KitKat as a snack. Because of this, KitKat in the United Kingdom was called 'Elevenses.' This type of break did not exist in any other country in Europe, so the break concept had to be 'translated' in a different way for the other countries. Continental Europeans do not have the same 'break' memory as do the British.

Language is much more important than many international advertisers realize. It is common knowledge among those who are bi- or trilingual that copy carrying cultural values is difficult to translate. Monolingual people generally do not understand this. If translations are needed, particularly for research purposes, the best system is translating and back-translating the questions to be sure that at least the questions have the same meaning. Yet the values included in the words cannot be translated, and often conceptual equivalence cannot be attained.

The view that language reflects culture is opposed to the Sapir-Whorf hypothesis, which states that the structure of language influences culture via perception and categorization. This would imply that the worldview and social behavior of people depend on the structure and characteristics of the language they speak.[36] The assumption is that certain thought processes are more likely to occur in one language than in another because of the structure of the language. A frequently found assumption is that there are systematic differences between Western and non-Western language and thinking.[37] This idea originated from the work by Bloom,[38] who suggested that in some cultures people use a more abstract form of reasoning, whereas in others forms of reasoning are more concrete, and that this phenomenon would be due to differences in language structure. He investigated reasoning in Hong Kong and concluded that English has a particular constellation of linguistic patterns encouraging a mode of abstract thinking among speakers of English that cannot be found in the Chinese language. Other studies have not supported this finding. It is unlikely that the Chinese are less capable of abstract thinking than Americans.

Language, Perception, and Memory

The structure of a language (e.g., its grammar and type of writing system) has consequences for basic consumer processes such as perception and memory. Structural differences, such as in scripts of Indo-European and Asian languages, seem to affect mental representations, which in turn influence memory. Chinese native speakers rely more on visual representations, whereas English speakers rely primarily on phonological representations (verbal sounds). Written Chinese contrasts with the Latin system because it is ideographic instead of alphabetic. Consumers who use ideographic languages evaluate brand names more in terms of visual features, while speakers of alphabetic languages view brand names with respect to their phonological codes.[39] In the English language, verbal sounds are most used to encode the brand name and facilitate memory. Explicit repetition of words enables consumers to encode and recall the brand name. An example is, 'If anyone can, Canon can,' used as pay-off in ads for Canon in the United Kingdom. Chinese and Japanese languages make it relatively easy for consumers to visually encode and remember the topic and theme (e.g., the brand's function).

Because of their own focus on sound and pronunciation, Western companies are inclined to adapt their brand names to other cultures more vocally than visually.

A first try to 'translate' the brand name Coca-Cola in China was *Ke-kou-ke-la* because when pronounced it sounded roughly like Coca-Cola. It wasn't until after thousands of signs had been printed that the Coca-Cola company discovered that the phrase could mean 'bite the wax tadpole' or 'female horse stuffed with wax,' depending on the dialect. Second time around things worked out better. After researching 40,000 Chinese characters, Coke came up with *ko-kou-ko-le* which translates roughly to the much more appropriate 'happiness in the mouth.'[40]

Chinese consumers are more likely to recall information when the visual memory rather than phonological memory trace is accessed. This information draws from a study by Schmitt et al.,[41] who found that Chinese native speakers were more likely to recall brands when they could write them down than when they generated a spoken response. The authors suggest that marketers, instead of translating Western brand names into Chinese via sound, should enhance the natural tendency of Chinese consumers to rely on visual representations. Visually distinct brand name writings or calligraphy and logo designs that enforce the writing should be more effective in China, whereas for English native speakers the sound qualities of brand names should be exploited by the use of jingles and onomatopoeic names (resembling the sound made by the object). One reason the written language is so important in Chinese is that there are more variations in writing than in sound. One sound can have different meanings that often can only be specified in the written words. This explains why Chinese people during a conversation sometimes write the words in their hands.[42]

In China a name is like a work of art, and the art of writing – *shu-fa* (calligraphy) – has a long tradition. A name should therefore 'look good' and be rendered in appealing writing. Associations with the brand depend on the way brand names are written. In Japan, specifically, brands that use the oldest writing system, *kanji*, are perceived to be 'traditional'; as a result, *kanji* may be appropriate for tea products but not for high-tech products. For high-tech products, the most 'modern' language system, *katakana*, is the best. *Hiragana*, written in the eleventh century by a courtesan, has a somewhat feminine image. It is used for beauty products, hair salons, and kimono stores.[43]

Most companies end up with suboptimal solutions. Some Western firms have kept the Western name and Western spelling. This approach may be appropriate in Japan, where consumers are familiar with the Roman alphabet, but it is less appropriate in a fast-growing market such as China, where only a minority of consumers know the Roman alphabet.

Language and Translations

The availability of specific linguistic devices or tools in a particular language can diminish the load on working memory. Western advertising tends to use efficient value-expressive language to help recognition and memory. But some trait terms that efficiently refer to specific behavior in one language do not exist in other languages. For example, in English, it is possible to combine a number of diverse behaviors under the adjectives *artistic* or *liberal.* These devices do not exist in Chinese. The separate behaviors referred to do exist in China, but there is no encompassing term for them.[44] Whenever in translations it is difficult to find a linguistically or conceptually equivalent word, it likely concerns a concept that represents culturally significant values that cannot be translated into copy for an ad in another culture without losing the value-expressive meaning. Differences between languages can go far beyond mere translation problems. In different cultures, people have different 'schemata.' These schemata are often linked with both a typical language concept and a specific product category.[45] This explains why copy for meaningful advertising concepts of one culture cannot easily be translated into other languages. One language represents only one cultural framework. Speakers of different languages not only say things differently, they experience things differently; the fact that there are rarely direct translations (especially for abstract words) is a reflection of this.[46] The ultimate consequence is that the more meaningful advertising is, the less it is translatable.

The international advertising consultant Simon Anholt says:

Translating advertising copy is like painting the tip of an iceberg and hoping the whole thing will turn red. What makes copy work is not the words themselves, but subtle combinations of those words, and most of all the echoes and repercussions of those words within the mind of the reader. These are precisely the subtleties which translation fails to convey. Advertising is not made of words, but made of culture.[47]

Translations can cause bias in value studies. The phenomenon that bilingual people express different values when using different languages is likely to influence translations of questions. The translation and back-translation system may not be able to correct for value-expression variations. Sometimes questions are simply untranslatable, such as the following two statements that appeared in the original VALS (values and lifestyles) questionnaire in the United States that cannot even be translated into UK English: 'I am a born-again Christian' and 'I like to think I am a bit of a swinger.'[48]

When translating an English brand name into Chinese phonetically, it matters how the Chinese word sounds. However, tonal sounds of Chinese words may sound similar to other Chinese words, but the meaning can be completely different and may be inappropriate.[49]

When adapting a brand name for another culture the choice often is between a semantic translation that transfers brand names into the local language by retaining the meaning of its original name irrespective of its sound, or a phonetic brand translation that transfers brand names into the local language by retaining the meaning of its original name irrespective of its sound. Preferences for the one or other method varies by culture, related to verbal or visual orientation.[50]

Foreign Language Speaking and Understanding

Although English is the most spoken second language in the world, fluency varies widely. Whereas in 2001, 79% of the Danish and 75% of the Dutch said they spoke English well enough to take part in a conversation, only 18% of the Spanish, 22% of the Portuguese, 32% of the French, and 44% of the Germans said they did. Of the British, only 11% speak French and 6% speak German.[51] Foreign language speaking correlates with low uncertainty avoidance. Both for the general public and young people, 58% of variance was explained by low uncertainty avoidance. In 2005 the percentages of people who said they could speak at least one language other than their mother language varied from 93% in Latvia and 91% in the Netherlands to 29% in Hungary and 30% in the United Kingdom.[52] In the high uncertainty avoidance cultures, if people do speak a little of a foreign language, they are reluctant to try because they are afraid to make mistakes.

In countries where large percentages of people say they understand English, this doesn't mean they really understand the meaning of everything said. This has consequences for international advertising. In countries like the Netherlands and Denmark, international advertisers assume understanding of English, in particular among young people, is enough to allow them to leave copy and speech untranslated, which is a dangerous thing to do. A study by Gerritsen and Jansen[53] among young people in the Netherlands showed that lack of English knowledge makes the use of English more popular, but also that Dutch young people (14–17 years old) do not know the meaning of many English language words that are regularly used in the Dutch language. Examples are words like *blazer, entertainment, image, research, sophisticated,* and *strapless.* The word *blazer* was thought to mean remote control or laser pistol; *entertainment*: working with a computer; *image*: energy, brains, health, appearance; *research*: rubbish; *sophisticated*: ugly, hysterical, aggressive; and *strapless* was thought to mean whorish. A former payoff by the electronics company Philips, 'Philips invents for you' was understood as *Philips invites you.* The watch brand Swatch used the term *boreproof,* which was understood as 'drill-proof.' In another study,[54] respondents had a high opinion of their understanding of the English language, but more than half could not write down what was said in the ads and only one third understood the meaning of English fragments in TV commercials. The claim by Fa 'The spirit of freshness' was understood as *the spirit of fitness.* Copy for L'Oreal's Studioline 'style and love for my hair, invisi'gel FX' was understood as *style grow of my hair* and *invisual terrifics.* A claim by Seiko 'lifetime precision without a battery' was understood as *goes slow.* Few Germans understand English language slogans like 'Be Inspired' (Siemens) or 'Impossible Is Nothing' (Adidas).[55]

Some advice about translating television commercials: whereas in large markets such as Germany, France, and Spain, people are used to dubbed television programs, in smaller markets such as the Netherlands, most foreign language programming is subtitled, so people are used to hearing and seeing the lip movements of the original language spoken. Even the best lip-sync looks fabricated to them. Hearing a well-known American soap star speak Dutch with another person's voice doesn't add to credibility. Whether subtitled or dubbed, viewers will note that the commercial is not made for them.

Categorization

How people categorize other people and objects varies with individualism/collectivism and with power distance. Because individualists focus more on individual objects when processing information, classifications based on rules and properties are preferred, whereas collectivists tend to classify events or objects according to relationships and family resemblance. Asking American and Chinese children to group together a cow, chicken and grass in pairs, American children grouped together the cow with the chicken because both were animals; the Chinese children grouped together the cow and grass because cows eat grass.[56] Chinese children will group items together that share a relationship, whereas Canadian children will group items together that share a category.[57] Ask an African to sort a few objects, say some tools, food items, and clothes, and he will put a knife in a potato, as a knife is needed to slice a potato.[58]

Categorization differences have implications for brand strategy. American consumers view a brand extension of a different product category not as fitting with the parent brand. A brand extension must fit, and this fit is judged on the basis of product class similarity. Collectivists view the parent brand in terms of the overall reputation of or trust in the company. So they perceive a higher degree of brand extension fit also for extensions in product categories far from those associated with the parent brand than individualists would.[59]

Whereas companies of individualistic cultures carefully select line or brand extensions that 'fit' the product category, companies from collectivistic cultures stretch their brands in wider directions. The American cola brands wouldn't think of stretching their brands beyond the soft drink and related food category products such as snacks, and if they would do so they would give them different brand names. The European brand Nivea has been careful to limit line extensions to related products and linked them all consistently to the core brand values 'purity' and 'value for money.' Japanese Shiseido, a cosmetics company, has extended its brand into the food category. The overall category they cover is 'beauty,' and both cosmetics and beauty food appear to fit this category. Examples of beauty food are sweets for shiny eyes, lollipops for full hair, and self-tanning chewing gum.[60] The Spanish brand Chupa Chups, characterized by the yellow-red logo designed by Salvador Dali, includes many different products, from lollipops to sunglasses, clothes, shoes, and stationery.

Categorization differences can explain variance of advertising formats and differences in presentation of goods in shops, by sort or by relationship, or by classifier. An example of categorizing by relationship is presenting food products together that are combined when cooking and/or eating, such as pasta with pasta sauce, herbs, or other ingredients and wine, versus presenting it according to the way they are packaged, for example, pasta sauces in pots together with other sauces in pots, pasta together with rice, and wine with wine.

Chinese department stores, unlike their US counterparts, typically offer products that share a classifier. For example, *tai* products (used for electric and mechanical equipment such as blow dryers, TVs, radios, washing machines, computers, and electric knives) are located on one floor.

Unlike Indo-European languages, Asian languages like Chinese, Japanese, and Korean are *classifier* languages. A classifier is a measure that is used in conjunction with numerals (one, two, three, etc.) or determiners (*a, the, that, this*) and that refer to common physical features of objects, such as shape, size, thickness, or length, as well as other perceptual or conceptual properties associated with objects, such as 'bendability' or 'graspability.' Classifiers categorize a given object into a larger set of objects and describe classes of objects. As such they are different from adjectives that describe specific instances within a class. Adjectives answer the question, 'What kind of object is it?,' whereas classifiers answer the question, 'What kind of object is this a member of?' The use of classifiers is found in Chinese, Japanese, Korean, and Thai languages as well as Navajo and Yucatan-Mayan languages. Some languages (e.g., Japanese) have classifiers that are generally of broader scope than classifiers of other languages (e.g., Chinese). Compared to English native speakers, Chinese speakers perceive objects that share a classifier as more similar than objects that do not share a classifier.[61] Chinese-speaking people have schematic organizations based on classifiers, so the Chinese are more likely to recall classifier-sharing objects in clusters than are English-speaking people.

In advertising in classifier languages, objects are more positively evaluated when they are combined with a visual cue related to the classifier. An example is the difference in judgment of pictures of 'graspable' objects (brush, cane, umbrella, broom) using the classifier *ba* in Chinese. A picture showing only the object is judged less positive than one showing the object with a hand. [62]

The classifier system has to be exploited carefully, as it can have positive and negative effects. For example, a classifier for pipe-like thick objects will lead to positive expectations for lipstick, but a classifier for long, thin objects can lead to negative expectations that it will provide less quantity and will not last long. When existing products are modified and change shape, inconsistency can occur. Classifiers used for telephones (objects standing on a frame) cannot be used for cellular phones.[63]

Perception

Perception gives us knowledge of the surrounding world. Perception of what a picture depicts, and that it means something, depends on both the picture and the perceiver. Failure to recognize a picture and its meaning are related to unfamiliarity with the picture itself and with the context.

Nearly all research on perception has been carried out in Western societies. If the development of visual perception depends on certain kinds of learning experiences, then it might be expected that there would be some important cross-cultural differences in perception. Evidence of a basic cross-cultural difference in perception was reported by Turnbull,[64] who studied a pygmy who lived in dense forests and so had limited experience looking at distant objects. This pygmy was taken to an open plain and shown a herd of buffalo a long way off. He argued that the buffalo were insects and refused to believe that they really were buffalo. When he was driven toward the buffalo, he thought that witchcraft was responsible for the insects 'growing' into buffalo. Presumably he had never learned to use depth cues effectively. Because only one person was studied, this study is limited. Moreover, the global spread of images of diverse societies would make such an experiment unrepeatable.

People learn the 'rules of seeing,' and these are not universal principles but are formed by the natural and social environments that teach us both what to look at and how to look.

> When developing algorithms for artificial intelligence through machine learning, machines may search for data patterns based on large numbers of pictures, but across cultures human beings design and recognize similar objects in different ways. An example is how people draw pictures of a chair: in Korea people draw a chair from above, in Brazil from the side and in Germany from the front.[65]

Some studies suggest that the integration of pictorial elements varies cross-culturally. The correct naming of elements of a picture does not predict ability to correctly perceive their mutual relationships.[66]

In perception studies the traditional concern is about *what* is perceived. Do people see or recognize pictures or colors? Next to this are the affective consequences of perception – do people like or dislike what they see?

Selective Perception

Perception can be a selective observation of reality. We actually see what we want to see and expect to see, even if it is not there. We do not see what we do not expect to see. The implication of *selective perception* is that people observe some aspects of reality and do not see other aspects. Selective perception is a universal phenomenon, but it is reinforced by culture. People who are used to behavior and phenomena in their own cultures tend to expect similar phenomena and behavior in other cultures, which may not exist or exist in limited ways. This selective perception process is stronger in individualistic cultures, where people are universalistic and tend to expect that everybody elsewhere has similar values. People tend to ignore the differences and only perceive the similarities. In individualistic cultures, reality is a subjective observation. In collectivistic cultures, more phenomena influence perception. In particular, the context influences what people see and hear. This can easily lead to miscommunication between members of individualistic and collectivistic cultures. When communicating in the different languages of individualistic and collectivistic cultures, the words can be the same, but the context in which the words are interpreted can be different and thus influence understanding.[67] What people hear can also depend on what the speaking person looks like.

Aesthetic Experience

Aesthetic experience refers to the experience of pleasure or displeasure caused by stimuli that are perceived as being beautiful or not beautiful, attractive or unattractive, and rewarding or unrewarding.[68] Many historical and geographical differences in styles and conventions in works of art point to cultural influences. The art of a culture is a symbolic representation of its social structure and social practices. In art and design, visual structures realize meanings as linguistic structures do. Visual language is culturally specific. Western visual communication, for example, is deeply affected by the convention of writing from left to right. Other cultures write from right to left or from top to bottom and as a result will attach different meanings to these dimensions of visual space. Whereas the composition of pages in Anglo-Western print media adheres to a basic left–right structure, others place the main stories and photographs in the top section or in the center. In Western visualization, central composition is relatively uncommon, but central composition plays an important role in the imagination of Asian designers. Centering is a fundamental principle in visual art in many Asian cultures. Although differences in composition and design are largest between East and West, differences are also found among Western countries. Composition of pages and images in the British media are characterized by the contrasting use of the left and right, whereas this is less usual in the Greek or the Spanish media.[69]

East Asians value decoration and the use of nature symbols such as waterfalls, mountains, spring blossoms, and autumn.[70] In East Asian advertising, nature symbols are ubiquitous. The Japanese psychiatrist Doi[71] explains that the Japanese turn to nature because there is something unsatisfying in the way they deal with human relations. Nature is neutral. Dealing with the complications of in- and out-group behavior in collectivistic cultures is much more complicated than human relations in individualistic cultures.

Variables found to influence aesthetic responses are complexity, novelty, uncertainty, and incongruity, but there is little empirical research on whether and how these variables vary across cultures.

Schmitt and Pan have summarized East Asian aesthetic expression as follows:

A general concern for aesthetics – i.e. for an attractive look, touch and feel, and attention to detail – is widespread in the Asia-Pacific Region; and despite regional variations, the region as a whole seems to share a common aesthetic style. Specifically, aesthetic expressions – whether in the arts or in the form of corporate aesthetic output (e.g. packaging, brochures, advertisements, store designs) – are guided by three aesthetic principles. First, Asians value complexity and decoration: they love the display of multiple forms, shapes and colors. This feature is most pronounced in Chinese, Thai, Malay, and Indonesian aesthetics. Second, beauty means balancing various aesthetic elements; harmony in aesthetic expression is seen as one of the highest goals. Third, Asian aesthetic expression values naturalism. In China, symbols and displays of natural objects – of mountains, rivers, and phoenixes – prevail and are frequently found in packaging and advertising … Finally, colors seem to have different meanings and aesthetic appeal in the Asia-Pacific Region than in the West.[72]

Color Perception

Colors represent different meanings and aesthetic appeals in different cultures. There are two major schools of thought relating color and human behavior that reflect the nature/nurture discussion. Color reactions could be innate or learned. The first school argues that color signals the brain to trigger an affective reaction directly, whereas others suggest that color preferences are learned over time as shared meanings or as result of past experiences or as conscious associations in language.[73]

Color categories are greatly determined by a culture's color language.[74] How people describe colors is related to the linguistic terms of their language and these terms vary by culture. Adult speakers of different languages show different patterns of discrimination and memory for the same set of colors. There are no cognitive color categories that are independent of the terms used to describe them.[75]

Cross-cultural studies of *color preferences* have found similarities and differences.[76] Red is the most preferred color by Americans, green by the Lebanese, and blue-green by Iranians and Kuwaitis. Red is found to be most strongly related to China, purple to France, green to both France and Italy.

Also, color associations vary across countries. In the United States, blue is associated with wealth, trust, and security; gray is associated with strength, exclusivity, and success; and orange denotes cheapness. Yellow, orange, and blue are connected with happiness, whereas red, black, and brown are sad colors. Dutch people designate red as the first color that comes to mind, whereas Americans nominate blue. Cross-cultural surveys of color meanings and associations have found that blue is the most highly evaluated color across cultures, followed by green and white. The most potent colors are black and red. In Japan, China, and Korea, purple is associated with expensive, whereas in the United States purple is associated with inexpensive. In India, Hindus consider orange the most sacred color, whereas the Ndembo in Zambia do not even consider orange a separate color. The pairing of colors shows more variation than separate colors. This is important knowledge when creating brand images and packaging across cultures, as often combinations of colors are used. A few examples are of pairing colors with green and red. The color best paired with green is yellow in Canada, Hong Kong, China, and Taiwan, blue in Colombia, and white in Austria. Only the Chinese and Taiwanese pair green with red. In Brazil and the United States people pair red with black, whereas in Colombia, Hong Kong, China, and Taiwan, red is paired with white. In Austria, Canada, and China, the preferred combination with red is yellow. The most selected color to pair with blue is white.[77]

Table 6.1 provides a summary of different color perceptions in 12 countries, based on an inventory by Aslam.[78]

According to the situation, color associations can vary. Although in China, white traditionally has been associated with mourning, young Chinese are pragmatic and have adopted the white wedding dress as a status symbol.

In marketing and branding, colors can have powerful effects. Colors can alter the meanings of the objects or situations with which they are associated and color preferences can predict consumers' behavior. Color is an integral element of corporate and marketing communications. It influences consumers' perceptions and behavior and helps companies

Table 6.1 Color associations for 12 countries

Associations with color	White	Black	Red	Yellow	Green	Blue	Purple
Germany		Sorrow	Lucky	Envy, Jealousy			
UK		Fear Anger					
Sweden		Sorrow				Warmth	
Denmark		Sorrow	Lucky				
Belgium		Sorrow			Envy		
France		Sorrow		Infidelity			
Russia		Anger, Fear		Envy, Jealousy			
USA	Happiness, Purity	Sorrow, Fear Anger, Expensive	Love	Warmth	Good taste, Adventure	Wealth, Trustworthy, Security, High quality	Inexpensive, Love
China	Mourning	Expensive, High quality	Love, Lucky	Pleasant, Happy, Good taste	Trustworthy		Expensive, Love
Japan	Mourning	Fear, Expensive	Love		Love, Happiness	Trustworthy	Expensive, Fear, Sin
India		Dullness, Stupidity	Ambition, Desire			Purity	
Korea	Mourning	Expensive	Love			Trustworthy	Expensive, Love

SOURCE: M.M. Aslam, 'Are you selling the right colour? A cross-cultural review of colour as a marketing cue,' *Journal of Marketing Communications*, 12, 1 (2006), pp. 15–30

position or differentiate from the competition. Color evokes strong product associations and category imageries. In the United States blue is associated with toys, health foods, dairy foods, desserts, and financial services; red is related to toys, pizzas, and some meat products.

The right choice of colors is important for package design. Van den Berg-Weitzel and Van de Laar[79] found that packages for deodorants for women used greater contrast and brighter colors in feminine cultures, whereas they used soft harmonious colors and low contrast in masculine societies to endorse female softness in societies with strong role differentiation.

Color communicates corporate position. In the United States, blue stands for solid, responsible, financial services; green for innovative, caring organizations; and yellow for young, bright, and exciting firms. Whereas blue is the corporate color in the United States, red is the winning business color in East Asia.

Aesthetic Preferences: Paintings and Music

Generally speaking, the little empirical evidence available suggests that with respect to aesthetics, people like most what they are used to. People prefer pictorial images that correspond to the aesthetic traditions of their culture. According to art historian Rudi Fuchs,[80] there is little globalization in art. Art remains linked with a geographic area with its own history.

Preferences for *landscapes* are influenced by the similarity of the landscapes to the living environments of the respondent. Chinese undergraduate students prefer Chinese landscape paintings to Western landscape paintings, whereas Western undergraduate students prefer Western landscape paintings.[81]

Several studies have suggested that people from East Asian cultures (e.g., China, Korea, and Japan) tend to pay greater attention to contextual information in art products than their counterparts in Western cultures. East Asian landscape paintings place the horizon higher than the horizons appearing in Western paintings. The high horizon broadens the space for context, which allows the painter to include more information about mountains, rivers, and other objects, including people.

Differences in aesthetic expression are based on culture-related, learned behavior. Findings from a study by Senzaki et al., suggest that children only after Grade 2 develop expressions unique to each culture. Children who have learned to understand the concept of horizon started to place it higher or lower in their pictures. The amount of contextual information varies with the degree of holistic versus analytical thinking.[82]

With respect to *music* preferences, some studies suggest cultural differences in the perception of consonance and dissonance, but little is known about the nature and extent of such differences. Western tonal music relies on a formal geometric structure that determines distance relationships within a harmonic or tonal space. It follows tonal stability, a consistent set of key notes. This consistency is lacking in African or Indonesian music, where focus is on changing tones, and fixed tone scales like the Western 12-tone scale are not found. A global comparison between the intervals found in Western and in African scales shows that African music does not conform to a fixed chromatic scale nor does it have another fixed scale.[83] Also rhythm in music follows the rhythm of the language of the composer.[84]

When designing products, some shapes can have undesirable associations. IKEA has standardized most of their product offerings. Chinese furniture stores have a broad range of tables with table tops made of glass, and these were also made available in IKEA in China. Figure 6.5 shows a table available at IKEA Shanghai, where you can see a circle surrounded by a square through the glass tabletop. To a Western consumer it looks like a normal small table, but for a traditional Chinese consumer it is not right. In China a circle represents the sky, while a square represents the earth. Putting the sky in the earth makes no sense.[85]

Figure 6.5   **IKEA China. Courtesy of Live Grønlien**

Field Dependency

Research from various areas suggests that members of individualistic and collectivistic cultures differ with respect to the degree to which they perceive objects either as single and independent entities (field independent) or as being related to the context in which they appear (field dependent). *Field dependent* people are influenced in their perception by characteristics of their physical and social environment. *Field independent* people will perceive an object separately from its environment.

The amount of field information is restricted in classic Western art – painters include field information only to the extent that it can realistically be observed given the perspective within a given scene. East Asians, in contrast, have employed various ways of emphasizing field information. The Chinese developed the scroll form to depict a panoramic view of landscape that could include a whole succession of mountain ranges, near and far. The bird's-eye view used in Japanese landscape depiction is another mode of representing field information. The artist's standpoint is higher than the objects depicted.

In Western portraits the intention is to distinguish the figure from the ground. For this reason, the model occupies a major fraction of the space. East Asian portraiture is unlikely to emphasize the individual at the expense of the context. For this reason, the size of the model is relatively small, as if the model is embedded in an important background scene. Analyses of paintings of groups of people show similar results: East Asian paintings of people place the horizon higher and present models smaller than do Western paintings of people. When making photographs, East Asians are more likely than Westerners to set the zoom function in order to make the model small and the context large.[86]

Figure 6.6. shows how this phenomenon applies to design. The traditional design of the package of Fruittella sweets features monsters with no background. This is unacceptable in China, so an exception was made and a landscape was added.[87]

If advertising is developed in collectivistic cultures, it is likely designed to be perceived field dependently. Information that can be perceived by the field-dependent target group cannot as easily be perceived by those who are field independent. Field dependents are likely to see more in a message than intended by the sender. This is further discussed in the section on processing visual images later in this chapter.

Figure 6.6   Fruittella packages in China

SOURCE: E. Visser, *Packaging Design: A Cultural Sign* (Index Book, Barcelona, 2009), s.l

The Creative Process

Artistic creativity refers to the creativity expressed in any aspect of the arts, including visual art, music, literature, dance, theatre, film, and mixed media. Several resources contribute to creativity: intelligence, knowledge, thinking style, personality, motivation, and the social environment. The extent to which a person or a product is judged as creative may be influenced by where the person or the product originates. The social environment can have a profound impact on judgments of the level of creativity of persons or products.[88] It is assumed that the Western conception of creativity is primarily concerned with innovation, whereas the Eastern conception of creativity is more dynamic, involving the reuse and reinterpretation of tradition rather than breaks in tradition.[89]

Two aspects of creativity are *creative expression* (i.e., production of creative products) and *judgment of creative products*. Several studies have measured judgment, but the number of cross-cultural studies measuring differences in production of creativity is limited. A general finding is that judges evaluate in-group creations more positively than out-group creations.[90]

A Western assumption is that the creative process is based on divergent thinking. If that were the core of creativity, the need for conformity in collectivistic cultures would inhibit the creative process. Several creativity tests that were developed in the West have been used to measure differences in creativity across Asian and Western cultures, some based on figurative expression (drawing tests), others based on verbal expression. The results of these studies, generally conducted with children or students, are mixed. Some have demonstrated that people of Western societies are more creative; others found that the Chinese are more creative.

An important difference is the Chinese inclination to perceive and to cognitively organize things holistically, suggesting that Chinese people see and interpret things in terms of wholes and context, which contrasts with an Anglo-American tendency to fragment, decompose, and decontextualize.[91]

> There is some variation in the ways creativity can be fostered in different cultures. And some influences can be explained with the cultural dimensions. For example, cultures high on uncertainty avoidance prefer creative individuals to work through organizational norms, rules, and procedures, and countries high on power distance prefer creative individuals to gain support from those in authority before action is taken. In individualistic cultures that are also low on uncertainty avoidance and power distance, creativity can best survive outside organizational constraints. High power distance means individuals are restricted in challenging others, and deviant ideas tend to be suppressed. In the Western sense, deviant ideas are viewed as a precondition of originality and creativity.

Cultures are creative and innovative within the context of their own systems. No one culture is best for innovation, and no one culture can claim a superiority of ideas. Conceptions and definitions of creativity in one culture should not be applied unthinkingly and uncritically to evaluate and judge creativity in another. The Western view of creativity as a break with tradition and movement beyond what exists contrasts with the Eastern notion of reinterpreting tradition. Classic Chinese visual art has pursued common stylistic and even topical forms for hundreds of years. The aim is not to create a new image or form but to reveal, or better still uncover, an essence through an exploration of or meditation on a long-standing theme. Africans are said to have a special liking for total art as most often a piece of sculpture is accompanied by movement and sound. The creative moment is like a state of grace. The Fon people of South Benin compare the creative process to an illness which comes in cycles and the outcome cannot be foreseen. Artists are as unpredictable as their works. A creative work is unique, but it ends up belonging to the collective process. The artist is the channel through which collective ideas are expressed.[92]

Also, photography is recognized as the product of cultural forces and is therefore particular to the culture that creates the imagery. There are two basic types of photojournalism: a descriptive approach and an interpretative approach. Whereas Korean newspapers use photographs with a more descriptive visual reporting approach, American photographs use a more interpretative approach.

For American photojournalists, self-expression is important, and creativity is a basic requirement. Subjectivity and objectivity are viewed as mutually supportive values. As individualists, they rely on their own individual interpretations, observe and document their subjects as individuals, and focus on distinctive individual personalities. For Korean photojournalists, however, objectivity appears to be the most important value, and subjective values are to be avoided. Artistic creativity is seen as a potential threat. They also adhere more strictly to their societal responsibilities. They are part of a larger group, either the journalistic community as a whole or their particular news organization. They act according to the group's interest rather than according to their own interpretations.

In terms of subject matter, Korean photojournalists tend to document people as part of larger groups. Education reflects or reinforces these culturally determined roles. American photojournalists are far more likely to have majored in journalism, where storytelling is taught, whereas Koreans are more likely to study history and politics. Another consideration concerns the workplace structure journalists inhabit. American photojournalists tend to work in collaboration with editors, writers, and others in the newsroom. Newsrooms in Korea, however, are strictly hierarchical and rigid. Editors demand particular types of photos following a specific assignment. Photographers are expected to return from assignments with the same shots their colleagues at other papers will have delivered to their editors. If a photographer doesn't have a 'required' shot, the photographer has failed, even if he produced a far more creative, innovative shot instead.[93]

Creativity in advertising is an applied form of art. A creative director at an advertising agency has to select properties from what the Canadian anthropologist Grant McCracken calls a culturally constituted world.[94] The selection process proceeds at unconscious and conscious levels. Directors are not always fully aware of how and why a selection is made, even when this selection presents itself as compelling and necessary. The director must decide how the culturally constituted world is to be portrayed in the advertisement. For the creative director, this process works as an automatic pilot. His or her own value system will automatically apply when developing concepts or appeals and when selecting or producing visuals. Generally good creative directors are very much ingrained in their own culture.[95]

Advertising serves as a lexicon of cultural meaning, and the viewer or reader who shares the culturally constituted world with the creator will be able to successfully decode the meaning transferred. The viewer or reader who does not do so may not be able to decode the meaning as meant by the designer of the ad.

Advertising is a reflection of the culture of the designer and his or her design training. In the West, design training generally gives the aspiring designer some insights into art and design history. The learning process, however, stops after school, when the Western designer-artist is required to be an instant genius. In contrast, as in most Asian cultures that favor a lifelong learning process, Japanese designers continue actively seeking out other influences.[96]

Attribution

Attribution theory is a theory about searching for causes of human behavior or phenomena. Causal attribution involves predicting and explaining the behavior of other people or finding causal explanations of events in order to predict similar ones in the future. Events can be explained as being due to either internal or external causes. Internal causes are those causes attributed to characteristics of individuals or groups, such as dispositions (efforts, ability of people) or personality traits. External causes are those causes attributed to situational constraints or to contextual factors. In individualistic cultures one's behavior or the result of one's behavior (e.g. success) is explained more by internal attributes than by situational factors, whereas the reverse is true in collectivistic cultures that focus on external, relational attributes such as social support or situational factors.[97]

There are particular differences with respect to attributing failure or success. In individualistic cultures, both attributions to success and failure are internal. In collectivistic cultures, the explanations of failure, but not of success, are more external, referring more to situation and context than to the ability of people. North Americans tend to give internal, dispositional explanations for behavior even when behavior is obviously caused by situational factors. For this phenomenon North American psychology uses the term *fundamental attribution error.*[98]

Another dimension involved in explaining internal versus external attribution is cultural masculinity.[99] In masculine cultures, people tend to take both their problems and their competencies more seriously, as compared with ego-effacing norms in feminine cultures.

When service providers fail to deliver, they want to respond positively to recover. The types and results of service recovery efforts vary across cultures. If service providers offer explanations for failing service, they may shift the American consumer's focus from blaming the service provider's personal characteristics (lazy, incompetent) to paying more attention to the situation as a cause of failure. East Asians are more apt to be aware of situational constraints and seek to maintain social harmony. So offering explanations is not the way to service recovery. Whereas North Americans want to be compensated for service failure, East Asians gain face in the eyes of family and friends by a genuine apology by top management, not just by front-line personnel.[100]

Locus of Control

A phenomenon related to attribution is *locus of control*, introduced by Julian Rotter.[101] Many attribution findings that indicate differences between the West and the East revolve around this locus dimension.[102] *Internal* or *external* locus of control refers to the degree to which persons expect that an outcome of their behavior depends on their own behavior or personal characteristics versus the degree to which persons expect that the outcome is a function of chance, luck, or fate, under the control of powerful others, or simply unpredictable.[103] At the culture level, the difference suggests that in some cultures people are more inclined to take social action to better their life conditions (also called *civic competence*), whereas in other cultures people are more dependent on institutions such as authorities and governments. Understanding the difference is important, because internal locus of control is part of the fundamental assumptions in consumer behavior, for example, in behavior intention models. North Americans tend to experience that they personally control events in their daily experience. They hold an exaggerated sense of control or mastery.[104] Roper Starch found that 84% of adult Americans believe that if you have an unhappy life, you can change it if you try.[105] They strongly believe that personal happiness is in their own hands and can be changed by force or will or effort. By contrast, the word happiness in Korean means 'fortunate or lucky blessing.'[106]

The dimensions involved in explaining internal and external locus of control are individualism, power distance, and uncertainty avoidance; the latter two usually are the most significant. However, Smith et al.[107] found a significant correlation between internal locus of control and individualism across 43 countries. Members of collectivistic cultures are controlled more externally than are members of individualistic cultures.

In 2005, Eurobarometer[108] asked the degree of influence people felt they had over things that happen to them. For 27 countries, the percentages agreeing with having little influence correlated with high power distance ($r = .55^{***}$), low individualism ($r = -.54^{***}$), and high uncertainty avoidance ($r = .54^{***}$). Figure 6.7 illustrates the correlation with power distance for 13 countries. The peaks in the chart are countries that score high on uncertainty avoidance

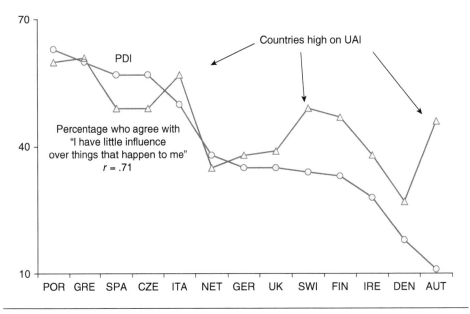

Figure 6.7   **Degree of perceived influence on life's happenings**

SOURCES: Hofstede et al. (2010) (see Appendix A); EBS 225 (2005) (see Appendix B)

Triandis[109] reported a 1985 study among American and Soviet students who were asked their opinions on two opposing statements: 'Human beings are unable to rule themselves and their government should rule them' versus 'Human beings should rule themselves, best government is least government.' The Soviet students, high on power distance and uncertainty avoidance, chose the first statement, whereas the American students, of low power distance and uncertainty avoidance, chose the second statement.

Locus of control is about expectations of authority versus the ability and wish of people to rule themselves. Thus, we find that reliance on the government for welfare[110] is related to high uncertainty avoidance, which explains 32% of variance. Reliance and dependence upon authorities also make people feel at the mercy of the authorities, which leads to lack of confidence in government institutions, such as the justice system, the police, and the civil service. Several data support these cultural relationships. Data from several Eurobarometer surveys show the relationship between trust in institutions or media and power distance and uncertainty avoidance. Table 6.2 shows examples of internal and external locus of control from various surveys.

Table 6.2 **Examples of internal and external locus of control**

Sources	Internal locus of control (Individualism, and low on power distance and uncertainty avoidance)	External locus of control (Collectivism, and high on power distance and uncertainty avoidance)
Social Values, Science and Technology (Special Eurobarometer 225, 2005)		People have little influence over things that happen to them
Eurodata, Reader's Digest Survey in 17 European countries (1991)		Reliance on the government for welfare
European Values Study (2005) Eurobarometer 69 (2008)		Lack of confidence in government institutions such as the justice system, police, and civil service
Standard Eurobarometer 88 (2017)	Trust public administration, national government, parliament	No or low trust in the media Trust online social networks
Cyber Security (Special Eurobarometer 464a, 2017)	When receiving fraudulent e-mails, contact no one, able to protect myself	When receiving fraudulent e-mails, contact police
Confidence in the Information Society (Flash Eurobarometer 250, 2009)	Feeling personally responsible for ensuring security on the Internet	
Globalisation (Flash Eurobarometer 151b, 2003)		Government should control globalization
Standard Eurobarometer 47 (1997)	Belief in cancer prevention by a better diet and healthy lifestyle	Belief in cancer prevention by regular medical check-ups

(Continued)

Table 6.2 **(Continued)**

Sources	Internal locus of control (Individualism, and low on power distance and uncertainty avoidance)	External locus of control (Collectivism, and high on power distance and uncertainty avoidance)
Attitudes of European Citizens Towards the Environment (Special Eurobarometer report 295, 2008)	Environmental problems related to our own consumption habits; my action can make a difference	Environmental problems related to natural disasters
Attitudes of European Citizens Towards the Environment. (Special Eurobarometer report 468, 2017)	As an individual I can play a role in protecting the environment; activities in the past done: cut down energy consumption, used car less, bought products with energy label	Worried about impact plastic products on your health

SOURCES: Hofstede et al. (2010) (see Appendix A); *European Value Study*, Eurodata and several Eurobarometer reports between 1997 and 2017(see Appendix B)

In cultures where external locus of control operates, the church – the moral authority – is trusted, but there is no confidence in the justice system, the civil service, or the police. In particular, low trust in the justice system is remarkable. In the wealthy, western part of Europe (15 countries), the relationship between no confidence in the justice system and power distance is even stronger. In some cases power distance explains 80% of variance.

In cultures where external locus of control prevails, people expect more from their governments than in cultures with internal locus of control, and governments can more easily influence people's attitudes. An example is how, across 12 countries in Europe, people answer the question when asked how globalization should be controlled.[111] The higher the countries score on power distance, the higher the percentage of people who say there should be more regulation by their governments to control globalization.

An example of differences in locus of control was acceptance of the European single currency (euro) before and after the introduction. Over time various surveys measured the acceptance of a single European currency. The relationships with culture demonstrate that being for a single currency has been a matter of external locus of control. In 1970, when the idea of a single currency was still an abstract concept, individualism explained variance. After 1990, it was related to large power distance and/or strong uncertainty avoidance. Large power distance means that people are used to others (e.g., government) making decisions for them. The idea that the single currency would be introduced over the heads of the people is something that was more difficult to accept in low power distance cultures than in high power distance cultures. This explains the strong and lasting opposition against the euro in Denmark, a country that scores very low both on power distance and on uncertainty avoidance. It is noticed that neither the young Europeans nor the wealthy target of EMS were very different from the mainstream in Europe in their attitudes to the single currency. Even after the actual introduction on 1 January 2002, in countries like Spain and Belgium many more people were for the euro than in the Netherlands and Finland. Being for the euro, however, didn't fit actual behavior. In the high uncertainty avoidance cultures, higher percentages of people said that they kept converting prices in their national currencies than in low uncertainty avoidance cultures. For example, 78.1% of the French said they converted prices versus 39.7% of the Irish.

With respect to Internet safety, locus of control differences operate. In individualistic cultures that are also low on power distance and uncertainty avoidance, more people feel personally responsible for ensuring security on the Internet. In the high power distance and collectivistic cultures, people are more inclined to not protect with the argument that antivirus products are too expensive or because security is too difficult to implement and use.[112] As a reaction to fraudulent e-mails the external locus of control cultures would contact the police, as compared with internals who say they are able to protect themselves. Externals have low trust in the media, but they trust online social networks.

Also related to locus of control are people's views about the degree to which they can influence their own health. In 1997, Eurobarometer asked questions about people's opinions about the possibility of cancer prevention. The differences between the European countries with respect to belief in prevention are large and culture bound. The questions were 'Do you personally think that cancer can be prevented, or not?' If Yes, 'How can it be prevented?' Answer possibilities were 'By a better balanced diet and a healthy lifestyle' or 'By regular medical check-ups.' Externals, who are dependent upon and trust experts and authorities, think that cancer can be prevented. They believe in regular check-ups (by experts). Internals believe they are able to influence their health themselves, for example, by a better diet. With respect to the environment, externals associate with natural disasters – beyond their control – and internals view environmental problems related to their own consumption habits.[113] They also think their own actions can make a difference (see Table 6.2).

Internal versus external locus of control can also be an instrument to explain differences in social and political attitudes or financial systems. External locus of control is likely to make people prefer government or company pension funds, whereas internal locus of control is likely to make people prefer individual pension insurance. In Great Britain, 75% of men of working age have some private pension provision, far more than in continental Europe.[114]

Figure 6.8 shows how countries can be clustered according to internal/external locus of control. This is a two-dimensional map of power distance and uncertainty avoidance. The countries in the left two quadrants are also mostly individualistic, and the countries in the right-hand quadrants are also mostly collectivistic, except France and Belgium that are individualistic.

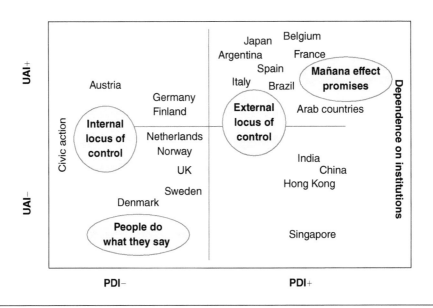

Figure 6.8   **Internal and external locus of control**

SOURCE: Data Hofstede et al. (2010) (see Appendix A)

Understanding the difference is important because internal locus of control is part of the fundamental assumptions in behavior intention models and in decision-making theories. When testing new product concepts, buying intent is regarded as one of the key performance indicators. In external locus of control cultures, people will be more inclined to express buying intention than internally driven consumers would. If one is used to fate or power holders interfering at any time in the realization of an expressed intention, it is easy to express a positive intention even when knowing reality may be different. This is reflected in the way buying intention is expressed. It will predict behavior less than it does in internally driven cultures. So it affects survey results.

Information Processing

Information processing theory is a psychological approach that analyzes how people acquire, organize, and use information to assist choice behavior. The underlying assumption is that people want to solve problems and choose rationally. Information may be viewed as reducing uncertainty in a decision making process, but there is a limit to the information people need or use. Uncertainty is not decreased by providing more information and it does not result in increased rationality of decision making. Yet, theories of consumer decision making, communication behavior and how advertising works are based on a universal assumption that in order to make a buying decision, consumers want to inform themselves, but this is not a universal process.

How people acquire information, if they do this consciously, and the importance of information varies with individualism/collectivism and power distance. In individualistic cultures, information is an all-encompassing need. No decision should be made without information. Information is the dominant factor that defines attitudes toward Internet advertising in the United States, as compared with trustworthiness as the dominant factor in Korea.[115] In collectivistic cultures people base their buying decisions on feelings and trust in the company and acquire information mostly via interpersonal communication, whereas in individualistic cultures people will actively acquire information via the media, friends, or organizations to prepare for purchases.

Eurobarometer[116] asked people to what degree they viewed themselves as well informed consumers. Across 14 Western European countries, the answers 'well informed' correlated with low power distance, low uncertainty avoidance, and individualism, which explains 61% of variance. Another question was which information sources (e.g., newspapers, TV, Internet, magazines, friends and relatives, consumer organizations) people consult to prepare for purchases.[117] The percentages of answers 'Normally I don't consult any information source' correlate with high power distance, which explains 58% of variance. Figure 6.9 illustrates the relationship for 12 countries.

Another example is from a Eurobarometer survey of 2010 on science and technology,[118] asking for levels of knowledge on a variety of scientific matters, showing significant negative correlations between individualism and the percentages of respondents who feel poorly informed about science, culture and the arts, politics, and sports news. These data show how, across cultures, information needs and perception of information vary, and this is not related to actual available information. Consistently, respondents in the more collectivistic south of Europe feel less informed than those in the individualistic North of Europe, and they also express a greater need for information, although objectively there is no lack of information. The percentage of British who feel well informed about sports news[119] is about three times as high as that of the Spanish. Yet the amount of sports news on Spanish television is about five times as high as on British television.[120] With respect to environmental issues, in the high power distance cultures, although people confirm the importance of eco labels in purchasing decisions, the percentages of people who say they never read any labels correlate with high power distance.[121] Asking for the need for information in cultures where knowledge is in the person because of a strong flow of interpersonal communication, people may not be aware of any need for information, and may answer survey questions accordingly.

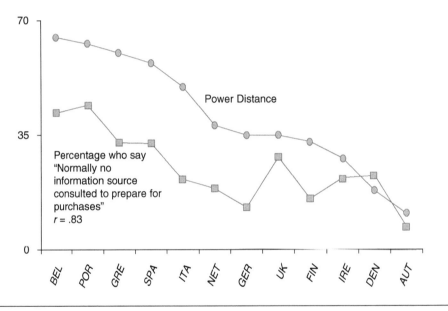

Figure 6.9   **Information behavior**

SOURCE: Hofstede et al. (2010) (see Appendix A); Flash EB 117 (2002) (see Appendix B)

Shelton Gunaratne, when analyzing Asian approaches to communication theory, has pointed at the *information seeking paradigm* as implicit in Western communication theory. In Western information processing theory the information-seeking paradigm 'assigns the communicational initiative to the receiver rather than the sender. It assumes several logical levels of knowledge including the receiver's knowledge about his/her lack of knowledge.'[122]

In most collectivistic cultures with much casual communication, where people talk a lot with each other, there is such an amount of exchange of oral interpersonal communication that people may not be aware of receiving information and they don't see the need to search for information, as it is readily available. It is like air, it is there without noticing it, like the water is for the fish that do not notice that the water is wet.

There is much human interaction, people meet their friends daily, they meet people in bars and restaurants, in the streets, they use the mobile phone more and blog more, so there is a constant flow of communication between people, also called *word of mouth*. In China, the major influence on purchase decisions is word of mouth.[123] Chinese youngsters rely on social networking sites as a source of electronic word of mouth (eWOM) in their decision-making process.[124]

If there are such strong flows of information between people, information is everywhere, and people cannot easily recall where they got the information from and whether they use it for making a buying decision. Theorists from individualistic cultures tend to call this *intuitive decision making*, suggesting it is not information based without understanding that the information is there, but the process is different.

Individualists of low power distance and low uncertainty avoidance actively search for information to make a buying decision. Across ten European countries the effect of online research on the brand chosen correlates with low power distance and low uncertainty avoidance.[125] The percentages of respondents that feel well informed about environmental issues across 23 countries in Europe correlate with low power distance, individualism, and low uncertainty avoidance.[126] Table 6.3 provides several other examples. Also across a group of seven Asian countries searching for information on products or services correlates with low power distance.[127] A number of such cultural relationships are presented in Table 6.3.

Table 6.3   **Information behavior**

	PDI	IDV	UAI	Predictor	R^2
Europe					
2002 – Feel well informed as consumer	−.57*	.78***	−.64**	IDV	.61
2002 – No information source consulted for buying decision	.76***			PDI	.58
2008 – Feel well informed about environmental issues	−.60***	.70***	−.55***	IDV	.49
2017 – Not well informed about the risks of cybercrime	.64***	−.49**	.76***	UAI IVR-	.57 .72

(Continued)

Table 6.3 **(Continued)**

	PDI	IDV	UAI	Predictor	R^2
2011 – Consider oneself well informed when choosing and buying goods and services	−.49**	.66***	−.63***	UAI-	.52
2012 – I will not make a decision if I am not well informed	.64***		.73***	UAI	.54
2008 – Internet related activities: search for information	−.49**	.49**		IDV	.24
2007 – I often recommend brands to others		−.51*			
2007 – People often ask my opinion about brands		−.48*			
2009 – Never read any labels when making a purchase decision	.35*				
2008 – Visit bar every day		−.76***	.52***	IDV-	.58
2008 – Meeting friends every day		−.41*			
Asia					
2008 – Internet: read blogs		−.89***		IDV-	.80
2008 – Internet: chat		−.95***		IDV-	.91
2008 – Activities via PC: search for information on products, services	−.74*				

SOURCES: Hofstede et al. (2010) (see Appendix A); *Europe*: 2002: Flash EB 117; 2008: EBS 295; 2007: *Reader's Digest* Trusted Brands; 2008: Flash EB 241; 2009: Flash EB 256; 2011: EBS 342; 2012: EMS 2012; 2017: EBS 464a; 2008: *Asia*: Synovate PAX Asia (see Appendix B)

Culture influences the way people process positive or negative information. In line with not displaying negative emotions (see Chapter 5), collectivists do not like negative communication and don't want to be confronted with problems. The problem-solving format of advertising that is so popular in the United States will be less effective in collectivistic cultures. Indians would be averse to buying a product category (e.g., deodorants) by which you implicitly admit you have a problem. Even being seen in a shop picking such a product from the shelf is a social risk. A positive approach like freshness or attraction, ignoring the problem, will be more effective.[128] Collectivists are more focused on ignoring negative information than attending to positive information. Because of the importance of face, which is easier lost than gained, avoidance of negative input is important for East Asians.

North Americans, however, because of the importance of high self-esteem, are used to focusing on positive self-characteristics to positively distinguish themselves from others.[129]

Processing Advertising

When consumers process advertising, either the information presented in an advertisement will fit existing schema or a new schema will be established. Most acquired information is organized in schemata that already exist in the memory. Often only the information relevant and important to the activated schema is selected; the rest is lost. Next, the meaning (semantic content) is interpreted so as to be consistent with the schema, to make it fit. Finally, schematically stored information can be used to make judgments, evaluations, and choices. However, the information must be retrievable before it can be used; it must be remembered.

Western information-processing theory generally states that distinctive (unusual) information is easier to remember than ordinary information. *Salient* (highly important) information is easier to remember than unimportant information. Many things can go wrong in this process. First, one's own cultural roots may inhibit the perception of stimuli coming from another cultural perspective. Second, interpretation of the meaning may not be as intended. Third, the evaluations and decision-making process may vary.

An example of advertising that did not fit the schemata of the target audience was an ad aimed at housewives in Finland that used quick cuts and short scenes that were associated exclusively with the youth ads the Finns saw on music channels such as MTV. Such styles were uncommon on Finnish terrestrial channels, where the housewives expected to see ads aimed at them. So an ad that used that style was dismissed as a commercial for young people. It might be thought that the ad's distinctiveness would make it stand out for the Finnish target, whereas in fact its execution cut it off from its audience by appearing to target others.[130]

The eternal dilemma of advertising is whether to follow the conventions of advertising for a particular product category in a particular culture or to be distinctive in order to raise awareness and find a place in people's memories. Within countries the danger of using distinctive, unusual information in advertising to attract attention is that it will not fit in consumers' schemata and will be discarded. This risk is even greater across cultures than within cultures because people's schemata vary. How people process information is related to the type of information people are used to processing. People of high-context cultures, used to symbols, signs, and indirect communication, will process information in a different way to people of low-context cultures who are used to explanations, persuasive copy, and rhetoric. Aaker and Lee[131] show that greater attention is associated with the processing of culture-compatible versus culture-incompatible messages. Briley and Aaker[132] suggest that this is modified by context. Compatibility effects may mostly arise when automatic, effortless processes guide judgments. Culture-based differences in processing arise when a person processes information in a cursory, spontaneous manner, but these differences decrease when a person's intuitions are supplemented by more deliberative processing.

Western Bias in Cross-Cultural Analysis of Advertising

The influence of Western information-processing theory has resulted in a biased approach to the way advertising is analyzed across countries. Information-processing research does not emphasize the meanings audiences might ascribe to advertising stimuli; it deals with the processing of details in advertisements, not with the holistically perceived meaning. It assesses, for example, the drawing power of proposed headlines or copy, it can indicate whether a celebrity spokesperson is perceived as credible, and it analyzes the copy points of an advertisement.[133]

Many cross-cultural advertising studies compare the information content of advertising. In order to operationalize the distinction between informative and noninformative content, a typology by Resnik and Stern[134] is often used. If at least one of 14 informational cues is present, an advertisement is considered to be informative. These 14 informational cues are price-value, quality, performance, components, availability, special offers, taste, nutrition, packaging or shape, guarantees and warranties, safety, independent research, company research, and new ideas. An informational cue generally is defined as 'a cue that is relevant enough to assist a typical buyer in making an intelligent choice among alternatives.' That doesn't make the procedure a proper one for cross-cultural research. What is informational for consumers in one culture may not be informational or relevant for consumers in another culture. In high-context cultures, relevance in advertising isn't even an issue. The type of information cues defined by Resnik and Stern also do not allow for measuring the influence of context. They cannot properly cover other types of information, such as indirect visual cues, which may be interpreted as informative by people of high-context cultures. It is the typical Western analytical system, which is not appropriate for measuring holistically developed Asian advertising. By the use of such Western scales, information of Eastern societies may be missed by forcing these communications to fit into the prescribed Western categories.[135]

Processing Visual Images

There are significant cross-cultural differences in pictorial perception and recognition. Visual language predominantly varies from one culture to another, much in the same way that textual language varies. When processing visual images, field (in)dependency plays a role. East Asians allocate their attention more broadly than Americans, and they are also slower at detecting changes in the center of a picture.[136]

Face recognition is facilitated if people are of the same ethnicity (discussed in Chapter 5). Complex visual images, relying on implicit meaning, can be better processed by members of collectivistic cultures, who are more used to deriving meaning from context, than by members of individualistic cultures, who are more used to simple visual images that carry explicit meaning. In low-context (individualistic) cultures, meaning often relies on explicit information; pictures speak for themselves. In high-context (collectivistic) cultures, much of the information derived from a message is present in the context. People have learned to decode implicit metaphorical messages and contextual language. This difference already exists at early age. Some indirect visual messages – in the English language called *mood metaphors* – are better understood by Chinese children than by British children.[137] When consumers have to quickly process complex information, such as visual information in advertising, familiarity will be a critical factor influencing the resulting brand preferences.[138] In Spain, advertisements including pictures (either alone or with text) are associated with higher levels of attitude toward the ad than those including only text.[139]

A picture that is very meaningful for members of one culture because it expresses important values of that culture can be completely meaningless to members of another culture. An example is the LG advertisement shown in Figure 6.10. East Asians recognize this picture as *continuity.* What the old man cannot finish in his life, the young one can. Most Westerners will not be able to recognize the meaning of this picture. Yet, the ad was placed in a Western business journal. Likewise, Asians may not be able to grasp the meaning of the frog-prince, a European fairy tale written by the German brothers Grimm.

Imagery is an important element of advertising, yet in research it is undervalued because of the historical focus on verbal communication in the United States. This bias is reflected in the use of the phrase 'copy theory' instead of 'advertising theory.' Also the terms 'copy research' and 'copy testing,' used for testing effectiveness of advertising, point at a bias toward thinking in verbal stimuli. As a result little is known about how consumers from different cultures process visual images in print advertisements. Visuals have been used for standardizing print advertisements worldwide with the underlying assumption that consumers from all around the world can 'read' a picture, whereas the copy of the advertisement often needs to be translated. However, these highly standardized visual campaigns do not always convey a uniform meaning among audiences. For example, Benetton's ad

Figure 6.10 **Advertisement for LG and Infonet**

with a black woman nursing a white baby won awards for its message of unity and equality in Europe. At the same time, the ad stirred up controversy in the United States, since many believed it depicted a black nanny in the subordinate role as a slave.[140] It is a misconception that visuals are understood across cultures. Pictures fit in schemata people have, and schemata vary by culture. A picture, meant in one culture to be associated with freedom (e.g., a lion), may be known in another culture to represent strength.

What may be thought to be a universal picture is likely to be interpreted in different ways. People can derive different meanings from the same message because contextual people will 'see' more in the message than was intended by the producer of the message. Because in high-context cultures people are used to contextual messages, they will read more into pictures and derive 'hidden' meaning from a visual image. Even for simple visual images with highly explicit information, the high-context audience may try to construct more abstract metaphorical meaning. This effect was demonstrated by Callow and Schiffman,[141] who tested image processing between the United States and the Philippines, countries that contrast strongly with respect to individualism and collectivism. Based on existing ads for perfume, variations were made with single persons or groups of people. The ability to derive implicit meaning from the visuals was measured by two associations, affiliation (collectivistic value) and achievement (individualistic value). The results showed that the higher-context Filipino respondents read higher levels of affiliation into the meaning of a man standing by himself and higher levels of personal achievement into the meaning of a group of women standing together as compared with their American counterparts.

Differences in perception and visual processing result in a range of differences in the use of pictures in advertising. A multi-country comparison in the United States, United Kingdom, France, Korea, and India[142] of visual components of print advertising found variations with respect to the size of the visual, frequency of usage of photographs and product portrayals, the size of the product, usage of metaphors, frequency of persons in general – and specifically women and children – depicted in advertising. When measuring the effects of visuals in advertising, visuals and words tend to be analyzed as separate items, with the role of visuals as a separate cue, suggesting that the use of an unexpected visual will grab the viewer's attention and get him or her to engage in more effortful and elaborative processing. However, visuals may have a direct and unconscious effect and, consequently, many studies of advertising visuals have not taken into account the context of the visuals or the likelihood of viewers treating the entire advertisement, no matter how incongruous, as information of some sort.[143]

Processing Foreign Words

The use of foreign words in advertising has two purposes. One purpose is to get *attention*. The assumption is that foreign words in advertising make the advertisement distinctive and raise curiosity. The other purpose is *efficiency* in international advertising. Using only one advertisement – usually in the English language – without translation is cheaper because no translation costs are involved. Foreign words in ads are supposed to raise attention and to be remembered as long as these expressions are perceived as unusual, unexpected, yet relevant information. However, the meaning of a foreign expression should be sufficiently apparent to the audience and the expression should add to, not detract from, the existing associations in consumer's schema for the advertised brand. Using French words in a wine advertisement aimed at an English-speaking audience is fine as long as such consumers regard 'Frenchness' as an important attribute of wines. If such foreign words are used in ads directed at monolingual audiences, only a limited number of words can be used, and only with the purpose of associating country of origin, for example, phrases like *pasta Italiano*. There is some evidence that to an English language audience product perceptions and evaluations change when the brand name is pronounced in French or English. French names produce a more hedonic perception than English names.[144] However, studies in the Netherlands showed that English language terms used in shop names, although liked, did not lead to more positive associations with the shops or more positive shop images.[145] Neither did the use of English lead to positive attitudes toward brands.

The purpose of English language in international advertising is to appeal to international segments. To young people, English language ads would be more appealing because they would represent the youthfulness and progressivity of the United States and thus add prestige to the brand. To Koreans, the fact that English is the language of international business may give brands expressed in English a cosmopolitan appeal. Among young Japanese, foreign symbols are considered to be exotic.[146]

Involvement Theory

Classic consumer behavior theory poses that people process information, in particular advertising, in what is called a *learning hierarchy*. People would be motivated to seek a lot of information, carefully weigh alternatives, and come to a thoughtful decision. Later theories include variations in a consumer's level of involvement in activating different cognitive processes when a message is received. One of the early sequences in how people were thought to process information and react to advertising was that people first should learn something about a product or brand, then form an attitude or feeling, and consequently take action, meaning purchase the product or at least go to the shop with the intention to buy. This sequence is called *learn–feel–do*. It was later seen as mainly applicable to processing information for products of 'high involvement,' such as cars, for which the decision-making process was assumed to be highly rational. This so-called *high-involvement* model assumes that consumers are active participants in the process of gathering information and making a decision. In contrast, there are low-involvement products, such as detergents or other fast-moving consumer goods, with related low-involvement behavior when there is little interest in the product. The concept of *low involvement* is based on Herbert Krugman's[147] theory that television is a low-involvement medium that can generate brand awareness but has little impact on peoples' attitudes. The low-involvement sequence was assumed to be *learn–do–feel*. Again, knowledge comes first, after that purchase, and only after having used the product would one form an attitude.

International advertising scholar Gordon Miracle[148] argued that for the Japanese consumer another sequence is valid: *feel–do–learn*. The purpose of Japanese advertising is not to sell or change attitude, like Western advertising. It is based on building a relationship between the company and the consumer. The purpose of Japanese advertising is to please the consumer and to build 'dependency' (*amae,* see Chapter 5), and this is done by the indirect approach. As a result, 'feel' is the initial response of the Japanese consumer, after which action is taken: a visit to the shop to purchase the product. Only after this comes knowledge. Miracle suggests that this sequence also applies to Korean and Chinese consumer responses. It may well apply to all collectivistic cultures.

According to Petty and Cacioppo's elaboration likelihood model (ELM),[149] information processing follows a central and/or peripheral route depending on the degree of involvement in the message. Within the central route, a person engages in thoughtful consideration (elaboration) of the issue-relevant information (= arguments) within a message. If the person lacks the motivation or ability to undertake issue-relevant thinking, processing follows a peripheral route. Actively thinking about the arguments in the message is the central route. When the person is not motivated to think about the arguments, the peripheral route is followed. In the theory, the peripheral route generally includes visual cues like the package, pictures, or the context in which the message is presented. The theory is embedded in Western advertising practice that uses pictures as illustrations of words. In many Western studies, visual cues are not viewed as informational but as emotional, in contrast to the rational aspects of advertising copy. However, because visuals are convention based, all pictures are interpreted according to learned patterns, just like reading words or recognizing numbers, and thus must be processed cognitively. Using pictures as peripheral stimuli becomes questionable under this theory. In collectivistic cultures, where people process information holistically instead of analytically, the theory may not apply at all. For properly processing an advertisement, the context is likely to be as important or even more important than the verbal message. If the information in the different cues of an advertisement (e.g., picture and words) is incongruent, North Americans tend to increase elaboration to resolve incongruity by discarding one of the incongruent pieces of information, whereas the more holistic East Asians are more likely to tolerate incongruity.[150]

Decision Making

The fundamental assumption in Western decision-making theory is that decisions do not 'happen'; someone 'makes them.' This is a Western view. Japanese are more likely to prefer events to shape whatever actions are required, to stand back from an event rather than attempt to control it by decision making.[151] Next to this, various aspects of decision making vary by culture, for example, the consumer need for information, preferences for quality, brand image, specific product features, and who influences the decision. The previous chapters have discussed these aspects.

American-based decision-making theory is based on internal locus of control. People are in control of their own destinies and are fully in charge of their own performance. In many cultures with a more fatalistic approach to life, various uncontrollable higher-order forces are assumed to shape people's acts and future. In cultures where external locus of control operates, people tend to postpone decisions more ('*mañana* syndrome') than in cultures where internal locus of control operates – cultures of the configuration of individualism and weak uncertainty avoidance.[152] Western thinking is that the chances of making an optimal choice are better when choosing among a large number of options. This cannot be generalized. Self-expression needs and ideals of uniqueness lead individualists to see greater value in having choices than collectivists do.

In marketing literature it is generally suggested that the decision-making process of consumers follows several stages, although not in all cases do all consumers pass through all stages. These stages are problem recognition, information search, evaluation of alternatives, purchase decision, and post-purchase behavior. Such models are based on the information-processing approach to consumer decision-making theory that suggests a rational consumer who thinks and evaluates consciously and rationally. The evaluation process is not universal. When presented with contradictory arguments, Americans tend to weigh them and choose the better one. The presence of a weaker argument only strengthens their conviction that they have made the right choice. Chinese often do the opposite. They may accept both options even if they seem mutually exclusive to Americans.[153] Also, the majority of consumer decisions are not based on a large degree of conscious thinking. A lot of information processing is unconscious – in particular in collectivistic cultures – and so is retrieval from memory. Many of these unconscious processes are 'automatic' cognitive processes.[154] There also is evidence that in Japan and more generally in Asia, different information is sought than in the West, and that it is used in different decision-making processes.[155] Asians, because of fear of losing face, are careful in ensuring that they know precisely what is on offer before deciding to commit. Due to their nonconfrontational nature, it is not easy for Asians to question certain aspects once they have made up their minds, so they are doubly careful that any decisions are based on close scrutiny and long deliberation.[156] In collectivistic cultures, it often is not information that drives choice behavior. Choices may be driven by loyalty or obligation, which is perfectly rational, although in Western views it may not be so.[157] There are several related influences on choice behavior that vary across cultures, such as price and quality. Chinese are very price conscious for personal use products, but for public use products a high price will enhance face. High quality may reduce the risk of losing face.[158]

Differences also exist with respect to the way people describe their own decision-making styles. Whereas Americans talk more often about the emotional nature of their buyer behavior, Japanese consumers provide more rational descriptions of their decision making.[159] This is likely due to the fact that Americans tend to attribute their behavior to their personal traits and related personal emotions, whereas Japanese are likely to refer to situational facts that in the eyes of the researchers are less 'emotional.'

The influence of group members on buying behavior will vary with various dimensions, as described in Chapter 5. In China, when it comes to the final decision about what to buy, friends and colleagues have more influence than advertisements or sales people. In cultures of high power distance with related dependency needs elders and superiors will have a more dominant role in decision making. In collectivistic cultures, children are taught to avoid social conflict and utilize parental standards in consumption, whereas in individual-istic cultures, where children are encouraged to have opinions and evaluate all sides of an argument, there is a tendency toward lower consumption dependence at a relatively young age (3–8 years). Japanese children make fewer purchases requests and exhibit lower levels of communication about consumption with their parents than American children do.[160] In the United States, household money decisions are often joint decisions, but in China and Japan usually the woman handles the household budget.[161]

In collectivistic cultures, decisions will be made in consensus with the group, so deci-sions are not individual decisions. Also, people will behave according to the expectations of group members. Consensus seeking is also important in feminine cultures. The degree of role differentiation influences the involvement of partners in decision making. An example is for buying cars. The EMS surveys asked who is involved in choosing the make and model in the purchase of one's main and second car. The answer categories were *you, your partner, another household member, your employer/business partner, someone else.* In 1995, 50% of variance of the answers 'your partner' was explained by low masculinity. In the feminine cultures, partners decide on this sort of purchase together, whereas in the masculine cul-tures selection of the make and model of car is likely to be the task of the male in the rela-tionship. This influence is likely to be noticeable in the decision-making process for many durable household goods.

Consumer Decision-Making Styles

Consumer decision-making style can be defined as 'a mental orientation characterizing a consumer's approach to making choices.'[162] The underlying thought of most Western con-sumer decision-making models is that consumers engage in shopping with certain funda-mental decision-making modes or styles, including conscious evaluations regarding brand, price, and quality. The search for a universal instrument that can describe consumers' decision-making styles across cultures seems to be problematic.

An approach that focuses on consumers' orientations in making decisions is the consumer characteristics approach of Sproles and Kendall,[163] who developed an instrument, analogous to the personality traits concept, to measure consumer decision-making styles, called the *consumer style inventory* (CSI). The CSI identifies eight mental characteristics of consumer decision making: (1) perfectionism or high-quality consciousness; (2) brand consciousness; (3) novelty-fashion consciousness; (4) recreational, hedonistic shopping consciousness; (5) price and 'value-for-money' shopping consciousness; (6) impulsiveness; (7) confusion over choice of brands, stores, and consumer information; (8) habitual, brand-loyal orientation toward consumption. Hafstrom et al.[164] applied the CSI to young Koreans and found similar decision-making styles. The brand conscious and perfectionist styles were among the top three decision-making styles. Lysonski et al.[165] tested the CSI among young people in Greece, India, New Zealand, and the United States and found that 6 of the 40 items that were used by Sproles and Kendall (e.g., price conscious and value-for-money) did not apply to the Greek and Indian samples. So, some of the original items had to be deleted. In the end, 34 items were used, which resulted in seven factors: perfectionist, brand-conscious, novelty-fashion conscious, recreational, impulsive, confusion over choice, and habitual, brand-loyal. Commercial research agencies use similar consumer characteristics to distinguish consumer decision-making styles. For example, in the lower-income countries, people were more brand loyal.

Business Decision Making

Businesspeople are generally considered to be a culture-free group because their decision-making process is assumed to be rational, as compared with more emotional consumer decision making. There is evidence that decision making by businesspeople is also culture bound. Because businesspeople are also part of their culture, they will exhibit similar differences as consumers. In addition to that, the culture of the company will influence cross-cultural differences.

In major purchases in all cultures, a number of people are involved. This is generally called the *decision-making unit* (DMU). This DMU can vary with respect to the number of people it contains. In business in Japan, intermediaries are used, such as bankers, accountants, or trade associations representatives, whereas American businesspeople tend to find their own way. Japanese firms tend to consult more personal sources than do American firms. Whereas American firms get their information about suppliers from the Yellow Pages or industry trade shows, Japanese find suppliers from information from good friends or municipal agencies and prefer to do business with 'someone the founder's family knows very well.'[166]

Finding the influence of others in decision making is not easy, as culture influences the degree to which people think they are involved in decision making (which may be different from actual decision-making power). Because of egalitarian values in low power distance cultures, more people think they are involved in decision making on corporate buying aspects than in high power distance cultures. Whereas in Denmark a secretary who assists the boss in gathering information on products to buy may view this as involvement in decision making, a secretary in France giving the same assistance probably will not view this as being involved in making the decision, because the boss implicitly makes all decisions.

This can be concluded from EMS, which asks the question, 'When decisions are made for business purchases several people may have responsibility for different aspects of the decision. Please indicate for each of the product or service areas below whether you have (a) responsibility (this could be for determining needs, choosing brands and suppliers, or authorizing purchase or finance); (b) some involvement (assisting in these decisions) or (c) no involvement.'

The questions referred to 26 product categories. Analysis of the mean answer scores shows that for 16 of 26 categories, the answers suggesting that people are involved in the decision-making process are related to low power distance.

Because of centralized decision making in high power distance cultures, the boss in a company more frequently has the final say in buying decisions than in low power distance cultures. This is a likely explanation of differences in the time it takes to pay invoices in Europe. In 1996 the differences between countries in Europe with respect to average agreed payment days and average actual payment days were significantly correlated with power distance (r = .69*** and r = .73***). In the high power distance cultures there is less delegation, lower-level employees do not have much decision making power, and payment decisions are likely to be carried to the boss through the layers of the organization, which takes more time.

In the sales process, what are considered to be positive influences on decision making vary. In high power distance cultures, seniority is preferred to skills and procedural discipline is preferred to trust. Personal relationships between seller and buyer are fine in individualistic and low power distance cultures, but personal favors are not.[167]

Conclusion

The mental processes relevant for understanding consumer behavior discussed in this chapter are cognition, learning, perception, creativity, attribution, information processing, communication, and decision making. All are processes that vary with culture. The basis of understanding is that culture is learned behavior. People who grow up in one culture have learned to see things in certain contexts that people in other countries have learned to see in different contexts. Our thinking and the way we process information defines what and how we communicate. Knowledge of the differences is of utmost importance to international marketers and advertisers. Communication is only effective if the receiver of the message understands the message as the sender intends it. Only recently cross-cultural psychologists and marketing researchers have found evidence of how culture influences these processes. The accumulated knowledge described in this chapter is only the beginning of a knowledge base that should further develop in the next decades.

Notes

1. L. Percy, J.R. Rossiter, and R. Elliott, *Strategic Advertising Management* (Oxford University Press, Oxford, UK, 2001), p. 22.

2. G.R. Semin and S. Zwier, 'Social cognition,' in J.W. Berry, M.H. Segall, and Ç. Kagitçibasi (eds), *Handbook of Cross-Cultural Psychology*, Vol. 3 (Allyn & Bacon, Boston, 1997), pp. 51–75, 61.

3. M.W. Eysenck, *Principles of Cognitive Psychology*, 2nd edn (Psychology Press, Hove, East Sussex, UK, 2001), pp. 1–2.

4. U. Kühnen, 'The semantic-procedural interface model of the self: The role of self-knowledge for context-dependent versus context-independent modes of thinking,' *Journal of Personality and Social Psychology*, 80 (2001), pp. 397–409.

5. N.K. Malhotra and J.D. McCort, 'A cross-cultural comparison of behavioral intention models,' *International Marketing Review*, 18 (2001), pp. 235–269.

6. S. De Oliveira and R. Nisbett, 'Beyond East and West: Cognitive style in Latin America,' *Journal of Cross-Cultural Psychology*, 48, 10 (2017), pp. 1554–1577.

7. I. Choi, R.E. Nisbett, and E.E. Smith, 'Culture, category salience, and inductive reasoning,' *Cognition*, 65 (1997), pp. 15–32.

8. R. Hicks, 'Back to the drawing board,' *M&M Europe* (March 2002), pp. 18–21.

9. J. Li, 'A cultural model of learning: Chinese "heart and mind for wanting to learn",' *Journal of Cross-Cultural Psychology*, 33 (2002), pp. 248–269.

10. R.C. Mishra, 'Cognition and cognitive development,' in J.W. Berry, P.R. Dasen, and T.S. Saraswathi (eds), *Handbook of Cross-Cultural Psychology*, Vol. 2 (Allyn & Bacon, Boston, 1997), pp. 143–175, 160.

11. S. Bulmer and M. Buchanan-Oliver, 'Advertising across cultures: Interpretations of visually complex advertising,' *Journal of Current Issues and Research of Advertising*, 28, 1 (2006), pp. 57–71.

12. T.J. Domzal, J.M. Hunt, and J.B. Kernan, 'Achtung! The information processing of foreign words in advertising,' *International Journal of Advertising*, 14 (1995), pp. 95–114.

13. Kühnen, 'The semantic-procedural interface model of the self.'

14. G. Christodoulides, J.W. Cadogan, and C. Veloutsou, 'Consumer-based brand equity measurement: Lessons learned from an international study,' *International Marketing Review*, 32, 3/4 (2015), pp. 307–328.

15. M.H. Hsieh, 'Measuring global brand equity using cross-national survey data,' *Journal of International Marketing*, 12, 2 (2004), pp. 28–57.

16. A. Koçak, T. Abimbola, and A. Özer, 'Consumer brand equity in a cross-cultural replication: An evaluation of a scale,' *Journal of Marketing Management*, 23, 1–2 (2007), pp. 157–173; B. Yoo and N. Donthu, 'Testing cross-cultural invariance of the brand equity creation process,' *Journal of Product and Brand Management*, 11, 6 (2002), pp. 380–398.

17. Available at: http://theinspirationroom.com/daily/2007/diesel-global-warming-ready/ (accessed 23 January 2010).

18. L. Scott, 'Images in advertising: The need for a theory of visual rhetoric,' *Journal of Consumer Research*, 21 (1994), pp. 252–273.

19. F.P. Peter, J.C. Olson, and K.G. Grunert, *Consumer Behaviour and Marketing Strategy*, European edn (McGraw-Hill, London, 1999), p. 39.

20. M.C. Cervellon and L. Dubé, 'Assessing the cross-cultural applicability of affective and cognitive components of attitude,' *Journal of Cross-Cultural Psychology*, 33 (2002), pp. 346–357.

21. G. Hofstede, *Culture's Consequences* (Sage, Thousand Oaks, CA, 2001), p. 229.

22. M. Solomon, G. Bamossy, and S. Askegaard, *Consumer Behaviour: A European Perspective* (Pearson Education, London, 1999), p. 96.

23. I. Choi, R.E. Nisbett, and A. Norenzayan, 'Causal attribution across cultures: Variation and universality,' *Psychological Bulletin*, 125 (1999), pp. 47–63.

24. J.L. Aaker and J. Sengupta, 'Additivity versus attenuation: The role of culture in resolution of information incongruity,' *Journal of Consumer Psychology*, 2 (2000), pp. 67–82.

25. W.B. Gudykunst, S. Ting-Toomey, B.J. Hall, and K.L. Schmidt, 'Language and intergroup communication,' in M.K. Asante and W.B. Gudykunst (eds), *Handbook of International and Intercultural Communication* (Sage, Newbury Park, CA, 1989), pp. 145–162, 145.

26. R.L. Munroe and R.H. Munroe, 'A comparative anthropological perspective,' in J.W. Berry, Y.H. Poortinga, and J. Pandey (eds), *Handbook of Cross-Cultural Psychology*, Vol. 1 (Allyn & Bacon, Boston, 1997), pp. 171–213, 183.

27. W.B. Gudykunst and S. Ting-Toomey, *Culture and Interpersonal Communication.* (Sage, Thousand Oaks, CA, 1988).

28. A. Macfarlane, *The Origins of English Individualism* (Blackwell, Oxford, UK, 1978).

29. H.C. Triandis, *Individualism and Collectivism* (Westview, Boulder, CO, 1995), p. 69.

30. H. Giles and A. Franklyn-Stokes, 'Communicator characteristics,' in M.K. Asante and W.B. Gudykunst (eds), *Handbook of International and Intercultural Communication* (Sage, Newbury Park, CA, 1989), pp. 117–144, 127.

31. E.S. Kashima and Y. Kashima, 'Culture and language: The case of cultural dimensions and personal pronoun use,' *Journal of Cross-Cultural Psychology*, 29 (1998), pp. 461–486.

32. G. Hofstede, personal communication, 1996.

33. P. Burger, 'Gaten in de taal,' *Onze Taal* (June 1996), p. 293.

34. J.P. Van Oudenhoven and B. De Raad, 'Eikels en trutten over de grens [Abusive behavior across eleven countries],' *Onze Taal*, 77, 9 (2008), pp. 228–231.

35. G.E. Miracle, H.K. Bang, and K.Y. Chang, *Achieving Reliable and Valid Cross-Cultural Research Results*, working paper panel of Cross-Cultural Research Design, National Conference of the American Academy of Advertising, San Antonio, TX (20 March 1992).

36. J.C. Usunier, *International Marketing: A Cultural Approach* (Pearson Education, Harlow, UK, 1996), p. 7.

37. Semin and Zwier, 'Social cognition,' pp. 51–75.

38. A.H. Bloom, *The Linguistic Shaping of Thought: A Study of the Impact of Language on Thinking in China and the West* (Lawrence Erlbaum, Hillsdale, NJ, 1981); Semin and Zwier, 'Social cognition,' p. 66.

39. F. Li and H. Cheng, 'Brand naming in China's globalized economy: Summarizing and elaborating power of key symbols,' in H. Li, S. Huang, and D. Jin (eds), *Proceedings of the 2009 American Academy of Advertising Asia-Pacific Conference*, American Academy of Advertising, in conjunction with China Association of Advertising of Commerce, and Communication University of China (2009), p. 256.

40. Available at: www.essentialaction.org/tobacco/funny.html and www.us-expatriate-handbook. com/chpt3.htm (accessed 1 September 2002).

41. B.H. Schmitt, Y. Pan, and N.T. Tavassoli, 'Language and consumer memory: The impact of linguistic differences between Chinese and English,' *Journal of Consumer Research*, 21 (1994), pp. 419–431.

42. G. Hofstede, personal communication, August 2002.

43. B.H. Schmitt and Y. Pan, 'Managing corporate and brand identities in the Asia-Pacific region,' *California Management Review*, 36 (1994), pp. 32–48.

44. Semin and Zwier, 'Social cognition,' p. 65.

45. W. Müller, 'Verlust von Werbewirkung durch Standardisierung [Loss of advertising effectiveness through standardization],' *Absatzwirtschaft*, 9 (1998), pp. 80–88.

46. S. García, 'When is a cat not a cat?,' *Admap* (October 1998), pp. 40–42.

47. S. Anholt, *Another One Bites the Grass: Making Sense of International Advertising* (Wiley, New York, 2000), p. 5.

48. J. Williams, 'Constant questions or constant meanings? Assessing intercultural motivations in alcoholic drinks,' *Marketing and Research Today* (August 1991), pp. 169–177.

49. P. Chao and S. Lin, 'Translating brand names effectively: Brand attitude reversal and perceived brand name translation relevance in an emerging market,' *Journal of International Consumer Marketing*, 29, 3 (2017), pp. 120–134.

50. H.T. Keh, C.J. Torelli, C.Y. Chiu, and J. Hao, 'Integrative responses to culture mixing in brand name translations: The roles of product self-expressiveness and self-relevance of values among bicultural Chinese consumers,' *Journal of Cross-Cultural Psychology*, 47, 10 (2016), pp. 1345–1360.

51. Standard Eurobarometer report 55 (2001); *The Young Europeans* (Special Eurobarometer report 151, 2001).

52. *Europeans and their Languages* (Special Eurobarometer report 243, February 2006).

53. M. Gerritsen and F. Jansen, 'Teloorgang of survival? [Loss or survival?],' *Onze Taal*, 2/3 (2001), pp. 40–42.

54. M. Gerritsen, I. Gijsbers, H. Korzilius, and F. Van Meurs, 'Engels in Nederlandse TV reclame [English in Dutch TV advertising],' *Onze Taal*, 1 (1999), pp. 17–19.

55. J. Paulick, 'Impossible is nothing, except understanding ads in English,' *Deutsche Welle* (16 November 2007). Available at: https://www.dw.com/en/impossible-is-nothing-except-under-standing-ads-in-english/a-2914472 (accessed 4 April 2019).

56. M.N. Kastanakis and B.G. Voyer, 'The effect of culture on perception and cognition: A conceptual framework,' *Journal of Business Research* (2013). Available at: http://dx.doi.org/10.1016/j.jbusres.2013.03.028.

57. S.J. Unsworth, C.R. Sears, and P.M. Pexman, 'Cultural influences on categorization processes,' *Journal of Cross-Cultural Psychology*, 36, 6 (2005), pp. 662–688.

58. A. Ramdas, 'Geef mij maar onzin kennis,' *NRC/Handelsblad* (10 March 2008), p. 7.

59. A.B. Monga and D. Roedder John, 'Cultural differences in brand extension evaluation: The influence of analytic versus holistic thinking,' *Journal of Consumer Research*, 33 (2007), pp. 529–536.

60. P. Gemmen, 'Eet u smakelijk [Enjoy the food],' *Adformatie* (12 September 2002), pp. 24–26.

61. B.H. Schmitt and S. Zhang, 'Language structure and categorization: A study of classifiers in consumer cognition, judgment, and choice,' *Journal of Consumer Research*, 25 (1998), pp. 108–122.

62. S. Zhang and B. Schmitt, 'Language-dependent classification: The mental representation of classifiers in cognition, memory and evaluations,' *Journal of Experimental Psychology: Applied*, 4 (1998), pp. 375–385.

63. Schmitt and Zhang, 'Language structure and categorization.'

64. C.M. Turnbull, *The Forest People* (Simon & Schuster, New York, 1961).

65. M. Hijink, 'Wat gebeurt er precies in de machinekamer van Google? [What exactly is happing in Google's engine-room?],' *NRC/Handelsblad IT Special*, E2-E5 (25 and 26 November 2017).

66. P.A. Russell, J.B. Deregowski, and P.R. Kinnear, 'Perception and aesthetics,' in J.W. Berry, P.R. Dasen, and T.S. Saraswathi (eds), *Handbook of Cross-Cultural Psychology*, Vol. 2 (Allyn & Bacon, Boston, 1997), pp. 107–142.

67. H. Giles and A. Franklyn-Stokes, 'Communicator characteristics,' in M.K. Asante and W.B. Gudykunst (eds), *Handbook of International and Intercultural Communication* (Sage, Newbury Park, CA, 1989), pp. 117–144, 133.

68. Russell et al., 'Perception and aesthetics,' p. 125.

69. G. Kress and T. Van Leeuwen, *Reading Images: The Grammar of Visual Design* (Routledge, London, 1996), pp. 4, 206.

70. B.H. Schmitt, 'Language and visual imagery: Issues of corporate identity in East Asia,' *Columbia Journal of World Business*, 3 (1995), pp. 28–37.

71. T. Doi, *The Anatomy of Self: The Individual Versus Society* (Kodansha International, Tokyo, 1985), p. 151.

72. Schmitt and Pan, 'Managing corporate and brand identities in the Asia-Pacific region.'

73. M.M. Aslam, 'Are you selling the right colour? A cross-cultural review of colour as a marketing cue,' *Journal of Marketing Communications*, 12, 1 (2006), pp. 15–30.

74. K.A. Jameson, 'On the role of culture in color naming: Remarks on the articles of Paramei, Kay, Roberson, and Hardin on the topic of cognition, culture, and color experience,' *Cross-Cultural Research*, 39, 1 (2005), pp. 88–106.

75. D. Roberson, 'Color categories are culturally diverse in cognition as well as in language,' *Cross-Cultural Research*, 39, 1 (2005), pp. 56–71.

76. T.J. Madden, K. Hewett, and M. Roth, 'Managing images in different cultures: A cross-national study of color meanings and preferences,' *Journal of International Marketing*, 8 (2000),pp. 90–107.

77. Ibid.

78. Aslam, 'Are you selling the right colour?'

79. L. Van den Berg-Weitzel and G. Van de Laar, 'Relation between culture and communication in packaging design,' *Brand Management*, 8 (2001), pp. 171–184.

80. K. Berkhout, 'Chinese storm. De hausse van de hedendaagse kunst uit China,' *NRC Handelsblad* (2 March 2007), p. 17.

81. W. Niu and R.J. Sternberg, 'Cultural influences on artistic creativity and its evaluation,' *International Journal of Psychology*, 36 (2001), pp. 225–241.

82. S. Senzaki, T. Masuda, and K. Nand, 'Holistic versus analytic expressions in artworks: Cross-cultural differences and similarities in drawing and collages by Canadian and Japanese school-age children,' *Journal of Cross-Cultural Psychology*, 45, 8 (2014), pp. 1297–1316.

83. P. Janata, J.L. Birk, J. D. Van Horn, M. Leman, B. Tillmann, and J.J. Bharucha, 'The cortical topography of tonal structures underlying Western music,' *Science*, 298 (2002), pp. 2167–2170; D. Moelants, O. Cornelis, and M. Leman, *Exploring African Tone Scales*, 10th International Society for Music Information Retrieval conference (2009).

84. B. Van Maris, 'Lettergreepritme,' *NRC Handelsblad/Wetenschap* (10 December 2006), p. 51.

85. L. Grønlien, *Understanding the Challenges of Entering the Chinese Market* (Department of Product Design, Norwegian University of Science and Technology, Trondheim, 2005).

86. T. Masuda, R. Gonzalez, L. Kwan, and R.E. Nisbett, 'Culture and aesthetic preference: Comparing the attention to context of East Asians and Americans,' *Personality and Social Psychology Bulletin*, 34, 9 (2008), pp. 1260–1275.

87. E. Visser, *Packaging Design: A Cultural Sign* (Index Book, Barcelona, 2009), s.l.

88. Niu and Sternberg, 'Cultural influences on artistic creativity and its evaluation.'

89. S.B.F. Paletz and K. Peng, 'Implicit theories of creativity across cultures,' *Journal of Cross-Cultural Psychology*, 39, 3 (2008), pp. 286–302.

90. C. Chen, J. Kasof, A.J. Himsel, E. Greenberger, Q. Dong, and G. Xue, 'Creativity in drawings of geometric shapes: A cross-cultural examination with the consensual assessment technique,' *Journal of Cross-Cultural Psychology*, 33 (2002), pp. 171–187.

91. R. Westwood and D.R. Low, 'The multicultural muse: Culture, creativity and innovation,' *International Journal of Cross-Cultural Management*, 3, 2 (2003), pp. 235–259.

92. J.C.E. Adande, 'The unique and the multiple in Africa,' *Diogenes*, 46, 3 (1998), pp. 25–39.

93. Y.S. Kim and J.D. Kelly, 'A matter of culture: A comparative study of photojournalism in American and Korean Newspapers,' *The International Communication Gazette*, 70, 2 (2008), pp. 155–173.

94. G. McCracken, *Culture and Consumption: New Approaches to the Symbolic Character of Consumer Goods and Activities* (Indiana University Press, Bloomington, 1988), pp. 78–79.

95. To find out whether creative directors at advertising agencies deviate from their own culture, I asked several to complete the Hofstede questionnaire. The resulting country scores usually mirrored Hofstede's scores for their country, suggesting their values were representative of national values.

96. M. Gagliardi, 'Alchemy of cultures: From adaptation to transcendence in design and branding,' *Design Management Journal* (Fall 2001), pp. 32–39.

97. M.J. Gelfand, D. Spurlock, J.A. Sniezek, and L. Shao, 'Culture and social prediction: The role of information in enhancing confidence in social predictions in the United States and China,' *Journal of Cross-Cultural Psychology*, 31 (2000), pp. 498–516.

98. S. Carpenter, 'Effects of cultural tightness and collectivism on self-concept and causal attributions,' *Cross-Cultural Research*, 34, 1 (February 2000), pp. 38–56.

99. Hofstede, *Culture's Consequences*, p. 304.

100. A.S. Mattila and P.G. Patterson, 'The impact of culture on consumers' perceptions of service recovery efforts,' *Journal of Retailing*, 80 (2004), pp. 196–106.

101. J.B. Rotter, 'Generalized expectancies for internal versus external control of reinforcement,' *Psychological Monographs*, 80, 609 (1966).

102. E. Lieber, K.S. Yang, and Y.C. Lin, 'An external orientation to the study of causal beliefs,' *Journal of Cross-Cultural Psychology*, 2 (2000), pp. 160–186.

103. J.B. Rotter, 'Internal versus external control of reinforcement,' *American Psychologist*, 45 (1990), pp. 489–493.

104. S. Yamaguchi, M. Gelfand, M.M. Ohashi, and Y. Zemba, 'The cultural psychology of control: Illusions of personal versus collective control in the United States and Japan,' *Journal of Cross-Cultural Psychology*, 36, 6 (2005), pp. 705–761.

105. Roper Starch Worldwide Conference, 'Has America changed as much as you think it has?,' *Brandweek* (1 November 1993), pp. 24–25.

106. K. Layous, H. Lee, I. Choi, and S. Lyubomirsky, 'Culture matters when designing a successful happiness-increasing activity: A comparison of the United States and South Korea,' *Journal of Cross-Cultural Psychology*, 44, 8 (2013), pp. 1294–1303.

107. P.B. Smith, F. Trompenaars, and S. Dugan, 'The Rotter locus of control scale in 43 countries: A test of cultural relativity,' *International Journal of Psychology*, 30 (1995), pp. 377–400.

108. *Social Values, Science and Technology* (Special Eurobarometer 225, June 2005), 27 countries.

109. Triandis, *Individualism and Collectivism*.

110. Data from *Reader's Digest*, 1991.

111. *Globalisation* (Flash Eurobarometer 151b, October 2003).

112. *Confidence in the Information Society* (Flash Eurobarometer 250, 2009).

113. *Attitudes of European Citizens Towards the Environment* (Special Eurobarometer report 295, March 2008).

114. *The Economist* (4 September 1999), p. 37.

115. D. An and S.H. Kim, 'Advertising visuals in global brands' websites: A six country comparison,' *International Journal of Advertising*, 26, 3 (2007), pp. 303–332.

116. *Consumer Survey* (Flash Eurobarometer Report 117, January 2002).

117. Ibid.

118. *Science and Technology* (Special Eurobarometer Report EBS 340, 2010).

119. Ibid.

120. B. Léon, 'Science related information in European television: A study of prime-time news,' *Public Understanding of Science*, 17 (2008), pp. 443–460.

121. *European's Attitudes Towards the Issue of Sustainable Consumption and Production* (Flash Eurobarometer 256, 2009).

122. S.A. Gunaratne, 'Asian approaches to communication theory,' *Media Development*, 1 (1991), pp. 53–55.

123. D.E. Schultz and M.P. Block, 'Understanding Chinese media audiences: An exploratory study of Chinese consumers' media consumption and a comparison with the USA,' in H. Li, S. Huang, and D. Jin (eds), *Proceedings of the 2009 American Academy of Advertising*

Asia-Pacific Conference, American Academy of Advertising, in conjunction with China Association of Advertising of Commerce, and Communication University of China (2009), pp. 1–12.

124. S.C. Chu and S.M. Choi, 'Use of social networking sites among Chinese young generations,' in H. Li, S. Huang, and D. Jin (eds), *Proceedings of the 2009 American Academy of Advertising Asia-Pacific Conference*, American Academy of Advertising, in conjunction with China Association of Advertising of Commerce, and Communication University of China (2009), pp. 50–57.

125. Mediascope Europe, *Online Shoppers* (EIAA, 2008). Europe, 10 countries.

126. *Attitudes of European Citizens Toward the Environment* (Special Eurobarometer Report 295, March 2008).

127. Synovate, *PAX Digital Life* (2008).

128. Information from Vivek Gupta, Senior Vice President IMRB BrandScience at Kantar Group, Bangalore, India.

129. T. Hamamura, Z. Meijer, S.J. Heine, K. Kamaya, and I. Hori, 'Approach–avoidance motivation and information processing: A cross-cultural analysis,' *Personality and Social Psychology Bulletin*, 35, 4 (2009), pp. 454–462.

130. L. Banister, 'Global brands, local contexts,' *Admap* (October 1997), p. 28.

131. J.L. Aaker and A.Y. Lee, '"I" seek pleasures and "We" avoid pains: The role of self-regulatory goals in information processing and persuasion,' *Journal of Consumer Research*, 28 (June 2001), pp. 33–49.

132. D. Briley and J.J. Aaker, 'When does culture matter? Effects of personal knowledge on the correction of culture-based judgments,' *Journal of Marketing Research*, XLIII (August 2006), pp. 395–408.

133. T.J. Domzal, J.M. Hunt, and J.B. Kernan, 'Achtung! The information processing of foreign words in advertising,' *International Journal of Advertising*, 14 (1995), pp. 95–114.

134. A. Resnik and B.L. Stern, 'An analysis of information content in television advertising,' *Journal of Marketing*, 41 (1977), pp. 50–53.

135. J.F. Mindy and J.U. McNeal, 'How Chinese children's commercials differ from those of the United States: A content analysis,' *Journal of Advertising*, 30 (2001), pp. 79–92.

136. A. Boduroglu, P. Shah, and R.E. Nisbett, 'Cultural differences in allocation of attention in visual information processing,' *Journal of Cross-Cultural Psychology*, 40, 3 (2009), pp. 349–360.

137. R.P. Jolley, Z. Zhi, and G.V. Thomas, 'The development of understanding moods metaphorically expressed in pictures,' *Journal of Cross-Cultural Psychology*, 29 (1998), pp. 358–376.

138. K. Bu, D. Kim, and S. Lee, 'Determinants of visual forms used in print advertising: A cross-cultural comparison,' *International Journal of Advertising*, 28, 1 (2009), pp. 13–48.

139. S. Salvador Ruiz and M. Sicilia, 'The impact of cognitive and/or affective processing styles on consumer response to advertising appeals,' *Journal of Business Research*, 5717 (2002), pp. 1–8.

140. M. Callow and L. Schiffman, 'Implicit meaning in visual print advertisements: A cross-cultural examination of the contextual communication effect,' *International Journal of Advertising*, 21 (2002), pp. 259–277.

141. Ibid.

142. B.D. Cutler, R.G. Javalgi, and M.K. Erramilli, 'The visual components of print advertising: A five-country cross-cultural analysis,' *European Journal of Marketing*, 26 (1992), pp. 7–20.

143.   S. Bulmer and M. Buchanan-Oliver, 'Visual rhetoric and global advertising imagery,' *Journal of Marketing Communications*, 12, 1 (2006), pp. 49–61.

144.   F. Leclerc, B.H. Schmitt, and L. Dubé, 'Foreign branding and its effects on product perceptions and attitudes,' *Journal of Marketing Research*, 31 (1994), pp. 263–270.

145.   J. Renkema, E. Hallen, and H. Hoeken, '*Tuinapparatuur* [garden equipment] or garden equipment?,' *Onze Taal*, 10 (2001), pp. 257–259.

146.   C.R. Taylor and G.E. Miracle, 'Foreign elements in Korean and US television advertising,' *Advances in International Marketing*, 7 (1996), pp. 175–195.

147.   H.E. Krugman, 'The impact of television advertising: Learning without involvement,' *Public Opinion Quarterly*, 29, pp. 349–356.

148.   G.E. Miracle, 'Feel-do-learn: An alternative sequence underlying Japanese consumer response to television commercials,' in F.G. Feasley (ed.), *Proceedings of the 1987 Conference of the American Academy of Advertising* (1987), R73–R78.

149.   R.E. Petty and J.T. Cacioppo, 'The elaboration likelihood model of persuasion,' in L. Berkowitz (ed.), *Advances in Experimental Social Psychology* (Academic Press, New York, 1986), pp. 123–192; and in L. Berkowitz (ed.), *Communication and Persuasion: Central and Peripheral Routes to Attitude Change*, Vol. 19 (Springer-Verlag, New York, 1986), pp. 123–205.

150.   Aaker and Sengupta, 'Additivity versus attenuation.'

151.   E.C. Stewart, 'Culture and decision making,' in W.B. Gudykunst, L.P. Stewart, and S.T. Ting-Toomey (eds), *Communication, Culture, and Organizational Processes* (Sage, Beverly Hills, CA, 1985), pp. 177–211.

152.   S. Abe, R.P. Bagozzi, and P. Sadarangani, 'An investigation of construct validity of the self-concept: Self-consciousness in Japan and the United States,' in L.A. Manrai and A.K. Manrai (eds), *Global Perspectives in Cross-Cultural and Cross-National Consumer Research* (International Business Press/Haworth Press, London, 1996), pp. 97–124.

153.   M. Minkov, *What Makes Us Different and Similar* (Klasika I Stil Publishing House, Sofia, Bulgaria, 2007), p. 181.

154.   K. Grunert, 'Research in consumer behaviour: Beyond attitudes and decision-making,' *European Research* (August 1988), pp. 172–183.

155.   J.C. Usunier, 'Atomistic versus organic approaches,' *International Studies of Management and Organization*, 26 (1996/1997), pp. 90–112.

156.   L. Simpson and K.S. Fam, 'Are Asian students' values similar across Asia? An empirical investigation,' ANZMAC 2000 *Visionary Marketing for the 21st Century: Facing the Challenge* (2000), pp. 1180–1184.

157.   D. Katzner, 'Culture and the explanation of choice behavior,' *Theory and Decision*, 48 (2000), pp. 241–262.

158.   Y. Cai, 'Investigating the relationship between personal values and mall shopping behavior: A generation cohort study on the new generation of Chinese and their previous generation,' *Proceedings of the Fourth Asia Pacific Retail Conference* (College of Management, Manidol University, Bangkok, 4–6 September 2007), pp. 62–87.

159.   W.J. McDonald, 'American versus Japanese consumer decision making: An exploratory cross-cultural content analysis,' *Journal of International Consumer Marketing*, 7 (1995), pp. 81–93.

160. G.M. Rose, D. Boush, and A. Shoham, 'Family communication and children's purchasing influence: A cross-national examination,' *Journal of Business Research*, 55 (2002), pp. 867–873.

161. D. Ackerman and G. Tellis, 'Can culture affect prices? A cross-cultural study of shopping and retail prices,' *Journal of Retailing*, 77 (2001), pp. 57–82.

162. S. Lysonski, S. Durvasula, and Y. Zotos, 'Consumer decision-making styles: A multi-country investigation,' *European Journal of Marketing*, 30 (1996), pp. 10–21.

163. G.B. Sproles and E.L. Kendall, 'A methodology for profiling consumer decision making styles,' *The Journal of Consumer Affairs*, 20 (1986), pp. 267–279; Lysonski et al., 'Consumer decision-making styles.'

164. J.L. Hafstrom, S.C. Jung, and S.C. Young, 'Consumer decision-making styles: Comparison between United States and Korean young consumers,' *The Journal of Consumer Affairs*, 26 (1992), pp. 146–158.

165. Lysonski et al., 'Consumer decision-making styles.'

166. R.B. Money, M.C. Gilly, and J.L. Graham, 'Explorations of national culture and word-of-mouth referral behavior in the purchase of industrial services in the United States and Japan,' *Journal of Marketing*, 62 (1998), pp. 76–87.

167. G.W. Calin Niculescu, 'Cultural differences in decision-making processes and their implications for companies operating in south Eastern Europe countries,' Master's thesis, European University Viadrina (2006). Countries covered were Austria, Bosnia, Bulgaria, Germany, Greece, Hungary, Romania, Serbia, and the Slovak Republic.

Culture, Communication, and Media Behavior

Many cross-cultural clashes result from the failure to recognize differences in communication. There is no such thing as a universal form of communication. Differences in cultural background, values and self-concepts may act as impediments to effective communication across cultures. We have learned that ways of expressing emotions, perceptions of self, others, and of phenomena differ, which also gives rise to miscommunication. Communication between people of different cultures is fraught with difficulties.[1]

Each culture has its own rules of communication. However, there are some patterns. One of the clearest distinctions is between high-context and low-context communication. Related to this distinction is how people process information and their expectations of the role, purpose, and effect of communication. Is advertising persuasive by nature, or can it have another role in the sales process? Understanding how advertising works across cultures is of great importance for international companies. People use different media across cultures and use them in different ways. With advanced information technology, new forms of communication have emerged. The way people use these and how the content is designed, such as websites, are also influenced by culture.

Communication

All living human beings communicate through sounds, speech, movements, gestures, and language. Communication involves many human activities: speaking, listening, reading, writing, viewing, and creating images. How people communicate is based on cultural conventions that are adhered to in interacting with other people, in producing and sending messages and in interpreting messages.

In Western communication studies since the 1960s, many definitions, theories, and models of communication have been developed, varying from process-oriented models to models that focus on signs, symbols, and the conveying of meaning. Scholars in other parts of the world have developed different theories of the purpose of communication and how communication works, but theories of marketing communication have mainly been derived from Western communication theory that defines communication more or less as a linear process. According to Asian scholars,[2] the Western process approach is not appropriate for understanding communication in most of Asia and in the past decades several scholars have argued against using theories that are not applicable to their culture.

'The discourse we have created on "human" communication is in fact a product of American (primarily Caucasian male) views rooted in American ideological values. … Our Western social science "human" communication research base has been heavily composed of Mid-western American college students, which represents a fraction of 1% of even the American population. As a result, the theoretical discourse that has been generated in the West and said to describe "human" communication has been severely skewed.'[3]

When studying communication and its effects, we have to understand how individuals communicate and their effects on others, in particular how communication and its effects are influenced and modified by the social systems in which they take place. Understanding interpersonal relationships across cultures also is important for understanding how forms of mass communication work and even more for understanding the recent electronic media that are hybrid forms of personal and mass communication. In order to understand communication, we have to be interested in people, their being, needs, motives, and so on. Many of the topics discussed in the previous chapters serve as the basis for understanding the differences in how people relate to each other across cultures that apply to cross-cultural communications.

In classic communication theory, communication in a broad sense includes all the procedures by which one mind may affect another. All communication is viewed as persuasive.[4] This tends to be illustrated by models of communication, as depicted in Figure 7.1, which include the source or sender of a message (person, organization, company, brand), the message itself (story, picture, advertisement), the channel or medium (any carrier of the message: a storyteller, newspaper, television, Internet), and the receiver of the message (person, consumer).

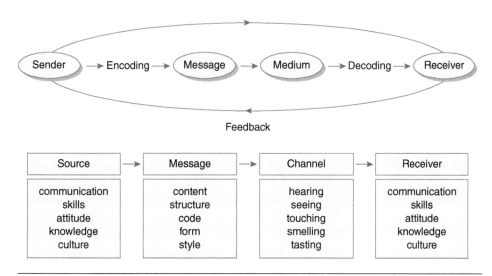

Figure 7.1   **Classic Western models of communication**

This model shows communication as a two-way process. The processes of encoding, interpreting and decoding are included both in the sender and receiver of the message. The process is circular: sender and receiver are in a continuous process of sending, interpreting and receiving messages as a two-way street, which may represent more interpersonal communication and interactive communication by the new communications means. The model is sender-oriented. Yet the sender of the message, after the message has been sent, wants to get feedback to find out if the message has been received and understood. The model doesn't include empathy with the receiver on the part of the sender of the message before or while sending a message. The second model in Figure 7.1 acknowledges the influence of the characteristics of sender and receiver of messages as well as the influencing variables of message and channel. These are all sorts of psychological characteristics of the persons who send and receive messages as well as their social environment.

The sender orientation of Western communication models is like a monologue and mostly relevant for North American and North European communication. In South and East Europe, the dialogue provides a different representation of the communication process, including empathy with the receiver of the message. For example, the Russian scholar Michael Bakhtin[5] views communication as a dialogue. In the dialogue, there is *utterance*, which refers to language spoken in context, so communication by definition is *contextual*. It includes the content of the conversation, the communicator's attitude toward the subject, and responsiveness on the part of the person being addressed. The speaker anticipates the viewpoint of the other and adapts communication to that anticipation. This anticipation or empathy that is also recognized in Asian communication is not found as an essential aspect in Western communication theory which generally is presented as a one-way process where feedback is mainly necessary to be certain that persuasion has taken place.

In Asia, next to empathy, several other aspects are central to communication, where, just as in most other collectivistic cultures, communication varies with roles and relationships, with concern for belonging to the community and fitting in and occupying one's proper place.[6] Included are the need for harmony in interpersonal relationships, causing indirectness in communication; distinction of in-group and out-group; adaptation to the different groups and to the context and situation; deliberation of the message in the mind of the sender of the message; and the ability of the receiver of the message to read the other's mind. The last two elements are more pronounced in East Asian communication than in communication in India and West Asian countries. As most Asian models describe a set of complex interactions between sender, message, receiver and context, according to Dissanayake[7] these models can be designated as *circular models*, which is in contrast to the Western *linear models*. The idea of exchange, as opposed to transmission is pivotal to such circular models and the emphasis is on production of communicative messages through the joint efforts of senders and receivers. The reading of available signs is a primary task of receivers. This view is reflected in an Asian model of human communication, as compiled from the various Asian models, but based on Ishii's *enryo-sasshi* model.

Basic to the preservation of harmony in East Asian communication is what Miike[8] describes as a *narrow exit* and a *wide entrance*. The 'exit' of the sender of a message is small

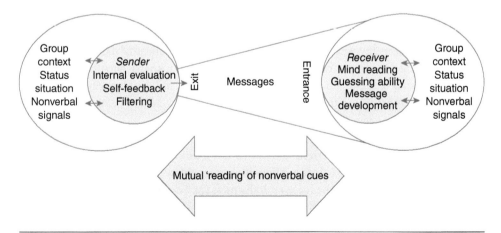

Figure 7.2 **Asian interpersonal communication model**

SOURCE: Adapted from S. Ishii, 'Enryo-Sasshi communication: A key to understanding Japanese interpersonal relations,' *Cross Currents*, 11, 1 (1984), pp. 49–58

as the message will exit only after careful internal evaluation filtering out undesirable elements. This is the process called *enryo* in the Japanese *enryo-sasshi* model, and *manas* in the Buddhist model. Potentially damaging ideas are filtered out during the internal self-feedback process. This careful deliberation may cause silences and pauses in conversation. The 'entrance' of the receiver of the message is wide open. Not only is the message indirect, but both parties also use nonverbal cues that have to be interpreted. This is the mind-reading process. There will be some periods of silence to help the internal evaluation and interpretation processes. Whereas in the Western communication model, the sender is responsible for effective communication, in the East Asian model, both receiver and sender are responsible. This model is illustrated in Figure 7.2.

Whereas the purpose of North American communication is persuasion and communication theory has been derived from Aristotle's rules for persuasive communication, in Asia, communication takes place according to rules for behavior inherited from the old Confucian and Buddhist philosophies.[9] Buddhism offers guidelines for how people should communicate, following the Buddhist ideal of social order.[10] Communication must be socially appropriate. Also in Hinduism, the positions of the sender and the receiver are not static. Communication is a two-way process resulting in mutual understanding. It does not emphasize dominance of the sender. Commonness of experience has to take place. The effectiveness of any message depends on the communication environment. The same message may have different meanings in different contexts.[11]

Of the differences between Western and Asian communication, *silence* is one of the most distinguishing elements of communication. Whereas in the United States each day on average time spent on conversation is 6 hours 43 minutes, it is 3 hours, 31 minutes in Japan. Silence as a form of speech in East Asian cultures is greatly influenced by both the Buddhist and Taoist emphasis on tranquility. It is the mind sounding inside, rather than the mouth talking outside. Silence, then, becomes an effective nonverbal expression for mutual understanding.[12] Silence in communication is found mostly in collectivistic cultures that are also long-term oriented. In collectivistic cultures that are short-term oriented, communication is a continuous stream of dialogue, of speaking and listening. For the Akan of Ghana, silence, unless requested for some sacred practices, is considered an insult. In Latin America, where in most areas the combination of collectivism and short-term orientation is found, speech is also more important than silence although in some areas silence is part of communication. Findings are also of elaborate greeting processes, body language, and use of prolonged silence.[13] The elaborate and sometimes extreme style of these cultures is recognized in the extreme response styles in survey research, which is very different from the moderate style of East Asians.[14]

In sum, in such collectivistic cultures as are found in Asia and Africa, but also Latin America, human communication is an exchange or interaction, more than merely a way that information moves from one place to another.[15] Yet there are important differences across collectivistic cultures with respect to long-/short-term orientation that are related to literacy and orality.

Orality and Literacy

The need to understand the difference between orality and literacy has grown with the electronic age because of the hybrid communication function of the various Internet and mobile media. The difference is more than that between writing and talking; orality or literacy influence our thoughts and verbal expressions.

Oral communication is simply said mouth to mouth communication, a speech or conversation, but derived forms are specific literary genres, such as legends, tales, and stories. Any nonliteral communication is a process where information is exchanged between individuals or groups through a common system of orality or visual features, such as symbols, signs, or behaviors. Today, primary oral culture hardly exists as every culture knows of writing and has some experience with its effects. Yet many cultures to varying degrees preserve much of the mind-set of primary orality. Oral cultures, even when becoming literate, tend to keep their oral style.[16] Oral literacy includes several forms of communication that are found less in textual or literate cultures, such as redundancy and repetition, use of metaphors and flowery and elaborate language.

Literacy generally points at writing, reading, learning, and developing knowledge. Reading and writing developed in a different way and at different places in the various parts of the world. In Northern Europe, literacy developed with the advent of Protestantism because individuals were expected to read the Bible personally or individually, not hear it read by others. Countries dominated by Catholicism, such as Spain and Italy lagged.[17] In East Asia, it was Confucianism which had emphasized written communication and de-emphasized oral communication.[18]

Generally, literacy is described as the ability to read and write, understand, interpret, create, communicate, compute, and use printed and written materials. In 2009, the 10 countries scoring highest on average reading ability of 15 year olds were in East Asia and Northern Europe. The degree of literacy as measured by UNESCO[19] correlates significantly with the long-term orientation dimension. Writing is the tool for permanent recording, whereas an oral utterance has vanished as soon as it is uttered. The new digital social media basically can be viewed as hybrid formats: they partly function as a conversation, but are written. Content, however, is not lost but can be preserved as long as the social media provider wishes.

Literate tradition has not replaced oral. No individual is either 'oral' or 'literate.' Rather, people use devices associated with both traditions in various settings. Oral residues have an impact on people's thinking patterns, people's mind-sets. People in an oral society had to rely on real situations for the understanding of abstract things. Concepts are used in situational, operational frames of reference that are minimally abstract and that are close to the living human world.[20] This may relate to the differences in abstract and concrete thinking and the differences found in information needs between different cultures. Knowledge is not necessarily gained by active information seeking, but is an implicit part of human communication flows. As literacy is said to influence all sorts of cognitive processes like categorization, and abstract and logical reasoning, in literate cultures, people may prefer searching for facts and data on the Internet whereas more oral cultures may get their information from interpersonal contacts and/or social media.

Communication and Culture

Several cultural dimensions explain variance in communication across cultures, of which individualism/collectivism is the most important. Personal communication styles vary across cultures, along with the self-concept. The independent self, when thinking about others, will consider the other's individual characteristics and attributes rather than relational or contextual factors. An interdependent self emphasizes status, roles, relationships, belonging and fitting-in, and occupying one's proper place.[21] The two types of communication distinguished by Hall – high-and low-context communication (as described in Chapter 2) – fit the differences in communication behavior of interdependent selves of collectivistic cultures and independent selves of individualistic cultures. Various other factors and cultural dimensions explain differences in communication style. Rapid speech rate, for example, suggests to Americans that the speaker makes true and uncensored statements, whereas for Koreans, slow speech implies careful consideration of others and context.[22]

In individualistic cultures, people are more verbal and textual oriented. They prefer e-mail to the telephone. In collectivistic cultures, people are more visual and oral oriented. They prefer face-to-face conversation or the telephone to e-mail. However, with respect to textual orientation, low uncertainty avoidance is the main explaining variable. In low uncertainty avoidance cultures people read more, write more, and use more textual means of communication.

Textual orientation is reflected in the degree to which people read books and newspapers and use e-mail and other textual devices. Over time, several data on book and newspaper readership have shown relationships with individualism, power distance, and uncertainty avoidance. Also across Asian countries that are collectivistic to varying degrees, low uncertainty avoidance explains differences in textual orientation. Table 7.1 sums up significant correlations between all sorts of textual behavior and individualism, power distance, and uncertainty avoidance. In particular, uncertainty avoidance explains various textual behaviors, like reading books, newspapers, use of teletext, e-mail, and the need for written information to protect consumers.

Table 7.1   **Textual orientation: Uncertainty avoidance, individualism, and power distance**

Written communication preferences	PDI	IDV	UAI	Predictor	R^2
Europe					
1970: More than 8 books read in past year	−.23	.58*	−.63**	UAI-	.40
1991: More than 12 books read in past year	−.31	.72***	−.68***	IDV	.52
1998: Reading a book at least once a month	−.89***	.62*	−.84***	PDI-	.79
2005: Average time spent reading newspapers	−.59***	.44*	−.75***	UAI-	.56
2007: Read 5 books in past year	−.43*	.57***	−.79***	UAI-	.63
2007: Teletext first source of information for new and current affairs	−.55*		−.63**	UAI-	.39
2008: Newspapers first source of information on environmental issues			−.74***	UAI-	.55
2008: Internet activities: e-mail or IM		.56***	−.36*	IDV	.31
2008: Clear written information best way to protect consumers		.34*	−.63***	UAI-	.40
2017: Read the written press every day	−.71***	.42*	−.54***	PDI-	.50
Asia					
2008: Mean hours per week reading newspapers	−.71*		−.86***	UAI-	.73
2008: Use e-mail			−.80*	UAI-	.64

SOURCES: Hofstede et al. (2010) (see Appendix A); *Europe*: 1970 and 1991: *Reader's Digest*; 1998: *Consumers in Europe* (2001), Eurostat; 2005: *European Social Survey*; 2007: EBS 278, EMS 2007; 2008: EBS 295, Flash EB 241, EBS 298; *Asia*: Synovate PAX Asia (2008) (see Appendix B)

The differences between cultures with respect to verbal and visual orientation are reflected in all aspects of marketing communications, such as corporate identity, brand name, package design, and advertising styles. Marketing communication styles are related to personal communication styles. Chinese-speaking consumers tend to judge a brand name based on its visual appeal, whereas English speakers judge a brand name based on whether the name sounds appealing. In Asia, visual symbolism is a key aspect of a firm's corporate identity.[23] A comparative study of package design across seven countries found that packages differ both in three-dimensional design and in the way they communicate through graphical design and vary in the use of textual information; use of color, shape, and symbolism; and degree of structure and detail in the package design. Culture appears to be of great influence on the noted differences.[24]

Whereas US advertising utilizes more copy, Japanese advertising uses more visual elements, and this applies to more Asian countries. Comparative analysis of 642 magazine advertisements of the United States and Korea showed that the proportion of indirect visual forms in Korean ads was significantly higher than in US ads.[25]

Communication Styles

Communication style is made up of verbal and nonverbal styles. Gudykunst and Ting-Toomey have best described the influence of the various dimensions of culture on verbal and nonverbal communication style.[26]

Verbal Styles

Verbal styles can be *verbal personal* or *verbal contextual* according to the degree of context. Another distinction is among elaborate, exacting, and succinct verbal style. *Verbal personal style* is individual-centered language, whereas *verbal contextual style* is role-centered language. Verbal personal style enhances the 'I' identity, is person oriented (e.g., English), whereas verbal contextual emphasizes the sense of a context-related role identity (e.g., Japanese, Chinese). The two styles focus on personhood versus situation or status. Verbal personal style is linked with low power distance (equal status) and individualism (low context), whereas verbal contextual style is linked with high power distance (hierarchical human relationships) and collectivism (high context). Verbal contextual style includes different ways of addressing different persons, related to their status. For example, the Japanese language adapts to situations where higher- or lower-placed people are addressed. *Elaborate* verbal style refers to the use of rich, expressive language. *Exacting* or *precise* style is a style where no more or no less information than required is given. *Succinct* or *understated* style includes the use of understatements, pauses, and silences. Silences between words carry meaning. High-context cultures of moderate to strong uncertainty avoidance tend to use the elaborate style. Arab cultures show this elaborate style of verbal communication, using metaphors, long arrays of adjectives, flowery expressions, and proverbs. Low-context cultures of weak uncertainty avoidance (e.g., United States, United Kingdom) tend to use the exacting style. The succinct style is found in high-context cultures of strong uncertainty avoidance (e.g., Japan).

Nonverbal Styles

There are four nonverbal style possibilities: *unique-explicit* and *unique-implicit* style, *group-explicit* and *group-implicit* style. Unique-explicit nonverbal behavior uses expressive nonverbal gestures to express one's unique identity as well as openness and accessibility. It is found in the configuration individualism, low power distance, and low uncertainty avoidance. Fashion models pose in a defiant way (see Chapter 5). Unique-implicit nonverbal behavior is meant to protect individual privacy while simultaneously using subdued nonverbal gestures to display relational liking, status positions, and power distance. Symbols are used to show position in society; there are behavioral norms that are recognized by the insider, implicit rules of how one should dress, eat, and so on, like French *etiquette*. Group-explicit nonverbal behavior must ensure group norms and regulate public face by the use of expressive nonverbal gestures. This is the style of cultures that combine collectivism with low uncertainty avoidance. Communication is more open. In collectivistic cultures of high uncertainty avoidance, group-implicit nonverbal style upholds group norms and public face, and subdued nonverbal behavior is to display relational liking and power distance. The latter behavior may be related to the extreme use of symbols that support group feelings, like status-enhancing fashion brands and cute characters like Hello Kitty.

The two basic dimensions used are *identity–communality*, which echoes the self-orientation of individualism versus the group orientation of collectivism, and *accessibility–inaccessibility*, which reflects the power distance and uncertainty avoidance dimensions. Accessibility–inaccessibility refers to the degree to which the home environment emphasizes the openness or closedness of occupants to outsiders. Strong uncertainty avoidance people perceive outsiders as more threatening than weak uncertainty avoidance cultures do, and power distance reinforces that. Together, verbal and nonverbal styles are reflected in advertising styles across cultures.

For individuals attempting to function effectively in a foreign cultural setting, nonverbal gestures are a critical facet of interpersonal communication that must be mastered to effectively navigate social situations. The skill to recognize nonverbal language is related to the number of years immigrants have lived in a country.[27]

Interpersonal Communication Styles

Together, verbal and nonverbal communication styles can explain how we communicate. Figure 7.3 clusters countries according to these styles and summarizes the different interpersonal communication styles.

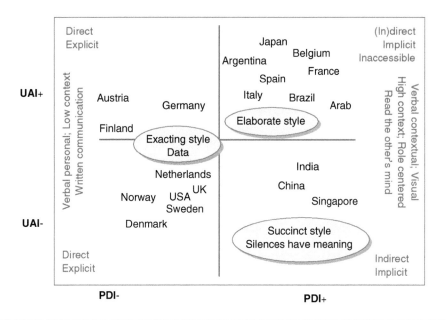

Figure 7.3   Interpersonal communication styles

SOURCE: Adapted from W. Gudykunst and S. Ting-Toomey, *Culture and Interpersonal Communication* (Sage, Newbury Park, CA, 1988), pp.99–133, Data from Hofstede et al. (2010) (see Appendix A)

Communication in the cultures in the two left quadrants of Figure 7.3 is direct, explicit, verbal, and personal. People like written communication. In business, they prefer using e-mail to using the phone. They use the exacting style and like data. The sender is responsible for effective communication. Communication in the mostly collectivistic cultures in the two right quadrants is more implicit and indirect. France and Belgium, which are individualistic, are exceptions, and communication can be both explicit and implicit. Communication is role centered. Particularly in Asia communication implies 'understanding without words.'[28] Children learn to 'read the other's mind,' to read subtle cues in the communication from others. They are expected to feel the mood or air of each interpersonal situation and improvise appropriate social behavior and communication depending on the reading of the contextual features.[29] So here the receiver is responsible for effective communication. In cultures in the top right quadrant, the elaborate style is used, and communication can be inaccessible. In the lower right quadrant, the succinct style is found. The difference between high and low uncertainty avoidance in Asia does have some implications for differences in explicitness and textual orientation.

In particular, the difference between the indirect style of the East and the direct style of the West can cause grave misunderstandings in international business.[30] In the direct style, wants, needs, and desires are expressed explicitly. Honesty and openness are the norm, and these are achieved through the use of precise, straightforward language behavior. The indirect verbal style refers to verbal messages that conceal the speaker's true intentions. In collectivistic cultures like Japan and Korea, where group harmony and conformity are so important, these are accomplished through the use of imprecise, ambiguous verbal communication behaviors. Wordings such as *absolutely* and *definitely* to express buying intentions are an example of the direct style, whereas *probably* or *somewhat* are examples of the indirect style. In indirect communication cultures, a direct mode of communication can be perceived as highly threatening, whereas in direct style communication cultures the indirect mode can be viewed as too ambiguous.

Digital Communication

How people use the Internet, e-mail, mobile phones and other technological means of communications reflects their interpersonal communication styles. One example is how people deal with the answering machine or voicemail. Japanese – because of stronger emphasis on the relational aspects of communication – find it more difficult than Americans to leave a message on an answering machine or voicemail. They use their answering machines less often and are more likely to hang up when they reach one than are American callers.[31]

In Asia, usage of technology is related to relationship and context. The mobile phone is used as a medium to communicate with people with strong ties, whereas texting is used as a group-talking tool.[32] But in most countries, the mobile phone has been adopted less for its talk function and more for its Internet-facilitating features. At the advent of the smartphone it was the key digital device for Japanese youngsters since they generally didn't have a PC until they went to college.

Social network services originated in the Western world, and Western services like Facebook are sender oriented; they employ individuals' needs to enhance the self. They do not allow for real dialogue. Yet people in collectivistic cultures have become the leaders in social networking on the Internet as they allow for continuous flows of information. However, people use social network services in different ways, and local services have adjusted to local cultural habits. The number of contacts (what in Western terms are called *friends*) vary enormously.[33] The numbers of friends people have across cultures correlate with short-term orientation. It is a manifestation of self-enhancement.

Chatting does not necessarily make global communities. It often is a group of existing relations that intensify their communication. Young people of the same city or even in the same street form closed groups that block out strangers with the argument that it is easier to talk to people one knows than to strangers.[34]

In individualistic cultures, social networks are viewed more as providing a path to resources, such as access to people who may have the right information to help deal with a health or medical issue.[35] In collectivistic cultures, Internet networks reinforce the sharing of feelings and ideas. They are a stronger media influence than the traditional media ever were. Of all media, the Chinese say blogs have the strongest influence on purchase decisions.[36] Chinese young generations rely on social networking sites as a source of electronic Word of Mouth (eWOM) in their decision-making process. For social networking sites users, people they communicate with every day, their friends and peers are significant and influential sources of opinions and information on products and services.[37]

Blogging has become a global phenomenon, but the degree to which people blog, their motives and topics vary by country. In 2006 there were more blogs in the Japanese language than in the English language, and the French spent five times as much time blogging as the Americans. For the French, the blog is like the café where they discuss everyday life and politics, fitting in with French argumentative culture.[38] Japanese tend to care less whether their blog influences others, and they are reluctant to reveal their identity, even with the use of aliases.

Whereas in the West the Internet provides an ideal context for self-disclosure, and people tend to release verbal emotions that they wouldn't do in a person-to-person context, self-disclosure has a negative connotation for East Asians. If one partner reveals too much about himself or herself, the other may take it as inappropriate or as an indicator of incompetence.[39] However, also for collectivists the Internet appears to be a context that allows for more self-disclosure than face-to-face relationships do. Yet, North Americans do not perceive East Asians as self-disclosing as much as East Asians perceive themselves to be.[40] Even when East Asians feel they cross their typical cultural constraints and engage in greater self-disclosure than they would do in face-to-face communication, North Americans still view their East Asian partners as indirect, without sufficient self-disclosure. At the same time East Asians feel that their North American partners are overexplicit and rude.[41]

The combination of talking and texting on the mobile phone (smartphone) makes it the most hybrid medium of all new technology. It allows illiterate people to connect with others who are not close by, and it also allows literary expressiveness. In many countries, the texting function has created a new type of language. Across cultures, people have also adopted the mobile phone to express themselves in their own culturally appropriate way. Whereas in individualistic cultures people use texting for efficiency reasons, in collectivistic culture, also those with oral literacy, people may use it to express themselves in style.

When people of different communication styles interact with each other online, they may encounter unexpected communication behaviors and barriers due to cultural differences. Across cultures, people construct culturally specific norms and patterns of online interactions and relationships and will continue to do so as the role of the Internet evolves and expands.

Mass Communication Styles

Three aspects determine mass communication styles: content, form, and style. Differences in form and style of mass communications reflect interpersonal communication styles as well as differences in orality and literacy. The influence of culture on these three elements can be recognized in literature, mass media programs, advertising, and public relations.

American television, for example, is more action oriented than Finnish television. Domestically produced Finnish video dramas are much more static. They sacrifice action and setting for dialogue and extreme close-ups.[42] Both the Russians and the Japanese depict boredom in their novels, whereas American novels do not do much with the theme. 'Fun is not a Russian concept,' says Moscow sociologist Maria Zolotukhina on the difficulties faced by the creators of a Russian version of the popular American children's television program *Sesame Street*.[43] The 'happy ending' is rare in Japanese novels and plays, whereas American popular audiences crave solutions. This is reflected in American TV dramas and commercials. The essence of much drama in Western, individualistic literature is an eternal struggle of the hero ('To be or not to be'). Chinese essayist Bin Xin has noted that real tragedy has never existed in Chinese literature because the Chinese have hardly any struggles in their minds.[44] Western readers of Chinese novels find lack of psychological depth and a plot, as most Chinese novels describe what happens without analyzing why it happens.[45] Also, how people behave in literature and what motivates them reflect cultural values. An example from literature is the Italian Carlo Collodi's *Pinocchio*, who is an obedient and dependent child, as compared with the nephews of Disney's Donald Duck, who are much more independent and less obedient. Strong uncertainty avoidance is reflected in the novel *Das Schloss* (*The Castle*) by Franz Kafka, in how the main character K. is affected by bureaucracy. *Alice in Wonderland*, where the most unreal things happen, is a typical work to originate in a culture of weak uncertainty avoidance: England. No surprise that in the same culture the Harry Potter books originated. US films have been found to be more successful in English-speaking countries, countries with values similar to the United States.[46] Press releases from American public relations agencies reflect US culture. They are short and to the point.

Advertising Styles

McCracken states:

> Advertising works as a potential method of meaning transfer by bringing the con-
> sumer good and a representation of the culturally constituted world together within
> the frame of a particular advertisement. The creative director of an agency seeks to
> conjoin these two elements in such a way that the viewer/reader glimpses an essential
> similarity between them. When this symbolic equivalence is successfully established,
> the viewer/reader attributes certain properties he or she knows to exist in the cultur-
> ally constituted world to the consumer good.[47]

Advertising has developed its own particular systems of meaning. These are by no means
universal across borders but rather are often culturally defined and frequently vary from
country to country. This suggests a difference in the way advertising is composed and read:
that is, a difference in advertising codes. It also suggests that where a different language is
spoken, there is likely to be a different set of symbolic references, including myths, history,
humor, and the arts. Any ad execution that does not tap into such references is likely to be
a blander proposition than one that does.[48]

Although some concepts might be somewhat universal, visual communication of them
is not. How the individual reads an advertisement depends on the uses the person has for
the interpreted meaning and on his or her unique life experiences and plans. Viewers produce unique interpretations of meaning, often interpreting advertisements in substantially
different ways than intended.[49]

Next to viewing advertising as transfer of meaning, in Western advertising theory it
is viewed as persuasive communication of which rhetoric is an integral part. *Persuasion*
means to 'cause someone to do something, especially by reasoning, urging or inducing.'
It is synonymous for 'to win over.' The persuasive communication function of advertising
is biased toward rational claims, direct address of the public, or 'hard sell.' All elements of
advertising, words and pictures, tend to be evaluated on their persuasive role in the sales
process. This is the typical approach of the individualistic–masculine cultural configuration
of the culture of origin of advertising theory. Although in other cultures sales will also be
the ultimate goal of advertising, advertising's role in the sales process is different. In collectivistic cultures the use of hard sell, or direct address of consumers, turns people off instead
of persuading them. Although US studies[50] have shown that persuasion tests (preference
shifting) are also adequate for measuring the effectiveness of emotional or image/mood
advertising in the United States, it seems inappropriate to use persuasion tests that are based
on rational, linear processing to test advertisements meant for people who have a different

information-processing system. The effects of advertising in collectivistic cultures in Asia, Latin America, the Arab world, as well as Russia cannot be understood without a thorough knowledge of local beliefs and assumptions.[51]

> Jean-Marie Dru, cofounder and Chairman of BDDP Group, writes, 'Ads are the mirror of societies, they reflect their respective cultures. ... Globalization changes nothing. On the contrary, the more sophisticated advertising gets, the more it takes on local colors.' Dru characterizes a few advertising styles as follows: 'while the British aim for cuteness and are sometimes funny, Americans have gone on to explore a lot of emotions like hunger, sex, fatherhood, etc.' In advertising, the Japanese share the French attraction to allegories, showing the brand in context. Half-words are second nature in Great Britain, the country of understatement. Spain makes a specialty of unexpected demonstrations and visual unforgettables. German advertising assumes responsibility for being advertising. German ads seek to sell, they strive to convince. Norwegian advertising is characterized by crazy, random humor. In Asia, there is humility and a humanity that gives messages a very particular sensibility.[52]

Both differences in information-processing and communication styles have resulted in specific advertising styles across cultures. Next to varying appeals and motives, communication styles, including aesthetic preferences, define advertising styles. The strongest distinction is between direct and indirect communication.

Direct Versus Indirect Communication in Mass Communication and Advertising

High-context communication involves transmitting implicit, indirect messages minimizing the content of the verbal message, whereas low-context communication involves being direct, precise, and open. Statements must be to the point and relevant, and people should avoid obscure expressions.

> On 16 July 2002, front-page news in India was the high price of the mango. Superficially, one would consider this to be non-news, but for the people in northern India it meant disaster. An expensive mango implied impending drought for 200 million people. Several years without a monsoon had aggravated the lack of water. The mango tree gets water from deep in the soil. If that last bit of water is gone before the fruit ripens, there are few mangos, and the price goes up. Indian journalists are not supposed to predict disaster; they just say that the price of the mango is high.[53]

In advertising the direct style uses the personal pronouns *you* or *we*, whereas the indirect style doesn't address people but uses indirect methods such as metaphors. There are, however, variations in indirectness among collectivistic cultures. Singapore Chinese are, for example, more direct than people from Taiwan.[54] This is confirmed by a study by Cutler et al.,[55] who examined advertisements from eight different countries (United States, United Kingdom, France, India, Japan, Turkey, Taiwan/Hong Kong, and Korea), measuring the use of a direct, personalized headline, addressing the public by *you* or *your*. The researchers viewed the singular form *you* as an expression of the direct approach, whereas the use of *we* was assumed to be an expression of collectivism. However, both the use of *you* and *we* are in fact reflections of the direct approach. A significant correlation was found between individualism and the measure 'personalized headline' used in the content analysis of magazine ads ($r = .62*$). Our own additional analysis of the data published in the article resulted in a more significant correlation with low uncertainty avoidance ($r = -.75***$). Among collectivistic cultures, the degree of uncertainty avoidance explains variation in directness in communications.

A distinction related to direct–indirect is *informational–transformational,* where *informational advertising* refers to advertising that focuses on providing meaningful facts to the consumer, whereas *transformational advertising* is the term used for advertising that uses emotions to move the consumer. Examples of transformational approaches are association, metaphor, storytelling, and aesthetics. Examples of informational approaches are description, comparison, argumentation or demonstration. Generally, cross-cultural comparisons of advertising find more informational approaches in individualistic cultures than in collectivistic cultures, where more transformational approaches are used.[56] This applies to print advertising, TV commercials or other moving content as well as brand pages on social media. A study comparing Facebook brand pages of a French cosmetics brand found the French brand pages argumentation oriented versus Saudi Arabian pages which were more visual and ludic (contests).[57]

Figures 7.4–7.7 show examples of direct and indirect advertising style. The direct ones use *you* or *we*. Figure 7.4 shows two examples of the direct approach, an ad for Centrum (UK) and an international ad for German Bayer. Figure 7.5 shows two examples of Belgian (Audi) and Spanish (Peugeot) car advertising that use the indirect metaphorical approach. The ad for Audi uses the skin care metaphor, saying 'We care,' and the Spanish ad for Peugeot uses the bull's horns as a metaphor for safety. Figure 7.6 shows two examples of what happens when you only translate the copy without changing the advertising style. The translation may be all right, but this is a direct style message for an indirect style culture. Two Asian examples in Figure 7.7 are ads for Thai Airways International and the Japanese company NSK, selling ball bearings.

Figure 7.4   **Direct style (United Kingdom, Germany/International)**

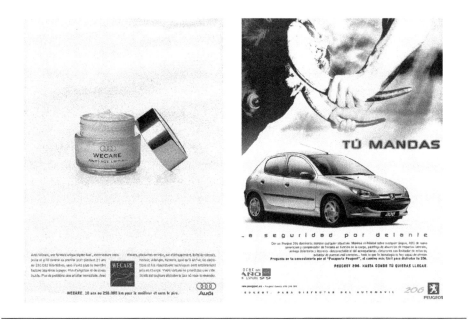

Figure 7.5   **Indirect style: Metaphor (Belgium, Spain)**

Figure 7.6   **Direct style ads in indirect style culture (France)**

Figure 7.7   **Indirect style: Symbolic (Thailand, Japan)**

Mapping Advertising Styles

For advertising styles countries can be mapped similar to the different elements of interpersonal personal communication style as in Figure 7.3. In particular power distance and uncertainty avoidance together explain differences in the use of aesthetics, drama, metaphors and symbolism in the PDI+ cultures and the use of humor in UAI- cultures versus structure in UAI+ cultures. However, for mass communication, the long-/short-term orientation data also appear to be a useful mapping tool, together with individualism–collectivism, because this dimension distinguishes between literate and oral styles that also explain differences in styles.[58] Cultures thus can be mapped as in Figure 7.8.

The advertising style in the two right quadrants, where cultures are individualistic, is direct and explicit, more verbal than visual, and it uses argumentation. Within this direct–explicit distinction, there are also differences, for example, with respect to the degree of self-enhancement and hard sell arguments for short-term effects. Within the quadrants, we find differences with respect to the other dimensions. For example, in individualistic cultures of strong uncertainty avoidance, advertising is more serious and structured.

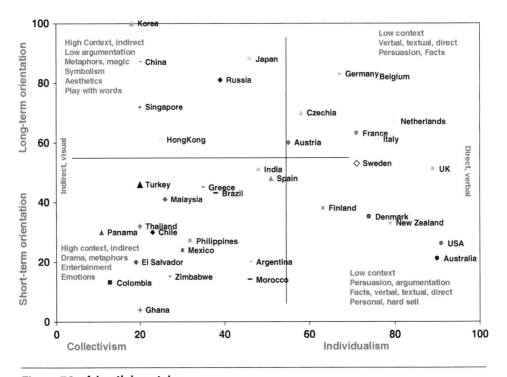

Figure 7.8 Advertising styles

SOURCE: Data Hofstede et al. (2010) (see Appendix A)

The execution of the visuals will be detailed, often including demonstration of how the product works. In the weak uncertainty avoidance cultures, where ambiguity is tolerated, more humor is used in advertising. Many centrally developed television commercials for Anglo-American brands in the household cleaning products category and personal products have used the personalized testimonial format. They are carefully directed to focus on the personality of the endorser and not to include any implicit nonverbal behavior. For the US market, the typical person endorser and spokesperson have a positive impact on recall.[59]

The two quadrants at the left where cultures are collectivistic include styles that are implicit and indirect using symbolism and visuals. The cultures in the upper left quadrant use less argumentation and more symbolism, metaphors, and aesthetics. These are also literate cultures, and playing with words and use of taglines in advertising is popular. But verbal expression is not direct and *double entendre* is appreciated.[60] An example of indirectness in Japanese advertising is saying 'These times exist in life, when someone wants to go somewhere very comfortable' instead of saying 'This car offers the most comfortable interior and the smoothest drive.'[61] Communication is subdued and works on likeability. The use of aesthetics and entertainment as an advertising form is characteristic of this communication style. Chinese consumers like visual and vivid ads with images. If celebrities are involved, they are not likely to address the audience directly. They play a more symbolic role and associate more with the product rather than endorsing it in a direct way. Visual metaphors and symbols are used to create context and to position the product or brand in its 'proper place.' They must ensure group norms and help maintain face. Next to the use of drama and metaphor, visuals, play with words (visually), songs, and symbolism are important in advertising in these cultures.

Moving to the lower left quadrant, we see India and Spain in the border area, where communication may be more direct, and a mix of Hispanic, African, and a few Asian cultures that are collectivistic as well as short-term oriented. Advertising style is mostly indirect and uses drama and metaphor although these cultures are more verbal in their communication. For India, a more direct communication style was noticed by Roland,[62] who states, 'Indian modes of communication operate more overtly on more levels simultaneously than do the Japanese.' In this cluster are mostly oral cultures with intensive interpersonal communication and dialogue as in soaps and other forms of drama. Drama is an indirect style based on dialogue that fits countries such as Spain as well as Latin American cultures. Variations are found between masculine and feminine cultures. In Italy, high on masculinity, show is favored, and the drama form tends to be theatrical and often not based on real life. In Spain, drama style is softer, and metaphorical stories are used to place the product in a context that provides meaning. Although in the United States the drama style is also used, it is even more popular in the countries in the lower left quadrant. Drama in the United States is more 'slice-of-life,' a form that demonstrates how a product is used in everyday life, whereas drama in the left quadrants is entertainment, meant to build a relationship between the consumer and the brand.

The Purpose of Advertising

The role and purpose of marketing communications and the way advertising works vary across cultures, in particular between individualistic and collectivistic cultures. In collectivistic cultures, the purpose of advertising is to build relationships and trust between seller and buyer, so positive feelings are included in communication and advertising is entertaining. Whereas the purpose of advertising in the United States is to sell, persuade, or change attitudes at short term, in collectivistic cultures the purpose of advertising is to build trust and relationships between company and consumer. The desire of Japanese consumers to establish trusting, in-group-like relationships with suppliers and their products is reflected in the tendency of Japanese advertising to focus on inducing positive feelings rather than to provide information.

Miracle[63] summarized the logic of advertising in two distinct ways. The logic of advertising in Western societies is basically to:

1. Tell the audience how you or your product is different.
2. Tell why your product is best, using clearly stated information and benefits.
3. Consumers then will want to buy, because they have a clear reason or justification for the purchase.
4. If they are satisfied, consumers will like and trust the brand, and make repeat purchases.

The logic of advertising in Japan, which is probably valid for most Asian collectivistic cultures, is essentially the reverse:

1. Make friends with the target audience.
2. Prove that you understand their feelings.
3. Show that you are nice.
4. Consumers will then want to buy, because they trust you and feel familiar with you, that is, the company.
5. After the purchase, consumers find out if the product is good or what the benefits are.

This difference is also recognized in Internet advertising. The dominant factor that defines attitudes toward Internet advertising in the United States is information, whereas in Korea the dominant factors are trustworthy and enjoyable.[64] The different purposes explain differences in advertising styles and related models of how advertising works. Persuasion is the model of the Anglo-Saxon world. Likeability is the model of collectivistic cultures, but also of feminine cultures. Likeability can be softness or pure entertainment.

Figure 7.9   **Dodot, Spain: Likeability**

Figure 7.10   **Nissin Cup Noodle, Japan: Entertainment**

The latter is the model of Asia. Figure 5.9 (Chapter 5) showed a US commercial, an example of the persuasion model – problem solving, argumentation, and comparison. Figure 7.9 shows a Spanish example of likeability and softness, and Figure 7.10 shows a Japanese example of pure entertainment. In the Spanish commercial, the children are the researchers to develop the driest nappy. When they have found it, they shout 'Eureka,' and they look very satisfied. The Nissin commercial is pure entertainment.

Along with different purposes of advertising, its effectiveness measurement methods should be different. Western measurements of advertising effectiveness use criteria like persuasiveness, attitude change, recall, recognition, brand linkage, message relevance, or likeability.[65] Because of varying mental processes of consumers and those who create advertising, none of these measures can be universal. Persuasiveness is a purpose of advertising mainly applicable to the Western world. The Western proposition is that likeability mediates brand attitude that in turn influences purchase intention.

Likeability will be a better effectiveness measurement for cultures where pleasing the consumer is an important objective of advertising. In most cultures where the purpose of communication is to raise trust between the company and the consumer or to build an emotional relationship between consumer and brand, likeability will be a better purpose and measurement criterion than persuasion. A comparative study across four Asian countries showed indeed that the more respondents like an advertisement, the greater the probability of buying the product.[66]

In Chapter 4 (section on attitude and behavior) we discussed the varying relationships among attitude–intention–behavior across individualistic and collectivistic cultures. Because of the importance of situational variables, the relationship is even weaker in collectivistic than it is in individualistic cultures. Relevance is not a condition for effective advertising in collectivistic cultures.

In a comparative study among young people in the Netherlands and Japan, Praet[67] found significant differences in advertising likeability of international ads for the global brands Nike, Adidas, Levi's and Diesel. However, the relationships between likeability and purchase intentions were different. Four measures were used to measure the effect of the ad on purchase intention: ad likeability, brand likeability, personal relevance, and appropriateness. Whereas ad likeability was the strongest predictor of purchase intention in Japan, it did not play a significant role in the Netherlands, where the personal appeal was much stronger. In Japan, ad likeability's main function is to create a favorable feeling toward the advertised brand, which will lead to purchase intention, whereas in the Netherlands the function of ad likeability should be primarily that of gatekeeper for further processing of an ad, which then has to present the viewer with personally relevant information to induce purchase intention. The importance of brand likeability in Japan reflects the strong brand consciousness of the Japanese, as compared with Dutch consumers who are less influenced by brand names and may use a brand's prestige less as a guiding principle for making purchase decisions. The two cultural dimensions at work for explaining the differences are individualism/collectivism and masculinity/femininity.

In sum, the advertising mechanisms that work best are subject to too many specific factors, reflecting market conditions, cultural differences, and brand history, to allow for only one method to measure the effectiveness of advertising across cultures.

Website Communication Styles

When the Internet became operational for the world, starting with e-mail and the potential to build websites to present a company or sell products, it looked as though its users were part of a global community with similar needs and communication styles, but people soon started to use it for different purposes and in different ways. The differences in communication behavior discussed before also apply to the new media. Subjects from low-context cultures possess a higher degree of information and convenience motivation, and there is more human-message interaction (click into deeper links, using search engine, stay longer for details), while subjects from high-context cultures demonstrate a higher degree of social interaction motivation and human–human interaction (that is, interacting with other people, for example by participating in customer discussions, or providing feedback). High-context communication consumers may trust the information they obtain from their online interpersonal communication, such as chat rooms or online forums, more than do low-context communication consumers who more rely on facts.[68] US citizens are more likely to be motivated to shop online and look for information online than Korean consumers. In contrast, Korean consumers are more motivated than US consumers to head online to fulfill social goals such as making friends, meeting people, and participating in newsgroups. With respect to communication style preferences, US citizens are found to have stronger preferences for verbal styles in comparison to Koreans.[69]

A review of 27 studies that analyzed culture's influence on website design showed that culturally congruent websites are more useful, easier to use, lead to positive attitudes and intentions and are overall more effective.[70]

For website design, the same laws operate as for other mass communications. There exists a creative process for generating messages that is independent of the medium and type of message. That is, website and banner designers are not that different from creative directors in the traditional advertising world.[71] Across cultures, people vary in the ways they want to be addressed. Values and motives vary as well as communication styles.

For example, university websites in feminine cultures have a softer approach and are more people oriented than websites of universities of masculine cultures that are more focused on achievement.[72] Belgian commercial websites reflect hierarchy and more frequent use of proper titles than do Dutch commercial websites.[73] Local websites of India, China, Japan, and the United States are very different and reflect their own cultural values. A striking feature of Chinese websites is the recurrent image of the family theme. Japanese websites exhibit clear gender roles and are rich in colors, aesthetics with pictures of butterflies, cherry blossoms, or other nature scenes. Indian websites prominently depict the titles of the employees to demonstrate hierarchy. US websites are low-context, direct, informative, logical, and success-oriented, with prominent independence themes.[74] In comparison with US websites, websites from Arab countries reflect collectivistic values like honor and hospitality and the importance of family; websites show company hierarchy as well as proper titles; more symbolism is used.[75]

Also, local websites for global brands distinguish between low- and high-context communication with more literal visuals in countries like the United States, United Kingdom, and Germany and more symbolic visuals in countries like Japan, Korea, and China.[76]

McDonald's has used culturally relevant approaches in their websites to profess its slogan 'I'm lovin' it': people alone or together, images of individuals separate or together with the product, more text, or more pictures. High-context cultures use more animation and images of moving people than low-context cultures, and the images promote values characteristic of collectivistic cultures.[77] The United Kingdom leads both in text-heavy layout and shorter pages, whereas South Korea leads both in visual layout and in longer pages. South Korea utilizes much more multimedia presentation than the United States and the United Kingdom, where presentation more often is based on text only.[78]

Generally high-context cultures use more animation and images of moving people in their websites than low-context cultures do, and the images promote values characteristic of collectivistic cultures. The United Kingdom leads both in text-heavy layout and shorter pages, whereas South Korea leads both in visual layout and in longer pages. South Korea utilizes much more multimedia presentation than the United States and the United Kingdom, where presentation more often is based on text only.[79]

There are significant differences between East and West in terms of interactive communication styles used by corporate websites. High-context Eastern websites employ less consumer–message and consumer–marketer interactivity than do low-context Western websites. High power distance explains less consumer–marketer interactivity, as communication between seller and consumer is more hierarchical versus more equal in low power distance cultures where the consumer is treated as a friend. Collectivism explains more group activities among consumers.[80] So in high-context cultures, where people are more motivated by social interaction, online marketers should generate more consumer interaction, such as discussion forums and chat rooms, whereas in low-context cultures, where people search more information, online marketers should emphasize information features such as keyword search and virtual product display.[81] The same applies to government applications of the Internet. In individualistic cultures of low uncertainty avoidance and low power distance, more people use the Internet for obtaining information from public authorities' websites.[82]

In sum, along with culture, there is variation in the way information is presented, the amount of data used, the use of extreme claims, rhetorical style, the use of visuals or animation, the degree to which information is explicit, precise, and direct, and the option to contact people.[83] Companies reaching their local customers through the traditional media do not have international customers to worry about, but the Internet is available for the world to see. Therefore it is critical for companies to develop culturally designed international websites.[84] The more the design of a website conforms to culturally familiar communication styles and cultural habits, the more trust is established and people appear to perform information-seeking tasks faster when using Web content created by designers from their own culture.[85] Cultural adaptation not only enhances ease of use on the website but also leads to more favorable attitudes toward the website, which in turn affects the intention to buy.[86]

Media Behavior Across Cultures

In Chapter 3, media data were used as examples of the convergence–divergence process. Although at macro level, some media converge, differences at micro level, or what people do with the media, are substantial. This section describes these differences for some of the traditional media television and newspapers as well as for the Internet. Generally it was expected that the Internet would be used at the cost of the traditional media, but it has become a medium that is used in addition to the existing media. People now use many media at the same time, which in the Western world is viewed as a negative development. Several words have been developed for this media behavior: *multitasking, parallel processing* or *perpetual partial attention* – watching television, working on the computer and using the mobile phone at the same time. In polychronic cultures like in Asia and Latin America, people have no problems with this and use all sorts of media at the same time with the TV set and computer next to each other. In particular, young people are using a wide variety of media and spending a good part of their time doing so. The biggest media junkies (15–24 years old) can be found in the Philippines (31.3 hrs a day) and Hong Kong China (26.6).[87]

Television

In Chapter 3 we saw that initially penetration of television sets converged across countries, but since 1997 it has been diverging. For a mix of poor and wealthy countries, TV viewing is negatively correlated with wealth, that is, in the poorer countries people watch more TV than in the richer countries. Although nowadays it is not only the TV set on which people watch TV, large percentages of people still watch broadcast TV on a television set. Everywhere broadcast TV has played a significant role in the leisure activities of people. Although penetration of television sets has converged across countries, differences in viewing time between countries are considerable, and these differences are more or less stable over time. Of all countries reported by Ofcom in 2016,[88] North Americans spend the most time watching television with 274 minutes per day. Also across Europe, differences in television viewing are large, varying from 264 minutes per person per day in Poland to 154 minutes in Sweden. In most countries in the past years, the time spent on watching TV has increased, but the relative differences have remained the same.

Over the years in the wealthy countries of the developed world, high power distance, uncertainty avoidance and masculinity have explained variance. In 1998, heavy viewing across 19 countries worldwide[89] was related to high masculinity and large power distance. In 2007, across 18 wealthy European countries, high power distance explained 38% of variance and masculinity an additional 16%.[90] In 2016 the Ofcom data on average minutes live broadcast TV viewing for 16 countries worldwide show significant correlations with uncertainty avoidance and masculinity, with uncertainty avoidance explaining 64%. In many countries television has increasingly become show and violence, to which people in masculine cultures obviously are more attracted than people in feminine cultures. In Europe in

2016 variance of watching TV on a TV set every day was explained by collectivism (32%) and additionally by masculinity (46%). Watching TV via Internet was explained by low uncertainty avoidance (39%), which tends to explain most of the differences in Internet usage.

In collectivistic, polychronic cultures, the TV set tends to be on the whole day, even more so in the masculine cultures. Across Latin American countries, the percentages of people who say they like having the TV set on while doing other things in the house correlate with masculinity.[91]

Across Europe, people hardly watch the programs of other countries, mainly because they do not understand the language. In 1997, 30% of the EMS respondents said they did not understand any foreign language well enough to watch TV news in another language; 54% of Europeans rarely or never watched the news in a foreign language; and 75% rarely or never watched soaps in a foreign language. Even within countries, different language groups will watch different programs. Analysis of People-Meter data from Germany and the three cultural regions of Switzerland showed substantial differences in television viewing.[92] In most countries people prefer watching local programs. The Los Medios y Mercados de Latinoamérica study of 1998 showed that in most Latin American countries, people are more interested in programs from their own countries than from the United States.[93] As a result of these local preferences, many international TV channels have localized language and content. CNN International and MTV started as global channels but have localized content and language.

How people watch TV – alone, with friends or family – is also related to culture, but these relationships have been changing with the advent of tablets and smartphones, on which in particular children and adolescents watch moving content. The degree to which parents give freedom to their children with respect to what they watch varies.[94] Chapter 5 discussed relationships between parents and children and differences in the levels of freedom parents allow to children for watching television. Generally in collectivistic cultures, also in Latin American countries, children have greater freedom, whereas in the more individualistic cultures both fathers and mothers decide which programs children may watch.[95]

The more visual orientation of collectivistic and high power distance cultures makes TV more attractive than print media, and within the print media magazines are more attractive than newspapers. High-quality print media are particularly popular among the Japanese, who are avid magazine readers. Magazines are important media for imported luxury brands. The main product categories that dominate the magazine industry in Japan are cosmetics, toiletries, fashion, accessories, automobiles, leisure, and beverage/tobacco.[96]

As more mobile devices have become available and integrated with IPTV, it has brought more interactivity and flexibility. In countries with limited TV channels, the Internet offers a great deal more.

Radio

Radio sets are available in most homes. Ownership of radios per 1,000 persons has been correlated with individualism for the last decades.[97] In individualistic cultures, everybody has his or her own radio or even more than one, whereas in collectivistic cultures one per family may be enough. Even across Latin cultures (Spain, Portugal, and nine Latin American countries) – all scoring more or less collectivistic – the numbers of radio receivers per 1,000 people correlated with individualism ($r = .64^{*}$).[98] Also the time spent on radio listening is related to individualism. For seven countries worldwide, weekly listening hours correlate with individualism ($r = .83^{***}$).[99] Data of 2016 for Europe[100] for listening to the radio everyday points at similar cultural relationships, but with low uncertainty avoidance explaining variance (34%). These data have become less useful as so many people nowadays listen to radio and music on all sorts of mobile hardware.

Yet, time spent on listening keeps varying. For example, in 2009 the Russians spent the most time listening to radio with 39 hours per person per week; the Japanese and Spanish spent the least with 12.6 hours.[101] In 2015 this was 29 hrs for the Russians, the Japanese spent 14 hrs listening and the Spanish 13 hrs. The data for average radio listening hours correlate negatively with IVR (restraint) and positively with uncertainty avoidance.[102]

Press Media

As we saw in the section on communication and culture earlier in the chapter, low uncertainty avoidance is the main explaining variable for differences in reading in general, which also explains differences in time spent reading newspapers. National wealth and low power distance explain differences in newspaper readership worldwide, whereas in Europe the configuration of power distance and uncertainty avoidance explains variance. In 1996, for the measurement 'Read a newspaper yesterday' for 31 countries worldwide, published by the advertising agency McCann Erickson,[103] 26% of variance was explained by low power distance, and an additional 15% by low uncertainty avoidance. In cultures of high power distance and high uncertainty avoidance, people read fewer newspapers than in cultures scoring low on these dimensions. The latter countries are more participative democracies where people want to be informed about politics and current affairs. The percentages agreeing with the statement 'I feel well informed about what is going on in politics and current affairs' are also correlated with low power distance ($r = -.57^{***}$) and low uncertainty avoidance ($r = -.51^{***}$).[104] Figure 7.11 illustrates the correlation between newspaper readership and power distance (r calculated for 26 countries) and the stability of the relationship over time for 14 countries in Europe.

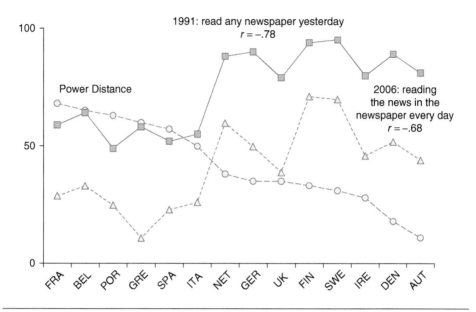

Figure 7.11 Newspaper readership and power distance 1991, 2006 and 2016

SOURCES: Hofstede et al. (2010) (see Appendix A); *Reader's Digest* 1991, EB 65 (2007) and EB 86 (2016) (see Appendix B)

The data of 1991 are from *Reader's Digest* Eurodata and are the percentages of answers to 'Read any newspaper yesterday,' a more general question than the Eurobarometer question that asks whether people read the *news* in the newspaper *every day*. So the percentages are lower. But the lines run parallel. Because the differences in newspaper readership across countries in Europe have existed for more than half a century, they are not likely to disappear.

In Latin America, press circulation also varies, and variance is partly explained by power distance. In 2007, for 15 Latin countries (Latin America plus Spain and Portugal), 69% of variance of press circulation was explained by GNI/capita and an additional 9% by power distance.[105]

Magazines have a different function. Differences in readership of news magazines or general interest magazines will be similar to newspaper and book reading. Glossy magazines that have an entertainment function might be compared to television. Across Asian countries, collectivism explains 73% of variance of the percentages of people who say they regularly read fashion or women's magazines.[106] In the 1990s, the magazine share of total advertising expenditures correlated with strong uncertainty avoidance and high power distance.

The Internet

The Internet by its very nature is a global communications channel with the potential to reach consumers anywhere in the world. Wealth and individualism have been the primary determinants of the structure of international hyperlink flows.[107]

Ownership and usage of many Internet-related products are still related to GNI/capita, but increasingly many differences are due to cultural values. Within the developed world, from the start, in the low uncertainty avoidance cultures people have adopted the Internet fastest, and there still are significant relationships between Internet penetration and usage and uncertainty avoidance. In 2004, whereas GNI per capita explained variance of the numbers of Internet users per 1,000 people for 55 countries worldwide, low uncertainty

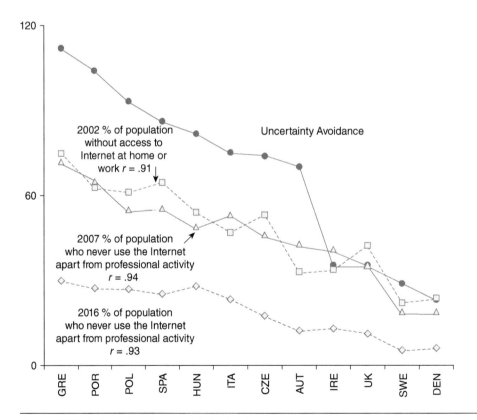

Figure 7.12   Internet and uncertainty avoidance

SOURCES: Hofstede et al. (2010) (see Appendix A); *European Social Survey* (2002); EBS 278 (2007) (see Appendix B)

avoidance explained 32% of variance in 26 wealthy countries.[108] This relationship has been very stable. In 2002, in Europe the percentages of people without access to Internet, neither at home nor at work were related to high uncertainty avoidance, which across 20 countries explained 46% of variance[109]. The relationship is illustrated in Figure 7.12 for 12 countries ($r = .91***$). The same chart illustrates data of 2007, the percentages of people who never use the Internet apart from professional activity.[110] For 24 European countries, uncertainty avoidance explains 59% of variance ($r = .77***$). For the 12 countries in Figure 7.12, $r = .94***$. In 2016 Eurobarometer[111] asked the same questions related to the Internet. For the same 12 countries the percentages were lower, but the differences still correlated with uncertainty avoidance ($r = .93***$).

Next to uncertainty avoidance, masculinity explains variance of Internet usage and some of its applications. Low masculinity often is a second or third predictor after GNI per capita and low uncertainty avoidance. For example, in 2007, for 23 countries in Europe and Asia, GNI per capita explained 47% of variance of Internet penetration and low masculinity an additional 14%.[112] In 2017 across Europe, GNI per capita explained 62% of variance of using Internet every day, with low masculinity explaining an additional 17% and low uncertainty avoidance another 10%.

In the masculine cultures people use the Internet more for business, to be more productive or competitive, and in the feminine cultures people will use it more for personal reasons, to enhance the quality of life. Time spent on the Internet is related to femininity. In 2007 in Europe, the percentages of people who said they used the Internet every day correlated negatively with masculinity.[113] Also in 2007, for 23 countries in Europe and Asia, the average monthly Internet hours per user correlated with low masculinity.[114]

Whereas Internet usage has increased with income in the United States, the relationship was not so clear in Japan, where people accessed the Internet mostly at work.[115] In Japan, the Internet has become more representative when new carriers were introduced, such as Internet services by mobile phone. Ownership of personal computers in Japan has been relatively low for several reasons. The configuration of high power distance, collectivism, and high uncertainty avoidance explains relatively low penetration of home computers in Japan. In this configuration there is a strong separation between home and work life; people don't take work home, so for that purpose they don't need home computers. Also, parents don't help children as much with homework, so for that purpose also there is no need for a home computer. Also across countries in Latin America, mostly of high power distance, the Internet was more used for education purposes in the relatively low power distance cultures. Whereas Americans use their computers for many things related to children and education, in developed Asian countries people are less likely to use computers for teaching or entertaining children or for school or college work. In Chapter 5, we discussed that in high power distance cultures parents participate less in the education of their children, and computer use for educational purposes will be in the schools.

The Internet supports a wide variety of uses; from simple communications, such as e-mail, chat, or twitter, to sophisticated real-time video and audio communications; from access to digital newspapers or information sources, buying goods or services, using online social networks to blogging, wikis, and other user-generated content; from educational and research purposes to online gaming or downloading music and videos; from accessing local government services to checking the bank account. ITU data on Internet activities across 25 countries plus an average for 27 countries of the European Union show great differences in usage of the various Internet possibilities. For example, the highest usage of the Internet for e-mail is in Chile; the highest usage for education is in Brazil; most use of Internet for reading and/or downloading newspapers, magazines, or books is in Hong Kong, China; and the highest use for interaction with governments is in EU countries.[116]

Table 7.2 summarizes a number of Internet activities and the significant correlations with the dimensions.

Table 7.2 **Use of Internet for various purposes**

	PDI	IDV	MAS	UAI	LTO
Internet use, % of total population, 2009	−.61***	.34*		−.36*	
% Households with Internet access, 2017	−.56***	.64***		−.63***	
% Individuals using the Internet for ordering goods or services, 2017	−.57***	.66***		−.69***	
% Individuals who use Internet every day, 2016	−.59***	.63***	−.48**	−.69***	
Online activities on the Internet, 2017:					
Banking	−.62***	.59***	−.46*	−.66***	
Buying goods and services	−.70***	.62***		−.78***	
Using online social networks			−.43*		−.34*
Sending or receiving e-mails	−.57***	.47**	−.35*	−.51**	
Reading news	−.43*		−.48**		
Watching TV	−.61***	.36*	−.71***	−.68***	
Selling goods and services	−.40*	.52**			

SOURCE: Hofstede et al. (2010) (see Appendix A); 1970 and 1991: Reader's Digest; 1998: Consumers in Europe 2001, Eurostat; 2005: European Social Survey; 2007: EBS 278, EMS 2007; 2008: EBS 295; 2008: Flash EB 241; 2008: EBS 298; 2017: EB88; Asia: Synovate PAX Asia 2008 (see Appendix B)

Quite a few Internet activities are positively correlated with long-term orientation, which indicates pragmatism. It looks like in long-term orientation cultures people adopt new technology to enhance a large number of existing activities and do these in a more intensive way than in the short-term oriented cultures that are more traditional.

Levels of interactivity vary across cultures. In low-context cultures, people search more for information and facts, clicking into deeper links and using search engines, whereas in high-context cultures, people are more interested in social interaction, interacting with other people and participating in customer discussions. In high-context communication cultures, people trust the information they obtain from their online interpersonal communication more than members of low-context communication cultures do.[117]

The Internet takes time from the old media or other activities. An example is Internet usage replacing book reading or time spent on sport or physical activity or other social activities. In Hong Kong, China time spent on the Internet doesn't take time from the amount of time spent on sociability. Generally, online relationships are weaker than those formed and maintained offline. People keep spending time on real-world social activities to enhance or maintain their social relationships.[118] In Latin American, mostly collectivistic and polychronic cultures, where people are used to doing more things at the same time, Internet usage and TV viewing are not mutually exclusive activities. In the home, the TV is placed next to the computer monitor so that people can watch the two things at the same time.[119]

For Internet users, privacy is a worldwide concern, but the importance people attribute to it varies. Whereas in the United States privacy is seen as a basic human right, entrenched in the constitution, the constitutions of Asian countries indicate little or no recognition of privacy. A survey among Internet users in Seoul, Singapore, Bangalore, Sydney, and New York found that in individualistic cultures Internet users were more concerned about privacy than those in collectivistic cultures.[120] In 2015 Eurostat[121] asked people about their Internet behavior related to privacy, finding that the percent of individuals who did not provide personal information correlated with collectivism and high uncertainty avoidance, but even stronger with restraint (low IVR). If you restrain yourself to give away personal information, you don't have to be concerned about privacy.

The Different Roles of the Internet

The basic roles of the Internet are *information* (search for information, compare, and buy products), *entertainment* (games, online video) and *social* (e-mail, social networks, and chat rooms).

The *information role* is more important in individualistic cultures, whereas the entertainment and social roles are more important in collectivistic cultures. Whereas in individualistic cultures people first try to find information via search engines, in collectivistic cultures, they will go to a discussion forum where people comment on and recommend various activities. Where upholding face is important, people can take part in discussion forums anonymously. Vuylsteke et al.[122] compared differences between Belgian and Chinese students with regard to their search for information on the Internet before making a buying decision. They found that Chinese search more frequently, but fewer base their final decision on information found online, as they rely more on recommendations from peers. Chinese often go directly to a forum or consumer website without doing other searching, and if they search, they do so in a more holistic way than Belgians do. Belgians tend to look at fewer results before they click on one, whereas Chinese may scroll down longer, to see the whole, before clicking for the first time. One measurement of the effectiveness of Internet advertising is by the number of online clicks. This search difference may influence comparison of effectiveness across cultures if based on numbers of clicks.

Instead of the expected globalization effects of the Internet there is a trend of 'hyperlocalism' or 'ultralocalism,' the trend of focusing on the immediate neighborhood. This applies to information retrieval as well as to online social networking. What people actually read on the Internet can be found by the number of clicks on stories, and such analysis shows that most clicked-on stories are local.[123] Also, social media increasingly have become local. Nigel Hollis[124] argues that what Facebook calls *global pages* is a misnomer as people get to see local content since Facebook automated the ability to serve a localized view of the site. Local versions of a brand's page are translated, and marketers can customize content.

The Internet has had a strong impact on *entertainment,* in particular by providing all sorts of games to be played on desktop computers or on portable devices such as tablets and smartphones. It has provided entertainment interactively with sound, motion and the live updating of content. Just like books and movies, there are also different genres of games that are played. The entertainment function, except TV or video watching, mostly merges with the social function because of the potential for interaction.

The creation of *social networking* and entertainment sites builds on the interactive power of the Internet. *Social network services* (SNS), or *social media* build online social networks for communities of people who share interests and activities or who are interested in exploring the interests and activities of others. Across cultures, people use social networks for different purposes, and because of that, network formats vary across cultures. For Brazilians, the main functions are communicating with friends and entertainment. For the Chinese, conversation, video content, and online gaming are most important. Russians are most drawn by file sharing of music and movies and online gaming, and in India, because of language differences, use is less textual and more directed at entertainment, watching videos, and listening to music.[125]

Social Media

Several comparative studies have found that everywhere the main usage of social media concerns contacts with friends and family. Social media in individualistic cultures show fewer connections between friends than in collectivistic cultures.[126] Chatting does not necessarily make global communities. It often is a group of existing relations that intensify their communication. Young people of the same city or even in the same street form closed groups that even block out strangers with the argument that it is easier to talk to people one knows than to strangers.[127] In collectivistic cultures, people prefer sharing experiences with known others and they make fewer contacts with strangers than in individualistic cultures, but fear of the unknown in high uncertainty avoidance cultures may have the same effect. A comparison of Hispanic students in Argentina, Chile, Colombia, the United States, and Uruguay showed that the main use of social media was to maintain contact with friends and family members. Most liked activities were sharing photos, reconnecting with old friends, and keeping in touch with others.[128] A comparison of such behavior across five other countries (United States, United Kingdom, Italy, Greece, and France) found that

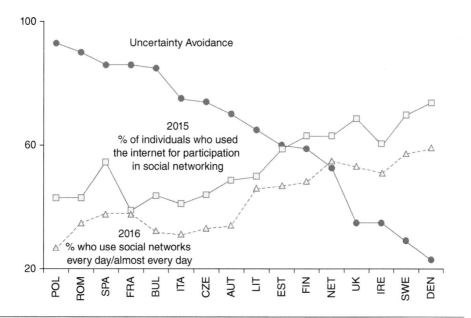

Figure 7.13   Social networks and uncertainty avoidance

SOURCES: Data from Hofstede et al. (2010) (see Appendix A); Eurostat 2015–2016 and Eurobarometer 86 (2016) (see Appendix B).

social browsing was more important for French and Italian users than for US users. For the French users, status updates and photographs were less important than for US users. In general, the largest differences were between US users on the one hand and UK, French, and Italian users on the other hand.[129]

Differences in social media usage in general vary with uncertainty avoidance, just like Internet usage in general. Figure 7.13 shows the relationship between uncertainty avoidance and different measurements of social media usage: individuals who used the Internet for participating in social networking and using online networks every day/almost every day (for both $r = -.90$***).[130]

The data are for a number of European countries, but also across Asia there are differences in adoption of social media. Indonesia, China and India boast above 60% penetration, but Japan only shows 35%.[131] Next to adoption of social media in general, there are also differences in usage and preferences. In individualistic cultures, social networks are viewed more as providing a path to resources, such as access to people who may have the right information to help deal with a health or medical issue.[132] In collectivistic cultures, Internet networks reinforce the sharing of feelings and ideas. Although collectivistic cultures are most motivated to use social networks, the ways they are used varies with long/short-term orientation. Across 25 countries worldwide the time spent on social networking is highest in short-term oriented cultures.[133]

To much of the English speaking world, it may appear that Facebook has become ubiquitous, but in many countries, local social networking sites generate more traffic than Facebook, for example, weibo, kaixin, and renren in China; Mixi in Japan; CyWorld in South Korea; and vkontakte.ru in Russia. Africa's biggest social network is MXit, but there are more than 30 other African social networks that are popular in various countries. MXit sells itself as a community network and includes a digital wallet that works via the mobile phone service provider.

Local SNSs were developed because the purpose of using social media varies with culture; consequently, the designs of local social network sites will also vary. Users of different social network services display different online practices, and even users of the same social media may use them in different ways and for different purposes. For example, users of Korean-based SNSs (e.g., Cyworld) have fewer but more intimate friends, keep their public profile anonymous, and use more nonverbal communication means, such as graphics or icons, as compared with users of American-based SNSs. Users of French SNSs like to carry out discussions that are not personal. And users of Chinese SNSs like to play more games. SNSs appear to be cultural systems in themselves.[134]

In Chapter 5, we described how in short-term oriented cultures, self-enhancement is important. One should show the best of oneself without much critical self-reflection, whereas in long-term oriented cultures, people are more modest, showing competence indirectly, and are more inclined to self-improvement which includes self-criticism. Facebook is the typical platform for self-enhancement.

Morozov[135] cites US psychologist Jean Twenge who says, 'Facebook rewards the skills of the narcissist, such as self-promotion, selecting flattering photographs of oneself and having most friends.' This also applies to other social networks of US origin, such as YouTube and Twitter. For 26 countries worldwide the percentages of Internet users who in 2015 had visited Facebook, YouTube or Twitter in the last month significantly correlated with short-term orientation; also the time spent on social media correlates with short-term orientation (25 countries, $r = -.55***$).[136]

In contrast to self-enhancement, the Japanese like to be anonymous. They use all sorts of mechanisms to disguise their true identity, such as pseudonyms and nicknames. Mixi is also less about interacting with friends and more about interacting on popular community pages where personal identity is not important, and it offers greater control of which friends get to see your personal information.[137] For East Asian collectivists, strong private in-group bonds may conflict with the public function of social networks. Korean CyWorld solved that problem by designing mini homepages where mainly existing personal relationships are consolidated.[138] In other Asian countries that are more short-term oriented, such as Thailand and the Philippines, Facebook is very popular. Unlike social media critics who cite it as intrusive, many Thais feel the opposite. They view Facebook and other platforms as an extension of their normal life.

A related phenomenon in long-term oriented and individualistic cultures, as in Germany, is the need for privacy. Online and offline privacy is a key concern to Germans, who have shown frustration with frequent privacy changes on Facebook.[139] Culturally, Germans tend to be very private and do not freely share personal information. Many still feel that their data are not safe online.[140] The differences in the degree of self-disclosure, as discussed in Chapters 5 and 7, can be recognized in social media behavior across countries. The Chinese say they are more open online than in real life. Being more easily open online refers to personal feelings, such as happy things or personal events, but also to unpleasant, embarrassing things. Although young Chinese often are hesitant to reveal deep emotions, especially sad feelings, in their blogs they do so, be it in a restricted way.[141] In Western eyes, they are not telling the 'truth.'

The numbers of friends users report vary greatly. In East Asia, social network users have fewer friends than in South Asia and in Latin America. In 2010 the number of friends varied from 233 in Malaysia to 63 in China and 29 in Japan. The United States and United Kingdom showed similar average numbers of friends with respectively 200 and 173 friends. Across Europe, the differences were large, with Russians having 89 friends, the French 95, and Italians 152. Latin American users score high, with Brazilians having 360 friends. [142]

The differences in numbers of friends are similar to those for professional membership networks that also correlate with short-term orientation. It is a manifestation of self-enhancement. Other cultural values also play a role, such as needs for prestige. In Brazil Googles's Orkut became popular because it was invite-only, implying you were 'well-connected,' which added prestige. Friends could rate you, based on how sexy you were, how cool, and how trustworthy. Also, one could amass 'fans.' Brazilians are very image-conscious, and carefully craft their online persona. Image and reputation are important parts of status, and guide online behavior.[143]

Because individualism/collectivism and long-/short-term orientation differentiate usage and design of social media, we can map countries according to these dimensions, as in Figure 7.14. It is the same configuration as used for mapping advertising styles, but it applies equally well to social media. In collectivistic culture, people use more social media than in individualistic cultures, and in the short-term oriented cultures, impression management is stronger.

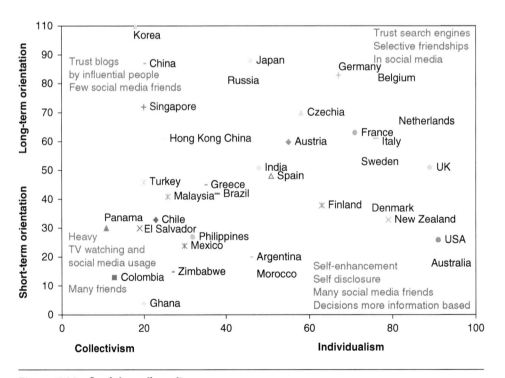

Figure 7.14 **Social media culture map**

SOURCE: Data from Hofstede et al. (2010) (see Appendix A)

Figure 7.14 shows four different quadrants that can be taken into account for understanding differences in using social media. Whereas in short-term oriented collectivistic cultures, people identify and present themselves in a self-enhancing way and are more interactive, in long-term oriented collectivistic cultures, people want to be anonymous and feel part of the larger community in a more passive way. Culture-related motives for social media such as self-enhancement and status are stronger in South America than in East Asia. Marketers therefore should consider using brand messages which emphasize self-expression to these short-term orientation cultures but emphasize group orientation and anonymity to long-term orientation countries that are also collectivistic. Across individualistic cultures in the two right-hand quadrants, long-/short-term orientation also explains differences with respect to the degree of privacy needs and self-enhancement, for example, as expressed by the difference in numbers of friends. In individualistic cultures, people search for information more by seeking facts than by discussion with others as decision making is more information and fact based, and they are also more interactive. In view of the different usages in collectivistic and individualistic cultures, marketers should consider using social media more in collectivistic cultures and using search engine marketing more in individualistic cultures, thereby further differentiating between short- and long-term oriented cultures.[144]

Social media have been adopted in marketing because they allow for precise targeting approaches (narrow audience targeting) by following people's habits and preferences and targeting related ads to them. They offer the opportunity to personalize messages with respect to demographics, interests, purchase history including culture-related attitudes and preferences, as well as communication styles. However, objections to this are complaints about privacy and buying very targeted small audiences also raises costs.

The Weblog or Blog

A *weblog* or *blog* is an online space regularly updated, presenting the opinions or activities of one or a group of individuals and displayed in reverse chronological order. As for social media, the degree to which people blog, their motives, and topics vary by culture. In terms of blog posts by language, in 2007, Japanese was the most used blogging language followed closely by English. There are more bloggers in collectivistic cultures than in individualistic cultures. Worldwide, the percentage who say they are involved in blogging correlates negatively with individualism ($r = -.83***$).[145] Blogging is often part of social media usage, and there are several comparative studies that also found differences in blogging.

Results from a study across 22 countries[146] comprising Southeast Asia, Japan, North America, and Europe suggest differences in topics covered as well as blogging motivations. Japanese blogs, for example, are dominated by hobby and recreational blogs, whereas personal blogs dominate in most other cultures. Australia has a large proportion of political blogs. Although more than half of North American blogs are personal, a large percentage can be categorized as political, hobby, and religious blogs. There is a notable lack of religious blogs across Asian cultures.

Sharing information about experiences with products or brands – also called eWOM has become an important element of consumer decision making. But how people respond to it varies with individualism–collectivism.[147] Also the role and acceptance of influencers on blogs or social media may vary across cultures. The degree of trust is an important issue: is the influencer just a celebrity earning money or an authentic user? The latter as a requirement may be more important in individualistic cultures than in collectivistic cultures where people are more used to celebrities in advertising.

The Internet has become part of everyday life. People routinely integrate it into the ways in which they communicate with each other, moving among phone, computer, and in-person encounters. Instead of social relationships disappearing, people's communities are transforming; however, people's networks continue to have substantial numbers of relatives and neighbors – the traditional bases of community – as well as friends and workmates. E-mail and social network services are indeed used for contacting distant friends and relatives, but even more frequently they are used to contact those who live nearby.

The effects of the Internet confirm the theory of McLuhan[148] who said that technological innovations are merely enhancements or extensions of ourselves. They are generally used by people to enhance current activities; they do not fundamentally change people's values or habits.

Responses to Marketing Communications

Responses to marketing communications are an important consumer behavior domain because expenditures on marketing communications tend to be high. Most research has been done on cross-cultural responses to advertising. This section of the chapter first touches on another marketing communication instrument, sales promotion.

Responses to Sales Promotions

Sales promotions vary across countries, and consumers generally respond positively to the type of sales promotions that they are used to. For example, attitudes toward coupons are influenced by familiarity with coupons. Other attitudes that play a role are attitudes of family and friends toward using coupons, fear of embarrassment or losing face when using coupons, as well as consumers' price consciousness. In the United States, where coupons are a frequently used promotional instrument, Hispanic Americans have negative attitudes toward coupons, partly because they view coupons as a sign of low class or inability to pay full price. Also Japanese and Korean consumers are embarrassed to redeem coupons, although coupons have been used in Japan for quite some time. Thai consumers appear to have the highest relative regard for coupons as compared with sweepstakes. To a lesser extent also consumers in Taiwan prefer coupons to sweepstakes. Malaysians respond least favorably to coupons.[149] What appeals to long-term orientation cultures are promotional activities that offer discounts or long-term saving opportunities, such as saving stamps that build longer-term relationships between consumers and brands. Responses to sweepstakes are likely to vary with the degree to which people like to or are allowed to gamble. Sweepstakes, like gambling, are submitted to varying legal constraints across cultures.

Responses to Advertising

Responses to advertising are related to various aspects: the purpose of advertising, general acceptance of advertising, consumers' relationships with the media, the specific advertising appeal, and executional styles.

Whereas the purpose of advertising in individualistic cultures is to persuade, in collectivistic cultures it is to build trust between buyer and seller, which results in different advertising styles, for example, direct address versus entertainment. Responses to direct style persuasion will be different to responses to entertainment, and thus, measurement of responses should not be the same. An example of a measurement item is 'relevance,' which in individualistic cultures is used to measure a viewer's affective reaction to a television commercial. The response item used is 'As I watched I thought of reasons why I would use the product.' For measuring the relevance of a TV commercial, thinking about the product is part of this process. For Asian recipients, no such relationship can be found. Generally, relevance may work in individualistic cultures, but the use for measuring affective response in collectivistic cultures is questionable.[150] In collectivistic, high-context cultures there is no direct link between a commercial and product usage in the mind of consumers because advertising works in a different way. Also, in individualistic cultures persuasion is likely to work differently. Psychological research indicates that external locus of control makes people more susceptible to being persuaded, socially influenced, and conform more than internal locus of control does.[151]

The importance of context when measuring responses to advertising is demonstrated by the limitations of neurophysiological methods. Measuring brain responses to advertising in individuals isolated in laboratory-based settings has been the standard. However, in the real world, consumers are never exposed to advertising messages in laboratory circumstances and advertising is not always experienced in complete isolation. Isolated laboratory settings provide suboptimal conditions for measuring responses to advertising, in particular in collectivistic cultures.[152]

Responses to advertising that are typically measured are attitude toward the ad and attitude toward the brand, assuming that consumers' reactions to products and brands are influenced by their evaluations of advertising. The attitude toward the advertisement (Aad) is defined as a predisposition to respond in a favorable or unfavorable manner to a particular advertisement during a particular exposure occasion. Aad is influenced by not only the particular ad but also by the viewer's attitude toward the advertiser and advertising as an institution. The latter is based on a general predisposition to respond in a consistently favorable or unfavorable manner toward advertising in general. The former is related to the credibility of the ad, attitude to the sponsor, and likeability of the ad. These measurement parameters are mostly valid for individualistic cultures. In collectivistic cultures, people's attitudes and behavior are not consistent, so the relationship between the parameters may be different.

La Ferle et al.[153] found that in collectivistic cultures people are less skeptical of advertising. This may be due to the fact that advertising is more entertaining in collectivistic cultures. Attitudes toward Internet advertising have become increasingly negative. Uncontrollable formats of Internet advertising tend to interrupt and irritate Internet users, thus negatively affecting their attitudes toward Internet advertising.[154]

Consumers' Relationships with the Media

In 2001, liking advertising on TV and radio in Europe was correlated with low individualism and high uncertainty avoidance.[155] In Spain 24% of respondents and in Germany only 6% liked TV advertising more than TV programs. If people prefer specific media, they also like advertising in these media or attribute an informative role to advertising. Across countries, reading the news in newspapers every day goes together with viewing advertising in newspapers as a source of new product information. Also EMS data show a positive correlation between heavy to medium press readership and viewing advertising in newspapers as a useful source of product information. For television we see similar relationships. Heavy TV viewing is related to a positive attitude toward advertising on TV. The percentages of heavy viewers correlate positively with the percentages of respondents saying that advertising on TV is a useful source of product information ($r = .66{***}$).

The overall explaining variables are cultural. Both a positive attitude to advertising in newspapers and newspaper readership are correlated with low uncertainty avoidance. Viewing advertising on television as a useful source of information correlates with low individualism, so for the more visually oriented collectivistic cultures, television has an informative role. This role is extended to advertising. A conclusion is that if people use specific media, they also like or attribute an informative role to advertising in these media.

Advertising Appeals

Advertising appeals generally reflect culture-bound motives or attitudes. Advertising appeals that are effective in one culture may result in different responses when used in another culture. Many American marketers assume Europe to be a homogeneous market with similar responses to their advertising. Also marketers targeting eastern European countries tend to select a region-centric approach without differentiating for the various countries in the area, but as in the West, across Eastern Europe countries are very different. Whereas the Polish like to show off, responses by the Romanians to status advertising tend to be negative.[156] Advertising produced in one culture often is not understood in another one. An example of how responses to specific advertisements across cultures vary is the Benetton campaign. In four different national cultures (British, Norwegian, French, and German), the intended messages that Benetton hoped to convey with the images used in their advertisements have not been interpreted as they had wished.[157]

Advertising appeals generally reflect buying motives that are related to the product category, and for each category these motives are culture specific. Chapter 5 provided several examples of category- and culture-specific motives. In cultures where advertising has a long history, the product-specific appeals are ingrained in the culture. Historically in the United Kingdom, beer advertising uses humorous appeals, and historically German car advertising uses technological appeals. But also such differences have been found in newly emerging markets. In China specific appeals exist for specific product categories. 'Modernity,' for example, is frequently found in service and automobile advertising. 'Family values' occur frequently in household appliance advertising, and 'tradition' is mostly found in food and drink commercials. In Hong Kong China, 'modernity' is found in service and automobile advertising, but 'enjoyment' is found more in food and drink advertising.[158] Important Chinese appeals are harmony between people, harmony between people and society and between people and nature. Also modesty and face are important values found in advertising.[159]

A word about sexual appeals in advertising. Studies searching for explanations of usage and acceptance of sexual appeals in advertising tend to assume cultural masculinity to be an explaining variable, but this is not the case. One study found that sexual appeals are more rejected in high than in low uncertainty avoidance cultures.[160] A major problem when measuring sexual appeals is the definition. Whereas in some countries a nude or scarcely dressed person in advertising is considered to have a sexual appeal, in other countries there is no such association.

Executional Styles

The previous sections of the chapter described how advertising styles follow interpersonal communication styles and different perceptual processes. The way an Asian perceives and evaluates writing differs significantly from the way an American views writing. Aesthetic expression is different, and so is the use of colors. This is reflected in advertising responses.[161] In particular, differences in high- and low-context communication will influence responses to advertising. Responses of members of high-context cultures to low-context communication are likely to be different from what is intended by the creator of a low-context communication advertisement. Like direct verbal address, the use of simple pictures is likely to be viewed as offensive by consumers who have learned to process more complex images. A high-context audience may over-read the meaning of a too simple visual image and develop a negative affective evaluation due to the message's apparent lack of metaphorical complexity. This type of audience is trained to read the metaphorical meaning of messages and will be uninspired by the lack of visual imagery in simple visuals that merely show the product.[162] Or people will take out information the creator of the advertisement has never meant to include.

If people are used to a specific advertising style, that is what they will expect from advertising. TGI[163] found that among Internet users 51.4% of Spanish respondents expected advertising to be entertaining, as compared with only 32.2% of Germans.

Part of advertising style is the basic form companies choose, for example, 'lesson,' 'drama,' 'entertainment,' the use of presenters, or comparative advertising. The culture of producers of advertising makes them prefer some basic forms to others. International advertisers sometimes use executional styles or basic forms of their own culture for other cultures than their own where they do not fit. Responses to advertising that uses basic forms that do not fit may not be as positive as responses to culture-fit executional styles. The result may be loss of effectiveness. The best example is the use of comparative advertising, which is basically a form that fits competitive (individualistic–masculine) cultures. Comparative advertising is not appreciated in most cultures that score low on individualism, low on masculinity, and high on uncertainty avoidance. In collectivistic cultures comparison with the competitor disturbs harmony. In low masculine cultures, modesty is a value that prevents you from saying that you are better than the other.[164]

In collectivistic cultures, more celebrities are used in advertising because advertisers like to link their brands to concrete personalities. But the roles of celebrities are different from those in individualistic cultures where generally celebrities endorse brands with argumentation. In collectivistic cultures, celebrities convey implicit rather than explicit messages and appeal to conformity rather than uniqueness.[165]

Some basic forms have become the property of specific advertisers. Examples are the testimonial format used by the household good producers Procter & Gamble and Unilever. Some brands (e.g., Ariel, Dove) seem to be exclusively linked to that format. Likewise, the use of humor is likely to be more related to the culture of advertising managers than to the degree to which people in some cultures have a greater sense of humor than in others. Humor doesn't travel because it plays with the conventions of societies that usually are historically defined. When people laugh at humorous advertising of other cultures, it often is for the wrong reasons.

Execution of Advertising

Differences that are generally pointed at as 'merely' executional aspects are also related to culture. Preferences for older people in advertising in China, for example, relate to high power distance. The consistent wish of advertisers in the United Kingdom to have a strong headline and pay-off in advertising is related to the direct communication style of that culture. The type of music, the pace of speaking and music, the frequency a brand name is mentioned in an ad, all are reflections of the culture of the country where the ad originates. Because the purpose of much Japanese advertising is to entertain the audience, it takes a long time before any mention is made of the brand or the advertiser. Often in commercials there is no benefit, no 'reason why,' because the Japanese tend to buy on the basis of their feelings of familiarity with the seller. Whereas in the United States elicited emotions are related to brand or seller from the start of the commercial, in Japan this relationship is absent, and identification with the company or brand comes only at the end of the commercial. Because of the importance of trust in the company as an advertising goal, the company name is more frequently shown in Korean and Japanese advertising than in US advertising. Whereas US advertisements often focus primarily on the brand, not including the company name in countries like Korea or China would be ill advised. In most Asian countries television commercials end with a shot of the company's logo. Procter & Gamble in Japan learned that their commercials worked much better when they incorporated a P&G 'talking cow' that conveyed the message that the products were made by a good, solid, credible, and trustworthy company.[166]

It is often said that a central idea or concept can be universal, but execution or executional details must be varied with culture. However, all details of an advertisement work together and, consequently, changing only some executional details will not have the desired result. Advertisements are wholes, not sets of headlines, pictures, and text. For some product attributes that are meaningful for different cultures, the central message may be similar, but for greater effectiveness, style and execution should be different. Examples of how the US brand Kellogg's ties into the various styles and execution of different cultures are presented in Figures 7.15 to 7.20. The US commercial displayed in Figure 7.15 is explicit about values that are typical of the United States. It starts with a field where wheat starts to grow and ends with a sports field. The voice over says, 'On the right field it is amazing what can grow. Things like self-confidence, friendship and values that last a lifetime. All it takes is someone to plant a seed. Kellogg's Frosted Flakes is building fields for your kids to play, to grow, to be their very best.'

Figure 7.15   **Kellogg's Frosted Flakes, United States**

Figure 7.16 shows pictures from a German Kellogg's Day Vita commercial. It shows a tough, independent woman who is repairing something in her kitchen. She is fit because she eats Kellogg's. The commercial shows pictures of how the product works and ends with a picture saying that the effect is proven.

Figure 7.16   **Kellogg's Day Vita, Germany**

Figure 7.17 shows pictures from a French commercial for Kellogg's Special K. This is soft drama. We see two women friends discussing the product and much more, and they keep talking while the husband of one of them is really getting annoyed. The product attribute here is slimming.

Figure 7.17   **Kellogg's Special K, France**

Figure 7.18 shows pictures from an Italian commercial for Kellogg's All-Bran. This commercial is like a thriller. Detectives barge into a house where a couple is sitting eating Kellogg's. There is some argumentation about the product, there are some pictures with details of how it works and in the end they all sit down eating Kellogg's.

Figure 7.18   **Kellogg's All-Bran, Italy**

Figure 7.19 shows pictures from a Japanese commercial for Kellogg's All-Bran, with Japanese fashion model Miyuki Koizumi. In an interview, Kellogg's marketing manager in Japan[167] states that Kellogg's adapts their products and marketing in each country, so not

Figure 7.19   **Kellogg's All-Bran, Japan**

only advertising, but also the product, ingredients, and taste. In Japan, for example, the product is less sweet. For Japan a special product was developed based on unpolished brown rice (*genmai*), and in India more iron is added as Indians tend to lack iron. In Japan mostly younger women eat cereals.

Figure 7.20 shows pictures from an Indian commercial for Kellogg's Special K. The product attribute is slimming, as in the French commercial. The woman picks out a dress for a party to be given in two weeks' time by the boss of her husband. She brings the dress to the tailor to make it smaller. He doesn't believe it will fit her in two weeks' time, but it does. We see her in the dress at the party, and all men admire her. In India the wish to be slim seems to catch on as a trend for young women, but more in the north than in the south of India. Slimming is mostly done by fasting, so this is a new way of slimming. The target group clearly is upper class, indicated by showing an occasion like a boss's party and showing the woman eating at a table. A large part of India still sits and eats on the floor, cross-legged, and not on a dining table.

Figure 7.20 **Kellogg's Special K, India**

Brand Communications Across Cultures

Chapter 6 discussed brands as association networks in the mind of the consumer. Cultural values are part of such association networks. Western brand managers select values consciously when formulating their brand strategies, whereas Asian marketers don't do this explicitly, but values are attached to brands by associating them with specific persons. Whether explicit or implicit, all marketing communication carries values. Values offer an opportunity to differentiate brands by going beyond attributes and benefits. Adding values creates association networks that distinguish the brand vis-à-vis the competitive brands in the category and thus can help build strong positions for brands. The attributes, benefits, and values of association networks can be used to develop value structure maps, including similarities and differences across cultures that can help develop a cross-cultural strategy.

Value Structure Maps

A tool for strategy is the *value structure map* (VSM), which describes how a particular group of subjects tends to perceive or think about a specific product or brand.[168] A value structure map links the product's attributes and benefits to values.

Attributes can be concrete or abstract, with variations. For example, in India objects have meanings at three levels – aesthetic, functional, and spiritual – whereas in Western cultures meanings are usually restricted to functional and symbolic.[169] Benefits can be functional or psychosocial consequences of the product's attributes. Values, as preferred states of being, can be the consequence of benefits. Both are culture-bound. The effects of some benefits can differ substantially across cultures, but some are similar across categories. This was found from a large study covering 25 nations with respect to four different benefits for five different product categories: quality, unique, leading, and growing in popularity. Some benefits may work universally well, but the connected values may differentiate.[170] Yet, these relationships will vary across product categories.

A 2016 Nielsen study of home cleaning attitudes around the world found global similarities of benefits and values for all-purpose cleaners, but also regional differences. For example effectiveness and ease of use are important globally, but in Europe the most sought benefit is effectiveness, while in Latin America ease of use, multipurpose, disinfectant and fragrance are most important. In the Asia-pacific region, disinfectant, fragrance, and ease of use are highly important. For North America most important are effectiveness, multipurpose and no scent/fragrance. For laundry detergents benefits sought also vary, with Asia-Pacific leading with respect to 'being best at getting stains out,' but also 'without harsh chemicals' and 'environmentally friendly.' Latin America leads with high efficiency, 'can be used for all types of items,' 'allows washing all colors together' and scent. Of all benefits lowest cost was most important in North America. For Europe high efficiency and lowest cost were most important.[171]

Value structure maps provide a structure of people's associations with a brand at the three levels: attributes, benefits, and values. They show the connections among the types of associations of people and a specific attribute of a product and its subsequent benefits and values. This connection, developed by Gutman,[172] was presented as the means–end chain model. Gutman formulated the essence as follows: means are objects (products) or activities in which people engage; ends are valued states of being such as happiness, security, accomplishment. A *means–end chain* is a model that seeks to explain how the choice of a product or service facilitates the achievement of desired end-states. Such a model consists of elements that represent consumer processes that link values to behavior.

The technique used to develop means–end chains is called *laddering,* an in-depth, one-on-one interviewing technique used to develop an understanding of how consumers translate the attributes of products into meaningful associations with respect to the self.[173] By using this laddering technique, sets of linkages can be determined among perceptual elements, which are then represented at different levels of abstraction. Figure 7.18 shows three levels of associations for toothpaste, and Figure 7.19 shows six levels of (hypothetical) associations for Coca-Cola. An example of a value structure map is one for automobiles in Figure 7.20, including values that appeal to different cultures.

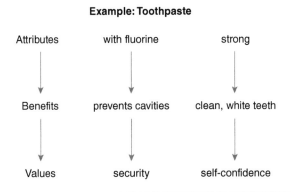

Example: Toothpaste

Attributes	with fluorine	strong
↓	↓	↓
Benefits	prevents cavities	clean, white teeth
↓	↓	↓
Values	security	self-confidence

Figure 7.21   **Levels of communication (VSM, laddering)**

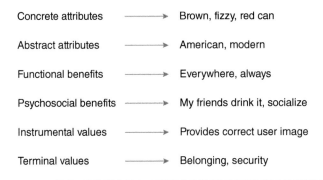

Concrete attributes ⟶ Brown, fizzy, red can

Abstract attributes ⟶ American, modern

Functional benefits ⟶ Everywhere, always

Psychosocial benefits ⟶ My friends drink it, socialize

Instrumental values ⟶ Provides correct user image

Terminal values ⟶ Belonging, security

Figure 7.22   **Levels of communication: Coca-Cola**

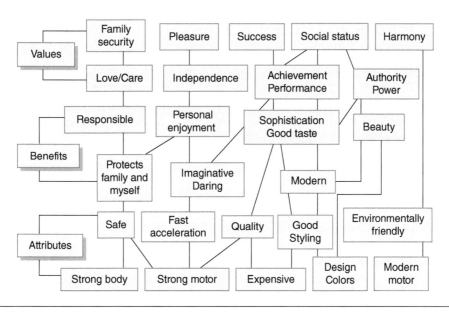

Figure 7.23   **Value Structure Map: Automobiles**

Advertisers who want to differentiate a brand can follow different routes via attributes and benefits to reach end values, as shown in Figure 7.21. In this system, the product attributes may be the same worldwide, yet different values may be connected to the attributes (to be found through research), reflecting different cultures. An example of a route in the VSM for automobiles is selecting, for example, one attribute, a Strong motor, and one end value, Pleasure, and following the route Fast acceleration → Imaginative → Daring → Personal enjoyment → Independence → Pleasure. Another route takes the same attribute as a starting point but continues via Safe → Protects the family and myself → Responsible → Love/Care → Family security. This could be an example of a route for a feminine culture. Volvo has used this route from the attribute Strong body. A route for cultures of the configuration collectivist–high power distance–high uncertainty avoidance would be Design/Colors → Good styling → Sophistication/Good taste → Authority/Power or achievement → Social status. Different routes can be followed, depending on the target group, the culture, and the competition. Even when similar abstract associations exist in such maps, they can have different links. Value for money, for example, was found to be positively associated with good acceleration and speed in China, but with good styling in Korea and France.[174] In a multinational campaign targeted at countries that are similar with respect to one or more dimensions, it may be possible to select one route with values that the different countries have in common. Yet, depending on the specific cultures, the communication style may have to be different.

The Future of Global Advertising

This book has presented information that can help readers to assess global advertising formats. Decisions on global uniform advertising are based on wrong assumptions and made for the wrong reasons. Short-term pressures on budgets make it tempting to reuse or modify material that has proved to be successful in one country for rollout in others, or a timing issue is involved, when an ad is used until a better one is developed. Supporting ineffective ads may result in waste of media expenditures or even damage the brand in the long term.[175]

Most assumptions underlying the choice of standard global advertising are based on the existence of global communities with similar motives and fundamental universal emotions. Even the Internet and ubiquitous social media have not led to the emergence of really global communities. In the twenty-first century the idea is outdated, although in some business schools or advertising agencies the concept is still central. In 2000, Sally Ford-Hutchinson, global director of planning of D'Arcy, a global advertising agency operating in 75 countries around the world, said, 'We have to look for similarities across the cultures and we come down to fundamental universal emotions like motherhood, teenage/parental relationships – these are the same in Cairo or Cologne. . . I believe that a good strategic idea will travel.'[176] In such statements 'a good creative idea' generally is a creative idea conceptualized in the home country of the person who makes the statement, which is made in abstract terms. Everybody agrees on abstract values or emotions like love or happiness, but made concrete they don't travel. Those who have read the previous chapters in this book know that the idea of universal emotions is based on ethnocentric research and on personal consistency needs of Western marketing managers that they extend to the strategies they develop. Mental and social processes and consumer behavior vary so fundamentally across cultures that global advertising is a true myth of the past century.

Conclusion

How people communicate varies with culture, and the different communication styles are reflected in advertising and the Internet. Different verbal and nonverbal communication styles can be recognized in both interpersonal and mass communication, and culture clusters can be defined where one or the other style prevails. People process information in different ways. For some, pictures contain more information than words; for others, the only way to convey meaning is verbal. These differences are also relevant for e-communications. Advertising styles follow interpersonal communication styles.

Knowledge of the differences is of utmost importance to international marketers and advertisers. Communication is only effective if the receiver of the message understands the message as the sender intends it. How advertising works, roles and function of advertising vary with culture. In one culture, advertising is persuasive by nature; in another, it must be liked in order to build trust between companies and consumers. Thus, models of one culture cannot be projected to other cultures. Marketers have had high expectations of the Internet as a new, interactive medium, unifying consumers worldwide. However it looks like the same principles of culture's influence apply to the new electronic media.

Notes

1. C.S. Craig and S.P. Douglas, 'Beyond national culture: Implications of cultural dynamics for consumer research,' *International Marketing Review*, 23, 3 (2006), pp. 322–342.
2. In particular, communication scholars Ronald Gordon, Yoshitaka Miike and Jing Yin of the university of Hawaii at Hilo, Wimal Dissanayake of the University of Hawaii at Mānoa, Guo Ming Chen of the University of Rhode Island and Molefi Kete Asante of Temple University have worked on the development of culturally relevant communication theory counter to the dominance of Eurocentric communication theory. They provided a host of literature about Asian and African communication theory when I wrote the book *Human and Mediated Communication Around the World* (2013, Springer), from which book I am drawing for this chapter. Yoshitaka Miike was particularly helpful by sending literature.
3. D. Gordon, 'Beyond the failures of Western communication theory,' *Journal of Multicultural Discourses*, 2, 2 (2007), pp. 89–107.
4. W. Schramm and D.F. Roberts, *The Process and Effects of Mass Communication* (University of Illinois Press, Urbana, 1974), p. 12.
5. M. Holquist, *Dialogism. Bakhtin and His World* (Routledge, London, 1990).
6. T.M. Singelis and W.J. Brown, 'Culture, self, and collectivist communication,' *Human Communication Research*, 21 (1995), pp. 354–389.
7. W. Dissanayake, 'Personhood, agency, and communication: A Buddhist viewpoint,' *China Media Research*, 9, 1 (2013), pp. 11–25.
8. Y. Miike, 'Enryo-Sasshi theory,' in R.L. Jackson II and M.A. Hogg (eds), *Encyclopedia of Identity*, Vol. 1 (Sage, Thousand Oaks, CA, 2010), pp. 250–252.
9. T. Kosaka, 'Listening to the Buddha's own words: Participation as a principle of the teachings of the Buddha,' *China Media Research*, 6, 3 (2010), pp. 94–102.
10. W. Dissanayake, 'Development and communication in Sri Lanka: A Buddhist approach,' *China Media Research*, 6, 3 (2010), pp. 85–93.
11. N.M. Adhikary, '*Sancharyoga*: Approaching communication as a *Vidya* in Hindu orthodoxy,' *China Media Research*, 6, 3 (2010), pp. 76–84.

12. S. Ishii and T. Bruneau, 'Silence and silences in cross-cultural perspective: Japan and the United States,' in L.A.Samovar, R.E. Porter, and E.R. McDaniel (eds), *Intercultural Communication: A Reader*, 7th edn (Wadsworth, Belmont, CA, 1994), pp. 246–251.

13. C. Beier, L. Michael, and J. Sherzer, 'Discourse forms and processes in indigenous Lowland South America: An areal-typological perspective,' *Annual Review of Anthropology*, 31 (2002), pp. 121–145.

14. P.B. Smith, 'Communication styles as dimensions of national culture,' *Journal of Cross-Cultural Psychology*, 42, 2 (2011), pp. 216–233.

15. R.S. Fortner, *Communication, Media, and Identity. A Christian Theory of Communication* (Rowman & Littlefield, Lanham, MD, 2007).

16. W.J. Ong, *Orality & Literacy. The Technologizing of the World* (Routledge, London, 1982).

17. M. Lyons, *A History of Reading and Writing in the Western World* (Palgrave Macmillan, Basingstoke, UK, 2010).

18. J.O. Yum, 'Korean philosophy and communication,' in D.L. Kincaid (ed.), *Communication Theory. Eastern and Western Perspectives* (Academic Press, San Diego, CA, 1987), pp. 71–86.

19. Unesco Institute for Statistics. Available at: www.uis.unesco.org/literacy/.

20. Ong, *Orality & Literacy*.

21. Singelis and Brown, 'Culture, self, and collectivist communication.'

22. D. Oyserman, H. Coon, and M. Kemmelmeier, 'Rethinking individualism and collectivism: Evaluation of theoretical assumptions and meta-analyses,' *Psychological Bulletin*, 128 (2002), pp. 3–72.

23. B.H. Schmitt, 'Language and visual imagery: Issues of corporate identity in East Asia,' *Columbia Journal of World Business*, 3 (1995), pp. 28–37.

24. L. Van den Berg-Weitzel and G. Van de Laar, 'Relation between culture and communication in packaging design,' *Brand Management*, 8 (2001), pp. 171–184.

25. K. Bu, D. Kim, and S. Lee, 'Determinants of visual forms used in print advertising: A cross-cultural comparison,' *International Journal of Advertising*, 28, 1 (2009), pp. 13–48.

26. W. Gudykunst and S. Ting-Toomey, *Culture and Interpersonal Communication* (Sage, Newbury Park, CA, 1988), pp. 99–133.

27. A.L. Molinsky, M.A. Krabbenhoft, N. Ambady, and Y.S. Choi, 'Cracking the nonverbal code: Intercultural competence and gesture recognition across cultures,' *Journal of Cross-Cultural Psychology*, 36, 3 (2005), pp. 380–395.

28. Y. Kobayashi and Y. Noguchi, 'Consumer insight, brand insight, and implicit communication: Successful communication planning cases in Japan,' in M.S. Roberts and R.L. King (eds), *The Proceedings of the 2001 Special Asia-Pacific Conference of the American Academy of Advertising* (2001), pp. 29–40.

29. A. Miyahara, 'Toward theorizing Japanese interpersonal communication competence from a non-western perspective,' in F.E. Jandt (ed.), *Intercultural Communication* (Sage, Thousand Oaks, CA, 2004), pp. 279–291.

30. J. Sanchez-Burks, F. Lee, I. Choi, R. Nisbett, S. Zhao, and J. Koo, 'Conversing across cultures: East–West communication styles in work and non-work contexts,' *Journal of Personality and Social Psychology*, 85, 2 (2003), pp. 363–372.

31. Y. Miyamoto and N. Schwarz, 'When conveying a message may hurt the relationship: Cultural differences in the difficulty of using an answering machine,' *Journal of Experimental Social Psychology*, 42 (2006), pp. 540–547.

32. H. Kim, G.J. Kim, H.W. Park, and R.E. Rice, 'Configurations of relationships in different media: FtF, E-mail, Instant Messenger, Mobile Phone, and SMS,' *Journal of Computer-Mediated Communication*, 12, 4 (2007), art. 3.

33. S. Van Belleghem, 'Social media around the world,' *InSites Consulting*. Available at: www.slideshare.net/stevenvanbelleghem/social-networks-around-the-world-2010 (accessed 22 February 2012).

34. A. Veilbrief, 'Chattend de puberteit door [Chatting through adolescence],' *NRC Handelsblad Maandblad* (January 2007), pp. 20–25.

35. J. Boase, J.B. Horrigan, B. Wellman, and L. Rainie, *The Strength of Internet Ties* (Pew Internet and American Life Project, Washington, DC, 25 January 2006). Available at: www.pewinternet.org.

36. D.E. Schultz and M.P. Block, 'Understanding Chinese media audiences: An exploratory study of Chinese consumers media consumption and a comparison with the USA,' in H. Li, S. Huang, and D. Jin (eds), *Proceedings of the 2009 American Academy of Advertising Asia-Pacific conference* (American Academy of Advertising, in conjunction with China Association of Advertising of Commerce, and Communication University of China, 2009), pp. 1–12.

37. S.C. Chu and S.M. Choi, 'Use of social networking sites among Chinese young generations,' in H. Li, S. Huang, and D. Jin (eds), *Proceedings of the 2009 American Academy of Advertising Asia-Pacific conference* (American Academy of Advertising, in conjunction with China Association of Advertising of Commerce, and Communication University of China, 2009), pp. 50–57.

38. R. Moerland, 'Frans weblog is een café [French weblog is a café],' *NRC Handelsblad* (20 August 2006), p. 18.

39. G.M. Chen, 'Differences in self-disclosure patterns among Americans versus Chinese,' *Journal of Cross-Cultural Psychology*, 26 (1995), pp. 84–91.

40. R. Ma, 'Computer-mediated conversations as a new dimension of intercultural communication between East Asian and North American college students,' in S.C. Herring (ed.), *Computer-Mediated Communication: Linguistic, Social, and Cross-Cultural Perspectives* (John Benjamins, Amsterdam and New York, 1996), pp. 173–185.

41. Y.O. Yum and K. Hara, 'Computer-mediated relationship development: A cross-cultural comparison,' *Journal of Computer-Mediated Communication*, 11, 1 (2005), art. 7. Available at: http://jcmc.indiana.edu/vol11/issue1/yum.html (accessed 3 March 2008).

42. R. Levo-Henriksson, *Eyes Upon Wings: Culture in Finnish and US Television News*, Doctoral dissertation (Oy. Yleisradio Ab., Helsinki, January 1994), p. 84.

43. 'Perspectives,' *Newsweek* (9 September 1996), p. 11.

44. Z. Li, *Cultural Impact on International Branding: A Case of Marketing Finnish Mobile Phones in China*, Dissertation (University of Jyväskylä, Finland).

45. S. Marijnissen, 'Onbegrepen diepgang,' *NRC Handelsblad Boeken* (20 June 2008), pp. 1–2.

46. C.S. Craig, W.H. Greene, and S.P. Douglas, 'Culture matters: Consumer acceptance of US films in foreign markets,' *Journal of International Marketing*, 13, 4 (2005), pp. 80–103.

47. G. McCracken, *Culture and Consumption: New Approaches to the Symbolic Character of Consumer Goods and Activities* (Indiana University Press, Bloomington, 1988), p. 77.

48. I. Becatelli and A. Swindells, 'Developing better pan-European campaigns,' *Admap* (March 1998), pp. 12–14.

49. S. Bulmer and M. Buchanan-Oliver, 'Visual rhetoric and global advertising imagery,' *Journal of Marketing Communications*, 12, 1 (2006), pp. 49–61.

50. K.E. Rosenberg and M.H. Blair, 'Observations: The long and short of persuasive advertising,' *Journal of Advertising Research* (July/August 1994), pp. 63–69.

51. G.M. Zinkhan, 'International advertising: A research agenda,' *Journal of Advertising*, 23 (1994), pp. 11–15.

52. J.M. Dru, *Disruption* (Wiley, New York, 1996), pp. 1–19.

53. A. Ramdas, 'Dure mango voorbode van paniek in Noord-India [Expensive mango predictor of panic in North-India],' *NRC Handelsblad* (16 July 2002), p. 4.

54. M.J. Bresnahan, R. Ohashi, W.Y. Liu, R. Nebashi, and C.C. Liao, 'A comparison of response styles in Singapore and Taiwan,' *Journal of Cross-Cultural Psychology*, 30 (1999), pp. 342–358.

55. B.D. Cutler, S.A. Erdem, and R.G. Javalgi, 'Advertiser's relative reliance on collectivism-individualism appeals: A cross-cultural study,' *Journal of International Consumer Marketing*, 9 (1997), pp. 43–55.

56. B.D. Cutler, E.G. Thomas, and S.R. Rao, 'Informational/transformational advertising: Differences in usage across media types, product categories, and national cultures,' *Journal of International Consumer Marketing*, 12 (2000), pp. 69–83.

57. H. Kefi, S. Indra, and T. Abdessalem, 'Social media marketing analytics: A multicultural approach applied to the beauty & cosmetic sector,' *PACIS 2016 Proceedings* (2016), Paper 176.

58. In previous editions of this book, for advertising styles we followed the interpersonal communication model. This was replaced by a map of the configuration IDV/COL and LTO.

59. H.A. Laskey, R.J. Fox, and M.R. Crask, 'Investigating the impact of executional style on television commercial effectiveness,' *Journal of Advertising Research* (November/December 1994), pp. 9–16.

60. J. Wang, *Brand New China. Advertising, Media, and Commercial Culture* (Harvard University Press, Cambridge, MA, 2008), p. 63.

61. Kobayashi and Noguchi, 'Consumer insight, brand insight, and implicit communication.'

62. A. Roland, *In Search of Self in India and Japan* (Princeton University Press, Princeton, NJ, 1988).

63. G.E. Miracle, 'Feel-do-learn: An alternative sequence underlying Japanese consumer response to television commercials,' in F. Feasly (ed.), *Proceedings of the 1987 Conference of the American Academy of Advertising* (1987), R73–R78.

64. D. An and S.H. Kim, 'A first investigation into the cross-cultural perceptions of internet advertising: A comparison of Korean and American attitudes,' *Journal of International Consumer Marketing*, 20, 2 (2007), pp. 49–65.

65. J. Wilkins, 'Why is global advertising still the exception, not the rule?,' *Admap* (February 2002), pp. 18–20.

66. A. Gazley, J. Krisjanous, K-S. Fam, and R. Grohs, 'Like it or not: Differences in advertising like-ability and dislikeability within Asia,' *Asia Pacific Journal of Marketing and Logistics*, 24, 1 (2012), pp. 23–40.

67. C.L.C. Praet, *The Role of Advertising Likability: A Cross-Cultural Study of Young Adults' Perception of TV Advertising*, Working paper (Otaru University, Sapporo, May 2000).

68. H. Ko, M.S. Roberts, and C.H. Cho, 'Cross-cultural differences in motivations and perceived interactivity: A comparative study of American and Korean Internet users,' *Journal of Current Issues and Research in Advertising*, 28, 2 (2006), pp. 93–104.

69. C. La Ferle and H.J. Kim, 'Cultural influences on internet motivations and communication styles: A comparison of Korean and US consumers,' *International Journal of Internet Marketing and Advertising*, 3, 2 (2006), pp. 142–157.

70. F. Vyncke and M. Brengman, 'Are culturally congruent websites more effective? An overview of a decade of empirical evidence,' *Journal of Electronic Commerce Research*, 11, 1 (2010), pp. 14–29.

71. M.P. Fourquet-Courbet, D. Courbet, and M. Vanheule, 'How Web banner designers work: The role of internal dialogues, self-evaluations, and implicit communication theories,' *Journal of Advertising Research* (June 2007), pp. 183–192.

72. C. Dormann and C. Chisalita, *Cultural Values in Web Site Design*, paper presented at the 11th European Conference on Cognitive Ergonomics, ECCEII, Catania, Italy (8–11 September 2002).

73. M. Brengman, *Cultural Differences Reflected on the Internet: A Comparison Between Belgian and Dutch E-Commerce Websites*, ECREA Symposium: The Myth of the Global Internet, Brussels (10 October 2007).

74. N. Singh, 'Analyzing the cultural content of web sites: A cross-national comparison of China, India, Japan, and US,' *International Marketing Review*, 22, 2 (2005), pp. 129–146.

75. W. Chun, N. Singh, R. Sobh, and M. Benmamoun, 'A comparative analysis of Arab and US cultural values,' *Journal of Global Marketing*, 28 (2015), pp. 99–112.

76. D. An, 'Advertising visuals in global brands' local websites: A six-country comparison,' *International Journal of Advertising*, 26, 3 (2007), pp. 303–332.

77. E. Würtz, 'A cross-cultural analysis of websites from high-context cultures and low-context cultures,' *Journal of Computer-Mediated Communication*, 11, 1 (2005), article 13.

78. M. Hermeking, 'Culture and Internet consumption: Contributions from cross-cultural marketing and advertising research,' *Journal of Computer-Mediated Communication*, 11, 1 (2005), article 10.

79. Ibid.

80. C.H. Cho and H.J. Cheon, 'Cross-cultural comparisons of interactivity on corporate websites,' *Journal of Advertising*, 34, 2 (2005), pp. 99–115.

81. Ko et al., 'Cross-cultural differences in motivations and perceived interactivity.'

82. Eurostat Statistics Database (2009).

83. Y. Husmann, 'Localization of website interfaces: Cross-cultural differences in home page design,' *Wissenschaftliche Arbeit zur Erlangung des Diplomgrades im Studiengang Sprachen-, Wirtschafts- und Kulturraumstudien* (Diplom-Kulturwirt) (Universität Passau, Germany, 2001).

84. N. Singh, V. Kumar, and D. Baack, 'Adaptation of cultural content: Evidence from B2C e-commerce firms,' *European Journal of Marketing*, 39, 1/2 (2005), pp. 71–86.

85. A. Faiola and S.A. Matei, 'Cultural cognitive style and web design: Beyond a behavioral inquiry into computer-mediated communication,' *Journal of Computer-Mediated Communication*, 11, 1 (2005), art. 18.

86. N. Singh, G. Fassott, M.C.H. Chao, and J.A. Hoffmann, 'Understanding international web site usage: A cross-national study of German, Brazilian, and Taiwanese online consumers,' *International Marketing Review*, 23, 1 (2006), pp. 83–97.

87. *Young Asians Survey* (Ipsos Hong Kong, 2010) (see Appendix B).

88. *Ofcom International Communications Market Report* (16 December 2016). Available at: www. ofcom.org.uk/research-and-data/multi-sector-research/cmr/cmr16/international (accessed 3 October 2017).

89. Austria, Belgium, Denmark, Finland, France, Germany, Greece, Ireland, Italy, Japan, Netherlands, Norway, Portugal, Spain, Sweden, Switzerland, Turkey, United Kingdom, United States. Source: Initiative Media (24 February 2008). Available at: http://initiativemedia.com/static/html_home2.htm.

90. IP Television, *TV Viewing Minutes* (2008). Available at: www.ip-network.com/tvkeyfacts (accessed 24 February 2008).

91. www.zonalatina.com. Posted by Ronald Soong (31 December 1998).

92. F. Krotz and U. Hasebrink, 'The analysis of people-meter data: Individual patterns of viewing behavior and viewers' cultural backgrounds,' *European Journal of Communication Research*, 23 (1998), pp. 151–174.

93. www.zonalatina.com. Posted by Ronald Soong (11 May 2000).

94. D. Pasquier, C. Buzzi, L. d'Haenens, and U. Sjöberg, 'Family lifestyles and media use patterns: An analysis of domestic media among Flemish, French, Italian and Swedish children and teenagers,' *European Journal of Communication*, 13 (1998), pp. 503–519.

95. X. Bringué Sala and C. Sádaba Chalezquer, *The Interactive Generation in Ibero-America: Children and Adolescents Faced with the Screens* (Colección Fundacion Telefónica, Madrid, 2008).

96. A. Voyiadzakis, 'Why magazines and newspapers are so important in the Japanese media mix,' *M&M Europe* (November 2001), pp. 41–45.

97. From 1980 onward, for 44 countries worldwide and for 15 developed countries in Europe, individualism explained between 40% and 72% of variance. Data UN statistical yearbooks.

98. Medios de Comunicacion Annuario de Medios, *El escenario Iberoamericano* [*The Ibero-American media scene*] (Fundacion Telefonica, Madrid, 2007).

99. Data Ofcom Telecommunications market 2006. United Kingdom, France, Germany, Italy, United States, Japan, China.

100. Standard Eurobarometer Report 86 (2017).

101. Ofcom (2010).

102. Ofcom (2016).

103. R.J. Coen, *The Insider's Report* (McCann-Erickson, New York, 1997).

104. *Social Values, Science and Technology* (Special Eurobarometer 225, June 2005).

105. Medios de Comunicacion Annuario de Medios, *El escenario Iberoamericano*.

106. *PAX Asia* (Synovate Asia, 2008).

107. G.A. Barnett and E. Sung, E. (2005). 'Culture and the structure of the international hyperlink network,' *Journal of Computer-Mediated Communication*, 11, 1 (2005), art. 11. Available at: http://jcmc.indiana.edu/v0111/issue1/barnett.html (accessed 3 March 2008).

108. World Development Indicators 2006, World Bank.

109. European Social Survey (2003).

110. *European Cultural Values* (EBS 278, 2007).

111. Eurobarometer report 86 (2016) (see Appendix B).

112. Comscore (2007) (see Appendix B).

113. *European Cultural Values* (2007). Europe, 24 countries; 43% of variance explained by low masculinity.

114. Comscore (2007).

115. C. La Ferle, S.M. Edwards, and Y. Mizuno, 'Internet diffusion in Japan: Cultural considerations,' *Journal of Advertising Research* (April 2002), pp. 65–79.

116. ITU (2011).

117. H. Ko, M.S. Roberts, and C.H. Cho, 'Cross-cultural differences in motivations and perceived interactivity: A comparative study of American and Korean Internet users,' *Journal of Current Issues and Research in Advertising*, 28, 2 (2006), pp. 93–104.

118. T-Q.Peng and J.J.H. Zhu, 'A game of win-win or win-lose? Revisiting the Internet's influence on sociability and use of traditional media,' *New Media & Society*, 13, 4 (2010), pp. 568–586.

119. *Los Medios y Mercados de Latinoamérica* (1998). Available at: Zonalatina.com, posted by Roland Soong (4 September 1999).

120. H. Cho, M. Rivera-Sánchez, and S.S. Lim, 'A multinational study on online privacy: Global concerns and local responses,' *New Media and Society*, 11, 3 (2009), pp. 395–416.

121. *Digital Economy and Society Statistics – Households and Individuals* (Eurostat, 2015–2016).

122. A. Vuylsteke, Z. Wen, B. Baesens, and J. Poelmans, 'Consumers' online information search: A cross-cultural study between China and Western Europe,' *Journal of Interactive Marketing*, 24, 4 (2010), pp. 209–331.

123. G. Berger, 'How the Internet impacts on international news: Exploring paradoxes of the most global medium in a time of "hyperlocalism",' *The International Communication Gazette*, 71, 5 (2009), pp. 355–371.

124. N. Hollis, 'The new Facebook global pages are really local pages,' [Blog] *Straight Talk*. Available at: www.millwardbrown.com/Global/Blog/Post/2012-11-05/The-new-Facebook-global-pages-are-really-local-pages.aspx (accessed 10 January 2013).

125. N. Hollis, *Straight Talk* [Blog] (2012). Blogs about how social media helps brand building: October 1: China; October 15: Brazil; November 8: Russia; November 26: India. All available at: www.millwardbrown.com/Global/Blog/Post/2012 (accessed 10 January 2013).

126. J. Na, M. Kosinski, and D.J.Stillwell, 'When a new tool is introduced in different cultural contexts: Individualism-collectivism and social networks on Facebook,' *Journal of Cross-Cultural Psychology*, 46, 3 (2015), pp. 355–370.

127. Veilbrief, 'Chattend de puberteit door [Chatting through adolescence].'

128. A.B. Albarran, C. Dyer, B. Hutton, and A. Valentine, *Social Media and Young Latinos: A Cross-Cultural Examination*, paper presented to the Media Management and Economics Division at the 2010 AEJMC Conference, Denver, Colorado (4–7 August 2010). Available at: www.allacademic.com/meta/p433602_index.html (accessed 25 February 2012).

129. A. Vasalou, A.N. Joinson, and D. Courvoisier, 'Cultural differences, experience with social networks and the nature of "true commitment" in Facebook,' *International Journal of Human-Computer Studies*, 68 (2101), pp. 719–728.

130. Data 2015 from Eurostat (2015–2016); data 2016 from Eurobarometer report 86 (2016).

131. W. Gong, R.L. Stump, R. L., and G.L. Zhan, 'Global use and access of social networking web sites: a national culture perspective,' *Journal of Research in Interactive Marketing*, 8, 1 (2014), pp. 37–55.

132. J. Boase, J.B. Horrigan, B. Wellman, and L. Rainie, 'The strength of Internet ties,' *Pew Internet & American Life Project* (Washington, DC, 2006). Available at: www.pewinternet.org/2006/01/25/the-strength-of-internet-ties/ (accessed 8 February 2019).

133. D. Chaffey, *Global Social Media Research Summary 2016*. Available at: www.smartinsights.com/social-media-marketing/social-media-strategy/new-global-social-media-research/ (accessed 4 February 2017).

134. L. Qiu, H. Lin, and A.K.-y Leung, 'Cultural differences and switching of in-group sharing behavior between and American (Facebook) and a Chinese (Renren) social networking site,' *Journal of Cross-Cultural Psychology*, 44, 1 (2013), pp. 106–121.

135. E. Morozov, *The Net Delusion. The Dark Side of Internet Freedom* (PublicAffairs, New York, 2011).

136. Partial correlations, controlling for income: Facebook $r = -.54$***; YouTube $r = -.47$**; Twitter $r = -.39$**. Data from: D. Chaffey, *Visitors to the Top Social Platforms By Country* (27 April 2015). Available at: www.smartinsights.com/social-media-marketing/social-media-strategy/ (accessed 8 February 2019).

137. P. Sawers, 'Why Twitter outguns Facebook in Japan,' *TNW Conference 2011*. Available at: http://thenextweb.com/socialmedia/2011/02/02/why-twitter-outguns-facebook-in-japan/ (accessed 25 April 2011).

138. K-H. Kim and H. Yun, 'Cying for me, Cying for us: Relational dialectics in a Korean social network site,' *Journal of Computer-Mediated Communication*, 13, 1 (2007), article 15. Available at: http://jcmc.indiana.edu/vol13/issue1/kim.yun.html.

139. T. Moore, 'Facebook under attack in Germany over privacy,' *Time.com* (13 April 2010). Available at: www.time.com/time/world/article/0,8599,1981524,00.html.

140. J. Williams, 'The growing popularity of social networking in Indonesia,' *Pronet Advertising* (11 February 2011). Available at: www.pronetadvertising.com/articles/the-growing-popularity-of-social-networking-in-indonesia.html.

141. Y. Sima, and P.C. Pugsley, 'The rise of a "me culture" in postsocialist China: Youth, individualism and identity creation in the blogosphere,' *The International Communication Gazette*, 72, 3 (2010), pp. 287–306.

142. S. Van Belleghem, *Social Media Around the World* (InSites Consulting, 2010). Available at: www.slideshare.net/stevenvanbelleghem/social-networks-around-the-world-2010 (accessed 22 February 2012).

143. N. Specht, *How Social Media is used in Germany, China and Brazil* (2010). Available at: http://blog.hubspot.com/blog/tabid/6307/bid/5948/3-Social-Media-Lessons-For-Global-Marketers.aspx

144. In this chapter examples have been given of the social media platforms existing at the time of writing the third edition of this book. As the existence, availability and working of social media are changing continuously, some of the platforms may have disappeared and others emerged.

145. *TNS Digital World* (2008), 16 countries.

146. M.N. Su, Y. Wang, G. Mark, G. Aiyelokun, and T. Nakano, 'A bosom buddy afar brings a distant land near: Are bloggers a global community?,' *Proceedings of the Second International Conference on Communities and Technologies* (C&T, 2005).

147. G. Christodoulides, N. Michaelidou, and E. Argyriou, 'Cross-national differences in e-WOM influence,' *European Journal of Marketing*, 46, 11/12 (2012), pp. 1689–1707.

148. M. McLuhan, *Understanding Media: The Extensions of Man* (McGraw Hill, New York, 1964).

149. L.C. Huff and D.L. Alden, 'An investigation of consumer response to sales promotions in developing markets: A three country analysis,' *Journal of Advertising Research* (May–June 1998), pp. 47–56.

150. M. Ewing, T. Salzberger, and R.R. Sinkovics, 'Assessing responses to standardized TV commercials: Using the Lastovicka "Relevance, Confusion and Entertainment-Scale": A cross-cultural perspective,' *Proceedings of the Australian and New Zealand Marketing Academy Conference, Auckland, NZ* (2001).

151. T.A. Avtgis, 'Locus of control and persuasion, social influence, and conformity: A meta-analytic review,' *Psychological Reports*, 83 (1998), pp. 899–903.

152. R. Pozharliev, W.J.M.I. Verbeke, and R.P. Bagozzi, 'Social consumer neuroscience: Neurophysiological measures of advertising effectiveness in a social context,' *Journal of Advertising*, 46, 3 (2017), pp. 351–362.

153. C. La Ferle, S.M. Edwards, and W.N. Lee, 'Culture, attitudes, and media patterns in China, Taiwan, and the US: Balancing standardization and localization decisions,' *Journal of Global Marketing*, 3, 21 (2008), pp. 191–205.

154. An and Kim, 'A first investigation into the cross-cultural perceptions of Internet advertising.'

155. R. Hielkema, 'Europa over reclame [Europe about advertising]. Results of the study Euro Life & Living by NFO Trendbox,' *Adformatie*, 24 (2001), pp. 54–56.

156. D.N. Lascu, L.A. Manrai, and A.K. Manrai, 'Value differences between Polish and Romanian consumers: A caution against using a regiocentric marketing orientation in Eastern Europe,' in L.A. Manrai and A.K. Manrai (eds), *Global Perspectives in Cross-Cultural and Cross-National Consumer Research* (International Business Press/Haworth Press, New York, 1996), pp. 145–168.

157. I.G. Evans and S. Riyait, 'Is the message being received? Benetton analysed,' *International Journal of Advertising*, 12 (1993), pp. 291–301.

158. K. Chan and H. Cheng, 'One country, two systems: Cultural values reflected in Chinese and Hong Kong television commercials,' *Gazette: The International Journal for Communication Studies*, 64 (2002), pp. 385–400.

159. D. Zhou, 'Harmony: Advertising situations in China,' in H. Li, S. Huang, and D. Jin (eds), *Proceedings of the 2009 American Academy of Advertising Asia-Pacific Conference*, American Academy of Advertising, in conjunction with China Association of Advertising of Commerce, and Communication University of China (2009), pp. 246–253.

160. E. Garcia and K.C.C. Yang, 'Consumer responses to sexual appeals in cross-cultural advertisements,' *Journal of International Consumer Marketing*, 19, 2 (2006), pp. 29–51.

161. B.H. Schmitt and Y. Pan, 'Managing corporate and brand identities in the Asia-Pacific region,' *California Management Review*, 36 (1994), pp. 32–48.

162. M. Callow and L. Schiffman, L. (2002). 'Implicit meaning in visual print advertisements: A cross-cultural examination of the contextual communication effect,' *International Journal of Advertising*, 21 (2002), pp. 259–277.

163. *TGI Europa Internet Report* (December 2001). Available at: www.tgisurveys.com.

164. This is described more comprehensively in M. De Mooij, *Global Marketing and Advertising: Understanding Cultural Paradoxes*, 5th edn (Sage, London, 2019).

165. N.H. Um, M.W. Kwon, and S. Kim, S. (2009). 'A cross-cultural comparison of creative characteristics of celebrity endorsement in Korea and US magazine advertisement,' in H. Li, S. Huang, and D. Jin (eds), *Proceedings of the 2009 American Academy of Advertising Asia-Pacific Conference*, American Academy of Advertising, in conjunction with China Association of Advertising of Commerce, and Communication University of China (2009), p. 178.

166. T. Taylor, 'Cracking Japan,' *M&M Europe* (1997), p. 41.

167. From the Kellogg's Japan website. Translated by Carlo Praet, 29 January 2010.

168. J.C. Olson and T.J. Reynolds, 'Understanding consumers' cognitive structures: Implications for advertising strategy,' in L. Perry and A.G. Woodside (eds), *Advertising and Consumer Psychology* (Lexington Books, Lexington, MA, 1983), pp. 77–90.

169. D. Singh, *Cross Cultural Comparison of Buying Behavior in India*, Doctoral thesis (University Business School, Panjab University, Chandigarh, 2007).

170. R. Van der Lans, Y. Van Everdingen, and V. Melnyk, 'What to stress to whom and where? A cross-country investigation of the effects of perceived brand benefits on buying intentions,' *International Journal of Research in Marketing*, 33, 4 (2016), pp. 924–943.

171. Nielsen, *The Dirt on Cleaning. Home Cleaning/Laundry Attitudes and Trends Around the World* (2016). Available at: www.nielsen.com/content/dam/nielsenglobal/eu/docs/pdf/Nielsen%20Global%20Home%20Care%20Report.pdf (accessed 3 May 2018).

172. J.A. Gutman, 'Means-end chain model based on consumer categorization processes,' *Journal of Marketing*, 46 (1982), pp. 60–72.

173. T.J. Reynolds and J. Gutman, 'Laddering theory, method, analysis, and interpretation,' *Journal of Advertising Research* (February-March 1988), pp. 29–37.

174. M.H. Hsieh and A. Lindridge, 'Universal appeals with local specifications,' *Journal of Product and Brand Management*, 14, 1 (2005), pp. 14–28.

175. J. Wilkins, 'Why is global advertising still the exception, not the rule?,' *Admap* (February 2002), pp. 18–20.

176. P. Vangelder, 'Market research for global advertising,' *ESOMAR Research World* (July/August 2000), pp. 16–17.

Consumer Behavior Domains

8

The previous chapters described how the mental and social processes that drive behavior vary across cultures. This chapter deals with various consumer behavior domains. The consumer behavior domains related to communication, such as responses to communication and the media, were discussed in Chapter 7. *Behavior* refers to the physical actions of consumers that can be directly observed and measured by others. It is also called *overt behavior* to distinguish it from mental activities.[1] A trip to a shop, usage and ownership of products involve behavior. All aspects discussed in the previous chapters, such as motivation, emotion, cognition, and affect, are involved in behavior, but they operate differently across the various consumer behavior domains, such as product acquisition, ownership and usage, shopping and buying behavior, complaining behavior, brand loyalty, and adoption and diffusion of innovations. These topics are discussed in this chapter.

Product Acquisition, Usage, and Ownership

There are substantial differences between countries with respect to product ownership and usage. People's values have a direct and an indirect effect on product ownership. A product has physical characteristics (attributes) that have functional or psychosocial consequences or benefits. A product can also express the (desired) values of the consumer. A car is not only a means of transportation; it also says something about its owner.

Many cross-country differences in product usage and ownership can be understood by the link between the product category and culture. Category-specific relationships can be found by correlating product category data to cultural dimensions and gross national income (GNI) per capita, thus finding the influence of income and product-specific cultural values. Such findings are presented in the following sections. For food and beverages, climate is also included as an explaining variable. The following categories are reviewed:

food and beverages, household cleaning products, cosmetics and personal care products, clothing and footwear, household appliances, consumer electronics, telecommunications, luxury articles, cars, leisure, and financial behavior.[2]

Food and Beverages

Food consumption varies with climate, historical, economic, and cultural factors. Food carries cultural meaning. Evidence is the variation of the percentages of household expenditures on food and beverages, even within the economically homogeneous Europe. Also with respect to consumption of specific food categories, there are fundamental differences in the patterns of consumption in the different European Union (EU) countries.[3] In Chapter 3 (section on Engel's law), the symbolic function of food was mentioned, which is stronger in collectivistic cultures than in individualistic cultures.

Different attitudes toward food can also be recognized in the presentation of food in shops. In most individualistic cultures, people shop for food in sterile supermarkets where meat is wrapped tightly in layers of plastics or processed into unrecognizable sandwich meat. In most collectivistic cultures, both in small shops and in large supermarkets, there are many counters with fresh food where people can touch, see, and recognize the texture of the food. This is related to differences in convenience needs with respect to food that are related to individualism and short-term orientation. Cultures also vary with respect to preferences for local traditions and heritage of food products as well as organic agriculture.

Countries in Europe differ with respect to associations people have with food. Whereas in collectivistic cultures people associate food with pleasure, in feminine cultures they associate food with conviviality and in masculine cultures more with taste.[4] The Germanic countries are health conscious. The Belgians, French, and Italians have sophisticated food cultures, and sensory enjoyment is important, whereas the Spanish prefer natural products. For the Portuguese, the meal is a social event and consists of small relatively light dishes, as it is in Greece. The British are fond of sweets and pastries as well as instant products. Convenience is important, as in Denmark and Norway, where people don't particularly enjoy cooking. The Swedes prefer heavy meals and have a weak preference for natural products.[5] In India, although young Indian consumers are passionate about visiting fast food outlets for fun and change, home food remains their first choice; they regard home food as better than fast food.[6]

In Chapter 3 (section on climate) the link between *calorie intake* and climate was discussed. Logic says that calorie intake is higher in cold than in warm climates, but national wealth and culture are better explaining variables. Worldwide GNI per capita is the explaining variable, but in the rich world individualism and masculinity explain variance.

Americans are the champions of calorie intake, and this has increased over time. In 1960, the average American ate 4 pounds of frozen French fries a year; in 2001 it was more than 30 pounds.[7]

Agricultural legacy of a country explains differences in individualism and collectivism, in particular the differences between rice and wheat farming areas. In China traditional paddy rice farmers had to share labor and coordinate irrigation in a way that most wheat farmers did not. Researchers observed people in everyday life to test whether these agricultural legacies gave rice-farming southern China a more interdependent culture and wheat-farming northern China a more independent culture. The more wheat growing North of China appeared to be more individualistic as compared to the rice growing South that was more collectivistic. The researchers checked the differences by observing large numbers of people sitting in cafes to see whether they sat alone or with more people, but also whether they moved chairs that were in the way as individualists tend to do trying to control their environment, or not doing so, to adjust the self to the environment.[8]

Worldwide climate explains between 20% and 52% of variance of consumption of 7 of 18 food product categories examined: meat, liquid milk, yogurt, cheese, canned foods, chocolate, and sugar confectionery.[9] In 2014 across Europe also high uncertainty avoidance explained 52% of per capita chocolate consumption in kgs.[10]

In Europe, most fresh fruit is consumed in Italy, Austria, and Spain. In the United Kingdom, people eat the least fruit. Also fish consumption varies enormously: in Spain, which has a long coast line, it is 10 times greater than in landlocked Austria. Modern distribution systems may have caused some convergence, but there still are considerable differences. These consumption habits have been established during the past centuries and are not likely to change in the foreseeable future.

Processed Food and Food Preferences

Worldwide GNI per capita and the cultural variables explain most of the differences with respect to processed foods. GNI per capita explains, for example, variance of the volume of consumption of chilled desserts and of soup, and individualism explains variance of frozen foods, biscuits (cookies and crackers), and savory snacks. Data on usage (not volume) of soup show a correlation with individualism that explains 21% of variance for 41 countries worldwide; later data show correlations with IDV ($r = .49^{***}$) and low PDI ($r = -.49^{***}$).[11]

The colder the climate, the more ice cream consumed. The strong explaining power of climate for the volume of ice cream consumption shows that ice cream is an energy provider in cold climates instead of a cooling mechanism in hot climates. It is basically sweet milk. How climate explains variance of food consumption in an indirect way and how it is related to trust in food products was discussed in Chapter 3 (in the section on climate). Processed food products are less trusted in cultures of high uncertainty avoidance, which explains variance of most processed foods. The LTO dimension explains several differences in usage of some processed food products, such as breakfast cereals, potato crisps, and colas.[12] These are all ready-to-eat or drink products that fit the convenience orientation of short-term orientation cultures.

Europe is an area where economic convergence has been paralleled by divergence of food habits. In 1997 the Norwegians, with 141 liters per capita, drank twice as much milk as the Belgians, who consumed 70.5 liters per capita. Milk consumption converged in the period 1970–1977[13] and diverged in later years. Also, ice cream consumption has diverged. In 1997[14] in Denmark, the sales volume of frozen food was 40.4 kilograms per capita; in the United Kingdom it was 30.6, and it was 10.3 in Spain. Low uncertainty avoidance explained 60% of variance. Originally, consumption of frozen food was related to penetration of deep freezers, but this relationship has disappeared. This may imply that much frozen food is not bought to keep for later use but to consume right after buying.

Individualism explains variance of biscuits (cookies and crackers) that represents a type of processed food that is rooted in history. Whereas in the individualistic cultures biscuits are consumed as between-meal snacks, they are consumed as breakfast items in countries like Spain.

Eurobarometer data of 2017 show differences of various food preferences. High uncertainty avoidance and high masculinity together explain most of variance of preferences for heritage (food products must come from a known geographical area), respect for local tradition, protected geographical indications, and a guaranteed traditional specialty on the package. Collectivism explains variance of preferences for organic agriculture products, think they are safer, better quality and taste better than other food products, but are more difficult to find in local supermarkets.[15]

Soft Drinks

In 1997 Americans consumed twice as many liters of soft drinks as the Dutch. Germans drank 164 liters per capita, nearly twice as much as the Norwegians, who consumed 86.1 liters per capita. The difference is explained by culture. In 2017 US consumption was still highest, with 154 ltrs/capita.

In Europe,[16] in 1997, cultural masculinity explained 60% of variance of soft drink consumption (liters per capita). One of the likely causes of this relationship was global advertising. The soft drinks market has for a long time been dominated by Anglo-American global brands (e.g., Coca-Cola, Pepsi-Cola, Fanta, Seven-Up, Sprite, Schweppes). These early global brands were the first to apply advanced marketing techniques. With growing global competition, the owners of these brands have standardized their marketing and advertising for increased efficiency. Because many global advertising campaigns are developed in London or New York, for decades the global campaigns for soft drinks have reflected Anglo-American values like masculinity, adventure, status, and success, which are not as appealing to all other cultures. Thus, the result of global advertising has been different than intended. Global advertising, instead of causing convergence, may have caused divergence. In countries with values that differ from Anglo-American values, standardized advertising campaigns have resulted in suboptimalization of sales. Consumption of soft drinks by young people varied in a similar way. The percentage of students age 15 years old who in 1998 said they drank soft drinks every day also correlated with masculinity.[17]

Looking not at volumes consumed but at the percentages of people who use colas and soft drinks, there also are large differences. Whereas in 2013 in the United States 75% of the people drank colas, in France it was 60%, in the Czech Republic it was 52%, in Canada 78%, and in Russia 35%.[18]

Mineral Water

Mineral water (and bottled water) consumption varies considerably across countries. The most important explaining variable is uncertainty avoidance, and this relationship has been consistent over time. In Chapter 3 (Table 3.3), mineral water consumption differences over time were used as an example of stability. Although in the past 30 years the quality of tap water has improved everywhere in Europe, the differences between countries have remained similar since 1970 or have become even larger. Since 1970, high uncertainty avoidance has explained between 44% and 53% of variance. In France, Germany, Italy, and Belgium, cultures of high uncertainty avoidance, people drink increasing volumes of mineral water, as compared to the United Kingdom and Scandinavia, cultures of low uncertainty avoidance, where people have different ideas about what is necessary for their health. Over time the differences have become more extreme. In 2015 in Sweden 10 liters of bottled water were consumed per person, 20 liters in Denmark and 33 in the United Kingdom as compared with 189 liters in Italy and 177 liters in Germany.

Coffee and Tea

The variable that best explains differences in volume of coffee consumption is climate. Consistently, about 35% of variance is explained by latitude.[19] In the colder countries people drink larger volumes of coffee. In Chapter 3 (section on climate), the theory of homeostasis explained the relationship between climate and stimulants such as coffee. Low masculinity also explains variance. In the feminine cultures in Europe that also have colder climates, coffee consumption is connected with the concept of *gezellig* (Dutch), *mysigt* (Swedish), or *hyggelig* (Danish), in particular in the Scandinavian countries. Although tea also is a stimulant, no such relationship with climate exists for tea consumption. There is however, a significant correlation between individualism and the percentages of populations who drink tea.[20]

Tea consumption varies from the typical British strong black tea with milk that is consumed during the morning break as well as in the afternoon to all sorts of herbal teas in Germany, to green tea in China, which is consumed with hot meals. Nowadays there are many types of tea, and tea is processed in many different ways. Next to black teas there are green teas, herbal teas, and a variety of chilled, ready-to-drink teas in cans or tetra packs. In Asian countries there are country-specific teas like oolong tea, as, for example, the Taiwanese Tao Ti brand that is very popular. The dominance of tea-based refreshments explains the low consumption of carbonated soft drinks in Taiwan. In Europe, the British and Irish have been drinking the most black tea (1,148 and 1,417 cups per person per year), while the Italians drink least (39.6 cups). Originally tea came from China. The Dutch introduced it to Europe in the seventeenth century. But the tea rituals of the Chinese or Japanese are far from what they are now in Britain.

Coffee and tea rituals are historically defined. Types of coffee consumed vary from various versions of black coffee to larger cups with milk, called *espresso* and *cappuccino* in Italy – names that have been adopted by other countries in Europe – and *solo* and *cortado* in Spain. The name *latte*, used in the United States, may suggest something continental European, but it is a typical American type of coffee mix. The Italian cappuccino is a drink for the morning in Italy, but the Danes have embraced it for use throughout the day. For them it is 'a coffee.' Whereas in the North of Europe most coffee is consumed in the home, in the south most is consumed in bars, where contact with people is as important as drinking coffee.

A large coffee café chain like Starbucks reflects American coffee culture. The type of coffee served is different from what people are used to in most other countries. Italian Illy café's owner Andrea Illy says, 'In the United States coffee is merely a hot beverage, not an elixir.'[21] Illy's aim is to create an exclusive destination with emphasis on quality and aesthetics, whereas Starbucks is more a place to communicate with other people.

Whereas to Americans, Starbuck's offers better coffee than they were used to, Europeans were used to a better coffee already. Also, the idea of a café as a meeting place is not new. In Vienna, as in many European cities, the café has been an important institution in the city's cultural and political life. It is the place to meet friends, to study for an exam, or to listen to Strauss music while reading the newspaper.[22]

In the section 'Readers Report' in *Newsweek* of 7 October 2002, an Italian reader reacts to an earlier *Newsweek* story about Starbucks ('Planet Starbucks,' the cover story on 9 September 2002).

> I was very amused by Starbucks Corp.'s claim that they will come to Italy one day. Automatic espresso machines? Most Italians go to the bar to chat with the cashier or the guy at the coffee machine about the latest actress or football match – hard to do with a machine, even with a Java-enabled one. And what about allowing customers to order their coffee via the Web? What if the customer meets somebody on the way to the bar? 'Happy to see you, but my coffee is ready, I'll send you an e-mail!' Come on. Prepaid cards? They've been around for ages here. What we want in Italy (and we have it already) is good coffee at a reasonable price, some nice food just in case, all served quickly but also with a human touch. Not one of these things is Starbucks able to deliver now. And they call themselves a 'coffee bar'? Brrrr . . .
>
> Alberto Canesi, Rome

Alcoholic Beverages

At the start of the twenty-first century variance of pure alcohol consumption was explained by GNI per capita, high uncertainty avoidance and individualism that altogether explained 46%, but there are differences with respect to consumption of beer, wine, and spirits. Whereas the Czechs and Irish drink most beer, the inhabitants of Luxembourg and France drink most wine, and in the Republic of Moldova, Reunion, and the Russian Federation they drink most spirits.[23] The data on pure alcohol consumption are based on recorded data and don't include home production or so-called cottage-produced alcoholic beverages such as a country liquor called *arrack* in India, corn liquor in Venezuela, rice wine called *tuak* or *tapai* in Malaysia, or home-brewed beers like *talla* in Ethiopia.

In Europe, countries converge with respect to alcohol consumption. This is due to convergence of wealth and to decreased consumption of wine in the wine-growing countries.

In the warmer countries people drink more wine, while in the colder climates people drink more beer. This is related to where the two types of alcoholic beverages are produced. A few specific alcoholic drinks are related to cultural variables. Data from EMS show that champagne, port wine, and vermouth are consumed more in high than in low power distance cultures. These drinks are obviously social status drinks. In some categories, such as brandy and whiskey some strong brands dominate the category with respect to added values like status.

Nondurable Household Products

Countries are becoming similar with respect to usage of washing powder and household cleaning products, and whatever other differences are related to wealth. Volume differences, however, are related to uncertainty avoidance, and this relationship can best be explained by the need for purity that also operates as a value for food preferences (see also Chapter 5). Just to be sure their clothing will be really clean, in high uncertainty avoidance cultures people are likely to throw more washing powder into their washing machines than will people in low uncertainty avoidance cultures. A strong argument found in advertising in high uncertainty avoidance cultures tends to be antibacterial effectiveness and whiteness as a result of washing.

Personal Care and Cosmetics

Usage of personal care products like creams, lotions and cleansers is mainly related to wealth. For cosmetics in Europe, there are clear cultural patterns for explaining differences in product usage, but this is not the case worldwide. In Europe, for example, in the past 30 years differences in use of lipstick, eye cosmetics, and deodorants have been correlated with low uncertainty avoidance and individualism, of which the relationships with uncertainty avoidance have been strongest. Worldwide these relationships are different. When analyzing the differences, measuring usage, volume, or value sales lead to different results. Data on usage cannot be compared with value or volume data, because for this product category price has a symbolic function. Whereas in some countries fewer people may use makeup, lipstick, or perfume, those who do use these products may prefer more expensive, branded products. Some products are used only in some areas: for example, skin lightening products are popular in Asia because, traditionally, darker skins have been associated with people who work outdoors, and lighter skins are considered more sophisticated. Across Asia, 30% of Chinese use skin lightening products either daily or weekly, followed by 20% of Taiwanese, and 18% of Japanese and Hong Kong Chinese.[24]

Worldwide differences between countries with respect to personal care and cosmetics use are substantial. GNI/cap explains differences of most personal care products, but often combined with low PDI and/or short-term orientation. Differences in usage of hair conditioners and hairstyling gels are explained by GNI and IVR. Deodorants are one of the few personal care categories that are not related to GNI.[25]

Different cultural relationships also point at differences in motives for using personal care products and cosmetics. The individualistic cultures are the ones where people want to distinguish themselves from others. Color cosmetics and perfume are a means to do so. In low power distance cultures, cosmetics are used to look young, but in high power distance cultures cosmetics are a social status means to uphold face. Going out into the streets without makeup implies not being properly dressed. In particular, in cultures of short-term orientation, high power distance, and high uncertainty avoidance, people want to look stylish at all times.

Color cosmetics can satisfy the need for female self-enhancement, to attract men, to look young, or to differentiate oneself from others, which is an individualistic motive. Cosmetics also are not natural; they are artificial. To accept the artificial, in high uncertainty avoidance cultures, scientific claims are used, found in particular in advertising for hair care, toothpaste, and personal care products, and the existence of 'scientific' brands such as Laboratoire Garnier in France. Scientific data and arguments are likely to be more effective in strong uncertainty avoidance cultures than in weak uncertainty avoidance cultures, where the results are more important than the process. An interesting relationship is between usage of cleansing cream and LTO ($r = .37^{**}$). By properly cleaning your skin it remains in better condition in the long term.

Figure 8.1 depicts four culture clusters for color cosmetics involving power distance and uncertainty avoidance that together best explain usage motives. As most low power distance cultures (expect France, Belgium, and Poland) are also individualistic, the map includes this dimension too.

In the lower right quadrant of Figure 8.1, people like variety; they will buy any new color, easily change brands, or buy unbranded products at the supermarket. The product or brand sells itself if it offers enough choice. In these cultures there is relatively little advertising by the expensive cosmetics brands. The top right quadrant includes different clusters of cultures that are all high on uncertainty avoidance, but some are low on power distance and some high. High uncertainty avoidance asks for scientific control in both clusters. Low power distance means people will use cosmetics to look young; high power distance means people use them for social status. Products or brands focusing on the natural and purity will sell best in the combination with low power distance and high quality; status brands

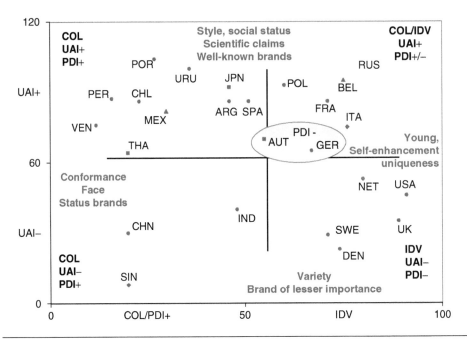

Figure 8.1 **Map color cosmetics**

SOURCE: Data Hofstede et al. (2010) (see Appendix A).

will sell best in the combination with high power distance. Big cosmetics brands like L'Oréal originated in this culture cluster.

In the culture cluster of the configuration collectivism, high power distance, and high uncertainty avoidance in the upper left-hand corner of Figure 8.1, people want to be stylish and are well groomed for social status reasons and for upholding face. They want to conform. Both the scientific approach and status brands are expected to sell best. Both quality and social recognition are important values. In the lower left-hand quadrant are collectivistic cultures of low uncertainty avoidance. Here conformance and status brands to uphold face are important, but scientific claims may be less relevant. China, Singapore, and India are in this quadrant.

An interesting relationship is between individualism and short-term orientation and deodorant use. Across 45 countries, use of deodorants is explained by short-term orientation, high uncertainty avoidance, and individualism, which together explain 50% of variance. Whereas the need for privacy makes people in individualistic cultures aware of the smell of other people, in collectivistic cultures they don't seem to care so much. In the hotter European countries, perspiration is viewed as the body's natural cooling mechanism; in the

United Kingdom they see it as an embarrassment. The relationship with short-term orientation may point at the fact that deodorants help to enhance the self, provide self-confidence.

Over time several Western companies have tried to sell deodorants to Asians, trying to induce social embarrassment or shame about wetness, sweat stains, and body odor. This negative approach inducing shame has not worked well in Asia, where people avoid negative information. People don't want to admit they have a problem. Indians, for example, would be reluctant to be seen buying a product that demonstrates they have a problem.[26] The positive approach, communicating freshness and attraction, making women more attractive to men or the other way around, is a better approach, which is also effective in other collectivistic cultures. In Russia, Unilever focused on the fact that Russian women spend heavily on cosmetics but not on deodorant. The message was that if you don't use a deodorant you won't look beautiful and will not be attractive to men.[27]

Clothing and Footwear

In lower-income countries, the percentage of household expenditure spent on clothing and footwear is higher than in the rich countries. In high power distance and collectivistic cultures, people have to be well groomed when going out into the streets, and they may spend more on clothing than in individualistic and low uncertainty avoidance cultures. Generally, people in high uncertainty avoidance cultures are also well groomed. It is one way of facing a threatening world. Spending money on clothing and footwear also serves needs for self-esteem and self-enhancement. In individualistic cultures, variety is important and the percentage of women who say they buy new clothes at least once a month correlates with individualism.[28] Status needs to show one's success can be another explaining variable, for example, in 1999 masculinity explained 46% of the mean household consumption expenditures on clothing and footwear. It also explained the separate expenditures on clothing (42%), garments (43%), and footwear (39%).[29] In Chapter 5 (section on appearance), the social processes were described that explain the varying needs for appearance.

Household Appliances

Generally, national wealth explains variance of ownership of large electrical household appliances. Of all product categories culture's impact on consumption behavior is weakest for appliances.[30] However, climate explains variance of ownership of deep freezers and the relationship with GNI/cap has been weakening. In 1970 GNI per capita explained 48% of variance of ownership of deep freezers; in 1991 it explained 57% of variance and in 1997 42%. As explained in Chapter 3 (section on climate), in countries where people used to keep food in the snow, they have embraced electric freezing technology most intensely.

Because of differences in food customs, housing, and cleaning, people will prefer different appliances. An example is the special Kimchi refrigerator developed in South Korea.

Korean *Kimchi* is a cabbage-based dish following century-old recipes. Koreans traditionally make a lot of Kimchi in winter and eat it the whole year, so they need special storage facilities. Koreans used to put Kimchi in a big jar and dig it in the ground, so the temperature was stable and the ground made a perfect ripening temperature for Kimchi. A special breathing brown jar kept the Kimchi fresh. People eat even two-year-old Kimchi. Because urbanization made it difficult to preserve Kimchi in a jar in the ground, a special Kimchi refrigerator was invented, which copies the conditions of the glazed pottery in the ground. If you put Kimchi in a regular refrigerator, it will go bad in one week because of varying temperatures when opening and closing it. By its construction, the Kimchi refrigerator is able to keep a constant temperature. At the beginning it was invented just for Kimchi, but nowadays some Kimchi refrigerators have various functions to keep fresh meat, vegetables, fruits, and so on.[31] Figure 8.2 illustrates the Kimchi jars and refrigerator.

Figure 8.2 **Kimchi pots and refrigerator. Courtesy of Eun Jee Hyun**

In 1997 low individualism explained 39% of variance of unit sales of food processors, and low masculinity explained an additional 19%. The link with collectivism explains preferences for slow food instead of fast food. Fast food and convenience are typical needs of individualistic and short-term oriented cultures, as discussed in Chapter 5 (section on convenience). In 2009, worldwide ownership of electric dishwashers and microwave ovens correlated with wealth, individualism, and low power distance.[32] Across 20 wealthy countries, however, where the influence of GNI per capita is weaker, dishwasher ownership is related to short-term orientation, which explains 36% of variance. In 2013 it was the combination of GNI/cap and low PDI that explained differences in ownership of dishwashers, together explaining 66% of variance. No such relationship is found for microwave ovens. Electric dishwashers are convenience products, but the microwave is not. Whereas convenience-oriented cultures may use a microwave for warming up precooked dishes, in the cultures where people like cooking, they use it to make more refined dishes. This is confirmed by the relationships found in 2013, when GNI/cap, together with high UAI explained 47% of variance.[33]

In 1999, 60% of expenditures on tools and equipment for the house and garden were explained by individualism.[34] This is understandable in view of the relationship between individualism and living in one-family houses as well as ownership of private gardens.

Consumer Electronics and Personal Computers

Many consumer electronics serve the individualistic need for variety and stimulation. Ownership of most audio and video consumer electronics correlates with GNI per capita and individualism. Worldwide music sales have been related to national income, and the richer countries have traditionally spent more on CDs, cassettes, and records than the poorer countries. Calculations from 1999 onward have shown relationships with individualism and low uncertainty avoidance.

The explaining variables for most audio and video electronics are individualism, low uncertainty avoidance, and low power distance. Ownership and sales of personal stereos, in 1991 first represented by the Sony Walkman, is related to the configuration of individualism, weak uncertainty avoidance, and small power distance. Listening to music all by yourself is an individualistic habit, and individualism explains variance of the whole personal stereo category. The more recent products tend to be related to low uncertainty avoidance. In these cultures people adopt innovations faster than in cultures of high uncertainty avoidance. With the advent of the Internet and the possibilities of downloading music cultural relationships have changed. In collectivistic cultures more music is downloaded from the Internet, both free and paid music. Ownership of DVD players for some time has been related to wealth, but in 2013 variance was mainly explained by IVR (34%).[35]

Ownership of television sets first converged and is now diverging. Radio ownership has diverged, as discussed in Chapter 3. Homogeneity of TV penetration masks heterogeneity at the micro level: numbers of television sets per household, types of television set, and viewing time vary. Television has become an integral part of life everywhere, but that doesn't mean people watch similar programs or use it in the same way. In Chapter 7 cultural differences with respect to TV viewing and radio listening were discussed. The role of television in social life varies. Whereas in individualistic cultures people mostly watch live TV in the home, in collectivistic cultures they may do so in public places like bars or cafes.

Radio listening has been an individualistic habit and still is, whether listening to radio on a radio set or via the Internet. In individualistic cultures everybody used to have his or her own radio or even more than one, whereas in collectivistic cultures one radio per household used to be enough. At the end of the twentieth century there were 1,432 radios per 1,000 people in the United Kingdom and 333 in Spain. There were nearly twice as many TV sets as radios in Spain and Portugal, whereas there were twice as many radios as TV sets in the United Kingdom. The best explanation is the difference between individualistic and collectivistic cultures with respect to verbal and visual orientation. Television is more visual and radio is verbal. Figure 8.3 illustrates the significant correlations between the number of radios per 50 people and individualism for 18 countries worldwide. The figure illustrates how these differences have become stronger over time and how they are related to individualism.

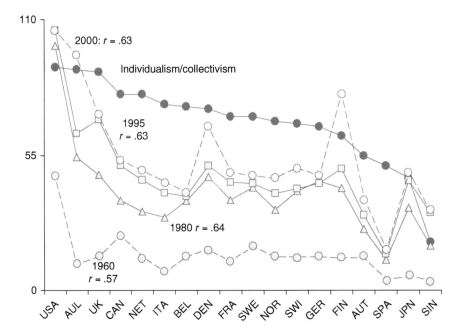

Figure 8.3 **Radios and individualism**

SOURCES: Hofstede et al. (2010) (see Appendix A); United Nations Statistical Yearbooks and World Development Indicators (see Appendix B)

In the year 2000, measurement of ownership of radio receivers stopped, because nowadays people listen to radio messages in many different ways, such as via their personal computers or mobile phones.

PC ownership is still a matter of wealth; in 2011 – even across the relatively wealthy countries of Europe – the percentages of households without a computer correlated negatively with GNI/cap.[36] Table 8.1 shows examples of how cultural relationships change over time. GNI keeps playing an important role, but next, in particular in the earlier years of existence of electronics, it is low uncertainty avoidance that explains variance. But also several relationships with IVR are found.

Table 8.1   **Video and audio electronics, and personal computers**

	GNI/cap	PDI	IDV	MAS	UAI	IVR
Music sales per person 2001[1]	.79***	−.62***	.61***		−.59***	
Recording media 1999, mean consumer expenditures[1]	.66***		.80***		−.65**	
CD players 1999, % owned[2]	.61**			−.65***	−.51*	
Personal stereos 1991, % owned[2]	.54*	−.44*	.56*	−.38	−.65***	
Personal stereos 1997, sales/person[3]		−.48*			−.63***	
VCR 1998, household penetration[4]	.65**	−.47*	.68***		−.73***	
VCR 2005, % households[9]	.78***	−.64***	.68***	−.46*		
DVD player 2000, household penetration[4]			.54*	−.47*	−.55*	
DVD player 2008, TV households with DVD player[9]	.74***	−.50**	.57**		−.41*	
DVD player 2013, % adult population[8]	.34**	−.31*				.58***
PCs per 1,000 people 2004[7]	.62***	−.44*	.38*		−.71***	

(Continued)

Table 8.1 **(Continued)**

	GNI/cap	PDI	IDV	MAS	UAI	IVR
PC at home, % of total population, 2008[5]	.78***	−.58***	.38*			
PC at home, % of total population, 2008, rich countries[6]	.41*			−.47*	−.46*	
Households (%) without computer, 2011[10]	−.69***	.51***	−.54***	.54***	.59***	−.69***
Percentage of individuals who own laptop computer, 2015[11]	.75***	-.60**	.51**		−.55**	.74***

SOURCES: Hofstede et al. (2010) (see Appendix A); 1) International Federation of the Phonographic Industry, worldwide, 22 countries; 2) *Reader's Digest* Eurodata 1991, Europe, 15 countries; 3) Euromonitor 1997, 15 countries; 4) Eurostat, 14 countries; 5) *TGI Product Book* 2009, worldwide, 38 countries; 6) *TGI Product Book* 2009, worldwide, 22 countries, GNI/capita > US$ 17,000; 7) World Development Indicators, 26 countries worldwide, GNI/capita > US$ 20,000; 8) *TGI Product Usage Guide* (2013); 9) IP Television, 25 countries Europe, USA and Japan; 10) EBS 362; 11) EBS 438 (see Appendix B)

People do all sorts of different things with their computers: read newspapers, play games, chat, e-mail, shop or buy via Internet, listen to radio, watch television or films, or work at home. These different activities have been discussed in Chapter 7. Most of such activities are not on a classic desktop computer, but most on the mobile phone, the smartphone.

Telecommunications

The quality of a country's infrastructure for transport, technology, and communication[37] depends on the country's wealth. In regions with increased homogenization of national wealth, the differences have decreased but not disappeared. Whereas in 2000 communication expenditures as a percentage of household expenditures still correlated with low GNI per capita, this relationship had disappeared in 2009. Between 1966 and 1998, GNI per capita explained between 95% and 70% of variance of telephone main lines per 1,000 people worldwide. In 1980 culture emerged as an explaining variable next to GNI per capita. After that year, worldwide individualism, and in Europe weak uncertainty avoidance, became additional explaining variables, but after 2006 the main explaining variables were GNI per capita, power distance, individualism, and LTO. This change is due to the advent of the mobile phone. At the start of mobile telephony, the general expectation was that mobile phones would penetrate faster in countries where communications infrastructure was weak, but this was not the case. Until 2002 there was a significant correlation between the numbers of fixed telephone lines per 100 inhabitants and mobile cellular subscriptions per 100 inhabitants ($r = .44*$), but this relationship disappeared. In many countries, the number of fixed lines has been declining slowly while the number of mobile subscriptions has been increasing. By 2007 in 48 countries, there were more mobile cellular phones than inhabitants and the numbers have been growing, but not everywhere as fast. By 2015 in Russia there were 175 mobile phone connections per 100 people, more than in the United States with only 117 per 100 people. The time spent calling also varies, with the United States 367 minutes per capita per month, Russia 321, India 141, Germany 118 and Nigeria at 70.[38]

Worldwide GNI per capita and individualism explain most of variance of ownership of mobile phones, but across a group of wealthy countries also a correlation with low individualism is found. The mobile phone is the typical product that appeals to collectivists to intensify and enhance interpersonal contacts. To facilitate this a subscription is preferred to prepaid, also for other intensive usage and applications like video viewing. In the collectivistic cultures, people use the mobile phone more intensively than in the individualistic cultures. Intensive usage is also related to short-term orientation, demonstrating its convenience function, but, next to uncertainty in the long-term-oriented cultures, where pragmatism is valued, all sorts of applications of the mobile phone have been embraced fastest. Also IVR plays a role in explaining differences, in particular ownership of an iPhone as compared with any other smartphone as well as several activities favored through the Internet function of the smartphone. The iPhone has become a matter of status, whereas other brands are for those who care less about status.

Table 8.2 presents data on usage of various applications and motives in different sets of countries.

Table 8.2 **Telecommunications**

	GNI/cap	PDI	IDV	UAI	MAS	LTO	IVR
Fixed telephone lines per 100 inhabitants, 2007[1]	.94***	.67***	.74***			.40**	
Mobile cellular subscriptions per 100 inhabitants, 2007[1]	.52***	-.26*	.38**				
Mobile connections per 100 people, 2016[2]	.60***						

(Continued)

Table 8.2 **(Continued)**

	GNI/cap	PDI	IDV	UAI	MAS	LTO	IVR
Mobile phone subscriptions with Internet, 2011[3]	.40*	−.49**	.38*	−.66***			.48**
Mobile phone subscriptions per 100 people, 2010[4]	.37***					.30**	
Percent who use mobile phone only occasionally, 2008[5]			.46*			.58**	
Percent who use mobile phone several times a day, 2008[5]			−.53*			−.67***	
Not using mobile: miss opportunity contact family and friends[5]						−.76***	
Main benefit mobile phone: possibility to be contacted at any place any time[6]	−.58*		−.51*			−.49*	
Global smartphone penetration, 2014[7]	.68***	−.32*		−.60***			.27*
Screen minutes smartphone, 2014[7]	−.59***		−.66***	−.44**		−.40*	
Smartphone share of video viewing, 2014[7]	−.52***	.47***	−.76***				
Own iPhone, 2012[8]	.49*	−.44*		−.58***			.73***
Own other smartphone, 2012[8]			−.41*		−.54*		
Regularly find news, 2012[8])	.52**	−.49*		−.73***	−.52**	−.38*	.80***
Read electronic newspaper, 2012[8])				−.52**	−.71***	−.40*	.49*

SOURCES: Hofstede et al. (2010) (see Appendix A); 1) ITU measuring the Information Society 2009, 44 countries worldwide; 2) Ofcom 2016, 18 countries; 3) EBS 362, 24 countries; 4) Worldbank, 2010, 66 countries; 5) Flash EB 241, 2008, 16 wealthy countries; 6) EBS 249, 2006, 14 wealthy countries; 7) Millward Brown, Adreaction 2014, 28 countries; 8) EMS 2012 (see Appendix B)

In particular, in collectivistic cultures people want to communicate continuously with the members of their in-groups, and all means of communication are used for that. For Japanese youth, the mobile phone is a means to feel connected (*tsunagatte iru*) with other members of their in-group all the time. So people use the new communications technology to satisfy existing needs more intensely.

> In 2002 a Japanese TV station conducted an experiment involving three secondary school girls who were close friends. All three had mobile phones that were used to stay in constant contact by SMS messaging. In the experiment, one of the three girls had to hand over her phone while the other two were allowed to keep theirs. The three girls were continuously followed by the TV station's camera team. At the end of the first day, the viewer could see the three friends singing together in a karaoke box. The two friends with the phones were receiving a continuous stream of SMS messages. Suddenly the girl without the phone started crying because she felt so lonely, although she was with her friends.[39]

So, in contrast to expectations that new technology would fundamentally change people's communication behavior, new technology has made people do more of what they used to do, to talk, write, chat, watch video, play games, gather information, do payments, etc. Countries vary with respect to usage for text messaging, e-mails, social networks, instant messaging, video calls and voice over IP. Whereas 89% of the French use it for text messaging, only 32% of the Japanese do so. Of the Swedes 60% use it for social networking as compared with 41% of the French and 38% of the Japanese.[40]

In cultures where interdependence is strong, parents use the mobile phone to stay in touch with their children. In Italy, children as young as 8 years old receive a mobile phone to take to school so that the parents can reach them. As a result, in Italy the mobile phone is called a 'communicative feeding bottle.'[41]

Many applications to the mobile phone were introduced much faster in Asia than in Europe or the United States. This was caused by the fact that PC and Internet penetration were much lower in Asia, and countries lagged with respect to digital leisure applications. Already in 2000, Japanese NTT DoCoMo introduced its i-mode service with subscriptions to Bandai – known for the Tamagotchi – services that allowed users to download popular cartoon characters and games. Also, in Asia, much faster than in Europe and the United States, a variety of fashionable models entered the market. The Japanese view their phones more as companions and personalize them with ring tones and distinctive images. This process was different from that in the United States, where the mobile phone was more viewed as an instrument for greater productivity.[42]

In Europe mobile phone producers kept standardizing their products and advertising for quite a long time, assuming similarity in behavior. Only in large developing markets like China did Nokia market its cellular phones with features that appealed to local tastes, such as greeting cards with popular Chinese astrological symbols.[43] However, Nokia did not develop specific handset designs for specific markets. Via a subsidiary, Nokia did offer an expensive luxury subbrand (Vertu) in gold or platinum that would appeal to the rich and famous of this world, and Siemens offered so-called fashion accessory phones under the name Xelibri.[44] In China a taste for faux diamond-studded handsets developed that was considered kitschy and thus bad taste in the West. As a result, in China handset brands such as TCL, Ningbo Bird, and Amoisonic quickly gained market share, and Nokia and Motorola were losing. Too late, Motorola started copying the diamond-studded phone designs so popular in China.[45]

With the advent of the mobile phone with Internet, the smartphone, intensity of usage increased. In 2014 global smartphone penetration correlated with low uncertainty avoidance, as found for all newly introduced technological and electronic products, but usage of the smartphone varied across cultures. For example in the collectivistic cultures people use it more for video viewing and in cultures that score low on masculinity, people use the smartphone more for finding news and reading newspapers. During the past century in these cultures people have been heavy newspaper readers, which supports the conclusion that people use the new electronic media for continuing doing what they did in other ways (see Table 8.2).

Luxury Articles

Many luxury articles serve status needs. Variance of buying or owning luxury articles is generally explained by masculinity or high power distance that explain the need to demonstrate one's success or social status. Ownership of real jewelry is correlated with cultural masculinity, worldwide ($r = .44^*$), in a group of developed countries worldwide ($r = .61^{***}$), and in Europe ($r = .51^*$). There is no significant correlation with national wealth. The wealthy, global target groups of travelers and business people are assumed to be homogeneous in their buying behavior, ownership, and preference for luxury products and brands, but data from EMS, covering the 20% highest-income groups of Europe, show a different picture, as illustrated in Table 5.1. One example is expensive wrist watches, usually highly branded to convey status value.

In the modern world everybody can afford to own a wristwatch, but differences in ownership of expensive watches are large. In 1999 low GNI per capita explained 50% of variance of ownership of relatively cheap watches, and low masculinity explained an additional 25%. The relationship between ownership of affordable watches and low income is a logical one. Low status needs explain high ownership of cheaper watches in the feminine cultures, whereas masculinity explains 29% of variance of sales of expensive watches. Of the Italian respondents of EMS, 11.9% reported that the value of their main watch was more than US$1,600, as compared with only 2.1% of the Swedes. In 2007, masculinity explained 38% of variance of ownership of a watch that was more expensive than €750.

In 1999 EMS also asked questions about ownership of specific watch brands. For four brands (Rolex, Seiko, Swatch, and Omega), meaningful relationships with culture were found. These are also the brands with a global positioning based on global advertising. There was no relationship with GNI per capita for any of these expensive watch brands. Judging from the relationship between individualism and ownership of a Rolex, this brand is likely a watch for those who want to distinguish themselves from others. The message of the advertising campaign for Rolex is that it is a brand for unique personalities, singers, musicians, scientists, sports people who have distinguished themselves in their profession. The values included in advertising for Rolex are not just material success, but unique achievement. The advertising campaign shows how the brand distinguishes the dedicated professional from ordinary people. Four examples of ads of the international Rolex campaign are shown in Figure 8.4. Seiko appears to be a no-nonsense brand for those who don't need material status. Ownership of a Seiko as a main watch correlated with low uncertainty avoidance ($r = -.66^{***}$) and with low masculinity ($r = -.61^{**}$).

Figure 8.4 **International advertising for Rolex, with opera singer Kiri te Kanawa, singers Tony Bennett and Diana Kroll, and with tennis player Roger Federer**

Now that people mostly make pictures with their mobile phones, the compact camera has nearly become extinct and analysis of cameras as a category is not interesting. How people use their camera varies. Historically heavy usage has been in the masculine cultures.

In the no-nonsense feminine cultures, people used them less frequently. The measurement 'number of films used in the past year' correlated with national income in 1991 and 1999,[46] but heavy usage is also related to masculinity. In 1999 GNI per capita explained 42% of variance, and masculinity explained an additional 36%.

As discussed in Chapter 5 the various motives for buying and owning luxury brands mostly vary with power distance, individualism–collectivism and masculinity–femininity, which can be used for mapping motives for luxury brands, as in the map in Figure 8.5.

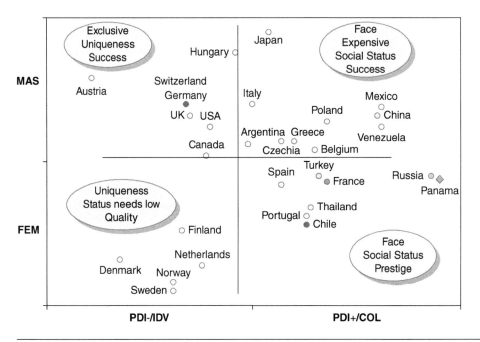

Figure 8.5   **Motives for luxury brands**

SOURCE: Hofstede et al. (2010) (see Appendix A)

Cars

Worldwide GNI per capita explains differences in car ownership in households, but differences across wealthy countries are explained by individualism.[47] Across wealthy countries individualism is the explaining variable.

High mobility in the individualistic cultures makes people use their cars more. Masculinity explains the differences in numbers of cars owned per family. In Italy, Germany, and the United Kingdom, there are more families with two cars than there are in feminine cultures such as the Netherlands and the Scandinavian countries. In these cultures, more people think one car is enough (although they may be able to afford two), and larger percentages of people than in the masculine cultures say they do not want a car. In the United States there are more cars per household than there are licensed drivers per household.[48] Across Europe, among business people differences in having more than three cars in the household are explained by GNI per capita (50%) and masculinity (explaining an additional 17%).[49] Ownership of more than one car is a matter of status. The different car buying motives have been discussed in Chapter 5.

In the feminine cultures people are less interested in technology than in the masculine cultures. Both the *Reader's Digest* Surveys and EMS have asked questions about the engine size of the car owned by respondents. The answers 'Don't know' can be viewed as a measurement of low interest in the engine size. The differences between countries in this respect are large. Of the respondents of EMS in 1999, 30.6% of the Swedes didn't know the engine size of their car, as compared with only 2.6% of the British.

Leisure

When examples of convergence in Europe are mentioned, a frequent example is convergence of expenditures on services such as leisure activities.[50] Leisure expenditures, however, do not converge. National wealth explains much of variance of leisure expenditures, in the developed world cultural variables are important explaining factors. The heavy spenders are Sweden and the United Kingdom; the low spenders are Spain and Portugal. Next to wealth much of variance is explained by individualism–collectivism. An explanation is that free time is spent with family and relatives in collectivistic cultures, whereas in individualistic cultures of low power distance and low uncertainty avoidance, people spend more time on paid leisure activities. Elements of low uncertainty avoidance that explain expenditures on leisure products and services are low anxiety, innovativeness, and a culture of fitness. Relevant individualistic values are pleasure, stimulation, variety, and adventure.

The most recent dimension indulgence versus restraint (IVR) is supposed to explain variance of leisure activities, but this is not the case. It is mainly variance of differences in attitudes toward the abstract notion of leisure that is explained. In 2005 the European Value Study[51] asked for the importance of leisure time, and IVR together with IDV explained 90% of variance. In 2007 Eurobarometer[52] asked the same question and IVR alone explained 72% of variance. However, leisure in general is an abstract notion; asking questions about concrete leisure activities leads to different cultural relationships, and IVR is mostly related to sports activities, as shown in Table 8.3. Also, some leisure activities may even be negatively related to leisure, as the percentage of leisure spent online, which correlates negatively with IVR ($r = -.69***$).[53]

Leisure Activities

Most of the different leisure activities, in particular sports, are related to wealth, next to varying cultural dimensions. Low power distance explains variance of visits to amusement facilities such as theme parks or the zoo. Individualism, low power distance and low uncertainty avoidance explain variance of active participation in sports activities and mean expenditures on sports and recreational services. Collectivism, high power distance, and high uncertainty avoidance tend to explain more passive leisure activities like watching TV, going to the cinema, visiting museums, or regularly dining out in restaurants. Gardening is the typical activity of individualistic cultures, but it is also related to long-term orientation. A few data on playing video games suggest that in masculine cultures people play more video games. However, the type of game may be related to culture. Some Japanese games have conquered the world, but some have not. Pachinko, for example, a gambling game played in nearly every street in Tokyo, has never become popular outside Japan.

For young people, both in Asia and Europe, shopping as a leisure activity is related to individualism.

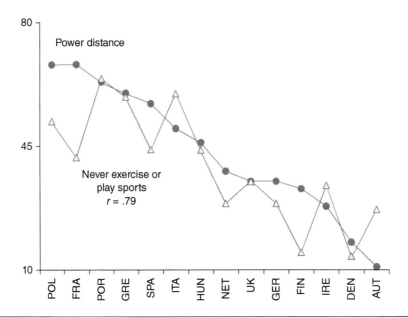

Figure 8.6   PDI and never exercise

SOURCES: Data from Hofstede (2001) (see Appendix A); Special Eurobarometer report *Sports and Physical Activity* (2014), EBS 412 (see Appendix B)

In the cultures of low power distance and low uncertainty avoidance, sports and fitness activities are a more important leisure activity than they are in the cultures of high power distance and high uncertainty avoidance, where people show relatively more interest in the arts. All sorts of activities are related to this 'art orientation,' varying from interest in interior design and painting, and buying books about it to regular visits to the cinema and doing a cultural tour as holiday activity.

In Europe, art orientation is most pronounced in Italy. The need for art and show can be traced back far into history. Luigi Barzini writes:

> Italians have always excelled in all activities in which the appearance is predominant: architecture, decoration, landscape gardening, the figurative arts, pageantry, fireworks, ceremonies, opera, and now industrial design, stage jewelry, fashions and the cinema. Italian medieval armor was the most beautiful in Europe: it was highly decorated, elegantly shaped, well designed, but too light and thin to be used in combat.[54]

Several examples of leisure activities and relationships with culture are presented in Table 8.3.

Table 8.3   **Leisure activities and motives in Europe and Asia**

	GNI/cap	PDI	IDV	MAS	UAI	LTO	IVR
Europe							
Recreation, culture % of total household expenditures[1]	.79***	−.66***	.59***		−.57***		
% who sport every day and % at least once a week[2]	.80***	−.61***			−.46**	−.42*	
% who never exercise or play sports[3]	−.74***	.50**	−.45**		.64***		−.67***
6+ visits to cinema in past 12 months[4]	−.55*	.68***			.56*	−.50*	

(Continued)

Table 8.3 **(Continued)**

	GNI/cap	PDI	IDV	MAS	UAI	LTO	IVR
6+ visits to museum or gallery in past 12 months[4]			−.47*	.53*	.54*	−.64**	
At least once a week:[5]							
Watch TV music channels	−.71***	.60***	.49**		.53*		
Watch TV movie channels	−.59***	.50***					
Major holiday motive/major attraction:[6]							
Wellness, health	−.49**			.50**	.34*		
Rest, recreation	−.55***	.42*			.60***		
Sports related	.50**	−.44*			−.51**		
Cultural heritage	.63*	−.43*			−.51**	−.45*	.72***
Europe leisure activities young people							
Watch TV[7]	−.50**	.38*	−.35*				
Internet, video games[7]	−.52***	.57***		.36*			
Participated in sports club[8]	.83***	−.50***	.37*		−.33*		.56***
Asia leisure activities young people[9]							
Listen to radio		.59*				−.89***	
Playing any sports				.62*			
Watching video						−.73***	
Shopping	.69**			.55*	.68*		
Camping	.51*				−.62*		

SOURCES: Hofstede et al. (2010) (see Appendix A); 1) Eurostat, *Structure of Consumption*, 2005; 2) Flash EB 241, 2008; 3) EBS 472, 2018; 4) EMS 2012; 5) Flash EB 199, 2007, Europe, Turkey and USA, 27 countries; 6) Flash EB 258, 2009, 25 countries; 7) Flash EB 202, 2007, Europe, 25 countries; 8) EBS 455, 2017, 26 countries; 9) Synovate *Young Asians*, 2009, 12 countries (see Appendix B)

In 2009, in Europe only 58% took a vacation, defined by a stay somewhere away from home for at least four consecutive nights for private reasons.[55] Expenditures on packaged holidays have been relatively high in the masculine cultures. In the feminine cultures people spend more on travel and less on accommodation. People have a greater connectedness to the home than in masculine cultures. This is reflected in the ownership of caravans (*trailers* in American English). Members of feminine cultures want to take a sort of home with them when they go on vacation. Across Europe in 1991, ownership of caravans[56] correlated with low masculinity ($r = -.57**$). Members of feminine cultures like staying in hotels for pleasure less than do members of masculine cultures. In 1997 masculinity explained 56% of variance of 21–30 nights spent in a hotel for personal reasons in the past year. In 2007 masculinity explained 66% of variance of more than 31 nights spent in a hotel for pleasure.[57]

What people want for their holidays varies. Whereas people of high uncertainty avoidance cultures search for rest, recreation, wellness, and health, in the low uncertainty avoidance cultures people search more for active sports or sports-related activities. Short-term-orientation cultures, where preservation of the status quo is important, like to visit museums, but cultural heritage, a motive for visting other countries was also related to IVR.[58] The numbers of museums per million people[59] are correlated with short-term orientation. An important value of short-term orientation is tradition, and what museums generally do is preserve the past.

People have very different ideas about requirements of facilities for their holidays, and these ideas are related to what they are used to at home. Americans and Asians want air-conditioned hotel rooms, whereas many Europeans think air conditioning is unhealthy. Northern Europeans like dining in the open air in the warm climates of southern Europe, whereas the Spanish will refuse to eat outside; it may spoil the food, or a fly may drop in your wine. Whereas in Asia, Westerners want a mix of sun, sea, and ethnic culture, and in the evening a beer at the poolside, the Japanese, Koreans, and Chinese will want their karaoke bars.

Pets

People mostly enjoy their pets in leisure time. Roles of dogs and cats vary across cultures. In particular the role of dogs in people's lives varies across cultures. In low power distance cultures dogs are companions, equals, and they join in fitness activities of humans. In high power distance cultures, what is appealing to people is that dogs can be trained to obey unconditionally. In high power distance cultures both dogs and cats can serve as status symbols. In individualistic and low power distance cultures, cats are companions and the fact that cats show individual minds fits individualistic cultures. Differences in cat ownership correlate with individualism, and differences in dog ownership correlate with high power distance.[60] Prepared pet food is correlated with wealth. In the lower-income countries, pets tend to be more fed with leftovers of human food.

In pet food advertising, the relationship between humans and pets reflect cultural differences that are similar to relationships between humans. In collectivistic cultures pets live with the family or are shown to be part of a pet family, whereas in individualistic cultures usually a pet is shown as a companion of a single individual. The two pictures in Figure 8.7 are from a German commercial for Sheba cat food, showing a woman alone with a cat, and the Japanese cat food brand Maruha, showing the extended cat family.

Figure 8.7 **Cat food advertising in Germany and Japan**

Finance

How people deal with their money is related to income, but also culture bound. Examples are insurance, banking, and private investments.

Insuring oneself and one's property is a habit of the wealthy, individualistic part of the world. Comparison of ownership of all sorts of insurance products over time shows convergence, but differences between countries have remained considerable. Worldwide, in Asia, in Latin America, and in greater Europe, income explains most of variance, although individualism tends to be a second predictor (except in Asia). At face value, one would expect that individuals in strong uncertainty avoidance cultures would own more insurance products than members of weak uncertainty avoidance cultures, but the relationship appears to be the opposite. This demonstrates that uncertainty avoidance is not the same as risk avoidance. Insurance products do eliminate risk, but in low uncertainty avoidance cultures where internal locus of control prevails, people take their future in their own hands by insuring themselves. In high uncertainty avoidance cultures where external locus of control operates, people are more inclined to wait until others take control. External locus of control also explains the relationship between public pension spending and high uncertainty avoidance, whereas private pension funds are related to low uncertainty avoidance, cultures where people save for their pension themselves instead of expecting the government to take care of their pensions. Several OECD data on public pension spending as a percentage of GNI correlate with high uncertainty avoidance.

Life insurances are sold more in individualistic cultures than in collectivistic cultures. In the former, should one die early, one cannot count on family to support one's dependants. Across Europe GNI/cap is the main explaining variable for life insurance, car insurance and private health insurance, together with low power distance and low masculinity. In the feminine cultures people are emotionally more sensitive to the needs of their dependants. In high power distance, people rely on their superiors to take care of them.[61] In many collectivistic cultures the children are responsible for supporting their parents. However, in some Asian countries, where originally children supported their elderly parents, but are not able or willing to do so anymore legislation has been introduced that spells out the children's duties in supporting their parents. In India the so-called *Maintenance and Welfare of Parents and Senior Citizens Act* is a legislation enacted in 2007, to provide more effective provision for maintenance and welfare of parents and senior citizens. Several other Asian countries have such laws. Involved are the traditional concepts of intergenerational fairness and reciprocity. For example, the common belief that, in adulthood, children should compensate their parents for the sacrifices that their parents made in supporting them to adulthood.[62]

A study comparing non-life insurances across 82 countries found similar cultural relationships: individualistic cultures of low power distance, and high uncertainty avoidance tend to have a relatively high level of non-life insurance consumption.[63]

Personal loans are more frequent in individualistic cultures than in collectivistic cultures where people save more for buying expensive products or loan from family and friends. Long-/short-term orientation is a dimension that explains differences in saving or borrowing money. In 2001, the percentage of respondents who tended to agree with the statement 'Buying on credit is more useful than dangerous,' correlated with short-term orientation.[64] The Chinese historically have saved much more than people in other countries, and they still do so. In 2009 China's households were saving 25% of their discretionary income, which is about six times the savings rate in the United States and three times the rate in Japan.[65] Yet, in Europe variance of personal loans is explained by low uncertainty avoidance.[66]

Credit card ownership and usage are more frequent in individualistic cultures, but the strongest relationship is with wealth. TGI data of 2013 for 48 countries worldwide show that GNI/cap and low power distance together explain 62% of variance of the percentages of population over 18 years old who use a credit card.[67] Across 26 European countries GNI/cap together with low masculinity explain 64% of variance.[68]

There used to be strong differences between cultures where clients asked for personal contacts with their banks, in particular in the more collectivistic cultures, but online banking has changed this. Online banking started in the feminine cultures, but Internet banking has spread across the world. This has not changed loyalty between clients and their banks everywhere. The degree to which people change providers is related to uncertainty avoidance. In 2016 changing providers of bank accounts, credit cards and car insurances correlated with low uncertainty avoidance.[69] Probably this is viewed as too strenuous in high UAI cultures.

Considerable differences exist between countries with respect to private investments. In 1970 and 1991, owning stocks and shares was a characteristic of wealthy societies. This relationship had disappeared by 1999, when low uncertainty avoidance explained variance. In 2007 the percentages of people who said they had traded stocks in the past 12 months correlated with long-term orientation. Across Europe 59% of variance of owning shares or bonds was explained by IVR, and combined with low UAI and low MAS this was 81%. Interestingly both having a savings account and a mortgage loan were related to high IVR, which explained 71% and 55% of variance. Obviously a mortgage loan is viewed as saving as in the end the house is yours.[70]

Shopping and Buying Behavior

Shopping and buying behavior concerns shopping activities, shopping purposes, who does the shopping and with whom, shopping frequency, buyer–seller relationships, retail preferences, and influences on buying decisions. In addition to the conventional retail options there is the Internet, which has introduced a new dimension to buyer–seller relationships.

Shopping activities and purposes in addition to buying can be *searching, learning* about product availability and quality, *bargain hunting, price bargaining, spending money, recreation*, avoiding *boredom*, and *self-gratification* to overcome a depressive mood. Shopping to overcome a depressive mood is not a likely phenomenon in collectivistic cultures where people are not aware of any depressive moods (see Chapter 5). Searching and price bargaining are activities common in collectivistic cultures. Widespread haggling is an important aspect of Chinese shopping behavior. Searching includes comparing shops, prices, and thoroughly inspecting the products, including touching and smelling. Chinese traditional values – related to long-term orientation – emphasize thrift, diligence, and value consciousness, so it is socially desirable to save money and be a meticulous shopper in China.[71] In individualistic and short-term-oriented cultures, saving time and convenience are more important, because extensive search takes time away from more important activities.[72] Convenience needs of short-term-oriented cultures make shoppers want to buy grocery as quickly as possible.[73]

In collectivistic cultures an important shopping distinction is between public and private consumption goods. People are more price conscious for personal goods than for public goods. For members of collectivistic and high power distance cultures where people are status conscious, for public consumption goods, and particularly for gifts, social norms are more important than price. Spending money as such can be a social value, demonstrating allegiance to friends and family. As individualists are more likely than collectivists to seek 'fun' situations, fun shopping is typical individualistic behavior. Individualistic Americans, for example, are more recreational and informational shoppers than Chileans, who score a low 23 on the individualism index. Whereas Americans will go to the mall more to look and browse, Chileans will go for a specific purchase, with a plan to buy.[74]

The term *recreational* covers shopping as leisure activity, but in collectivistic cultures some shopping activities also are a social activity, both for grownups and young people, which is not exactly the same as recreation in the individualistic sense. Donquixote, a Japanese discount retail chain, decided to extend shopping hours in 2002 because young people out on dates were visiting the store late at night.[75] So recreational shopping may have different purposes in the United States and in Japan. In India shopping has become a leisure activity for urban nuclear family women. They love visiting various retail formats and comparing prices and bargaining.[76] In Malaysia, shopping malls offer all sorts of entertainment, like cinemas, bowling, ice skating, and other indoor entertainment, which makes visiting shopping malls a leisure activity.[77]

Both in the search and buying process social relationships between buyers and sellers vary among individualistic and collectivistic cultures. In collectivistic cultures buyers want a relationship with the seller and involve in-group members more than in individualistic cultures.

Triandis describes a high-involvement purchase in a collectivistic culture as follows:

> Consider the situation of buying a carpet for the house. Most individualists will shop around, will find one or two carpets that are within the price range they are willing to pay, and will consult one or two members of their family and buy the carpet. Most collectivists are likely to proceed in a more elaborate way. First, they are likely to establish a personal relationship with a storekeeper. Ideally, they will find a member of their kin group who sells carpets, or a friend of a member of the kinship group who does that. They will tell this person about their needs and give details of their income and family life. Having established trust with this merchant, they will examine the stock and find a number of carpets that may be suitable. They will then invite a large portion of their in-group to view the carpets and express their opinions. Finally, after extensive consultations, they will purchase the carpet. Whereas the individualist primarily has an exchange relationship with the merchant – I pay my money and receive the carpet – the collectivist fosters a personal relationship, allowing the merchant to learn a great deal in order to arrive at the best decision.[78]

The importance of in-group members doesn't imply that people always go shopping with their in-group members. Although teenagers may shop in groups when shopping as a leisure activity, for some purposes Chinese prefer to shop anonymously, attracting little community and extended family attention to avoid any resulting gossip and the risk of losing face. They prefer crowded places. The Chinese concept of *renao* – meaning lively, bustling with noise and excitement, opposite to a negative state of being alone – explains preference for crowded and noisy shopping places like markets.[79]

Living conditions influence shopping habits. Whereas in the United States or the United Kingdom, or even in France, people go to a mega-store once a week to do bulk buying, Japanese housewives make it their routine to visit a familiar nearby supermarket where their friends gather. One reason is the social influence; another is that refrigerators and storage space at Japanese homes are limited.[80] In Europe, in the individualistic and low uncertainty avoidance cultures, important influencing factors for food choice are convenience and availability.[81] People who work full-time will have fewer shopping time opportunities than people who work part-time, so it will influence the number of visits they make to the shop. In low power distance cultures, more women work part-time ($r = -.61^{***}$) than in high power distance cultures.[82] The degree of male–female role differences measured by the masculinity–femininity dimension explains why in some cultures more males do the shopping chores or fathers shop with their children.

Table 8.4 shows data that demonstrate how in masculine cultures women do more of the shopping and in the feminine cultures men also go shopping.

Table 8.4 **Shopping behavior**

	GNI/cap	PDI	IDV	MAS	UAI	LTO
Shopping						
Women's share of total time spent on shopping[1]			.83***	.72*		
Men's share of total time spent on shopping[1]			−.83***	−.72*		
Proportion of men who spend any time on shopping activities[1]	.62*			−.72*		
Buying grocery as quickly as possible[6]						−.53*
Young people in Asia who enjoy the fun of shopping[7]			.70**			

	GNI/cap	PDI	IDV	MAS	UAI	LTO
Mail order/Internet shopping						
Purchased goods by post, mail order[4]	.35*	−.39*	.43*		−.44*	.47**
Bought by post, phone, Internet[2]	.78***	−.55***	.58***		−.72***	
Bought via Internet[2]	.76***		.61***		−.66***	
Bought goods via Internet in past 12 months[4]	.71***	−.57***	.64***		−.67***	
Bought on Internet in the past month:[5]	.39*	−.44**	.43*			.33*
Grocery			−.33*	.39*		.64***
Event tickets	.51***	−.48***	.38*			−.43*
Video games, DVDs	.40***	−.56***	.61***			−.33*
Prefer shopping[2]			−.44*		.37*	
Percent individuals who ordered goods or services over the Internet last 12 months[8]	.81***	−.61***	.71***		−.73***	
Compared on Internet, did not buy[4]	.50**	−.45*	.54***	−.42*	−.71***	
Compared on Internet, bought in shop[4]	.65***	−.47*	.47**	−.45*	−.59***	
Online shopping 10–18 yrs old, Latin America[3]					−.87**	

SOURCES: Hofstede et al. (2010) (see Appendix A); 1) Eurostat 2002, *How Europeans Spend their Time*, 9 countries; 2) *Consumer Empowerment*, EBS 342, 2011, 25 countries; 3) Ibero-America Interactive Generation, 2008, 7 countries; 4) EBS 298, 2008, 25 countries; 5) Data Nielsen, 2007, 28 countries worldwide. In: Goodrich and De Mooij, 2010; 6) Future Foundation, *Trends in Clothes Shopping and Fashion*, 2009, Europe, 12 countries; 7) Synovate *Young Asians*, 2009, 12 countries; 8) Eurostat 2015, 28 countries (see Appendix B)

Other differences in buying behavior are between *planned buying* and *impulsive buying*. Impulsive buying is involved when a person has no intention to buy a product, yet buys it. A consumer can also intend to buy a product and decide only in the shop which brand to buy. A completely planned purchase occurs if both the product and the brand purchase were planned. If impulsive buying were related to the personality trait 'impulsiveness,' it should be correlated with strong uncertainty avoidance, but there is little evidence that impulsive buying is related to the overall personality trait impulsiveness. Impulsive buying is likely more related to thrill, variety, and sensation seeking as well as stimulation, traits that are related to individualism and low uncertainty avoidance. A comparison of impulsive buying behavior across five Western and Asian countries[83] showed that the individualistic emphasis on the self, individual needs, and desires encourage impulsive buying behavior.

Collectivistic notions of the self that emphasize interdependence, emotional control, and moderation tend to discourage impulse buying behavior. For a group of seven countries in Latin America[84] there is a relationship between low uncertainty avoidance and the percentages of answers 'Agree' to the question 'I often buy products on impulse' ($r = -.70^*$). Chileans tend to make more planned purchases than Americans, who rely more on spur-of-the-moment decisions.[85]

Out-of-Home Shopping and Buying

Next to the physical retail environment – also called *brick-and-mortar retailing* – there are various means for out-of-home shopping and buying: mail order, television shopping, and Internet shopping.

Mail order buying by catalogue has existed for a long time, and the Internet is partly a replacement of the printed catalogue. Internet shopping has not replaced brick-and-mortar shopping. Between 51% (Poland) and 81% (Hungary) of Europeans prefer shopping personally. These differences are not related to either income or culture. Variance of the percentages of people who purchased goods by post is explained by long-term orientation and low power distance. Across Europe there is a significant correlation between buying by mail and by Internet ($r = .57^{***}$),[86] so basically the Internet is a new medium for out-of-home shopping. Internet buying is, as yet, more commonplace in individualistic cultures of low uncertainty avoidance and low power distance (see Table 8.5). One would expect more out-of-home buying in rural areas than in cities with more physical shops available, but that is not the case. In 2016 Eurostat[87] presented cross-Europe differences in the proportions of individuals who bought goods and services over the Internet. For three categories the Internet was used more in the cities than in rural areas, except in the United Kingdom: for buying clothes and sports goods, films and books, or booking a travel or holiday accommodation.

Several studies show that the main driver of Internet shopping is income, but this has been declining. Across Europe the percentage of individuals who said in the last 12 months they had ordered goods or services over the Internet for private use[88], correlated most significantly with GNI/cap, but when controlled for income, low uncertainty avoidance was the most important variable.

What people buy online across cultures reflects differences of products or services people buy in regular stores. For example, more event tickets or video games are bought online in the individualistic cultures. The relationship between grocery buying via the Internet and long-term orientation and collectivism reflects historical habits of having grocery products delivered to the home in Asian countries.[89] The Internet offers the opportunity to compare products. Across Europe, in the individualistic, low uncertainty avoidance, and low power distance cultures where decision making is more information based, more people tend to search for information and compare products on the Internet even when they do not buy online or buy in the shop. In cultures scoring high on the long-term orientation dimension, people trust the typical literate Internet features, such as search engines and product reviews, whereas in the short-term oriented cultures, people have more trust in their family and friends.[90] As in collectivistic cultures social influences are more important than in individualistic cultures; social media sites are more used for making a purchase decision in collectivistic cultures than in individualistic cultures, as illustrated in Figure 8.8.

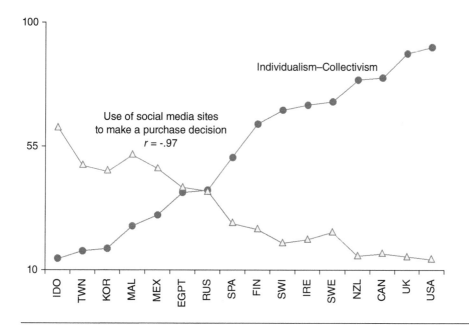

Figure 8.8   IDV–COL and use of social media

SOURCE: Data from Hofstede (2001) (see Appendix A); *Nielsen Global Online Consumer Survey 2010* (see Appendix B)

In low power distance and individualistic cultures people depend less on other people and base decision making more on facts and data, consciously gathering information throughout the decision-making process. Personal contacts serve more as a source of infor-mation, whereas in collectivistic and high power distance cultures, personal contacts tend to serve to form opinions, and people rely more on online forums and social media. In col-lectivistic and high power distance cultures, individual utility is less important than sharing with others, so new electronic media are used more for sharing ideas and opinions than for personal information search. People rely more on personal sources of recommendation, are more active opinion seekers, and are less active in information seeking via impersonal sources. In collectivistic cultures, social media also reinforce word-of-mouth communi-cation about products and brands. In China, the major influence on purchase decisions is word-of-mouth.[91] This is intensified by the various discussion opportunities offered by the Internet.

Also long-term orientation plays a role in understanding the differences. Consum-ers from short-term oriented cultures rely more on the human factor and prefer to get their information from people, whereas in long-term oriented cultures, consumers rely more on facts and data. Significant correlations were found between long-term orien-tation and both trust in search engines ($r = .50***$) and trust in online product reviews ($r = .41***$). Short-term orientation uniquely explains 36% of variance in trust in family. These cultural differences might also apply to various other online purchase decision sources.[92]

There is a variety of platforms that are used to access websites that help make a choice, but not all are equally preferred across cultures. An example is the mobile phone: the per-centage of people who do not use the mobile phone to browse shopping websites and apps correlates with short-term orientation.[93] Analysis of data from 43 countries showed that consumers' adoption and usage of mobile commerce services are influenced by different cultural dimensions. While uncertainty avoidance is a consistent predictor for the adoption of mobile commerce across different services, masculinity and indulgence seem to be the most important drivers of usage intensity for mobile shopping.[94]

Although online sales have been most pervasive in the United States, Chinese consumers, although relatively new to the Internet, are very active online shoppers and buyers. They are willing to make high-risk purchases (e.g., medical, health) and buy high-involvement prod-ucts such as cosmetics, beauty aids, and travel online.[95] In particular social networking helps them to make better comparisons,[96] and Chinese websites show collectivistic community activities like group buying that you find less on US websites.[97]

To many, Internet buying is still considered to be risky, so trust in the seller is import-ant. Across Europe, however, the identity of the supplier is of lesser importance than other influences, such as safety, the country of origin where the product was made, and the brand.[98] Several problems like insecurity and privacy are associated with online buying. A study among respondents from the United States, Canada, Germany, and Japan showed differences between countries with respect to concerns about payment security, company legitimacy, and assurance. The Japanese in particular note telephone follow-up as desirable because it is more personal than e-mail. In general people prefer local website design features.[99]

Retail Design

Because of shopping differences, retail design varies across countries with respect to the products offered, variety, shop design, product presentation, shopper behavior, personnel, and service. Consumer preferences for supermarkets or shopping centers vary, and these differences change only slowly over time.[100]

In collectivistic and high power distance cultures, freshness of food is very important. What is considered fresh varies. For the Dutch, prepacked cut lettuce is considered to be fresh, but not so for the Belgians, to whom fresh means you have to cut it yourself. A whole fish is fresh, not so some prepacked bits and pieces. In high uncertainty avoidance cultures, more product information is provided on the shelves. Personnel are better dressed and cleanliness is demonstrated, for example, by white floors and thongs or plastic gloves to pick fresh food products that you don't see so frequently in low uncertainty avoidance cultures.

Figure 8.9   **Delhaize, Belgium, and Albert Heijn, the Netherlands**

To symbolize freshness of food products or the offer of the day, handwritten information may be provided instead of well-designed, consistent printed information that cannot be produced instantaneously.

Figure 8.9 shows two in-store sales messages. The one on the left, which reads 'Suggestion from the Chef,' is from the Belgian supermarket Delhaize; the second one is from the Dutch supermarket Albert Heijn, and it says in a much more egalitarian way, 'What do we eat today?' The pictures also show how the Belgian supermarket communicates freshness by handwritten text, whereas consistency needs of the Dutch will always have everything printed with the right logo, colors, and type font.

A difference related to individualism and power distance is how products are categorized: by sort or by relationships or even by color, as discussed in Chapter 6. Belgian supermarkets tend to present more products by relationship, whereas in the Netherlands products are categorized by sort. Other differences are visual routing signs versus verbal routing signs.[101] In Belgium, personnel are presented by specialization and hierarchy, whereas in the Netherlands they wear the same uniform to suggest they are all equal. For shoppers in Belgium, it is clear by name and picture who is the manager. In the Netherlands, the manager doesn't make him- or herself known. In supermarkets in feminine cultures more men do food shopping, even with children. This influences the type of shopping carts offered to the public. In low power distance cultures where independence of children is important, small shopping carts are available for children so they can learn to shop independently.

> The IKEA formula is based on self-assembly, which is not attractive to high power distance cultures where people want service from human beings. However, IKEA offers total concepts – living rooms, bedrooms – which is attractive to collectivistic and high power distance cultures where people think more holistically. Although Russia scores high on power distance, IKEA is very successful in that country.

Several studies have highlighted the crucial role of retail employees in collectivist cultures. A study comparing what determines store patronage in China and Spain found that Chinese consumers emphasize the relationship with sales personnel in determining their store patronage.[102] Relationships between sales personnel and customers vary mostly with power distance.

Whereas service personnel in retail in the United States learn to be friendly and personal and present themselves at equal level with the customer by conducting some small talk, this is different in Asia. Consumers in Japan look to salespeople to explain a product's attributes without any direct messages. Communication is not personal and small talk can be perceived as artificial or even intrusive. Americans can find the Japanese emphasis on formality and hierarchy (with the retailer on a lower footing) cold.[103] Taiwanese consumers expect service personnel to perform tasks because they genuinely wish to gratify consumer preferences. Service personnel should be willing, enthusiastic, and respectful in fulfilling their service tasks, and Taiwanese consumers expect a genuine attitudinal regard for the 'master–servant relationship.' Giving and/or preserving a consumer's face is of great importance.[104] Figure 8.10 shows an example of courtesy to the customer in China.

Figure 8.10   **China: Courtesy to the customer. Photograph by Gerard Foekema**

TV sales channels follow cultural preferences and are analogous to department store shopping. In the United States discussions are personalized, and hosts address guests as friends. In Japan little emphasis is placed on any personal details, and each product is shown in detail with extreme close-ups. Conversations stay close to the product.[105]

> Because of differences in shopping behavior retail mergers and acquisitions often fail. There are little advantages of economies of scale because both the product offer and retail design have to be local. Dutch Ahold failed in Spain, British Boots failed in Japan, French Carrefour failed in Japan, British Marks & Spencer failed in continental Europe, German C & A failed in the United Kingdom, and British Tesco failed in Taiwan. One of the reasons of failure of the latter was unclear communication about Tesco's own brands. In Asia retail brands are viewed as cheap and poor quality.[106]

Not all countries have the large shopping malls that exist in the United States or some Asian countries. Across Europe the hypermarket format is not equally available in all countries. Hypermarket penetration is lowest in Austria (1%) and highest in Romania (31%). GNI/cap explains 50% of variance. Sales of total grocery products per capita from modern grocery retailers varies between 5,300 in Norway and 1,000 in Romania. The two explaining variables were high power distance and low masculinity that together explained 38% of variance.[107] In many Western countries a shopping center tends to have a variety of stores selling different product categories to a variety of consumers. In collectivistic cultures shops selling the same category are often located in one area to facilitate comparison and price negotiating. Motives for shopping in supermarkets also vary. Whereas in Western societies supermarkets are characterized by a large variety of packaged goods, in Thailand shoppers say they are attracted to supermarkets because of the quality of fresh food and the cleanliness. Because of the importance of fresh food, wet markets continue to dominate shopping behavior in Thailand.[108] Also in the south of Europe, fresh food markets are popular. In Spain only 40% of food is bought in the supermarket, as compared with 59% in the rest of Europe. Across Europe other retailing types vary with consumer preferences. In Germany 'hard discounters' like Aldi and Lidl have a far bigger market share than in other European countries. They account for around 30% of food sales, as compared with only 10% that such firms have in Britain and 8% in France.[109] The degree to which supermarkets offer products under private label varies with individualism. In collectivistic cultures private label products are less popular because they don't contribute to upholding face (see also Chapter 5).

Complaining Behavior

Consumer complaining behavior can be classified into three categories: (1) voice response to the party directly involved in the complaint; (2) negative word of mouth or brand switching; (3) legal action.[110] With varying concepts of self, perceptions of others, and levels of social activity, consumers across cultures are likely to vary with respect to these three types of responses. Because of harmony needs, collectivistic consumers, compared with individualists, are relatively loyal and are less likely to voice complaints when they experience post-purchase problems. They are more likely than individualists to engage in negative word of mouth to in-group members. Moreover, when collectivists do exit, it is particularly difficult for the offending supplier to regain them as customers.[111] There is evidence that compared with Australians the Chinese are less likely to lodge a formal complaint for a faulty product.[112] Consumers in individualistic cultures tend to demand redress and practice speaking to others about their dissatisfaction, but less so speak to the firm itself, whereas collectivists would avoid the product or might inform the firm of their dissatisfaction.[113] American consumers may view complaining as a positive reflection on themselves, Koreans view it as a negative reflection, so they prefer to keep it private.[114]

Across Europe the percentages of people who say they have made any kind of formal complaint by writing, by telephone or in person, to a seller or provider in the past 12 months vary from 4% in Bulgaria to 25% in the Netherlands. The differences are correlated with GNI per capita, individualism, and low uncertainty avoidance. The percentages of people who took no further action when the complaint was not dealt with in a satisfactory manner varied from 38% in Denmark to 84% in Romania. These differences are related to high power distance and collectivism.[115]

A phenomenon that may only work in collectivistic cultures is a boycott of products. Chinese consumers nowadays are increasingly using boycotts to express their discontent with foreign brands. In 2005 there was a nationwide boycott of Japanese brands after the Japanese prime minister refused to cancel his worship of Yasukini Juja, the burial place of the most notorious Japanese war criminals of the Second World War.[116]

An aspect of American culture is the frequent use of legal action. It may be related to the configuration individualism and masculinity, which makes people want to get the most out of life. This explains the high use of litigation in the United States. Also consumers will take more legal action. For years the cigarette industry has been sued for damaging smokers' health. In 2002 in the United States, obese people even started suing fast food chains, holding them responsible for their gaining weight.

Fear of legal action has made many companies in the United States and the United Kingdom include all sorts of warnings on label instructions on consumer goods. On a bar of Dial soap: 'Directions: Use like regular soap.' On a Sears hair dryer: 'Do not use while sleeping.' On packaging for a Rowenta iron: 'Do not iron clothes on body.' On Nytol sleep aid: 'Warning: May cause drowsiness.' On a child's Superman costume: 'Wearing of this garment does not enable you to fly.' On Sainsbury's peanuts: 'Warning: Contains nuts.' On Marks & Spencer bread pudding: 'Product will be hot after heating.' On Boot's child's cough medicine: 'Do not drive a car or operate machinery after taking this medication.' On a toner cartridge of a photocopying machine: 'Do not eat.'

Service firms are especially susceptible to cultural influences because of the high level of interaction. Some marketing philosophies – in particular the 'Customer is King' philosophy – do not travel well across cultures. In particular in cultures high on power distance customers may feel superior in social hierarchy compared to the service providers, and develop a sense of entitlement that infringes on the rights of the service providers. Other examples are of individualistic cultures that score low on power distance and high on uncertainty avoidance where customers have higher quality expectations. Collectivists of high uncertainty avoidance do not easily complain or switch after poor service.[117] A study comparing company executives' judgments of various service quality aspects in the United States and Chile found that in both countries reliability and responsiveness were the most important dimensions of service quality, but reliability was found to be more important in Chile and responsiveness in the United States.[118]

Brand Loyalty

Conformance and harmony needs make collectivists relatively brand loyal. Purchasing products that are well known to the in-group may help to decrease uncertainty about in-group approval of the purchase.[119] Choosing a brand other than the group members' brand or changing brands distinguishes a person from the group. It is preferable to choose the popular or perceived popular brands. This will be reinforced by uncertainty avoidance. Trying a new product or brand involves the willingness to change, and it may also satisfy a variety-seeking motive.[120] Variety seeking and stimulation are elements of individualistic cultures. Change, on the other hand, may cause unexpected results, which is less desired in high uncertainty avoidance cultures.

There is little fundamental cross-cultural research on brand loyalty. The 1991 Frontiers[121] study by the Henley Center, conducted in Germany, the Netherlands, Italy, United Kingdom, France, and Spain, asked people of several age categories whether they would replace their car with one of the same brand. For the age group 45–59 years, this study showed a significant relationship between brand loyalty for cars and cultural masculinity ($r = .90^{***}$). Data for seven countries worldwide by the market research agency TGI[122] show a relationship between the wish to stick to a brand and long-term orientation. These findings must be viewed as indicative only, as the number of countries surveyed is limited. Data from *Reader's Digest* surveys seem to confirm the relationship with long-term orientation in view of the relationships between short-term orientation and the percentages of people who say they are among the first to try new brands. In 2005, short-term orientation explained 40% of variance.[123]

Analysis of mean switching rates for service providers of all sorts of services (banking, insurance, telecom, energy, etc.) in 2009 showed for the average of all services across 25 European countries correlations with high GNI per capita, low power distance, and low uncertainty avoidance. Also across 18 of the richest countries wealth explains variance. Maybe at that time mainly the rich countries had better switching facilities for services like energy, banking, and Internet.[124] Yet, in 2016 the percentages of people who changed providers mainly correlated with low uncertainty avoidance. For changing providers of one's current bank account the correlation was significant, but weak ($r = -.37^*$). For other financial services the relationships were stronger. Variance of changing provider of one's savings account was explained by low uncertainty avoidance and low masculinity together (39%), for credit card and car insurance by low uncertainty avoidance (respectively 22% and 28%).[125]

Generally the concept of brand loyalty may vary with different brand types, like product brands or company brands. It makes a difference if one is loyal to a product brand, to a store, or to a company.

Large power distance implies respect for the status quo, the 'proper place' of the power brand, the brand with the highest market share. In Asia, big market share brands are the kings of their 'brand world,' and consumers in Asia believe in them implicitly.[126] This is the reason brands like Coca-Cola, Nescafé, and San Miguel have such high and sustained market shares in a number of Asian countries. Being big automatically promotes trust. This trust, combined with harmony and conformance needs of collectivistic cultures, leads to high brand loyalty. Consequently, it will be difficult for new entrants in these markets to gain market share.

Sales of private label products have remained relatively low in high power distance cultures, but has now been growing, in particular in these cultures. Examples are Russia, Indonesia and Argentina. In Europe, in particular for cleaners, branded product growth has been higher than private label growth.[127]

Brand credibility is an important motive for brand loyalty in collectivistic and high uncertainty avoidance cultures.[128] For consumers in East Asian cultures, the reputation of the firm contributes to customer loyalty more than in individualistic and low uncertainty avoidance cultures.[129] This is particularly important for e-commerce, when customers don't have personal contacts as they do in shops.

Companies develop loyalty programs to increase customers' repeat purchase behavior. Cultural differences significantly influence consumer loyalty program choice. For example, consumers from collectivistic cultures of high power distance prefer loyalty programs that offer related rewards, whereas consumers from countries low in uncertainty avoidance and masculinity prefer unrelated rewards.[130]

Adoption and Diffusion of Innovations

Understanding why and how fast people adopt new products and the differences across countries is important for marketers because new product success is linked to profitability. Consumer innovativeness can be defined as the predisposition to buy new and different products and brands rather than remain with previous choices and consumption patterns.[131] As innovativeness is related to tolerance for ambiguity and deviant ideas, members of weak uncertainty avoidance cultures are more innovative than are members of strong uncertainty avoidance cultures, and new products take off faster. Several studies have demonstrated the relationship between uncertainty avoidance and consumer innovativeness[132] and new product take-off across wealthy countries.[133] High power distance and high uncertainty avoidance are found to hinder the acceptance of new products, so in these cultures it takes longer for new products to penetrate. Individualism has a positive effect because initiating new behavior independently from others is a characteristic of innovativeness.

It is best not to view innovativeness as a general disposition, but to distinguish between consumers' general innovativeness and domain-specific innovativeness as motives for innovativeness vary by product category.[134] For example, there are differences between technological and design innovations. Adoption of the former are related to the dimensions high uncertainty avoidance and indulgence, adoption of the latter to individualism and indulgence.[135]

Lynn and Gelb[136] also found that innovativeness is domain specific. They developed an index of national innovativeness based on ownership of a number of consumer electronics, which was found to be significantly correlated with individualism, low uncertainty avoidance, and purchasing power. However, they also found that consumers who are likely to adopt the latest new product in one field may be laggards in another. Adoption of one new product reinforces adoption of others in the same category. New product innovators will be drawn from the heavy users of other products within the product category.[137] This also applies to the culture level.

Rogers[138] identified five categories of (American) consumers according to the degree of acceptance of new products. They are called innovators, early adopters, early majority, late majority, and laggards. The *innovators* represent 2.5% of (American) society; they are described as venturesome individuals who are willing to take risks. *Early adopters* (13.5%) are the ones to take up new ideas that are taken up by the innovators who serve as role model. *Early majority* (34%) are risk avoiders; *late majority* (34%) are skeptical and cautious of new ideas; and *laggards* (16%) are very traditional. A two-category distinction is between *innovators* and *imitators*. Figure 8.11 illustrates the curve.

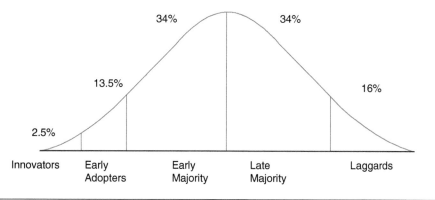

Figure 8.11   **Adoption of innovations, United States**

Steenkamp[139] calculated percentages of adoption categories for packaged goods in five countries in Europe (see Table 8.5). These were based on household panel data on the occurrence and timing of first purchases for 239 new consumer packaged goods over a 52-week period after introduction for a large sample of consumers. Correlations with the cultural variables confirm the relationships with uncertainty avoidance and individualism. The category innovators for the five European countries plus the United States is correlated with low uncertainty avoidance and individualism, whereas the category late majority is correlated with high uncertainty avoidance and collectivism.

Table 8.5   **Adopter categories across countries**

	Innovators (%)	Early Majority (%)	Late Majority (%)	Laggards (%)
United States	16.0	34.0	34.0	16.0
United Kingdom	23.8	43.4	26.4	6.4
France	15.1	25.5	35.6	23.8
Germany	16.8	26.1	34.2	22.9
Spain	8.9	34.1	43.9	13.1
Italy	13.4	30.8	41.0	14.8
Correlation coefficients				
IDV	.75*		−.74*	
UAI	−.83*		.83*	

SOURCES: Rogers (1962); J.B. Steenkamp, *Global Consumers*, presentation at Tilburg University (17 November 2002). Based on *Consumer and Market Drivers of the Trial Probability of New Consumer Packaged Goods*, working paper

Also, in Latin America, where all countries are high on uncertainty avoidance, the percentages of early adopters tends to be lower than in the United States. A Target Group Index (TGI) study in Chile found that 7.5% of the average population could be viewed as early adopters of technological innovations.[140]

Diffusion is the process by which an innovation is communicated through certain channels over time among the members of a social system. The channels are the mass media and word-of-mouth communication. The *adoption rate* is the relative speed with which members of a social system adopt an innovation. New products diffuse at significantly different rates in different countries. For example, in the United States new products diffuse more slowly than in Asia or Europe, but also across Europe there are differences.[141] In Japan, a collectivistic culture of high uncertainty avoidance, adoption of new ideas and products takes long, but the need for conformity leads to fast diffusion as soon as opinion leaders have taken the lead. Cultures of low uncertainty avoidance in Asia adopt innovations faster. Analysis of adoption rates of Japanese, Chinese, Korean, and American consumers showed that the Japanese (high uncertainty avoidance) are cautious until the facts about a novel product are known, whereas the Chinese (low uncertainty avoidance) are the least cautious.[142] A study across 13 European countries found a relationship between diffusion rates of technological innovations with high power distance, collectivism, and masculinity. The explanation was that in these cultures more interpersonal communication causes faster diffusion, and power holders serve as opinion leaders.[143] The measurement and comparison of diffusion across cultures is difficult, because diffusion rates must be compared over longer time periods. The most difficult problem of time-series research across countries is the availability and accuracy of data. If available at all, early data may not be accurate and/or not comparable with later data.

Several studies have used the *coefficients of innovation* (p) and *imitation* (q) developed by Bass[144] to measure the effects of the media on diffusion of innovations.

The Bass model predicts the spread of innovation, the number of adopters of a new product, and at which time they will adopt it. It assumes that there are two groups in the diffusion process: the innovators and imitators, and two ways a new product diffuses: via the mass media and word-of-mouth. The model is based on Western practice where the innovators are the first ones to buy a product and are mainly affected by the media or advertising. The effects of these influences are captured by the coefficient of innovation, p. The imitators are influenced by their peers and are mainly influenced by word-of-mouth, whose effect is captured by the coefficient of imitation, q. Diffusion occurs within a system and therefore is a culture-specific phenomenon. The coefficient of innovation is high in countries that are high on individualism, low on uncertainty avoidance, and low on power distance. The coefficient of imitation is high in countries that are low on individualism (word-of-mouth communication is strong) and high on uncertainty avoidance.[145]

Takada and Jain,[146] who have conducted several studies on diffusion of innovations, believed that the coefficient of imitation would represent cross-country differences more clearly and distinctly than the coefficient of innovation, because the latter represents small parts of populations of any country. The innovators are a relatively small segment in the market, and they play a rather limited role in diffusing the innovation to other segments. The imitators, in contrast, play the major role in diffusion of innovations in the marketplace and are a substantially larger segment.

An important conclusion is that culturally similar countries have similar diffusion patterns. Some countries, for some products, will be leaders while others lag. As a result of global media, there is a learning effect between leading and lagging countries. Consumers in a lag country can potentially learn about the benefits of a product from the experience of adopters in the lead country, and this learning can result in a faster diffusion rate in the lag markets.[147] For industrial new products, the learning effect is substantial. It took 17 years for the adoption of scanners (in retail) to peak in the United States, whereas it peaked much faster in the lag markets. Within Europe, the adoption peaked in 9 years in Germany and Belgium, where it was introduced in 1980, whereas in Denmark and Spain it peaked within 4 years, where it was introduced in 1986.[148]

Culture also influences the development of new products. In the new product development process, two stages are important: initiation and implementation. Cultures whose strengths center on initiation are high in individualism but low in power distance, masculinity, and uncertainty avoidance. Cultures whose strengths center on implementation are low in individualism but high in power distance, masculinity, and uncertainty avoidance.[149]

Predicting Market Development Across Cultures

Understanding the role of culture can lead to better predictions of how markets will develop, and new products and services diffuse and thus help develop marketing strategy. Although in some cultures people adopt a new innovation or habit quickly, people of other cultures may not. Let's take the Internet as an example. At the end of the twentieth century, expectations were that the Internet would cause greater productivity everywhere and make all societies more egalitarian. Instead, people have adopted it for their specific culturally defined purposes.

For better predictions, countries can be mapped according to cultural similarity. An example is a culture map for the development and effects of the Internet. The Internet first penetrated the economically developed markets of low to medium uncertainty avoidance where people adopt innovations faster than in markets of high uncertainty avoidance. These markets are in the lower two quadrants in Figure 8.12.

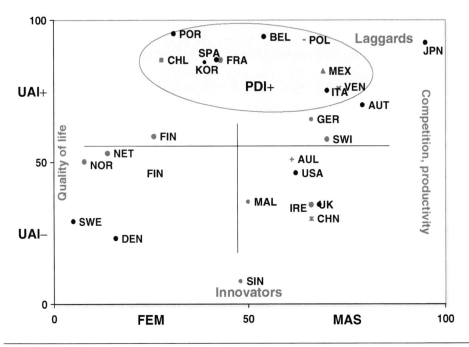

Figure 8.12 **Mapping cultures for the Internet**

SOURCE: Data Hofstede et al. (2010) (see Appendix A)

In the upper two quadrants of Figure 8.12 are the lagging markets, the high uncertainty avoidance cultures. When the Internet became more common in all developed markets, purposes of usage varied. Whereas in the low masculine markets people have adopted the Internet to enhance the quality of life, using it more frequently, and more for leisure and educational purposes, in the high masculine markets the Internet was initially and most importantly expected to enhance productivity for greater competitiveness.

A third dimension that explains variance of adoption rates is power distance. In the high power distance cultures, governments can exert greater power to influence new developments. In France the government had an early influence on information technology by backing the Minitel system. In Spain the government pushed Internet usage by sponsoring its use in schools. In South Korea the government has pushed broadband communications. As a result, already in 2001 South Koreans spent more time online than the people of any other nation in the world, which also had a beneficial effect on the Korean economy.[150] South Korea is one of the countries with the highest broadband penetration in the world.

Conclusion

This chapter showed that differences exist between countries with respect to ownership and usage of many products. Many data on product consumption, ownership, and usage are available in the public domain and can be submitted to correlation and regression analysis to understand the differences. This chapter provided many examples of how culture explains variance. Many differences are stable over time, and with increased wealth the relationships between GNI per capita and the various cultural dimensions change. In particular, new technology shows different patterns over time. Whereas generally national income combined with low uncertainty avoidance explains variance of new products first, after some time, when new products have penetrated, other dimensions explain variance of usage.

Several aspects of buying and shopping behavior are related to culture. The different concepts of self are reflected in shopping activities and motives. Whether people complain and how they complain is mainly related to individualism and collectivism. The diffusion-of-innovations process and the adopter categories defined by Rogers are based on American culture. Although similar adopter categories do exist across cultures, the distribution across populations varies by culture, and so do the rates of diffusion.

Notes

1. J.P. Peter, J.C. Olson, and K.G. Grunert, *Consumer Behaviour and Marketing Strategy*, European edn (McGraw-Hill, London, 1999), p. 19.
2. Cigarettes as a category in the 2nd edition was deleted in this edition. Various government measures to prevent smoking tobacco such as high taxes or smoking bans will cause biased results.
3. F.M. Magrabi, Y.S. Chung, S.S. Cha, S.J. Yang, *The Economics of Household Consumption* (Praeger, New York, 1991), pp. 210–234, 245–248.
4. *Risk Issues* (Special Eurobarometer report 238, 2005).
5. S. Askegaard and T.K. Madsen, *European Food Cultures: An Exploratory Analysis of Food Consumption in European Regions*, MAPP working paper no. 26 (September 1995). Available at: http://130.226.203.239/pub/mapp/wp/wp26.pdf (accessed 18 December 2009).
6. D. Singh, *Cross Cultural Comparison of Buying Behavior in India*, Doctoral thesis (University Business School, Panjab University, Chandigarh, 2007).
7. A. Nagorski, 'Hold the French fries,' *Newsweek* (26 February 2001), pp. 50–51.
8. T. Talhelm, X. Zhang, and S. Oishi, 'Moving chairs in Starbucks: Observational studies find rice-wheat cultural differences in daily life in China,' *Science Advances*, 4, 4 (2018), eaap8469.
9. Data Euromonitor (1997).

10. www.confectionerynews.com.

11. *TGI Product Book* (2009); *TGI Product Usage Guide* (2013), 45 countries worldwide. TGI data are of usage of a product category, not volume, which results in indications of relationships that in some cases are different from correlations with volumes.

12. *TGI Product Book* (2009). 41 countries worldwide; *TGI Product Usage Guide* (2013), 45 countries worldwide.

13. *Social Indicators* (Eurostat, 1980).

14. Euromonitor (1997).

15. *Europeans, Agriculture and the CAP* (Special Eurobarometer report 473, 2018).

16. Euromonitor (1997).

17. *Consumers in Europe* (Eurostat, 2001), p. 73.

18. *TGI Product Usage Guide* (2013).

19. Data on fresh coffee consumption 1998–2008 from Sara Lee/Douwe Egberts, courtesy of Leo van Deutekom.

20. *TGI Product Usage Guide* (2013).

21. G. Edmondson, 'Basta with the venti frappuccinos,' *BusinessWeek* (7 August 2006), pp. 42–43.

22. G.O. Rettenbacher, 'Vienna's café culture,' *Newsweek* (8 January 2007), Letters, p. 8.

23. *Status Report on Alcohol* (World Health Organization, 2004). Available at: www.who.int/sunstance_abuse/publications/global_status_report_2004_overview.pdf (accessed 18 December 2009).

24. *Health, Beauty and Personal Grooming*, a global Nielsen report (March 2007). Available at: www.acnielsen.com (accessed 30 December 2007)

25. *TGI Product Usage Guide* (2013).

26. Information from Vivek Gupta, Sr. Vice President Brand Science, IMRB International, Bangalore, India.

27. C. Mortished, 'Sorry, Asia, you smell: The not-so-subtle sales ploy as Unilever scents profits,' *Timesonline* (26 May 2008).

28. *Trends in Clothes-Shopping and Fashion-Following* (Future Foundation, London, 2009).

29. *Consumers in Europe* (2001), p. 96.

30. M. Cleveland, J.I. Rojas-Méndez, M. Laroche, and N. Papadopoulos, 'Identity, culture, dispositions and behavior: A cross-national examination of globalization and culture change,' *Journal of Business Research*, 69 (2016), pp. 1090–1102.

31. Story and illustration courtesy of Eun Jee Hyun, student Master of Retail Design at the Willem de Kooning Academy, Rotterdam, the Netherlands (Autumn 2009).

32. *TGI Product Book* (2009).

33. *TGI Product Usage Guide* (2013).

34. *Consumers in Europe* (2001), p. 135.

35. *TGI Product Usage Guide* (2013).

36. *E-Communications Household Survey* (EBS362, 2011).

37. *Structure of Consumption* (Eurostat, 2009).

38. Ofcom (2016).

39. C. Praet (personal communication, January 2003).

40. Ofcom (2016).
41. G. Graziella, as quoted from the *Corriere della Sera*. Translated in *NRC Handelsblad* (18 January 2003), p. 4.
42. S. Levy, 'The next new thing,' *Newsweek* (17 December 2001), pp. 60–63.
43. Y. Cai, 'Design strategies for global products,' *Design Management Journal* (Fall 2001), pp. 59–64.
44. 'The origins of Vertu,' *The Economist* (22 February 2003), pp. 66–67.
45. 'The local touch,' *The Economist* (8 March 2003), p. 62.
46. Data 1991 *Reader's Digest*; data 1999 EMS.
47. *World Development Indicators* (2006). Number of passenger cars per 1,000 population. For 48 countries worldwide, GNI/capita explains 72% of variance, but for 25 countries with GNI/capita over US$20,000, individualism explains 37% of variance. TGI data of 2013 for 48 countries worldwide also show a significant correlation with IDV ($r = .62^{***}$).
48. K. Naughton, 'Three for the road,' *Newsweek* (15 December 2003), p. 40.
49. *European Media and Marketing Survey* (Synovate, 2007). 15 countries. One car in the household correlates with low uncertainty avoidance, low power distance, and low masculinity. Low uncertainty avoidance explains 46% of variance with low masculinity explaining another 19%. High power distance explains variance of having two cars in the household. Variance of more than three cars in the household is explained by GNI/capita (50%), and an additional 17% is explained by masculinity.
50. P.S.H. Leeflang and W.F. Van Raaij, 'The changing consumer in the European Union: A "meta-analysis",' *International Journal of Research in Marketing*, 12 (1995), pp. 373–387.
51. *European Value Study*, 2005.
52. *European Social Reality* (Special Eurobarometer report 273, 2007).
53. *TNS Digital World* (2010), 16 countries.
54. L. Barzini, *The Italians* (Penguin Books, London, 1964), p. 111.
55. *Survey on the Attitudes of Europeans Towards Tourism* (Flash Eurobarometer report 258, 2009), 25 countries.
56. *Reader's Digest* (1991).
57. EMS (1999, 2007).
58. *Survey on the Attitudes of Europeans Towards Tourism*.
59. Data UNESCO (1992), Europe, 12 countries.
60. Data courtesy of Pets International, Netherlands. For 23 countries worldwide with GNI/capita > US$15,000, 2005. Cats per 1,000 people IDV: $r = .59^{***}$; dogs per 1,000 people PDI: $r = .42^{*}$.
61. A.C.W. Chui and C.C.Y. Kwok, 'National culture and life insurance consumption,' *Journal of International Business Studies*, 39 (2008), pp. 88–101.
62. R. Serrano, R. Saltman, and M-J. Yeh, 'Laws on filial support in four Asian countries,' *Bulletin World Health Organization*, 95,11 (2018), pp. 788–790.
63. A. Treerattanapun, *The Impact of Culture on Non-Life Insurance Consumption*, Wharton Research Scholars Project (2011). Available at: http://repository.upenn.edu/wharton_research_scholars/78.
64. *Views on Financial Services* (Eurobarometer report 56, December 2001).

65. R. Dobbs, A. Grant, and J. Woetzel, 'Unleashing the Chinese consumer,' *Newsweek* (14 September 2009), pp. 42–44.

66. *Financial Products and Services* (EBS 446, 2016).

67. *TGI Product Usage Guide* (2013).

68. *Financial Products and Services* (EBS 446, 2016).

69. Ibid.

70. Ibid.

71. Y. Cai, 'Investigating the relationship between personal values and mall shopping behavior: A generation cohort study on the new generation of Chinese and their previous generation,' in E. Howard (ed.), *Proceedings of the Fourth Asia Pacific Retail Conference* (Said Business School, Oxford and Manidol University, Bangkok, 4–6 September 2007), pp. 62–87.

72. D. Ackerman and G. Tellis, 'Can culture affect prices? A cross-cultural study of shopping and retail prices,' *Journal of Retailing*, 77 (2001), pp. 57–82.

73. *Trends in Clothes-Shopping and Fashion-Following*. 12 countries, LTO: $r = -.53^*$.

74. J.A.F. Nicholls, T. Mandakovic, F. Li, S. Roslow, and C.J. Kranendonk, 'Are US shoppers different from Chilean? A comparative study of shopping behaviors across countries,' in *Proceedings of the Seventh Cross-Cultural Consumer and Business Studies Research Conference* (1999). Available at: http://marketing.byu.edu /htmlpages/ccrs/proceedings99/nicholls.htm (accessed 9 July 2010).

75. G. Botting, 'Buyers be wares – shopping consumes Japan,' *The Japan Times* (23 May 2002). Available at: www.japantimes.co (accessed 16 September 2002).

76. A. Mishra and R. Vishas, 'Classification and store affiliation of Indian retail consumers: A case study with Bangalore women,' in *Proceedings of the Fifth Conference on Retailing in Asia Pacific* (Institute for Enterprise, The Hong Kong Polytechnic University, and Oxford Institute of Retail Management, 25–27 August 2009), pp. 248–274.

77. Y. Kamarulzaman and A. Madun, 'Attracting patrons to shopping malls: A case of Malaysia,' in *Proceedings of the Fifth Conference on Retailing in Asia Pacific* (25–27 August 2009), pp. 174–185.

78. H. Triandis, *Individualism and Collectivism* (Westview, Boulder, CO, 1995), p. 8.

79. C.A. Warden, S.C.T. Huang, T.C. Liu, and W.Y. Wu, 'Global media, local metaphor: Television shopping and marketing-as-relationship in America, Japan, and Taiwan,' *Journal of Retailing*, 84, 1 (2008), pp. 119–129.

80. M. Tanikawa, 'French supermarket struggles to fit in,' *International Herald Tribune* (5 October 2001). Available at: www.iht.com.

81. *Risk Issues* (2005).

82. OECD data (2001).

83. J. Kacen and J.A. Lee, 'The influence of culture on consumer impulsive buying behavior,' *Journal of Consumer Psychology*, 2 (2002), pp. 163–176.

84. Argentina, Brazil, Chile, Colombia, Mexico, Peru, Venezuela. *Source*: TGI, 2001.

85. Nicholls et al., 'Are US shoppers different from Chilean?'

86. *Consumer Protection in the Internal Market* (Special Eurobarometer report 298, 2008), 25 countries.

87. *Digital Economy and Society* (Eurostat regional yearbook, 2017).

88. Eurostat, 2015–2016

89. K. Goodrich and M. De Mooij, 'New technology mirrors old habits: Online buying mirrors cross-national variance of conventional buying,' *Journal of International Consumer Marketing*, 23, 3-4 (2011), pp. 246–295.

90. K. Goodrich and M. De Mooij, 'How "social" are social media? A cross-cultural comparison of online and offline purchase decision influences,' *Journal of Marketing Communications*, 20 (2013), pp. 103–116.

91. D.E. Schultz and M.P. Block, 'Understanding Chinese media audiences: An exploratory study of Chinese consumers media consumption and a comparison with the USA,' in H. Li, S. Huang, and D. Jin (eds), *Proceedings of the 2009 American Academy of Advertising Asia-Pacific Conference* (American Academy of Advertising, in conjunction with China Association of Advertising of Commerce, and Communication University of China, 2009).

92. Goodrich and De Mooij, 'How "social" are social media?'

93. Ofcom (2016).

94. T. Mandler, R. Seifert, C-M. Wellbrock, L. Knuth, and R. Kunz, *The Impact of National Culture on Mobile Commerce Adoption and Usage Intensity*, proceedings of the 51st Hawaii International Conference on System Sciences (2018). Available at: http://hdl.handle.net/10125/50347.'

95. H. Kwak, G.M. Zinkhan, Y. Pan, and T.L. Andras, 'Consumer communications, media use, and purchases via the Internet: A comparative, exploratory study,' *Journal of International Consumer Marketing*, 20, 3–4 (2008), pp. 55–68.

96. L.M. Maddox and W. Gong, 'Online buying decisions in China,' in H. Li, S. Huang, and D. Jin (eds), *Proceedings of the 2009 American Academy of Advertising Asia-Pacific Conference* (American Academy of Advertising, in conjunction with China Association of Advertising of Commerce, and Communication University of China, 2009), p. 261.

97. H. Ahn, M.W. Kwon, and L. Yuan, L. (2009). 'When talking about global brands in cyberspace, cultural-free or cultural-bound? A cross-cultural study of the US and Chinese brand community web sites,' in H. Li, S. Huang, and D. Jin (eds), *Proceedings of the 2009 American Academy of Advertising Asia-Pacific Conference* (American Academy of Advertising, in conjunction with China Association of Advertising of Commerce, and Communication University of China, 2009), p.117.

98. *Consumer Protection in the Internet Market* (Special Eurobarometer report 298, 2008).

99. D. Cyr, C. Bonanni, J. Ilsever, and J. Bowes, *Trust and Design: A Cross-Cultural Comparison* (ACM Conference on Universal Usability, Vancouver, BC, 2003).

100. V. Severin, J.J. Louviere, and A. Finn, 'The stability of retail shopping choices over time and across countries,' *Journal of Retailing*, 77 (2001), pp. 185–202.

101. These are examples of findings by students of the Master of Retail Design at the Willem de Kooning Academy at Rotterdam, 2006, 2007, 2008, and 2009. They compared the Dutch supermarket Albert Heijn and the Belgian supermarket Delhaize, of the same size in similar neighborhoods.

102. G. Kan, G. Cliquet, and M. Puelles Gallo, 'The effect of country image on hypermarket patronage intention. A cross-cultural study in China and Spain,' *International Journal of Retail & Distribution Management*, 42, 2 (2014), pp. 106-130.

103. Warden et al., 'Global media, local metaphor.'

104. B.B. Imrie, J.W. Cadogan, and G. Durden, 'The Confucian relational ethic: Respecifying the role of relational norms within service quality evaluation,' *Visionary Marketing for the 21st Century: Facing the Challenge* (ANZMAC, Melbourne, 2000), pp. 574–579.

105. Warden et al., 'Global media, local metaphor.'

106. C.W. Ho and J. Temperley, 'Consumers' reactions to Tesco's market entry in Taiwan. A comparison with the UK experience. Attracting patrons to shopping malls: A case of Malaysia,' in *Proceedings of the Fifth Conference on Retailing in Asia Pacific* (25–27 August 2009), pp. 24–50.

107. *European Grocery Retailing* (Data PlanetRetail, 2014). Data 2013, 28 countries.

108. 'Shopping habits die hard in Thailand,' *Insights Asia Pacific*, 92 (April 2000), p. 11.

109. 'German retailing: Cheap and cheerless,' *The Economist* (2 September 2000), pp. 65–66.

110. P. Chelminski, 'The effects of individualism and collectivism on consumer complaining behavior,' *Proceedings of the Eighth Cross-Cultural Research Conference*, Kahuku, Hawaii (2001).

111. H.S. Watkins and R. Liu, 'Collectivism, individualism and in-group membership: Implications for consumer complaining behaviors in multicultural contexts,' in L.A. Manrai and A.K. Manrai (eds), *Global Perspectives in Cross-Cultural and Cross-National Consumer Research* (International Business Press/Haworth Press, New York/London, 1996), pp. 69–76.

112. A.C.T. Lowe and D.R. Corkindale, 'Differences in "cultural values" and their effects on responses to marketing stimuli: A cross-cultural study between Australians and Chinese from the People's Republic of China,' *European Journal of Marketing*, 32 (1998), pp. 843–867.

113. O. Chapa, M.D. Hernandez, Y.J. Wang, and C. Skalski, 'Do individualists complain more than collectivists? A four-country analysis of consumer complaint behavior,' *Journal of International Consumer Marketing*, 26 (2014), pp. 373–390.

114. P. Sharma, R. Marshall, P.A. Reday, and W. Na, 'Complainers vs. non-complainers: A multinational investigation of individual and situational influences on customer complaint behavior,' *Journal of Marketing Management*, 26, 1-2 (2010), pp. 163–180.

115. *Consumer Protection in the Internal Market*.

116. F. Liu, A. Kanso, W.W. Wang, and X. Li, 'Negative emotions, attribution, and attitudes towards boycotting a foreign brand in China,' in H. Li, S. Huang, and D. Jin (eds), *Proceedings of the 2009 American Academy of Advertising Asia-Pacific Conference* (American Academy of Advertising, in conjunction with China Association of Advertising of Commerce, and Communication University of China, 2009), p. 48.

117. C.S. Kim and P. Aggarwal, 'The customer is king: Culture-based unintended consequences of modern marketing,' *Journal of Consumer Marketing*, 33, 3 (2016), pp. 193–201.

118. R. Guesalaga and D. Pitta, 'The importance and formalization of service quality dimensions: A comparison of Chile and the USA,' *Journal of Consumer Marketing*, 31, 2 (2014), pp. 145–151.

119. J.A. Lee, 'Adapting Triandis' model of subjective culture and social behavior relations to consumer behavior,' *Journal of Consumer Psychology*, 2 (2000), pp. 117–126. Countries studied were Australia, United States, Hong Kong, Singapore, and Malaysia.

120. H. Baumgartner and J.-B.E.M. Steenkamp, 'Exploratory consumer buying behavior: Conceptualization and measurement,' *International Journal of Research in Marketing*, 13 (1996), pp. 121–137.

121. L. Stockmann, 'Frontiers geeft Euromarketeers grip op de toekomst [Frontiers offers grip on future to Euromarketers],' *NieuwsTribune* (7 November 1991).

122. Data TGI (2001). Copyright TGI, all rights reserved.

123. *Reader's Digest* Trusted Brands reports 2005 and 2007, 14 countries. See Appendix B.

124. *Consumers' View on Switching Service Providers* (Flash Eurobarometer 243, 2009), 25 countries.

125. *Financial Products and Services* (EBS 446, 2016).

126. C. Robinson, 'Asian culture: The marketing consequences,' *Journal of the Market Research Society*, 38 (1996), pp. 55–66.

127. *Planet Retail* (2013). Available at: www.planetretailrng.com/.

128. T. Erdem, J. Swait, and A. Valenzuela, 'Brands as signals: A cross-country validation study,' *Journal of Marketing*, 70 (2006), pp. 34–49.

129. B. Jin, J.Y. Park, and J. Kim, 'Cross-cultural examination of the relationships among firm reputation, e-satisfaction, e-trust, and e-loyalty,' *International Marketing Review*, 25, 3 (2008), pp. 324–337.

130. F. Mattison Thompson and T. Chmura, 'Loyalty programs in emerging and developed markets: The impact of cultural values on loyalty program choice,' *Journal of International Marketing*, 23, 3 (2015), pp. 87–103.

131. J.B. Steenkamp, F. Ter Hofstede, and M. Wedel, 'A cross-national investigation into the individual and national cultural antecedents of consumer innovativeness,' *Journal of Marketing*, 63 (1999), pp. 55–69.

132. S. Yeniurt and J.D. Townsend, 'Does culture explain acceptance of new products in a country?,' *International Marketing Review*, 20, 4 (2003), pp. 377–396.

133. G.J. Tellis, S. Stremersch, and E. Yin, 'The international take-off of new products: The role of economics, culture and country innovativeness,' *Marketing Science*, 22, 2 (2003), pp. 188–208; S. Singh, 'Cultural differences and influences on consumers' propensity to adopt innovations,' *International Marketing Review*, 23, 2 (2006), pp. 173–191.

134. W. Kim, C.A. Di Benedetto, and J.M. Hunt, 'Consumer innovativeness and consideration set as antecedents of the consumer decision process for highly globalized new products: A three-country empirical study,' *Journal of Global Scholars of Marketing Science: Bridging Asia and the World*, 22, 1 (2012), pp. 1–23.

135. D.A. Griffith and G. Rubera, 'A cross-cultural investigation of new product strategies for technological and design innovations,' *Journal of International Marketing*, 22, 1 (2014), pp. 5–20.

136. M. Lynn and B.D. Gelb, B. D. (1996). 'Identifying innovative national markets for technical consumer goods,' *International Marketing Review*, 13 (1996), pp. 43–57.

137. H. Gatignon and T.S. Robertson, 'A propositional inventory for new diffusion research,' *Journal of Consumer Research*, 11 (1985), pp. 849–861.

138. E.M. Rogers, *Diffusion of Innovations* (Free Press, New York, 1992).

139. J.B. Steenkamp, *Global Consumers*, presentation at Tilburg University (17 November 2002). Based on *Consumer and Market Drivers of the Trial Probability of New Consumer Packaged Goods*, working paper.

140. *Early Adopters of Technological Innovations* (TGI Chile, 2003). Available at: www.zonalatina.com/Zldata99.htm (accessed 5 November 2004).

141. T. Tellefsen and H. Takada, 'The relationship between mass media availability and the multi-country diffusion of consumer products,' *Journal of International Marketing*, 7 (1999), pp. 77–96.

142. A.C. Samli, *International Consumer Behavior* (Quorum, Westport, CT, and London, 1995), p. 106.

143. S. Dwyer, H. Mesak, and M. Hsu, 'An exploratory examination of the influence of national culture on cross-national product diffusion,' *Journal of International Marketing*, 13, 2 (2005), pp. 1–28.

144. F.M. Bass, 'Empirical generalizations and marketing science: A personal view,' *Marketing Science*, 14 (1995), G6–G19.

145. I.S. Yaveroglu and N. Donthu, N. (2002). 'Cultural influences on the diffusion of new products,' *Journal of International Consumer Marketing*, 14, 4 (2002), pp. 49–63.

146. H. Takada and D. Jain, 'Cross-national analysis of diffusion of consumer durable goods in Pacific Rim countries,' *Journal of Marketing*, 55 (1991), pp. 48–54.

147. J. Ganesh, V. Kumar, and V. Subramaniam, 'Learning effect in multinational diffusion of consumer durables: An exploratory investigation,' *Journal of the Academy of Marketing Science*, 25 (1997), pp. 214–228.

148. J. Ganesh and V. Kumar, 'Capturing the cross-national learning effect: An analysis of an industrial technology diffusion,' *Journal of the Academy of Marketing Science*, 24 (1996), pp. 328–337.

149. C. Nakata and K. Sivakumar, 'National culture and new product development: An integrative review,' *Journal of Marketing*, 60 (1996), pp. 61–72.

150. N. Drewitt, 'Korea opportunities,' *M&M Europe* (June 2001), pp. 15–22.

Appendix A

Hofstede Country Scores and Gross National Income (GNI)/Capita at Purchase Power Parity 2016, for 66 Countries

Country	Abbreviation	GNI/cap at PPP 2016, US$	IDV–COL	PDI	MAS–FEM	UAI	LTO	IVR
Argentina	ARG	19,480	46	49	56	86	20	61
Australia	AUL	45,970	90	36	61	51	21	71
Austria	AUT	49,990	55	11	79	70	60	62
Bangladesh	BAN	3,790	20	80	55	55	47	19
Belgium	BEL	46,010	75	65	54	94	81	56
Brazil	BRA	14,810	38	69	49	76	43	59
Bulgaria	BUL	19,020	30	70	40	85	69	15
Canada	CAN	43,420	80	39	52	48	36	68
China	CHI	15,500	20	80	66	30	87	23
Chile	CHL	23,270	23	63	28	86	30	68
Colombia	COL	13,910	13	67	64	80	13	83
Croatia	CRO	22,880	33	73	40	80	58	33
Czech Republic	CZE	32,710	58	57	57	74	70	29
Denmark	DEN	51,040	74	18	16	23	34	69
Ecuador	ECA	11,070	8	78	63	67	n.a.	n.a.
Estonia	EST	28,920	60	40	30	60	82	16
Finland	FIN	43,400	63	33	26	59	38	57
France	FRA	42,380	71	68	43	86	63	47
Great Britain	GBR	42,100	89	35	66	35	51	69
Germany	GER	49,530	67	35	66	65	82	40

(Continued)

427

(Continued)

Country	Abbreviation	GNI/cap at PPP 2016, US$	IDV–COL	PDI	MAS–FEM	UAI	LTO	IVR
Ghana	GHA	4,150	20	77	46	54	4	72
Greece	GRE	26,900	35	60	57	112	45	49
Guatemala	GUA	7,750	6	95	37	101	n.a.	n.a.
Hong Kong, China	HOK	60,530	25	68	57	29	60	16
Hungary	HUN	25,640	80	46	88	82	58	31
Indonesia	IDO	11,220	14	78	46	48	61	37
India	IND	6,490	48	77	56	40	50	26
Iran	IRA	17,370	41	58	43	59	13	40
Ireland	IRE	56,870	70	28	68	35	24	64
Israel	ISR	37,400	54	13	47	81	37	n.a.
Italy	ITA	38,230	76	50	70	75	61	29
Japan	JPN	42,870	46	54	95	92	87	41
Korea Rep.	KOR	35,790	18	60	39	85	100	29
Latvia	LAT	26,090	70	44	9	63	68	12
Lithuania	LIT	28,840	60	42	19	65	81	15
Malaysia	MAL	26,900	26	104	50	36	40	57
Mexico	MEX	17,740	30	81	69	82	24	97
Malta	MLT	35,720	59	56	47	96	47	65
Morocco	MOR	7,700	46	70	53	68	14	25
Netherlands	NET	50,320	80	38	14	53	67	68
Nigeria	NIG	5,740	20	77	46	54	13	84
Norway	NOR	62,510	69	31	8	50	34	55
New Zealand	NZL	37,860	79	22	58	49	32	74
Pakistan	PAK	5,580	14	55	50	70	49	0
Panama	PAN	20,990	11	95	44	86	n.a.	n.a.
Peru	PER	12,480	16	64	42	87	25	46
Philippines	PHI	9,400	32	94	64	44	27	41
Poland	POL	26,770	60	68	64	93	37	29
Portugal	POR	29,990	27	63	31	104	28	33
Romania	ROM	22,950	30	90	42	90	51	19
Russia	RUS	22,540	39	93	36	95	81	19
(El) Salvador	SAL	8,220	19	66	40	94	19	88
Serbia	SER	13,680	25	86	43	92	52	28
Singapore	SIN	58,050	20	74	48	8	71	45
Slovak Republic	SLK	29,910	52	104	110	51	76	28

Country	Abbreviation	GNI/cap at PPP 2016, US$	IDV–COL	PDI	MAS–FEM	UAI	LTO	IVR
Slovenia	SLV	32,360	27	71	19	88	48	47
Spain	SPA	36,340	51	57	42	86	47	43
Sweden	SWE	50,000	71	31	5	29	52	77
Switzerland	SWI	63,660	68	34	70	58	73	66
Taiwan1	TAI	n.a.	17	58	45	69	92	49
Thailand	THA	16,070	20	64	34	64	31	45
Turkey	TUR	23,990	37	66	45	85	45	49
Uruguay	URU	21,090	36	61	38	100	26	53
USA	USA	58,030	91	40	62	46	25	68
Venezuela	VEN	n.a.	12	81	73	76	15	99
Vietnam	VIE	6,050	20	70	40	30	57	35

SOURCES: Hofstede et al. (2010); Latvia and Lithuania: M. Huettinger 'Cultural dimensions in business life: Hofstede's indices for Latvia and Lithuania,' *Journal of Baltic Management* (2006). Data for Ghana and Nigeria for four dimensions are Hofstede's scores for West Africa, LTO and IVR are from Minkov, in Hofstede et al. 2010. GNI/capita 2016 (at Purchasing Power Parity): World Development Indicators database, World Bank national accounts data, available at: http://data.worldbank.org/indicator/NY.GNP.PCAP.CD. [1]) GNI/capita Taiwan from CIA World Factbook

Key

IDV–COL individualism–collectivism
PDI power distance
MAS–FEM masculinity versus femininity
UAI uncertainty avoidance
LTO long-term versus short-term orientation
IVR indulgence versus restraint

Appendix B

Data Sources

Many secondary data sources were used for the cultural analysis in this book. Databases are of several types.

1. Consumer surveys sponsored by the media that ask questions about consumption of products and media usage. The surveys used are the *Reader's Digest* Surveys, *A Survey of Europe Today 1970* and *Eurodata 1991,* and the *European Media and Marketing Surveys* (EMS) of 1995, 1997, 1999, 2007, and 2012.
2. Statistical data on sales of various products measured in value and liters or kilograms per capita from commercial sources like *Euromonitor*. Several global market research companies publish data on the Internet. Examples are TNS, Ipsos, and TGI.
3. Economic statistics published by governmental or nongovernmental organizations: World Bank, United Nations, OECD, and Eurostat.
4. Surveys of opinions and habits of citizens of countries, published by governmental organizations. The major studies used are the Eurobarometer reports published by the European Commission Directorate.
5. Academically driven value studies. Examples are the *World Values Survey* and the *European Value Study.*
6. Industry driven studies, for example, by the tourism trade, car industry, or telecommunications industry. The latter is represented by the ITU (International Telecommunications Union) that offers data on telephones, Hotrec on tourism, and the Beverage Marketing Corporation of New York.
7. Studies on specific areas of consumer behavior conducted and published by market research agencies, media, or companies, for example, studies by Roper Starch or TGI, the 'Trusted Brands' study by *Reader's Digest,* and the study of environmental attitudes by the tire company Goodyear.

In this appendix the major studies of categories 1 through 7 are described. In addition to these, the notes at the end of each chapter mention various other studies from which data were drawn.

1. Media-sponsored consumer surveys

The *Reader's Digest* Surveys (*Reader's Digest* Association Limited, London), studies of the lifestyles, consumer spending habits, and attitudes of people in 17 European countries, published in 1970 and 1991. The data of the survey 1970 were the results of a probability sample representative of the national population aged 18 and over. Comparable sample surveys were conducted in 16 Western European countries in early 1969. Approximately 24,000 personal interviews were involved. Eurodata 1991 was based on comparable sample surveys conducted in the early summer (May/June) of 1990. Approximately 22,500 personal interviews were involved. The study was commissioned by The *Reader's Digest* Association, Inc. in cooperation with its editions and offices in Europe. With the exception of Sweden, it was conducted by the Gallup-affiliated companies and institutes in Europe and was coordinated by Gallup, London. Probability samples were employed in each of the 17 countries, representative of the population aged 18 and over, living in private households. Countries surveyed were Austria, Belgium, Denmark, Finland, France, Germany, Greece, Ireland, Italy, Luxembourg, the Netherlands, Norway, Portugal, Spain, Sweden, Switzerland, and the United Kingdom.

Another survey by *Reader's Digest* is the annual *Reader's Digest Trusted Brand*TM *Survey* that, in cooperation with Ipsos, measures the degree of trust people have in brands worldwide. Available at: www.rdtrustedbrands.com

The *European Media and Marketing Survey* (EMS) was conducted by Inter/ View-NSS, Amsterdam, the Netherlands, which was later owned by Synovate, and in 2013 by Ipsos, which continues conducting the surveys (www.ipsos.com). Data used are from surveys of 1995, 1997, 1999, 2007, and 2012. EMS is a European 'industry' survey (later extended to other world regions), which measures national and international media usage as well as ownership of some products and services. EMS covers the main income earners living in the top 20% of households in 36 survey countries across Europe, Africa and the Middle East, an estimated population of almost 54 million affluent consumers. Data are based on interviews and self-completion questionnaires. Reports are available to subscribers only. In

2012, in Europe 21 countries were surveyed: Austria, Belgium, Czech Republic, Denmark, Finland, France, Germany, Greece, Hungary, Ireland, Italy, Luxembourg, the Netherlands, Norway, Poland, Portugal, Spain, Sweden, Switzerland, Turkey and the United Kingdom.

Synovate PAX is the Asia-Pacific Cross-Media Survey that offers continuous tracking data on media, product, and brand consumption from a sample of over 20,000 high-end consumers. It covers large cities in Asia: Bangkok, Hong Kong, Jakarta, Kuala Lumpur, Manila, Singapore, Taipei, Seoul and Tokyo; in India, Mumbai, New Delhi, and Bangalore; in Australia, Sydney and Melbourne. PAX Digital Life provides data on digital media usage.

Synovate *Young Asians Survey* (2008) and Ipsos *Young Asians Survey* (2010) provide data on digital media consumption of young people aged 15–24 in Asia. The 2010 survey was based on a sample of 13,708 in China, Hong Kong China, India, Indonesia, Korea, Myanmar, Philippines, Singapore, Taiwan, Thailand, and Vietnam.

The data are not in the public domain and were provided by Reinier Schaper, Marlies van Oudheusden, Ipsos MediaCT, and for the Asian studies by Susanna Lam of Ipsos in Hong Kong.

2. Commercial statistical databases and market research

Euromonitor. *Consumer Europe 1997*. A compendium of pan-European market information on sales in value and volume of a large number of products, and Consumer International 1997, by Euromonitor PLC, London. Euromonitor publishes databases on consumption and ownership of products worldwide (*Consumer World*) and category specific data reports (www.euromonitor.com). Countries included in *Consumer Europe 1997* were Austria, Belgium, Denmark, Finland, France, Germany, Greece, Ireland, Italy, Luxembourg, the Netherlands, Norway, Portugal, Spain, Sweden, Switzerland, United Kingdom.

TNS *Digital World* (2008) and *Digital Life* (2011) are global reports by tns-global, published on the website www.tnsdigitallife.com. TNS is a research company that is part of a consultancy firm (Kantar). In 2008, the company interviewed 27,522 people aged 18–55 in 16 countries around the world about online behavior, trust in online sources, or preferences for recommendations by friends; and in

2011 in 60 countries, 72,000 people were asked about what they do online and why they do it.

TGI (www.globaltgi.com) annually publishes its TGI product book with data on product consumption; in 2012, data were published for 62 countries worldwide.

3. Economic statistics

World Bank (New York). Annual World Development Reports include economic data and data on infrastructure; separate reports on World Development Indicators. Data on most countries in the world (see: http://econ.worldbank.org/wdr/). Income data from Table 1. Key Indicators of Development include data on daily newspapers, Internet, PCs, etc.

United Nations (New York). UN Statistical Yearbooks include economic data and data on product ownership and media. Data on most countries in the world (see: http://unstats.un.org/unsd/methods/inter-natlinks/refs3.htm). UN Demographic yearbooks 2008 (data 2006), 2009 (data 2007), and 2016 (data 2014–2015) – https://unstats.un.org. Special report: *United Nations World Population Prospects*, 2017 (see: AgegroupsWPP2017_KeyFindings.pdf). The United Nations World Tourism Organization publishes UN Tourism Reports.

World Health Organization (WHO). Data on physicians and pharmacists per 100,000 population (www.who.org). *British Heart Foundation*, 2015 also publishes data beyond Great Britain.

OECD is the Organization for Economic Co-operation and Development. They publish several statistics on social indicators, such as income, population developments, labor, etc. but also some special reports such as on risky behavior, leisure time, and time spent eating, e.g. *Society at a Glance* (2009, 2016) including data on health care, leisure time, and eating time. Data on literacy are provided by the OECD Programme for International Student Assessment (PISA).

Eurostat. (1) Annual Reports include demographic data and data on consumption. Data cover the member states of the European Union. (2) Social Indicators reports. (3) Family Budgets. The report *Consumers in Europe: Facts and Figures* (2001) covers data 1996–2000. Published by the Office for Official Publications of the European Communities, Luxembourg (http://eur-op.eu.int/general/en/index_en. htm). Data are for Austria, Belgium, Denmark, Finland, France, Germany, Greece, Ireland, Italy, Luxembourg, the Netherlands, Portugal,

Spain, Sweden, United Kingdom, Bulgaria, Cyprus, Czech Republic, Estonia, Hungary, Latvia, Lithuania, Malta, Poland, Romania, Slovakia, Slovenia, and Turkey. The report *How Consumers Spend their Time* (2002) covers data from 1998–2002. A later report on time use is *Harmonised European Time Use Survey* (2007). The report *Cinema, TV and Radio in the EU*, with data 1980–2002, covers statistics on audiovisual services. A report covering the young is *Youth in Europe, A Statistical Portrait* (2009). A later report is *Being Young in Europe Today* (2015). A general report on household expenditures is *Household Expenditures by Consumption Purpose, Share of Total Expenditures* (2016). A report on the digital economy is *Digital Economy and Society Statistics. Households and Individuals* (2015–2016).

4. Governmental opinion surveys

Eurobarometer. The standard Eurobarometer reports cover the resident populations (aged 15 years and over) of the European Union member states. The basic sample design applied in all member states is a multistage, random (probability) one. The results of Eurobarometer studies are reported in the form of tables, data files, and analyses and published by the European Commission Directorate, Brussels. Until 2004, separate surveys were conducted for the EU member states and for the EU candidate countries. After the EU enlargements in 2004 and 2007, the candidate countries were included in the standard Eurobarometer. Since 2007, surveys cover 24 or 27 countries. Some go beyond the EU and add countries like Switzerland, Turkey, and Israel. The results are published on the Internet server of the European Commission: http://ec.europa.eu/commfrontoffice/publicopinion/index.cfm. Each year standard reports are published including specific questions that are repeated every year, such as the degree of satisfaction with life in general. Several special reports are published, and some are repeated in the years after, which makes comparison possible. Examples are *Measuring the Information Society* (1997 and 2000); *The Young Europeans* (1997, 2001, and 2007); and *Trend Variables 1974–1994* (November 1994). One series of surveys is called Special Eurobarometer (EBS), another Flash Eurobarometer. Data from the following Standard, Flash and Special Eurobarometer surveys were used for this book:

- Eurobarometer (1976) *European Consumers, their Interests, Aspirations and Knowledge of Consumer Affairs* (EBS 007)

- Eurobarometer (1997) *Standard Eurobarometer Report* (47)
- Eurobarometer (2000) *How Europeans See Themselves*, European Documentation Series
- Eurobarometer (2000) *Measuring Information Society* (53)
- Eurobarometer (2001) *Standard Eurobarometer Report* (55)
- Eurobarometer (2001) *Young Europeans* (151)
- Eurobarometer (2002) *Standard Eurobarometer Report* (57.1)
- Eurobarometer (2002) *Consumer Survey* (Flash Eurobarometer 117)
- Eurobarometer (2003) *Globalisation* (Flash Eurobarometer 151b)
- Eurobarometer (2003) *Antibiotics* (Special Eurobarometer Report EBS 183.3)
- Eurobarometer (2004) *Citizens of the European Union and Sport* (EBS 213)
- Eurobarometer (2005) *Social Values, Science and Technology* (EBS 225)
- Eurobarometer (2006, 2008, 2011) *E-Communications Household Survey* (EBS 249, 293, and 362)
- Eurobarometer (2007) *European Social Reality* (EBS 273)
- Eurobarometer (2007) *European Cultural Values* (EBS 278)
- Eurobarometer (2007) *Young Europeans: A Survey Among Young People Aged Between 15–30 in the European Union* (Flash Eurobarometer Report 202)
- Eurobarometer (2008) *E-Communications Household Survey* (EBS 293)
- Eurobarometer (2008) *Information Society as Seen by EU Citizens* (Flash Eurobarometer 241)
- Eurobarometer (2008) *Attitudes of European Citizens Towards the Environment* (EBS 295)
- Eurobarometer (2008) *Towards a Safer Use of the Internet for Children in the EU – A Parents' Perspective* (Flash Eurobarometer 248)
- Eurobarometer (2009) *Confidence in the Information Society* (Flash Eurobarometer 250)
- Eurobarometer (2010) *Science and Technology* (EBS 340)
- Eurobarometer (2010) *Food-related Risks* (EBS 354)
- Eurobarometer (2011) *E-Communications Household Survey* (EBS 362)
- Eurobarometer (2011) *Consumer Empowerment* (EBS 342)
- Eurobarometer (2011) *Youth on the Move* (Flash Eurobarometer 319)
- Eurobarometer (2013) *How Companies Influence our Society, Citizens' View* (Flash EB 363)
- Eurobarometer (2014) *E-communications and Telecom Single Market Household Survey* (EBS 414)
- Eurobarometer (2014) *Gender Equality* (EBS 428).
- Eurobarometer (2016) *European Youth in 2016* (Special Eurobarometer of the European Parliament, European Parliamentary Research Service PE582.005)

- Eurobarometer (2016) *Standard Eurobarometer Report* (86)
- Eurobarometer (2017) *Public Opinion in the European Union* (87)
- Eurobarometer (2010 and 2017) *Food-related Risks* (EBS 354, 2010 and EB88, 2017).

5. Academically driven value studies

World Values Survey. A study of values via public opinion surveys was started in the early 1980s as the European Values Study. In 1981, it was carried out in 10 EU member states. In 1990, a second round was started, and 16 countries were added. It was renamed the World Values Survey (WVS). Six waves have been conducted: in 1981–1984, 1990–1993, 1995–1997, 1999–2004, 2005–2007, 2010–2014, and a seventh started in 2017. It eventually covered over 65 countries, representing about 70% of the world's population, with a questionnaire including more than 360 forced-choice questions. Examples of areas covered are ecology, economy, education, emotion, family, health, happiness, religion, leisure, and friends.

The 1990 data are published in R. Inglehart, M. Basañez, and A. Moreno, *Human Values and Beliefs: A Cross-cultural Sourcebook* (University of Michigan Press, Ann Arbor, 1998). Data for Europe of 1999/2000 are published in the following: *European Values Study: A Third Wave* (Contact: Loek Halman, Tilburg University, PO Box 90153, 5000 LE Tilburg, The Netherlands (evs@uvt.nl)).

Countries covered by the European Values Study are Austria, Belarus, Belgium, Bulgaria, Croatia, Czech Republic, Denmark, Estonia, Finland, France, Germany, Greece, Hungary, Iceland, Ireland, Italy, Latvia, Lithuania, Luxembourg, Malta, Netherlands, Northern Ireland, Poland, Portugal, Romania, Russia, Slovakia, Slovenia, Spain, Sweden, Ukraine, United Kingdom.

Another survey is the *European Social Survey* (R. Jowell and the Central Co-ordinating Team, Centre for Comparative Social Surveys, City University, London). The European Social Survey (the ESS) is a biennial multi-country survey covering over 30 nations. The first round was fielded in 2002/2003, with seven more rounds following. The latest data are of 2016. The project is funded jointly by the European Commission, the European Science Foundation and academic funding bodies in each participating country. Website: http://www.european socialsurvey.org. The questionnaire includes two main sections, each consisting of approximately 120 items; a 'core' module, which will remain relatively constant from round to round, plus two or more 'rotating' modules, repeated at intervals. The core module aims to monitor change and continuity in a wide range of social variables, including media use, social and public trust; political interest and participation; sociopolitical orientations, governance, and efficacy; moral, political, and social values; social exclusion, national, ethnic, and religious allegiances; well-being, health, and security; demographics and socioeconomics. In addition, a supplementary questionnaire is presented to respondents at the end of the main interview. The first part of this questionnaire is a human values scale (part of the core), while the second is devoted to measures to help evaluate the reliability and validity of items in the main questionnaire.

Interactive Generation in Ibero-America. In 2008 Telefonica, the University of Navarra (Spain) and the Inter-American Organization for Higher Education founded the 'Interactive generations Forum,' an initiative that is open to public and private corporations, with the aim to foster and promote a responsible and safe use of the new technologies by children and young – the people that constitute the new 'interactive generation.' See: www.generacionesinteractivas.org. The first findings were published in X. Bringué Sala and C. Sádaba Chalezquer, *The Interactive Generation in Ibero-America: Children and Adolescents Faced with the Screens* (Collección Fundación Telefónica, Madrid, 2008). Countries included are Argentina, Brazil, Chile, Colombia, Mexico, Peru, and Venezuela.

6. Industry-driven organizations

International Telecommunications Union (ITU) offers data on telephony worldwide (www.itu.org). Data for several years.

The Beverage Marketing Corporation of New York sells worldwide data on soft drinks (www.beveragemarketing.com). Data for Europe are from the *European Federation of Bottled Water* (EFBW).

Comscore, Inc. is a Global Internet Information Provider. It maintains proprietary databases that provide a continuous, real-time measurement of the myriad ways in which the Internet is used and the wide variety of activities that are occurring online (www.comscore.com).

Ofcom – Office of Communication, is an independent organization that regulates the UK's broadcasting, telecommunications, and wireless communications sectors. Publications are communication market reports providing data on television, radio, and telecommunications for several countries (www.ofcom.org.uk). Especially relevant are the *Ofcom International Telecommunications Market Reports* (2010, 2016).

Mediascope Europe is the media consumption study of the European Interactive Advertising Association (EIAA) that provides insight into the evolution of TV, Internet, radio, newspaper, and magazine consumption across Europe, and the role the Internet plays in people's lives. Several studies are published, on the Internet at www.eiaa.net/index.asp. Used for this book was the report *Online Shoppers* (2008).

7. Various Survey Data and Reports Published by Market Research Agencies, Media, or Data Companies

Global TGI is an international network of harmonized market and media research surveys, present in more than 60 countries around the world. Several free data can be downloaded from http://tgisurveys.com. For this book, several years' data on product ownership and usage were used, for example, *TGI Global Surveys 2001* and *2003/2004* and from *Product Book 2009*. Specialized surveys are, for example, *TGI Europa Internet Report*, December 2001; *TGI European Women* report (see: www.bmrb.co.uk. womensreportch2.htm); *Early Adopters of Technological Innovations* (TGI Chile, 2003).

Synovate Asia. Young Asians is a syndicated study that covers 8- to 24-year-olds in 12 markets across the region in 2008 (China, Hong Kong China, India, Indonesia, Japan, Korea, Malaysia, Philippines, Singapore, Thailand, and Vietnam). It covers media consumption and digital lifestyles, as well as favorite brands and singers, climate change, and even who's happiest. Data courtesy of Clare Lui.

Nielsen is a worldwide operating marketing and media information company. They measure and analyze how people interact with digital platforms, traditional media and in-store environments – locally as well as globally. The company is active in more than 100 countries, with headquarters in New York. They publish summaries on the Internet. Examples are reports on *Trust in Advertising* (October 2007), *Consumers and Designer Brands* (May 2006), *Health, Beauty and Personal Grooming* (March 2007), *The Power of Private Label* (2005) and Nielsen Global Online Consumer Survey (2010). See: www.nielsen.com.

Index